Japanese/Korean Linguistics
Volume 10
Volume 10

In Memory of James D. McCawley 1938-1999

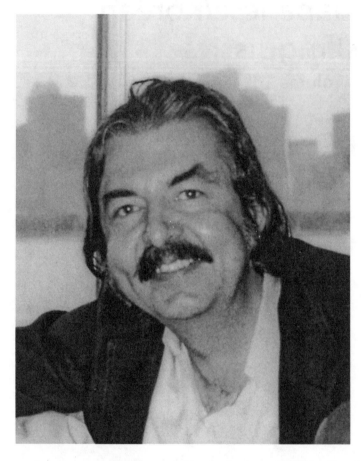

Jim was the teacher, colleague, and friend of many people in linguistics who admired him greatly for his deep humanity and decency, his intellect, and the wide spectrum of things he loved and loved to share. He was the Andrew McLeish Distinguished Service Professor of Linguistics and East Asian Languages at the University of Chicago, and a scholar of an enormous range of subjects, including "syntax and semantics, Chinese, Japanese, Spanish, and miscellaneous other subjects, ranging from writing systems to philosophy of science," as he put it.

The photograph and prose were excerpted from the University of Chicago website dedicated to the memory of James D. McCawley: http://humanities.uchicago.edu/humanities/linguistics/McCawley.html.

Japanese/Korean Linguistics

Volume 10

Edited by
Noriko M. Akatsuka &
Susan Strauss

Published for the
Stanford Linguistics Association by
CSLI Publications
Center for the Study of Language and Information
Stanford, California

Copyright © 2002
Center for the Study of Language and Information
Leland Stanford Junior University
Printed in the United States
06 05 04 03 02   5 4 3 2 1

Library of Congress Cataloging-in-Publication Data

Conference on Japanese/Korean Linguistics (1st : 1989 : University of Southern
        California)
                Japanese/Korean Linguistics / edited by Hajime Hoji
                p.   cm.
                Includes bibliographical references and index.
                ISBN 1-57586-343-X
                ISBN 1-57586-342-1 (pbk.)
    1. Japanese language—Congresses. 2. Korean language—Congresses.
3. Japanese language—Grammar, Comparative—Korean—Congresses.
4. Korean language—Grammar, Comparative—Japanese—Congresses.
5. Linguistics—Congresses. I. Hoji, Hajime. II. Stanford Linguistics Association.
III. Center for the Study of Language and Information (U.S.) IV. Title.
PL503.C6   1989
495.6–dc20   90-2550
                                                                        CIP

∞ The acid-free paper used in this book meets the minimum requirements of the American
National Standard for Information Sciences—Permanence of Paper for Printed Library Materi-
als, ANSI Z39.48-1984.

CSLI Publications reports new developments in the study of language, information, and
computation. In addition to conference proceedings, our publications include lecture
notes, monographs, working papers, revised dissertations, and Studies in Logic, Language
and Information. Our aim is to make new results, ideas, and approaches available as
quickly as possible. Please visit our website at
http://cslipublications.stanford.edu/
for comments on this and other titles, as well as for changes and corrections by the
author and publisher.

Contents

Part II
Discourse and Conversation   119

Part III
Historical Linguistics and Grammaticalization   235

Part IV
Phonetics and Phonology   335

Part V
Syntax and Semantics   449

Preface

This volume is doubly significant: Not only does it commemorate the 10th anniversary of what now has become an international conference on Japanese and Korean linguistics, it also commemorates the everlasting spirit of James D. McCawley, one of the giants of 20th century general linguistics.

Jim was truly a pioneer in East Asian scholarship, even though his area of specialization does not center necessarily on East Asian linguistics--this was just one of the dozens of interests and passions that drove him. Jim 's 1965 MIT dissertation was on Japanese phonology. His research interest in phonological theory was soon to be overshadowed by his passionate inquiry into the relationship between grammar and meaning, but his deep commitment to the study and analysis of the Japanese language never faded. Upon examining the list of his course offerings, we find that from the winter of 1965 as a beginning assistant professor, just one year after his Fall '64 appointment at the University of Chicago, until his untimely death in 1999, he taught Japanese linguistics courses more frequently than any other course, except courses on linguistic logic. We list below the Japanese-related course titles and quarters in which he taught them.

Structure of Japanese	W 65, W 66, W 67, W 68, W 69, S 71, W 72,
Japanese Syntax:	Su 71, W 84, F 89, F 91, S 95,
Topics in Japanese syntax:	F 90, W 96,
Seminar in J Syntax	W 92,
Japanese phonology:	W 75, S 86, F 93
History of the J language:	S 74, 77
English-Japanese	
Comparative Vocabulary:	W 76, Su 77, S 93

We cannot overemphasize Jim's dedication and contribution to the area as a revered teacher and mentor throughout his career at the University of Chicago. Moreover, he was an early member of the American Association for Teachers of Japanese (AATJ) and published articles in the AATJ Newsletter, the predecessor of the current journal JATJ (Journal of he Association of Teachers of Japanese); he maintained his membership in the organization for the duration of his career. While not a language pedagogue per se, Jim considered himself both a linguist as well as a teacher of Japanese.

The Japanese/Korean Linguistics Conference, now in its tenth year, is one of the few linguistic meetings in which formalists, functionalists, discourse analysts and cognitive linguists gather together within a single forum to examine typological, syntactic, semantic, phonological, pragmatic, and even cultural aspects of these two languages, analyzing a variety of topics from different perspectives. From its very inception, one of the most significant contributions of this conference and of its proceedings is the fact that scholars from all disciplines engage in dialogues and discussions on current issues.

UCLA has played a dynamic and creative role in establishing an academic community for this forum, having hosted the conference during its first, fourth, fifth, seventh, and tenth years. The conference began as a joint endeavor among a handful of scholars and graduate students between UCLA and USC. The current standing committee consists of Noriko Akatsuka (UCLA), Patricia Clancy (UCSB), Hajime Hoji (USC), Shoichi Iwasaki (UCLA), and Sung-Ock Sohn (UCLA).

The tenth Japanese/Korean linguistics conference was held at UCLA between October 13-15, 2000, and consisted of a total of 48 papers that were delivered--12 by invited speakers and 36 by contributors representing the United States, Germany, Japan, and Korea. This year, we received a total of 146 abstracts and the 36 papers were rigorously refereed with each paper evaluated by 6 experts in the field.

The 12 invited speakers were all Jim's long-time friends and former students. They are Sukjin Chang, Wes Jacobsen, Susumu Kuno, S.-Y. Kuroda, Chungmin Lee, Seiichi Makino, Naomi McGloin, Kat Momoi, William O'Grady, Masayoshi Shibatani, Yoko Sugioka, and Tim Vance.

This volume contains 45 papers: 12 by the invited speakers in addition to 33 of the 36 competitively selected papers that were delivered at the conference. It is an exciting collection of articles and the entire volume is dedicated to the memory of our great friend, teacher, and scholar as his legacy for having inspired us so deeply.

We specifically chose the weekend of October 13-15 to host the conference because it is the weekend of Hangul Day (October 9th), an especially meaningful Korean 'holiday' to Jim McCawley. In the years before his passing, Jim celebrated Hangul Day by cooking and serving Korean food to his students, friends, and colleagues at the University of Chicago. It is noteworthy that one of Jim's last papers includes "Hangul and Other Writing Systems" which appeared in the Proceedings of the Conference commemorating the 600th anniversary of King Sejong's birth.

In the spirit of Jim's hospitality and culinary appreciation, the organizers of the 10th J/K Conference also hosted a sumptuous Korean feast, catered by one of the leading restaurants in the Koreatown area. During the banquet, the 12 invited speakers briefly shared their personal memories of Jim, most of which centered on his love for linguistics, music, ethnic food, travel, and above all, friends. Because of its combined intellectual and gastronomic excitement, we are sure that Jim would have enjoyed this event tremendously.

Papers for the 10th J/K Conference were selected in the following manner:

1) We required both hard copies as well as electronic versions of the abstract. We expect to accept only electronic versions in the future.

2) Once received, the abstracts were classified according to the following general categories:

a) Formal framework (e.g., formal syntax, semantics, phonetics, phonology)

b) Discourse/Functional framework (e.g., discourse analysis/discourse linguistics, conversation analysis, cognitive linguistics, functional linguistics, pragmatics, historic linguistics, grammaticalization).

3) The Organizing Committee determined the six most suitable referees according to the specific field.

4) For the sake of fairness, we took the utmost care in assuring that referees did not read their own abstracts or those of their intimate colleagues or their students.

We are fortunate to have had the following scholars as our referees this year, many of whom also served in the previous years as well. Some referees have chosen to remain anonymous, and those referees' names, therefore, will not appear in our list:

Formal Framework:
Jun Abe (Nagoya, Japan), Young-mee Yu Cho (Rutgers), Stanley Dubinsky (U South Carolina), Danny Fox (Harvard), Naoki Fukui (UCI), Bruce Hayes (UCLA), Hiroto Hoshi (U London), Sun-Ah Jun (UCLA), Chris Kennedy (NWU), Soowon Kim (U Washington), Satoshi Kinsui (Osaka U, Japan), Yoshihisa Kitagawa (Indiana U), Haruo Kubozono (Kobe U), Chungmin Lee (Seoul National, Korea), Anoop Mahajan (UCLA), William McClure (CUNY), Michiko Nakamura (U Hawaii), Taisuke Nishigauchi (Kobe Shoin Women's U), Toshiyuki Ogihara (U Washington), David Pesetsky (MIT), Mamoru Saito (Nazan U, Japan), Barry Schein (USC), Peter Sells (Stanford), Donca Steriade (UCLA), Yuji Takano (Kinjo U, Japan), Yukinori Takubo (Kyoto U, Japan), Christopher Tancredi (Tokyo U, Japan), Koichi Tateishi, Satoshi Tomioka (U Delaware), Ayumi Ueyama (Kyoto U of FS), Rachel Walker (USC), Akira Watanabe (Tokyo U, Japan), James Yoon (U Illinois UC).

Discourse/Functional Framework:
Noriko Akatsuka (UCLA), Young-mee Yu Cho (Rutgers), Patricia Clancy (UCSB), Yoko Collier-Sanuki (UBC), Haruko Cook (U Hawaii), Pamela Downing (U Wisconsin, Milwaukee), Noriko Fujii (U Oregon), John Haig (U Hawaii), Yoko Hasegawa (UC Berkeley), Bruce Hayes (UCLA), Kaoru Horie

(Tohoku, Japan), Shoichi Iwasaki (UCLA), Wesley Jacobsen (Harvard), Sun-Ah Jun (UCLA), Kyu-Hyun Kim (Kyung Hee U, Korea), Satoshi Kinsui (Osaka U, Japan), Chisato Kitagawa (U Mass), Chungmin Lee (Seoul National, Korea), Hyo-sang Lee (Indiana U), Samuel Martin (Yale), Yoshiko Matsumoto (Stanford), Senko Maynard (Rutgers), Naomi H. McGloin (U Winsconsin, Madison), Junko Mori (U Winsconsin, Madison), Hiroyuki Nagahara (U Hawaii), William O'Grady (U Hawaii), Toshio Ohori (Tokyo U, Japan), Shigeko Okamoto (CSU Fresno), Tsuyoshi Ono (U Arizona), Yong-Yae Park (Seoul National, Korea), Charles Quinn (OSU), Katsue Reynolds (U Hawaii), Leon Serafim (U Hawaii), Yasuhiro Shirai (Cornell), Ho-min Sohn (U Hawaii), Sung-Ock Sohn (UCLA), Susan Strauss (Penn State), Tim Vance (U Arizona).

The Organizing Committee this year consisted of the standing Organizing Committee in addition to Chungmin Lee, of Seoul National University.

We are extremely grateful to the Center for Japanese Studies at UCLA for its consistently generous support of our hosting of the 1st, 4th, 5th, 7th, and 10th conferences. We were also fortunate to have received funding from the Department of East Asian Languages and Cultures (UCLA), the Department of Linguistics (UCLA), Korea Research Foundation, and the Japan Foundation.

We express our deep gratitude to our secretary, Ms. Mee-Jeong Park for her dedication and hard work throughout the entire process. We are also grateful to the graduate students from UCLA's Departments of East Asian Languages and Cultures and Applied Linguistics for their warm hospitality and enthusiastic participation.

And finally, we are grateful to Jim's family, especially his sisters Monica and Caroline, who have provided us with the refreshing text of Jim's most recent entry in their family newsletter of December, 1996. Here, Jim recounts his travels through Germany and Holland, and through his words we see just how Jim was able to fully integrate and savor all the joys of life, with his love of linguistics at the absolute center.

Noriko Akatsuka Susan Strauss
UCLA Penn State University

August 18, 2001

Jim McCawley, field reporter for Daily Planet (December 1996) Travels to Europe - Jim reports:

This summer I made two 3-weeks trips, one in June to Germany & Holland, one in September to Korea & Japan, both for lectures & conferences & whatever sightseeing I could fit in. I left on the 1st trip just a few hours after my last class of the Spring quarter, flying from O'Hare to Frankfurt & arriving on Friday 6/6 around noon.

Frankfurt airport has a nice convenient arrangement with a railway station inside the airport, on a main line from Koln to Munchen, & less than an hour after I got off the plane, I was on a train to Wurzburg, 1 of 2 places that I visited before starting my lectures. Wurzburg is a lovely old city on the banks of the Main, in the heart of the Frankish wine country (there are old Vineyards on the hills adjacent to the railway station), parts of which look very like Prague: one of the bridges over the Main looks like the Charles Bridge in Prague (it has statues every 50 feet of so), & on the other side of the bridge there are very steep hills with a huge castle on top, as in Prague.

I spent the Friday afternoon & all day Saturday walking around Wurzburg, visiting the castle, the palace, & some museums, & going to an open-air concert in the palace grounds Sat. evening. I spent most of Sunday in Nurnberg, visiting the castle, a streetcar museum & the Germainsches Museum (which has a marvelous musical instrument collection as well as an art collection), & then went by train to Tubigen (changing in Stuttgart).

In Tubingen (an old university town on the Neckar), I spent Monday morning visiting yet another castle & walking around the very hilly old town, then met some friends from the university for lunch, gave my lecture in the afternoon, had dinner with them & took the train to Stuttgart, where I stayed with friends (a Swedish linguist & his Israeli linguist wife, who had studied at the U. of Massachusetts & gave a lecture on Tuesday at the university).

In Stuttugart I was able to spend a couple of hours at the superb art museum. On Weds, I went by train to Leipzig, getting there in time to have lunch with a linguist friend at Auerbachs Keller (one of the scenes in Goethe's "Faust" is set there) & then spent the afternoon visiting the marvelous musical instrument museum they have there. I then visited the Thomas-Kirche (where J.S. Bach was the director of music; he's buried there) & shopping at an excellent 2nd-hand music store across the street. On Tuesday I gave a lecture at the university in the late morning & then in the afternoon went by train to Berlin, where I was for the next 5 days.

The visit to Berlin included lectures at Humboldt Univ. (in what had been East Berlin) the Free University and the University of Potsdam. I was straying at Humboldt U.'s guesthouse. I visited San Souci (Frederick the Great's palace in

Postdam), a visit to a museum that had a really nice Picasso exhibition, followed by an afternoon playing violin & piano music with a linguist friend (him on a violin, me on piano) who teaches at the Univ. of Potsdam, a concert by the Minsk Chamber Orchestra, & a lot of walking around what had been East Berlin, which was changed enormously (mainly for the better) in the last few years.

On Tuesday, I took a morning train to Hamburg. The Univ. (where I gave an early evening lecture that day) provided me with a room in a hotel that was very close to the Dammtor railway station & to the university which made it very convenient to get around and see quite a bit of Hamburg before I left the following day at around 4pm. Also, in Hamburg you can buy for about $7 a card that is good for 1 day's unlimited use of the commuter trains, subways, and buses & discounts or free admissions to a lot of museums. I got full value from it with visits to the Kunsthalle (a superb art museum) & a great arts & crafts museum. Hamburg is also a wonderful city for seafood, of which I took full advantage, including some take-out food to eat on the train going to Leiden, Holland (changing in Duisburg & Utrecht).

The visit to Leiden was the main reason for the trip; the annual international conference on Chinese Linguistics, so I spent 3 days in Leiden attending the conference & walking around Leiden between & after the sessions (it's a lovely old city, with lots of canals & old Dutch-style drawbridges). After the conference was over, I took the train to Amsterdam & visited with friends there for the rest of the weekend; I found time forevisits to the Stedelijk Museum (a superb museum of modern art) & the museum of the history of Amsterdam. On Monday morning, I took a train to Nijmegen, where a friend had recruited me to serve as an outside examiner at a very theatrical Dutch-style PhD thesis defense (the faculty involved in the ceremony wear black robes & hats and march together into & out of the hall).

The following morning I took a train to Koln, where I had another lecture that evening. I was in Koln from Tuesday noon to Wednesday early evening, so I was able to do quite a lot of sightseeing, including several large segments of the old town wall, several exquisite churches (most of them severely damaged in WWII & rebuilt, some of them with lovely modern stained glass in place of that destroyed in the war) & a spectacular art museum.

I then went to my last stop Dusseldorf, where I did a lecture on Thursday evening. I got to another really interesting art museum there, one particularly nice part of which is a huge & very diverse collection of glass objects. The hotel where my friends at the university got me a room was a great location; a few minutes walk from a streetcar line that goes to the university & from a railway station that's just one stop from the Central Station where I was able to change to the train to the Dusseldorf airport for my flight back to Chicago.

Editors' Note: Jim was supposed to report on his September trip to Korea and Japan in the next issue of the family newsletter, but unfortunately he did not have that chance.

Part I

Cognition and Grammar

On the Interaction of Temporal and Modal Meaning in Japanese Conditionals

WESLEY M. JACOBSEN
Harvard University

1. Introduction

Conditional sentences in Japanese are known to have not only hypothetical uses like those typical of conditionals in English, but also non-hypothetical uses involving events which are believed to have actually occurred or to be certain to occur. In an earlier paper (Jacobsen 1999), I discussed a set of semantic parameters which correlate with the relative presence or lack of hypothetical meaning in Japanese conditionals.[1] In the current paper, I will propose an account for one of the correlations observed there: the tendency for aspectually stative conditional clauses to be given a hypothetical interpretation.

The fundamental insight presented here is that stative meaning, and imperfective aspect in general, is characterized by a property of non-uniqueness whereby the set of times over which a situation is seen to hold is not limited to a single point in time, but implicitly contains multiple points in

---

[1] I will not provide arguments in defense of the view taken here that morphological conditionals with non-hypothetical interpretations are rightfully included in the class of conditional sentences in general. Readers interested in that question are referred to Jacobsen (1999), where arguments are presented that the defining property of conditional meaning is not hypothetical meaning itself, but rather a relationship between two states of affairs where one is seen to be temporally contingent on the other.

time. States asserted of the moment of speech, or other instantaneous points of reference are, as a result, seen to encompass points in time other than the time of speech or time of reference. This property can easily be extended to the case of multiple worlds as well, so that stative and imperfective clauses become capable of encompassing worlds external to the real world of the speaker, analogously to the way they encompass times external to that of the speech act. The temporal function of stative meaning is thereby extended in a natural way to a modal function. Considered in this way, imperfective aspect has an inclusive character which is complementary to that of the past tense marker, argued in Iatridou (2000) to exclude the time or world of the speaker from the topic under discussion. The co-occurrence of past tense morphology and imperfective aspect commonly observed in counterfactual constructions across a wide range of languages can be seen as the natural outcome of an interaction between these complementary functions of including versus excluding worlds or times.

2. Degrees of hypothetical meaning in Japanese conditionals

Examples (1)-(6) illustrate the range of hypothetical and non-hypothetical meanings exhibited by one of the conditional verb auxiliaries in Japanese, the TARA form. The examples are ordered according to the degree of hypothetical meaning exhibited, from a high degree in (1) to a total absence of such meaning in (5), with intermediate stages representing a gradual decrease in the presence of such meaning. The presence of hypothetical meaning is roughly proportional to the degree to which the hypothetical adverb *mosi* "if" co-occurs naturally with the conditional clause, and is also reflected in the degree to which "if" is more appropriate as an English gloss of the Japanese conditional than "when."

> (1) *Ame ga hutTARA siai wa tyuusi ni naru.* (*mosi* OK)
>   If it rains, the game will be canceled.
> (2) *Tanaka-kun ni atTARA yorosiku tutaete-kure.* (*mosi* OK)
>   If/when you see Tanaka, say hi to him for me.
> (3) *Kono sigoto ga owatTARA nomi ni iku.* (?*mosi*)
>   If/when this job gets finished, I'm going drinking.
> (4) *Raisyuu ni natTARA motto hima ni naru.* (*mosi)
>   When next week comes, I'll have more time.
> (5) *Kusuri o nonDARA genki ni natta.* (*mosi)
>   When I took the medicine, I got better.

For our purposes, we may define a hypothetical proposition as one whose truth value is, at the time of speech, either indeterminate or contrary to what is known to be the case. The proposition *ame ga huru* "it rains" embedded in the TARA clause in (1), for example, is hypothetical in the sense that, at the time of speech, the speaker does not know whether or not it constitutes a true proposition at some relevant time in the future of the real world of the speaker. Expressed in terms of possible worlds, a hypothetical proposition is one which is seen to be true in one or more members of a set of possible worlds which may include, but does not necessarily include, the real world of the speaker. This set of possible worlds is typically defined by differing courses of events (histories) branching out from the present into the future, as in examples (1)-(4) above, but may also be conceived in terms of differing courses of events branching out from some point in the past, constituting alternative, though unreal, histories to what is known to have actually occurred in the past of the real world. The latter is what we find in counterfactual constructions, a special case of hypothetical constructions, illustrated in (6).

(6) *Kuru to sitteiTARA tyanto sita syokuzi no yooi o siteageta noni.*
If I had known that you were coming, I would have prepared a proper meal for you. (*mosi* OK)

The propositions making up the antecedent and consequent clauses of a counterfactual conditional are thus hypothetical propositions with the special property that the set of possible worlds in which they are seen to be true specifically excludes the real world of the speaker.

3. Lexical aspect and hypothetical meaning

Whether a future conditional of the sort seen in (1)-(4) is interpreted as more or less hypothetical is dependent on a variety of factors. These include, certainly, pragmatic and contextual factors which determine the degree of confidence the speaker is able to place in the likelihood of occurrence of the event in the conditional clause. Pragmatic and contextual factors are not, however, the only factors responsible for the occurrence of hypothetical meaning. I shall be concerned here, specifically, with a semantic factor that plays a role in the occurrence of such meaning, and that is lexical aspect. In general, for a conditional clause to receive a non-hypothetical, or low hypothetical, interpretation, its predicate must express an event where some sort of change in state is prominently featured. Stative predicates, by contrast, can only receive a hypothetical interpretation in conditional clauses. This contrast is illustrated in the following pair of future conditionals.

(7)(a) *Hima ga atTARA asobi ni iku.* (stative predicate)
If I have some free time I'll come over for a visit.
(b) *Hima ni natTARA asobi ni iku.* (non-stative event predicate)
If/when my time frees up (I become free), I'll come over for a visit.

(7a), involving the stative clause *hima ga aru* "have free time" receives a purely hypothetical interpretation in contrast to *hima ni naru* "become free" in (7b), an event clause associated with a much higher certainty of realization. Stative clauses are, furthermore, excluded totally from the conditional clause of past-tense non-hypothetical conditionals such as (5), which permit only actual states of affairs occurring at a unique point of time in the past.

    (8) **Hima ga atTARA otikonde-simatta.* (compare (5))[2]
        (Intended reading) When I had free time, I got depressed.

This observation bears one qualification: not all stative situations are the same in terms of their permanence. Following the well-known distinction made in Carlson (1989), stage-level predicates, which express less permanent, more changeable states, are typically acceptable in non-hypothetical past conditional contexts, illustrated in (9) and (10). To the extent that a predicate takes on the character of an individual-level predicate, it is disallowed in such contexts, as illustrated in (12).

    (9) *Eki no hoomu de densya o matteiTARA 30sai gurai no zyosei ga hanasikakete-kita.*
        When (as) I was waiting on the platform for a train, a woman of about age thirty started talking to me.
    (10) *Okane ga nakute komatteiTARA aru hi negattemo nai sigoto ni arituita.*
        When (as) I was out of money and feeling down, I stumbled one day onto a job like none I could have asked for.
    (11) ??*Tyuugokugo ga hanaseTARA minna kansin site-kureta.*
        When I was able to speak Chinese, everyone was impressed.
    (12) **Kanemoti datTARA ippai tomodati ga dekita.*
        (Intended meaning) When I was wealthy, I made many friends.

The semi-grammatical character of (11) can be attributed to the possibility of interpreting *tyuugogoku ga hanaseru* "be able to speak Chinese" not simply as the state of possessing an ability, but as a particular, overt performance exhibiting that ability. To the degree that states approach the characteristics of events in terms of their changeability and low permanence, then, they become acceptable in past-tense non-hypothetical contexts.

---

[2] (8) would be open to a past counterfactual interpretation, given an appropriate sentence-final modal auxiliary such as *daroo* "probably," or, marginally, to a past iterative interpretation, "whenever I had spare time, I would get depressed," but could in no case be interpreted as a unique one-time occurrence parallel to (5).

4. States and modality in main clauses

On first glance it might appear that the correlation we have seen between stative and hypothetical meaning is limited to conditional clauses, and is perhaps in some way an artifact of the conditional construction itself. It is certainly possible for stative meaning to occur in main clause constructions without any apparent hint of a hypothetical interpretation.

> (13) *Teeburu no ue ni hon ga nisatu aru.*
> On the table there are two books.

Yet there is an important class of main-clause constructions involving verb auxiliaries which impart various meanings of a modal nature, and these auxiliaries are consistently stative in their aspect. These include clauses with the desiderative auxiliary –TAI "want to," the potential auxiliary –E(RU) "be able to," and the negative auxiliary –NAI "not."

> (14) *Moo tukareta. Uti e kaeriTAI.*
> I'm tired. I want to go home.
> (15) *Kinyoobi no gogo wa zyugyoo ga nai kara hayaku uti e kaerERU.*
> Friday afternoons I don't have any classes, so I can go home early.
> (16) *Yoru ni nattemo kodomo ga gakkoo kara kaette-koNAI kara sinpai ni natta.*
> My child did not return from school even after night fell, so I became worried.

Space does not permit elaboration here, but the stative character of these auxiliary constructions can easily be demonstrated on the basis of various standard tests for stativity.[3] As to their modal character, note that each of these auxiliaries makes reference in some fashion to one or more of a set of possible worlds, which may or may not include the real world, in which the accompanying proposition is true. (14), for example, makes reference to a set of possible worlds, having the specific characteristic of being desirable ones for the speaker, in which the proposition *uchi e kaeru* "(I) return home" is true. It may turn out that the real world is included in this set; the meaning of –TAI does not overtly exclude that possibility. In the case of the negative auxiliary, by contrast, the real world is explicitly excluded from the set of possible worlds in which the accompanying proposition is true—in the case of (16), the proposition *kodomo ga gakkoo kara kaette-kuru* "my child returns from school."

---

[3] The negative auxiliary –NAI exhibits certain complexities, but can nevertheless be shown to have a fundamentally stative character. For a fuller discussion, see Jacobsen (1996).

We may conclude, then, that while stative meaning in main-clause predicates does not always involve reference to non-actual possible worlds, it is nevertheless the case that when such reference is made, the aspect tends toward a stative quality.

5. Counterfactuals and aspect

Counterfactual conditionals are, as noted earlier, a special case of hypothetical conditionals where the set of possible worlds in which the antecedent and consequent events are seen to be true specifically excludes the real world of the speaker.[4] They bear a similarity in this respect to negative constructions, which also have the function of excluding the real world from the set of possible worlds under consideration. Counterfactual conditionals may occur in past, present, and future contexts, expressing, respectively, situations counter to what the speaker believes to have occurred in the past, counter to what s/he believes to be the case in the present, and counter to what s/he believes to be certain to occur in the future. These are illustrated in (17)-(19).

(17) *Motto hayaku uti o dereBA/deTARA densya ni ma ni atta noni.*
   If we had left home earlier, we would have made the train on time.
(18) *Kumotte-inakereBA/inakatTARA hosizora ga mieru noni.*
   If it weren't cloudy we would be able to see the starry sky.
(19) *Kusuri o nomeBA/nonDARA genki ni naru noni.*
   If he took the medicine, he would get better.

Two features of the morphology of Japanese conditionals bear explanation here. The first is in regard to the conditional auxiliary form marking the conditional clause. As seen above, either of two conditional auxiliaries is possible in counterfactual conditional clauses, one being the TARA auxiliary introduced earlier, and the other the auxiliary BA. Neither of these is unique to counterfactual constructions, but BA is more restricted in its range of usage than TARA, as it can occur only in hypothetical contexts.[5] In future conditionals, for example, BA forces a specifically hypothetical reading

---

[4] Or, at least, does so in typical uses of counterfactual conditionals. I will not consider here cases where the falsity of the antecedent and consequent propositions in the real world appears to be cancelable. Examples of such cases are well known in the literature. See, for example Comrie (1986).

[5] BA also differs from TARA in conveying the sense that the consequent event is a desirable one for the speaker, whereas TARA is neutral in this regard. I will not be concerned with this difference in the current paper, although some of the examples of counterfactuals cited in this paper, such as (25) and (26), do not allow BA for this reason. For further discussion, see Jacobsen (1992).

even in contexts where TARA might otherwise allow a non-hypothetical, or low hypothetical, reading.

(20)(a) *Kono sigoto ga owatTARA nomi ni iku.* (*?mosi*) (=(3))
     If/when this job gets finished, I'm going drinking.
   (b) *Kono sigoto ga owareBA nomi ni iku.* (*mosi* OK)
     If this job gets finished, I'm going drinking.

BA may never be used, morevoer, in past-tense non-hypothetical contexts such as (5) and (9)-(11). This means that in a past-tense construction, BA will force a counterfactual reading, as in (17) above.[6]

The second feature to be noted about counterfactual conditionals is that they are typically marked by a sentence-final modal auxiliary predicate or particle, such as *noni* in (17)-(19). *Noni* has no exact lexical counterpart in English, but conveys that the speaker considers the counterfactual outcome expressed in the consequent clause to be a desirable one, in contrast to the undesirable state of affairs which actually obtains (obtained) in the real world. This explicitly counterfactual character of *noni* figures centrally in the Japanese counterpart to the English "wish" construction.

(21) *Monku bakkari iwanakereBA ii noni.*
     I wish you wouldn't complain all the time.
     (Lit., It would be good if you didn't complain all the time.)

As seen in this example, the "wish" construction is in reality a special case of a counterfactual construction where the consequent clause consists of the predicate *ii* "(be) good," followed clause-finally by *noni*.

Other modal auxiliaries which may appear sentence-finally in counterfactual constructions include *daroo* "(will/would) probably," *ni tigainai* "(will/would) undoubtedly," and *hazu da* "is/would be expected that." Unlike *noni*, none of these are explicity counterfactual in force, although their use in past or present conditional contexts such as (17) or (18) will, due to independent factors, typically be associated with a counterfactual interpretation. In future hypotheticals, by contrast, where such factors are not normally at work, these modal auxiliaries are typically free of any counterfac-

---

[6] There exists one important class of exceptions to this: BA may be used to express actual events iterated in the past. For examples, see Jacobsen (1999). The correlation between iterativity and hypothetical meaning may be seen as a further manifestation of a broad correlation between multiple times and multiple worlds of which the correlation between stativity and hypothetical meaning is but a special case.

tual force. Compare, for example, the use of *daroo* "probably" to *noni* in a context such as (19), repeated here as (22a).

(22)(a) *Kusuri o nomeBA/nonDARA genki ni naru noni.*
      If he took the medicine, he would get better.
  (b) *Kusuri o nomeBA/nonDARA genki ni naru daroo.*
      If he takes the medicine, he will (probably) get better.

The use of *daroo* does not exclude the possibility of the antecedent event *kusuri o nomu* "(he) takes medicine" being realized in the real world, whereas this possibility is excluded, or at least treated as remote, in the case of *noni*. A rough approximation to this distinction can be seen in the English use of differing tenses in the future conditional: the past tense, as in (22a), denotes a less likely, more remote hypothetical possibility in such cases. *Noni* is, in summary, always associated with a counterfactual interpretation, although not all counterfactuals require the occurrence of *noni*.

The grammatical expression of counterfactual meaning in Japanese is thus achieved through an interplay of morphological elements, including tense, conditional clause marker, and sentence-final modal auxiliary. To this we add one further element: the role played by the aspectual form of the predicate in the conditional clause. This is most clearly seen in the use of the stative affix *te-i(ru)*[7] in counterfactual constructions to effect a less vivid, more remote hypothetical interpretation—to heighten, that is, the counterfactual force of such constructions. Alongside, the earlier (15), repeated here as (23a), for example, exists the version in (23b), where both the antecedent and consequent predicates occur in their augmented *te-i(ru)* form, resulting in a heightened sense of remoteness from the real world of the speaker.

(23)(a) *Motto hayaku uti o dereBA/deTARA densya ni ma ni atta noni.*
      If we had left home earlier, we would have made the train on
        time

---

[7] The *te-iru* affix normally functions to impart one of two main interpretations to the predicate to which it is attached: progressive or perfect (resulting state), depending on the aspectual semantics of the attached predicate. Both of these interpretations can be treated as varieties of stative meaning, but the use of *te-iru* in counterfactual constructions may be considered closer in affinity to the perfect (resulting state) reading, as it commonly appears on predicates in such constructions which would not be capable of a progressive interpretation with *te-iru* (as is the case, for example, in (23b), (25) and (26)).

(23)(b) *Motto hayaku uti o deTE-IREBA/deTE-ITARA densya ni ma*
          ni atTE-ITA noni.

   If we had left home earlier, we would have made the train on
   time.

Whether or not to opt for one or the other form of counterfactual expression,
with or without the inclusion of *te-i(ru)*, will be governed by various pragmatic and contextual factors that determine whether a relatively more remote
or less remote form of expression is appropriate or desirable. I will not attempt an anlysis of such factors here, except to note that a first-person context such as (23), dealing as it does with events directly experienced by the
speaker, may be expected to at least allow for a less remote form of expression. Contexts such as those involving third-person subjects or a more objective reporting style will, by contrast, typically favor counterfactual expression with the use of *te-i(ru)*, consonant with a decreased level of involvement of, and greater remoteness from, the speaker in such cases. The
following examples illustrate the use of *te-i(ru)* in such contexts. (25) and
(26), in particular, are actually attested examples from written texts, cited as
representative of the use of this affix in the objective style typical of such
discourse.[8]

(24) *Motto benkyoo siTE-IREBA/siTE-ITARA siken ni ukatTE-ITA*
       daroo ni.[9]

       If he had studied more he would probably have passed the exam.

(25) *Kore wa Kyooto no ryakuzu de, mosi genbaku ga tookasareTE-*
       ITARA donoyoo na bubun ga eikyoo o ukeTE-ITA ka o simesu.

       This is a map of Kyoto showing what parts would have been af-
       fected if the atom bomb had been dropped (there).

(26) *Hooryuuzi ga mosi hinoki igai no ki de tukurareTE-ITARA,*
       osoraku ima no yoo ni mukasi no sugata o tutaeru koto wa deki-
       nakatta daroo.

       If Horyu Temple had been made of wood other than Japanese cy-
       press, it would probably have been unable to keep its ancient
       form as it does today.

---

[8] These examples are cited, with slight modification, from the following sources: (25) from
the Japanese translation of "Mr. Stimson's 'Pet city'--The Sparing of Kyoto, 1945", by Otis
Cary, *Moonlight Series No. 3* (1975, Kyoto: Amherst House, Dooshisha University); (26)
from from *Ki no Bunka*, by Jiro Kohara (1972, Tokyo: Kajima Kenkyuujo Shuppankai).

[9] The modal form *daroo ni* occurring sentence-finally in this example may be seen as the
result of combining the two modal forms *daroo* and *noni*.

We see, then, further evidence in counterfactual constructions of a correlation between stative aspect and hypothetical meaning. The effect *te-i(ru)* has of heightening the sense of remoteness of a conditional event from the real world of the speaker in such constructions can be seen to support a scalar conception of hypothetical meaning, measured in terms of varying distances at which possible worlds may be subjectively perceived to lie relative to the real world.

6. A bridge between temporal and modal meaning in statives

We turn now to the question of what temporal property of statives it is that lends itself so easily to hypothetical interpretation in the way we have seen. Consider first the well-known flexibility states exhibit in their ability to occur in a variety of time frames, including both intervals and instants of time, as illustrated in (27a) and (27b).

(27)(a) I was in my room from 3:00 until 5:30 yesterday afternoon.
    (b) I was in my room at 3:30 yesterday afternoon.

States are inherently homogeneous in quality: for any interval over which a state is seen to hold, such as the interval 3:00 to 5:30 in (27a), the same state is seen to hold of any subinterval of that interval, no matter how small, down to any and every instant encompassed by the interval. As the interval of time imposed on a stative clause becomes smaller and smaller, it ultimately approaches a single point in dimension, making it possible to speak of a state holding at an instant of time, as in (27b). Even in such cases, however, the state is not asserted to hold uniquely at that instant, as would be the case with an achievement-type event as in (28) .

(28) I arrived at the hotel at 3:30 yesterday afternoon.

A state asserted of an instant is, in fact, typically understood to hold of an interval, however small, which contains, but is not limited to, that instant.[10] This is true of states occurring in a variety of guises, including those expressed by simple stative predicates as in (29), as well as resulting state constructions and progressive constructions, as in (30) and (31), all of which exhibit the basic homogeneous quality of states.

---

[10] There are, to be sure, cases where the context imposes narrow constraints making it impossible to conceive of a state as holding for longer than a single instant, as when saying of an airplane climbing at a constant velocity *It was at 30,000 feet when the engine malfunction occurred.* The uniqueness of the instant in question here does not, however, arise from any property inherent in states; it is simply a limit imposed on the time frame of a state by outside factors.

(29) *Teeburu no ue ni hon ga <u>aru</u>.*
There is a book on the table.

(30) *Doa ga <u>aite-iru</u>.*
The door is open (lit., in the state of having become open).

(31) *Taroo wa puuru de <u>oyoide-iru</u>.*
Taroo is swimming in the pool.

To use (30) as an illustration, the resulting state *aite-iru* "be open," while asserted only of the instant of speech, is not, in any but the most marked of contexts, understood to hold exclusively of the instant of speech. In the unmarked situation in which this sentence is used, the instant of speech is rather understood to constitute part of a surrounding interval, at every moment of which the state *aite-iru* "be open" is seen to hold. The same can be said, mutatis mutandis, of (29) and (31). Whether asserted of instants of time or intervals of time, therefore, states by their very nature partake in a property of non-uniqueness: the temporal domain over which they are seen to hold is not inherently limited to a single point in time, but extends to multiple times inclusive of, but not limited to, the instant of speech or other temporal point of reference.

It is this property of non-uniqueness which, we submit, provides a bridge between temporal and modal meaning in stative constructions. Reference to multiple times (temporal non-uniqueness) has a direct parallel in reference to multiple worlds (modal non-uniqueness), which is the defining characteristic of hypothetical meaning. The same character of statives which allows their domain of temporal reference to extend to points of time other than the time of speech makes it possible, that is, for their domain of modal reference to extend to possible worlds distinct from the real world of the speaker.

7. Counterfactuals and past tense: Iatridou's exclusion feature

Based on data from a variety of languages, including English, modern Greek, Hindi, and French, Iatridou (2000) observes that there is a cross-linguistic tendency for counterfactual conditional meaning to be marked by a combination of past tense and imperfective aspectual morphology. Examples (32)-(34) are examples from modern Greek cited by Iatridou to illustrate these morphological features. I have added Japanese counterparts in each case for comparative reference. Examples (32) and (33) are future hypothetical conditionals, distinguished in Greek morphology by nonpast tense (NPST) and perfective aspect (PRF) in the former and past tense (PST) and imperfective aspect (IMP) in the latter. As indicated in the gloss, this difference correlates with a less vivid, more counterfactual-like reading in the case of (33). (34) is a past counterfactual where, in both English and Greek, the antecedent clause is marked by pluperfect (past of a past) tense.

(32) *An pari*   *afto to siropi θa* γ_1ini *kala.*
    If   take/NPST/PRF this   syrup FUT become/NPST/PRF well
    "If he takes this syrup, he will get better." (future neutral vivid)
    Japanese: *Kono siroppuzai o nomeBA genki ni naru (daroo).*

(33) *An eperne*   *afto to siropi θa* $\gamma_1inotan$ *kala.*
    If   take/PST/IMP this   syrup FUT become/PST/IMP well
    "If he took this syrup, he would get better." (future less vivid)
    Japanese: *Kono siroppuzai o nomeBA genki ni naru noni*

(34) *An iχ$_1$e pari to siropi θa iχ$_1$e $\gamma_1$ini kala.*
    If   had taken the syrup FUT had   become better.
    "If he had taken the syrup, he would have gotten better." (past counterfactual)
    Japanese: *Kono siroppuzai o nonDE-IREBA genki ni natTE-ITA noni.*

Of these two morphological ingredients, tense and aspect, only tense, according to Iatridou, makes a semantic contribution to the counterfactual construction. The imperfective morphology in examples such as (33) is, she suggests, "fake aspect," lacking, presumably, any well-defined semantic role in such constructions. The meaning contributed by the past tense is defined by an "exclusion feature" formulated as in (35).

(35) Topic(x) (the x that we are talking about) excludes C(x) (the x of the speaker at time of utterance), where x ranges over both times and worlds.

Past tense contributes to counterfactual meaning, that is, by means of a feature that specifically excludes the world of the speaker from the range of possible worlds under consideration. In future conditionals such as (33), this leads to a more remote reading. In past counterfactuals such as (34), the pluperfect morphology involves two past tenses, one functioning as a "true" temporal past, and the other as a modal past excluding the real world by virtue of this exclusion feature.[11]

A similar use of the past tense in future hypothetical contexts can be observed in Japanese as well, and, as Iatridou's analysis would predict, carries counterfactual force in such cases, as seen in (36).

---

[11] In the English version of (34), the two past tenses are realized together in the form *had taken*, one as the lexical verb *have* itself, the other as the past tense morphology on this verb, yielding *had*.

(36) *2zikan mae ni kusuri o nonDE-IREBA, 2zikan-go ni kiiTE-ITA daroo ni.*[12]

If he had taken the medicine two hours ago, it would have taken effect two hours from now.

Such usage of the past tense is limited, however, to the consequent clause, as antecedent clauses in Japanese conditionals, at least of the TARA and BA variety we have considered here, are non-finite and unmarked for tense. Furthermore, such usage appears to occur in Japanese only in contexts where the consequent event expresses a future outcome of a past event in the antecedent clause, unlike the English and Greek cases in (33), where both the antecedent and consequent events express future events.

The more common device for heightening counterfactual meaning in Japanese is in fact through the use of aspectual marking, as our discussion of the role of the stative affix *te-i(ru)* in counterfactual conditionals has shown. It is evident, furthermore, that the class of constructions we have referred to under the rubric of stative in Japanese, including simple states, progressive states, and resultative states, are the aspectual counterparts to what have been traditionally referred to as imperfective constructions in many Indo-European languages. This suggests that imperfective aspect, far from contributing vacuously to modal meaning, constitutes an equally viable alternative for bridging temporal and modal meaning as past tense does in languages such as Greek and English. Based on our analysis of the temporal character of statives in Section 6, we propose that the particular mechanism by which it does so can be described as a feature of inclusion, complementary to the exclusion feature proposed by Iatridou for past tense:

(37) Topic(x) (the x that we are talking about) includes non-C(x) (x that are not of the speaker at time of utterance), where x ranges over both times and worlds.

Imperfective meaning in any of its forms—stative, habitual, generic, or progressive—may be predicted to exhibit this feature, as long as it shares in the temporal non-uniqueness property discussed in Section 6. Which of these forms are actually exploited for modal purposes in particular languages is, of course, an empirical question that can only be answered through detailed investigation language by language.

Past tense morphology and imperfective aspect are thus both capable of having their temporal meaning exploited for the purposes of accessing worlds external to that of the speaker, albeit in a complementary fash-

---

[12] I am grateful to Satoshi Kinsui (personal communication) for this example.

ion—past tense by specifically excluding the world of the speaker, imperfective aspect by making possible the inclusion of worlds other than that of the speaker. The fact that (37) does not explicitly exclude the world of the speaker leaves open the possibility of modal uses other than purely counterfactual ones: recall that the correlation between hypothetical meaning and statives in Japanese includes future contexts where the conditional event is not assumed to be a non-actual one. For the purposes of expressing counterfactual meaning proper, though, the complementary functions of accessing a set of multiple worlds and then excluding the real world from that set combine in an ideal way to express the desired meaning. The fact that past tense and imperfective aspect are commonly observed to occur together in counterfactual constructions across a wide range of languages would seem to be a natural outcome of this.

8. Conclusion

This paper has presented an account of one semantic parameter which correlates positively with the presence and degree of hypothetical meaning in Japanese conditionals: stative aspect. I have argued that stative meaning, as a special case of imperfective aspect, is characterized by a property of non-uniqueness by which states implicitly bear reference to multiple points in time and, by extension, multiple worlds which may include, but are not limited to, the world of the speaker.

There is abundant evidence that the correlation we have observed between reference to multiple times and multiple worlds extends well beyond the stative predicates and auxiliaries which have been our focus in this paper. The combination of iterative and hypothetical functions in a range of conditional auxiliaries in Japanese, including BA, TEMO, and TEWA, can also be attributed to this correlation. The behavior of the conditional form NARA, which expresses a contingency relationship between speech acts, as opposed to events, and which is consistently hypothetical, can, as well, be seen to exhibit signs of this correlation in the copular, and therefore stative, meaning it imposes on the clause preceding. A full treatment of these phenomena will, however, have to await another occasion.

References

Akatsuka, Noriko. 1997. On the co-construction of counterfactual reasoning. *Journal of Pragmatics* 28: 781-794

Carlson, Gregory. 1989. On the semantic composition of English generic sentences. *Properties, Types and Meaning*, vol. 2, ed. G. Chierchia, B. Partee, R. Turner, 167-92. Dordrecht: Kluwer.

Comrie, Bernard. 1986. Conditionals: a typology. *On conditionals*, ed. E. Traugott, A. Ter Meulen, J. Reilly, C. Ferguson, 77-102. Cambridge: Cambridge University Press.

Fujii, Seiko Yamaguchi. 1990. Counterfactual concessive conditionals in Japanese. *Japanese/Korean Linguistics*, ed. H. Hoji, 353-367. Stanford: Stanford Linguistics Association.

Hasada, Rie. 1997. Conditionals and counterfactuals in Japanese. *Language Sciences* 19:3:277-288.

Iatridou, Sabine. 2000. The grammatical ingredients of counterfactuality. *Linguistic Inquiry* 31:2:231-270.

Jacobsen, Wesley M. 1992. Are conditionals topics? The Japanese case. *The Joy of Grammar--A Festschrift in Honor of James D. McCawley* , ed. D. Brentari, G. Larson, and L. MacLeod, 131-160. Amsterdam: John Benjamins.

Jacobsen, Wesley M. 1996. Time, reality, and agentivity in Japanese negation. *Japanese/Korean Linguistics* , vol. 6, ed. N. Akatsuka, S. Iwasaki, S. Strauss, 169-186. Stanford: Center for Study of Language and Information.

Jacobsen, Wesley M. 1999. Aspects of hypothetical meaning in Japanese conditionals. *Function and Structure*, ed. A. Kamio and K. Takami, 83-122. Amsterdam: John Benjamins.

Lewis. 1973. *Counterfactuals*. Cambridge: Harvard University Press.

Masuoka, Takashi. 1993. Zyooken hyoogen to bun no gainen. *Nihongo no Zyooken Hyoogen*, ed. T. Masuoka, 23-39. Tokyo: Kurosio Publishers.

McCawley, James D. 1981. *Everything that Linguists Have Always Wanted to Know about Logic* (*but Were Ashamed to Ask)*. Chicago: University of Chicago Press.

Takubo, Yukinori. 1993. Danwa kanri riron ni yoru nihongo no hanzizitu zyookenbun. *Nihongo no Zyooken Hyoogen*, ed. T. Masuoka, 169-183. Tokyo: Kurosio Publishers.

Processing Japanese and Korean: Full Attachment versus Efficiency

WILLIAM O'GRADY, MICHIKO NAKAMURA & MISEON LEE
University of Hawaii at Manoa

1. Introduction

It is widely agreed in the literature on parsing that English sentences are built from 'left to right', more or less one word at a time (see, e.g., Frazier 1998:126 and the references cited there). In the words of Frazier (1987:561), 'perceivers incorporate each word of an input into a constituent structure representation of the sentence, roughly as [it] is encountered.' When it comes to SOV languages, however, there are two competing views. On the one hand, it has been suggested (e.g. Fodor & Inoue 1995:27) that each incoming word must be attached, as it is encountered, into the current phrase marker for the sentence. Fodor and Inoue refer to this as the Full Attachment Hypothesis.

18

(1)   The Full Attachment Hypothesis
       Each incoming word is attached, as it is encountered, into the
       whole current partial phrase marker for the sentence.

One way to implement this idea is to assume that an X-bar schema or
similar architectural blueprint defines a skeletal tree into which words and
phrases can be incorporated as they come into the processor (Yamashita
1997:184 considers such an idea). The example below helps illustrate how
a simple Korean/Japanese sentence might be formed in this manner.

(2)   Gakusei-ga hon-o   yon-da. (J)
       Haksayng-i chayk-ul ilk-ess-ta. (K)
       student-Nom book-Acc read-Pst
       'The student read a book.'

(3)   *Step 1*: Insertion of the subject argument into the X-bar template:

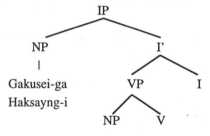

       Step 2: Insertion of the direct object into the X-bar template:

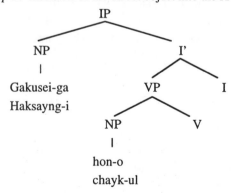

Step. 3: Insertion of the verb into the X-bar template:

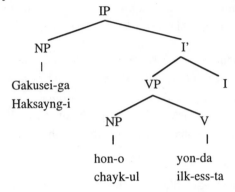

A contrasting view, which we favor, holds that there is no X-bar template and that arguments in SOV languages cannot be incorporated into the syntactic representation until the relevant functor (here the verb) becomes available. This is illustrated below.

(4) *Step one*: storage of the subject and direct object arguments until the verb becomes available:

N	N
gakusei-ga	hon-o
haksayng-i	chayk-ul

Step two: combination of the verb with its direct object argument. (For the sake of exposition, we take clauses to be verbal projections; our node labels indicate category membership, but not 'bar level'.)

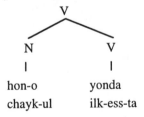

Step three: Combination of the resulting verbal phrase with the subject argument.

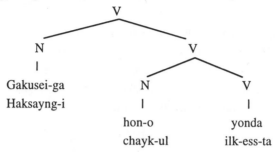

The intuition here is that pre-verbal arguments and adjuncts cannot be immediately incorporated into the syntactic representation, for the simple reason that there is not yet anything for them to combine with. This view, which is associated with so-called 'head-driven parsers', has previously been advocated for Japanese by Pritchett (1991), among others.

Notice that we do not require that ALL combinatorial operations be postponed until the end of a sentence in SOV languages. Rather, we propose only that elements are held 'in storage' until a category that they can combine with becomes available. Let us refer to this as the Efficiency Hypothesis.

(5)   The Efficiency Hypothesis
       The computational system prefers to carry out combinatorial
       operations at the first opportunity.

In the case of the simple sentence that we have been considering, the first opportunity to carry out a combinatorial operation happens not to occur until the end of the sentence, when the verb is encountered, so it is at this point that the sentence formation process commences. However, in sentences such as (6), an opportunity to carry out a combinatorial operation arises much earlier—since the genitive can combine with a nominal argument right after the noun to its right becomes available.

(6)   John-no tomodachi-ga sat-ta. (J)
       John-Gen friend-Nom   leave-Pst
       'John's friend left.'

The Efficiency Hypothesis allows—indeed prefers—that this particular operation take place at this point and not be postponed until the end of the sentence.

Fodor & Inoue (1995) offer several arguments in favor of the Full Attachment Hypothesis in Japanese, but their observations are in fact fully consistent with the Efficiency Hypothesis. For instance, they note that there is a 'rather strong' preference for the two adjectives in the following sentence to be interpreted as modifiers of the first noun *kutsu*.

(7)   toshitotta   takai   kutsu-no shuurinin
        old (animate) expensive shoe-Gen repairer

This in turn leads to a momentary surprise, since the inanimate *kutsu* 'shoe' cannot be modified by *toshitotta* 'old'. Crucially, however, this is also what the Efficiency Hypothesis would predict in this case, since the noun *kutsu* is the first element with which the sentence-initial adjectives could combine.

Along similar lines, Fodor & Inoue note that the (a) reading of (8) is preferred over the (b) reading.

(8)   kawaii shoojo-ga daiteita   ningyoo
        pretty girl-Nom was. holding doll
        a. 'the doll that the pretty girl was holding'
        b. 'the pretty doll that the girl was holding'

This too is expected on the Efficiency Hypothesis, since the first opportunity to combine the adjectival modifier *kawaii* 'pretty' with an argument arises when the nominal *shoojo* 'girl' is encountered.[1]

We believe that it is possible to do more than just defend the viability of the Efficiency Hypothesis, however. In the remainder of this paper, we will seek to provide evidence that actually favors this view of sentence building in SOV languages over the Full Attachment Hypothesis.

---

[1] Kamide & Mitchell (1999) put forward a different sort of argument in favor of full attachment for Japanese, following work by Koh (1997) for Korean. We address this argument in work currently in progress.

2. Quantifier Structures

As we see it, the best test of the competing claims made by the Full Attachment Hypothesis and the Efficiency Hypothesis comes from clausal structures in which the verb is preceded several dependents. If the Full Attachment Hypothesis is right, the verb's dependents should be incorporated into the syntactic representation as soon as they are encountered; on the other hand, if the Efficiency Hypothesis is right, this cannot happen until the verb becomes available.

In order to investigate this matter more deeply, we set out to examine the manner in which particular contrasting pairs of structures are processed. We will focus our attention on the contrast illustrated in (9).

(9) a. Genitive quantifier
Senshuu **sannin-no** kodomo-ga machi-de jitensha-o nusunda.
last.week three-Gen children-Nom town-in bike-Acc stole
'Last week, three children stole a bike in the town.'

  b. Floated quantifer
Senshuu kodomo-ga machi-de **sannin** jitensha-o nusunda.
last.week children-Nom town-in three bike-Acc stole
'Last week, three children stole a bike in the town.'

The structure of the (a) pattern in these examples is, as far as we know, uncontroversial: the genitive-marked quantifier combines with the nominal to its right, forming a phrase with which the verbal projection eventually combines.

(10)   [**Sannin-no** kodomo-ga] [machi-de jitensha-o nusunda].
    three-Gen children-Nom town-in bike-Acc stole

The analysis of the (b) pattern is also straightforward if we assume that floated quantifiers are dependents of the verb, as proposed by Dowty & Brodie (1984) and O'Grady (1991:211ff), among others. (Independent evidence for this view comes from the fact that floated quantifiers can bear the nominative and accusative case in Korean—a sign that they combine with a verbal projection (O'Grady 1991, Sells 1995).)

(11)   [Kodomo-ga [machi-de **sannin** jitensha-o nusunda]].
        children-Nom town-in three bike-Acc stole

This in turn leads to an interesting prediction. If the Efficiency Hypothesis is right in predicting that dependents of the verb must be held in storage until the verbal functor becomes available, then at the point at which the verb is encountered in the first pattern, three combinatorial operations must be carried out.

(12) i: Combination of the verb with its direct object argument:
         jitensha-o [nusunda]
           bike-Acc stole

    ii: Combination of the resulting verbal phrase with the locative:
         machi-de [jitensha-o nusunda]
         town-in bike-Acc stole

    iii: Combination of the resulting verbal phrase with the subject phrase:
          [**Sannin-no kodomo-ga**] [machi-de jitensha-o nusunda].
            three-Gen children-Nom town-in bike-Acc stole

In contrast, FOUR combinatorial operations are required in the case of the floated quantifier pattern, as (13) helps illustrate.

(13) i: Combination of the verb with its direct object argument:
         jitensha-o [nusunda]
           bike-Acc stole

    ii: Combination of the resulting verbal phrase with the floated quantifier:
         sannin [jitensha-o nusunda]
         three bike-Acc stole

iii: Combination of the resulting verbal phrase with the locative:
      machi-de [sannin jitensha-o nusunda].
      town-in   three   bike-Acc   stole

iv: Combination of the resulting verbal phrase with the subject:
      Kodomo-ga [machi-de sannin jitensha-o nusunda].
      children-Nom town-in   three   bike-Acc   stole

In principle, these differences—if indeed they exist—should be detectable: combinatorial operations must take place in real time and there are psycholinguistic techniques for measuring the amount of time that it takes to compute syntactic representations. One such widely used technique makes use of a self-paced word-by-word reading task (e.g. Yamashita 1997). Words are presented one at a time on a computer screen, and subjects press a key when they are ready for the next word or sentence. The computer automatically measures the amount of time that is spent on each word, giving a rough measure of processing time for each item in the sentence. If the Efficiency Hypothesis is right, the final position in floated quantifier patterns should require more processing time than the final position in genitive quantifier patterns, since one more combinatorial operation is required.

No such effect is expected if the Full Attachment Hypothesis is correct, however. Since this theory predicts that the major components of a sentence are incorporated into the syntactic representation as they are encountered, there is no reason to expect the sentence-final position to be associated with greater processing time in the floated quantifier pattern. Indeed, all other things being equal (see below), there should be no difference at all in the manner in which the latter part of the sentence is processed.

3. The Experiment

In an attempt to test the predictions of the Efficiency Hypothesis, we carried out a self-paced reading task with the help of PsyScope software (Cohen et al. 1993) run on a Macintosh G3 laptop computer. The test session began with procedural instructions that appeared on the computer screen. Subjects were instructed to read the sentences that were to follow as quickly as permitted by the demands of comprehension. They were also informed that they could not go back to earlier parts of the sentences and that there were no incomplete or ungrammatical sentences. They were then given three practice sentences before the actual test session began.

The key contrast involved the structure types illustrated in (14), corresponding to (9) above.

(14)a. Genitive quantifier
Senshuu **sannin-no** kodomo-ga machi-de jitensha-o nusunda.
last.week three-Gen children-Nom town-in bike-Acc stole
'Last week, three children stole a bike in the town.'

 b. Floated quantifer
Senshuu kodomo-ga machi-de **sannin** jitensha-o nusunda.
last.week children-Nom town-in three bike-Acc stole
'Last week, three children stole a bike in the town.'

There were five tokens of each type, which were interspersed among sentences of other types in order to guard against possible habituation effects.

In order to ensure that subjects were processing the test sentences, each item was immediately followed by a probe statement. Subjects were then asked to evaluate the truth of the probe statement against the test sentence.

Fifty-one Japanese-speaking subjects participated in the study. Only the results from the forty-six subjects who responded correctly to the probe statement at least 80% of time were used for subsequent analysis.

4. Results

Table 1 presents the mean processing profiles for the two quantifier patterns. (In reporting our results, we ignore the processing time associated with the sentence-initial time adjuncts that occur in each of our test items. W = word)

	W1	W2	W3	W4	W5	W6
Gen. Quant.	764	784	814	746	653	**611**
Floated Quant.	760	850	795	745	725	**660**

TABLE 1 Response times (in msecs.) for each position in the test sentences

As can be seen here, more processing time was required at the position of the verb in the floated quantifier pattern than in the genitive quantifier pattern. A one-way repeated measures ANOVA (within-subjects) revealed that this difference was significant ($F=5.05$, $df(45,1)$, $p=.03$). This accords with the predictions of the Efficiency Hypothesis, but runs against the expectations of the Full Attachment Hypothesis.[2]

An especially interesting feature of this contrast is that it apparently cannot be attributed to a frequency or markedness effect. Indeed, Kim (1995:223) reports that the floated quantifier pattern in Japanese is more frequent than the genitive quantifier in colloquial discourse, although the situation is reversed in 'formal writing'. Yet, the floated quantifier pattern requires significantly greater processing time, as we have seen. This is just what one would expect if its formation requires an additional combinatorial operation after the verb becomes available, as the Efficiency Hypothesis predicts.

Of course, there is always the danger that there is something about the semantics of the floated quantifier pattern that accounts for the greater processing time—after all, as is commonly observed, the genitive quantifier and floated quantifier patterns differ subtly in meaning.

One way to guard against this possibility is to consider a variety of structural pairs that differ in the number of combinatorial operations that take place when the verb is encountered. Although these other structural contrasts may well be associated with semantic differences of their own, the precise nature of these differences will vary from structure to structure.

---

[2]As far as can see, neither theory offers an explanation for why a significant difference between the two patterns is also manifested in the preverbal position (W5).

Thus, the more often we find the predicted processing contrast, the less likely that it can be attributed to a particular semantic effect.

Our work in this area is ongoing, but we are able to discuss here one other structure which lends itself to the sort of comparison that is relevant to our thesis. Consider in this regard the well known genitive/nominative alternation illustrated in the following example.

(15)   Hanako-**no/ga**   taichoo-ga   warui(-koto).
        Hanako-Gen/Nom health-Nom bad
        '(the fact that) Hanako's health is bad.'

On standard assumptions, the genitive-marked possessor combines directly with the nominal to its right, so that only one combinatorial operation is required to form the clause when the verb becomes available.

(16)   The verb combines with the previously formed subject phrase:
        [[**Hanako-no taichoo-ga**] warui](-koto).
        Hanako-Gen health-Nom   bad

In contrast, as the case marking and other tests help show (see, e.g., Saito 1985 and many others), the nominative-marked possessor is a clause-level dependent. It therefore has the structure illustrated in (17).

(17)   [Hanako-ga [taichoo-ga warui]](-koto)

This in turn implies that two combinatorial operations are needed to form the double nominative sentence after the verb becomes available.

(18)i.   The verb combines with the closer nominal:
        taichoo-ga [warui(-koto)].
        health-Nom   bad

   ii.   The resulting verbal phrase combines with the more distant nominal:
        Hanako-ga [taichoo-ga warui(-koto)].
        Hanako-Nom   health-Nom   bad

We therefore predict that more processing time will be required at the position of the verb in the case of the 'double nominative' pattern than in the case of the 'genitive-nominative' pattern. Working with the same technique and the same subjects, we found this to be true—significantly greater processing time was required at the clause-final position in the double nominative pattern (F=11.45, df(45m1), p=.001).[3]

On the other hand, we feel compelled to report that we have thus far been unable to replicate our quantifier pattern results in Korean. In considering Korean, we focused on sentence types such as the following, in which the contrast between a genitive quantifier and a floated quantifier is manifested in the first conjunct of a coordinate constructions. (This was to allow us to investigate processing time contrasts with verbs that do not occur sentence-finally.) There were five tokens of each type, interspersed among twenty-five other sentences not relevant to the current study.

(19)a. Genitive quantifier

[Eceyspam-ey sey myeng-uy chinkwu-tul-i   wuli cip-eyse
  last.night-at three person-Gen friend-Pl-Nom our house-at
yenghwa-lul po-ko] [pamnuckey swukcey-lul   hay-ss-ta].
movie-Ac see-and   night.late homework-Ac do-Pst-Decl
'Last night three friends watched a movie at our house and did
their homework late at night.'

b. Floated quanitifer

[Eceyspam-ey   chinkwu-tul-i wuli cip-eyse sey myeng-i
  lastnight-at   friend-Pl-Nom our house-at three person-Nom
yenghwa-lul po-ko] [pamnuckey swukcey-lul   hay-ss-ta].
movie-Ac see-and   night.late   homework-Ac do-Pst-Decl
'Last night three friends watched a movie at our house and did
their homework late at night.'

---

[3]It should perhaps be noted, however, that the double nominative pattern is more marked in Japanese than its genitive nominative counterpart and that this too may be reflected in our processing time data.

Using the same technique employed for Japanese, we carried out a self-paced reading task with thirty-three Korean-speaking subjects. Although the floated quantifier patterns manifested a slightly longer processing time at the position of the verb in the first clause, the difference was not statistically significant.

5. Conclusion

If the results reported here for Japanese stand up and are eventually extended to other languages and other patterns, then the processing of SVO languages and the processing of SOV languages are alike in certain respects and different in certain respects. They are alike in that sentence formation in both types of languages is 'efficient'; that is, the computational system prefers to carry out combinatorial operations at the first opportunity. However, the two types of languages differ in terms of when this opportunity arises. In the case of SVO languages, the relatively early occurrence of the verb in the clause allows immediate incorporation of its arguments and modifiers into the syntactic representation in most sentences. In contrast, the head-final character of SOV languages forces a delay in the computation of syntactic structure. Although this delay can perhaps not be discerned intuitively, it is manifested in the processing profiles associated with self-paced reading tasks, as we have seen.

We look to further research involving this and other paradigms for additional insights in the manner in which the world's two major language types are processed and the possible relevance of these findings for our understanding of how language in general works.

References

Cohen, J., B. MacWhinney, M. Flatt & J. Provost. 1993. PsyScope: An Interactive Graphic System for Designing and Controlling Experiments in the Psychology Laboratory using Macintosh Computers. *Behavior Research Methods, Instruments and Computers* 25:257-271.

Dowty, D. & B. Brody. 1984. A Semantic Analysis of Floated Quantifiers in Transformationless Grammar. *Proceedings of the West Coast Conference on Formal Linguistics* 3.

Frazier, L. 1987. Sentence Processing: A Tutorial Review. *Attention and Performance XII: The Psychology of Reading*, ed. M. Coltheart, 559-86. Hillsdale, NJ.

Frazier, L. 1998. Getting there (slowly). *Journal of Psycholinguistic Research* 27:123-46.

Inoue, A. & J. D. Fodor. 1995. Information-Based Parsing of Japanese. *Japanese Sentence Processing*, eds. R. Mazuka & N. Nagai, 9-63. Erlbaum.

Kamide, Y. & D. Mitchell. 1999. Incremental Pre-Head Attachment in Japanese Parsing. *Language and Cognitive Processes* 14:631-62.

Kim, A. H.-O. 1995. Word Order at the Noun Phrase Level in Japanese. Word order in discourse, eds. P. Downing & M. Noonan, 199-246. Philadelphia: Benjamins.

Koh, S. 1997. The Resolution of the Dative NP Ambiguity in Korean. *Journal of Psycholinguistic Research* 26:265-73.

O'Grady, W. 1991. *Categories and Case: The Sentence Structure of Korean*. Philadelphia: Benjamins.

Pritchett, B. 1991. Head Position and Parsing Ambiguity. *Journal of Psycholinguistic Research* 20:251-70.

Saito, M. 1985. Some Asymmetries in Japanese and Their Theoretical Implications. Doctoral dissertation, MIT.

Sells, P. 1995. Korean and Japanese Morphology from a Lexical Perspective. *Linguistic Inquiry* 26, 277-325.

Yamashita, H. 1997. The Effects of Word Order and Case Marking Information on the Processing of Japanese. *Journal of Psycholinguistic Research* 26:163-88.

Japanese and Korean Causatives Revisited*

MASAYOSHI SHIBATANI & SUNG YEO CHUNG

*Center for Advanced Studies in the Behavioral Sciences, Kobe University &
Japan Society for the Promotion of Science, Osaka University*

1. Introduction

Controversies over Japanese and Korean causatives have centered on two major
issues. On the Japanese side, there has been a continuing debate between
Miyagawa (1980, 1989) and Kuroda (1981, 1990) whether productive *sase*
causative derivation is best treated as a syntactic phenomenon or as a case of
lexical word formation. On the Korean side, the controversy has centered on the
semantics of the two types of causative form, the lexically restricted *-i/-hi/-li/-ki*

---

*During this tenth anniversary meeting of the J/K Conference dedicated to James D.
McCawley, we learned that Professor In-Soek Yang also passed away this spring. We were
deeply saddened by the news, as Professor Yang was one of the pioneer Korean linguists who
worked on Korean causatives and other topics in the generative framework, and who inspired
our work, especially Shibatani's early work, on Korean. We wish to dedicate this work to the
memories of Jim McCawley and In-Seok Yang, to whom we are greatly indebted both profes-
sionally and personally. This paper was prepared while the first named author was a Fellow at
the Center for Advanced Study in the Behavioral Sciences at Stanford, California. We are
grateful for the financial support provided by Center general funds.

forms and the productive periphrastic *–key ha-ta* forms. The issue here has been whether these two types of causative form can be considered synonymous or not. This paper directly addresses the issues relating to the controversy on the Korean side, but the discussion has important implications for the proper interpretation of the phenomena relevant to the general treatment of Japanese causatives. A new analysis of these relevant phenomena is proposed.

2. Direct vs. indirect causation

Shibatani (1973b) distinguished two principal types of causative situation. Manipulative causation involves an agentive causer and a patient causee; the causer typically has to bring about the caused event by physically manipulating the causee. Directive causation, on the other hand, involves two agents, both causer and causee being agentive. In this paper, we shall use the more popular terms of direct and indirect causation by unambiguously defining them in terms of the nature of the causee involved in a causative situation, as we have done above. That is, the term 'direct causation' is used in reference to a situation where an agentive causer and a patient causee are involved, and the term 'indirect causation' in reference to a situation involving an agentive causer and an agentive causee.

One of the major points made by Shibatani (1973a, 1973b, 1973c, 1976) was that in both Japanese and Korean, lexical causatives convey direct (i.e., manipulative) causation, whereas the productive *sase*-forms in Japanese and the periphrastic *-key ha-ta* forms in Korean express indirect (i.e., directive) causation. This generalization obtains true to a large extent, as indicated by the following contrastive pairs of examples and their English translations:

(1) a. Hahaoya-ga kodomo-ni huku-o   kise-ta.
     mother-NOM   child-DAT   clothes-ACC put on-PAST
     'Mother put the clothes on the child.'
   b. Hahaoya-ga kodomo-ni huku-o   kisa-se-ta.
     mother-NOM child-DAT clothes-ACC put on-CAUS-PAST
     'Mother made the child put on the clothes.'
(2) a. emeni-ka   ai-eykey pang-eyse os-ul   ip-hi-ess-ta.
     mother-NOM child-DAT room-in   clothes-ACC wear-CAUS-PAST-IND
     'Mother put the clothes on the child in the room.'
   b. emeni-ka   ai-eykey pang-eyse os-ul   ip-key   ha-yess-ta.
     mother-NOM child-DAT room-in   clothes-ACC wear-COMP do-PAST-IND
     'Mother made the child put on the clothes in the room.'

Evidence of this kind was the basis for Shibatani's (1973c) argument against Yang's (1972) claim that Korean lexical causatives (Yang's short-form causatives) and periphrastic causatives (Yang's long-form causatives) are synonymous and that both forms are accordingly to be derived from the same embedding underlying structure. Although presumably no one seriously accepts Yang's synonymy hypothesis anymore (see Song's (1988) summary of various opinions on this issue), Shibatani's original framework based on the manipulative-directive (or the direct-indirect) contrast is insufficient in explicating the nature of the following kind of Korean expressions, where lexical causatives express situations clearly involving two agents.

(3) emeni-ka   khun ai-lul   kel-li-ko   cakun ai-nun
     mogther-NOM big   child-ACC walk-CAUS-CONJ small   child-TOP
     tung-ey   ep-ko   cang-ey   ka-ss-ta.
     back-LOC carry-CONJ market-LOC go-PAST
     'Mother went to the market making the big child walk and carrying the
     younger child on her back.'
(4) emeni-ka   ai-eykey   kulca-lul   hanahana ciphe-ka-mye
     mother-NOM child-DAT letter-ACC one-by-one point-go-while
     chayk-ul   ilk-hi-ess-ta.
     book-ACC read-CAUS-PAST
     'Mother made the child read the book by pointing to the letters one-by-one.'

These examples unambiguously show that the equation of 'lexical causatives = direct (or manipulative) causation' breaks down.[1] It is on the basis of these examples that Yang (1974, 1976) and Song (1988) make a claim that Korean lexical causatives do express indirect causation (hence they are synonymous to the periphrastic counterparts according to Yang). In this paper we will argue that these expressions are in fact not a case of indirect causation, and that they represent another category of causative situation that is intermediate between direct and indirect causative situations.

3. Sociative causation

Examples (3) and (4) describe situations in which the causer agent participates in or attends to the activity of the causee agent in a more direct way than in indirect causative situations. The typical situation (3) represents is the one where the mother takes the child's hand and walks with him. By the same token, example (4) depicts a situation where the mother sits next to the child and

---

[1] See Shibatani (1973a, 1976) for other cases in which this equation and the other equation of 'productive causatives = indirect causation' break down.

makes the child read under her supervision. The contrast between these cases and typical indirect causative situations can be clearly seen in the following pair of lexical and periphrastic causative sentences.

(5) a. sensayngnim-i   haksayngtul-ul yek-kkaci kel-li-ess-ta.
       teacher.HON-NOM students-ACC   station-to walk-CAUS-PAST-IND
       'The teacher walked (marched) the students to the station.'
    b. sensayngnim-i   haksayngtul-ul yek-kkaci ket-key   ha-yess-ta.
       teacher.HON-NOM students-ACC   station-to walk-COMP do-PAST-IND
       'The teacher made the students walk to the station.'

The situation most aptly described by (5a) is the one where the teacher actually leads the students all the way to the station. Even if the teacher does not walk himself, he is still likely to be accompanying the students on a bicycle or in a car with a watchful eye on them. In the case of (5b), on the other hand, the teacher only needs to make sure that the students walk to the station; he may stay at school after giving the instructions to the students.

Although some Korean -i/-hi/-li/-ki forms do express situations involving an agentive causer and an agentive causee, they represent well-definable situations that are distinct from the typical indirect causative situation, in which the causing event and the caused event need not show spatio-temporal overlap. The causative situations under discussion are both similar to and distinct from direct and indirect causation. They are similar to indirect causation in that they involve two agents—an agentive causer and an agentive causee—but are distinct from it in that the causer actively participates in the execution of the caused event. They are similar to direct causation in that the causing event and the caused event typically show spatio-temporal overlap, but are distinct from it in involving two agents.

This intermediate causative situation was first recognized by Pardeshi (1999) and was christened 'sociative causation' by Shibatani and Pardeshi (to appear), where the three types of causative situation (direct, sociative, and indirect causation) were given theoretical status as the three focal points along the continuum of the directness dimension of the causative semantics. In this paper we attempt to establish the significance of this intermediate causative type in the description of Japanese and Korean causatives. Particularly important is the bearing it has on the adverbial modification pattern and on the antecedent-reflexive construal pattern, phenomena that have played an important role in the description of causative constructions. Before going into detail, let us distinguish the three types of sociative causative below, which can be recognized in Korean as well.

(6) Hahaoya-ga kodomo-o asoba-se-te   i-ru. (Joint-action)
     mother-NOM child-ACC   play-CAUS-CONJ be-PRES
     'Mother is making the child play.'
(7) Hahaoya-ga kodomo-ni osikko-o sa-se-te   iru. (Assistive)
     mother-NOM child-DAT   pee-ACC do-CAUS-CONJ be-PRES
     'Mother is making the child pee.'
(8) Hahaoya-ga kodomo-ni hon-o   yoma-se-te   i-ru. (Supervision)
     mother-NOM child-DAT   book-ACC read-CAUS-CONJ be-PRES
     'Mother is making the child read a book.'

In (6), it is most likely that the mother is also playing with the child, though the supervision reading is also possible. (7) depicts a situation where the mother is helping the child to pee by pulling the pants down or by holding the child, when it is still small. (8) conveys a situation where the mother is supervising the child, who is reading. Although the mother is not as physically involved in the execution of the caused event as in the case of the joint-action and the assistive sociative, she is most likely physically close to the child reading a book. There is, however, a possibility of long-distance supervision. For example, in (8) the mother could be sitting at the door outside the room.

As the discussion above makes clear, sociative causatives themselves form a continuum along the directness dimension of the causative semantics. The joint-action sociative is closer to direct causation in that the causer is totally involved in the execution of the caused event. The assistive causative entails partial involvement of the causer in the achievement of the caused event. On the other hand, the supervision sociative is closer in meaning to indirect causation in that here the causer plays a more detached role in the execution of the caused event. Sociative causatives, thus, provide a gradual transition from direct causation to indirect causation.

Notice that in Japanese it is the productive *sase*-causatives that express sociative causation, whereas in Korean it is the lexically restricted *-i/-hi/-li/-ki* forms that are used in the expression of sociative causation. This difference will turn out to be significant in the subsequent theoretical discussion.

3. Aspectual correlates

Though the productive *sase*-forms are used in Japanese for both sociative and indirect causation, the sociative/indirect distinction manifests clearly when the *–te iru* progressive form is used. The forms in (6)-(8) are unambiguously interpreted as sociatives. The *ni*-causative in (9a) below is likely to be interpreted as a case of indirect causation (see next section on the relevance of case marking). Converting it to the progressive form results in an odd sentence if interpreted as a normal indirect causative sentence, as seen in (9b).

(9) a. Hahaoya-wa kodomo-ni kooen-de asoba-se-ta.
　　　mother-TOP　child-DAT　park-at　play-CAUS-PAST
　　　'Mother had the child play in the park.'
　　b. ??Hahaoya-wa kodomo-ni kooen-de asoba-se-te　　　iru.
　　　mother-TOP　child-DAT　park-at　play-CAUS-CONJ be-PRES
　　　'Mother is having the child play in the park.'

It the case of sociative causation, it is possible and natural for a causer to be engaged for a prolonged time in the causing activity, e.g., undertaking the caused event jointly or supervising the causee. Notice here that the causee is simultaneously executing the caused event, and thus a causative situation obtains as the causer performs the causing activity. In the case of indirect causation, however, the caused event typically takes place after the causing event of direction-giving is completed. One can imagine a situation where a causer is giving long directions to a causee, which can conceivably be repre-sented by the progressive aspect. But it is not possible to construe such a situation as causative, because the caused event has not been realized at the time of direction giving. This prevents the causative progressive expression –sase-te iru from conveying indirect causation.

The only possible interpretation of the –te i-ru form as expressing indi-rect causation is a generic one, where the causation takes place as a routine over a certain period of time. Under this interpretation (9b) sounds natural, especially together with an adverb like *saikin* 'recently' in sentence initial position. In other words, while the –te i-ru form allows both progressive and generic interpretations when sociative causation is involved, it allows only the generic reading when indirect causation is expressed.

A similar pattern appears to obtain in Korean, as indicated by the fol-lowing contrast:

(10) a. emeni-ka　　ai-lul/-ekey　　chayk-ul　ilk-hi-ko　　　　iss-ta.
　　　mother-NOM child-ACC/DAT book-ACC read-CAUS-CONJ be-IND
　　　'Mother is making the child read the book.'
　　b. ??emeni-ka　　ai-lul/ekey　　chayk-ul　ilk-key　　ha-ko　　iss-ta.
　　　mother-NOM child-ACC/DAT book-ACC read-COMP do-CONJ be-IND
　　　'Mother is having the child read the book.'

4. Case marking of the causee nominal

Traditionally differential case marking of the causee nominal in terms of the dative and the accusative case was analyzed in relation to the nature of the causee. The dative case is used to mark a willing causee, whereas the accusative marks a coercively induced causee (see Kuroda (1965) and Shibatani (1973a)). Yet, it is clear from the following pairs of sentences that the *o/ni* distinction in Japanese correlates significantly with the sociative/indirect distinction.

(11) a. Hahaoya-wa kodomo-o kooen-de asoba-se-ta. (Sociative)
      mother-TOP   child-ACC park-in   play-CAUS-PAST
      'Mother made the child play in the park.'
  b. Hahaoya-wa kodomo-ni kooen-de asoba-se-ta. (Indirect)
      mother-TOP   child-DAT park-in   play-CAUS-PAST
      'Mother had the child play in the park.'

The fact that the *–te iru* progressive form requires the *o*-causative also corroborates our finding here (cf. (6) and (9b)). Korean also seems to reflect the distinction in point, as indicated below, where the sociative version prefers the accusative marking, but both dative and accusative marking are equally natural in the case of indirect causation.[2]

(12) a. emeni-ka   ai-lul/$^{??}$-eykey   kongwuen-eyse kel-li-ess-ta.
      motherNOM child-ACC/-DAT park-in   walk-CAUSE-PAST-IND
      'Mother made the child walk in the park.' (Sociative)
  b. emeni-ka   ai-lul/-eykey   kongwuen-eyse ket-key   ha-yess-ta.
      mother-NOM child-ACC/-DAT park-in   walk-COMP do-PAST-IND
      'Mother had the child walk in the park.' (Indirect)

5. Adverbial modification

The pattern of adverbial modification was important in Shibatani's (1973a, 1973b, 1973c, 1976) arguments against deriving lexical causatives from a complex embedding underlying structure and for deriving the *sase-* and *-key ha-ta* causatives from an embedding underlying structure. The argument was based on a contrast similar to the one observed in the following and the parallel Korean examples:

---

[2] In the case of transitive based *–i/-hi/-li/-ki* forms, the distinction is less clear. In Japanese the *o/ni* contrast does not obtain in transitive-based causatives.

(13) Frequentive adverb

a. Hahaoya-wa kodomo-o yonaka-ni san-kai   okosi-ta. (Direct)
   mother-TOP   child-ACC night-at   three-times wake up-PAST
   'Mother woke up the child three times at night.'

b. Hahaoya-wa kodomo-ni yonaka-ni san-kai   oki-sase-ta. (Indirect)
   mother-TOP   child-DAT night-at   three-times wake up-CAUS-PAST
   'Mother had the child wake up three times at night.'

The difference in the scope of adverbial modification would be easily accounted for if an embedding underlying structure were posited for the *sase*-indirect form, as shown below:

(14) a. [hahaoya-ga yonaka-ni san-kai [kodomo-ga oki-] sase-ta]
     b. [hahaoya-ga [kodomo-ga yonaka-ni san-kai oki-] sase-ta]

If a simplex structure were assumed for the lexical, direct causative form, we would not expect the ambiguous interpretation of adverbial modification to obtain. But the problem is that it is not always the case that *sase*-causatives permit ambiguous readings. For example, both joint-action and assistive sociatives necessarily require place and time adverbs to specify that the causing and the caused event both take place in the same location and at the same time. The normal supervision sociative also exhibits the same pattern of modification, whereas a long-distance supervision sociative permits a place adverb to modify only the caused event as in the following example.

(15) Hahaoya-wa kodomo-ni attino   heya-de hon-o   yoma-se-te
     mother-TOP   child-DAT over.there room-in book-ACC read-CAUS-CONJ
     i-ru.
     be-PRES
     'Mother is making the child read the book in the room over there.'

As for manner adverbs, joint-action sociatives behave differently from the assistive and the supervision sociatives. In the former, the causer and the causee are engaged in a joint action, and accordingly a manner adverb cannot modify the causing event and the caused event separately. The adverb in an assistive form is most likely to be interpreted as modifying the manner of the causer, whereas the one in a supervision sociative form can modify the caused event. Frequentive adverbs also show different readings depending on the type of sociative causative. They modify both the causing and the caused event in both joint-action and assistive sociative types, whereas in the supervision type they may modify either both the causing event and the caused event or only the caused event.

The discussion above shows that the pattern of adverbial modification is not uniform throughout all the *sase*-causative forms. This by itself is not a problem for the embedding analysis of these forms. One only needs to stipulate that the adverbial modification works differently depending on the type of causation expressed and that the existence of an embedded clause does not automatically guarantee that an adverb can modify that clause separately from the main clause. The situation is more problematic in Korean, however, where the lexical causatives express sociative causation.

The standard arguments, as advanced by Shibatani (1973c) for example, have it that while periphrastic *–key ha-ta* forms allow the reading in which the relevant adverbs modify either both the causing and the caused event or only the caused event, lexical *–i/-hi/-li/-ki* forms do not allow the interpretation where the adverbs modify only the caused event, for in the latter there is claimed to be no embedded clause for the adverbs to be uniquely associated with. This contrast obtains in the standard direct and indirect causatives, as observed in (2a) and (2b).

As pointed out by Song (1988), however, there are lexical causatives that allow the interpretation where an adverb modifies only the caused event. Song (1988: 195, 197) gives the following examples, among others.[3]

(16) a. ku i-ka   halwu-ey ney pen ssik yak-ul
      that person-NOM one day-in four times each medicine-ACC
      mek-i-ess-ta.
      take-CAUS-PAST-IND
      'He/She made [the patient] take the medicine four times a day.'
   b. emeni-ka   ai-lul   kilka-eyse ocwum-ul nwu-i-ess-ta.
      mother-NOM child-ACC road side-at urine-ACC pee-CAUS-PAST-IND
      'Mother made the child urinate at the roadside.'

As for (16a), Song tells us that if *ku i* 'that person' is understood as a nurse, it is likely that she helps the patient take the medicine four times a day. But if *ku i* 'that person' is understood to be a physician, the most likely interpretation is that the adverb modifies only the caused event of the pa-

---

[3] Song (1988) also uses duration adverbs to make his point that lexical causatives allow adverbs to modify the caused states. But this is a well-known fact from the discussion of generative semanticists, who have shown that lexical causatives allow a duration adverb to modify the resulting state with an example such as *The sheriff of Nottingham jailed Robin Hood for three years.*

tient's taking the medicine. (16b) also allows similar interpretations—both the mother and the child could be at the roadside, or only the child. Rather than interpreting these expressions as a case of indirect causation, as Song (1988) does, we would interpret these as cases of sociative causation. When a nurse is involved in (16a), it is a case of assistive sociative, and we expect the frequentive adverb to modify both the causing event and the caused event. On the other hand, when a doctor's involvement is stipulated, we have a case of long-distance supervision sociative, which allows an adverb to modify only the caused event, as we saw earlier with Japanese examples. (16b) is similar.

Although our interpretation of the fact differs from Song's (1988) and although we maintain that lexical *–i/-hi/-li/-ki* forms do not express the normal indirect causation, the fact that these lexical causatives do allow an adverb to modify the caused event is a serious challenge to the analysis of the adverbial modification pattern in terms of simplex vs. embedding structure. That is, it undermines the arguments for the embedding analysis of *sase-*causatives and *–key ha-ta* causatives based on the adverbial modification pattern. The upshot is that the forms of the causatives do not correlate with the pattern of adverbial modification straightforwardly and that what is crucial is the types of causative situation different forms express. A similar conclusion can be drawn from the construal pattern of the reflexives.

6. Construal of the reflexives

In the history of the generative study of causative constructions, the pattern of antecedent-reflexive relations has played a significant role. It provided important data for Shibatani (1972, 1973c), for example, for analyzing lexical causatives and productive causatives (*sase-* and *–key ha-ta* forms) differently. As in the case of the adverbial modification pattern, the phenomenon is straightforward when a maximum distinction between direct and indirect causation obtains, as in the following examples.

(17) a. Ai-ga   Hana-ni   zibun-no heya-de huku-o   kise-ta. (Direct)
        Ai-NOM Hana-DAT self-of   room-at clothes-ACC put on-PAST
        'Ai$_i$ put the clothes on Hana$_j$ in self's$_{i/*j}$ room.'
     b. Ai-ga   Hana-ni· zibun-no heya-de huku-o   ki-sase-ta. (Indir.)
        Ai-NOM Hana-DAT self-of   room-at clothes-ACC put on-CAUS-PAST
        'Ai$_i$ made Hana$_j$ put on the clothes in self's$_{i/j}$ room.'

With the understanding that only a grammatical subject antecedes the reflexive *zibun* 'self' in Japanese, the fact observed above is accountable straightforwardly if we posit the following structures for the respective sentences.

(18) a. [Ai-ga Hana-ni zibun-no heya-de huku-o kise-ta] (17a)
    b. [Ai-ga [Hana-ga zibun-no heya-de huku-o ki-]sase-ta] (17b)

Again, sociative causatives present situations where *sase*-forms do not align with indirect causatives in a straightforward manner, despite the fact the same morphology is involved. Observe the contrast between the indirect causative and the joint-action sociative form below:

(19) a. Ai-ga   Hana-ni   zibun-no heya-de asoba-se-ta. (Indirect)
       Ai-NOM Hana-DAT self-of   room-at play-CAUS-PAST
       'Ai$_i$ made Hana$_j$ play in self's$_{i/j}$ room.' (Ai told Hana to go play.)
    b. Ai-ga   Hana-o   zibun-no heya-de asoba-se-te
       Ai-NOM Hana-ACC self-of   room-at play-CAUS-CONJ
       i-ru. (Joint-action; Ai is playing with Hana.)
       be-PRES
       'Ai$_i$ is making Hana$_j$ play in self's$_{i/*j}$ room.'

The joint-action sociative form in (b) above does not permit the interpretation in which *zibun* 'self' refers to the causee Hana.

    Joint-action and assistive sociatives pattern alike in not allowing the causee nominal to antecede the reflexive.

(20) Assistive sociatives
a. Hana-wa Ken-ni zibun-no heya-de gohan-o tAbe-sase-te   i-ru.
   Hana-TOP Ken-DAT self-of   room-in meal-ACC eat-CAUS-CONJ be-PRES
   'Hana$_i$ is making Ken$_j$ eat the meal in self's$_{i/*j}$ room.'
b. Hana-wa Ken-ni   zibun-no kutu-o   haka-se-te   i-ru.
   Hana-TOP Ken-DAT self-of   shoes-ACC put on-CAUS-CONJ be-PRES
   'Hana$_i$ is making Ken$_j$ put on self's$_{i/*j}$ shoes.'

    One must take care in interpreting the assistive forms above, because they are also construable as supervision sociatives. For the assistive interpretation, one must imagine a situation where the causer is manually helping the causee to execute the caused event; e.g., a situation in which Hana was physically helping Ken to eat the meal for (20a). Under such an interpretation, the causer nominal is the only one that can antecede *zibun*. But if this sentence is understood as a long-distance supervision sociative, where Hana simply supervises Ken to eat at some distance, either the causer or the causee nominal can antecede the reflexive. A clearer supervision sociative is given below where, unlike joint-action and assistive sociatives, either the causer or the causee nominal can control the reflexive.

(21) Supervision sociative
    Hana-wa Ken-ni   zibun-no asi-o   teineini   arawa-se-te
    Hana-TOP Ken-DAT self-of   foot-ACC meticulously wash-CAUS-CONJ
    i-ru.
    be-PRES
    'Hana$_i$ is making Ken$_j$ wash self's$_{i/j}$ feet meticulously.'

The data above show the alignment of direct causatives, joint-action so-ciatives, and assistive sociatives on the one hand, and indirect causatives and supervision sociatives on the other. What is interesting and problematic for morphologically based analysis of Japanese causatives is the fact that this alignment crosses the lexical/*sase*-causative boundary. The division here harkens back to our earlier discussion on the directness continuum. Joint-action and assistive sociatives, though they both involve the *sase*-form, are similar to direct causation, expressed by lexical causatives, in that they all entail direct physical involvement of the causer in the execution of the caused event. The caused event here is not an autonomous event free of the direct involvement of the causer. Supervision sociatives, on the other hand, are like indirect causation in that they both entail an autonomous caused event free of physical intervention by the causer. The distinction drawn here can be seen more clearly in the following event structure diagrams.

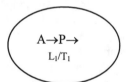

Fig. 1 Direct causation

Fig. 2 Joint-action/assistive
sociatives

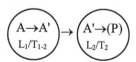

Fig. 3 Supervision sociatives

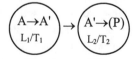

Fig. 4 Indirect causation

An arrow in the diagrams above represents an event segment, which is a potential unit for an autonomous event to be encoded by a verb. Representation $A{\rightarrow}A'{\rightarrow}P$ indicates a transitive action chain, such that A's action carries over to the event segment involving A' and P. This is in fact what happens when A engages himself in direct causation or joint-action or assistive sociative causation. For example, if A kills P ($A{\rightarrow}P{\rightarrow}$), A's causing action carries over to P's dying event ($P{\rightarrow}$). Similarly, if A assists A' to act on P in an assistive situation, A's causing action ($A{\rightarrow}A'$) carries over to the caused event by A' ($A'{\rightarrow}P$). This spatio-temporal overlap between the causing and the caused event is indicated by the L_1/T_1 specification shared by the relevant event segments.

In the case of supervision causation, it is typically the case that the causer is in the causee's proximity (unless it is long-distance supervision). Despite this physical proximity between the causer and the causee, the caused event is accorded its own spatial specification, as there is a physical separation between the causer and the caused event. There is, however, a partial temporal overlap between the two relevant events here. In indirect causation the causing and the caused event are accorded with their own temporal and spatial specifications, though it is possible that they overlap spatially.

In this paper we propose to analyze the reflexive phenomenon in terms of the event structures associated with different types of causation. In doing so, we must define possible protagonists that can control the reflexive. All event participants such as A (agent) and P (patient) are potential reflexive-controlling protagonists. But there is a dominance relation such that when A and P co-occur in an event segment, the former outranks the latter. When two A's are involved as in the first segments in Figs. 3 and 4, the initial A is dominant. Although the second segments in Figs. 1 and 2 have potential protagonists P and A', they are dominated by the initial A, as it is also involved in these segments because of the transitivity of A's actions. On the other hand, the second event segments in Figs. 3 and 4 are autonomous in the sense that they are not dominated by the initial A; hence the A' participant in these event segments functions as a protagonist capable of controlling the reflexive. In other words, whereas there is only one reflexive-controlling protagonist in Figs. 1 and 2, there are two such protagonists in Figs. 3 and 4.

The hierarchy determining the dominance relation reflects degrees of cognitive salience different event participants have. The initial agent of an action chain is most salient since it is responsible for the occurrence of the entire event. An agent of an event segment is more salient than a patient because the former also holds the key to the realization of that sub-event.

Thus P is least salient among these event participants. With these under-standings, we can now formulate the rule of reflexive construal.

(22) <u>Reflexive construal rule (first approximation)</u>
A protagonist controls the reflexive unless it is dominated by a more salient protagonist.
(•Protagonist salience hierarchy: Initial $A > A' > P$[4]
•A protagonist is dominated by a more salient protagonist when both occur in the same event segment.)

In direct causative and joint-action sociative as well as assistive causative expressions, there is only one controller of the reflexive, namely the initial agent of the entire action chain corresponding to the causer; hence in these expressions, the reflexive form is uniquely controlled by the causer nominal (see (17a), (19b), and (20)). In supervision and indirect causative expres-sions, on the other hand, there are two protagonist candidates for the con-troller of the reflexive; hence the possibility of an ambiguous reading arises in these expressions (see (17b) and (21)).

One of the most interesting aspects of the reflexive phenomenon is con-cerned with the notion of autonomous event segment. In both supervision and indirect causation, the caused event is normally autonomous in the sense that it is free from the most dominant protagonist, the initial agent; and thus its protagonist (the causee) controls the reflexive, as in (17b) and (21). Nev-ertheless, it is possible that a dominant protagonist (the causer) involves himself in the caused event, when, for example, he stays in a specific loca-tion where the caused event takes place. Under such circumstances, the caused event is not free of a dominant protagonist, and accordingly it ceases to be an autonomous event segment. As predicted, the protagonist (the causee) of such an event segment fails to control the reflexive. Observe the following sentence:

(23) Ken-ga   Ai-ni   zibun-no heya-de piano-o   hika-se-ta.
Ken-NOM Ai-DAT self-of   room-in piano-ACC play-CAUS-PAST
'Ken made Ai play the piano in self's room.'

Understood either as describing a normal indirect causative or as a long-distance supervision sociative situation, the sentence above is ambiguous, as the possibility of interpreting the reflexive antecedent could be either Ken or Ai. Now imagine that Ken was in Ai's room and made her play the piano. If

---

[4] A refers to an agentive protagonist subsuming both A and A'. P, a patient protagonist, likewise subsumes both P and P'.

Ken had told Ai to go play the piano in his room, then (23) would go through with the interpretation that the reflexive refers to Ken. But if Ken had told Ai to play the piano in her own room, then (23) would not describe such a situation. Diagrammatically, this situation looks:

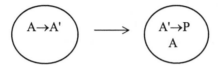

Fig. 5 Where a caused event is not free of a dominant protagonist

Fig. 5 represents a case where the caused event is not free of a dominant protagonist rendering it a non-autonomous event segment. The rule of the reflexive construal given in (22) disallows the causee nominal (A') of such a non-autonomous event segment from controlling the reflexive.[5]

In some other circumstances a dominant protagonist is 'automatically' involved in the caused event, rendering it non-autonomous. Most easily imaginable situations are those involving body parts. Observe the following:

(24) a. Ken-wa Ai-ni   zibun-no heya-de hige-o   sora-se-ta.
      Ken-TOP Ai-DAT self-of   room-in beard-ACC shave-CAUS-PAST
      'Ken$_i$ made Ai$_j$ shave his beard in self's$_{i/*j}$ room.'
   b. Ken-wa Ai-ni   zibun-no heya-de kami-o   kira-se-ta.
      Ken-TOP Ai-DAT self-of   room-in hair-ACC cut-CAUS-PAST
      'Ken made Ai cut the hair in self's room.'

Normally sentence (24a) forces the reading where the beard belongs to Ken. When Ai is to shave Ken's beard in her room, Ken would necessarily be in her room. This is similar to the situation depicted in Fig. 5, where the caused event is not autonomous, as it is not free of a dominant protagonist. Sentence (24b) allows the interpretation that the causee Ai controls the reflexive only if we understand that the hair in question was hers and that Ken was not present in her room. If we understand the hair to belong to Ken, then *zibun* unambiguously refers to the causer Ken, because under such a circumstance Ken would be involved in the caused event; the latter accordingly is not free of a dominant protagonist.

We must ascertain the nature of a dominant protagonist in our account more thoroughly, especially in relation to passive constructions, but let us

---

[5] An expression corresponding to Fig. 5 requires a pronominal form, e.g., *kanozyo-no heya* 'her room'.

now take stock of the implications of our discussion of the reflexive phenomenon so far. The problem of the reflexive interpretation discussed here has serious implications to the analysis that posits embedding structure for *sase*-causatives and that refers for the grammatical subject as a possible candidate for anteceding the reflexive. Such an analysis cannot account for the fact that sentences (19b) and (20) do not show ambiguity in the interpretation of the reflexive form; i.e., the subject of the embedded clauses cannot antecede the reflexive in these sentences. A further problem for such an analysis is the fact that lexical causatives in Korean allow a non-subject nominal to antecede the reflexive *caki* 'self'. If lexical causatives are analyzed as having a simplex structure, and if it is assumed that only a grammatical subject can antecede the reflexive, then there is no way of accounting for the fact that in the following example the causee nominal *hwanca* 'patient' can antecede the reflexive form.

(25) kanhosa-ka hwanca-eykey caki chimtay
    nurse-NOM   patient-DAT   self bed
    wuy-eyse yak-ul   mek-i-ko   iss-ta.
    top-on   medicine eat-CAUS-CONJ be-IND
    'The nurse is making the patient take the medicine on self's bed.'

This sentence can represent two distinct causative situations. In one, the nurse is assisting the patient to take the medicine on the bed. Under this assistive causative interpretation, the reflexive *caki* refers uniquely to the nurse. But the sentence is also construable as representing a supervision causative situation, where the nurse does not herself get physically involved in the execution of the caused event. Under this interpretation, the sentence is ambiguous because *caki* can be controlled by either the causer nominal or the causee nominal.

Our account above indicates that it does not matter whether we have productive (i.e., non-lexical) causatives as in the Japanese case, or lexical causatives as in the Korean case above. Reflexive construal operates in terms of the event structure according to the rule in (22). This predicts that Korean periphrastic *-ke ha-ta* constructions also show the relevant facts about the reflexive *caki*. That is, whereas this construction normally expresses indirect causation in which the caused event constitutes an autonomous event segment free of a dominant protagonist, there can be situations in which the caused event is rendered non-autonomous because of the involvement of the causer. Again, situations involving body parts present themselves as a test case.

(26) yengsiki-ka   kyenghi-eykey caki pang-eyse meli-lul
    Yengsiki-NOM Kyenghi-DAT   self room-in   hair-ACC
    calu-key   ha-yess-ta.
    cut-COMP do-PAST-IND
    'Yengsiki made Kyenghi cut the hair in self's room.'

Just like Japanese example (24b), this sentence is ambiguous only if the hair in question is understood to belong to Kyenghi. If it is understood to belong to Yengsiki, then the sentence is unambiguous, barring the construal of *caki* as the causee Kyenghi.

A number of additional constructions support the analysis of the reflexives presented above. Among them are the Japanese construction of *–te morau* 'to get something done' and passive constructions. Though the latter require some modifications of the Reflexive Construal Rule, these constructions provide further evidence pointing to the soundness of the approach explored here. [6]

8. Conclusion

By examining the causative type intermediate between the direct and the indirect causative type, this paper has shown the indeterminacy of morphology in the analysis of causative constructions. Although crossing of form-meaning correspondences between the lexical and the productive causatives was noted by Shibatani (1973a) and others, sociative causatives provide, especially in a Japanese-Korean comparative light, a clear picture in which there is a mismatch of form and meaning. In Japanese the productive *sase*-causatives express sociative causation, whereas the lexically restricted *–i/-hi-/-li/-ki* forms convey the sociative meanings in Korean.

We have shown that the case-marking pattern, the pattern of adverbial modification, and the construal pattern of the reflexive are all sensitive to the properties of different types of sociative causative, demanding an analysis that has direct recourse to the relevant event structure. We predict that in a coherent framework that directly relates a clause structure to the corresponding event structure, various syntactic explanations hitherto attempted may reduce to straightforward semantic explanations, obviating various abstract syntactic structures posited in order to account for semantic phenomena syntactically.

---

[6] On these modifications of the Construal Rule, see the longer version of this paper, which appears in *Kobe Papers in Linguistics 3* (Department of Linguistics, Faculty of Letters, Kobe University).

References

Chung, S. Y. 1999. *Transitivity and Voice: A Korean-Japanese Contrastive Study of Semantic Transitivity and Syntactic Transitivity.* Doctoral Dissertation, Kobe University.

Kuroda, S.-Y. 1965. Causative forms in Japanese. *Foundations of Language.* 1: 30-50.

Kuroda, S.-Y. 1981. Some recent issues in linguistic theory and Japanese syntax. *Coyote Papers* 2. 103-122. Department of Linguistics, University of Arizona.

Kuroda, S.-Y. 1990. Sieki-no zyodoosi-no ziritusei-ni tuite. *Bunpoo-to Imi-no Hazama.* Tokyo: Kurosio Publishers. 93-104.

Miyagawa, S. 1980. *Complex Verbs and the Lexicon.* Doctoral dissertation. University of Arizona, Tucson.

Miyagawa, S. 1989. *Structure and Case Marking in Japanese* (Syntax and Semantics 22). New York: Academic Press.

Pardeshi, P. 1999. *Transitivity and Voice: A Marathi-Japanese Contrastive Perspective.* Doctoral Dissertation. Kobe University.

Shibatani, M. 1972. Three reasons for not deriving 'kill' from 'cause to die' in Japanese. *Syntax and Semantics Vol. 1,* ed. J. Kimball, 125-137. New York: Academic Press.

Shibatani, 1973a. Semantics of Japanese causativization. *Foundations of Language.* 9: 327-373.

Shibatani, M. 1973b. *A Linguistic Study of Causative Constructions.* Doctoral dissertation. University of California, Berkeley.

Shibatani, M. 1973c. Lexical versus periphrastic causatives in Korean. *Journal of Linguistics.* 9: 281-297.

Shibatani, M. 1976. The grammar of causative constructions: A conspectus. *The Grammar of Causative Constructions* (Syntax and Semantics 6), ed. M. Shibatani, 1-42. New York: Academic Press.

Shibatani, M., and P. Pardeshi. to appear. The causative continuum. The Eighth Biennial Rice University Symposium on Linguistics. April 6-9, 2000.To appear in the proceedings from John Benjamins.

Song, S. C. 1988. *Explorations in Korean Syntax and Semantics.* Berkeley: Institute of East Asian Studies, University of California.

Yang, I-S. 1972. *Korean Syntax: Case Markers, Delimiters, Complementation, and Relativization.* Seoul: Paekhap Publishing Company.

Yang, I-S. 1974. Two causative forms in Korean. *Language Research.* 10.1:83-117.

Yang, I-S. 1976. Semantics of Korean causation. *Foundations of Language.* 14. 1: 55-87.

Characteristic Lexicalization Patterns of Motion Events in Korean

SUNG-CHOOL IM

State University of New York at Buffalo

1. Introduction

This paper is an attempt to account for the characteristic 'lexicalization' patterns of motion events in Korean, using the conflation patterns of semantic elements in cognitive semantics.[1] The major focus of this paper is to show how Path is expressed.

Motion events, in general, consist of four major semantic elements (Talmy 2000: 53-56):

> Figure (F) is a moving or conceptually movable object, Ground (G) is a reference-frame, or a reference object stationary within a reference-frame, with respect to which the Figure's path or site is characterized, Path (P) is the path/course followed by the Figure, and Motion (M) is the presence *per se* of motion or locatedness in the event.

In this study, however, we are only concerned about the actual translational motion, not about the locatedness of an object. Consider the examples in (1):

(1) a. He ran into the room.

---

[1] 'Lexicalization' here is not interpreted in a strict sense but in a broad sense: it applies to both monomorphemic and multimorphemic motion verbs.

b. ku-nun pang-ey   tali-e-tule-ka-ass-ta.
he-TOP room-LOC run-C-into/entering-go-PST-DEC²
'He ran into the room.'

In (1a), *he* is the Figure, *ran* is the Motion verb including both Motion and Manner, *into* is the Path, and *the room* is the Ground. (1b) is the equivalent of (1a) in meaning. *ku* is the Figure, *pang* is the Ground, *tali-* is the Manner verb, *tul-* is the Path verb, which functions as a Path satellite, and *ka-* is the Deictic verb in the Motion event.³ In (1b), however, the Motion component is not conflated with Manner but with Path, so Manner is expressed separately. Thus, *tali-* only expresses Manner of the Motion and the final Deictic verb *ka-* contains both Motion and Deixis.⁴ Like the Manner verb *tali-*, the Path verb *tul-* only expresses the Path of the Motion event.

My arguments on Korean motion events are: First, in Serial Verb Constructions (SVCs), Motion conflates with Deixis in a Deictic verb and Path combines with the Deictic verb as a Path satellite. Second, in Sino-Korean Motion Light Verb Constructions (LVCs), Path is conflated into a Motion-containing morpheme, which exactly corresponds to the typology of monomorphemic motion verbs (MMVs). Third, therefore, MMVs, SVCs, and LVCs all have the same Motion conflation pattern.

This paper will proceed in the following way. In Section 2, Typology of Lexicalization Patterns of Motion Verbs will be presented. In Section 3, Serial Verb Constructions for Motion Events will be discussed. In Section 4, Sino-Korean Light Verb Constructions for Motion Events will be considered. Last, Section 5 will summarize the conclusion and the remaining issues of this paper.

2.   Typology of the Lexicalization Patterns of Motion Verbs

The languages of the world are classified into three major types, depending on the semantic element that is conflated with Fact of Motion in the verb root (Talmy 1985, 1991, 2000). The first type is a Co-event language. In this type, the Co-event such as precursion, enablement, manner, cause or

---

² An asterisk [*] indicates that the sentence is ungrammatical and a question mark [?]/[??] is used to indicate the awkwardness of the sentence. Following abbreviations are used throughout this paper: ACC (ACCUSATIVE), CAU (CAUSATIVE), DEC (DECLARATIVE), lit. (literal meaning), LOC (LOCATIVE), NOM (NOMINATIVE), PRS (PRESENT), PST (PAST), and TOP (TOPIC).

³ In this paper, only the Path verbs which function as Path satellites before a Deictic verb will be treated. 'Satellite' is the grammatical category of any constituent other than a noun-phrase or prepositional/postpositional-phrase complement that is in a sister relation to the verb root. It relates to the verb root as a dependent of a head (Talmy 2000: 102).

⁴ Later in Section 2, I argue that the Deixis component contained in a Deictic verb is also one type of Path.

concomitance is conflated with Fact of Motion in the verb root. Languages or language families that seem to be of this type are Indo-European (except for post-Latin Romance languages), Finno-Ugric, Chinese, Ojibwa and Walpiri. The second type is a Path language, in which the Path notion is conflated with Fact of Motion in the verb root. Languages of this type include Romance, Semitic, Korean, Japanese, Turkish, Tamil, Polynesian, etc. Last, the third type is a Figure language. In this type of language, the moving object, i.e. the Figure, is conflated with Fact of Motion in the verb root. The typical examples of this type are American Indian languages such as Atsgewi and Navajo. Consider a motion event consisting of a Framing event and a Co-event as in (2):[5]

(2) Framing event and Co-event (Talmy 2000: 228)

    [I $_A$MOVED the ball into the box] WITH-THE -CAUSE-OF [I kicked it]
    a. English: I *kicked* the ball into the box.
    b. Spanish: Metí la pelota a la caja de una patada.
            'I inserted ($_A$MOVED-in) the ball to the box by a kick.'
    c. Korean: na-nun kong-ul baks-ey *cha*(-se)   *neh*-ess-ta.
            I-TOP ball-ACC box-LOC *kicking*(-by) *put.in*-PST-DEC
            'I inserted ($_A$MOVED-in) the ball in the box by kicking it.'

In English, the Co-event, i.e. CAUSE here, is conflated with Fact of Motion in the verb root *kick* but the Path is expressed separately as *into* as in (2a). In Spanish, however, Path is conflated with Fact of Motion and the Manner notion is expressed separately as an adverbial phrase as in (2b). Similarly, in the Korean example of (2c), Path is conflated with Fact of Motion in the verb root *neh-ta*. Instead, Manner is separately expressed as a gerundive form *cha* 'kicking' before the Path verb. Thus, English is a Co-event language, whereas Spanish and Korean belong to a Path language group. The following is an example of Atsgewi, which shows that the Figure is conflated with Fact of Motion in the verb root -*staq́*-:

(3) Atsgewi (Talmy 2000: 58-59)
    /'-w-ca-*staq́*-ičt-ᵃ/ => [čwa*staq́*ičta]
    Verb root: *staq́*- 'for runny icky material (e.g., mud, manure, rotten tomatoes, guts, chewed gum) to move/be-located'
    Directional suffix: -ičt 'into liquid'
    Cause prefix: ca- 'from the wind blowing on the Figure'
    Inflectional affix-set: '-w-ᵃ '3rd person subject, factual mood'

---

[5] A framing event conceptually relates to Fact of Motion and the co-event relates to the event through which the motion is performed.

Literal: 'Runny icky material moved into liquid from the wind blowing on it'
Instantiated: 'The guts blew into the creek.'

From a typological point of view, Korean is basically classified as a Path language (Talmy 1985, 1991, 2000, Choi & Bowerman 1991, Kim 1997), which was shown by example (2c). But we can raise the following questions with regard to motion verbs in Korean:

First, is Path always realized within the verb root together with Motion?
Second, in SVCs including Path and Deictic verbs, which verb is the main verb, i.e. the verb expressing Path or the verb expressing Deixis?
Third, is there any difference in lexicalization patterns between Native-Korean motion verbs and Sino-Korean motion verbs?

Consider the first question. In Korean, Path is not always conflated with Fact of Motion in the verb root. I will classify motion verbs into three typical lexicalization patterns as in (4) (Im 2000a):

(4) Lexicalization patterns of motion verbs in Korean
- Type 1: Path and Motion are conflated in a monomorphemic verb root (see example (2c)).
- Type 2: A Path verb as a satellite may precede a Deictic verb in an SVC (see example (5)).
- Type 3: In Sino-Korean Motion LVCs, Path is expressed together with Motion in the same morpheme but, unlike Type 1, this morpheme must accompany another bound morpheme like Ground or Path (see example (6)).

In example (5) below, *tule-* is a Path satellite that has only a Path notion without a Motion component:

(5) ku-nun pang *an-ulo*   *tule*-ka-ass-ta/(*tul-ess-ta).
     he-TOP room inside-toward *into*-go-PST-DEC/(*move.in-PST-DEC)
     'He went into the room.'

In the light verb *kwi-hyang-ha-* in (6), the first morpheme *kwi-* contains both Motion and Path notions and that morpheme is followed by *hyang-*, which is a Ground:

(6) ku-nun *kwi-hyang*-ha-ess-ta.
     he-TOP *return/come.back.to* (M&P)-*hometown* (G)-do-PST-DEC
     'He came back to his hometown'

Type 1 is a monomorphemic motion verb, and Type 2 and Type 3 are multimorphemic motion verbs. In Korean, multimorphemic motion verbs are more productive and preponderant. In the following section, the answer to the second question above is addressed.

3. Serial Verb Constructions for Motion Events

In SVCs including a Manner verb, a Path verb and a Deictic verb, the most typical order is [Manner][Path][Deixis] as in (7a) (Kim 1997). (7a) has the right order but (7b,c,d) have the wrong order, hence they are ungrammatical.

(7) a. ttwi-e- tul-e- o-
    run-C- move.in-C-come
    [Manner] [Path]   [Deixis]
    'Run into a place toward the speaker'
  b.*ttwi-e- o-a-   tul-
    [Manner][Deixis][Path]
  c.*o-a-   tul-e- ttwi-
    [Deixis][Path][Manner]
  d.*tul-e- ttwi-e- o-
    [Path][Manner][Deixis]

    Then, what is the main verb in SVCs including both a Path verb and a Deictic verb? In other words, which verb is the Motion notion conflated with? Choi & Bowerman (1991) claim that Korean has a mixed conflation pattern in motion events: In a spontaneous motion, Motion is conflated with Deixis as in (8a) and in a caused motion, it is conflated with Path as in (8b):

(8) Choi & Bowerman (1991: 88-90):
  a. Spontaneous motion (intransitive)
    John-i   pang-ey   (ttwui-e) tul-e- o-   ass-ta
    J.-NOM room-LOC (run-C) enter-C come-   PST-DEC
    [Figure] [Ground] ([Manner])[Path] [Motion+Deixis]
    'John came in(to) the room (running).'
  b. Caused motion (transitive)
    neh-ta
    put in-DEC
    [Motion+Path]
    'put in/insert'

Korean can represent both Path and Deixis concurrently in nonagentive sentences. In this case, the Deicitc verb is the main verb and the Path verb appears in a gerundive constituent, and a Manner verb can still appear in a further gerundive constituent (Choi & Bowerman 1991: 88-89). In their analysis, however, they do not include Deixis within Path notion and so claim separate patterns for spontaneous motion and caused motion: for the former, the conflation of Motion with Deixis and for the latter, the conflation of Motion with Path.

Unlike Choi & Bowerman (1991), however, Kim (1997) claims that Korean employs the same motion-conflation pattern for expressions of spontaneous and caused motion: In either case, Motion is conflated into Path verbs and the final Deictic verb in SVCs adds only Direction to the preceding Path verb as in (9):

(9) Kim(1997):
    ttwi-e-   tul-e-   o-
    run-C-   move in-C-   come
    [Manner] [**Path+Motion**] [**Deixis**]
    'run into a place toward the speaker'

In her analysis above, both the Manner verb and the Deictic verb modify the Path verb with Manner and Deixis notions respectively without a Motion component: Only the Path verb contains a Motion component. With reference to Lee (1992), she suggests the 'Se-Insertion' rule as evidence for her analysis.[6] Her point is that the Deictic verb after a Path verb is an auxiliary verb because it rejects 'se-insertion' as in (10a) but that the Deictic verb after a Manner verb is the main verb because it allows 'se-insertion' as in (10b).

(10) Lee(1992): 'Se-Insertion':
    a. [Type 1: *ka*- expresses direction]
        ku-nun san-ey   oll-a-*se-ka-ss-ta.
        he-TOP mountain-LOC move.up-C-SE-go-PST-DEC
        'He went up the mountain.'
    b. [Type 2: *ka*- expresses motion]
        ku-nun cip-ey   kel-e-*se* ka-ass-ta.
        he-TOP house-LOC walk-C-by go-PST-DEC
        '(lit.) He went home by walking/He walked home.'

This analysis, however, has two problems: First, in (10b) also, the Deictic verb *ka* expresses direction, i.e. 'in a direction other than toward the

---

[6] Attached to the suffixes such as -*ko*, -*a*, and –*e* of a verb, the suffix '-se' makes the meaning of the verb clearer with the meaning like 'by/by means of' or 'and', depending on the context.

speaker'; second, Path verbs also allow 'se-insertion' in some contexts as in
(11).

(11) a. ku sonyen-un cha-eyse *nayli-e-se*/*se   o-ass-ta.
     the boy-TOP   car-from move down-C-and/by come-PST-DEC
     'The boy got off the bus and came (to me). (≠ (for *se) The boy got
     off the bus.)'
    b. ku sonyen-un ku kenmwul-ul   *tol-a-(se)*   o-ass-ta.
      the boy-TOP   the building-ACC turn.round-C-(by) come-PST-DEC
      '(lit.)The boy came by turning round the building.'

      Of course, a Deictic verb may be used as an auxiliary verb as in
(12). In this use, the verb *ka*- does not express direction of a motion event
but indicates an aspectual meaning like continuity/duration of an action or a
state that is in process. In this case, 'se-insertion' is rejected because the
verb preceding the Deictic verb is the main verb and the Deictic verb is an
auxiliary verb.

(12) a. sagwa-ka pwulk-key ik-e(*-se) ka-n-ta.
     apple-NOM red-C   ripen-C go-PRS-DEC
     '(lit.)Apples are ripening into red.'
    b. nal-i   etwu-e(*-se) ka-n-ta.
      day-NOM be.dark-C   go-PRS-DEC
      'It's getting darker.'
    c. ce   namwu-nun cwuk-e(*-se) ka-n-ta.
      that tree-TOP   die-C   go-PRS-DEC
      '(lit.) That tree is dying/That tree is withering and going to die.'

      Like Choi & Bowerman (1991) and Talmy (2000), I argue that in
SVCs the final Deictic verb contains Motion as a main verb. In my analysis,
however, this is because the Path verb has changed into a Path satellite before a Deictic verb, losing the Motion component and containing the Path
notion alone as in (13). For this analysis, first we consider the Path notion
again. There are three main subcomponents of Path: the Vector, the Conformation and the Deictic (Talmy 2000: 53-56):

> The Vector comprises the basic types of arrival, traversal, and departure
> that a Figural schema can execute with respect to a Ground schema. The
> Conformation component of the Path is a geometric complex that relates
> the fundamental Ground schema within a Motion-aspect formula to the
> schema for a full Ground object. The Deictic component of Path typically
> has only two member notions 'toward the speaker' and 'in a direction
> other than toward the speaker'.

Based on this subclassification of Path, we can make the analysis of a SVC as in (13).

(13) Im (2000a)
    ttwi-e-   *tule-*   *o-*
    run-C-   into   come
    [Manner] [Path(Conformation)]   [Motion+Path(Deixis)]
    'run into a place toward the speaker'

In the analysis of (13), both *tul-* and *o-* have Path notions, the former containing the Conformation Path and the latter including the Deictic Path. Thus, we can find that even in a complex spontaneous motion verb, Motion is conflated with Path in the verb root. Therefore, we can make the conclusion that Korean has only one conflation pattern of motion verbs, i.e. the conflation of Motion with Path in the verb root.

    My assumption here is that originally both a Path verb and a Deictic verb in SVCs were Path verbs but later the Motion notion included in a Path verb preceding a Deictic verb was lost. As a result, this Path verb has changed into a Path satellite. Like the Manner verb preceding a Deictic verb, it just modifies the final Deictic verb with an additional Path concept. Then, what is the evidence for this argument? The most typical evidence for this analysis is *na-* 'out': it used to be used as a full motion verb as in (14).

(14) ptut   moll-a   mot *na*-ni (*Yongpiechenka*).[7]
     meaning not know-C not *go out*-C
     '(lit.) Since (I) do not know the meaning, (I) don't *go out...*'

Thus, in the modern Korean language, *na-* has completely changed into a Path satellite before a Deictic verb as in (15).[8]

(15) a. ku-ka   wuntongcang-ulo   *na*-ka-ass-ta.
       he-NOM playground-toward   *out*-go-PST-DEC
       'He went out to the playground'
    b. *ku-ka   wuntongcang-ulo   *na*-ass-ta.
       he-NOM play-ground-toward   ?-PST-DEC

    tul- is another piece of evidence which supports the Path satellite analysis. Consider the following examples.

---

[7] *Yongpiechenka* is a movement of music, which was written by the scholars such as Kwen Cey, Ceng Inci, and An Ci in accordance with the order by King Seycong in 1445. It is the first literature written in the Korean alphabet.
[8] *na-* is mostly used with metaphorical senses or with specialized meanings in the modern Korean.

(16) a. *ku-ka   kyosil-ey   *tul*-ess-ta.
      he-NOM classroom-LOC ?-PST-DEC
  b. ku-ka   kyosil-ey   *ttwi-e-tul*-ess-ta.
      he-NOM classroom-LOC run-C-?-PST-DEC
      'He suddenly/surprisingly/threateningly ran into the classroom.'
      (not for 'He came into the classroom (by) running.')
  c. ku-ka   kyosil-ey   *ttwi-e-tule-o*-ass-ta.
      he-NOM classroom-LOC run-C-into-come-PST-DEC
      'He came into the classroom (by) running.'

As is shown in the examples of (16), *tul-* cannot stand alone in a motion event. It must be combined with a Deictic verb.[9] The Path satellites such as *na-* 'out' and *tule-* 'into' in SVCs have historically developed from Path verbs (see Im 2000a).

4. Light Verb Constructions for Motion Events

In Korean, LVCs have several subtypes. But in this study, the discussion is limited only to Sino-Korean (hereafter SK) LVCs with motion-related morphemes. These SK Motion LVCs are very common in Korean but little attention has been paid to their lexicalization patterns. In general, SK Motion LVCs are composed of one SK verbal noun plus a light verb *ha-* 'do':

(17) Sino-Korean Motion LVCs in Korean: 'Verbal Noun - ha-'

      This study posits a new interpretation of SK Motion LVCs, in which their most typical lexicalization pattern is 'M&P+G': In the bimorphemic SK verbal noun, Motion and Path are conflated into the same morpheme and Ground separately in another morpheme within a verb root as in (18) and (19). These two morphemes are bound to each other, so they cannot stand alone.

(18) a. *ip-cang-ha*-ta.   'enter'
     enter-place-do-DEC
     M&P-G
  b. *ip-ha-ta.

---

[9] *tul-* can be used in a non-motion event, in which this verb has metaphorical meanings. When *tul-* is combined with a manner verb, the complex form does not exactly have the meaning of 'come in by running'. In general, *ttwi-e-tul-* is used for two uses: ① plunge into water from a high place, e.g., *patasmwul-ey ttwi-e-tul-ta* 'plunge into the sea'; ② come in moving quickly or appear suddenly/surprisingly/threateningly, e.g., *catongcha-ka into-lo ttwi-e-tul-ess-ta* 'A car moved onto a sidewalk suddenly and surprisingly.'

In this example, Motion and Path are conflated into the same morpheme *ip* and Ground is expressed in another morpheme *cang*. Example (19a) shows the same phenomenon.

(19) a. *to-kang*-ha-ta.　　　　　　　'cross a river'
　　　 move across-river-do-DEC
　　　 M&P-G
　　 b. *to-ha-ta.

　　　 The Ground combined with the Motion-containing morpheme defines the general category for the Ground of the motion event. Thus, an additional Ground, which gives specific information on the Ground, may be mentioned as in (20). In (20a), *cang* defines the general category of the Ground of the motion and *kangtang* is the specific Ground that belongs to that general category. The same is true of (20b).

(20) a. ku-ka　　 *kangtang*-ey　　ip-cang-ha-ess-ta.
　　　 he-NOM auditorium-LOC enter-place-do-PST-DEC
　　　 F　　　　　 G　　　　　　 M&P-G
　　　 'He entered the auditorium.'
　　 b. kutul-i　　 *hankang*-ul　　　to-kang-ha-ess-ta.
　　　 they-NOM hankang.river-ACC move across-river-do-PST-DEC
　　　 F　　　　　 G　　　　　　　　 M&P-G
　　　 'They crossed the Hankang.'

　　　 Instead of Ground, an extra Path satellite may precede an 'M&P' morpheme as in (21): These two Paths must be of the same kind in meaning. In this case, since that morpheme is not followed by a Ground morpheme, a Ground must be expressed separately as in (22):

(21) a. *ha*-kang-ha-ta.
　　　 downward-move down-do-DEC
　　　 P　　　　 M&P
　　　 'move down'
　　 b. *sang*-sung-ha-ta.
　　　 upward-move up-do-DEC
　　　 P　　　　 M&P
　　　 'move up'
(22) a. ku-ka　　 *tolo*-lul　　 hoyng-tan-ha-ess-ta.
　　　 he-NOM road-ACC horizontally-move across-do-PST-DEC
　　　 F　　　 G　　　　 P　　　　　　 M&P
　　　 'He crossed the road.'

b. ku-ka   *kwuktho*-lul cong-tan-ha-ess-ta.
   he-NOM country-ACC vertically-move across-do-PST-DEC
   F   G   P   M&P
   'He crossed the whole country from north to south/from south to north.'

A Path satellite must precede a Motion-containing morpheme in case the Path conflated with Motion is neutral to the direction as in (23). Thus, the morpheme *cin* in (23a,b) has the Path notion which is either 'forward' or 'backward'.

(23) a. *cen*-cin-ha-ta
        forward-move *forward/backward*-do-DEC
        P   M&P
        'move forward'
     b. *hwu*-cin-ha-ta
        backward-move *forward/backward*-do-DEC
        P   M&P
        'move backward'

In any case of SK Motion LVCs, the motion-containing morpheme must accompany another morpheme, which is either G or P. In general, P precedes M and G follows M.

5. Conclusion and Remaining Issues

The most contributory findings of this study are:

- Korean has three typical lexicalization patterns of motion verbs. Monomorphemic native-Korean motion verbs, multimorphemic native-Korean motion verbs, and multimorphemic Sino-Korean motion verbs.
- Path is conflated with Motion in the verb root in simplex Path verbs, whereas in SVCs Conformation Path combines with Deictic verbs as a Path satellite and Deixis Path is conflated with Motion in the verb root. Thus, in the complex form of a Path and a Deictic verb, the main verb is the final Deictic verb and the Path verb has changed into a Path satellite before a Deictic verb.
- In LVCs, Path is expressed within a Motion-containing morpheme, which is followed or preceded by Ground or Path.
- In conformity with the typology of Korean monomorphemic motion verbs, Path is conflated with Motion in Sino-Korean Motion LVCs, too.
- Therefore, all types of motion verbs in Korean have the same Motion conflation pattern, i.e., the conflation of Motion with Path.

Remaining issues:

- Is there any difference in the degree of change of Path verbs into Path satellites among Conformation Path verbs?
- Do the present speakers of Korean treat the complex forms of 'Path Satellite+Deictic verb' as one single unit or two separate units in their cognition?

References

Choi, S., & M. Bowerman. 1991. Learning to express motion events in English and Korean: The influence of language-specific lexicalization patterns. *Cognition, 41*, 83-121.

Im, S. 2000a. *Lexicalization Patterns of Motion Verbs in Korean.* Unpublished MA thesis, State University of New York, Buffalo.

Kim, Y. 1997. Verb Lexicalization Patterns in Korean - with Focus on Motion Conflation in Complex Verb Constructions, In *Japanese/Korean Linguistics*, VI, Sohn and Haig (eds.), 495-511. Stanford: Stanford Linguistics Association.

Lee, S. 1992. *The Syntax and semantics of serial verb constructions.* Unpublished doctoral dissertation, University of Washington.

Slobin, D. 1996b. Two ways to travel: Verbs of motion in English and Spanish, In *Grammatical Constructions: Their Form and Meaning*, Shibatani and Thompson (eds.), 195-217. Oxford: Oxford University Press.

Talmy, L. 1985. Lexicalization patterns: Semantic structure in lexical forms. In *Language Typology and Semantic Description, Vol 3: Grammatical Categories and the Lexicon*, Timothy Shopen (ed.), 36-149. Cambridge: Cambridge University Press.

Talmy, L. 1991. Path to realization: A typology of event conflation, In *Proceedings of the Seventeenth Annual Meeting of the Berkeley Linguistics Society*, 480-519. Berkeley: Berkeley Linguistics Society.

Talmy, L. 2000. *Toward Cognitive Semantics.* Volume 1: *Concept structuring systems*; Volume 2: *Typology and process in concept structuring*. Massachusetts: MIT Press.

Wienold, G. 1992. Up and Down: On some concepts of path in Korean motion verbs, *Language Research* (Seoul) *28*, 15-43.

Wienold, G. 1995. Lexical and Conceptual Structures in Expressions for Movement and Space with Reference to Japanese, Korean, Thai, and Indonesian as Compared to English and German, *Current Issues in Linguistic Theory 114*, Egli et al.(eds.), 300-340. John Benjamins Publishing Co.

The Processing of Wh-phrases and Interrogative Complementizers in Japanese

EDSON T. MIYAMOTO & SHOICHI TAKAHASHI

Kanda University of International Studies & University of Tokyo

1. Introduction

Researchers in sentence processing are concerned with how people read (or hear) words in a sentence and produce an appropriate mental representation. Emphasis is on the process of incorporating each word into a partial representation until the end of the sentence is reached and a complete representation is obtained. Assuming that the constraints proposed by syntacticians are relevant during parsing, the question is how people compute mental representations that conform with such constraints. In particular, one should ask how knowledge of the grammar interacts with other sources of information (e.g. world knowledge) and with cognitive resources (e.g. working memory capacity) as each word is processed. We also have to consider where cross-linguistic parameterization is necessary. Clearly, grammars have to be parameterized, but the more interesting question is whether the parsing algorithm (that presumably uses grammars as one of its knowledge sources) has to be different for each human language as well.

The present paper argues that, despite their syntactic differences, wh-phrases in English and Japanese present similar processing properties supporting the assumption that a single mechanism along the lines of Gibson (1998) may be at work in both cases. Thus, the parameterization is restricted to the grammars: In English, fronted wh-phrases require an associated gap, whereas in Japanese, in-situ wh-phrases require a question particle. Given the dependencies required by a grammar, cognitive mechanisms keep track of the constituents that are still needed as the sentence is read. Moreover, because of working memory constraints, shorter dependencies are favoured over longer ones, in other words, required constituents are preferred to occur early rather than late in the input string. Under these assumptions, we also discuss how certain types of movements without phonological effect (LF movement, Huang, 1982; May, 1985; and null-operator movement, Watanabe, 1992) may be computed by people.

2. The processing of wh-phrases

The fact that people read one word at a time and attempt to create a partial representation without delay may seem unsurprising and is supported by various experimental results (Marslen-Wilson & Tyler, 1980, *inter alia*). However, we immediately face problems in the processing of fronted wh-phrases in languages such as English. For example, in (1) below, the wh-phrase who is fronted to the beginning of the sentence and, therefore, it must be associated with a gap (i.e. an empty argument or adjunct position)[1] in order for its relation with a predicate to be determined. But how is the representation built incrementally if the position of the gap only becomes clear at the end of the sentence?

(1) Who did the children sing for <gap>?

Moreover, if a uniform account of wh-phrases across languages is to be attained, there are clear differences that need to be taken into consideration. While languages such as English require wh-phrases to be fronted,[2] East Asian languages allow wh-phrases to remain in situ. Thus, in a question such as (2a), Japanese allows the wh-phrase what kind of computer to occur in the same position as a lexical NP such as computer in (2b).

---

[1]It will not be crucial in the present discussion how the gap is encoded (e.g. as a trace left by movement, Chomsky, 1981; as a slash feature, Gazdar, et al., 1985).

[2]We will not address the processing of sentences with multiple wh-phrases in this paper.

(2) a. senmu-ga   donna-pasokon-o   tukatteiru-no?
      director-Nom what-kind-computer-Acc using-is-QP
      'What kind of computer is the director using?'

   b. senmu-ga   pasokon-o   tukatteiru.
      director-Nom computer-Acc using-is
      'The director is using the computer.'

It is possible that fronted wh-phrases in English and in-situ wh-phrases in Japanese are too different to be handled by a single processing mechanism. In fact, if we only consider the position where they occur, in-situ wh-phrases are more likely to be processed in the same manner as lexical NPs such as computer in (2b). However, the processing of in-situ wh-phrases cannot be reduced to the processing of lexical NPs because the former have a further requirement, namely, wh-phrases in Japanese have to be licensed by a question particle such as no in (2a) (Cheng, 1991; Nishigauchi, 1990). In the following, we will draw a parallel between this requirement and the gap-search process triggered by wh-phrases in English.

3. Fronted wh-phrases in English

One common assumption in the literature on the processing of fronted wh-phrases in English is that a wh-phrase triggers a search process for a gap (see Fodor, 1989, for a summary). This can be expressed as a dependency that is still pending; the constituent (namely a gap) that will complete this dependency has yet to come in the input string. The expectation generated by this process modulates the way how people process the following up-coming words. A successful line of work has suggested that people try to posit the required gap as soon as grammatically possible, in other words, people favour positing a gap rather than expecting an overt constituent (de Vincenzi, 1991; Frazier & Clifton, 1989; and references therein). Supporting this proposal, experimental evidence suggests that native speakers of English have difficulty when a potential position for a gap turns out to be unavailable because of an overt NP. For example, in the sentence below (adapted from Crain & Fodor, 1985), readers insert a gap immediately after force as indicated by the ∧ sign. Next, people slow down when the pronominal us is read because it is incompatible with the gap previously posited. The search is resumed and the eventual position of the gap is found after the preposition for.

(3) Filled gap effect (FGE)
     Who did the children force ∧ us to sing the songs for <gap>?

This type of phenomenon, in which a gap posited too early turns out to be filled by a lexical NP, is known as the *filled gap effect* (FGE).

The preference to posit a gap as soon as possible has been explained in terms of a requirement to minimize the length of chains (the *minimal chain principle*, MCP; de Vincenzi, 1991). One of the advantages of the MCP is that it provides a uniform account for the processing of wh gaps as well as other types of empty positions (e.g. pro taken as a singleton chain).

4. In-situ wh-phrases in Japanese

One problem with the MCP is that it does not easily generalize to constructions without gaps. For example, the MCP does not apply to the processing of in-situ wh-phrases in East-Asian languages because they do not involve a chain with an empty position (but see discussion below for a possible extension of the MCP).

In an alternative proposal, it has been suggested that the preference for early gaps in English is an instance of a more general preference for required constituents to come as soon as possible in the input string (Gibson, 1998). In this case, whether a chain is involved or not is irrelevant, and any type of predicted constituent should preferentially occur as soon as possible. This model can be extended to East-Asian languages as it predicts that people would prefer a constituent required by in-situ wh-phrases to occur early rather than late in the input string.

The question then is whether in-situ wh-phrases predict an upcoming constituent. It has been observed that East-Asian languages and various other languages with in-situ wh-phrases require a question particle in order to indicate that a sentence should be typed as interrogative (Cheng, 1991). Moreover, in-situ wh-phrases have been argued to require unselective binding by a relevant element in complementizer position (Pesetsky, 1987, and references therein). In Japanese, in particular, wh-phrases require a question particle such as ka or no in order to be licensed.[3] Thus, following Gibson (1998), Japanese speakers should prefer such a particle to occur as soon as possible after a wh-phrase. If the parallel with the processing of fronted wh-phrases in English holds, we should be able to produce in Japanese an effect similar to the FGE. The rest of this section describes a phenomenon which we will argue to be the in-situ counterpart of the FGE.

In the following sentence, the wh-phrase donna-pasokon requires a

---

[3]The actual requirement is for a particle that can determine the force of the wh-phrase (as interrogative, existential or universal; Nishigauchi, 1990). For example, a non-interrogative particle such as mo could also license the wh-phrase, in this case, as a universal quantifier.

question particle, whose earliest possible position would be immediately after the verb using-is. Therefore, Japanese speakers should slow down when they read the complementizer to because its affirmative typing clashes with the expectation for a question particle and gives rise to a *typing mismatch effect* (TME).

(4) Typing mismatch effect (TME)

senmu-ga   donna-pasokon-o   tukatteiru ∧   **to**
director-Nom   what-kind-computer-Acc   using-is   Comp(aff)

kakarichoo-ga   ittano?
supervisor-Nom   said-QP

'What kind of computer did the supervisor say the director is using?'

In order to test whether Japanese readers slow down at the affirmative complementizer, we conducted a non-cumulative moving-window self-paced reading experiment (Just, Carpenter & Woolley, 1982; the segmentation used is indicated with spaces in the example sentences). We compared the sentence above (repeated as (5a) below) with the sentence in (5b). In the latter sentence, the embedded verb is followed by the question particle ka, thus providing a base-line reading time for the embedded verb with the affirmative complementizer in (5a).

(5) a. Wh/Aff

senmu-ga   donna-pasokon-o   tukatteiru-to
director-Nom   what-kind-computer-Acc   using-is-Comp(aff)

kakarichoo-ga   ittano?
supervisor-Nom   said-QP

'What kind of computer did the supervisor say the director is using?'

b. Wh/Int

senmu-ga   donna-pasokon-o   tukatteiru-ka
director-Nom   what-kind-computer-Acc   using-is-QP

kakarichoo-ga   kiitano?
supervisor-Nom   asked-QP

'Did the supervisor ask what kind of computer the director is using?'

However, there is the possibility that the affirmative complementizer to is always read more slowly than the question particle ka, independent of the environment in which these two types of particles occur. In order to counter this possibility, we created two more conditions in which the wh-phrase was replaced with a lexical NP, new-computer, as shown in

(6ab).

(6) a. NP/Aff

senmu-ga   atarasii-pasokon-o tukatteiru-to
director-Nom new-computer-Acc   using-is-Comp(aff)

kakarichoo-ga   itta.
supervisor-Nom   said

'The supervisor said that the director is using the new computer.'

b. NP/Int

senmu-ga   atarasii-pasokon-o tukatteiru-ka
director-Nom new-computer-Acc   using-is-QP

kakarichoo-ga   kiita.
supervisor-Nom   asked

'The supervisor asked whether the director is using the new computer.'

If the wh-phrase is indeed predicting a question particle, we should expect a slow-down in the third region (the embedded verb and the complementizer) of (5a) in comparison to the corresponding region in (5b). In contrast, there should be no such a difference between the NP conditions in (6) because new computer does not require a question particle. The results of the experiment supported our claims (see Figure 1). The Wh/Aff condition was slower than the Wh/Int condition; whereas, the NP/Aff condition was faster than the NP/Int condition (interaction Wh/NP × Aff/Int: $F_1(1,24) = 5.39$, $P < 0.05$; $F_2(1,23) = 5.36$, $P < 0.05$; see Miyamoto & Takahashi, 2000, for further details). The difference between the two NP conditions can be explained if we assume that the lexical NP does not require a question particle, and furthermore, that the affirmative typing is the default. Under those two assumptions, the slow-down in the NP/QP condition occurs because some extra processing is required when the question particle is detected; in other words, the question particle is the first constituent that indicates that the sentence must be typed as interrogative, contradicting the default affirmative typing that was probably assumed up to that point.

The present result supports the assumption that there is a TME taking place at the affirmative complementizer in the Wh/Aff condition, (5a). The parallel with the FGE in (3) suggests that a similar process is taking place in both cases: a wh-phrase is read and requires a certain type of constituent, and a slow-down is observed when the required constituent does not occur at the earliest possible position.

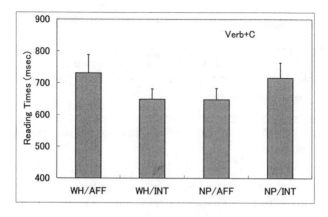

FIGURE 1   Reading times (msec) for the embedded verb and
complementizer.

5. Grammars and cognitive resources

The previous section suggests that parameterizations can be restricted
to the grammars, allowing the processing algorithm to be characterized
uniquely for both types of languages at least with respect to wh-phrases.

As observed earlier, the syntactic properties of wh-phrases in English and Japanese are so different that, at first sight, it would seem
more natural to propose two separate mechanisms to deal with their
processing. The FGE and the TME certainly differ in many respects. In
the FGE, the fronted wh-phrase is not associated with a predicate, consequently, its thematic role remains uncertain until the gap is found. In
the TME, by contrast, the in-situ wh-phrase is associated with a local
predicate in order to get a thematic role, but its scope is undetermined
until the question particle is found.

The model we are adopting here implies that the processing mechanism may be blind to the fact that, at the grammar level, thematic
relations are distinct from scope relations. Even though linguists have
various reasons to keep those two types of relations separate, the present
model suggests that the only relevant aspects for the processing algorithm are the positions that have to be associated and how far apart
they are from each other.

More precisely, a syntactic model has to account for two aspects of
wh-phrases — their requirements for a thematic role and for a scope
position. In most cases, it is not possible to satisfy both requirements
locally; one of them has to be encoded as a long distance dependency.
As observed earlier, fronted wh-phrases indicate their scope position

based on where they are pronounced in a sentence, but their thematic role has to be determined through a long distance dependency with a gap. In contrast, the thematic role of in-situ wh-phrases is indicated by the position where they are pronounced, whereas their scope is expressed as a long distance dependency with a question particle. In our processing model, the long distance dependency is the factor that exposes the cognitive bottleneck which is being measured in experimental settings. The presumable bottleneck is the restricted capacity that working memory has to hold various items (in the present case, various unresolved dependencies) for relatively long periods of time. Clearly, it is entirely possible that future experimental techniques will uncover more intricate patterns that will require differentiated treatments of these dependencies even at the processing level.

Note that, in the present model, even if the exact nature of the dependencies is not crucial, nevertheless, the grammar is strictly obeyed during parsing as people do not make random predictions in order to circumvent working memory constraints.

6. Extending the minimal chain principle

The minimal chain principle (MCP) was originally proposed for chains with empty positions, in other words, for constituent omission (e.g. instances of pro) or overt movement (de Vincenzi, 1991). We contended that the MCP cannot apply to the processing of in-situ wh-phrases because these constructions do not involve a gap. However, an extended version may be possible, in which chains generated by movement without phonological effect may also be subject to the MCP. The present section discusses how such movements may be processed by people as they read a sentence, and whether such a proposal could explain the TME.

6.1 Movements without phonological effect

Two types of syntactic movements have been proposed in order to explain in-situ wh-phrases. In one proposal, in-situ wh-phrases move covertly at the level of *logical form* (LF; Huang, 1982). In another proposal, a phonologically-null operator associated with wh-phrases moves to the relevant CP Spec before LF (Watanabe, 1992). In either case, movement does not have any phonological effect and a crucial question is when people compute such types of movements. Take LF movement, for example. In syntax, LF movement is assumed to take place after spell-out, or after S-structure has been sent to the phonological component. Thus, one possibility in processing is that people only compute LF movements at sentence end, after all overt movements have taken place. However, coupled with the MCP, this proposal does not explain the TME. If LF chains are only computed at the end of the sentence, they cannot be related to the mid-sentence slow-down observed at the affirmative complementizer in (5a).

Alternatively, it can be argued that the steps in the processing of a sentence (i.e. in the performance module) do not have to mirror the order in the grammatical formalization (i.e. the order observed in the competence module). In this case, the computation of LF movement may occur at any point during the processing of a sentence; in particular, given the general processing preference for relations to be asserted as soon as possible (some sort of *don't procrastinate* policy in psycholinguistics), LF movement may be processed as soon as it is clear that such a movement is required. (A similar rationale is true for null-operator movement.) The earliest point in which it is clear that movement is necessary is at the wh-phrase. In the sentences below, assume that covert movement occurs as soon as the wh-phrase is detected. As observed earlier, such a movement does not have phonological consequences, and is represented in (7a) with the null operator $\wedge$ in Spec of CP_1.[4]

(7) a. $[_{CP_1}$ $\wedge$ senmu-ga   donna-pasokon-o
            director-Nom wh-computer-Acc

     b. $[_{CP_2}$ $\wedge$ $[_{CP_1}$ senmu-ga   donna-pasokon-o tukatteiru-to]
            director-Nom wh-computer-Acc using-is-Comp(aff)

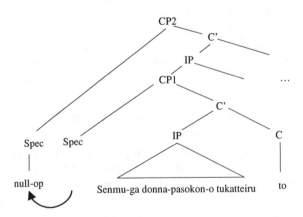

FIGURE 2 The TME as reanalysis of a null operator.

When the affirmative complementizer to is read, an outer clause

---

[4] We crucially assume in the present analysis that the specifier in Japanese is on the left of the complementizer, thus preceding the IP node.

is created (as indicated by CP_2 in (7b); see also the tree structure in Figure 2). Because the null operator in Spec of CP_1 is not compatible with the affirmative to, reanalysis must take place and the null operator is shifted to Spec of CP_2 indicating that the wh-phrase takes scope in the higher clause, CP_2, and not in the embedded CP_1. Consequently, the slow-down observed at the affirmative complementizer is predicted to have been caused by the mismatch between the null operator and the complementizer, or by the reanalysis process necessary to change the scope of the wh-phrase.

6.2 The processing of LF movement: QR in English

As discussed above, the extended MCP may account for the TME, but it requires a number of unattested assumptions about the computation of movements without phonological effect. It would be desirable to obtain independent evidence that LF chains or null-operator chains are computed on-line and influence processing time. The present section discusses potential evidence in support of the processing of LF movement during on-line parsing; the next section considers the same discussion for null-operator chains.

If LF chains are relevant during processing, in other words if they can add difficulty to the processing of a sentence, then the extended MCP should predict that the direct object in (8a) would take less time to process than the direct objects in (8bc) because the latter NPs require quantifier raising (QR; May, 1985) to a position adjoined to IP, as indicated by $\wedge$.

(8) a. Object NP without quantifier
A man bought *the painting.*

b. Object NP with quantifier, near its scope position
$\wedge$ A man bought *every painting.*

c. Object NP with quantifier, far from its scope position
$\wedge$ A man who the reporter talked about bought *every painting.*

The NP the painting does not contain a quantificational feature and, consequently, does not involve LF movement. In contrast, every painting and other NPs with a quantifier require QR. If QR is computed as soon as the quantificational feature is detected, we should expect the direct objects in (8bc) to take longer to process than the direct object in (8a). Moreover, if longer LF chains are harder to process than shorter LF chains, the direct object in (8b) should be easier to process than the direct object in (8c). However, intuitive judgements suggest that there are no noticeable differences between the sentences in (8). One possible confound in this case is that discourse complexity factors may be masking the LF-chain effect given that each determiner requires a different set of presuppositions in those sentences (Crain & Steedman, 1985, *inter alia*).

In related work, it has been proposed that the more elements in a chain, the more complex is the syntactic representation perceived to be (the *representational theory of complexity*, RTC; Pritchett & Whitman, 1995). The RTC was proposed as an updated version of the *derivational theory of complexity* (see an extensive critique of the DTC in Fodor, Bever & Garrett, 1974). It applies to chains in S-structure as well as in LF, and it is supposed to explain preferences in the interpretation of ambiguous sentences in English and Japanese. However, the RTC runs into a number of conceptual and empirical problems. Like its predecessor, it fails to give an explicit parsing algorithm and consequently only provides an off-line measure of complexity, in other words, the RTC only makes predictions of people's preferences at sentence end and does not explain the word-by-word process. Moreover, the examples provided by Pritchett and Whitman seem to be explained by independent factors, making the contribution of the RTC unclear. Finally, and perhaps most problematic is the assumption that only the number of chain elements influences processing difficulty, whereas the distance between two consecutive elements in a chain does not (Pritchett & Whitman, 1995, pp73-6), given that, at least in S-structure chains, it is well known that both measures are relevant (de Vincenzi, 1991; Gibson, 1998).

In short, we would argue that the influence of LF chains during online parsing is dubious at this point. But this is a little explored area and further work is clearly necessary.

6.3 The processing of null-operator movement

If it is eventually shown that LF chains for QR do not involve a processing cost, it will be harder to argue for the processing cost of LF chains in Japanese wh-phrases. However, independent of the conclusion about QRs, it should still be possible to argue that null-operator movement (Watanabe, 1992) has some processing impact. This type of movement was originally proposed for the level of S-structure and is not directly related to LF chains.

As a corollary of the MCP, assume that longer chains take longer to be processed than shorter chains. Thus, a wh-phrase should take longer to process, the farther it is from the CP Spec containing its null operator. For example, the null operator $\wedge$ in CP Spec is closer to the the subject wh-phrase in (9a) than to the object wh-phrase in (9b).

Consequently, it should take longer to read the wh-phrase in (9a) than the wh-phrase in (9b). Sentence (9c) is given as a possible baseline for each wh-phrase in the first two conditions.[5]

(9) a. Subject wh

∧ dono-senmu-ga   pasokon-o   tukatteiru-ka...
which-director-Nom computer-Acc using-is-QP

b. Object wh

∧ senmu-ga   dono-pasokon-o   tukatteiru-ka...
director-Nom which-computer-Acc using-is-QP

c. Lexical NPs

senmu-ga   pasokon-o   tukatteiru-to...
director-Nom computer-Acc using-is-Comp(aff)

The distance between the null operator and the question particle ka is the same in (9ab), thus the extended MCP should not predict any differences at the particle. Moreover, in this model, an in-situ wh-phrase has a dependency with a null operator, which in turn is associated with a question particle; but there is no direct dependency between the wh-phrase and the question particle.

In the original explanation we provided for the TME, the crucial dependency is between the wh-phrase and the question particle; there is no null operator in Spec of CP serving as an intermediary. In this case, there should not be any differences in the processing times of the wh-phrases in (9ab), because no null operator is posited. However, the question particle should be read more slowly in (9a) than in (9b) because it is farther from the wh-phrase in the former sentence.[6]

We are currently investigating the extended MCP and the TME in a number of different environments. As a long term project, we would like to explore other possible constructions in which LF movement or null-operator movement may affect processing times.

Conclusion

The present paper argued that the processing of in-situ wh-phrases in Japanese can be explained by the same procedure that underlies the processing of fronted wh-phrases in English. In this model, cognitive mechanisms attempt to satisfy as early as possible the dependencies

---

[5]This example could also be explained with LF chains.

[6]We are adopting a linear distance metric here (according to Gibson, 1998, the crucial measure should take into account the number of intervening discourse referents). A structural metric would yield different predictions because, in a tree structure, the question particle in complementizer position is closer to the subject than to the object NP.

dictated by the grammar of a given language (Gibson, 1998). The proposal was supported by the results of a reading time experiment which revealed a typing mismatch effect similar to the filled gap effect previously reported for English (Frazier & Clifton, 1989, *inter alia*). An alternative explanation was also discussed, which takes into consideration chains created by LF movement (Huang, 1982; May, 1985) or null-operator movement (Watanabe, 1992).

Acknowledgements and contact information

The experimental result reported in the present paper was supported by a Grant-in-Aid for COE Research (08CE1001) from the Japanese Ministry of Education, Science and Culture granted to Kanda University of International Studies.

Correspondence should be sent to the first author at etm@is.s.u-tokyo.ac.jp or University of Tokyo, Faculty of Science, Dept of Information Science, Tsujii Lab., 7-3-1 Hongo Bunkyo-ku Tokyo 113-0033 JAPAN.

References

Cheng, L. L. S. 1991. On the Typology of Wh-questions. Doctoral dissertation, MIT.

Chomsky, N. 1981. *Lectures on Government and Binding*. Dordrecht: Foris.

Crain, S., & Fodor, J. D. 1985. How can grammars help parsers? *Natural Language Parsing*, eds. D. R. Dowty, L. Karttunen, & A. M. Zwicky, 94-128. Cambridge, UK: Cambridge University Press.

Crain, S., & Steedman, M. 1985. On not being led up the garden path: the use of context by the psychological syntax processor. *Natural Language Parsing*, eds. D. R. Dowty, L. Karttunen, & A. M. Zwicky, 320-58. Cambridge, UK: Cambridge University Press.

de Vincenzi, M. 1991. *Syntactic Parsing Strategies in Italian*. Dordrecht: Kluwer Academic Publishers.

Fodor, J. A., Bever, T. G., & Garrett, M. F. 1974. *The Psychology of Language*. New York: McGraw-Hill.

Fodor, J. D. 1989. Empty categories in sentence processing. *Language and Cognitive Processes* 4:155-209.

Frazier, L.,& Clifton, C. 1989. Successive cyclicity in the grammar and the parser. *Language and Cognitive Processes* 4:93-126.

Gazdar, G., Klein, E., Pullum, G., & Sag, I. 1985. *Generalized Phrase Structure Grammar*. Cambridge, Mass: Harvard University Press.

Gibson, E. 1998. Linguistic complexity: Locality of syntactic dependencies. *Cognition* 68:1-76.

Huang, C.-T. James. 1982. Logical Relations in Chinese and the Theory of Grammar. Doctoral dissertation, MIT.

Just, M. A., Carpenter, P. A., & Woolley, J. D. 1982. Paradigms and processes in reading comprehension. *Journal of Experimental Psychology: General* 3:228-38.

Marslen-Wilson, W., & Tyler, L. K. 1980. The temporal structure of spoken language understanding. *Cognition* 8:1-71.

May, R. 1985. *Logical Form — Its structure and derivation*. Cambridge, Mass: MIT Press.

Miyamoto E. T., & Takahashi, S. 2000. Wh-phrases and typing mismatch in Japanese. In preparation.

Nishigauchi, T. 1990. *Quantification in the Theory of Grammar*. Dordrecht: Kluwer Academic Publishers.

Pesetsky, D. 1987. Wh-in-situ: movement and unselective binding. *The Representation of (In)definiteness*, eds. E. J. Reuland, & A. G. B. ter Meulen, 98-129. Cambridge, Mass.: MIT Press.

Pritchett, B. L., & Whitman, J. B. 1995. Syntactic representation and interpretive preference. *Japanese Sentence Processing*, eds. R. Mazuka, & N. Nagai, 65-76. Mahwah, NJ: Lawrence Erlbaum.

Watanabe, A. 1992. Subjacency and S-structure movement of wh-in-situ. *Journal of East Asian Linguistics* 1:255-91.

On Sound Symbolism in Japanese and Korean

REIJIROU SHIBASAKI
University of California, Santa Barbara

1. Introduction

Sound symbolism has long attracted the attention of anthropologists and linguists at least throughout this century. Therefore, there are various approaches with different technical terms.[1] Yet roughly speaking, the main approaches to sound symbolism are divided into two types: negative and positive. As an extreme negativist, for example, Newmeyer (1992: 758) argues that 'the number of pictorial, imitative, or onomatopoetic words in any language is vanishingly small' (see Saussure 1983: 69). On the other hand, Swadesh (1972: 162), a positivist, suggests that 'they (=people) make language express many and very important things that are not necessarily implicit in the words themselves'.

---

* I am grateful to Matthew Gordon, Sun-Ae Lee, Marianne Mithun, Pat Clancy, Joseph Park, Junghee Ahn and Edmundo Luna for their invaluable comments and supports. Also, much helpful input came from discussions with Seiichi Makino, Jee Tauber and anonymous JK-reviewers. The remaining faults are all my own.
[1] For example, see Taylor and Taylor (1962) which displays a cross-linguistic analysis of nonsense words in English, Japanese, Korean and Tamil. The result is that the Japanese and Korean speakers tend to have the same impression about a given nonsense word more than the English and Tamil speakers do. Some well-known terms are as follows: *onomatopoeia* (appeared in English in 1577); *Ecoism* (by Jespersen); *Phonaesthetic* (from Firth 1957; originally in 1930); *Ideophone* (from Doke 1935 who used it for Bantu languages). Of course, these terms are slightly different in usage.

For convenience, we will start from the following working hypothesis based on the negative view of sound symbolism, as in Chart 1. Also, we will continue to use the term 'sound symbolism' (=SS) or 'sound symbolic words' (=SSW) because this study centers on sound symbolism in general, including vowel ablaut, consonantal changes and others.

System	Non-Organized
Quantity	Small
Motivation	None / Arbitrary

CHART 1: The Working Hypothesis

2. Data and Categorization

The data sources are illustrated in this section. The Korean SSW are from Lee (1992), Sohn (1994) and my native consultants, and all examples are presented in the Yale system of romanization. The Japanese SSW are from Asano (1978) and my native consultants. The sources of examples from other languages are specified whenever referred to.

The number of SSW examined for this study amounts to 1500 on average (Japanese: 1800; Korean: 1300, approximately), and these are phonologically and semantically analyzed, divided into three subcategories:[2]

(1) Categorization of SSW:[3]
a. *Phonomimes*: imitation of human, animal or natural sounds;
b. *Phenomimes*: depiction of manner, look, shape, …etc. in the external world;
c. *Psychomimes*: expression of internal feelings, conditions, or sensations

3. Methodology

This study consists of two experiments: psychological and phonological. The psychological experiment goes through the following three steps: 1) a non-linguistics student randomly chooses SSW from each subcategory; 2) a Japanese consultant checks the Korean SSW and a Korean consultant checks the Japanese SSW; 3) if s/he almost completely understands the

---

[2] Note that some interjections in both languages were illustrated at the conference, yet they are omitted here because of limitations of space.

[3] According to these definitions, the numbers of SSWs in each subcategory are approximately: Phenomimes 60~70%, Phonomimes 25~35%, and Psychomimes 2~3% in both languages. Of course, many SSW cannot be categorized into one subcategory, so this is very difficult to calculate. What is worse, definitions vary from one researcher to another (see note 10).

meaning of a given SSW, I rate it two points; when s/he cannot understand it, I explain to her/him a certain situation where it is used. Then if s/he understands it with my explanation, I rate it one point; if s/he cannot understand it even with my explanation, I rate it zero.[4] For example, my Korean consultant completely understands a Japanese SSW 'sala-sala' (a rustling sound of wind), and I rate it two points. A similar scenario is provided for all the selected SSW. Note that 40 phonomimes (20 animal sounds and 20 nature sounds), 30 phenomimes, and 10 psychomimes are chosen from both languages.

The phonological experiment is built on the analysis of whether there are certain cognitive or physiological relations of sound to meaning for both vowels and consonants in Japanese and Korean. The result of this experiment will address our working hypothesis in Chart 1.

We can regard these two experiments as follows. The psychological experiment is a kind of 'macro' analysis because it is based on Gestalt perception of SSWs. On the other hand, the phonological experiment is a kind of 'micro' analysis because the focus is narrowed down to each vowel and consonant in SSWs.

4. Analysis 1: A Psychological Experiment

In this section, the three types of SSW subcategorized in (1) are illustrated in 4.1 through 4.3, and the results are summarized in 4.4. Note that because of limitations of space, only part of the selected data is demonstrated. 'N=20' in the parentheses means that the examples given are from a total of 20. The number to the right of each example in Japanese and Korean indicates the rating of comprehension as explained in section 3. (K→J) means that Korean consultants check the Japanese SSW, and (J→K) means the reverse. A sign '<' means degrees of intensity.

4.1 Phonomimes in Japanese and Korean[5]

In this subsection, we will see two types of phonomimes: animal and nature sounds, and these results are separately illustrated in Charts 2 through 4.

Let us first look at the examples in (2). The important thing is that the phonomimes listed are felt to be really similar to my consultants of Japanese and Korean, irrespective of whether the correlation of sound to meaning is completely transparent to them or not. Interestingly, the cries of relatively familiar animals like cats and dogs seem to be conventionalized in

---

[4] In short, this is a simple version of the 'semantic differential' analysis set forth, for instance, by Osgood et al. (1975: 40-41).

[5] Examples from other languages, including English, KiVunjo-Chaga, Punjabi, Seneca and Tamil are available. Yet not all of them are illustrated here because of limitations of space.

similar sequence of sounds, not only in Japanese and Korean, but also in some other languages.

(2) The Animals Sounds (N=20):

	Japanese (K→J)		Korean (J→K)	
Dog	*wan-wan*	1	*meng-meng*	1
Cat	*nyaon-nyaon, nyan, nyaa*	2	*yaong-yaong*	2
Bird (small)	*ciik-ciik* *pii-cik*	2	*ccik-ccik* *ccayk-ccayk*	2
Crow	*ka:-ka:*	1	*kkawuk-kkawuk* *kkak-kkak*	1
Rooster	*kokekokko:, kokkoo*	1	*kkokkiyo, kkokkyo*	2
Cuckoo	*kakkoo-kakkoo*	1	*ppekkwuk-ppekkwuk*	0
Cow	*moo-moo, um(m)oo*	1	*ummey*	1
Frog	*kero-kero* *gweeko-gweeko*	2	*kaekol-kaekol* *kaekul-kaekul*	2
Locust	*miin-miin*	1	*maym-maym*	2
Pig	*buu-buu*	1	*kkwul-kkwul*	0
Owl	*hoo-hoo*	1	*pueng-pueng*	0
Horse	*hin-hin, hihiin*	2	*hiig-hiing*	2

For example, it seems that the barking of dogs has an initial bilabial sound, as in 'waŋwaŋ' (Chinese), 'bau-wau' (English), 'pàù-pàù' (Punjabi from Bhatia 1993), 'vaalvaal' (Tamil from Asher 1985), ...etc. And the crying of cats seems to have an initial nasal sound, as in 'mjao-mjao' (Chinese), 'miau' or 'mjau' (English), 'miyaaüü' (Punjabi), ...etc.[6] On the other hand, some animal sounds are not similar as in pigs and owls. Yet any

---

[6] Matsumoto and Kato (1993) give an interesting sound-spectrographic analysis of SSW in Chinese, English and Japanese. Their analysis is based on a naive question: which onomatopoeia is most similar to the real crying sound. The results are in the following orders:

Dog: 1.English (bau-wau) 2.Chinese (waŋ-waŋ) 3.Japanese (wan-wan)
Cat: 1.English (miau) 2.Japanese (nyaa-nyaa) 3.Chinese (mjao-mjao)
Horse: 1.Chinese (hui-hui) 2.Japanese (hihiin) 3.English (nei)

Their comment on this result is that the crying of dogs and cats is very similar to the real sound, yet the crying of horses is far from the real sound in the three languages. In addition, the crying of horses is different form each other in three languages. However, the important thing related to our analysis is that the crying of horses is conventionalized in a similar sequence of sounds in Japanese and Korean. This gives support for the opinion by Taylor and Taylor (1962) as in note 1, and implies that Japanese and Korean share something common (see also note 8).

others are not so different, like frogs[7] and locusts, therefore the comprehension of animal sounds by the Japanese and Korean consonants is high.

Nature sounds are relatively similar, and the comprehension of them is not so low in both languages, as in Chart 2. I cannot show all the data here, but in many cases, the initial sounds (and sometimes, initial CV clusters) tend to be analogous in Japanese and Korean. Let us take a look at (3).

(3) The Nature Sounds (N=20):

	Japanese (K→J)		Korean (J→K)	
clinking	*calin* < *calan*, *(kachin)*	2	*callang* < *celleng* *ccallang* < *ccelleng*	2
boiling, bubbling	*puku-puku* < *buku-buku* < *boko-boko*	1	*pokul-pokul* *pwukul-pwukul* < *(ppwukul-ppwukul)*	2
rustling (wind)	*sala-sala*, *saja-saja*, *sojo-sojo*	2	*sal-sal* < *sol-sol* < *swul-swul*	1
gulping	*goku-goku* < *gubi-gubi*	1	*kkolkkak* < *kkwulkkek*, *kkolttak* < *kkwulttek*	0
rattling	*kata-kata*, *kara-kara*, etc.	1	*talkak* < *telkek* *ttalkak* < *ttelkek*, etc.	1

Whether the initial consonants are voiceless or voiced, their sounds are comparable to each other. If compared to other languages, the similarity would be more obvious. For example, the sounds of boiling or bubbling are 'baṛ' or 'baṛaaṇaa' in Punjabi (from Bhatia 1993), and 'taḷa-taḷa-ṇṇu' in Tamil (from Asher 1985). None of these are understandable to either Japanese or Korean consultants. In short, the Japanese and Korean speakers can associate a similar sound with the same meaning, though not always. Of course, there are some complex cases, for example, where Japanese and Tamil happen to have similar sequences of sounds in SSW like 'gatu-gatu' in Japanese and 'gaṭ-gaṭ' in Punjabi; however, they are different in meaning. The former indicates a manner of eating rapidly or hungrily, but the latter a sound of gulping. We cannot make any full analyses of the sound-and-meaning correlation here, although this is necessary. Our findings are summarized in (4).

---

[7] In Seneca, frogs croak like 'krŏkrŏk' (Mithun 1982: 53), and two Japanese consultants completely associated it with the croaking of frogs 'kero-kero' in Japanese.

(4) The Findings from Phonomimes:

a. Phonomimes in J/K are similar, compared to other languages;

b. Basically, vowel ablaut/consonantal change is rare in J/K;

c. Animal/nature sounds are physically the same as in the external world: the external basis of SS (weak language-universal?);

d. Animal/nature sounds are perceived as being relatively fixed (see Lee 1992: 110);

e. Rating: K→J 67.5% (animal sounds); 57.5% (nature sounds);
    J→K 57.5% (animal sounds); 37.5% (nature sounds).

The findings in (4b) through (4d) are important. They indicate that human beings cannot control animal/nature sounds, which tend to be perceived as fixed expressions, basically with no vowel/consonant change. As a result, the comprehension rating of phonomimes is relatively higher than that of phenomimes or psychomimes. In sum, the correlation of sound to meaning in phonomimes is iconic across Japanese and Korean.

4.2 Phenomimes in Japanese and Korean

As in note 3, phenomimes make up a greater part of SSW in Japanese and Korean. Yet there are some problems with this. For example, quite a few phenomimes are semantically developed from nature sounds (at least in Japanese), whereas some are extended into psychomimes and already conventionalized in various ways. Therefore it is very difficult to categorize phenomimes. Moreover, some phenomimes can perhaps be considered to derive from nouns.[8] Of course, it may be possible to discover the original functions of SSW and to see their semantic developments; however this is beyond the realm of this study.

Now let us consider the phenomimes in (5). The first three examples are relatively similar, therefore understandable to the speakers of Japanese and Korean, while the rest are so different that my consultants could not associate them with their respective meaning. On the whole, phenomimes are more or less language-specifically motivated, as far as can be judged from those examined for this study. The rating of comprehension goes down slightly as shown in Chart 2.

---

[8] In my opinion, for example, the Japanese phonomime/phenomime 'doki' in (5) derives from a noun 'douki' (beating/palpitation) through phonological reductions and reduplication processes. In addition, my Korean consultant told me an interesting episode that a Korean phenomime 'muk-muk' (being silent) was developed from Chinese 'mò' (being silent as V and Adj.), and is written 黙 in both languages. Interestingly, this word came to Japanese with the same form 黙; however it is used as a verb or compound word, not as a phenomime. This kind of geographical correlation of SSW is also important.

(5) Manner, Look, Shape, ...etc. (N=30)

	Japanese (K→J)		Korean (J→K)	
pitapat	*dokun-dokun* < *dokkun-dokkun* *(doki-doki* < *dokkin-dokkin)*	2	*twukun-twukun,* *(pelttek* < *phelttek* < *ppelttek)*	2
trembling, shivering	*pulu-pulu* < *bulu-bulu*	2	*(pal-pal* < *pel-pel* <*)* *pwul-pwul*	1
frozen hard	*kachin-kochin,* *kon-kon*	2	*kkong-kkong*	1
(burning) lively	*mera-mera,*	0	*ikul-ikul*	0
plump, chubby	*puku-puku* < *buku-buku* *pukkun-pukkun* < *bukkun*	0	*photong-photong* < *phutwung-phutwung*	0
stealthily	*koso-koso,* *sorori-sorori*	0	*salkum-salkum* < *sulkum-sulkum*	0

It should be noted, however, that we can find more similar SSW in Japanese and Korean than in other languages. For example, the SSW of trembling or shivering in Japanese and Korean are analogous to each other, but the corresponding SSW 'thar' or 'tharaaṇaa' in Punjabi seems not.[9] In fact, my consultants of both languages could not make out the meaning of the latter sound. At any rate, there is still something common at work in Japanese and Korean. Our findings are summarized in (6).

(6) The Findings from Phenomimes:
a. Phenomimes in J/K are rarely if ever the same or similar, but some are recognizable;
b. Basically, vowel ablaut/consonantal change is abundant in J/K;
c. Rating: K→J 31.7%; J→K 33.3%.

In comparison to phonomimes, especially animal sounds, there are much more varied SSW for one meaning. In addition, the shades of meaning are expressed usually with consonantal change in Japanese and with both consonantal and vowel changes in Korean. This is quite

---

[9] These Punjabi phenomimes 'thar' or 'tharaaṇaa' are from Arabic as seen in Persian too. I am grateful to Jees Tauber for this comment.

systematic, counter to our working hypothesis (see section 5 and K.-O. Kim 1977). However, the correlation of sound to meaning in phenomimes is often language-specific, so iconicity seems limited to each language.

4.3 Psychomimes in Japanese and Korean

The number of psychomimes is very small in Japanese and Korean; in some cases, a corresponding or similar SSW does not exist. Lee (1992: 90) states, following Hamano (1986/1998), that Korean SSW (like Bantu languages) play broader roles in all aspects of grammar than Japanese. However, judging from my data and its categorization as in (1), Japanese seems to have many more psychomimes than Korean. Yet the number of SSW varies from one researcher to another (see note 3 and 10); therefore this opinion must be researched further. Let us turn to the psychomimes in (7).

(7) Internal Feelings, Conditions, Sensations, …etc. (N=10):

	Japanese (K→J)		Korean (J→K)	
disturbedly, uneasily	*ira-ira* *sowa-sowa*	0	*swulleng-swulleng*	0
pricking, sticking, irritating	*ciku-ciku,* *muka-muka,* *ira-ira*	0	*kkalkkum-kkalkkum* < *kkelkkum-kkelkkum*	0 ~ 1
chilly	*zoku* < *zoku-zoku*	0	*samul* < *senul*	0
sudden burst of anger	*kka, kacin, (pakiin)*	0	*palkkun* < *pwulkkun* *pelkkun*	0
in total chaos	*?moya-moya,* *?mowa-mowa*	0	*twicwukpakcwuk*	0
terribly pitiful	*? / … … … …*	…	*cicili (< Adv.)*	0
losing one's composure	*musyakusya(-suru)*	0	*?kwucil-kwucil(-hata)*	0

The correlation of sound to meaning is almost completely limited to each language, never across languages. This is the most crucial finding. Actually, one Korean consultant and I needed several meetings to comprehend the shades of nuance of psychomimes inherent in each language. However, we could not find good examples with any similar meaning and sound. Importantly, it is also reported that phenomimes differ from dialect to dialect in Japanese (Asano 1978: 8-9); therefore psychomimes may be more different. For dialectal variations in Korean SSW see Kim-Renaud (1976:409, note 9). The findings are summarized in (8).

(8) The Findings from Psychomimes:
a. No SSW are similar enough: the internal-basis of SS (language-specific);
b. In both languages, the number of psychomimes is small;
c. Sometimes, a corresponding SSW does not exist (language-specific);
d. Basically, vowel ablaut/consonantal change is not so abundant in both languages;
e. Rating: K→J 0%; J→K 5%.

4.4 Summary of the Psychological Analysis

Finally in this section, I will explain about Charts 2 through 4. The rating of comprehension is summarized in Chart 2, which clearly shows a continuum of transparency between sound and meaning as in Chart 4. The stimulus-and-response relation is illustrated in Chart 3. As explained in the above subsections, phonomimes are relatively fixed, while phenomimes have various expressions, for example, with consonantal change in Japanese and vowel ablaut in Korean for one meaning. This implies that human beings can control relatively proximal things, but not distal things. The physically distal SSWs, phonomimes, are in the domain of higher sensory modalities (sight and hearing) whose stimuli are relatively stronger; therefore they are perceived as being fixed. Yet the physically proximal SSWs, phenomimes, are in the domain of not higher, but lower sensory modalities; therefore their stimuli are not so strong that their realization tend to be language-specific and diversified, as in (5) and Charts 3 and 4. This fact is reflected in the quantity of phonomimes vs. phenomimes. How about psychomimes? Psychomimes are depictions of internal feelings and conditions whose stimuli are not visual and basically soundless: in other words, we cannot perceive them in an objective way.[10] Their small quantity accounts for this view. In addition, Japanese and Korean often do not have any corresponding SSW for a psychomimetic phenomenon. Therefore, internal feelings, conditions, etc. tend to be more language-specifically realized than phenomimes, as summarized in Charts 2 through 4. All in all, our three charts can explain these facts, illustrating a continuum of transparency from language-specific to weak language-universal.[11]

---

[10] Masataka (1999: 217) reports that Japanese tend to use gesture with phenomimes, though they do not usually use gesture. According to Masataka, approximately 40% of phenomimes tend to occur with gesture. (In his opinion, psychomimes seem to be included in phenomimes) This fact suggests that the more abstract expressions are, the more they need visual explanatory support like gesture, perhaps in order to make transparent the correlation of sound to meaning.

[11] Of course, morpho-syntactic structures (like reduplications) are important for the realization of SSW, so this is never a strong language-universal. I am grateful to Soohee Kim and Emily Curtis for this comment.

	PHONO I (Animal Sounds)	PHONO II (Nature Sounds)	PHENO	PSYCHO
K → J	67.5%	57.5%	31.7%	0%
J → K	57.5%	37.5%	33.3%	5%

CHART 2: The Rating of Comprehension

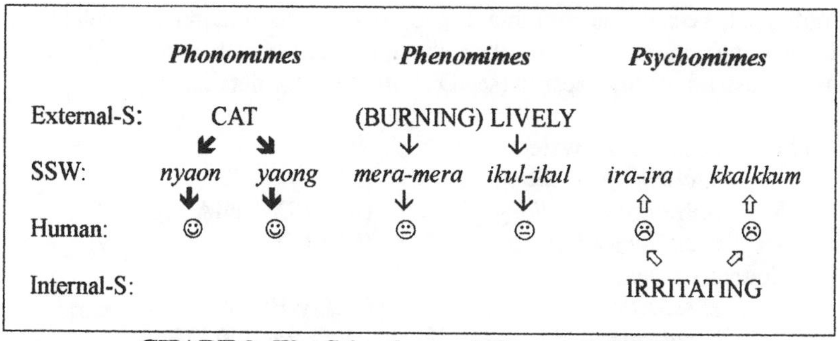

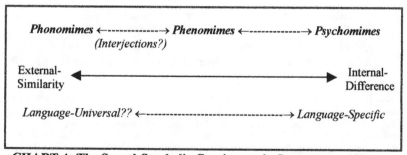

CHART 3: The Stimulus-and-Response Relation

→ : Visual & Sound stimuli, and both are strong
→ : Visual stimulus is strong, but Sound stimulus is weak
⇨ : Basically, Visual & Sound stimuli are weak.
S : Stimulus

Phonomimes ←-------------→ *Phenomimes* ←-------------→ *Psychomimes*
            (Interjections?)

External-Similarity ◄────────────────────► Internal-Difference

Language-Universal?? ←----------------------------------→ *Language-Specific*

CHART 4: The Sound-Symbolic Continuum in Japanese and Korean

5. Analysis 2: A Phonological Experiment

In this section, we will briefly see how vowels and consonants influence the shades of meaning of SSW in Japanese and Korean. Because of limitations of space, I will focus here on vowels, although my sound-spectrographic analyses of consonantal burst tension provide additional evidence. The main point in this section is to see how sounds are physiologically motivated and language-specifically realized at the same time.

5.1 Vowel Motivation in Korean

We will investigate the five vowels from standard Korean, based on Sohn (1994). The Korean vowels can be viewed as language-specifically motivated, because as in Table 1, the vowel [i] is semantically related to bigness, heaviness, ...etc. most of which are related rather to [a] than to [i] as in cross-linguistic research (see Diffloth 1994 for details).

(9) Slopping sounds of water:

	a. *challang-challang*:	(LESS)
	b. *chollong-chollong*:	(INTERMEDIATE)
	c. *chilleng-chilleng*:	(MORE)

(10) Sounds of wind:

	a. *sal-sal*:	(SLOWEST)
	b. *sol-sol*:	(INTERMEDIATE)
	c. *swul-swul*	(FASTEST)

Korean:	vowels [i, u, e]:[12]	BIGNESS, HEAVINESS, DULLNESS, THICKNESS, QUICKNESS, ... etc.
	vowels [a, o]:	SMALLNESS, (LIGHTNESS), SHARPNESS, THINNESS, SLOWNESS, ... etc.
		(cf. Sohn 1994: 500)

Table 1: The Relation of Vowel to Meaning in Korean

In the psychological experiment, every example in (9) and (10) is rated '2' by all Japanese consultants, so the gestalt (or macro) perception of SSW

---

[12] The semantic interpretation of the vowel [i] is problematic. A Korean consultant (a Seoul speaker) explains that it does not always indicate bigness or heaviness. However, his wife (also, a native Korean) says that it is closely related to bigness and heaviness. In my opinion, this semantic ambiguity is rooted in some socio-cultural aspects (see Kim-Renaud 1976: 408; 409, notes. 2 and 9). Moreover, the vowel [i] passed through a complex historical process in Middle through Modern Korean (K.-O.Kim 1977: 70-72), so it is hard to define its implicated meaning. Note that even Sohn (1999) avoids referring to this vowel, though explaining it in Sohn (1994). I think that this is because the semantic interpretation of [i] in Korean is still controversial. The other vowels reached a consensus among my Korean consultants as in Table 1.

is transparent, at least in these examples. Yet how about micro-perception? Japanese consultants felt strange about this correlation of vowels to meanings, while some did not care for the vowel ablaut. We have to avoid any immediate decisions; however the latter opinion would reflect usual impressions of vowel ablaut by Japanese. This is because the semantic contrast of SSW is basically due to the voiced/voiceless change of consonants, not to vowel ablaut.[13] At any rate, the correlation of sound to meaning in Korean SSW is systematically motivated as in Table 1, which clearly goes against our working hypothesis.

5.2 Vowel Motivation in Japanese
In this subsection, the three Japanese vowels [i, a, o] are examined. In contrast to Korean, the vowel [e] is extremely rare in Japanese SSW,[14] and the vowel [u] seems not to show a clear semantic contrast in SSW, unlike (10). Let us consider (11) and (12).

(11) A quick sound of rotation as heard in winding screws:
    a. *kiri-kiri*   (smooth and light sounds)
    b. *giri-giri*   (hard and heavy sounds)
(12) A continual sound of rolling as heard in the motion of balls:
    a. *koro-koro*   (small round balls)
    b. *goro-goro*   (heavy balls, but not always round)

Japanese: vowel [i]:	SMALLNESS, QUICKNESS, ... etc.
vowels [a, o]:	BIGNESS, SLOWNESS, ... etc.
	(cf. Asano 1978: 19)

Table 2: The Relation of Vowel to Meaning in Japanese

The pair (11a) and (12a) shows vowel contrast, but the semantic contrast is not so clear. The pair (11b) and (12b) is the same. As explained in 5.1 and note 13, the shades of nuance of Japanese SSW are explained by the voiced/voiceless change of consonants, not vowel ablaut. Therefore, the semantic contrast is clearer in (11a) vs. (11b), and (12a) vs. (12b). However,

---

[13] This fact may be related to the loss of vowel harmony (=VH) in Japanese. Japanese VH had already disappeared in the 9th century, so almost nothing remains, even in SSW (Ohno 1974:197). On the other hand, Korean VH existed until the 17th century (*ibid.*), and has almost disappeared in present day standard Korean, except in SSW. Also see Kim-Renaud (1976:408) for brief comments on Korean VH.

[14] In the history of Japanese, the sounds [ï (=ɯ), ě, e] seem to have developed later than other vowels (Ohno 1974: 162-63): ai > ě, ia > e, ui > ï, ŏi > ï. This may be the reason why the vowel [e] is rare in Japanese SSW. See also Asano (1978: 19).

it is also true that all Japanese consultants agree to the vowel contrast in Table 2. The findings from vowels are summarized as follows.

Similarity:	i) [i] sound tends to indicate QUICKNESS in J/K;
	ii) [a, o] tend to indicate SLOWNESS in J/K;
Difference:	i) the Japanese [i] sound tends to indicate SMALLNESS, while the Korean [i] indicates BIGNESS;
	ii) [a, o] in both languages are impossible to compare, or completely different in meaning

Table 3: The Summary of Vowel Motivation in Japanese and Korean

Basically, vowel contrast is language-specifically motivated, but is systematic. The semantic contrast of vowels [i, u, e] to [a, o] in Korean is accounted for uniquely by the height of tongue. The semantic contrast of [i] to [a, o] vowels in Japanese is also explained in the same way, but sometimes motivated in the converse way. Certain contrasts are illustrated in Charts 5 and 6. This study represents a starting point for this kind of iconic analysis. From the examination thus far, it can be concluded that SSWs are physiologically motivated and language-specifically realized in vowel systems, at least in Japanese and Korean.[15] A full typological analysis awaits further research.

Korean	[a, o]	[i, u, e]
Size	LESS ←---------------------------→ MORE	
Speed	LESS ←---------------------------→ MORE	
Weight	LESS ←---------------------------→ MORE	
Thickness	LESS ←---------------------------→ MORE	
Quickness	LESS ←---------------------------→ MORE	

CHART 5: The SIMPLEX Iconicity of Vowel in Korean

Japanese	[a, o]	[i]
Size	MORE ←---------------------------→ LESS	
Speed	LESS ←---------------------------→ MORE	

CAHRT 6: The COMPLEX Iconicity of Vowel in Japanese

---

[15] For strong evidence of physiological motivation of sound to meaning see Gouffé (1966). That study reports that in Hausa, the lip-rounding sounds [kw, gw, 'kw] are always associated with round objects. Of course, both Japanese and Korean SSW are also systematically and physiologically motivated in consonantal systems as I presented at the conference.

6. Concluding Remarks

This study suggests that SSWs are rich in quantity, systematically organized, and motivated either (weakly) language-universally or language-specifically: in other words, they are fully iconic. Thus, our working hypothesis was wrong, and is reformulated in Chart 7.

System	Organized
Quantity	Large
Motivation	Exists

CHART 7: The Japanese and Korean SSW

References (partial)

Asano, T. (1978) *Giongo Gitaigo Jiten*. Tokyo: Kadokawa-shoten.
Asher, R.E. (1985) *Tamil*. London and Sydney: Croom Helm.
Bhatia, T. K. (1993) *Punjabi*. London: Routledge.
Diffloth, G. (1994) *i*: big, *a*: small. *Sound Symbolism*, eds. Hinton, L., J. Nichols, and J.J.Ohara, 107-114. Cambridge: Cambridge UP.
Doke, C. (1935) *Bantu Linguistic Terminology*. New York: Green & Co.
Firth, J.R.(1957) *Papers in Linguistics 1934-1951*. London: Oxford UP.
Gouffé, C.(1966) Noms d'objets "rond" en haussa. *Comptes Rendus du Groupe Linguistique d'Etudes Chamito-Sémitique* 10: 104-13.
Hamano, S. (1998) *The Sound-Symbolic System of Japanese*. Stanford, CA: CSLI Publications. (originally, Doctoral dissertation, University of Florida, 1986)
Kim, K.-O. (1977) Sound Symbolism in Korean. *Journal of Linguistics* 13: 67-75.
Kim-Renaud, Y.-K. (1976) Semantic Features in Phonology: Evidence from Vowel Harmony in Korean. *CLS* 12: 397-412.
Lee, Jin-Seong (1992) *Phonology and Sound Symbolism of Korean Ideophones*. Doctoral dissertation, Indiana University.
Masataka, N. (1999) Kotoba: Tanjoo-no Imi. *Gakumon-no Kakutou*, ed. Yourou Takeshi, 206-229. Tokyo: Nikkei Sience.
Matsumoto, H. and Kato, H. (1993) 'Bow-wow' or 'Wan-wan'. *Gengo* 22 (6). Tokyo: Taisyuukan-shoten.
Mithun, M. (1982) The Synchronic and Diachronic Behavior of Plops, Squeaks, Croaks, Sighs, and Moans. *IJAL* 48(1): 49-58.
Newmeyer, F. J. (1992) Iconicity and Generative Grammar. *Language* 68: 756-96.
Ohno, S. (1974) *Nihongo-no Kigen*. Tokyo: Iwanami.
Osgood, C.E., May, W.H. and Miron, M.S. (1975) *Cross-Cultural Universals of Affected Meaning*. Urbana and Chicago: University of Illinois Press.
de Saussure, F. (1983) *Courses in general linguistics*. La salle Illinois: Open Court.
Sohn, Ho-Min (1994) *Korean*. London: Routledge.
Sohn, Ho-Min (1999) *The Korean Language*. Cambridge: Cambridge UP.
Swadesh,M.(1972) *The Origin and Diversification of Language*. London:Routledge.
Taylor, I.K and Taylor, M.M (1962) Phonetic Symbolism in Four Unrelated Languages. *Canadian Journal of Psychology* 14 (4): 344-56.

A Cognitive Account of Extraction Asymmetry in Japanese Relative Clauses

Mitsuaki Shimojo
State University of New York at Buffalo

1. Introduction

Since the proposal of so-called island constraints by John Ross (1967), the constraints have become central issues in syntactic theories. While the formalist's theories continue to reformulate the constraints, there have been proposals from functional perspectives (e.g. Erteschik-Shir & Lappin 1979, Kuno 1987, Van Valin 1996), and particularly over the past ten years, island effects have been studied from a cognitive perspective, in terms of the attention and working memory mechanism (e.g. Deane 1991, 1992). The primary goals of this paper are to demonstrate that observed island effects in relative clauses in Japanese are due to processing difficulties and to account for why extraction is more restricted in so-called internally-headed relative clauses, that are claimed to be more matrix-like than the externally-headed counterparts.

A cognitive theory of island phenomena used in this study assumes the following theoretical premises. In order for knowledge to be identified and utilized, information relevant to the task must be activated in one's consciousness. However, when information is activated, certain activation costs are involved.

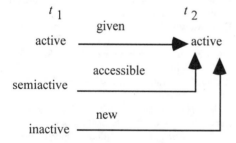

Figure 1: Activation states, activation costs, and time (Chafe 1994: 73)

Chafe (1994) shows in Figure 1 that already activated concepts, i.e. concepts in one's focus of attention, are readily available for current processing, but previously semiactivated concepts requires some activation cost, and nonactive concepts require an even greater activation cost to be available for processing. Thus, when a referring expression is encountered in discourse, if it has not been activated, the mental representation of the referent must be activated or reactivated, requiring some activation cost. Secondly, it is assumed that our working memory capacity is limited so that only a limited amount of information may be focused at one time (see Anderson 1983). Therefore, activation of particular information causes deactivation of the other that has been active, unless these pieces of information are related to each other so that activation spreads from one to the other and thus both are kept activated.

With the assumption above, Deane (1992) illustrates the mechanism of island effects, as summarized as follows:

(i) Extraction is an intrinsically difficult processing task since the extracted phrase and its extraction site are discontinuous but must be processed together. ...

(ii) Intrinsically difficult tasks may be impossible to perform except under conditions which optimize performance. If the problem with extraction is an attentional overload, then optimal performance should occur when the extracted phrase and the extraction site attract attention automatically. ...   (ibid, 30)

The optimal performance is attained if the extracted phrase is potentially topical, hence has already been salient in the hearer's mind, and the extraction site is the information focus, which attracts the hearer's focus of attention. For example:

(1) a. What was John willing to live without?
    b. What did John fight against?
    c. *What did John eat salad without?
    d. *Which parent's wishes did you get married against? (Deane 1991)

In (a) and (b), the extracted element is a part of the VP, which is the natural focus element; therefore, both the wh-expression and the extraction site naturally attract attention. In (c) and (d), on the other hand, the VP is independent of the following PP; hence, the VP competes with the extraction site for attention.

The processing difficulties may be described in terms of the bridging elements for extraction, as Kluender (1990: 188) summarizes as follows:

Open-class, low frequency, referentially specific constituents are the best candidates for extraction but simultaneously difficult to extract over... Conversely, closed-class, high frequency, referentially nonspecific constituents are relatively easy to extract over.

Naturally, open-class, low-frequency, referentially specific elements require more processing load to be activated and presumably to be maintained in the cognitive focus as well; hence, these are not suitable as bridging elements. In (2), for example, as the referential specificity of the 'picture' increases, from (a) to (e), the extraction out of the NP becomes increasingly difficult.

(2) a. Who did you see pictures of? >
    b. Who did you see a picture of? >
    c. Who did you see the picture of? >
    d. Who did you see his picture of? >
    e. Who did you see John's picture of? (Erteschik-Shir & Lappin 1979)

2. High matrixhood of IHRCs

The two types of relative clause constructions, that will be discussed throughout, are shown in (3).

(3) a. Externally-headed relative clause [EHRC]
    [Mary ga ___i tutta] sakanai o   John ga   ryoorisita
        NOM   caught fish   ACC   NOM cooked
    'John cooked the fish which Mary caught.'
    b. Internally-headed relative clause [IHRC]
    [Mary ga   sakana o   tutta]   no   o   John ga   ryoorisita
        NOM   fish   ACC   caught   NMZ   ACC   NOM cooked

It has been suggested in the literature that IHRCs are more matrix-clause like than the externally-headed counterparts. There is a semantic and conceptual basis for this contrast. In the linear processing of an IHRC, the proposition represented by the relative clause is processed without singling out a particular referent of the proposition. Then the proposition is related to another proposition expressed by the matrix clause. This contrasts with EHRCs, which single out a referent of the proposition to modify. Figures 2 and 3 illustrate the conceptual structure for each type.

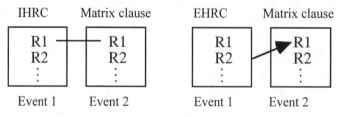

| IHRC | Matrix clause | | EHRC | Matrix clause |

Event 1 relates to Event 2 via the shared referent and "relevancy" (Kuroda 1976).

Event 1 as a whole modifies the referent in Event 2.

Figure 2: IHRC

Figure 3: EHRC

Figure 2 shows that IHRCs denote an event without singling out a particular referent to modify. The two separate events are linked with each other by the shared referent and pragmatically *relevancy*, as Kuroda (1976) argues, or more specifically Event 1 enables Event 2 to occur, as Ohara (1996) claims. On the other hand, Figure 3 depicts that the whole event described by the EHRC is simply an attribute for the singled out referent. Therefore, Event 1 is conceptually more dependent on Event 2 in this type.

This argument is favored by a semantic relation between an IHRC and its matrix clause. It has been claimed (e.g. Silverstein 1976) that different semantic relations between syntactic units may be ranked in a continuum, based on the extent to which the units represent a single event or discrete events. Van Valin & LaPolla (1997) list the major semantic relations in the form of Interclausal Semantic Relations Hierarchy, as shown in Figure 4.

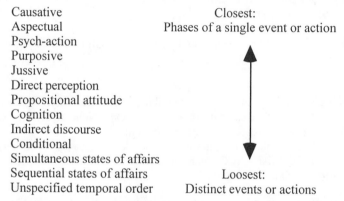

Causative   Closest:
Aspectual   Phases of a single event or action
Psych-action
Purposive
Jussive
Direct perception
Propositional attitude
Cognition
Indirect discourse
Conditional
Simultaneous states of affairs
Sequential states of affairs   Loosest:
Unspecified temporal order   Distinct events or actions

Figure 4: Interclausal Semantic Relations Hierarchy (Van Valin & LaPolla 1997: 480)

The two events represented by an IHRC and its matrix clause resemble sequential states of affairs, in which one event establishes a condition for the other to occur. As shown in Figure 4, sequential states of affairs are represented by loosely-connected syntactic units cross-linguistically. In fact, a sentence with an IHRC is easily translated into a coordinated sentence in English. For example, the sentence in (3b) could be translated into 'Mary caught fish and John cooked them'; however, this translation does not fit (3a).

Ohara (1996) claims a morphosyntactic basis for the higher matrixhood of IHRCs. In particular, she argues that IHRCs function to be *event-reporting* in the sense that the whole proposition expressed represents assertion, hence, the sentence-focus in Lambrecht's (1994) sense. Ohara bases the claim on her observation such as the following. First, *ga*-coordinated clauses and IHRCs both disallow wh-questions, while the corresponding wh-questions in EHRCs are generally acceptable (Ohara 1996: 71-72).

(4)
a. EHRC
    [dare ga   kattekita] ringo o   Hanako ga   tabemasita ka
    who NOM buy.came apple ACC   NOM ate   Q
    Lit. 'Hanako ate the apple which who bought?'
b. S1 of *ga*-coordinated clauses
 * [dare ga   ringo o   kattekita] ga,   Hanako ga   tabemasita ka
    who NOM apple ACC buy.came CONJ   NOM ate   Q
    Lit. 'Who bought the apple, and Hanako ate it?'
c. IHRC
 * [dare ga   ringo o   kattekita] no   o Hanako ga   tabemasita ka
    who NOM apple ACC buy.came NMZ ACC   NOM ate   Q
    Lit. 'Who bought the apple, and Hanako ate (it)?'

Furthermore, Ohara (1996: 76) argues that IHRCs disallow the use of the topic marker *wa*.

(5)
a. [haha ga/*wa   seetaa o   okuttekureta] no ga   kyoo todoita
    mother NOM/TOP sweater ACC sent   NMZ NOM today arrived
    'Mother sent me a sweater, and (it) arrived today.'
b. [tuma ga/*wa   sakana o   tuttekita] no   o   otto ga ryoorisita
    wife NOM/TOP fish   ACC catch.came NMZ ACC   hus. NOM cooked
    'The wife caught a fish, and the husband cooked (it).'

However, the argument which I have reviewed so far raises a paradox. On one hand, IHRCs are claimed to be more matrix-clause like, due to the semantic, conceptual, and morphosyntactic basis discussed above. On the other hand, IHRCs are claimed to disallow extraction such as wh-question formation and relativization, which is cross-linguistically a matrix phenomenon. If IHRCs are matrix like, then its high matrixhood should facilitate extraction. In what follows, I will demonstrate that this paradox does not apply for two reasons: (i) relativization and topicalization are in fact allowed in both types of relative clauses under the same conditions, and (ii) the restriction on wh-questions in IHRCs is an epiphenomenon which results from attentional overload and the intrinsic information structure of wh-questions.

3. Relativization and Topicalization out of IHRCs

The topicalization out of IHRCs is in fact observed. For example:

(6) **wakamono**_i **wa** [__i kyooki noyooni ryoote o hirogete
    young.man TOP   craziness like   both.hands ACC spread

hune ni kakeyorootosuru] no o kinzyo ni iawaseta
ship to try.to.run   NMZ ACC nearby in happened.to.exist

sanyonin no hito ga awatete hikitomeru...
3.or.4 GEN people NOM in.a.hurry stop
'The young man, who tries to run to the ship with his arms spread
crazily, three or four people nearby stop (him) in a hurry...'
                (Takeo Arishima, "Aru onna")[1]

    Likewise, it is possible to relativize as well as topicalize the target NP
of the IHRCs, as shown in the constructed examples below.

(7)

a. [[__i sara no ue ni atta] no o Taro ga totta] ringo_i
       plate GEN top on existed NMZ ACC   NOM took apple
    'the apple which Taro took that was on the plate'

b. sono ringo_i wa [__i sara no ue ni atta] no o Taro ga totta
    the   TOP
    'The apple, Taro took (it) which was on the plate.'

(8)

a. [[haha ga   __i okuttekureta] no ga kyoo todoita] seetaa_i
    mother NOM   sent   NMZ NOM today arrived sweater
    'the sweater which mother sent me that arrived today'

b. sono seetaa_i wa [haha ga __i okuttekureta] no ga kyoo todoita
    the   TOP
    'The sweater, (it) which mother send me arrived today.'

It is not surprising that the extraction of a target NP is acceptable since the
NP is functionally a matrix argument as well. However, the extraction may
be acceptable even if the displaced NP is not the target of the IHRC.

(9)

a. [[__i __j katta] kuruma_j ga   kowaretesimatta]   gakusei_i
       bought car   NOM ended.up.breaking.down student
    'the student who the car that (he) bought broke down'

b. [[__i kuruma o katta] no ga kowaretesimatta] gakusei_i

---

[1] The corpus examined for this study consists of 20 sources (17 novels, 2 essays, and 1 newspaper article), containing 46 IHRC tokens in total. I would like to thank Hidematsu Miura for his help in compiling the texts.

c.   sono gakusei$_i$ wa   [___$_i$ ___$_j$ katta] kuruma$_j$ ga kowaretesimatta
      the   TOP
     'The student, the car which (he) bought broke down.'
d.   sono gakusei$_i$ wa [___$_i$ kuruma o katta] no ga kowaretesimatta

(10)
a.   [[___$_i$ ___$_j$ dasita] tegami$_j$ ga   todokanakatta] hito$_i$[2]
               mailed letter   NOM did.not.reach person
     'person who the letters that (he) mailed did not reach (the addresses)'
b.   [[___$_i$ tegami o dasita] no ga todokanakatta] hito$_i$
c.   sono hito$_i$ wa [___$_i$ dasita] tegami ga todokanakatta
      the   TOP
     'The person, the letters which (he) mailed did not reach (the addresses).'
d.   sono hito$_i$ wa [___$_i$ tegami o dasita] no ga todokanakatta

In (9) and (10), the extracted NP is not a target but it represents a referent which is potentially topical in the sense that the whole unit is *about* the referent of the extracted NP. In this regard, Kuno's Topichood Condition, as cited in (11), is relevant.

(11) Topichood Condition for Extraction (Kuno 1987: 23)
Only those constituents in a sentence that qualify as the topic of the sentence can undergo extraction processes (i.e., *Wh*-Q Movement, *Wh*-Relative Movement, Topicalization, and *It*-Clefting).

    In order to define the aboutness relationship, I suggest a diagnostic as follows. If there is a semantic/pragmatic link between the extracted NP and the bridging clause, the whole unit remains acceptable even if the lower clause containing the gap is truncated, as shown in (9') and (10').

(9')
a.   [kuruma ga   kowaretesimatta]   gakusei
     car   NOM ended.up.breaking.down student
     'the student who the car (that (he) bought) broke down'
c.   sono gakusei wa kuruma ga kowaretesimatta
     'The student, the car (which (he) bought) broke down.'

(10')
a.   [tegami ga   todokanakatta] hito
     letter NOM did.not.reach   person
     'person who the letters (that (he) mailed) did not reach (the addresses)'

---

[2]This example is from Kuno (1973: 240).

  c.   sono hito wa tegami ga todokanakatta
      'The person, the letters (which (he) mailed) did not reach (the
      addresses).'

In (9'a), for example, the truncation is acceptable because the link between
the referent 'student' and the proposition 'the car broke down' is easily
imaginable in the way that the car belongs to the student. Thus, it is
possible to interpret that the proposition is about the student.
     In (12) and (13), on the other hand, it is unacceptable to relativize or
topicalize out of either type of relative clauses.

(12)
a.* [[__$_i$ __$_j$ nusunda] otoko$_i$ o   keisatu ga   taihosita] kuruma$_j$
              stole   man ACC police NOM arrested car
    'a car which the police arrested the man who stole (it)'
b.* [[otoko ga __$_j$ nusunda] no o keisatu ga taihosita] kuruma$_i$
c.* sono kuruma$_i$ wa [__$_j$ __$_i$ nusunda] otoko$_j$ o keisatu ga taihosita
    'The car, the police arrested the man who stole (it).'
d.* sono kuruma$_i$ wa [otoko ga __$_i$ nusunda] no o keisatu ga taihosita

(13)
a.* [[__$_i$ __$_j$ kattekita] tyokoreeto$_j$ o   Hanako ga   tabetesimatta] John$_i$
             bought chocolate   ACC   NOM ate.up
    'John, who Hanako ate up the chocolate that (he) bought'
b.* [[__$_i$ tyokoreeto o kattekita] no o Hanako ga tabetesimatta] John$_i$
c.* John$_i$ wa [__$_i$ __$_j$ kattekita] tyokoreeto$_j$ o Hanako ga tabetesimatta
    John, Hanako ate up the chocolate that (he) bought.'
d.* John$_i$ wa [__$_i$ tyokoreeto o kattekita] no o Hanako ga tabetesimatta

The unacceptable examples above have in common that there is no obvious
connection between the extracted NP and the bridging clause, which is
shown by the unacceptable truncation of the EHRCs in (12') and (13').

(12')
a.* [otoko o   keisatu ga   taihosita] kuruma
     man ACC police NOM arrested   car
    'a car which the police arrested the man (who stole (it))'
c.* sono kuruma wa otoko o keisatu ga taihosita
    'The car, the police arrested the man (who stole (it)).'

(13')
a.* [tyokoreeto o   Hanako ga   tabetesimatta] John
     chocolate ACC   NOM ate.up
    'John, who Hanako ate up the chocolate (that (he) bought)'

c.* John wa tyokoreeto o Hanako ga tabetesimatta
    'John, Hanako ate up the chocolate (that (he) bought).'

The examples from Ohara in (5a, b) are unacceptable for the same reason, as one cannot easily imagine a proper semantic/pragmatic link between the displaced NP and the bridging clause. As shown in (14b, c) and (15b, c), the corresponding EHRCs and the truncated versions are both unacceptable.

(14)
a.* haha$_i$ wa [__$_i$ seetaa o   okuttekureta] no   ga   kyoo todoita
    mother TOP   sweater ACC sent   NMZ NOM today arrived
    'Mother, the sweater which (she) sent me arrived today.'
b.* haha$_i$ wa [__$_i$ __$_j$ okuttekureta] seetaa$_j$ ga kyoo todoita
c. * haha wa seetaa ga kyoo todoita

(15)
a.* tuma$_i$ wa [__$_i$ sakana o   tuttekita] no   o   otto   ga
    wife TOP   fish   ACC catch.came NMZ ACC husband NOM
    ryoorisita
    cooked
    'The wife, the husband cooked the fish which (she) caught.'
b.* tuma$_i$ wa [__$_i$ __$_j$ tuttekita] sakana$_j$ o otto ga ryoorisita
c.* tuma wa   sakana o otto ga ryoorisita

To summarize, the two types of relative clauses are analogous in relativization and topicalization and I state the principle in (16). The principle predicts that it is acceptable to relativize and topicalize the target NP of an IHRC because the target NP is functionally the matrix argument, and therefore, the NP is potentially topical.

(16) Relativization and topicalization out of EHRCs and IHRCs are possible if there is a relevant semantic/pragmatic link between the extracted NP and the bridging clause.

Then, how does the principle in (16) relate to the cognitive theory which I discussed earlier? I argue that if the bridging clause does not have a relevant link with the extracted unit, the activation of the bridging clause does not spread to the topical element (since they are conceptually discontinuous) and therefore, activation of both the bridging clause and the extracted NP overloads the working memory. The conceptual structure for (9) and (12) are shown in Figures 5 and 6 respectively. In the former, the two propositions share the topical element 'the student', while in the latter the two propositions have disjunctive topical referents which need to be kept in the cognitive focus, while processing the whole unit. Hence, the shift in the pattern of salience, from 'the car' to 'the police', negatively affects the performance.

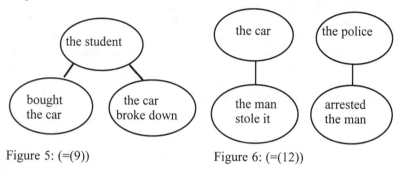

Figure 5: (=(9))   Figure 6: (=(12))

4. Wh-question Formation in IHRCs

Wh-question formation points to an asymmetry between IHRCs and EHRCs, as we saw in (4); wh-questions in IHRCs are more restricted than in EHRCs. Some additional examples are shown in (17) and (18).

(17)
a. [__$_i$ nani o   nusunda] otoko$_i$ o   keisatu ga   taihosita no?
        what ACC stole   man   ACC police NOM   arrested FP
     Lit. 'The police arrested the man who stole what?'
b.* [otoko ga nani o nusunda] no o keisatu ga taihosita no?

(18)
a. [dare ga   __$_i$ kattekita] tyokoreeto$_i$ o Hanako ga   tabetesimatta no?
      who NOM   bought   chocolate   ACC   NOM ate.up   FP
     Lit. 'Hanako ate up the chocolate which who bought?'
b.* [dare ga tyokoreeto o kattekita] no o Hanako ga tabetesimatta no?

However, there are some factors which boost the acceptability. In the case of (17) and (18), the corresponding relativization and topicalization are not acceptable either, as we saw in (12) and (13); thus the questioned noun phrases are not potentially topical. On the other hand, more speakers find it more acceptable if the questioned noun phrase is potentially more topical. For example, in (19), the questioned NP is the target of the relative clause, and in (20), the questioned NP is both the target and the subject of the relative clause.

(19) ? [Hanako ga   nani o   okutta] no   ga   todokanakatta no?
            NOM what ACC sent   NMZ NOM did.not.reach FP
     Lit. 'What that Hanako sent did not reach (the addressee)?'

(20) ? [dare ga   kuruma o   nusunda] no   ga   taihosareta   no?
       who NOM car   ACC stole   NMZ NOM   was.arrested FP
Lit. 'Who that stole the car was arrested?'

The pattern that potentially topical elements are favored as questioned NP mesh with the cognitive theory. The questioned NP remains salient so that the overall structure of salience remains the same while the whole question is processed. In addition, in IHRCs, it is typically the salient entity of the relative clause that is identified as target. For example:

(21)

a. [**norainu** ga Hanako o   kamituita] no   ga   niwatori mo osotta
    stray.dog NOM   ACC bit   NMZ NOM   hen   also attacked
   'The stray dog which bit Hanako attacked the hen too.'

b.* [Hanako ga   **norainu** ni kamitukareta] no   ga   niwatori mo
            NOM stray.dog by was.bit   NMZ NOM   hen   also
    osotta
    attacked
   'The stray dog by which Hanako was bit attacked the hen too.

c. [Hanako ga __ᵢ kamitukareta] **norainu**ᵢ ga   niwatori mo osotta
           NOM   was.bit   stray.dog NOM   hen   also attacked
   'The stray dog by which Hanako was bit attacked the hen too.

In (21a), the subject of the IHRC 'stray dog' is case-matched with the matrix clause. In (b), on the other hand, the referent is represented by the oblique NP; so it is potentially less topical than the subject referent. Note that the EHRC counterpart, which is shown in (c), is acceptable. Subject referents are more topical in default and in the speaker's *viewpoint* in Kuno & Kaburaki's (1977) sense; therefore, it is easier for them to be identified as the target of IHRCs.[3]

    Furthermore, I observe in my corpus that it is typically the subject of the IHRC that is case-matched as target, as shown in Table 1. Given the mechanism that a salient referent is typically identified as target, it is not surprising that the processing of a wh-question is easier if the questioned NP is the target NP. Otherwise, two salient elements, the target NP and

---

[3]Similarly, an asymmetry in target identification for IHRCs has been observed. Ohori (1995) points out that the generally-recognized accessibility hierarchy for relativization (subject > direct object > indirect object > oblique NP > others) (cf. Keenan & Comrie 1977) applies to Japanese IHRCs also. Ohori states that subjects and direct objects are possible targets, and with indirect object, etc., the acceptability is increasingly degraded. This accessibility hierarchy certainly has bearing on my argument. If the subject of an IHRC is favored as a target and a wh-expression is favored as a target, it then follows that a wh-expression is favored as a subject of an IHRC.

the questioned NP, must be kept in the cognitive focus, and therefore, it overloads the processing task.

NP of IHRC case-matched as target / Matrix case	# of tokens (%)
Subject / Nominative	11 (24%)
Subject / Accusative	32 (70%)
Object / Nominative	1 (2%)
Object / Accusative	2 (4%)
Total	46 (100%)

Table 1: # of IHRCs in the corpus in terms of target and matrix case

5. Information Structure of IHRCs

The discussion given so far raises a question: why wh-questions in IHRCs remain awkward to many speakers, even if the questioned NP is the target of the relative clause, as we saw in (19) and (20)? I argue that it is due to the obligatory pragmatic focus on the predicate of an IHRC. As widely assumed (e.g. Kuno 1972), wh-questions carry presuppositions which satisfy the question. For example, the wh-question in (19) pragmatically presupposes a proposition that something which Hanako sent didn't reach the addressee. This obligatory presupposition conflicts with the intrinsic function of IHRCs, presenting the event as new. In this regard, I support Ohara's (1996) claim that IHRCs function to be event reporting. To be precise, however, IHRCs do not have to represent the sentence-focus. Arguments of IHRCs are often previously activated, as in the topic sentences which we have seen in (6)-(10). Likewise, I observe in my corpus that the arguments of an IHRC are often given in the preceding context, therefore, ellipsed in the IHRC, as shown in (22).

(22)
a. [Ø$_i$ obon ni okasi o zyuuman noseta] no o mottekosasete...
        tray on cake ACC fully   put   NMZ ACC have.bring
    '(I) had (the maid) bring the cakes which (she)$_i$ put on the tray full...'
                                    (Akiko Yosano, "Watashi no oitachi")

b. [Ø$_i$ Ø$_j$ kamitukootosuru] no o osinoketa
        tried.to.bite   NMZ ACC pushed.away
    '(He) pushed away (Sato's wife)$_i$ who tried to bite (him)$_j$.'
                                    (Takeo Arishima, "Kain no matsuei")

Table 2 summarizes the token distribution of IHRCs in the corpus in terms of the three focus-structure types (see Lambrecht 1994: 221-235). An IHRC may represent either the sentence-focus, in which the whole IHRC represents the information focus, or the predicate-focus, in which the subject previously activated information. Whether the sentence-focus or the predicate-focus, the predicate of the clause must carry the information focus. Therefore, as we saw in (19) and (20), wh-questions, which represent the argument-focus, are never perfectly acceptable in IHRCs, even if the questioned NP is the target of relativization.

Focus structure of IHRC	# of tokens (%)
Sentence focus	27 (59%)
Predicate-focus	19 (41%)
Argument-focus	0
Total	46 (100%)

Table 2: # of IHRCs in the text database in terms of focus structure types[4]

6. Conclusion

The discussion above are summarized as follows. (i) The two types of relative clauses are analogous in relativization and topicalization. The filler, i.e. the topical element, must be kept salient while processing the whole sentence. (ii) Wh-questions in IHRCs are considerably more restricted than in EHRCs, due to the saliency requirement for the IHRC target and the intrinsic focus placement on the IHRC predicate. Since the island effects are due to the cognitive and pragmatic factors, the paradox raised in Section 2 is an epiphenomenon that results from the factors above. Overall, the cognitive-based account explains why there are island effects in Japanese, which is structurally "island-free", relative to many other languages in which long-range extraction is structurally more constrained.

References

Anderson, J. R. 1983. *The Architecture of Cognition*. Cambridge, MA: Harvard University Press.

Chafe, W. 1994. *Discourse, Consciousness, and Time*. Chicago: University of Chicago Press.

Deane, P. 1991. Limits to Attention: A Cognitive Theory of Island Phenomena. *Cognitive Linguistics* 2: 1-63.

Deane, P. 1992. *Grammar in Mind and Brain: Explorations in Cognitive Syntax*. Berlin: Mouton de Gruyter.

Erteschik-Shir, N, and S. Lappin. 1979. Dominance and the Functional Explanation of Island Phenomena. *Theoretical Linguistics* 6: 41-86.

---

[4]The three focus types are defined in terms of *referential distance* (Givón ed. 1983) of the subject and the open proposition of each IHRC. In the predicate-focus, for example, the referential distance for the subject is smaller than that for the open proposition. See Shimojo (1995) for a detailed discussion of a similar corpus analysis.

Givón, T. ed. 1983. *Topic Continuity in Discourse: A Quantitative Cross-Language Studies*. Amsterdam: John Benjamin.

Keenan, E. L., and B. Comrie. 1977. Noun Phrase Accessibility and Universal Grammar. *Linguistic Inquiry* 8, 63-99.

Kluender, R. 1990. A Neurophysiological Investigation of *Wh*-Islands. Proceedings of the 16th annual meeting of the Berkeley Linguistics Society, 187-204.

Kuno, S. 1972. Functional Sentence Perspective: A Case Study from Japanese and English. *Linguistic Inquiry* 3, 269-320.

Kuno, S. 1973. *The Structure of the Japanese Language*. Cambridge, MA: MIT Press.

Kuno, S. 1987. *Functional Syntax: Anaphora, Discourse and Empathy*. Chicago: University of Chicago Press.

Kuno, S. and E. Kaburaki. 1977. Empathy and Syntax. *Linguistic Inquiry* 8: 627-672.

Kuroda, S.-Y.. 1976. Headless Relative Clauses in Modern Japanese and the Relevancy Condition. Proceedings of the 2nd annual meeting of the Berkeley Linguistics Society, 269-279.

Lambrecht, K. 1994. *Information Structure and Sentence Form: Topic, Focus, and the Mental Representations of Discourse Referents*. Cambridge: Cambridge University Press.

Ohara, K. H. 1996. A constructional approach to Japanese internally headed relativization. Doctoral dissertation. University of California, Berkeley.

Ohori, T. 1995. Problems of Japanese IHRCs: Argument Linking and Reference Tracking. *Language, Information, Text* 2: 89-108.

Ross, J. R. 1967. Constraints on Variables in Syntax. Doctoral dissertation. MIT.

Silverstein, M. 1976. Hierarchy of Features and Ergativity. *Grammatical categories in Australian languages*, ed. R. M. W. Dixon, 112-171. Canberra: Australian Institute of Aboriginal Studies.

Shimojo, M. 1995. Focus Structure and Morphosyntax in Japanese: Wa and Ga, and Word Order Flexibility. Doctoral dissertation. State University of New York at Buffalo.

Van Valin, R. D., Jr. 1996. Toward a Functionalist Account of So-called Extraction Constraints. *Complex Structures: A Functionalist Perspective*, eds. B. Devriendt, L. Goossens, J. van der Auwera, 29-60. Berlin: Mouton de Gruyter.

Van Valin, R. D., Jr. and R. J. LaPolla. 1997. *Syntax: Structure, Meaning and Function*. Cambridge: Cambridge University Press.

Grammar, Cognition and Procedure as Reflected in Route Directions in Japanese, Korean and American English

SUSAN STRAUSS, HANAE KATAYAMA & JONG OH EUN
The Pennsylvania State University

1. Introduction

Describing in words how to get from one location to another seems like a commonplace and rather simple task, requiring little more than familiarity with the destination and a basic idea of how to reach that location. When someone asks for directions, we typically consider the request to be non-intrusive and the task easy to accomplish, provided of course, we know the way; we gauge distances, visualize landmarks, count blocks, traffic signals, stop signs, and ultimately envisage their arrival--And we do this generally without regard for how lexical choice and grammar combine to verbally represent both our conceptualization of the trajectory as well as our attempt at making our instructions readily understood by our interlocutor.

This paper, which is part of a larger, on-going project (See Strauss, Katayama, and Eun (under review)), investigates how and to what degree language and grammar influence the overall linguistic output of a designated task--in this case, the provision of route descriptions in Japanese, Korean, and American English. Our findings indicate that despite the consistency and relative simplicity of the task itself, the responses tend to vary and reflect certain specific patterns in the descriptions, with these variations appearing to be largely language specific.

---

* While none of the authors really knew Jim McCawley personally, we feel he was a kindred spirit and we are honored to be able to have our paper published in this volume which is dedicated to his memory.

In this paper, because of the severe space constraints, we will limit our discussion to two areas: expressions of visual perception and basic perspective taking within the route descriptions themselves.

II. The data

The data consist of a corpus of 75 spontaneously produced route directions: 25 in Japanese, 25 in Korean, and 25 in American English. In all cases, we asked native speaker subjects to explain how to get from a designated location on the campus of a large Northeastern university to a well known destination that required a travel distance of approximately five miles and a series of turns. The requests were made in the subjects' respective language and the responses in turn were given in that same language.

The task was designed such that the subjects and route inquirers were not at the starting point of the trajectory when the request was made. Rather, the departure point was a location on campus that both parties knew well, such as the student union building or some other familiar building on campus. This way, the entire route, from start to finish, would have to rely on the respondents' imagination of the entire trajectory without appealing to streets, buildings, or other landmarks that would be within both parties' visual field. This is in contrast with Klein (1982) whose work on German route descriptions (Wegauskunft) begins with a departure point where both parties do, in fact, utilize features of their perceptual field at the initial stages of the interaction.

III. Findings--General Discussion

What makes the provision of route directions so linguistically interesting is the fact that it necessarily involves the progressive mental imaging of and along a particular trajectory as well as the ability to clearly communicate that trajectory and what to do along the way in order to successfully reach the desired destination. It requires the visualization of concrete and recognizable landmarks and sign posts (both literal and figurative), the general sequential order in which these signposts distribute themselves, approximate distances relevant to such markers, as well as explicit procedural instruction with respect to how to navigate around and through them until the final one is reached; the provider of the directions must rely upon his/her own memory of visual images, as well as on information that may or may not be shared with the interlocutor. Ultimately, what is conceptualized and communicated is some actual displacement through time and space involving the Figure, or person traveling along the route, and a series of Grounds, or the landmarks along that route, including the final destination[1].

Thus, the nature of the task provides a ripe environment for an analysis of how speakers of the languages in question employ expressions of visual

---

[1] See Talmy (1978, 1982, 1985) for a full discussion of the concepts of Figure and Ground as they relate to verbs of motion, paths, and destinations.

perception and how they both imagine and communicate the actual trajectory and the arrival at the final destination. Sections IV and V will briefly address these issues[2].

IV. Findings--Expressions of visual perception

What is immediately noticeable in the data is the use, distribution, and frequency of expressions of visual perception across the three languagaes, all of which pertain to designated landmarks along the particular route. Figure 1 below provides an inventory of these expressions including the number of tokens, for each language.

Korean:

poita:	be visible	41
naota	appear	67
pota:	look, see	15
katapota:	go and see/look	30
palapota:	look up	1
sayngkita:	be formed	9
nwun aphey twuta	put in front of your eyes	1
TOTAL:		**164**

Japanese:

mieru / miete kuru:	be visible	30	mieru (24) miete kuru (6)
dete kuru:	appear	10	
miru:	look, see	1	
wakaru:	understand, tell	2	
me no mae no	in front of your eyes	1	
miotosu koto wa nai	can't miss	1	
TOTAL:		**46**	

English:

see:	16
look:	2
can't miss:	3
TOTAL:	**21**

Figure 1.   Expressions of visual perception

Here, it is clear that native speakers of Korean tend to use the largest number of different types of expressions with a far greater frequency than Japanese or English speakers, though the number of Japanese types nearly

---

[2] Strauss, Katayama, and Eun (under review) provides a more detailed analysis and discussion of these and other linguistic (semantic, syntactic, pragmatic, socio-cultural) and pedagogical issues which emerged in the three corpora.

equals that used in the Korean data. The English data reveals both the least number of expression types (predominantly 'see') and the least number of tokens.

A careful look at the most frequent of these expressions in all three languages will reveal the workings of a more complex cognitive process than the simple envisioning and communication of that landmark by the speaker to the interlocutor. Rather, what we will witness in addition to visual perception is the speaker's distinction in landmarks between those that are close, less specific and less expected, and those that are distant, more specific, and more expected. Examples (1) and (2) below will illustrate, using the Japanese expressions *dete kuru* 'appear' and *mieru/miete kuru* 'be visible,' 'become visible.'

As indicated in (1), the general meanings of these two verbs seem to be rather similar. When asked to distinguish between the two, native speakers generally respond that the expressions are indeed similar and in many cases interchangeable.

(1) <u>Japanese</u>:   *dete kuru* ('appear')   vs.   *mieru / miete kuru*   ('be visible')
General meaning of both verbs: 'appear,' 'be seen,' 'come into view,' 'be/become visible'

In looking at the Japanese corpus, we find that the subjects occurring with *dete kuru* 'appear' are all streets, roads, nameless buildings (e.g., *shoppingu sentaa* 'shopping center'), and general areas (e.g., *michi ga kou hutatsuni wakarete iru tokoro* 'place where the street splits like this into two'). This is illustrated in the two examples in (A) below:

(A) subjects with *dete kuru* ('appear')
(i) (from dataset #10)
shootolijji tte iunoga <u>detekurunde</u>, soko de migi ni magatte kudasai.
'<u>you'll see</u> a street called Shortlidge (lit. 'a street called Shortlidge will be seen/appear'), so turn right there.'

(ii) (from dataset #8)
san mairu gurai ikuto, waiji wai ji no michi ga <u>detekimasu</u>.
'if you go for about 3 miles, you'll see a "y" shaped street (lit. 'a "y"-shaped street will be seen/appear').'

In contrast, subjects which co-occur with the verb *mieru* or *miete kuru* tend to be referents which are clearly recognizable to both the speaker and the hearer, as indicated in the three examples in (B):

(B) subjects with mieru / miete kuru ('be seen/visible, become visible')
(i) (from dataset #1)
hidarite ni nitanii mooru ga miemasu.
'on the left you'll see the Nittany Mall (lit. 'will be seen/ become visible').'

(ii) (from dataset #8)
nittani mooru no mein no iriguchi ga hidari gawa ni miemasu.
'you'll see the main entrance to the Nittany Mall on the left (lit. 'will be seen/become visible').'

(iii) (from dataset #3)
shoumen ni nitanii mooru ga miete kurundakedo
'in the front you'll see the Nittany Mall, (lit. 'will be seen/ become visible') but..'

In all three examples, it is the final destination (i.e., the Nittany Mall) that is marked with *mieru* or *miete kuru*. Other referents occurring with these verbs include specific buildings that are referred to by name as in *hidari no hou ni moobiru toka miemasu* ('toward the right you'll see the Mobil [station] and stuff') and *hidarigawa geetowei apaatomento tte iu no ga miete kimasu* ('you'll see the Gateway Apartments on the left.'). Further, of the 30 tokens of *mieru/miete kuru*, 23 or (77%) co-occur with an expression of more specific location such as *hidari ni* 'on the left,' in contrast with *dete kuru*, where only one token (10%) appears with such an expression.

Based on these results, we begin to realize that Japanese verbs of visual perception actually mark very distinct types of objects that come into view. This becomes especially salient when we consider the opposition between *dete kuru* and *mieru/miete kuru*. Example (2) below presents the semantic distinctions which seem to more precisely characterize each of these expressions.

(2) **Precise meanings** of *dete kuru* and *mieru/miete kuru* beyond general meanings of 'appear,' 'be or become visible, etc.

dete kuru:	PROGRESSION RELEVANT	
	SPECIFICITY / EXPECTEDNESS RELEVANT:	LOW
	DISTANCE RELEVANT:	PROXIMAL
mieru:	progression not relevant	
	SPECIFICITY / EXPECTEDNESS RELEVANT:	HIGH
	DISTANCE RELEVANT:	DISTAL
miete kuru:	PROGRESSION RELEVANT	
	SPECIFICITY / EXPECTEDNESS RELEVANT:	HIGH
	DISTANCE RELEVANT:	DISTAL

As indicated in (2), in the case of *dete kuru*, what is seen tends to emerge in a less expected way, it tends to appear within the immediate vicinity of the Figure or person seeking the destination, and it tends to mark entities which might fall into the set of more indefinite referents. *Mieru* and *miete kuru*, on the other hand, seem to mark visually perceived entities that are more expected, more physically distant, and more specific; in other words, entities that could be considered more definite referents. With respect to the use of the V-*te kuru* auxiliary, as in *dete kuru* and *miete kuru*, we also note that the notion of progression is relevant, as if it entailed some kind of visual change of state, with that change being either gradual or punctual. In the case of the simple lexical verb *mieru*, progression is then not a relevant characterization.

The fact that *dete kuru* tends to signal objects that are physically proximal, that are arrived at less expectedly, and that are more indefinite is illustrated in the sentence pairs in (3a) and (3b). (3a), excerpted from the data, is a prototypical example of the use of *dete kuru*. It occurs toward the latter part of the trajectory description and the entity signaled by the verb is something that the hearer would have come quite close to in an unexpected way. Further, and more importantly, the referent is decidedly an indefinite one.

(3)   (a) *san mairu gurai ikuto, waiji wai ji no michi ga <u>detekimasu</u>.*
       'if you go for about 3 miles, you'll see a "y" shaped street.'

If we replace the verb with *miete kuru*, as in (3b) below,

       (b) *?san mairu gurai ikuto, waiji wai ji no michi ga <u>mietekimasu</u>.*
       'if you go for about 3 miles, you'll see **the** "y" shaped street.'

The utterance becomes pragmatically odd within the context, capturing the idea that the referent has already been talked about, hence definite, is expected to be seen, and finally, that its relative location vis à vis the hearer would be more physically distant than in the case of *dete kuru*.

For the Korean corpus, the two most frequent verbs of visual perception are *naota*, which is the general functional equivalent of Japanese *dete kuru*, and *poita*, the general functional equivalent of Japanese *mieru*. Example (4) below sets up the same opposition between *naota* and *poita* as we saw earlier in (1), which contrasts *dete kuru* and *mieru*. That is, both verbs generally signal the meaning of 'be seen,' 'come into view,' 'be/become visible,' and so forth, and both verbs tend to be considered by native speakers of Korean as being largely interchangeable in many cases.

(4) <u>Korean</u>: *naota* ('appear') vs. *poita* ('be visible')
General meaning of both verbs: 'appear,' 'be seen,' 'come into view,' 'be/become visible'

Like Japanese *dete kuru,* Korean *naota* tends to co-occur overwhelmingly with subjects such as streets and roads, traffic lights, and stop signs. The two examples in (A) will illustrate.

(A) subjects with *naota* ('appear')
(i) (from dataset #1)
khaymphes pakkulo nakamyen, sinhotungi naonuntey,
'if you go out of the campus, you'll see a traffic light (lit. 'a traffic light will be seen/appear'), and...'

(ii) (from dataset #19)
tasi oynccokey mwe nongcang kathun ke naocyo,
'again on the left, you'll see a farm or something like that (lit. 'a farm or something like that will be seen/appear').'

One notable difference between Japanese *dete kuru* and Korean *naota* is that *naota* tends to appear often with more specific expressions of location such as *oynccokulo* 'on the left' and *olunccokulo* 'on the right,' whereas *dete kuru* generally does not.

The examples in (B) below represent typical subjects occurring with *poita,* and again, as in the case of Japanese *mieru/miete kuru* from (1B), these subjects frequently represent the final destination, in this case, the Barnes and Noble bookstore.

(B) subjects with *poita* ('be visible,' 'become visible')
(i) (from dataset #6)
ccokumman kamyenun, oynccok phyenulo pancu eyn nopulcu ka poye.
'if you go a little, you'll see Barnes and Noble (lit. 'will be seen/ become visible') on the left.'

(ii) from dataset #5
siaphing moli aphulo poimyenun, olun- e- oynccokulo pancu eyn nopulcuka poyeyo.
'if you see the shopping mall straight ahead, you'll see Barnes and Noble (lit. 'will be seen/ become visible').on the righ- on the left'.

Example (5) below outlines the basic semantic characteristics of the *naota* and *poita* opposition, where we posit very similar types of distinctions as we saw in the schema in (2) for Japanese. Different from the Japanese, however, are the concepts of the relevance of progression (captured in the Japanese by the use of the V-*te kuru* auxiliary) for Korean *poita* as well as the overall specificity level of the entity co-occurring with *naota*; that is, in Japanese, the verb 'be seen/become visible' can appear as either *mieru* (in which the progression with which an object comes into view is not a relevant factor) or *miete kuru*, in which it is. For Korean *naota*, since we have evidence of it frequently co-occurring with other, more specific location descriptors, we consider that the level of specificity of the entity that it designates is slightly higher than its general Japanese counterpart *dete kuru*, and have indicated that it marks LOW to MEDIUM specificity, rather than simply LOW.

(5) **Precise   meanings** of <u>naota</u> and <u>poita</u> beyond general meanings of 'appear,' 'be or become visible, etc.

naota   PROGRESSION RELEVANT, BUT NOT REQUIRED
           SPECIFICITY RELEVANT: LOW > MEDIUM
           EXPECTEDNESS RELEVANT: LOW
           DISTANCE RELEVANT: PROXIMAL

poita: progression not relevant
           SPECIFICITY / EXPECTEDNESS RELEVANT: HIGH
           DISTANCE RELEVANT: DISTAL

Again, the most significant feature in the *naota* vs. *poita* opposition, similar to the *dete kuru* vs. *mieru* opposition, is the fact that with *naota*, referents tend to be physically close, less specific, and less expected, while with *poita*, they tend to be more distant, more specific, and more expected. The tendency for *naota* to signal indefinite entities and for *poita* to signal definite entities is illustrated in the example pairs (6a) and (6b) below. Example (6b), with *naota*, is taken from the actual data.

(6)   (a)   *khaymphes pakkulo nakamyen, sinhotungi <u>naonuntey,</u>*
              'if you go out of the campus, you'll see a traffic light and..'

When we change the visual perception verb from *naota*   to *poita*, the sentence remains grammatically well formed, but pragmatically strange, given the context of the utterance.

      (b)   *?khamphes pakkulo nakamyen, sinhotungi <u>poinnuntey,</u>*
             'if you go out of campus, you'll see **the** traffic light.'

That is, by substituting the verb *poita*, as in (6b), the conceptualization of the referent *sinhotung* 'traffic light' seems to shift from something indefinite and unexpected to something that is at the same time expected and potentially recognizable by the hearer. Conversely, in (7a) and (7b), the referent, Barnes and Noble bookstore, being the final destination of the route, is signaled with *poita* in the actual data segment from (7a), as both an expected an recognizable entity, i.e., the very bookstore that the person is looking for.

(7) (a) *oynccokey __poinun__ ku kenmwuli pancu eyn nopulsu*
          ku pwuksuthoa ipnita.
          'the building that you see on the left is the bookstore, B & N'

In view of the context and purpose of the talk, the utterance in (7b), altered to substitute *naota* for the original *poita*, sounds odd since the entity here is now framed as being less expected as well as less specific.

(b) *?oynccok ey __naonun__ ku kenmwuli pancu eyn nopulsu*
     ku pwuksuthoa ipnita.
     'the building that you see on the left is the bookstore, B & N'

The opposition of proximality and distality signaled by *naota* and *poita*, respectively, is illustrated in (8). Here, the speaker is describing the path along which the hearer must go to find the Barnes and Noble bookstore. Along the way, there is a Dunkin Donuts shop. This speaker indicates in the first clause that the hearer will see and also come close to the Dunkin Donuts, using *naota* as a marker of proximality. In the very next clause, he says the equivalent of 'once you begin to see the Dunkin Donuts shop, that is, from a far away distance, that means that you're almost at your destination'.

(8) *e: tto ilehkey ccokum kasimyen, oynccokey tenkhin tonesi __nawayo__.*
     kutaumey incey tenkhin tonesi __poiki sicakul__ __hamyen__, keui ta on
     keyeyyo mwe, pancu eyn nobulcuey
     'and if you go a little more, you'll see Dunkin Donuts. And once you begin you see Dunkin Donuts, you're almost there, I mean AT B & N.'

The sentence pairs in (9a) and (9b), further illustrate that *naota* underscores proximality. (9a), an actual excerpt from the data, contains the adverb *mak* 'right there' together with the verb *naota*.

(9) (a) *ccwuk katapomyenun **mak** icey moli __naokey twenuntey__*
          'if you keep going straight, the mall is about to appear,
          (i.e., right in front of you.)'

(9b) has been modified by using the verb *poita*. Here, in keeping the rest of the utterance identical to (9b), we derive an odd sounding statement, with the semantic clash occurring because of the mismatched collocation of *mak* with *poita*, the latter of which carries with it a sense of physical distality.

(b) *?ccwuk katapomyenun **mak** icey moli __poikey twenuntey__*
     'if you keep going straight, the mall is about to appear,
     i.e., right in front of you).'

As we noted in the early part of this section, the English corpus contains the fewest number of tokens of verbs of visual perception overall. Predictably, the most frequent verb is 'see,' comprising 16 of the 21 total tokens, or 76% of the total number of visual perception verbs in the corpus. Example (10) below contains the entire set of nouns occurring as objects of this verb. Interestingly, where Japanese and Korean tend to distinguish between indefinite, non-specific, and unexpected entities on the one hand, from definite, specific, and expected entities on the other, English seems to make no such distinction whatsoever with the verb 'see.' Note the types of objects or object complements that follow 'see' in English:

(10)   English: "see" -- 16 tokens:
you'll see some buildings, you'll see the Giant on the right, you'll see a MacDonald's, you'll see the Nittany Mall, you'll see lots of houses, you'll see signs for 550, you'll start seeing signs for the 150 toward Bellefonte, you'll see signs for 26, you'll see that the road is going ta split inta two, you'll see a "y"- you'll come to a "y" in the road

However, beyond explicit expressions of visual perception, we note one construction in English which seems to pattern in a very similar manner as both Japanese *dete kuru* and Korean *naota*--and that is expression is 'come to' or 'come across.' Example (11) indicates a total of twelve tokens of this expression, together with an itemization of the types of referents with which it co-occurs. These referents are strikingly similar to those co-occurring with *dete kuru* and *naota*. And, like the verbs in Japanese and Korean, not only do these referents constitute the more unexpected landmarks, they also represent landmarks that are arrived upon with some type of progression as well as entities within a relatively close spatial distance to the person traveling along the path.

(11)   English: "come to" / "come across"
you'll come to a "y" in the road: 7
you'll come to a 4-way stop: 1
you'll come across two lights: 1
you'll come to the signs for the bypass: 1
you'll come to the next stop light: 1
you'll come to a stop light: 1
TOTAL: **12**

And so here we can see that notions such as definiteness/indefiniteness, specificity/non-specificity, and expectedness/unexpectedness do not seem to affect English speakers' use of the verb 'see,' though the proximal/distal distinction may indeed be relevant, since the verb appears to designate objects or Grounds that are relatively far from the Figure. In this light, we see that English 'come to' and 'come across' tend to pick out entities that are less definite as well as more proximal, as illustrated in (10) and (11).

What is also interesting is that Japanese V-*te kuru* and Korean *naota* both contain overt semantic elements which mean 'come' (i.e., *kuru* in Japanese and *ota* in Korean). One major distinction between the Japanese and Korean usages of these verbal constructions and the English use of 'come to' or 'come across' is that the English excerpts in (11) underscore a clear focus on the Figure as the entity which moves along the trajectory, in sharp contrast with the Japanese and Korean examples in (1) - (9), all of which focus on the Ground, especially given that in all cases it is the Ground itself that is the sentential subject (cf. *x ga dete kuru/mieru/miete kuru; x ka naonta/pointa* vs. 'you'll see x,' 'you'll come across x').

V. Findings--Figure - Ground perspectives

Along the lines of Figure - Ground perspective taking, we have noted an overwhelming preference for Japanese and Korean grammar to highlight the Grounds or the various stationary landmarks that distribute themselves along the path from the departure point up to and including the destination. This is especially salient in the visual descriptions discussed in Section IV, where the landmarks in question are framed in such a way that they seem to be the predominant entities of focus, in contrast with the English data which highlights instead the movement of the Figure toward the Ground.

Interestingly, we find the same preference in perspective taking in the final few utterances of the speakers as they describe the route inquirer's arrival at the desired destination. Example (12) below outlines these endings or arrival descriptions: (A) contains the English descriptions, (B) the Japanese, and (C) the Korean.

(12)   ENDINGS--ARRIVAL DESCRIPTIONS:

(A)   English:
    you'll be...   6
    (there you are; then you're in the mall parking lot, I'd
    just drive about three blocks and be there)
    go in: 9   **16**
    (then you make a right into the mall, ya just hafta
    look for the place where ya turn in)
    get to: 1
    (and ya can get to ta the mall from eether the left er the right)
    the mall is there: 6
    (right there is the mall, it'll be on your right side)
    hybrid: the mall is there / you'll see it   3
    (after you follow 26 the mall will be there. I mean you'll see it)

arrival description **foregrounding the Figure:** 16/25 = **64%**

Note in the (A) excerpts from English that 16 of the 25 speakers describe the arrival with a motion verb (go, get to, turn in, reach) or the verb 'be', used here as a motion verb as well ('you'll be there, you're there). In other words, it appears that the tendency in the English corpus is to focus on the Figure as sentential subject traveling toward the Ground destination.

Conversely, in both the Japanese (12B) and Korean (12C) corpora, we find instead a clear focus on the Ground as a stationary location that is framed either as being visible as the recognizable and desired end point (using *mieru* for Japanese and *poita* for Korean), as being situated in a particular location, or as being deictically indicated (e.g., *sorega nitanii mooru desu* 'that's the NM;' *keki pansu eyn nopul pwuksuthoa ipnita* 'that's the Barnes & Noble bookstore'). In these cases, it is the Ground which emerges as the sentential subject as prominent to the Figure. In other words, it appears that English grammar highlights the perspective of the Figure while de-emphasizing the perspective of the Ground, where Japanese and Korean grammar clearly highlight the Ground and de-focus the Figure.

This inverse tendency is quite striking when we compare the English and Japanese results in (12A) and (12B) respectively. That is, in English, 64% of the arrival descriptions center on a moving Figure, with the remaining 9 speakers or 36% focusing on the Ground (e.g., 'right there is the mall'). In Japanese, 64% of the arrival descriptions focus on the Ground ('the mall is there'), with the remaining 36% focusing on the motion of the Figure arriving at the Ground (*nitanii mooru ni ikitsuku wake desu* 'so you'll arrive at the Nittany Mall').

(B) Japanese:

nitanii mooru ga mieru (the mall will be visible) 8
(Nitanii mooru ga miemasu, tabun soko ni ikuto NM ga
mieru to omoimasu, moo ookiku mou NM ga miemasu)
NM desu (it's/that's the mall) 6
(dokomade massugu ikuno kana NM nanode, sorega NM desu)
NM ga aru (the mall is there) 2
(soshitara arimasu)

<u>16</u>

NM ni tsukimasu (you arrive) 5
(juu mairu gurai ikeba mooru ni tsukimasu,
NM ni ikitsuku wakedesu)
haitte kudasai (go in) 2
(jiyuu ni soko no mooru no naka ni haitte kudasai)
hybrids: 3
you'll see the entrance, it'll be the mall please go in
(sugu iriguchi ga miemasu node, hidarigawa sono NM ni narimasunode
hidarini sasetsu shite, NM ni haitte kudasai)

arrival description **foregrounding the Ground** 16/25 = <u>64%</u>

What we find in the Korean arrival descriptions is an even stronger emphasis on the perspective of the Ground, with 18 of the 25 speakers (72%) choosing to empahsize the desired location as the sentential subject through verbs of existence (*issta* 'to be/exist') or visual perception (*poita*), or through a deictic indexical plus copula construction (e.g., *keki pansu eyn nopul pwuksuthoa ipnita* 'that's the Barnes & Noble bookstore).

With respect to the use of the verb 'to be' in English and its functional counterparts in both Korean and Japanese, we find the identical tendency in terms of the Figure - Ground perspective and its patterning across the three languages. That is, while in English, the verb 'be' can and does co-occur with the Figure as sentential subject (e.g., 'you'll be at the mall;' 'and then you're in the mall parking lot'), Japanese *aru* and Korean *issta* co-occur only with a stationary subject referent. In the case of Japanese, the grammar requires that *aru* co-occur with a non-moving entity (see Strauss, 1993, ms). However, Korean grammar allows for a broader usage of *issta* such that its subject referents may be either moving and animate or non-moving and inanimate; in spite of this flexibility of the Korean counterpart, *issta* only co-occurs with a Figure referent in these data.

(C) <u>Korean:</u>

issta (it's there)	8
(kullo tulokasimyen ku palo kuncheey ku chaykpangi isseyo, kulemyen oynccokey pancu ayn nopulcuka issci)	
B & N ka poita (B & N will be visible)	6
(han yelsi panghyangulo pomyenun, ku pancu eyn nopuli poikedunyo, oynccok phyenulo pancu eyn nopulcuka poye)	
B & N ipnita (it's/that's B & N)	4
(keki pansu eyn nopul pwuksuthoa ipnita, pancu eyn nopul iyeyyo)	
tulekamyen tweyyo (you can go in/enter)	2
(kekise cwahoycen heyse tulekasimyen twayyo)	
tochakhakey twepnita (you'll arrive)	1
(keysok hamyenun pancu eyn nopuley tochakhakey twepnita)	
chacakaseyyo (find it)	
(kulehkey chacakaseyyo)	1
hybrids:	3
you go in and it's there/it'll be there	
(tulekamyenun pancu eyn nopuli palo ku welmas- talun welmas hako palo i- kuncheey isskittaymweuney)	

The first three entries (8, 6, 4) are braced together totaling <u>18</u>.

arrival description **foregrounding the Ground:** 18/25 = <u>72%</u>

Essentially, what we have noted in the latter part of Section IV and in Section V is that language typology plays an important role in the conceptualization and subsequent communication of procedural information in terms of entity highlighting.

VI. Conclusion

In sum, we hope to have demonstrated that a cross-linguistic analysis of an identical language-eliciting task such as this one could shed significant light on how we view language as an overt and analyzable manifestation of both cognitive behavior and explicit communicative endeavors. In taking an apparently simple and straightforward communicative behavior such as the provision of route descriptions and eliciting the identical task in three languages, we feel that we have been able to uncover certain tendencies in the grammar of each language which reflect deeper levels of human cognition that would otherwise be unavailable for inspection. We have found, for example, that concepts such as definiteness, specificity, expectedness, and even spatial proximity as they relate to concrete nouns are encoded in the systematic uses of and alternation between verbs of visual perception, especially in Japanese and Korean. We have also found clear patterns in how the various entities involved in such route descriptions are emphasized or de-emphasized, and that this notion of emphasis is largely influenced by typology, grammar and grammatical preferences.

We hope that this paper and the larger version of which it is a part will contribute to our understanding of Japanese, Korean, and English in particular as well has the broader area of human language in general, especially with respect to how language, lexical choice, and grammar, all intersect to shape how we conceptualize, how we communicate, how we interact, and what we expect in terms of informational as well as interactional styles and preferences.

References

Klein, W. 1982. Local Deixis in Route Directions in *Speech, Place, and Action*, ed. J. Jarvella and W. Klein, 161 - 182. New York:John Wiley & Sons

Strauss, S., Katayama, H., and Eun, J. (under review) The Intersection of Grammar, Cognition, and Procedure in Route Descriptions in Japanese, Korean, and American English.

Talmy, L. 1978. Figure and Ground in Complex Sentences in *Universals of Human Language, Vol. 4: Syntax.*, eds. J. H. Greenberg, C. Ferguson, and E. Moravesik, 625-649. Palo Alto:Stanford University Press.

Talmy, L. 1983. How Language Structures Space in *Spatial orientation: theory, research, and application* eds. H. Pick and L. Acredolo, New York:Plenum Press.

Talmy, L. 1985. Lexicalization Patterns: Semantic Structure in Lexical Forms in *Language Typology and Syntactic Description.* ed. T. Shopen, 57-149. New York:Cambridge University Press.

Part II

Discourse and Conversation

When Does Communication Turn Mentally Inward?: A Case Study of Japanese Formal-to-Informal Switching

SEIICHI MAKINO
Princeton University

1 Introduction

This paper addresses an issue of formal–to–informal switching in Japanese discourse. However, before I discuss formal–to–informal switching at discourse level, let me discuss an issue of choice between informal and formal forms at sentence level. In every sentence the final predicate ends either informally or formally depending on a given social context. If the final predicate is a complex predicate that consists of verbal (that is, the term that combines verbs and adjectives) + dependent form (mostly modality forms) , verbals cannot be marked formal even if the dependent form is marked as formal, because of its morphological tightness, as shown in (1).

(1)   a.   やがては、韓国と北朝鮮との統一が {出来る/*出来ます}
             でしょう。
             'Sooner or later South Korea and North Korea will
             probably be united.'

       b.   韓国語と日本語の比較対照文法の本を書いて {いる/*いま
             す} んです。
             'I'm writing a book on contrastive grammar of Korean
             and Japanese.'

       c.   この秋、久しぶりに韓国に {行く/*行きます} つもりです。
             'This fall I intend to go to Korea after a long interval.'

       However, if the verbal appears not sentence-finally but
in a dependent clause there are cases when it can be marked either
informal or formal. In all the example sentences of (2) the
sentence-final predicate is marked formal, but since there the
verb and the final predicate are not found in the same clause, the
verb can be marked formal, if the speaker wants to be hyper-
polite.

(2)   a.   先生がお書きに {なった/なりました} ご本は全部読ませてい
             ただいております。
             'Professor, I have been reading all the books that you
             have written.'
       b.   私が留守を {している/しております} 間に何かございました
             ら、恐れ入りますが、この電話番号にご連絡ください。
             'If something happens while I'm away, please call me at
             this telephone number.'
       c.   ここをまっすぐ１０分ぐらい {いらっしゃる/いらっしゃい
             ます} と駅に出ます。
             'If you go down here straight you will come to the
             station.'

In Makino (1996) I referred to the informal form and formal forms as UCHI-form, and SOTO-form, respectively because the former (i.e., the informal form) is primarily used when speaking with a person or persons in UCHI space, a space in which casual communicative interactions take place, whereas the former (i.e., the formal form) is primarily used when speaking with a person or persons in SOTO space, a space in which formal interactions take place. However, the distinction between UCHI and SOTO should not be understood to be dichtomous but rather continuous. A person in UCHI-space, that is, UCHI-person (to use my coined grammatical term in Makino (1996)) includes the speaker himself and any person the speaker can empathize with, whereas a person in SOTO-space, that is, SOTO-person is anyone other than UCHI-person. As we noted earlier in connection with (2), the verb within a dependent clause is an informal-form in a normal situation. To explain this fact in spatial terms, a position within a dependent clause is spatially UCHI and is a position at which the speaker's attention is directed not outwardly but inwardly. To use my terms I used in Makino (1983), the inward communicative direction can be called 'speaker-orientation',and the outward communicative direction, 'listener-orientation'.

Now, if I were giving this talk in Japanese all the sentence-final predicates would have to be marked formal, except the forms in dependent clauses, because I am talking to SOTO-persons. The communicative direction has to be listener-oriented. Now let us further suppose that a bee came into this auditorium and stung my pate. Which sentence do I have to use, (3a) or (3b)? And why?

(3)　　a.　あ、痛いです！　'Ouch!'
　　　　b.　あ、痛い！

Under such an excruciating circumstance I have to use the informal version (3b), because the communication is not really directed to the audience, rather it is essentially directed to myself. It is simply a self-directed exclamation, although I would be successful in conveying a message that I am experiencing awful pain. Such formal-to-informal switching within formally marked discourse is just a tip of the iceberg in Japanese discourse. In other words, it is not the case that all the sentences are marked formal in a SOTO-oriented talk or writing. The remainder of my talk will be devoted to analysis of such switching that occurs in SOTO-oriented discourse data.

The first linguist who dealt with the formal-to-informal switching was Nomoto (1977:85). After giving a rhetorical statement that each discourse has to be consistently marked as to formal/informal distinction in order to maintain stylistical unity, he recognized that some mixing of the marking can take place in discourse. His example and his explanation follow.

(4)   私たちはことばにたいして、つねに無意識の信頼をいだいて
        おります。ことばを通じて、自分の意図が他人に伝わり、また
        他人の意図が自分に伝わると<u>思い込んでいる</u>。もっともそう思
        わなければ、うかうか口をきく気にもならぬでしょう。なるほ
        ど、そういう信頼感の上に安心してよりかかっていて不自由を
        感じない世界というものは<u>ありうる</u>。
        (福田恒存　出典不明　下線筆者)
        'Unconsciously we trust language. We <u>are convinced</u> that
        we can convey our intention to others and that others'
        intention can be conveyed to us. Come to think of it, we
        don't feel like speaking with others unless we are
        convinced that way. It is true that there <u>can be</u> a world in
        which we securely lean on such feeling of trust and feel no
        loss of freedom. '

Nomoto makes a very brief but interesting discussion on the mixing of the formality marking using the example (4): He says: "It seems to me that Fukuda used informal markings when he as the writer becomes less conscious of the existence of the reader, in other words, he is writing the parts to himself. If my assumption is correct, it means that we can read into his psyche by means of such mixing, thereby enabling us to read his writing more deeply. " As far as I know no linguists except Nemoto have done research on how Japanese communication turns inward by using the formal-to-informal switching. Nemoto's brief analysis has instigated me to analyze the phenomenon further to see how the switching works in Japanese SOTO-oriented discourse. My research on the switching is intended to make clear that "concisousness of the existence of the reader" alone cannot explain complex manifestations of the switching phenomena.

2. Contrast between Dependent Clause and Discourse Phenomena

Let me start with cases that are very close in nature to cases that happen in a dependent clause. Pay your attention to the underlined parts in the examples. Note that in all this the unmarked speech level is formal. (I am not interested here in the reversed switching, that is, the informal-to-formal switching that occurs in the UCHI-oriented discouse.)

(5) a. 受験勉強で休みどころでは<u>ない</u>。就職がまだ決まってい<u>ない</u>。部活動が<u>ある</u>。アルバイトの予定が<u>つまっている</u>。そんなさまざまな理由で、休暇を楽しむどころではない、という人が多いことでしょう。(朝日 7/20/2000 社説)
'Study for entrance examination <u>hardly allows</u> us to take rest. A job is <u>yet to find</u>. <u>There are</u> club activities. The schedules for part-time job <u>is very tight</u>. There may be a lot of people who say, for one reason or another that there is no time for vacation.'

   b. お客を迎えて、ではデザートをどの皿で出そうかと考えた時に、末娘のことを描いた天使の器とよんでいる小鉢をつくっ

たんです。食事をするときに美しい食器をみて気持ちがふわっ
と明るくなる。日常と違う次元の中で、食べるものもおいし
く話もはずむ。器をつくる時、そういう感覚がとても大事だ
なと思います。(座談会「家庭で伝えたい食卓の文化」婦人
之友　1992 10月号, 20-31)

'When we have decided to invite people and started to
wonder which plate we should use for desert, I made
a small plate called an angel's plate on which I painted
my youngest daughter. When you eat you take a look at
the plate and you feel sort of cheerful. In a dimension
different from that of daily life you can enjoy eating and
can talk rhythmically. I feel that it is important to have
that kind of consciouness when one makes utensils.'

Notice that all these connected sentences can be
rephrased as a single sentence with a dependent structure,
because each sentence includes an anaphoric pronoun such as
'sonna' in (5a) and 'soo iu' in (5c). For example, the second, third
and fourth sentences in (5b) can be rephrased as (6).

(6)　食事をするときに美しい食器をみて気持ちがふわっと明るく
　　なり、日常と違う次元の中で、食べるものもおいしく話もはず
　　むような感覚が、器をつくる時、とても大事だなと思います。

As I stated earlier, a dependent clause is a space where
UCHI-forms are normally used, unless one is
hyper-conscious of the listerner's higher status. UCHI-forms
indicate UCHI-information — information deeply internalized in
the mind of the speaker/writer. UCHI-information can be
information known to both the speaker/writer and the
listener/reader as in (5a,b,d) or the information only known to
the speaker/writer, as in (5c). The deeply internalized information
is a chunk of 'backgrounded' information not exactly in the sense
of Hopper (1979)'s notion of 'backgrounded' information, but

very close to it, because UCHI-information serves to 'support, amplify, or comment' on the 'forgrounded' information presented in the main clause. Or to put it in other words, UCHI-information is speaker-oriented information which indicates that for some reasons the on-going communicative direction turns mentally inward.

3. Informal Forms Expressing Psychological, Historical, Cultural, Scientific, Political Facts

Now let me discuss a wider range of cases of formal-to-informal switching which Nomoto didn't dealt with. In (7) the speaker is using UCHI-forms to express facts, that is, psychological facts as in (7a,b), a historical fact as in (7c), a cultural fact as in (7d) , scientific facts as in (7e, f) or a political fact as in (7g). Those facts are presented as indespensable background information. More importantly the facts are all irrevocable fait accompli which nobody can change. Those facts may be known to both the speaker/writer and the listener/reader or may be known only to the speaker/writer. In the latter's case the speaker/writer seems to cherish facts as real UCHI-information.

(7) a. 佐藤：「．．．．。真正面を向き合って話をするとどうしても感情的に<u>なる</u>。ところが一緒に歩くと、お互いに冷静に前向きの話が<u>できる</u>。韓国と日本もそういう関係になるべきだということで意気投合しました。」(「２１世紀を元気にあと一歩」朝日 7/9/2000)

'Sato: When we talk face to face we tend to <u>become</u> emotive. But when we walk together we <u>can talk</u> calmly in a forward-looking way. We have enthusiastically agreed that the relationship between Korea and Japan should be like that.)

b. 昔は自分の街から出て働きに行くということはほとんど<u>な</u>
    <u>かった</u>。テレワーク（在宅勤務）という形態によって、そ
    ういう昔に<u>戻れる</u>。昔に戻ることがいいか、どうか分かり
    ませんが、様々なライフスタイルを選択できるようになる
    ということなんです。（「在宅勤務　足音そこまで」朝日
    7/5/2000）

    'In olden times people <u>seldom went</u> to work out of
    their own town. The system of the tele-work (work at
    home) makes it possible for them to <u>go back</u> to the
    good old days. I don't know if it is a good thing for us
    to go back to the olden days, but the bottom line is
    that we can now choose all sorts of life styles.)

c. 「. . . . . 。例えば、日中は薬剤師や検査技師がいても、夜は
    看護婦しか<u>いない</u>。点滴の準備をしている時もナースコール
    で呼ばれて中断すると、どうしても集中力が途切れて確認が
    不十分になりがち。いつもヒヤヒヤしているのが現実です。」
    （「医療事故続発、どう防ぐ」　読売　7/1/2000）

    'For example, during the daytime there are pharmacists and
    lab technicians, but at night there <u>are only</u> nurses. When a
    nurse who is preparing for an intravenous drip receives a
    nurse call she temporarily loses attention and will become
    careless about confirmation. To tell you the truth, we are
    always nervously fearful.)

d. 清水：「生き物でも人間でも、子は親に<u>る似る</u>。この伝わって
    　　　　いく基は、DNA しかないと考えていました。これは
    　　　　別のことばで言えばゲノムです。」　　（ibid.）

    Shimizu: 'Both animals and humans <u>resemble</u> their parents.
    　　　　　We thought the foundation of heridity is nothing
    　　　　　other than DNA. To say it in another word, it is
    　　　　　GENOM.'

3. Informal Forms Expressing Visual Images

Some of the deeply internalized information realizes linguistically as visual images as in (8). The images are close to flashback techniques in film making. The visual images that are expressed by the UCHI-forms are so deeply embedded in the speaker's/writer's consciousness that he or she cannot negotiate that part of information semantically with the listener/reader, nor vici versa. The listener has to just view the chunk as if it were a piece of frozen image. In fact, my extensive examination of the so-called *zadankai* (round table discussion) — a kind of conversation not for listening but for reading — provides evidence that the listener usually cannot make a turn-taking while the speaker is switching from formal SOTO-mode to informal UCHI-mode.

Note that all the example (8) is a storiy that narrates about the speaker's past experience. As noted in Miura (1776), Soga (1983) and Makino (1981 & 1983), Japanese past tense switches to non-past tense in narrative discourse on past events. My research on the tense switching has shown that such tense switching occurs when the narrator talks about backgrounded information. It is very intriguing that the tense switching and formal-to-informal switching interface in all the examples of (8). It is not accidental that those two switchings occur similtaneously when the speaker wants to revive pictorial images out of his past experience, using often the progressive Vte *iru* form.

(8) うちでは、おふくろがお饅頭ふかしたり、柏餅をつくっていたし、味噌や醤油は村で共同で作るんですよ。またお客さんが来ますと、そばを<u>打つ</u>。そして必ずその日には、鶏が一羽<u>いなくなる</u>。あれはうちのおやじのごちそうだったんですね。(座談会「家庭で伝えたい食卓の文化」婦人之友　1992 10 月号, 20-31)

'At our home my mother steamed buns and tice cakes., and the villag ersjointly made *miso* and soy sasuce. When we had

4. Formal-to-Informal Switching for Expressing One's Conviction

Now in the examples of (9) the formal-to-informal switching is used to express the speaker's conviction that may or may not convince the listener. One's emotive conviction is often expressed by negation, so the switching frequently occurs when the final prediate is in the negative, as shown by examples (9a). If the informally marked verb happens to be the verb 'omou' (which means "for s.o. to spontaneously perceive s.t. in one's mind") the listener will find it hard to verbally react to it. However, if it is replaced by the formal versions 'omoimasu ga', 'omotte iru n desu ga", then the listener can freely negotiate the meaning with the speaker.

(9)　a.　榊：「国としてゲノムにどう対応するのか、いろいろ議論が
　　　　　あるところです。アメリカとは国の投資額が一桁違い
　　　　　ますが、我が国とスケールの似ているフランスやドイ
　　　　　ツと比較して、日本の体制が非常におかしいかってい
　　　　　うと<u>そうではない</u>。(「「ヒトゲノム」がこんなによ
　　　　　くわかる」文芸春秋 2000 年, 8 月号, 262-273)

　　　　'Sakaki: How to deal with GENOME as a nation is
　　　　　　　convtroversial.The Japanese investment is
　　　　　　　different from that of U.S. by one digit,
　　　　　　　but if you compare it with that of France or
　　　　　　　Germany, a country comparable to Japan,
　　　　　　　Japanese system is not that unusual. '

　　b.　　大脇：「......。私は、これからは平和外交と信頼醸成こ
　　　　　　そが２１世紀の「人間の安全保証」だと<u>思う</u>。武
　　　　　　力では平和は絶対につくれないことは歴史が証明
　　　　　　していますよ。」
　　　　　　(「各党の憲法調査会委員にこの結果を論じていた
　　　　　　だきました」通販生活　6 月号, 2000,
　　　　　　114-119)

Owaki: 'I <u>feel</u> that peaceful deplomacy and forstering
trust among nations are 'the security of human
beings'. History has proven that peace can never
be created by military powers.'

5. Formal-to-Informal Switching for Expressing One's Personal Feelings

Next, as shown in examples in (10) the
formal-to-informal switching also tends to occur when the
speaker expresses his personal feelings as a part of his   true
feeling as in (10a) , that is, 'HONNE to use one of the cultural
keywords in Japan or as an exclamation as in (10b) which I have
already discussed in connection with Example (3).   HONNE
naturally is easier to be expressed in Japanese casual speech in
which practially all the predicates are marked informal, but it can
be also expressed in SOTO-oriented communicative context by
employing the switching rule.   As a matter of fact, HONNE
expressed through the switching is more acutely felt than
HONNE expressed in only UCHI-oriented context. One can argue
that the switching is one of the most effective pragmatic
strategies available to Japanese language which serves to give
psychological or modal depth to a propositional message.

(10) a. 私の場合は、若いころから苦労をともにした姉への思い
が支えでした。レコードの吹き込みの前日、私の伴奏で姉
が稽古をしたなんて本当に<u>懐かしい</u>。そんな思い出の中で、
最後の5年を一緒に過ごせたのは幸いだったんでしょうね。
(「淡谷とし子さんのケアノート」9. 読売 7/2/2000)'
'In my case I have been supported by my love for my
big sister with whom I shared difficut time since my
younger days. She practiced her singing with my
piano accompanyment on the day before her
recording. Just to think of it <u>makes me so nostalgic!</u>
I've been no doubt very lucky that I was able to spend

her last five years with her.'

b.　　佐藤：「......。体重１０３キロの私はその雑誌で歩い
　　　　　　てやせる生体実験をすることになっています。」
　　辻：　「そりゃ面白い。どの程度やせるんですか。」
　　（「二十一世紀を元気に、あと一歩」朝日　7/9/2000）
　　'Sato: "I weigh 103 kil grams, so I am subjecting myself
　　　　　to an experiment of reducing my weight."
　　Tsuji: "That's interesting! I wonder how much you can

6.　Non-Controllability Expressed by Formality -to-Informality Switching

　　　Practically all the cases of UCHI-forms in the formal-to-informal switching express something that is beyond human control. In other words, the speaker/writer is dealing with a chunk of reality that cannot be humanly changed. Facts as explained in (7) , pictorial images in (8), convictions in (9), and personal feelings in (10) are not easily subject to change. It is not accidental that the verbals are mostly stative verbals. Actually my exhaustive examination of the switching in one *zadankai* (「「ヒトゲノム」がこんなによくわかる」文芸春秋　2000 年，8 月号，262-273) confirmed that the majority of the verbals are, in fact, stative verbals such as *~nai, aru, dekiru , niru, omou, kangaerareru, ~te kuru,* Vstem + *yasui,* among others. Behind such use of UCHI-forms lies a sense of resignation percieved by the speaker. Examples given in (11) are proto-typical cases of non-controllability, often with connotated sense of resignation.

(11)　a.　森：「私も含め、医療者は昔からミスをおかしてきたので
　　　　　　す。ここ数年、私の病院でミスの既遂、未遂の事例
　　　　　　を報告させていますが、想像以上に数が多い。（
　　　　　　「医療事故続発、どう防ぐ」読売　7/1/2000)
　　'Mori: "Including myself, people engaged in medical field
　　　　　　has committed errors. During the past few years

I have made it mandatory to report cases of consummated or attempted errors, but they <u>are more than</u> I had imagined.

b. 辻：「その通りです。日本は世界でも未曾有の高齢化が進行
していて、二十一世紀の前半に人口の三分の一が六十
五歳以上という社会に<u>なる</u>。いかにして元気で寝たき
りにならずにトシをとるかというのが、基本テーマな
のです。（「二十一世紀を元気に、あと一歩」朝日
7/9/2000）

Tsuji: "That's right. Japanese society is getting old at the
fastest speed in the world, and by the end of the
first half of the 21st century, it <u>will become</u> a
society in which more than one third is over 65
years old. The basic theme for Japan is how
people grow old healthy without becoming
bed-bound.)

売り手も買い手も非常にスキルがあるわけですね。朝
早い時間に<u>行われる</u>。築地で<u>行われる</u>。スキルと時間
の壁が<u>ある</u>。それを乗り越えることを可能にするのが、
インターネットであろうと考えます。」（「テレワー
ク JAPAN 2000 シンポ」朝日　7/5/2000）

6.　Conclusion

Taxnomy of formal-to-informal switching may be more multi-faced and more complex than I have shown above, but it is about time I should come up with a generalization on what is going on in the switching in Japanese discourse, more specifically in reading conversation (*zadankai*, that is) and essays. All my data and my foregoing discussion seem to indicate that it has crucially to do with informational calassification, that is to say, backgrouding information which is essentially UCHI-oriented and foregrounding information which is essentially SOTO-oriented. Japanese morphology of UCHI-forms and SOTO-forms serves to overtly index such informational classification, when they are used at sentence-final position within a SOTO-context. Such informational classification is useful not only to explain formal-to-informal switching, but also to explain the tense switching, as I discussed it in connection with examples of (8). On the basis of my findings in this paper I belive I can say that the formal-to-informal switching signals that the speaker/writer turns his communicative direction inwardly. In more concrete temrs the formal-to-informal switching is used in discourse to express:

a.   Backgrounding information.
b.   Speaker/UCHI-oriented information or inwardly directed information.
c.   Non-controllable matters such as 'facts', 'pictorial images', 'personal feelings', 'convictions', and 'fait a complit'.
d.   Psychological depth to a propositional information.
e.   UCHI-oriented discourse with SOTO-oriented discourse.
f.   Psychological situation rather than social situation.

What is interesting about the switching is that it is a pragmatic and cognitive rule which the speaker may or may not want to use. If he wants to express discourse functions stated above to give depth to his communication he will use it; otherwise he simply doesn't use it without damaging the acceptablity of discourse. I don't believe that the rule is a universal rule but not Japanese-specific rule either. If a language has dual verbal morphology , that is, informal and formal forms the language should have the conversion rule very similar to Japanese. As a matter of fact, according to my Korean colleague at Princeton Dr. Eun Joo Kim, the formal-to-informal switching occurs in Korean language, too. It is now on the shoulder of Korean linguists to prove or disprove the existence of Formal-to-Informal Switching with functions comparable to those for the Japanese version.

References

Hopper, Paul J.   1979.   Aspect and Foregrounding in Discourse. *Syntax and Semantics* Vol.12. *Discourse and Syntax.* New York: Academic Press, 213–59

Makino, Seiichi. 1981. Tense Switching in Japanese Written Narrative Discourses. *Papers From The Middlebury Symposium On Japanese Discourse Analysis*, (ed. by Makino), University of Illinois, 125–50

Makino, Seiichi.   1983. Monogatari no Bunshoo ni okeru Jisei no Tenkan [Tense Switching in Narrative Discourse] *Gekkan Gengo* 12:12 Tokyo: Taishukan.   109–17

Makino, Seiichi . 1996. *Uchi to Soto no Gengo-Bunkagaku— Bunpoo o Bunka de Kiru* . [Culturo-Linguistics of Inside and Outside — Intersection between Language & Culture] Tokyo: ALC

Miura, Akira (1974) The V–u Form vs. the V–ta Form. *Papers in Japanse Linguistics*. 3. 95–121

Nomoto, Kikuo. 1977. Buntai o Kangaeru Tame ni [A Note on Styles] *Amata mo Bunshoo ga Kakeru*, Tokyo: Gakutosha. 69–99

Soga, Matsuo. 1983. *Tense and Aspect in Modern Colloquial Japanese*, Vancouver: Univeristy of British Columbia Press

Markers of Epistemic vs. Affective Stances: *Desyoo* vs. *Zyanai**

Naomi Hanaoka McGloin
University of Wisconsin-Madison

1. Introduction

It has long been recognized that languages are responsive to the speaker's needs to express an affective stance as well as an epistemic stance. Ochs (1988:217), for example, defines affective disposition as 'feelings, moods and attitudes of participants toward some proposition' and epistemological disposition as 'some property of the participants' belief or knowledge vis-a-vis some proposition.' Ochs, furthermore, suggests that affective and epistemological dispositions are two contextual dimensions which are directly evoked by linguistic features.

In Japanese, such stances are characteristically expressed by various sentence-final forms. The present paper focuses on two such sentence-final expressions, *desyoo* (and its informal variant *daroo*) and *zyanai* (and its variants *zyanai desu ka* and *zyan*).[1] *Desyoo* is generally said to be an epis-

---

* An earlier version of this paper was read at the AILA '99 in Tokyo, Japan. I am grateful to the panelists and the discussant, Kim Jones, for useful comments and observations.
[1] *Zyanai desu ka* is used in situations where formality is required. *Zyanai* is an informal variant and is used among friends and family members. *Zyan* is also an informal variant, but it is used primarily by younger speakers of Japanese.

temic modality marker, as in (1), and *zyanai* a rhetorical question marker, as in (2).

(1) Asita   wa   ame   ga   furu   **desyoo.**
    Tomorrow TOP   rain NOM   rain
    'It will probably rain tomorrow.'

(2) Oisii   **zyanai (ka).**
    delicious
    '(It isn't delicious?) It's delicious!'

In (1), *desyoo* indicates that the proposition is probable. In (2), *zyanai* is rhetorical in that this form does not negate the proposition nor ask for information from the addressee. So, *desyoo* and *zyanai* seem to have inherently very different functions. In some situations, however, these two forms are almost interchangeable. Observe (3a) and (3b).

(3) a.   Kono aida   ageta **desyoo.**
       The other day   gave
       'I gave it to you the other day, right?'

    b.   Kono aida ageta **zyanai.**
       'I gave (it) to you the other day, right?'

Here, the speaker assumes that the interlocutor shares the propositional knowledge. Both *desyoo* and *zyanai* function very much like the English 'tag-question'. The main goal of this paper is to examine subtle differences involved in cases like (3). Specifically, we will try to show that *desyoo* indexes the speaker's epistemic stance and *zyanai* the affective stance. Hence, *desyoo* tends to be a more objective expression and *zyanai* a more subjective expression.

The data used for analysis in this paper consist of ten audio-taped informal conversations among friends (ranging from five minutes to thirty minutes each) and two audio-taped semi-informal conversations between a professor and a graduate student.[2] I have also used my field observation notes of conversations among the Japanese around me.

---

[2] The recorded conversations were transcribed either by myself or by the graduate students in my Seminar in Japanese Linguistics course. The transcription convention follows Psathas (1995), which follows Gail Jefferson's transcription convention with a few exceptions.

2. Preliminary Look at *Desyoo* and *Zyanai*

The usage of *desyoo* has generally been classified into three types. Tano-mura (1990), for example, recognizes 'simple inference,' 'request for con-firmation of an inference,' and 'request for confirmation of a fact,' of which the first is generally considered to be the basic meaning of *desyoo*. These usages are illustrated by the following examples, respectively.

(4) Tabun   kuru desyoo.
    Probably come
    '(He) will probably come.'

(5) Tukareta   desyoo.
    Got tired
    'You must be tired./You are tired, aren't you.'

(6) Eki   ya   tikagai   ni yoku iru   daroo,
    station and underground market in often exist

    aa yuu   otoko   ga.   (Tanomura 1990:71)
    that kind   man   NOM

    'They are often in the station and underground markets, aren't they. Those kinds of men.' (Translation by Szatrowski 1994)

In (4), the speaker is making an inference about something he/she does not know for certain. In the second usage, *desyoo* is predicated to a proposition about which the hearer has direct knowledge but which the speaker can only infer. So, in (5), the speaker infers that the hearer is tired and asks if that inference is correct. In the third usage, *desyoo*, as in (6), is predicated to information which the speaker believes/knows is a fact. It is in the third usage where *desyoo* is interchangeable with *zyanai*.

    As for *zyanai*, there are two types. The first type (*zyanai*$_1$) occurs both with verbs/adjectives and nouns. The other type (*zyanai*$_2$) occurs only with nouns and noun phrases. These are illustrated by (7) and (8).

(7) Ame ga   hutteru   zyanai.
    rain NOM is raining
    'It's raining, you know.'

(8) Ame ga   hutteru   n   zyanai?
    rain NOM is raining NML
    'Isn't it raining?'

In (7), which is a case of *zyanai*₁, the speaker knows that it's raining. (8) is a case of *zyanai*₂. Here, *n* nominalizes the preceding sentence, and the speaker is simply inferring that it might be raining. *Zyanai*₁, moreover, is generally uttered with a falling intonation, while *zyanai*₂ is accompanied with a rising intonation. Our concern in this paper is *zyanai*₁. Hence, we will restrict our discussions to *zyanai*₁.[3]

In McGloin (1999), I have identified three functions of *zyanai*₁--a strongly expressive function; a less expressive, tag-like function; and a textual function. (9) and (10) are examples of a strongly expressive function.

(9) (Two speakers are talking about American football. After the first speaker said that her school had a team but it wasn't very good, the second speaker asks which school it was. The first speaker answers that it was *Kangaku*, and the second speaker then says:)
Kangaku　tuyoi　　zyanai desu ka.
　　　　　strong
'Kangaku is strong.'

(10) (After viewing a video segment where an American student's speech was dubbed in an unnatural Japanese.)
Nihon no　ima　no　gakusei wa　anna hanasikata　　suru
Japan LK　now　LK　student　TOP　such way of talking　do

hazu　　　　ga　　nai　　zyanai.
Likelihood　NOM　NEG
'There is no way a young Japanese student talks like that!'

In its strongly expressive function, *zyanai* presents the speaker's point of view or evaluation very strongly. It is thus very persuasive and expresses a 'nonchallengeable' attitude.

Furthermore, it is not accidental that *zyanai* is in a negative form. *Zyanai* often occurs in a context where a certain contrast or opposition is implied, e.g., when someone holds an opposing view/opinion or when the speaker holds an expectation which is contrary to the fact. Its strongly assertive power can be said to derive from negation of the implied or observed

---

[3] Since *zyanai*₂ indicates 'inference,' it is interchangeable with *desyoo*, when it indicates 'inference,' as in (i).
　(i)　(a) henna mono demo tabeta n zyanai?
　　　　(b) henna mono demo tabeta n desyoo.
　　　　'(He) must have eaten/probably ate something bad.'
However, as was stated earlier, *zyanai*₂ is distinguished from *zyanai*₁ both in its meaning and intonation contour. Cases like (i), therefore, are not examined in this paper.

contrast/opposition.[4] So, in (9), the speaker presents her view, which is in direct opposition to that of the interlocutor. In (10), what the speaker thinks is in opposition to the observed fact--the way a teenager's speech was portrayed in a video.

Zyanai also has a less expressive, tag-like function, as in (11).

(11) (Three women are talking about a theft in T's dorm.)
   T: sore ga sa: ryoo tte (0.1) MON mo kugirareteru **zyan**?=
       then   dorm TOP   gate also separate-passive
       'Then, the dorm is separated (from the street) by the gate, right?'

   K: u::n
       'uh-huh'

   T: =iriguti datte nakanaka zen'in ga haireru wake
       entrance even   not easily everyone NOM enter-can

       zya nai **zyan**?
       COP-NEG
       'Even the entrance to the building, not everyone can pass through, right?'

Here, T is not trying to persuade K concerning this information--how access to the dormitory building is restricted. It is not clear whether K actually knows the information that T presents. However, T, by presenting it as if it were shared information, creates a sense of rapport and seeks understanding/empathy from K.

So, in its basic function, *desyoo* indicates the speaker's epistemic stance, from simple inference to strong assumption of knowledge on the part of the interlocutor. On the other hand, *zyanai* relates to the speaker's affect, such as emotional emphasis, surprise, etc.

3. *Zyanai* vs. *Desyoo*

In general, when the proposition is about what the speaker can only infer, such as the interlocutor's feelings or the interlocutor's affairs which the speaker is not certain about, *desyoo* is appropriate but not *zyanai*.

(12) B: kekkoo, turai n   desu kedo ne.
         fairly   tough NML COP   but   FP

---

[4] A similar view was independently advanced in Uehara, Fukushima & Kitano (1999); they also observed that what they call a 'modal' *zyanai* typically occurs when there is 'kotonatta ninshiki (a differing view/understanding).'

'It is fairly difficult.'

A: n:. demo, omosiroi   desyo? (*zyanai)
    But   interesting
    'Yeah, but it's interesting, right?'

In (12), speakers A and B are talking about B's studies. B began college later than usual and comments that it is not easy. A then says that it must be interesting. However, whether B finds it interesting or not concerns B's internal feeling, and thus this information is accessible only to speaker B (A's interlocutor). Here, *zyanai* is unacceptable.

However, in some situations, *zyanai* is acceptable even when the speaker can only form an inference about the proposition.

(13) (A and B have been talking about A's recent trip to Europe. After A talked about his trip, B says:)
   B: zya, zuibun kyookoogun **zyanai desu ka.**
      then quite   hard trip
      'Then, it's a pretty hard schedule, *zuanai desu ka.*'

(14) (A, who teaches a craft to B and C, is talking about her trip to Northern Honshu.)

A: Fukusima de ne, sono otomodati ga   kudamono ippai
           at FP   friend   NOM fruit   a lot

   katte   notte kita wake. de watasitati wa Tookyoo
   buy-and get on came   and we   TOP

   kara   notta n   desu. Hanamaki ni iku toki ni
   from   got on NML COP   to go time at

   de, so- senmenzyo de ne sono toki wa   budoo
   and   wash room in FP that time TOP grapes

   o   aratte
   ACC   wash-and

'At Fukushima, our friend came on board carrying a lot of fruit. We were on the train from Tokyo. We were on the way to Hanamaki, and she washed grapes in the washroom,'

B: [aa

'I see.'

A: [araootte yuu wake na no. sore ga ne   araenai   no
   try to wash   FP but   FP wash-can't   FP
   '(She) tried to wash them, but she couldn't.'
   (laugh)
C: zya zenbu   mae nuretyau **zyanai desu ka**,   ne,   sensee.
   then all   front get wet   FP   teacher
   'Then, (she/one) gets completely wet in front, right?'

In (13) and (14), the statement appended by *zyanai desu ka* pertains to what
the interlocutor experienced and hence what the speaker can only infer.
This is the domain of *desyoo*. However, here, only *zyanai* is acceptable. If
the sentences are put into the past tense, however, *desyoo* is fine, as in
(13B') and (14C').

(13) B': zuibun kyookoogun datta **desyoo**.
        'It must have been a pretty hard schedule.'

(14) C': zya zenbu mae nuretyatta **desyoo**.
        'Then, she must have gotten completely wet in front.'

There are some differences, however. With *zyanai desu ka*, the speaker
expresses the sentiment that the idea has just entered her consciousness at
the discourse site and is not something which has been previously expected.
So, in (13B), the idea that the trip was fairly stringent was a newly formed
judgment at the discourse site, and hence carries a sense of surprise/ discov-
ery. (13B') with *desyoo*, on the other hand, indicates that the speaker had
prior knowledge about how hard the schedule of the trip would be. In (14),
speaker C, after hearing that someone had a great deal of difficulty trying to
wash fruits on a moving train, makes a comment that she might have gotten
wet all over. The use of *zyanai desu ka* adds a great deal of emotional
tone—it sounds as if speaker C was quite taken by surprise at the prospect
of someone getting wet. The use of *desyoo*, on the other hand, presents the
prospect of getting wet as an obvious and expected consequence.

The fact that *desyoo* implies that the speaker has prior knowledge or
has expected the proposition/information to be true can be further illustrated
by the following examples.

(15) (S and K are talking about S's telephone bill.)

S: kooraa aidii de, (.) soo. juudoru   izyoo   torareteru
    caller ID   yes ten dollar more than take-passive

  [yo.
  FP
  'For a caller ID service, I am paying more than ten dollars.'

K: [kanari kitui ne.
  'pretty tough.'

S: **desyoo**, [nanka bakabakasii-
      kind of stupid
  'Right? It's kind of stupid.'

(16) (Three women are talking about women and applying makeup.)

H: demo nanka koosyuukai toka ikanakatta?
  but like workshop like go-NEG-PST
  'Didn't you go to a makeup session?'

B: itta itta.
  'I did. I did.'

H: itta **desyo** watasi sore itta.
  went   I   that went
  'You did, right? I did.'

In these cases, *desyoo*, but not *zyanai*, is acceptable. In (15), S and K are talking about how much it costs to have a caller ID service. K comments that the cost is a bit steep. S then says 'desyoo' implying that she agrees with K's comments. By using 'desyoo', S implies that the assertion is not something which has just entered her consciousness but something which she has previously thought of. In (16), H and B are talking about workshops on how to apply makeup. H asks if B went to one of those workshops and B answers that she did. So, H is certain of this fact. In this case, then, H is not asking the interlocutor to confirm this fact, but she is confirming that this is something which she has previously expected to be the case. So, *desyoo* presents a proposition matter-of-factly as something which was expected/known, while *zyanai* carries an emotional tone such as surprise.
  Let's look at example (17).

(17) (The speaker N is talking about an old convertible sports car that she
   was given free of charge.)

1 N: kumottyatte:, (0.9) kumottyatte mienakatta no
    get fogged up   get fogged up couldn't see FP

2   usiro ga.
      back NOM
      'It got fogged up. It got foggy, and I could not see through the back.'

3 O: a:: untensiteru toki ni?
       is driving   time at
       'When you drove?'

4 N: mono sugoku kowai **desyo**.
       extremely   scary
       'It's really scary, right?'

5 O: u::n.
       'uh-huh.'

6 N: de   ano::: (1.5) zu:to   ne?   itinitizyuu saa
       and   all the time FP   all day   FP

7   akete:, (.) nee [untensiteru wake ni wa ikanai **zyanai**. [
      open   FP   is driving   can't very well
      'And, you can't really drive with the top down all the time, right?'

8 O: [un.   [u::n

9 N: dakara, kinzyo   tama:ni   notta kedo:,
       so   neighborhood once in a while drove but

       bureeki kowareteru si: moo   kowai si:,
       brakes be broken   and   really scary   and
       'So, I drove it occasionally around the neighborhood, but the brakes didn't work, and it was scary, so ....'

On lines 1 and 2, N says that she could not see out the back of the car because the vinyl cover was worn out. The whole point of N's utterances on lines 1 to 7 is to give reasons for line 9--that she could not drive the car that much. On line 4, she says 'kowai desyo' and tries to get the interlocutor to share her view--that it is scary to drive the car without being able to see through the back window. The use of *desyoo* indicates that the speaker presents this proposition as something which she can naturally expect the interlocutor to share. O then gives a minimum response. N then presents another reason with *zyanai*--that one cannot drive the car with the top down all the time. The use of *zyanai* indicates that somehow N felt the need to emphasize this proposition. Perhaps she felt that driving with the top down is rather an unusual thing to do and hence needs to be highlighted. Or, it might be because, after line 4, the interlocutor only gave a minimum response and hence the speaker N felt the necessity to emphasize this reason, to justify her saying that the car was more or less useless.

So, *zyanai*, more than *desyoo*, tends to be associated with situations where the speaker wants to justify his/her opinion or position.

4. Textual Functions

Now, I would like to briefly comment on the textual functions of *desyoo* and *zyanai*. Both *desyoo* and *zyanai* have been going through functional changes in a manner very similar to what Herring (1991) describes for Tamil rhetorical questions. Szatrowski (1994:543-544) observes that *desyoo* is 'undergoing a reanalysis from semantic-pragmatic to textual uses,' and recognizes three textual functions of *desyoo*: 'to retrieve information for further predication,' 'to provide a focus/theme for subsequent utterances,' and 'to provide a basis for subsequent discourse.' Similar textual functions are also observed for *zyanai* in McGloin 1999.

(18) and (19) are examples of 'to retrieve information for further predication.'

(18) ... de   baribari no   kyariaa uuman   na n   da   kedo.
         and   hard working career woman   NML COP   but

     de   singuru no zassi   ga   aru   **desyoo**. de
     and   single   magazine NOM   exist   and

     asoko ni kookoku   o   nosete, sorede
     there in advertisement   ACC   publish that way

     deeto o   sita gurai datta   n   da.
     date   ACC did   extent was   NML COP

'And she is quite a career woman. And, there is a magazine for singles, right? She went so far as to place an ad in it, and went on dates that way.'

(19) (S and K are discussing telephone rates.)

S: he:	nanka,	kooringu kaado	toka	aru	**zyan,**	**are**
really?	like	calling card	like	exist		that

o	tukau	to	yasui	toka	tte.
ACC	use	if	cheap	something like	I hear

'Really? Like, there is a calling card, right? If you use that, it's really cheap, I hear.'

K: honto ni?
     'Really?'

In (18) and (19), sentences predicated with *desyoo* and *zyan* introduce 'magazine' and 'calling card' into the listener's consciousness and provide referents for the following anaphoric pronouns *asoko* and *are*.

In the next two examples, sentences predicated with *desyoo* and *zyanai* 'provide a basis for subsequent discourse.'

(20) tadane	nanka	mizu	dake	nomu	wake ni	yatara
except		water	only	drink		too much

nomu	wake ni ikanai	**desyoo.**	**dakara**	mada	sono mama ni
drink	can't very well		so	still	as it is

site	arimasu	kedo	ne.
leave		but	FP

'Except, you can't just drink water, right? So, I still keep it as it was.'

(21) (TA talking to a professor)

kono aida	wa	watasitati	ga	inakatta	**zyanai desu ka.**
the other day	TOP	we	NOM	exist-NEG-PST	

Sorede	donna	bideo	mita	ka	kiite	mita
	what kind	video	see-PST	Q	ask	see

n	desu	yo.
NML	COP	FP

'We weren't here the other day, right? So, we asked (the students) to tell us the story of the video they saw.'

In (21), both the TA and the faculty member know that the TAs were not in class the other day. The use of *zyanai desu ka* here is not expressive. It simply provides a basis for the following sentence.

There are some noteworthy differences between textual usages of *desyoo* and *zyanai*. First, the textual use of *zyanai* is a relatively recent phenomenon. Table I gives a breakdown of various usages of *desyoo* and *zyanai* in some of my data.

	desyoo			**zyanai**		
	conf. of inference	conf. of fact	textual	expressive	tag	textual
Data 1	8	11	16	1	0	0
Data 2	5	9	14	9	1	1
Data 3	20	13	2	44	15	25

Table 1[5]

It is significant that in data 1 from the early 80's, *desyoo*, regardless of its function, was the predominant form: only one instance of *zyanai* was observed. Data 2 (recorded in the early 90's) and Data 3 (recorded in the late 90's) are fairly comparable in that they both involve speakers in their 20's. As we can see, however, there are significant differences between the use of *desyoo* and *zyanai*. In data 2, *desyoo* was still predominantly used for its textual usage, while, in data 3, *zyanai* is overwhelmingly preferred over *desyoo* in its textual function.

Furthermore, while the use of *desyoo* is restricted to a higher-status person in talking to a lower-status person, or among equals, *zyanai* does not have such a restriction. *Zyanai desu ka* is also used by someone lower in status to someone higher in status and also between two strangers.

This type of *zyanai desu ka* has been tagged as one of the features which characterize the speech of the younger generation. Inoue (1998:151-152) cites the *Bunkacho* opinion survey where people were asked if they utter a sentence such as (22).

---

[5] Data 1 (50 min) is a conversation among housewives in their 30's to 60's and was recorded circa 1983. Data 2 (62 min) consists of conversations between graduate students in their 20's which were recorded in 1991. In data 3 (100 min), conversation participants are graduate and undergraduate students in their 20's to early 30's, and they were recorded in 1997-99.

(22) Neru mae ni ha   o   migaku zyanai desu ka. Sono toki ni
     sleep before teeth ACC brush   that   time at
     'I brush my teeth before going to bed, right? When I do that, ...'

According to this survey, this expression is overwhelmingly accepted by speakers in their teens and 20's, and especially among the student population living in Tokyo.

Why is *zyanai desu ka* an acceptable utterance toward superiors while *desyoo* is not? As we observed earlier, *desyoo* assumes that the listener already knows or should know a certain fact, and thus sounds somewhat imposing or presumptuous. Maynard (1990:144) goes so far as to say 'Using these phrases gives the impression that you are challenging the depth and the extent of your superior's knowledge; it carries a condescending tone.' *Zyanai*, on the other hand is an expression which carries a strong emotion, thereby evoking listener involvement. In its strongly expressive function, it also tends to have an effect of strongly impressing a piece of information on the listener, persuading the listener or justifying one's view point. The development of the textual function is a result of 'pragmatic unmarking, or the gradual diminishing of its expressive impact' (Herring 1991:277-278). I believe the popularity of the textual *zyanai desu ka* is due to its 'weakened affect.' It is thus used simply to appeal for the listener's attention, and to seek emotional rapport with the listener, which is not incompatible with a lower-status person speaking toward a superior.

5. Conclusion

In this paper, we have examined subtle differences which exist between *desyoo* and *zyanai* based on naturally occurring conversations. Both *desyoo* and *zyanai* are used to evoke common ground between the speaker and the interlocutor. Both *desyoo* and *zyanai* have also developed a textual function in discourse. Although I was not able to give a full range of examples in limited space, I hope to have shown that the subtle difference between *desyoo* and *zyanai* reflects *desyoo* as a marker of an epistemic stance and *zyanai* as a marker of an affective stance.

List of abbreviations

ACC	Accusative	NML	Nominalizer
COP	Copula	NOM	Nominative
FP	Final Particle	PST	Past
IMP	Imperative	Q	Question
LK	Linking Nominals	QT	Quotation
NEG	Negative	TOP	Topic marker

References

Hasunuma, Akiko. 1992. Nihongo no danwa maakaa 'daroo' to 'zyanaika' no kinoo--kyootuu ninsiki kanki no yoohoo o tyuusin ni. *Koide kinen nihongo kyooiku kenkyuukai ronbunsyuu*, ed. Shigeko Imada, Tazuko Ueno, Michiko Sasaki, Taeko Nakamura and Suzuko Nishihara, 39-58. Tokyo: Nihongo kyooiku kenkyuukai.

Herring, Susan C. 1991. The grammaticalization of rhetorical questions in Tamil. *Approaches to Grammaticalization*, ed. Elizabeth Traugott and Bernd Heine, 253-284. Amsterdam: John Benjamins.

Inoue, Fumio. 1998. *Nihongo Watching*. Tokyo: Iwanami-shoten.

Maynard, Senko. 1990. *An Introduction to Japanese Grammar and Communication Strategies*. Tokyo: The Japan Times.

McGloin, Naomi Hanaoka. 1999. Pragmatic and Discourse Functions of the Rhetorical Negative Question Form, *Zyanai desu ka*. *Linguistics: In Search of the Human Mind—A Festschrift for Kazuko Inoue*, ed. M. Muraki and E. Iwamoto. Tokyo: Kaitakusha.

Moriyama, Takuro. 1992. Nihongo ni okeru 'suiryoo' o megutte. *Gengo Kenkyu* 101:64-83.

Ochs, Elinor. 1988. *Culture and Language Development*. Cambridge: Cambridge University Press.

Psathas, George. 1995. *Conversation Analysis: the study of Talk-in-Interaction*. Thousand Oaks: Sage Publications.

Szatrowski, Polly. 1994. Discourse functions of the Japanese epistemic modal DESYOO. *BLS* 20:532-546.

Tanomura, Tadaharu. 1988. Hitei gimonbun syoo koo. *Kokugogaku* 152:16-30.

_____. 1990. *Gendai Nihongo no Bunpoo--NO DA no Imi to Yoohoo*. Izumi-shoin.

Uehara, Satoshi, Etsuko Fukushima & Hiroaki Kitano. 1999. *Soo janai n janai n desu ka*?: A conversation-based study of *janai* in Japanese. *Gengogaku to Nihongo Kyooiku*, ed. Yukiko Sasaki Alam. Tokyo: Kurosio.

The Social Meanings of the Japanese Plain Form

HARUKO MINEGISHI COOK
University of Hawaii at Manoa

1. Introduction

From the perspective of indexicality (Agha 1993; Hanks 1999; Levinson 1979; Lyons 1977; Silverstein 1976), which sees language as "social action," this study examines one of the Japanese verbal forms, the plain form (also known as the abrupt form, direct form or *da-tai*) and offers a unified account on how the plain form can index diverse contexts.

Hanks (1999: 124) defines indexicality as "the pervasive context-dependency of natural language utterances." Indexical signs point to some aspect in the immediate communicative context. This paper considers the Japanese plain form as an indexical sign and examines what contextual aspects it foregrounds.

2. Background

The plain form has been invariably referred to in the literature as the informal or casual form when it occurs in the main clause predicate. This is in contrast with the addressee honorific, the *masu* form, which marks formal contexts (e.g., Ikuta 1983; Maynard 1993; Niyekawa 1991). However, this analysis has only limited validity, for it is a well-known fact that the plain form is also used in impersonal contexts such as expository writing, newspaper articles and textbooks. This paradox has rarely been addressed.

Studying casual conversations and written narratives, Maynard (1993) makes a distinction between the plain form with a discourse marker such as a final particle (i.e., non-naked *da* style) and that without any (i.e., naked *da* style). She points out that the plain form without a final particle tends to occur when the speaker has low awareness of the addressee, and it indicates i) immediacy and directness in expression, ii) a narrative internal perspective, and iii) an expression not deliberately addressed to the addressee. Maynard's proposal to make a distinction between the plain form with and without a discourse marker is insightful. Her study focuses on the mixed use of the plain and *masu* forms but does not address the question of why the plain form indexes the impersonal style as well. To date, there is no adequate account on how the plain form indexes such a variety of contexts.

3. Data

The data for this study consist of a newspaper article and naturally occurring interactions from three different social contexts, namely a multi-party casual family conversation, an elementary school classroom interaction, and a TV interview. The participants of these interactions are speakers of standard Tokyo Japanese.

4. Foregrounding Functions

Maynard (1993) notes that the plain form rarely occurs without a final particle or the like attached. My family conversation data are consistent with her observation. Consider the following example from the adult family conversation. Here H is asking his high school son T what was the most interesting thing when he was visiting the U.S. T talks about his American host family's dog, and then the other participants, C and A, also talk about C's cousin's dog. In all the examples in this paper, the plain form is indicated by a single underline, affect keys by a double underline, and the *masu* form a dotted line.

(1)

1 H: Nani ga   ichiban omoshirokatta?
       what SUB most   interesting
       'What was most interesting?'

2 T: Sakki   hanashita <u>yo</u>.
       just now spoke   FP
       'I just now told you, you know'

    ((several lines are omitted.))

3 T: Deree to shite ne, bunnagutte mo okon   <u>nai</u> <u>no</u>.
       slouching   FP even if I hit   get angry not FP
       'The dog is slouching, and does not get angry even if I hit him.'

4 SEVERAL: ((laugh))

5 C: Haa
       'uhuh'

6 H: <u>Hidee</u> inu <u>da</u>   <u>na</u>.
       terrible dog COP FP
       'It's a terrible dog!'

7 C: Yuu-chan toko   itta   toki mo
                   place went when also
       'When we went to Yuu-chan's house'

8 A: Aa dakkusufundo
       'Uh dachshund'
          [
9 T: Dakkusufundo
       'dachshund'

10 ALL: ((laugh))

11 C: Sore de <u>ne</u>, neteru toko haitte <u>kichatta</u> <u>no</u> <u>yo</u>, <u>Ako-chan to futari de</u>.
     and   FP sleep when enter come FP FP   with two
     'And when we were sleeping, the dog came in, when the two of us,
     Ako-chan and I (were sleeping).'

12 A: Kao o   pero pero pero <u>nameru</u> <u>no</u>.
     face OBJ   lick   FP
     'He licked our faces.'
   [
13 C: <u>Soide</u> <u>nee</u> ofuton ni <u>mogurikomu</u> <u>no</u> <u>yo</u>=
     then   FP cover in crawl   FP FP
     'Then he crawled into our beds.'

14 A: =Betto no   naka ni haitte <u>kun</u> <u>no</u> issho ni
      bed   GEN inside in enter come FP together
      'He comes into the bed, together.'

Here we observe that the plain form co-occurs with a final particle, postposed information, rising intonation, lengthened vowel and coalescence. In lines 2, 3, 6, 11, 12, and 13, the plain form co-occurs with the final particles *yo, no, na, nee* and *no yo*. The final particles index an interpersonal relationship between the speaker and the addressee in on-going talk (Maynard 1989; Cook 1990, 1992). In this sense, final particles are what Ochs (1988) calls 'affect keys', which index the speaker's moods, attitudes, feelings, and dispositions toward the addressee or the referent. Final particles are not the only affect keys. Rising intonation, postposing information, vowel lengthening, and coalescence also serve as 'affect keys'. In line 1, rising intonation is used to ask a question. According to Bolinger (1989), intonation conveys 'emotion and attitude.'[1] In this sense, intonation is an affect key. Rising intonation indexes the speaker's uncertainty: uncertainty about listener comprehension or a contribution to conversation (Lakoff 1975; Guy 1986; Ochs 1996). It demands a response from the addressee. Postposing information also functions as an affect key. According to Hirokawa (1995), postposing information in Japanese conversation can function as a turn exit signal. In this sense, it is a floor management device. The current speaker surrenders the floor to the next speaker, which is the speaker's display of his/her concern for the next speaker. Postposing information occurs in line 11. Here C continues, but A takes the floor in line 12, which indicates that A expects C to surrender the floor at this point. In general, a lengthened vowel is an affect intensifier (Ochs 1996). In line 13, C lengthens the vowel [e] in the final particle *ne* as in *nee,* which intensifies C's affective stance toward the story. C's utterance in line 13 is the climax of the story in the sense that the dog finally even crawled into the bed. Notice that there is a progression to the dog's behavior in this story. Before he crawled into the bed, he first came into the bedroom and then licked the speakers' faces. In line 14, A rephrases what C has just said. Then several turns after line 14, C elaborates on how they tried to get the dog out of the bed. The *nee* in *soide nee* 'and then *nee*' intensifies the excitement of the story that will unfold. Coalescence also indexes the speaker's affective state. In lines 6, 11, 13, and 14, we see *hidee* from *hidoi,*

---

[1] . Bolinger (1989:1) states, '... intonation manages to do what it does by continuing to be what it is, primarily a symptom of how we feel about what we say, or how we feel *when* we say.'

chatta from *te shimau*, *soide* from *sorede* and *kun* from *kuru*. *Chatta* involves palatalization, and *soide* involves vowel raising from a mid front vowel to a high front vowel. Crosslinguistically, palatalized sounds and the high front vowel [i] are typically associated with smallness, and childishness in expressions such as *Johnny,* which comes from *John* (Hamano 1998). Thus, *chatta* and *soide* here index the speaker's informality and intimacy. *Hidee* indexes the speaker's rough attitude toward the referent. When *no* immediately follows a verb ending with *-ru,* the last vowel [u] drops, and the liquid [r] assimilates to the dental nasal [n] for ease of pronunciation. Thus, *kun* (from *kuru*) 'to come' indexes relaxed, informal speech. Affect keys are not limited to those that appear in (1). They include a large number of various features. Rough words such as *umai* 'tasty'and *meshi* 'meal', modulated voice, and laughing are among these features.

Newspaper articles, on the other hand, are written in the plain form without affect keys. Consider (2), which comes from Nihon Keizai Newspaper.

(2) Nihon Keizai Newspaper

1 Natsu ni naru to   karada no   fuchoo o   uttaeru hito
  summer come when body GEN disfunction OBJ complain people

  ga   ooi.
  SUB   many
  'When summer comes, there are many people who experience physical disorder.'

2 Darukute nani mo suru ki   ni narenai.
  dull   nothing do desire   become NEG
  'They feel dull and do not feel like doing anything.'

3 Shokuyoku mo naku,   tsukare yasui.
  appetite   also not exist tired   easy
  'They have no appetite and easily get tired.'

4 Tada de sae atsusa de   yowatte iru no   ni,
  usual even heat   with weakened NOM on
  'On top of the fact that they are weakened by the heat,

5 shokuyoku fushin, nebusoku   ga   kuwawaru kara
  appetite   dull   lack of sleep SUB added   because

because of loss of appetite and lack of sleep

6 joobu na hito   de mo <u>kotaeru</u>.
  healthy person   even suffer
  even normally healthy people suffer.'

The above text completely lacks affect keys. Due to their absence, it is interpreted as an impersonal text. Table 1 summaries the features of the plain form used in conversations and newspapers. (The list in Table 1 are not exhaustive.)

Table 1: Collocation of linguistic features co-occurring with the plain form

Linguistic form: Affect keys	Conversation	Newspapers
Final particle (interpersonal relation marker)	+	-
Postposing information (floor management device)	+	-
Rising intonation (uncertainty, request for information)	+	-
Vowel lengthening (emotional Intensity marker)	+	-
Coalescence (various affective states)	+	-

From table 1, it is clear that the presence or absence of the co-occurring affect keys is responsible for informality and impersonality. The plain form with an affect key indexes informality because it foregrounds the speaker's affective involvement with the addressee or the referent. However, it is not the effect of an affect key alone that gives rise to the social meaning of informality. The addressee honorific, the *masu* form, at times also co-occurs with affect keys. However, it foremost foregrounds formality or the presentational mode of self and does not foreground informality. This fact indicates that the plain form has a specific indexical function that foregrounds an affect key if there is one or more. Otherwise, the plain form foregrounds the informational content of an utterance or text. When the plain form is devoid of affect keys, it is interpreted as impersonal, and it makes sense that it is used when the speaker has low awareness of the addressee as discussed by Maynard. The basic function of indexes is to point to something in the context. In the case of the plain form, what it points to is an affect key if any. Otherwise, it points to the informational content.

5. The Plain Form as a Linguistic Resource for Social Interaction

Henceforth, I will refer to the plain form without an affect key as the naked plain form and the plain form with an affect key as the non-naked plain form.

The consistent use of the naked plain form indexes impersonality as seen in the newspaper article in (2). In speech, while the non-naked plain form occurs frequently, the naked plain form neither occurs frequently nor does it always index impersonality. In speech, what does it index and in what specific speech context does it occur? This section investigates these questions in two institutional speech events, namely an elementary school classroom interaction and a TV interview program.

There is a high correlation between the occurrence of the naked plain form and a particular turn type in these speech events. In the TV interview program, the naked plain form tends to occur in the interviewer's summary turn, and in the elementary school classroom interaction, it occurs in the student's response turn in the *happyoo* 'presentation' activity.[2] In the TV interview program, the interviewer mostly uses the *masu* form but often switches to the naked plain form in the summary turn. Consider (3). While in line 1 the interviewer asks a question in the *masu* form, in lines 3 and 6, he summarizes in the naked plain form the interviewee's statement. If one of the important responsibilities of the interviewer is to convey clearly the content of the interviewee's opinion to the TV audience, the use of the naked plain form to foreground the informational content in the summary turn makes sense.

---

[2] . In some classes the students consistently use the *masu* form in *happyoo*. In other classes, the mixed use of the *masu* and naked plain forms are observed. In Cook (1998), I found that in *happyoo*, students use the naked plain form 94.2 % of the time when simply stating an answer whereas they use the *masu* form 73.9% of the time when framing the answer as a personal opinion with the hedging verb *to think* (*omoimasu*). This fact indicates that students use the *masu* form when they are more concerned with the interpersonal relationship with the class members and the teacher and that they use the naked plain form when they focus more on the content of the lesson.

(3) The interviewer is interviewing a few clients in a yakitori restaurant.
I= Interviewer, C1= male customer, C2 & C3=female customers

1 I: Ano yakitori no   miryoku wa   doo iu toko desu ka?
   uh   yakitori GEN appeal TOP what kind   COP Q
   'Uh what is yakitori's appeal?'

2 C2: A, yappari yasukute oishii   n   de,   oishii   kara.
     uh after all cheap   delicious   NOM COP delicious because
     'Uh it's after all inexpensive and delicious, 'cause it's delicious.'

3 I: →Yasukute oishii.
    cheap   delicious
    'It's inexpensive and delicious.'

4   Jibun de anoo tsukuchaoo nante ki   wa?
    self   by uh   make   what desire TOP
    'Don't you want to make it yourself?'

5 C2: Arimasen.
     exist NEG
     'I don't.'

6 I:→ Nai.
    exist NEG
    'You don't.'

      In the *happyoo* activity, the naked plain form occurs in the
students' response turns together with other features copresent in the speech
context. Consider (4).

(4) Mr. K poses a review question as to what one should do in writing a
poem and nominates a student.

1 T: Hai, Katoo-san
    'Yes, Katoo-san'

2 Katoo: ((stands up))
    →Hai nani ni tsuite kaku ka kimeru.
    yes what about   write Q decide
    'Yes, we decide what to write about.'

3 T: ((writes on the board.))

   ((one line is omitted))

4   Tsugi. Hashimoto-kun
     next

5 Hashimoto: ((stands up))
             →Hai, shi   o   tooshite tsutaeru koto o   <u>iu</u>.
              yes poem OBJ through convey thing OBJ say
              'Yes, we say things we want to convey.'

6 T: ((writes on the board))
   Kishiro-san.

7 Kishiro: ((stands up))
          →Kanjita koto, kizuita koto o   memo ni <u>toru</u>.
           felt   thing noticed thing OBJ memo in take
           'Jot down what we felt and noticed.'

The plain forms in (4) are naked forms since they are said with neither
rising nor falling intonation. The turns in lines 2, 5 and 7 are responses to
Mr. K's question regarding the content of the lesson (i.e. how to create a
poem), and it is in these turns the students use the naked plain form. It
makes sense for the students to use the naked plain form to foreground the
informational content in answering a question concerning the content of the
lesson. Note here that their turns are selected by the teacher, and they stand
up when giving their responses. In this sense, the naked plain form
constitutes the *happyoo* activity together with those features copresent in
the speech context. In other words, the naked plain form does not index the
happyoo activity by itself. This fact is demonstrated in (5).

(5) A student has just read the textbook and the class is asked to evaluate
her performance.

1 Kawamura: Masuda-kun.

2 Masuda: Hai. ((stands up))
          'yes'
          →Yumiko no hitotsu dake, tte yuu tokoro ga (   ) kanji ga <u>dete ita</u>.
           Yumiko GEN one   only place SUB   feeling SUB showed
           'When Yumiko said "just one", the feeling was expressed.'

3 ((Two students raise their hands))

4 Kawamura: Tenjin-kun.

5 Tenjin: ((stands up)
  →Machigae ga   nakutee, yokatta   to   omoimasu.
    mistake   SUB   not exist was good QUO think
    'It was good that there was no mistake.'

6 S7: ((seated))
  →Ikkai atta.
    once was
    'There was one mistake.'

Here both Masuda and Tenjin are acting as players of *happyoo*. They are
selected to speak by the student in charge of the *happyoo* activity, and their
turns are response turns to the question posed in *happyoo*. In line 2 Masuda
uses the naked plain form while in line 5 Tenjin uses the *masu* form. In
contrast, S7 self-selects to speak, and his turn is not a response turn. In
addition he is sitting at his desk. Thus, although it foregrounds the
informational content, S7's naked plain form does not index the *happyoo*
activity but a casual interjection to Tenjin-kun's statement. In this particular
context, the seated posture and self-selection for the next turn function like
affect keys. Therefore, S7's utterance sounds informal. This example shows
that the naked plain form indexes the *happyoo* activity only when it occurs
in the response turn in the pre-allocated turn-taking system, and the student
is standing.

    As discussed above, the TV interviewer uses the naked plain form
in the summary turn to clearly convey the content of the interviewee's
statement to the TV audience. In addition, in the interview program in
which the participants mostly use the *masu* form, the interviewer uses at
times the non-naked plain form, which makes the interview fresh and alive.
Consider (6), which includes example (3).

(6) The interviewer is interviewing a few clients in a yakitori restaurant.
I= Interviewer, C1= male customer, C2 & C3=female customers

1 I: Oo ano yappari nomu to   iu to   yakitoriyasan desu ka?
    Oh uh expected drink QUO say QUO yakitori shop COP Q
    'Oh, uh so when it comes to drinking, is it a yakitori restaurant?'

2 C1: Ee soo desu nee.
    yes so COP FP

'Yes, that's right.'

3 Yakitori ga yappari nee, natsu wa ichiban ii desu ne.
 yakitori SUB still FP summer TOP best COP FP
 'Yakitori is still the best in summer.'

4 I: Aa
 'Oh'

5 C2: Shotchuu kimasu.
 often come
 'I come here often.'

6 I: Shotchuu kichau.
 often come end up
 'You come here often.'

7 C2 & 3: ((laugh))

8 I: Ano yakitori no miryoku wa doo iu toko desu ka?
 uh yakitori GEN appeal TOP what kind COP Q
 'Uh what is yakitori's appeal?'

9 C2: A, yappari yasukute oishii n de, oishii kara.
 uh after all cheap delicious NOM COP delicious because
 'Uh it's after all inexpensive and delicious, 'cause it's delicious.'

10 I: Yasukute oishii.
 cheap delicious
 'It's inexpensive and delicious.'

11 Jibun de anoo tsukuchaoo nante ki wa?
 self by uh make what desire TOP
 'Don't you want to make it yourself?'

12 C2: Arimasen.
 exist NEG
 'I don't.'

13 I: Nai.
 exist NEG
 'You don't.'
  [

14 C2: <u>Taberareru</u> kara ((laugh))
      can eat   because
      'Cause I can eat (it at the restaurant.)'

15 I: <u>Shooganai.</u>   Nihon no   shoorai wa   <u>kurai.</u>
     Can't be helped   Japan GEN   future   TOP   dark
     'Can't be helped   The future of Japan is dark.'

16 C2&3: ((laugh))
       [
17 I: Soo <u>desu</u> ka.
       so   COP Q
       'Is that so.'

     In line 6, his summary is in the non-naked plain form. It has the coalescence, *chau* (from *te shimau* 'end up'), foregrounding the affective stance rather than the informational content. The laugh by C2 and C3 that immediately follows indicates that the addressees take the interviewer's utterance in line 6 to be funny. Thus, the effect of the interviewer's non-naked plain form here is comical. The comical effect must come from the *chau* form. If he said it in the naked plain form as in *shotchuu kuru* 'often come' or *shotchu kite shimau* 'often end up coming', it would not be so funny and would probably not induce a laugh. Here the use of the non-naked plain form *kichau* lightens the interview. In line 15, the interviewer uses the naked plain form to express his own evaluative reaction to the opinion of the female customer, C2'. The unstated cultural assumption here is that women should be good cooks. Apparently, the future of Japan does not depend upon one female customer who does not want to make *yakitori* at home. In Gricean terms, the comment in line 15 flouts the Maxim of quality. It is what Grice calls hyperbole or an exaggeration, and adds a comical touch to the interview while the interviewer displays a male chauvinist point of view. The naked plain form in line 15 foregrounds the exaggerated informational content and helps enhance the comical effect. In line 17, he then acknowledges in the *masu* form C2's utterance in line 14. As seen above, both the naked and non-naked plain forms are tools to index the interviewer's professional responsibility as well as create a comical interaction that will not bore the TV audience.
     In sum, the above examples demonstrate that the interpretation of both the naked and non-naked plain forms depends upon various factors such as turn-taking system, activity, and cultural assumptions among others. The plain form functions as a resource available to the participants to

construct an activity and/or social role in on-going talk, and indexes various shades of meaning.

6. Conclusion

This paper has examined the use of the plain form in various natural spoken and written data. The contributions of the present proposal are three-fold.

First, the present paper accounts for the informal and impersonal uses of the plain form without setting up two different categories. A microanalysis of the data reveals that the plain form foregrounds an affect key if there is one or more present in the utterance (non-naked plain form); otherwise it foregrounds the informational content (naked plain form). Thus if the plain form co-occurs with affect keys, it foregrounds the speaker's affective stance toward the addressee or the referent and is an indicator of informality and/or intimacy. When the informational content is systematically foregrounded as in newspaper articles, the style is perceived as the impersonal style.

Secondly, this paper demonstrates that occurrence of the naked plain form in speech is not random in at least institutional settings. It accounts for a high correlation between the naked plain form and a certain turn type in the two different speech events. The foregrounded informational content of the naked plain form is in line with the goal the specific turn tries to achieve. This paper has shown that the plain form serves as a resource to create a social role and/or social context, and that the type of activity and assumptions in the speech context affect the interpretation of the naked plain form.

Thirdly, the analysis presented in this paper accounts for why the naked plain form often appears in what Maynard calls 'low awareness situations'. When the informational content is foregrounded, it is likely that the speaker's attention is not directed toward the addressee.

Finally, intonation is one of the major affect keys (Bolinger 1989) and plays an important role in interpreting social meaning. Future studies on the Japanese plain form need to investigate a wider range of intonation patterns that function as affect keys.

References

Agha, A. 1993. Grammatical and Indexical Conventions in Honorific Discourse. *Journal of Linguistic Anthropology* 3: 131-163.
Bolinger, D. 1989. *Intonation and its Uses: Melody in Grammar and Discourse*. Stanford, CA: Stanford University Press.

Cook, H. M. 1990. An Indexical Account of the Japanese Sentence-final Particle *No*. *Discourse Processes* 13: 401-439.

_____. 1991. The Japanese Sentence-final Particle *Yo* as a Non-referential Indexical. Second International Cognitive Linguistics Conference. University of California at Santa Cruz, CA, July 29-August 2.

_____. 1992. Meanings of Non-referential Indexes: A Case of the Japanese Particle *Ne*. *Text* 12: 507-539.

_____. 1998. Students' Use of the Impersonal Style in a Japanese Elementary School Classroom. *Crossroads of Language, Interaction and Culture* 1: 43-58.

Guy, G. 1992. Explanation in Variable Phonology: An Exponential Model of Morphological Constraints. *Language Variation and Change* 3: 1-22.

Hamano, S. 1998. *The Sound-symbolic System of Japanese*. Stanford, CA and Tokyo: CSLI Publications and Kuroshio Shuppan.

Hanks, W. 1999. Indexicality. *Journal of Linguistic Anthropology* 9: 124.

Hirokawa, K. 1995. The expression of culture in the conversational style of Japanese and Americans. Doctoral dissertation, University of Michigan.

Ikuta, S. 1983. Speech Level Shift and Conversational Strategy in Japanese Discourse. *Language Science, 5*, 37-53.

Lakoff, R. 1975. *Language and Women's Place*. New York: Harper and Row.

Levinson, S. 1979. Pragmatics and Social Deixis. *Proceedings of the Fifth Annual Meeting of the Berkeley Linguistic Society*, 206-223.

Lyons, J. 1977. *Semantics*. Cambridge: Cambridge University Press.

Maynard, S.1993. *Discourse modality: Subjectivity, Emotion and Voice in the Japanese Language*. Amsterdam: John Benjamins

Niyekawa, A. 1991. *Minimum Essential Politeness: A Guide to the Japanese Honorific Language*. Tokyo: Kodansha International.

Ochs, E. 1988. *Culture and Language Development*. Cambridge: Cambridge University Press.

_____. 1996. Linguistic Resources for Socializing Humanity. *Rethinking linguistic relativity*, eds. J. Gumperz, and S. Levinson, 407-437. Cambridge: Cambridge University Press.

Sacks, H., Schegloff, E., & Jefferson, G. 1974. A Simplest Systematics for the Organization of Turn-taking in Conversation. *Language* 50: 696-735.

Silverstein, M. 1976. Shifters, Linguistic Categories, and Cultural Description. *Meaning in anthropology*, eds. K. Basso and H. Selby, 11-56. Albuquerque: University of New Mexico Press.

Listener Responses in Telephone and Face-to-face Conversations: How do Non-verbal Behaviors Affect Japanese and English Interactions?

HIROKO FURO
Illinois Wesleyan University

1. Introduction

This study compares telephone and face-to-face conversations in Japanese and U.S. English for the purpose of investigating how listener responses are expressed verbally in each language. In particular, this study explores how frequently and at what points listener responses are verbalized in telephone and face-to-face conversations in order to examine how nonverbal cues, such as gestures and head nods, affect social interaction. In addition, verbal listener responses in telephone and face-to-face conversations are compared cross-culturally in Japanese and U.S. English in order to study how culture affects verbal and non-verbal listening behaviors.

---

[1] I would like to express my sincere appreciation to Becky Fredericks, who helped me edit this paper. Also, I appreciate valuable comments from the audience of Japanese / Korean Linguistics Conference 10. Nevertheless, any remaining errors are my responsibility.

2. Previous Studies

Many previous studies on listener response behaviors in Japanese have been examined comparatively with those in U.S. English. For example, Clancy, Thompson, Suzuki, and Tao (1996) define a reactive token as "a short utterance produced by an interlocutor who is playing a listener's role during the other interlocutor's speakership," and find that there is not a great difference in the frequency of reactive tokens between Japanese and English conversations; however, Japanese conversations have far more backchannels than English conversations. They also find that reactive tokens in English conversations occur at grammatical completion points at a high rate, whereas those in Japanese conversations occur at grammatical completion points at a low rate. White (1989) finds that vocal backchannels take place more than twice as often in Japanese as in U.S. English. Whereas many of these cross-cultural studies on listeners' behaviors focus on verbal listener responses, Maynard (1986, 1989) defines Japanese backchannel responses as "turn-internal listeners' responses" and includes nonverbal cues such as head nods, head shakes, and laughter. She finds that backchannels take place approximately three times more frequently in Japanese conversations than in U.S. English conversations. Furthermore, Saft (1996) argues that Americans use various other resources besides verbal backchannels to express their listenership. He suggests that although the Japanese use verbal listener responses more than Americans, if we count non- or para- linguistic elements, the number of listener responses in English may increase. In summary, previous studies find that the Japanese use more verbal listener responses than Americans and that Americans may use other types of listener responses to express their listenership.

3. Hypotheses

This study is conducted based on the following two hypotheses. First, if nonverbal elements, such as eye gazes and head nods, function as listener responses, telephone conversations, in which people cannot employ these nonverbal cues, must have a greater number of verbal listener responses than face-to-face conversations. Second, if Americans employ more non-verbal behaviors as listener responses, the difference in the frequency of reactive tokens between telephone and face-to-face conversations in English must be greater than that in Japanese since they have to verbalize all the non-verbal cues used in face-to-face conversations when they talk on the phone.

4. Data

This study employs a total of eighty minutes of conversations, consisting of four kinds of data sets; (1) five four-minute telephone conversations in Japanese, (2) five four-minute face-to-face conversations in Japanese, (3) five four-minute telephone conversations in U.S. English, and (4) five four-minute face-to-face conversations in U.S. English. Each conversation takes place between a pair of female friends who are native speakers of either Japanese or English. Both Japanese and American participants are university students studying at Midwestern universities. However, the Japanese participants' stay in the U.S. has been less than one year, so U.S. culture seems to have had little influence on their Japanese conversation styles.[2] The topics of the conversations are ordinary, varying from the participants' friends to the courses that they are taking at their universities. The conversations were both video- and audio- recorded, and the four minutes after the greeting in each data set is the focus of the data analysis for this study.

5. Data Analysis

The data analysis includes the following procedures. First, all the data sets are transcribed, and the transcription conventions presented by Du Bois (1991) are adopted with some modifications. Each language data set is transcribed and/or checked by at least three native speakers of each language. Second, the discourse length of the four data sets are compared, focusing on the number of intonation units and words that take place in the data. Third, the frequency of reactive tokens is compared in the four data sets. Fourth, verbal listener responses are categorized into five types, and the number of each type of reactive token is compared in the four data sets in order to identify how listener responses are expressed verbally. The five types of reactive tokens are as follows; 1) backchannels, 2) reactive expressions, 3) collaborative finishes, 4) repetitions, and 5) laughter. This categorization follows Clancy et al. (1996) and Furo (1998, 2000) in many respects. The five types of reactive tokens that are adopted in this study are discussed in turn.

First, backchannels are audible vocal sounds produced by an interlocutor who plays a listener role. They are fragments smaller than a lexical form. The following are examples of backchannels used in the data sets of this study.

---

[2] Other factors, such as gender and generation, may affect the results of the data analysis. However, they are beyond the scope of this study.

Japanese	English
un	hum hum
heee	humm
uuun	mhuum
aaa	oh
huuun	wow

The second type of reactive token, reactive expressions, are lexical expressions smaller than a sentential or clausal level. Following are examples of reactive expressions that take place in the data of this study.

Japanese	English
uso	really
hontoni	yeah
sou (ne)	ok
maji	oh cool

Thirdly, collaborative finishes are the sentences finished with or by an interlocutor who plays a listener role (See Learner 1987). An example of this type is as follows.

```
     734   Susan:   I have a test Monday Tues-I have-
     735            ( )
     736            [Bio next Monday.
->   737   Lissa:   [Bio Monday.
```

In the excerpt above, Susan talks about her schedule for that week. While Susan is recalling Monday's schedule, Lissa finishes her sentence along with her in line 737. The following is an example of a collaborative finish from the Japanese data.

```
     822   Tomo:   Sou wakattan    da    jibun no,
                   right understood COP   my  of
     823           ( )
->   824   Kane:   yowasa  ga,
                   weakness SP
[Translation]
     822   Tomo:   Right, I understand my-
     823           ( )
->   824   Kane:   weakness,
```

Tomo is talking about the movies that make her cry. Kane finishes Tomo's sentence in line 824, adding the word 'yowasaga' (weakness) to Kane's sentence in line 822. These examples of collaborative finishes refer to clauses or sentences finished by an interlocutor singly or along with the collaborated speaker.

The fourth type of reactive token, repetition, takes place when the listener repeats a part of the primary speaker's utterance. The following is an example from the English data.

```
     520   Nata:   Do you know who Sarah Johnson [is?
->   521   Anne:                                [Sarah Johnson?
     522   Nata:   She has like long brown hair.
```

Natalie is talking about a friend of hers, whose name is Sarah Johnson. In line 521, Anne repeats the person's name, Sarah Johnson, with a rising intonational contour. Responding to Anne's repetition, Natalie explains what Sarah Johnson looks like in line 522. The following is an example of repetition from the Japanese data.

```
     673   Yumi:   Demo Un-university demo ammari ii      no yatte [nai.
                   but                  even  any   good PP show N

->   674   Yayoi:                                                [un yatte
                   nai  na.
                                                                 yes show
                   N   SP
[Translation]
     673   Yumi:   But there are not any good movies at Un-University (Theater).
->   674   Yayoi:  Not any good movies.
```

Yumi is talking about a movie theater that she thinks does not show any good movies. In line 674, Yayoi repeats a part of Yumi's utterance to show agreement to Yumi.

The fifth and last category of reactive tokens adopted in this study is laughter, which is considered a response to the previous utterance that is perceived as humorous. They are transcribed as 'Hahaha' or 'Huhuhuhu' in both Japanese and English data sets. This method of transcription allows us to understand how the laughter is delivered and how long it lasts.

As the last stage of data analysis, onset places of reactive tokens are examined in relation to grammar and intonation in order to understand at what points a listener responds verbally to the primary speaker. The discussions of grammatical and intonational completion points are based on the studies by Oreström (1983), and Ford and Thompson (1996). The point that is grammatically complete is determined by the following three criteria: 1) grammatically well formed clauses, 2) increments, and 3) recoverable predicates. For example, in the sentence, "She wasn't feeling well last night," the clause, "She wasn't feeling well," is considered grammatically complete since it is a grammatically well formed clause. The whole clause,

"She wasn't feeling well last night," is also considered grammatically complete since it is also a grammatically well formed sentence. The phrase, 'last night,' is, therefore, considered an increment, and grammatical completion points are marked before and after it. Grammatical completion points are marked by '/' as follows.

She wasn't feeling well / last night./

In addition, if a clause does not have complete clausal structure, but is recoverable from the context, it is considered grammatically complete. The following excerpt includes the recoverable predicate.

```
       255  Laura:   Well we went to Blockbuster / and lost [her./
       256  Sarah:                                           [Oh you did really?/
 ->    257  Laura:   Well just in the store./
```

Laura's comment in line 257 is not complete as a clause, but it is recoverable from the context and can be interpreted as 'we lost her just in the store.' Thus, it is considered grammatically complete, and a grammatical completion point is marked after it.

As for Japanese clauses, since the canonical word order in Japanese is SOV, predicates are considered the indicators of grammatical completion points, and all the words and phrases after predicates are considered increments. Grammatical completion points are therefore marked before and after these increments. In addition, since the Japanese allow implicit arguments as well as flexible word order to a great extent, clauses that are recoverable from the context are considered grammatically complete even if some arguments are not verbally produced. The following is an example of an increment from the Japanese data.

```
       62 Aki:    Tomodachi ni,
                  friend     by
       63         ( )
       64         te    de yattemoratta,/
                  hand by pierce-have-Past
       65 Naka:   Heee.
 ->    66 Aki:    tongatta      piasu  de,/
                  sharp-pointed piercer by
[Translation]
       62 Aki:    By hand,
       63         ( )
       64         (I) had my friends pierce my ear,/
       65 Naka:   Heee.
 ->    66 Aki:    with a sharp-pointed piercer./
```

Although there is no explicit subject, Aki's sentence in lines 62 to 64 is considered grammatically complete because of the predicate, 'yattemoratta' (have my friends do), which indicates a possible end of the clause. The phrase in line 66, 'with a sharp-pointed piercer,' is considered an increment, as it appears after the predicate, and grammatical completion points are marked both before and after the increment of her utterance.

The feature of intonation is first marked in terms of intonation units, which are segments of utterances divided by a pause for inbreath (See Chafe 1993). The contour of intonation units is characterized in five ways. First, falling intonational contour is marked by '.'. The rising intonational contour is marked by '?'. The continuing intonational contour is marked by ',', and the continuous, but slightly rising, intonational contour is marked by ',?'. The abrupt drop-off is marked by '-'. Following are examples of the five ways to designate intonational contours.

1) falling intonational contour:
    40   Tracie: They spend all their time together.
2) rising intonational contour:
    88   Cindy: You're positive with this?
3) continuing intonational contour:
    97   Tracie: Maybe we-well when we go back,
4) continuing, but rising, intonational contour:
    271   Sarah: We should bake or something,?
5) drop-off intonational contour:
    82   Cindy: Are you sure like this is all like set like with-

Of the five types of intonational contours, the first two types, the falling and rising intonational contours, are considered intonationally complete.

6. Results

6.1 Discourse Length

The data sets are first analyzed regarding discourse length, focusing on words and intonation units (IUs). The results on discourse length are illustrated in Chart 1. In Chart 1, 'J' stands for Japanese data, 'A' for U.S. (American) English data, 'phone' for telephone conversation data, and 'face' for face-to-face conversation data.

Chart 1: Discourse Length

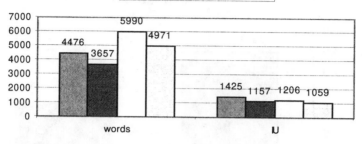

Chart 1 shows that telephone conversations have more words and intonation units than face-to-face conversations in both language data sets. Namely, the Japanese telephone conversation data have 4476 words (versus 3657 in the Japanese face-to-face data) and 1425 intonation units (versus 1157 in the Japanese face-to-face data). The English telephone data have 5990 words (versus 4971 in the English face-to-face data) and 1206 intonation units (versus 1059 in the English face-to-face data). This result shows that the participants talk more in the telephone conversations than in the face-to-face conversations. This makes sense since people in telephone conversations can only rely on verbal cues and therefore have to verbalize non-verbal interactional cues, which results in longer discourse length in telephone conversations. Secondly, Chart 1 shows that the English data, both telephone and face-to-face conversations, have more words, but fewer intonation units, than their Japanese counterparts. This result indicates that the English conversations have more words per intonation unit, and therefore are more dense and faster paced than the Japanese conversations.

6.2 Frequency of Reactive Tokens

The total numbers of reactive tokens are examined in order to investigate how frequently reactive tokens are used in the data. Since the length of the four data sets varies, the frequency of reactive tokens is compared in relation to the number of intonation units in each data set. Chart 2 illustrates, for comparison, the frequency of reactive tokens relative to intonation units in each data set and graphs each figure as a percentage.

Chart 2: Frequency of Reactive Tokens

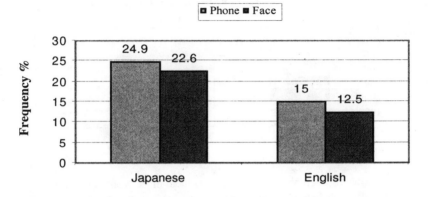

Chart 2 shows that telephone conversations have a higher frequency of reactive tokens than face-to-face conversations in both Japanese and English. That is, 24.9 reactive tokens per 100 intonation units take place in the Japanese telephone data compared with 22.6 in the Japanese face-to-face data while 15 reactive tokens per 100 intonation units appear in the English telephone data compared with 12.5 in the English face-to-face data. This result implies that nonverbal cues are used to express listenership in face-to-face conversations in both Japanese and English. Secondly, the Japanese data sets, both telephone and face-to-face conversations, have more frequent occurrences of reactive tokens than their English counterparts. This result suggests that the Japanese employ more verbal listener responses than Americans. Thirdly, the difference in frequency between telephone and face-to-face conversations in the English data is similar to that in the Japanese data, although the difference within the English data is slightly higher than that of the Japanese data. Namely, the ratio of reactive tokens between telephone and face-to-face conversations in the Japanese data sets is 1 to 0.91, while that in the English data is 1 to 0.83. This result may suggest that nonverbal elements are used at a similar rate in Japanese and English conversations.

6.3 Reactive Token Types

This section examines the kinds of reactive tokens used in the four data sets. The reactive tokens are categorized into five types: backchannels, reactive expressions, collaborative finishes, repetitions, and laughter. The number of times each of these five types is used in the four data sets is compared in Chart 3. In Chart 3, 'BC' stands for backchannels, 'RE' for reactive expressions, 'CF' for collaborative finishes, 'RP' for repetitions, and 'LT' for laughter.

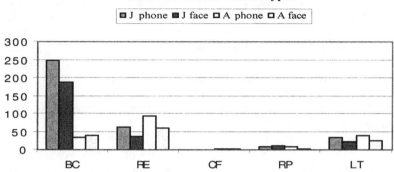

Chart 3: Reactive Token Types

Chart 3 shows the number of reactive tokens used in the four data sets. However, since the discourse length varies in the four data sets, in order to examine the frequency of each type of reactive token in relation to the other types in each data set, the distribution of each type of reactive token is demonstrated in Chart 4.

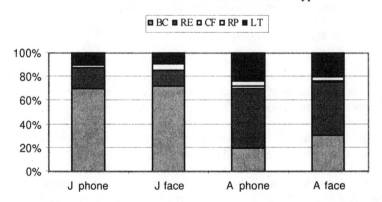

Chart 4: Distribution of Reactive Token Types

Charts 3 and 4 show that collaborative finishes and repetitions are rarely used in the four data sets. In addition, backchannels are used more frequently in the Japanese data, in both telephone and face-to-face conversations, i.e., 71% of all the reactive tokens in the Japanese data are backchannels while 20 % are backchannels in the English data. In contrast, reactive expressions and laughter are used more often in the English data, i.e., in the English data, 48% are reactive expressions, and 21.5% are laughter, while, in the Japanese data, 16% are reactive expressions, and 9.5% are laughter. In other words, the Japanese verbally express their listenership primarily with backchannels, while Americans generally do so with reactive expressions and laughter. Reactive expressions and laugher are more vigorous forms of listener responses, whereas backchannels are the least intrusive forms of all types of reactive tokens. Thus, this result may indicate that Japanese listenership is more passive, while listeners play an active role in English conversations.

Secondly, Chart 4 shows that, in both language data, the telephone conversations have a slightly greater distribution of reactive expressions and laugher than the face-to-face conversations, but a smaller distribution of backchannels. Namely, in the Japanese data, of all reactive tokens observed within the telephone conversations, 70% are backchannels, 18% are reactive expressions, and 10% are laughter, while within the face-to-face conversations, 72% are backchannels, 14% are reactive expressions, and 9% are laughter. In contrast, in the English data, within the telephone conversations, 19% are backchannels, 51% are reactive expressions, and 23% are laughter, while within the face-to-face conversations, 31% are backchannels, 45% are reactive expressions, and 20% are laughter. This result may imply that listenership is expressed slightly more actively in telephone conversations than in face-to-face conversations in order to compensate the limited access to non-verbal cues in telephone conversations.

6.4 Onset Places of Reactive Tokens

This section discusses the onset places of reactive tokens in order to examine how grammar and intonation project the turn transition points of reactive tokens. The onset places of reactive tokens are examined in relation to grammar and intonation and are categorized into the following five points: (1) grammatical completion points, represented as GCP, (2) intonational completion points, ICP, (3) concurring points of grammatical and intonational completion points, GICP, (4) ending points of intonation units, IU, and (5) neither grammatical and intonational completion points nor ending points of intonation units, None. The frequency of reactive tokens set out at these five points (out of the total number of reactive tokens in each data set) is illustrated in Chart 5.

Chart 5: Onset Places of Reactive Tokens

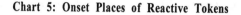

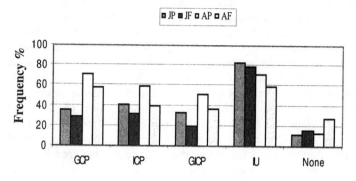

Chart 5 shows that the reactive tokens in the telephone conversations start at completion points, both grammatical and/or intonational completion points, at a higher rate than in the face-to-face conversations. Since telephone conversations do not communicate nonverbal cues, people on the phone may pay closer attention to linguistic cues and start their reactive tokens at completion points, which can be considered transition relevance places (See Sacks, et al. 1974). Additionally, the English conversations have a higher rate of onset places at both grammatical and intonational completion points, as well as at the concurring points of the two completion points, than their Japanese counterparts. Since the American participants use reactive expressions and laughter more often than the Japanese participants, and since these listener responses are more intrusive than backchannels, the American participants may more frequently start reactive tokens at transition relevance places. In contrast, the Japanese verbal listener responses start at the end of intonation units at a higher rate than those in English. This result may suggest that the Japanese participants express their listenership by using a great number of backchannels, which are less intrusive than any other type of reactive token. These participants generally place the backchannels at the pauses between intonation units, rhythmically collaborating with the primary floor-holder.

6.5 Discussion

The results from the data analysis show that there are differences between telephone and face-to-face conversations regarding discourse length, frequency, type, and onset places of reactive tokens. Namely, compared with the face-to-face conversations, the telephone conversations in both Japanese and English have more words and intonation units and a greater frequency of overall reactive tokens. These reactive tokens are set out at transition relevance places that are projected by grammar and intonation at a higher rate than those in the face-to-face conversations. These differences between the telephone and face-to-face conversations may primarily result from the fact that people cannot use contextual cues other than verbal elements to express their listenership on the phone. Therefore, we can conclude that nonverbal elements, such as eye gazes and head nods, play an important role in the ways people verbalize their listenership in social interaction.

Secondly, the results of this study have shown that the use of reactive tokens differs in Japanese and English. Namely, the Japanese data have more frequent overall reactive tokens and more backchannels, specifically. Furthermore, these reactive tokens are placed at pauses between intonation units at a high rate. On the other hand, the English data have less frequent overall reactive tokens. Among those reactive tokens that take place, however, are many reactive expressions and laughter. These reactive tokens are often set out at transition relevance places that are projected by grammar and intonation. This finding agrees with many previous studies, which claim that the Japanese give more listener responses, especially bakchannels, at non-linguistic completion points (See Muzutani 1983, Maynard 1989, Clancy et al. 1996). These previous studies explain the frequent use of Japanese listener responses in relation to a Japanese cultural orientation that places a high value on harmony in interpersonal relationships. Tannen (1989) describes American culture as high involvement and Japanese culture as high consideration. In order to show consideration to the primary speaker, the Japanese frequently give listener responses as interactional support. However, they do so with careful consideration, using the least intrusive form of reactive tokens, backchannels, at pauses between intonation units in order to cooperate harmoniously with the primary speaker. The American participants, on the other hand, express their active listenership with reactive expressions and laughter frequently at linguistic completion points, which are regulated by linguistic projectability. Therefore, we may argue that the use of listener responses reflects harmonious and considerate interaction in Japanese versus active collaboration in English.

The differences in the frequency of reactive tokens between telephone and face-to-face conversations are similar in Japanese and English conversations. This result implies that the Japanese and Americans may employ nonverbal cues as listener responses at a similar rate. In other words, nonverbal cues may play a similarly important role in social interaction in Japanese and English conversations.

7. Conclusion

This study shows that nonverbal cues influence social interaction in both Japanese and English, but little quantitative differences in the degree of influence are observed between the two languages. Therefore, we can conclude that nonverbal cues affect Japanese and English conversations to a similar degree.

References

Chafe, W. 1994. Discourse, Consciousness, and Time: The Flow and Displacement of Conscious Experience in Speaking and Writing. Chicago: University of Chicago Press.

Clancy, L. M., S. A. Thompson, R. Suzuki, and H. Tao. 1996. The Conversational Use of Reactive Tokens in English, Japanese, and Mandarin. *Journal of Pragmatics* 26: 355-387.

Du Bois, J. W. 1991. Transcription Design principles for Spoken Discourse Research. *Pragmatics* 1: 71-106.

Furo, H. 2000. Reactive Token in Japanese and English Conversations: Gender and Social Interaction. *Social and Cognitive Factors in Second Language Acquisition,* ed. B. Swierzbin, F. Morris, M. E. Anderson, C.A. Klee, and E. Tarone, 445-457. Somerville, MA: Cascadilla Press.

Furo, H. 1998. Turn-taking in Japanese Conversation: Grammar, Intonation, and Pragmatics. *Japanese/Korean Linguistics 7,* ed. S. Iwasaki, 41-57. Stanford: Stanford Linguistic Association.

Lerner, G. H. 1987. Collaborative Turn Sequences: Sentence Construction and Social Action. Doctoral dissertation, University of California, Irvine.

Maynard, S. K. 1986. On Backchannel Behavior in Japanese and English Casual Conversation. *Linguistics* 24: 1076-1108

Maynard, S. K. 1989. Japanese Conversation: Self-contextualization through Structure and Interactional Management. Norwood, NJ: Ablex.

Mizutani, N. 1983. Aizuchi to Ootoo [Backchannels and Responses]. Hanashikotoba no Hyoogen [Expression in Spoken Language], ed. O. Mizutani, 37-44. Tokyo: Chikuma Choboo.

Oreström, B. 1983. *Turn-taking in English Conversation.* Gleerup: Lund.

Saft, S. L. 1996. Reassessing Cross-cultural Comparisons of Backchannel Behavior in Japanese and English: Arguments for an Expanded Notion of Context. *Linguistics and Language Teaching: Proceedings of the Sixth Joint LSH-HATESL Conference.* 169-187.

Sacks, H., E. Schegloff, and G. Jefferson. 1974. A simplest Systematics of the Organization of Turn-taking in Conversation. *Language* 50: 696-735.

Schegloff, E. A. 1982. Discourse as an Interactional Achievement: Some Uses of 'Uh huh' and Other Things that Come Between Sentences. Analyzing Discourse: Text and Talk. (Georgetown University Round Table on Language and Linguistics 1981.), ed. D. Tannen, 71-83. Washington, DC: Georgetown University Press.

Tannen, D. 1989. Talking Voices: Repetition, Dialogue, and Imagery in Conversational Discourse. Cambridge: Cambridge University Press.

White, S. 1989. Backchannels across Cultures: A Study of Americans and Japanese. *Language in Society* 18: 59-76.

Where Korean and Japanese Differ: Modality vs. Discourse Modality

KAORU HORIE & KAORI TAIRA
Tohoku University

1. Introduction

Modality, 'the grammaticization of speaker's (subjective) attitudes and opinions' (Bybee et al. 1994: 177) has been intensively studied by typologists (e.g. Palmer 1986, Bybee and Fleischman 1995). However, compared to the typological studies of other grammatical categories, e.g. tense, aspect, typological studies of modality apparently have not been equally successful. As Kiefer (1999) stated, it is not entirely clear 'what the typological universals are, or if there are any: the typology of modality is still in its infancy' (p. 227).

The difficulty inherent in the typology of modality stems from the fact that it is difficult to give a proper characterization/definition of 'modality'. It is not surprising, therefore, that grammaticalization pathways of modality 'grams' (grammatical morphemes) are far more varied than those of tense and aspect grams. In fact, Horie's (1997) examination of the grammaticalization pathways proposed in Bybee et al. (1994) based on data on Japanese modality grams did not yield confirmatory results as satisfying as those put forth for the development of tense and aspect grams.

These findings suggest the possibility that the manifestation of modality meanings can vary even between two languages having very similar typological profiles such as Korean and Japanese (see, for instance, Tsukamoto 1990).

This study is intended to highlight the nature of cross-linguistic differences between modality systems in Korean and Japanese from a cognitive and functional-typological perspective.

The organization of this paper is as follows. Section 2 presents a contrastive linguistic analysis of modality systems in Korean and Japanese. Section 3 explores cognitive-functional foundations of the cross-linguistic differences presented in Section 2. Section 4 summarizes the findings.

2. Modality Systems of Korean and Japanese in Contrast

As mentioned in Section 1, typology of modality systems in the world's languages is still in its preliminary stage. The following preliminary generalization, which concerns formal expression of modality grams in the world's languages, serves as a good starting point (Kiefer 1999):

> Languages have at least the following means at their disposal to express modality: (a) modal verbs, (b) verbs denoting (various degrees of) knowledge and belief, (c) modal adverbials, (d) modal particles, (e) evidentials, (f) grammatical mood. Languages do not make equal use of all these means. Moreover, some of them may be completely lacking in some languages. (p. 227)

Among the above-mentioned modality grams, we will select two grams, i.e. (f) grammatical mood, and (d) modal particles, which are expected to highlight subtle cross-linguistic differences between Korean and Japanese, and will present a contrastive linguistic analysis of them in turn.

2.1 'Grammatical mood' in Korean and Japanese

'Mood' is distinguished from 'modality' in that 'modality is the conceptual domain, and mood is its inflectional expression' (Bybee et al. 1994: 181). While the definition of mood as verbal inflectional category may not be directly applicable to agglutinative languages like Korean and Japanese, Palmer (1986) suggested the following:

> The term "inflection" (…) should be used in a wide sense to include the features of agglutinative languages, where by definition there will be a one-to-one correspondence between the modal marker and its semantic function (…). (p. 43-44)

In what follows, we will consider what kind of modality meanings are expressed inflectionally in Korean and Japanese.

It is a controversial issue in Korean linguistics what kind of phenomena are to be identified as 'mood' (e.g. Ko 1965). It is customary to divide inflectional suffixes into 'non-terminal suffixes' and 'sentence enders'. According to Sohn (1994: 8), a sentence-ender, 'consisting of one or more suffixes, denotes not only one of the sentence types but also one of the six speech levels (or styles) and a mood (such as indicative, requestive or restrospective)'. The two types of inflectional suffixes encode modality meanings, i.e. what Sohn (1994) calls 'Mood' (we will continue to refer to this inflectional category as 'Mood' with a capital letter in order to distinguish it from 'mood' as employed in general linguistics and typology) and 'Sentence-Type' (henceforth abbreviated as 'S-type'). The former indicates whether the state of affairs expressed in a sentence is presented as an objective fact ('indicative'), a directly experienced past event ('retrospective'), or a request ('requestive'), while the latter signals the type of speech act a sentence is used to perform, e.g. assertion ('declarative'), question ('interrogative'), proposal ('propositive'), or command ('imperative').

Table 1 presents a list of Korean indicative-mood sentence enders wherein Mood and S-type (as well as Addressee Honorific at deferential speech level) are manifested in a fairly complex manner:

	Declarative	Interrogative	Imperative	Propositive
plain	**-n/nun**-ta	**-ni**?/**-nu**-nya?	-ela/-ala	-ca
intimate	-e/-a	-e?/-a?	-e/-a	-e/-a
familiar	**-ney**	-na?/**-nu**-nka?	**-key**	**-sey**
blunt	-(s)o	-(s)o?	-(u)o	-(u)p-**si**-ta
polite	-e.yo/-a.yo	-e.yo?/-a.yo?	-e.yo/-a.yo	-e.yo/-a.yo
deferential	-(su)p-**ni**-ta	-(su)p-**ni**-kka?	-(u)si-p-**si**-o	-(u)si-p-**si**-ta

Table 1. Indicative-Mood Sentence-Enders in Korean (based on Sohn 1999: 355; partially modified)

Indicative and requestive Mood suffixes are overtly present where indicated in bold; otherwise they merge with S-type suffixes occurring sentence-finally.

The identification and segmentation of inflectional endings has also been a matter of much controversy in Japanese linguistics (see Shibatani 1990 for the details of the controversy). Table 2, adapted from Shibatani (1990), presents inflectional categories in Modern Japanese and their endings, attached to a consonant stem *sin* (< *sin-u* 'to die') and a vowel stem *mi* (< *mi-ru* 'to look at'):

Mizen (Irrealis)	sin-a	mi- ϕ
Renyoo (Adverbial)	sin-i	mi- ϕ
Syuusi (Conclusive)	sin-u	mi-ru
Rentai (Attributive)	sin-u	mi-ru
Katei (Hypothetical)	sin-e	mi-re
Meirei (Imperative)	sin-e	mi-ro/yo
Sikoo (Cohortative)	sin-o	mi-yo

Table 2. Standard inflectional categories and their endings for Modern Japanese (Shibatani 1990: 232; the paradigm for the copula is omitted)

Some of the inflectional endings clearly encode modality-related meanings, e.g. 'imperative', 'cohortative', which belong in the domain of 'speaker-oriented modality' (Bybee et al. 1994). Others like 'irrealis' and 'hypothetical' endings have some connection with modality in that they can co-occur with a negative auxiliary *nai* and a hypothetical conjunctive particle *ba* ('if') respectively (e.g. *sin-a-nai* 'don't/doesn't die', *sin-e-ba* 'if (one) dies'). However, it is not entirely clear whether the rest of the inflectional endings, i.e. 'adverbial', 'conclusive', and 'attributive' endings, encode any kind of modality meaning at all.

To summarize Section 2.1, we can see that Korean has a very elaborate system of grammatical mood sensitive to the manner in which a state-of-affairs is conceived of and presented (e.g. indicative) as well as to the type of speech act the sentence is intended to express (declarative, interrogative, imperative, propositive). In contrast, Japanese has only a handful of inflectional endings which positively encode modality meanings and hence can be regarded properly as 'grammatical mood'.

2.2 'Modal particles' in Korean and Japanese and the notion of 'Discourse Modality'

It has been noted that some languages express modality meanings by elements that are relatively independent of predicate structure referred to as 'modal particles', which 'fit the content of an utterance to the content of speech' and 'have no lexical meaning and contribute nothing to the propositional meaning of a sentence' (Bussmann 1996: 307, emphasis added).

These particles arguably encode certain modality meanings. However, as can be envisaged from the above definition, the type of modality meaning conveyed by modal particles appears to be radically different from the types of modality meaning encoded by grammatical mood discussed in Section 2.1, which are more closely related to the propositional content of the sentence. The type of modality meaning encoded by modal particles is clearly discourse-oriented. Modal particles thus instantiate a close relationship between discourse and modality, as noted by Palmer (1986):

> (…) in discourse we often express opinion, draw conclusions, etc.; and no doubt, in "evidential" language speakers regularly indicate in their conversations and arguments the evidential basis for what they are saying. Not surprisingly then, it is by no means always possible to make a clear distinction between a discourse and a modal feature. (p. 91, emphasis added)

The close relationship between 'a discourse and a modal feature' led to the Japanese linguist Senko K. Maynard to propose the notion of 'Discourse Modality' as follows:

> Discourse Modality refers to information that does not or only minimally conveys objective propositional message content. Discourse Modality conveys the speaker's subjective emotional, mental or psychological attitude toward the message content, the speech act itself or toward his or her interlocutor in discourse. Discourse Modality operates to define and to foreground certain ways of interpreting the propositional content in discourse (…). (Maynard 1993: 38-39, emphasis added)

Maynard contrasts 'Discourse Modality' with two related concepts, 'proposition' and 'modality', the latter referring to 'functional aspects mostly realized by English modal auxiliary verbs, and modal manipulations such as declarative, interrogative, imperative, exclamatory, and so on' (p. 39). According to Maynard, '(m)odality operates primarily within a sentential boundary and has less impact on the discourse structure within which Discourse Modality primarily operates' (p. 39). Maynard's view on the relationship between proposition, modality, and Discourse Modality is schematized as follows:

[Discourse structure: [Sentence structure: [proposition] [**modality**]] [**Discourse Modality**]]

Figure 1. Maynard's (1993) view on the relationship between proposition, modality, and Discourse Modality

The typological implications of Maynard's notion of Discourse Modality are not immediately obvious. Her proposal of the notion is primarily based on an in-depth analysis of discourse-pragmatic phenomena in Japanese apparently without paying much attention to typological studies of modality (for instance, Palmer 1986 is not cited in the references). However, from the viewpoint of Korean-Japanese contrastive linguistics, it may be worthwhile to examine whether the two languages differ in terms of the relative degrees of prominence given to two types of modality, i.e. modality versus Discourse Modality. To this end, we will analyze counterparts to 'modal particles' in the two languages, which are expected to encode Discourse Modality.

2.2.1 Japanese sentence-final particles

As discussed by Maynard (1993) as an instance of 'Discourse Modality indicators', Japanese has a set of sentence-final morphemes referred to as 'sentence-final particles' or 'syuuzyosi' that have the function of 'expressing the speaker's judgment and attitude toward the message and the partner' (Maynard 1997: 87).

While the discourse-oriented functions of Japanese sentence-final particles have long been recognized, research interest in their pragmatic information-related functions is rather recent, owing primarily to the theory of 'Territory of Information' developed by Akio Kamio (e.g. Kamio 1994). Kamio's theory clarifies the information-pragmatic functions of Japanese sentence-final particles, listed below:

zo, ze, sa, yo	'to impart information which belongs to the speaker's territory to an addressee' (p. 25)
	'not used if the information belongs to the hearer's sphere of knowledge or feeling' (p. 25)
na, ne	'can be used when talking about information which belongs to the hearer's territory' (p. 26)

Table 3. Information-territorial characterizations of Japanese sentence-final particles (based on the descriptions in McGloin 1990)

These characterizations account for the acceptability differences between (1) and (1'):

(1) *Omae   wa   kinoo   yasun-da   *zo/ze/sa/yo*.
    you   TOP   yesterday   be absent-PAST   SFP
    'You were absent yesterday, I tell you.' (McGloin 1990: 26)

(1') Omae   wa   kinoo   yasun-da   *na/ne*.
      you   TOP   yesterday be absent-PAST   SFP

     'You were absent yesterday, weren't you.' (ibid: 26)

The information of the hearer's absence, which belongs to the hearer's informational territory, cannot be felicitously conveyed by the first group of particles (1), but can be appended by the second group of particles (1') (unless of course the addressee in (1) is denying his/her actions).

    Through the pragmatically oriented studies of Japanese sentence-final particles (See Kamio 1994; also Maynard 1993, 1997), it has become increasingly obvious that two particles, i.e. *yo* and *ne*, exhibit an intricate division of labor in Japanese conversational interaction. Incorporating Kamio's theoretical insights, Maynard (1997) proposes the following analysis of *yo* and *ne*:

(2) Discourse-information functions of *yo* and *ne* in contrast (Maynard 1997: 88)

    Yo: (I) indicates the speaker's assumption that the addressee 'has more access to and/or possession of the information and wants to focus on the information conveyed in the utterance';   (II) 'information-oriented'

    Ne: (I) indicates the speaker's assumption that the addressee 'has less (or about the same amount of) access to and/or possession of the information and wishes to concentrate on feelings and attitude more than on information';

        (II) 'interaction-oriented'

The choice of *yo* or *ne* in (3) indeed brings about the kind of discourse-pragmatic differences that can be captured along the lines of the greater versus lesser access to the information, as well as of the focus on information versus on interaction:

(3) Kore to   itte   gen'in ni naru   yoo na   dekigoto ga   atta
    this QUOT say:GER cause to become such as incident-NOM happened
    wake   dewanai   to   omoimasu   {(a) Ø/ (b) *yo* / (c) *ne* }.
    reason COP:NEG   QUOT   think:POL   SFP   SFP

    'I don't think there was a specific reason that caused the incident {(a) (straightforward assertion). (b) as I'm telling you. (c) and I hope you agree with me.}' (example (3c) is taken from Maynard 1997: 121; (3a, b) added)

While (3a) is a straightforward assertion, (3b) and (3c) clearly convey additional discourse-pragmatic meanings. Both *yo* and *ne* are oriented toward the addressee, but with *yo* (3b), the speaker conveys her/his conviction, which the addressee may not have enough information to be able to judge or share. In contrast, with *ne* (3c), the speaker not only conveys her/his conviction but expects and encourages the addressee to share it. *Yo* and *ne*, which are representative of Japanese sentence-final particles presented in Table 3, thus clearly serve as indicators of what Maynard (1993) calls 'Discourse Modality'.

2.2.2 Korean sentence-final suffixes

Korean also has a set of morphemes that occur sentence-finally and serve some pragmatic-informational functions:

(4) Ku salam-i   ka-ss-{*ta/ci/kwuna/ney/e*}.
    that person-NOM   go-PAST-SE
    'The man went.' (K. Lee 1993: 9; gloss added)

K. Lee states that the sentences carrying each sentence-final suffix 'have the same propositional content, but the speaker expresses different attitudes toward each of the propositional content and makes different assumptions about the listener' (p. 10).

Unlike their Japanese counterparts, however, they are normally referred to as 'suffixes' rather than as 'particles' (H. Lee 1991), implying their greater degree of morphological boundedness. While there is agreement among Japanese linguists as to the membership of sentence-final particles, the representative members of which are listed in Table 3, there appears to be less agreement among Korean linguists regarding the membership of sentence-final suffixes. Table 4 is a list of sentence-final suffixes commonly listed in H. Lee (1991), K. Lee (1993), and Choi (1995), three recent cognitive-functional studies of Korean sentence-final suffixes:

-ta	newly perceived information for the speaker, new information for the listener
-e	assimilated information, unmarked form
-ci	certainty of proposition, shared information
-kwun	newly made inference
-ney	information based on factual evidence

Table 4. Sentence-final suffixes in Korean and their pragmatic-information functions

The pragmatic-information functions presented in Table 4 were taken from Choi

(1995: 171), whose observations of Korean sentence-final suffixes owe a lot to the pioneering work of Hyo Sang Lee (H. Lee 1991). It should be noted that two of the five sentence-final suffixes, i.e. *–ta* and *–e*, were observed to constitute part of the grammatical mood system in Korean respectively as plain-level declarative sentence ender and intimate-level sentence ender in Section 2.1 and encode sentence-level modality meaning (cf. Table 1). This suggests that these two suffixes, unlike Japanese sentence-final particles, are not to be considered as indicators of Discourse Modality proper.

Among the rest of the sentence-final suffixes, as noted by H. Lee (1991), *-kwun* and *–ney* clearly encode 'evidential' meaning, as shown in (5) and (6):

(5) (touching one's hand)

    Son-i   cham   ttattusha-si-*kwun*-yo.

    hand-NOM   really   warm-HON-SE-SE:POL

    'Your hand is really warm.'

    (SBS drama *Coha Coha* http://like.sbs.co.kr/script.htm)

(6) (After tasting the meal)

    Um,   mas-to   kwaynchanh-*ney*.

    Yeah,   taste-also good-SE

    'Yeah, it tastes good.' (Taira 2000: 39)

In (5), suffix *–kwun* indicates the speaker's newly made inference that the addressee's hand is warm, whereas *–ney* in (6) encodes the speaker's factual realization that the taste is good. These two sentence-final suffixes, clearly encoding evidential meaning, have been referred to as 'apperceptive mood' markers (Sohn 1994). As such, it may be more appropriate to consider them to be part of the evidential system rather than to be indicators of Discourse Modality proper.

After this process of elimination, the list of sentence-final suffixes in Table 4 has come down to a sentence-final suffix *–ci*. The discourse-pragmatic characteristics of sentence-final suffix *-ci* has been most comprehensively investigated by Hyo Sang Lee (H. Lee, 1991, 1999), who proposed that '(t)he invariant meaning underlying these contextual meanings is that <u>the speaker believes in the conveyed message</u>, a meaning I shall term "commital"'(H. Lee, 1999: 243, emphasis added).

(7) (a) Wuli   kotunghakkyo colepha-kwu   chem-i-*ci*?

      we   high school graduate-CONJ first time-COP-SE

    '(This) is the first time we (met) since graduation from high school, right?'

(b) Chem-i-*ci*.   Ya,   ne   hana-twu an   pyenhay-ss-ta.

first time-COP-SE   VOC you one-even NEG   change-PAST-DECL

'(It) is the first time. Hey, you haven't changed a bit.'

(SBS drama *Coha Coha*; http://like.sbs.co.kr/script.htm)

By using –*ci*, the speaker can convey her/his commitment to the message that it is indeed the first time they met after graduation (7b). The speaker can also ascertain that the addresses shares her/his commitment (7a).

Korean sentence-final suffix –*ci* is thus shown to encode a Discourse Modality meaning positively, in comparison to other sentence-final suffixes, i.e. –*ta* and –*e*, which are more deeply embedded in the system of grammatical mood, and –*kwun* and –*ney*, which may be more properly situated in the evidential system. It is interesting to note that –*ci* shows certain semantic/functional resemblance to Japanese sentence-final particles *yo* and *ne* discussed in Section 2.2.1.

To summarize Section 2.2, it has been demonstrated that Japanese has a system of sentence-final particles that encode what Maynard (1993) refers to as Discourse Modality, wherein two particles *yo* and *ne* are particularly prominent in terms of complementary pragmatic-information functions they serve in discourse. In contrast, though Korean has a set of sentence-final particles apparently comparable to Japanese sentence-final particles, it has been shown that the majority of these suffixes may be integrated into other modality systems (i.e. grammatical mood, evidentials) instead of properly belonging to the domain of Discourse Modality. Suffix –*ci*, which apparently encodes Discourse Modality meaning in a similar fashion to Japanese particles *yo* and *ne*, can be regarded as the indicator of Discourse Modality proper among the Korean sentence-final suffixes.

3. Modality Systems in Korean and Japanese: Where Do the Differences Come from?

The contrastive linguistic analysis of modality systems in Korean and Japanese in Section 2 suggests that the two languages prioritize rather different kinds of 'modality' meanings in their grammatical systems. The type of modality more systematically grammaticalized (or encoded in the grammatical structure) in Korean directly affects the propositional content of the sentence, most typically evidenced by its intricate grammatical mood system discussed in Section 2.1. In contrast, the type of modality more elaborately manifested in Japanese grammar is what Maynard (1993) calls

'Discourse Modality', whose relationship to the propositonal content is more indirect and whose function is more interactionally oriented, most typically evidenced by its system of sentence-final particles. These cross-linguistic differences can be illustrated in Figure 2:

[Discourse structure: [Sentence structure: [proposition] **[modality]**] **[Discourse Modality]**]
K > J   J > K

Figure 2. The two types of modality and their relative degrees of grammaticalization in Korean and Japanese

It seems to be no coincidence that Korean and Japanese exhibit different priorities in the type of modality meanings encoded in their grammatical systems (Horie 2000). As discussed in Horie (1998) and Horie and Sassa (in press), Korean tends to 'spell out' the propositional content of the sentence in a more unambiguous manner than Japanese, and thus to avoid potentially ambiguous surface structures more consistently. This contrast is manifested in various domains of grammar (e.g. case-marking particles, nominalized embedded clauses, formal distinction between adnominal (attributive) and sentence-final predicate forms). For instance, as noted by Tsukamoto (1997), Korean requires that the adnominal past tense verb form *ha-n* be present in the verbal noun construction (8a), in keeping with the presence of the accusative case particle *ul*. In contrast, Japanese does not require overt tense marking in the corresponding construction (8b). The past tense interpretation of the verbal noun *syuppatu* ('departure') in (8b) is arrived at only pragmatically, not structurally.

(8) (a) Ku yelcha-nun, tokhyo-yek-**ul**   **chwulpal-{han/**   ***?Ø}-hwu**,
    that train-TOP   Tokyo-station-ACC departure- do:PAST:ADN   after
    kot   phokpalhay-ss-ta.
    soon explode-PAST-DECL

  (b) Sono ressya-wa,   tookyoo-eki-**o**   **syuppatu-go**,   sugu bakuhatusita.
    that train-TOP   Tokyo-station-ACC departure-after   soon exploded
    'That train exploded soon after it left Tokyo station.'

It has been argued in the literature (Du Bois 1985, Haiman 1985) that there is an inherent tension between the two fundamental principles governing form-meaning correspondence in natural languages, i.e. 'isomorphism' and 'economy'. Prioritizing the former may lead to the proliferation of forms for every meaning to be spelled out, while prioritizing the latter can lead to an increase in surface structural ambiguities. Each language strikes a balance between the two principles in a delicate manner, but it has been argued (Hawkins 1986) that some languages (e.g. German), apparently giving priority to isomorphism, tend to keep form-meaning correspondence more straightforward than other languages (e.g. English), which are more tolerant of potential structural ambiguities and resolve them pragmatically.

We argue, following the discussion in Horie (1998) and Horie and Sassa (in press), that a similar contrast is manifested between Korean and Japanese, with Korean prioritizing isomorphism while Japanese lays greater emphasis on economy. If Korean tends to encode the propositional content of the sentence more faithfully than Japanese, it is natural that the type of modality meaning directly affecting the propositonal content ('modality' in Figure 2) is more elaborately grammaticalized in Korean. Conversely, if Japanese tends to utilize pragmatic ambiguity resolution more extensively than Korean, it is natural that the type of modality meaning more relevant to the discourse structure ('Discourse Modality') is more systematically developed in the grammatical system of Japanese. Though we need a systematic contrastive discourse analysis to substantiate this point, we suspect that this contrast is correlated with the often-cited differences in communicative style between the two societies.

4. Conclusion

It has been argued in this paper that modality systems in Korean and Japanese, though superficially very similar, turn out to exhibit remarkable differences on closer scrutiny. The type of modality meaning more closely related to the propositonal content of the sentence is elaborately encoded in Korean, whereas the type of modality meaning more interactionally oriented (i.e. Discourse Modality) is systematically manifested in Japanese. It has also been suggested that these cross-linguistic differences, which are in keeping with the contrast observed in different areas of the respective grammars, are motivated by the different priorities given to the competing cognitive-functional norms in two linguistic communities.

Abbreviations

ACC (accusative); ADN (adnominal); CONJ (conjunctive); COP (copula); DECL (declarative); GER (gerund); HON (honorific); NEG (negative); NOM (nominative); POL (polite); QUOT (quotative); SE (sentence ender); SFP (sentence final particle); TOP (topic); VOC (vocative).

Acknowledgement

This work was supported in part by a grant from the Matsushita International Foundation. The authors thank Jung Hye Choi, Jae Yong Jung, Sun Young Lee, Kyung Soon Oh, and Hee Young Ryu for assistance in data collection, and Noriko Akatsuka, Andrew Barke, Shoichi Iwasaki, Stephen Nolan, Debra Occhi, Sung Ock Sohn, and Masakazu Wako for comments and constructive criticism.

References

Bussmann Hadumod (ed.) 1996. *Routledge Dictionary of Language and Linguistics*. Translated and edited by Trauth, Gregory P., and Kerstin Kazzazi. London: Routledge

Bybee, Joan, Revere Perkins, and William Pagliuca. 1994. *The Evolution of Grammar. Tense, Aspect, and Modality in the Languages of the World*. Chicago: University of Chicago Press.

Bybee, Joan, and Suzanne Fleischman. (eds.) 1995. *Modality in Grammar and Discourse*. Amsterdam: John Benjamins.

Choi, Soonja. 1995. The Development of Epistemic Sentence-Ending Modal Forms and Functions in Korean Children. In Bybee and Fleischman, 165-204.

Du Bois, John W. 1985. Competing Motivations. In Haiman, John (ed.), *Iconicity in Syntax*, 343-365. Amsterdam: John Benjamins.

Haiman, John. 1985. *Natural Syntax*. Cambridge: Cambridge University Press.

Hawkins, John A. 1986. *A Comparative Typology of English and German*. London: Croom Helm.

Horie, Kaoru. 1997. Form-Meaning Interaction in Diachrony: A Case Study from Japanese. *English Linguistics* 14: 428-449.

Horie, Kaoru. 1998. Functional Duality of Case-Marking Particles in Japanese and its Implications for Grammaticalization: A Contrastive Study with Korean. In Silva, David (ed.), *Japanese/Korean Linguistics 8*, 147-159. Stanford: CSLI.

Horie, Kaoru. 2000. Complementation in Japanese and Korean: A Contrastive and Cognitive Linguistic Approach. In Kaoru Horie (ed.), *Complementation. Cognitive and Functional*

Perspectives, 11-31. Amsterdam: John Benjamins.

Horie, Kaoru, and Yuko Sassa. In press. From Place to Space to Discourse: A Contrastive Linguistic Analysis of Japanese *Tokoro* and Korean *Tey*. In Nakayama, Mineharu, and Charles J. Quinn (eds.), *Japanese/Korean Linguistics 9*. Stanford: CSLI.

Kamio, Akio. 1994. The Theory of Territory of Information: The Case of Japanese. *Journal of Pragmatics* 21: 67-100.

Kiefer, Ferenc. 1999. Modality. In Brown, Keith, and Jim Miller (eds.) 1999. *Concise Encyclopedia of Grammatical Categories*, 223-229. Oxford: Elsevier.

Ko, Yeng Kun. 1965. Hyentaykwukeuy sepep cheykyeyey tayhan yenkwu (A Study of the Modern Korean Mood System). *Kwukeyenkwu* 15: 4-5.

Lee, Kee Dong. 1993. *A Korean Grammar on Semantic-Pragmatic Principles*. Seoul: Hankwukmwunhwasa.

Lee, Hyo Sang. 1991. *Tense, Aspect, and Modality. A Discourse-Pragmatic Analysis of Verbal Affixes in Korean from a Typological Perspective*. Doctoral Dissertation, UCLA.

Lee, Hyo Sang. 1999. A Discourse-Pragmatic Analysis of the Committal –*Ci* in Korean: A Synthetic Approach to the Form-Meaning Relation. *Journal of Pragmatics* 31: 243-275.

Maynard, Senko K. 1993. *Discourse Modality*. Amsterdam: John Benjamins.

Maynard, Senko K. 1997. *Japanese Communication*. Honolulu: Hawaii University Press.

McGloin, Naomi Hanaoka. 1990. Sex Differences and Sentence-Final Particles. In Ide, Sachiko, and Naomi Hanaoka McGloin (eds.), *Aspects of Japanese Women's Language*, 23-41. Tokyo: Kurosio publishers.

Palmer, F. R. 1986. *Mood and Modality*. Cambridge: Cambridge University Press.

Shibatani, Masayoshi. 1990. *The Languages of Japan*. Cambridge: Cambridge University Press.

Sohn, Ho Min. 1994. *Korean*. London: Routledge.

Sohn, Ho Min. 1999. *The Korean Language*. Cambridge: Cambridge University Press.

Taira, Kaori. 2000. *Kankokugo no setzuzi* ney *no kaiwa sinkoo kinoo ni kansuru kenkyuu: modaritii ron no kanten kara* (A Study of Conversation-Advancing Function of Korean *Ney*: From the Perspective of Modality Studies). M.A. thesis, Tohoku University, Japan.

Tsukamoto, Hideki. 1990. Nittyoo tasiyoo kenkyuu to nihongo kyooiku (Japanese-Korean Contrastive Study and Japanese Language Education). *Nihongo Kyoiku* 72: 68-79.

Tsukamoto, Hideki. 1997. Goitekina gokeisei to toogotekina gokeisei: nihogo to tyoosengo no taisyoo kenkyuu (Lexical Word Formation and Syntactic Word Formation: A Contrastive Study of Japanese and Korean). In *Nihongo to tyoosengo* (Japanese and Korean), Vol. 2., 191-212. Tokyo: Kurosio publishers.

Demonstratives as Prospective Indexicals: *ku* and *ce* in Korean Conversation

KYU-HYUN KIM & KYUNG-HEE SUH

Kyung Hee University & Hankuk University of Foreign Studies

1. Introduction

In this paper, we examine some interactional aspects of the Korean demonstratives used as prospective indexicals in spontaneous conversation (Goodwin 1996). Prospective indexicals, as defined in this paper, refer to deictic expressions cataphorically pointing ahead to a referent or a proposition which is to be explicated in the subsequent context. It subsumes instances of demonstratives deployed as fillers, which speakers use to hold the turn-in-progress momentarily while searching for a word or a proposition.

The system of Korean demonstratives is based on a tripartite distinction. The basic morphemes are thus three elements; the proximal form *i* 'this', the medial form *ku* 'that (near the hearer)' and the distal form *ce* 'that (far from both speaker and hearer)'. In their prototypical deictic use, the choice of one form over the others is thus determined by the relative distance of an entity *vis-à-vis* the speaker and/or the hearer. These three morphemes are combined with various elements, forming tripartite paradigms such as demonstrative adverbs *yeki* 'here', *keki* 'there', and *ceki* 'there'.

---

* This work was supported by the Brain Korea 21 Project in 2000.

This paper aims to explicate some of the differences between these demonstratives in the context where they are used as prospective indexicals. We are particularly interested in examining differences between *ku/keki* and *ce/ceki*, both translated into 'that/there' in English, which predominantly occur as prospective indexicals in Korean conversation (Suh & Hong 1999).

The methodology we have used in this paper is conversation analysis (Sacks *et al.* 1974). In analyzing these forms in spontaneous conversation, we will mainly concern ourselves with the analytic task of explicating the way in which the use of a particular demonstrative is occasioned by a particular type of sequential orientation displayed by the participants. It will be proposed that *ku* and *ce* constitute distinct types of trouble source which sequentially project different forms of resolution in terms of the extent to which the interlocutor's co-participation is solicited for the given task of referent identification. Differences between *ku* and *ce* are further explicated in terms of whether or how they are employed not only for identifying a referent but also for situating a referent in the context of a projected action.

The data analyzed in this paper consist of tape-recorded face-to-face conversations between graduate students studying in the U.S. and their families. Also included are segments of overheard conversations that have been written down immediately after hearing each of the fragments.

This paper is organized as follows. Section 2 discusses the functions of *ku* in terms of its tendency toward eliciting the hearer's uptake. Section 3 presents the analysis of *ce* in terms of its predisposition to project speaker explication of the projected referent. In Section 4, we further explore the discourse-organizational function of *ce* with reference to its function of framing the action in which the projected referent is situated.

2. Functions of *ku*: Eliciting the hearer uptake

In examining the function of *ku* and *ce* as prospective indexicals, we will first look at their differences with reference to the extent to which the hearer's uptake is solicited. We will also examine how the speaker treats the hearer's attempt to co-identify the referent. Let us first discuss some of the sequential aspects associated with *ku*. Consider example (1):[1]

---

[1] The transcription notation used for this paper was adapted from Sacks *et al.* (1974):

//	Interruption	=	Contiguous utterances
[ ]	Simultaneous utterances	--	Cut-off
(0.0)	Intervals between utterances	.	Falling intonation
(.)	Micro-pause	,	Continuing intonation
( )	Words unclear	?	Rising intonation
(( ))	Transcriber's remarks	°	Portions quieter than the surrounding talk
:	Sound stretch	__	Emphasis

(1) (After Dinner)
```
1   Y:  salam  -tul -i     cwungangilpo -lul   ceki
        person-PL-NOM Jungang Daily-ACC there
2       hankwukilpo -pota manhi po -nun    iywu  -cwung-uy
        Hankuk Daily-than many see -ATTR reason-among-POSS
3       hana-ka  -yo,  kwuin      kwangko-hako,
        one -NOM-POL employment ad      -with
```
        "One of the reasons why there are more people subscribing to the
        Jungang Daily than the Hankuk Daily is because of its job sec-
        tion and,"
```
4   S:  ung::
        yes
```
        "Yes."
```
→ 5 Y:  ku:: ku -ke   iss -cian    -ayo. phan//may:::
        that that-thing exist-ASSERT-POL sale
```
        "**That,** you know **that thing.** The sales section."
                                               [
```
→ 6 S:                                         Ah  phanmay ung.
                                               DM sale    yes
```
        "Oh, the sales section. Right."
```
7   Y:  ku -ke  -ttamey phanmay pwuswu-ka
        that-thing-because sale      number-NOM
8       manh-un  -ke  -lay  -yo.
        many-ATTR-NOML-QUOT-POL
```
        "They say it's because of those two sections that so many people
        read it."

This segment shows a context in which Y is comparing two Korean
newspapers, and in line 3, she brings up two reasons why more people read
the Jung-Ang Daily than *the Hankwuk Daily*. The item she proposes as the
first reason for why the former is more popular than the latter is a better job
ad section (*kwuin kwangko* 'job ads'). As suggested by the particle -*hako*
'and' attached to the first item in line 3, Y projects that a second item is
forthcoming in the format of 'A and B'.[2] It is here that Y, observably engaged in a word search, produces two prospective indexicals *ku* 'that' and
ku-ke 'that thing' pointing to the second item. Note that these demonstratives are used in the confirmation-seeking expression, *ku:: ku-ke iss-cyan-
ayo* 'that, you know that thing', which indexes the speaker's belief that what
is being pointed to by *ku* is something that can be identified by the hearer.
We thus find that, even though the speaker of *ku* (Y) ends up identifying the

---

[2] As Lerner (1995) observes, such a list-in-progress opens the possibility of recipient involvement by providing an opportunity for anticipatory completion.

second item (*phanmay* 'the sales section') in line 5, she formulates her utterance in such a format that the hearer's involvement is actively elicited.

Note that this hearer-involving practice is demonstrably oriented to and reciprocated by the hearer (S) who promptly acknowledges the referent by producing a change-of-state token *ah* 'oh' in overlap with Y's turn, thus showing that she has realized what the referent is even before Y's explication is completed. She then affirms the referent by repeating it and produces the post-recognition acknowledgment marker *ung* 'I see'. This three-part responsive move triggered by Y's *ku*-utterance strikingly shows how keenly speaker S is oriented toward grasping the projected referent collaboratively.

The function of *ku* eliciting the hearer's uptake in identifying the referent is also shown in example (2):

(2) (After Dinner)
1 Y: *kuliko kay   -nun (.) apple ha -myen   -un (0.2) chak*
       and   that child-TOP   apple say-COND-TOP   right away
→ 2   *nao   -ntay ku-*
          come out-QUOT that
          "And when one says 'apple' to that child, it comes out right away, **that-**"
3   (0.8)
→ 4 S: *spelling-i,=*
          spelling-NOM
          "(You mean) its spelling (comes out right away)."
5 Y: *=spelling-i.*
          spelling-NOM
          "(Right.) Its spelling (comes out right away)."

Note that, in this segment, S, in line 4, identifies the referent projected by *ku*. This fragment could be analyzed as an instance of an other-initiated repair sequence (see discussions below); S initiates repair and collaboratively completes Y's preceding utterance by producing a candidate understanding of the referent pointed to by *ku*, which is then confirmed by Y. From a slightly different perspective, we also find a sense in which Y, the speaker of *ku*, invites S to join the collaborative search for the projected referent. In this respect, this fragment might be taken as an instance of self-initiated other repair, where the speaker of *ku* initiates repair in such a way that the hearer is invited to repair the problem (i.e. identify the projected referent) for her.

This hearer-involving property of *ku* is observed in a more indirect and elaborate way in other-initiated repair sequences (Schegloff *et al.* 1979).[3] As

---

[3] Other-initiated repair sequences are composed of three turns: trouble-source turn, repair-initiating turn, and repair turn. In the repair initiating turn, the interlocutor raises the problem of

Kim (to appear) has noted, the demonstrative *ku* predominantly occurs in trouble-source turn, particularly in the context in which it is used in a topic-initial question. Example (3) is a case in point:

(3) (North Campus Talk 1)
→ 1 H: *min yengswun -ssi -hanthey °ku pili   -ess -eyo?*   ←(a)
        Min Youngsoon-Ms-to   that borrow-PST-POL
  2   *chayk?*
      book
      "Have you borrowed **that** from Ms. Min Youngsoon? The Book?"
  3   (.)
  4 S: *mwe -yo?*   ←(b)
      What-POL
      "What?"
→ 5 H: *ki//m sangho kyoswunim.*   ←(c)
      Kim Sangho professor
      "(The book written by) Prof. Kim Sangho."
      [
→ 6 S: <u>*ah:::*</u> *pillye -tal -la   kulay-ss -te   -ni,*
      DM borrow-give-QUO say -PST-RETROS-CONN
      "Oh! I asked her to lend (it) to me and,"

In lines 1 and 2, H asks S whether she borrowed something from Ms. Youngsoon Min. Here he uses the demonstrative *ku* as a filler, filling in the syntactic slot for the object of the verb 'borrow' (cf. Kitano 1999). This utterance is immediately tagged upon by the noun *chayk* 'book', which is produced as a post-positional phrasal unit explicating the projected referent. Note, however, that H is still being vague in identifying which book he is talking about, which leads S to initiate repair in line 4 (*mwe-yo?* 'what?'). H, facing S's repair initiator, still does not fully identify the book, but only provides the name of the author in line 5 (*kim sangho kyoswunim* 'Prof. Kim Sangho'). As noted in Kim (to appear), this repair structure displays a 'clue-giving' pattern, in which the speaker of *ku* goes about providing the hearer with clues instead of a full explication, which prompts the hearer to identify the referent. As such, it serves as a piece of empirical support for the observation that *ku* actively involves the hearer in referent identification.

We can make two additional points in example (3) which further evidence that the participants are demonstrably oriented to mutually affirming

---

hearing or understanding with regard to the preceding trouble-source turn and prompts the speaker of the trouble-source turn to repair the problem in the repair turn (Schegloff *et al.* 1979). In the fragments analyzed in this paper, the trouble-source turn, the repair-initiating turn, and the repair turn are marked by (a), (b), and (c) respectively.

the expectation (indexed by *ku*) that the hearer is able to identify the projected referent. First, note that the hearer (S) responds to the speaker of *ku* (H) with the change of state token *ah* 'oh'. The tendency of *ku* to elicit a change-of-state token, which was also observed in example (1), shows that the hearer of *ku* is keenly oriented to acknowledging the referred-to-entity identified by the speaker. Second, we find that the repair turn (line 5), where the speaker of *ku* addresses the trouble source, is overlapped by the interlocutor's subsequent turn acknowledging the success of repair even before the repair is completed (line 6). This sequence-organizational feature could be accounted for as a structural manifestation of the repair recipient's collaborative uptake geared to displaying a successful grasp of the trouble-source meaning projected by *ku*.[4]

3. Functions of *ce*: Projecting an explication by the speaker

Unlike *ku*, which is massively used in topic-initial 'questions' as in (3), *ce* is predominantly used in topic-initial 'statements'. In such a context, *ce* offers little room for the hearer to involve or volunteer himself/herself in identifying what it refers to. Consider example (4). This conversation takes place in the context where H recommends to the other participants a series of candidate research topics:

(4) (Lunch Discussion)
→ 1 H: *na-nun* **ce** *-ke*   *caymiiss -ulkeskat-te*   *-lakwu*   ←(a)
              I -TOP that-thing interesting-seem   -RETRO-QUOT
  2   *-yo, (2.2) social interaction (0.6) -ulo*   *hay-ya*
              -POL   social interaction   -INSTR do -NECESS
  3   *toy -nun*   *-ke*   *-cyan*   *-ayo ku//-ci*   *-yo.*
              OK-ATTR-NOML-ASSERT-POL that -COMM-POL
              "I think **that thing** might be interesting. So the research topic should be related to social interaction, right?"
  4 K: *ney.*
          yes
          "Yes"
  5   (0.8)

---

[4] The use of *ku* observed in (1), (2), and (3), while projecting an explication, gives the sense of referring back to some shared knowledge or interactional history shared by the participants. In this sense, *ku* used as a prospective indexical could be analyzed as a type of discourse deixis that conceptually locates a referent in some shared prior text evoked as a demonstrative space (cf. Matras 1998); it invites the hearer to join the collaborative search for a given referent by way of evoking a shared interactional history.

→ 6 H: *kuntey bilingual ha-nun   salam -tul -i,*
　　　　 DM   bilingual do-ATTR person-PL-NOM
　　　　 "And bilingual people,"

　 7 　 (1.6)

→ 8 K: *code switching-i   -yo?*　　　　　　　← (b)/(a')
　　　　 code switching-COP-POL
　　　　 "You mean code switching?"

→ 9 H: *yey?*　　　　　　　　　　　　　　　　← (b')
　　　　 yes
　　　　 "Huh?"

　10 K: *code s//witching-i   -yo?*　　　　　← (c')
　　　　 code switching -COP-POL
　　　　 "You mean code switching?"

　11 H: *yey.*　　　　　　　　　　　　　　　← (c)
　　　　 yes
　　　　 "Yes."

→ 12 H: *malha-taka, (.) konlanhan -ke*
　　　　 talk   -TRANS troublesome-thing

　13 　 *yaykiha-l   -ttay -myen yenge -lo   hay.*
　　　　 talk   -ATTR-time-COND English-INSTR do:IE
　　　　 "while talking, if they say something troublesome, they use
　　　　 English."

In line 1, H uses the demonstrative *ce* cataphorically referring to a candidate research topic. After some intervening talk of parenthetical nature, H,
in line 6, begins to offer an explanation identifying the referent, producing
the subject of the projected utterance (*bilingual people*). Before H produces
the rest of the projected utterance, K takes the intervening pause as the opportunity to propose his candidate understanding of the referent (*code-
switching*) projected by the prospective indexical *ce-ke* 'that thing'.

K's proposal of the candidate understanding of the referent projected by
ce-ke 'that thing' is subsequently constituted as trouble source by H's repair
initiator (*yey?* 'huh?') in line 9, which suggests that H did not expect K's
voluntary identification. Furthermore, note that K's proposal of a candidate
understanding and the repair sequence it initiates (lines 8-11) are eventually
deleted by H in a subtle tying operation (Kim 1999); H resumes his own
explication in line 12 in such a way that his turn-initial utterance (*malha-
take* 'while talking') is retroactively linked back to the noun phrase in line 6
as its predicate. By doing so, he deletes out the whole embedded repair sequence (lines 8-11) as an 'interruption' and continues his own explication in
spite of K's successful identification of the referent.[5]

---

[5] Throughout the overall sequence of talk containing the segment in example (4), H has been

We find a similar pattern in example (5), where the hearer's identification of the referent projected by filler *ceki* interrupts the current turn in-progress:

(5) (After Dinner)

1 Y: *yey payk-myeng-pwun ha-nta   -kulay-se*
            yes 100 -CL   -serving do-QUOT-say -CONN

2   *kalbiccim   -ul   cikum phalsipphal pound-ey   -ta//ka,=*
          steamed short-rib-ACC now 88   pound-LOC-TRANS
          "Yes. They are preparing 100 servings, and in addition to 88 pounds of steamed short-ribs,"

3 S: *huh:::*
          EXCL

4 K: *=eyu   menu-ka   coh -a   -ci   -ess -ney, hh*
          EXCL menu-NOM good-CONN-INCHOA-PST-FR
          "Wow, the menu has got better."

5   (.)

6 S: *ani kuntey ku -ttay -twu cwungkwuk umsikcem-ey//se*
          no but   that-time-also Chinese   restaurant -LOC

7 K: *(kuntey) kuciman (   )*
          DM   but
          "Well, but (   )"

→ 8 S: *taylyang   -ulo   **ceki** hay-ss -e kwuiphay-kaciko*
          large quantity-INSTR there did-PST-IE purchase -CONN

9   *(.) //iman won--*
            20,000 won
          "But, last time, too, from a Chinese restaurant we did **that** in large quantities. We purchased food and, with 20,000 won-"
            [

→ 10 Y: *(-ttay) catering-to   hay-se   mek-ss -ta*
            -time catering-also do -CONN eat -PST-DECL

11   *-kule-tay   -yo,*
          -say -HEARSAY-POL
          "They say that they once ordered catered food." (Literal translation: "They say that they did catering.")

12 S: *e::. e::. ((in a subdued tone))*
          yes yes
          "Right. Right."

taking the role of the expert who gives advice to one of the participants (S) in response to the latter's request for help in finding an appropriate research topic. In this participation structure, H may have perceived K's early successful grasp of the projected referent as undermining his position as the expert.

In this fragment, the interlocutors have been talking about the party that the graduate student Bible study group is planning to throw, and in the preceding context one of the interlocutors mentioned that one of the wives of the student members is single-handedly preparing the food for the party. After several exchanges, in line 8, interlocutor S, who attended the Bible study group party the previous year, says that in the previous year they ordered food from a Chinese restaurant. Here she initially uses *ceki* as a filler which is placed in the object position in the form of *ceki hay-ss-e* 'we did that', and in explicating what 'that' means, she proceeds to recount what they did, saying that they collected money and took out food from a Chinese restaurant (lines 8-9). It is just at this point that Y interrupts S's turn-in-progress and says that she has also heard that they once ordered catered food (lines 10-11). As illustrated in the literal translation of this utterance, Y's proposed term 'catering' is formulated as the object of the verb 'do' (*did catering*) (line 10), just as S's *ceki* occurs as the object of the verb 'do' (*did that*) in her preceding utterance (line 8). This formal affinity strengthens the sense in which Y has proposed the term *catering* as a candidate understanding of the referent projectively referred to by *ceki* in S's preceding turn.

In both (4) and (5), we find that the candidate understanding proposed by the hearer of *ce/ceki* interrupts the speaker's turn in-progress. The candidate understanding is formulated as a single word gisting the projected explication[6] and is produced interruptively to the effect that the speaker's ongoing narrative-style explication of the projected referent is curtailed. In both cases, the hearer of *ce*, by proposing his/her candidate understanding, seriously undermines the tellability of the speaker's on-going explication (Sacks 1992:13).[7]

As in (4), there is a sense in (5) that the speaker of *ce* did not invite or expect the hearer to volunteer her candidate understanding, and this orientation is displayed by the way she responds to Y's candidate understanding. Note in line 12 that S produces two bits of acknowledgment tokens in a rather subdued tone (*Right. Right*), which could be taken as a *pro forma* agreement with Y's candidate understanding. This suggests that she is experiencing a momentary state of disorientation and an unexpected adjustment following Y's successful, but uninvited, attempt to identify the referent projected by *ceki* that she has been in the middle of explicating.

---

[6] It is to be noted in passing that, in both (4) and (5), the candidate understanding proposed by the hearer of *ce/ceki* happens to be a foreign word (i.e. *code-switching* and *catering*).

[7] Note that Y's candidate understanding in example (5) undermines speaker S's position as a member of the bible study group who is supposed to be more knowledgeable than Y about the past event sponsored by the group (cf. footnote (5)). This observation suggests that *ce* tends to be employed in the context where the speaker asserts his/her own knowledge in such a way that the hearer is positioned as a passive recipient of the explication to be offered by the speaker.

These observations suggest that the speaker of *ce* does not encourage (or even resists) the hearer's uptake in co-identifying the referent at issue. In contrast with *ku*, the use of *ce* orients the hearer toward the speaker's explicating action through which the projected referent is identified (e.g. advicegiving in (4) and story-telling in (5)). Such an action implicativeness of *ce*-utterances seems to have the significant interactional consequence of leading the hearer to take the stance of a *recipient* of the forthcoming action, hence the speaker's reluctance or even potential aversion to soliciting the hearer's involvement.

4. *Ce/ceki* as a filler: Framing an action

As we have analyzed in the preceding section, *ce/ceki* in natural conversation tends to be used when the speaker initiates an action while observably searching for a referent or a proposition. Often, *ce/ceki* is used for framing an action disjunctively shifting the hearer's orientation.[8] Consider example (6), which is a segment from a conversation between father, mother, and their 14-year-old son:

(6) (Overheard Conversation)
1 Son: *kapcaki lamyen   mek-kosip-ta*
        suddenly instance noodles eat -want -DECL
        "Suddenly I feel like eating instant noodles."
2 Father: *((shaking head))*
→ 3 Mother: *emma -ka   ce -ke   hay-cwu-lkkey.*
        mother-NOM that-thing do -give-MOD:IE
4   *ccacangmyen*
        Chinese-style noodles
        "I will make **that thing** for you, Chinese-style noodles"
5 Son: *ccacang?*
        Chinese-style noodles
        "Chinese-style noodles?"

As the son says that he wants to eat instant noodles, his father nonverbally displays his negative response by shaking his head. In line 3, the

---

[8] It is to be noted in this respect that *ce* or *ceki* is often used for marking the beginning of a new discourse unit by framing a pre-sequence or what Schegloff (1980) calls a 'pre-pre', which is routinely followed by further preliminaries inserted before the projected action. A case in point is the pre-request expression 'let me ask you a question', which is not usually followed by a question but by further preliminary information. The corresponding Korean expression often includes the utterance-initial *ce* or *ceki*, as in *ce/ceki malssum com mwut-keyss-nuntey-yo*, '**That/There**, I'll ask you a question.' This feature of *ce* is also observed in example (4) where H's pre-advice-giving *ce*-utterance is followed by a parenthetical knowledge check (lines 2-3).

mother proposes an alternative option, which is initially referred to by *ce-ke* 'that thing' and subsequently explicated by the post-positional noun phrase *ccacangmyen* 'Chinese-style noodles'. Note that the mother's use of *ce-ke* is situated in the context where she *makes an offer* to the child, and what it refers to is an alternative to what the son chose (i.e. instant noodles). With *ce-ke* pointing to an alternative to the son's choice, we find that it is embedded in the context where the mother attempts to persuade her son to eat Chinese-style noodles rather than instant noodles.

Example (7) is another context where *ceki* projects a referent embedded in an action context. This conversation takes place at a dinner table. M (mother) and D (daughter) are preparing to eat with other family members:

(7) (Overhead Conversation)
        ((M, standing in front of the sink, is holding a cup of water.))
    1 M: *mek -nun   mwul-i   -ye, swuto   mwu l-i   -ye,*
            drink-ATTR water-COP-IE tap   water-COP-IE
            "Is this bottled water or tap water?"
    2 D: *swuto mwul-i   -ya.*
            tap   water-COP-IE
            "It's tap water."
    3 M: *((pours the water in the sink.))*
 → 4 D: *nay-ka   ceki mantu-llyek//o*
            I   -NOM there make -INTENT
            "In order to make **that**,"

                                            [
    5 M: *ung ((sitting at the dinner table))*
                                            yes
            "I see."
    6 D: *((pointing to a dish on the table)) yeki-eta   neh -ullyeko*
                                            here-LOC put in-INTENT
    7   *ha-n   -ke   -ya.*
            do-ATTR-NOML-COP:IE
            "(That's) what I was going to put in here."

In this fragment, M notices a cup of water next to the sink, and in line 1 she asks D if it is bottled water or tap water. As D responds that it is tap water, M pours the water in the sink. In line 4, D produces an utterance in which she uses *ceki* as a filler holding the syntactic slot for the object of the verb phrase (*ceki mantu-llyeko* 'in order to make **that**'), explaining that it was the water that she was going to put in the particular dish being deictically pointed to in line 6. Note that what D is doing here is to *provide an account* for why she has left the cup of tap water next to the sink.

Given the function of *ceki* situating the projected referent in the context where the speaker (D) initiates the action of providing an account, it is noteworthy that M, the hearer of *ceki*, responds and acts in line 5 *before D completes her explication*. She produces an acknowledgement token (*ung* 'I see') in overlap with D's *ceki*-utterance containing the adverbial clause marking her intention (*ceki mantu-lleyko* 'In order to make that') and sits down to eat before D finishes the rest of her account explicating the referent of *ceki*. This suggests that M, the hearer of *ceki*, is oriented not so much toward receiving complete information about the identify of the referred-to-referent of *ceki per se* as toward grasping the general *upshot* of the action being initiated by D, i.e. the action of providing an account (cf. Kitano 1999); by monitoring the adverbial clause of D's utterance in line 4, M would be able to see that what D is doing with her on-going *ceki*-utterance is providing an account.

Overall, even though many of the observations made above are preliminary in nature, they suggest that *ce* orients the hearer toward the action being initiated. The function of *ce* situating a referent in the context of a newly initiated action is saliently observed as being distinct from the function of *ku* focusing on referent identification *per se*. Consider example (8):

(8) (Overhead Conversation)
→ 1 S: *acham. **ceki** paci ip -e -la. (.) **ku** europe*
        DM   there pants put on-IE-IMPER that Europe
  2   *ka-ss -ul -ttay ip -ess -te -n ku paci.*
        go-PST-ATTR-time pet on-PST-RETRO-ATTR that pants
        "Oh, by the way, put on **those** pants, **those** pants you wore when we went to Europe."

As signaled by the discourse marker *acham* 'Oh, by the way', S's *ceki*-utterance in line 1 is disjunctively produced topic-initially, and it performs a speech action as a directive (*Put on those pants*). Note that *ceki* is used here as a sort of adnominal form modifying *paci* 'pants', setting a vague categorical domain relevant to the question of 'which pants' are being referred to. Note that *ku* is subsequently used as the speaker narrows down the reference domain and points to a more specific referent. We thus find that *ceki* is initially used in the context where the speaker disjunctively initiates the action of direction-giving while pointing to a general reference domain and then moves on to the use of *ku* in the course of specifying the projected referent within the given domain of the action context. This observation serves another piece of evidence suggesting that *ku* concerns referent identification *per se* and *ce* concerns the task of explicating a referent with reference to the action context where the referent is to be situated.

5. Conclusions

Both *ku* and *ce* are used as prospective indexicials signaling that the speaker has a momentary difficulty retrieving, selecting, or constructing a lexical item or a proposition. However, *ku* and *ce* generate distinct sequential shapes, which manifest a different degree of accessibility from the hearer. The use of *ku* focuses on identifying the projected referent in such a way that the hearer's co-identificational effort is solicited. It tends to presuppose intersubjectivity with the interlocutor by way of evoking a prior shared experience and encourages the hearer to locate the referent (cf. Cheshire 1996, Matras 1998). In contrast, *ce* is often employed in the context in which the speaker initiates a disjunctive action in such a way that the hearer is positioned as a passive recipient of the explication to be offered by the speaker. These distinct discourse features associated with *ku* and *ce* are structurally manifested and designedly produced as interactional accomplishments by the participants who index their orientations in formally describable, methodic ways.

On the basis of the preceding analysis, we may summarize the major differences between *ku* and *ce* used as prospective indexicals as follows. *Ku* specifies a referent by *presuppositionally proposing a referential domain as common grounds shared with the hearer*. Its use is mainly oriented to inviting the hearer to affirm the domain as a shared ground from which the projected referent is to be retrieved. In contrast, *ce* negotiates a preliminary ground and guides the hearer's attention toward it by way of *evoking a referential domain and action context to be shared by the hearer*. It points to a referent in such a way that the hearer is constituted as the recipient of the action being initiated as a context for introducing the referent.

These distinct features of *ku* and *ce* could be related to differences in referential intensity (Kirsner 1979, Matras 1998). With a greater extent of referential intensity, *ku* would be predisposed to pointing to a specific/discrete referent, and *ce*, indexing a lower degree of referential intensity, would be predisposed to pointing to a vague, not-yet-materialized action-relevance of the projected referent.[9] These and other related observations presented above serve as points to be further examined in future research.[10] A detailed analysis of how demonstratives serve as grammatical

---

[9] These contrasting features are strikingly observed if we compare the place terms *keki* and *ceki*, 'there'. *Keki* tends to refer to a specific place, while *ceki* tends to be somewhat vague in terms of whether it points to a specific location, a specific referent, or even a speech act (see examples (5), (7), and (8)).

[10] One research question that suggests itself for further research would be how the proximal form *i* 'this' would be different from or similar to either *ku* or *ce*. Preliminary observations suggest that *i* 'this', while not frequently used as a prospective indexical, shares a number of interactional properties with *ce*.

resources for organizing interaction will shed light on the interactional dimension of the deictic use of prospective indexicals and provide a solid basis for cross-linguistic comparisons.[11]

References

Cheshire, J. 1996. That jacksprat: An interactional perspective on English *that*. *Journal of Pragmatics* 25:369-93.

Cook, H. M. 1993. Functions of the filler *ano* in Japanese. *Japanese/Korean Linguistics*, vol. 3, ed. S. Choi, 19-38. CSLI, Stanford University.

Goodwin. 1996. Transparent vision. *Interaction and Grammar*, ed. E. Ochs, E. A. Schegloff and S. A. Thompson, 370-404. Cambridge: Cambridge University Press.

Kim, K.-H. 1999. Phrasal unit boundaries and organization of turns and sequences in Korean conversation. *Human Studies* 22:425-46.

Kim, K.-H. to appear. Confirming intersubjectivity through retroactive elaboration: Organization of phrasal units in other-initiated repair sequences in Korean conversation. *Studies in Interactional Linguistics*, ed. M. Selting and E. Couper-Kuhlen. Amsterdam: John Benjamins.

Kirsner, R. S. 1979. Deixis in discourse: An exploratory quantitative study of the Modern Dutch demonstrative adjectives. *Syntax and Semantics 12: Discourse and Syntax*, ed. T. Givón, 355-75. New York: Academic Press.

Kitano, H. 1999. On interaction and grammar: evidence from one use of the Japanese demonstrative *are* ('that'), *Pragmatics* 9:383-400.

Lerner, G. H. 1995. Turn design and the organization of participation in instructional activities. *Discourse Processes* 19:111-31.

Matras, Y. 1998. Deixis and deictic oppositions in discourse: Evidence in Romani. *Journal of Pragmatics* 29:393-428.

Sacks, H. 1992. *Lectures on Conversation*, vol 2, ed. G. Jefferson. Oxford: Blackwell.

Sacks, H., Schegloff E. A., and G. Jefferson. 1974. A simplest systematics for the organization of turn-taking for conversation. *Language* 50:696-735.

Schegloff, E. A. 1980. Preliminaries to preliminaries: "Can I ask you a question". *Sociological Inquiry* 50(3-4):104-52.

Schegloff, E. A., Jefferson, G. and H. Sacks. 1977. The preference for self-correction in the organization of repair in conversation. *Language* 53:361-82.

Suh, K.-H. and J.-H. Hong. 1999. "Ikey palo ku-ke-ya": wenkun cisi-eyse thayto cisi-lo ("This is it": From spatial to speaker-stance deixis). *Discourse and Cognition* 6(2):1-22. The Discourse and Cognitive Linguistics Society of Korea.

---

[11] An interesting research area, in this respect, would be the comparison of the Korean and Japanese medial and distal forms, given that some of the functions served by the Korean medial form *ku* seem be covered by the Japanese distal forms *ano* or *are* (Cook 1993, Kitano 1999).

The Switching Between desu/masu Form and Plain Form: From the Perspective of Turn Construction

MAERI MEGUMI

University of Southern California

1. Introduction

The idea of politeness being a universal phenomenon has been spotlighted since Brown and Levinson's (1987) theory of politeness[1]. In their book "Politeness: Some universals in language usage," the Japanese *keigo* system, particularly referent honorifics, is considered to be one of the negative politeness strategies; Japanese *keigo* is said to be used to "give deference," which is classified as one of the negative politeness strategies in their theory. They additionally claim that some referent honorific forms "originate as productive outputs of face-preserving strategies" (1987: 278), thereby suggesting that their theory is applicable to the Japanese language.

However, Ide (1989) and Matsumoto (1988, 1989) point out that Brown and Levinson's theory of politeness is not quite applicable to the Japanese language, because it neglects the aspects of social conventions which play a crucial role in the use of *keigo* in Japanese. Ide argues that *keigo* is not merely used as a politeness strategy in terms of Brown and Levinson, but it has a role to

---

[1] They discuss "politeness" in relation to the notions of "face" and "face threatening acts(FTAs)." "Face" is divided into "positive face" and "negative face" where the former is the desire to be approved by others, and the latter is that of not being impeded by others. Corresponding to these notions of face are "positive politeness strategies" and "negative politeness strategies" where the former are used in order to attain the hearer's positive face, and the latter for satisfying the hearer's negative face. FTAs are acts that "run contrary to the face wants of the addressee and/or the speaker." (Brown and Levinson 1987:65)

206

demonstrate that the speaker "knows his or her expected place in terms of group membership (in-group and out-group), role structures (relative status, power relationship, specific role relationship such as selling and buying), and situational constraints (formal and non-formal settings)" (1989: 241). She proposes that it is "discernment" rather than the speaker's volition to use politeness strategy that governs the speaker's choice of the use of *keigo* in Japanese. Matsumoto also rightly points out that "no utterance in Japanese can be neutral with respect to social context," (1989: 208) sharing the same view as Ide that Japanese *keigo* system should be considered in the framework of social settings and conventions rather than from the perspective of politeness strategy. Other scholars such as Hinds (1976), Mizutani and Mizutani (1987), and Niyekawa (1991) also investigated the Japanese keigo system extensively, and the indication is that the use of keigo is primarily determined by external social factors.

Those static factors are, however, not sufficient when looking at the phenomenon of the switching between honorific and non-honorific forms. Several studies attempted to explain the switching between honorific form and plain form from various perspectives. For example, Ikuta(1983) uses the idea of communicative distance, and Maynard (1991b,1993) approaches it from the perspective of discourse modality. Cook (1996), through a close examination of children's switching patterns between different forms, observes that the alternation seems to correspond to the awareness of public and private self. Most recently, Okamoto (1999) proposes that the mixture of honorific and non-honorific forms is to adjust the right degree of formality or deference. However, none of these studies investigates the pattern of the alternation from the perspective of turn construction.

In this paper, the speaker's alternation between non-honorific form, particularly desu/masu form, and plain form is closely examined using the methodology of conversation analysis. It will be argued that there is a pattern in the way the speaker mixes the two forms. Specifically, the speaker initially uses desu/masu form to reply to other participants, then switches to plain form as he starts expanding his presentation. Additionally, if he asks for some feedback from other participants, he switches back to desu/masu form.

2. Data and subjects

The data for this paper are from a naturally occurring conversation, which lasted for about six and half minutes. It was held among three native speakers of Japanese, T, N, and K in a TA (Teaching Assistant) office in the United States. T and N are female and K is a male speaker. At the time of the recording, T and N were TAs as well as graduate students, while K was an exchange (undergraduate) student. T and N were older than K (their age difference is at most five years). N had worked for a few years before she came to the United States after graduating from Z university in Japan. T had graduated from the same university

(Z university) but she came to the US immediately after graduation. K, on the other hand, still belonged to Z university and he was in the US as an exchange student at the time of this conversation. Although they have common ground in that they were either a graduate or a student of the same university in Japan, the three of them had never met one another prior to coming to the US.

3. Data Analysis

From Table 1 (see appendix), it is clear that while T and N use plain form almost entirely, K uses both desu/masu form and plain form. T and N's use of plain form throughout the conversation can be explained by the classic approaches which emphasize the influence of social factors, such as Hinds who says "the speaker does not use formal expressions with those people falling within a loosely defined group known as ingroup" and "a social superior does not use the formal style when speaking to a social inferior" (1976: 121). Since T and N were TAs in the same department, they were colleagues, and thus were considered to be in the same group (*uchi*). Therefore, they do not have to use formal expressions (desu/masu form) to each other. From T and N's point of view, K is their *koohai*, which is a "social inferior." Therefore, T and N do not have to use desu/masu form while talking to each other or while talking to K.

Explanations of social factors, however, cannot explain K's mixed use of plain form and desu/masu form. Hinds says "a social inferior is required to use the formal style when speaking to a social superior" (1987:121). However, K not only uses desu/masu form but also uses plain form. Other explanations such as Ikuta's idea of empathy and discourse coherency do not seem to be able to provide an adequate account for the observed switching pattern between desu/masu form and plain form either[2]. As we look at the data closely, however, there are some tendencies regarding when and where K uses desu/masu form, and in what circumstances K uses plain form.

In this paper, I will argue that K's switching between desu/masu form and plain form has a pattern. Namely, K initially uses desu/masu form in a short reply (such as "soo desu ne", "soo desu ka") to remarks made by T and/or N. Then, when he develops or elaborates on his opinion after providing a short reply, he tends to use plain form. Also, if he tries to get some feedback or to seek an agreement from T or N, then he again employs desu/masu form.

3-1. Desu/masu form in short replies

---

[2] Ikuta(1983) claims that the place where the switching between different forms occurs corresponds with the transition of context spaces, where "context space" is defined by Reichman (1987:47) as "a group of utterances that refers to a single issue or episode." However, the data analyzed here indicates that it is not necessarily the case.

When K speaks to other speakers (T/N) in the form of relatively short replies (e.g., "soo desu ne" (that's right), "soo desu ka"(is that so?/is that right?), etc.), K never uses plain form. There are twelve instances of his short answer to T and/or N in the data; all of them have desu/masu form. (line 25, 66, 116, 118, ,174,181, 192, 219, 224, 260, 269) Within these twelve instances, six instances are his use of "soo desu ne" (in line 26, 66, 179, 181, 192, and 219). The phrase "soo desu ne" is usually interpreted as a reply of agreement: "soo desu" meaning "that is so", and "ne" being a marker of seeking an agreement[3]. In fact, at least two different functions of "soo desu ne" can be distinguished in K's speech in our data. One is a reply showing an agreement to the question or inquiry from other speakers, and the other functions more like a filler.[4]

For example, we observe K's "soo desu ne" in line 26 as a reply to T's question in line 15, 16,19 and 22-24.

```
15    T:                                                      [demo
16          kekkyoku tatoeba kimurakun ga sa:=
            "but, after all, for example, if you(Kimura-kun)..."
17    K:                  un
18    K:    =hai=
            "yes"
19    T:    =sooyuu no mo mitashi amerika ni kite soojanai no mo=
20    K:                                              hai
21    K:    =hai
22    T:    mita wake desho?
            "(you ) saw those (types of Japanese women) and those who are not like that, after you
            came to America, right?"
23    T:    demo yappari ketu sakki yappari jyosee wa nihon[jin
24          desu yo tte yuu ketsuron
            "but, after all, your conclusion is that, as for women, (you prefer) Japanese women?"
25    K:                                                    [SSS
26->        SSss::: Soo: desu ne=
            "Well... yeah.../let me think"
27    T:    =yappari ne [(sorya sooyone)
            "As I thought, (that's so, isn't it?)"
28    K:              [toyuuka maa (.) ss:: Nnn: (.) nanteen
29          desu ka sore wa (.5) yappari (1.5) NNuun betsumni
            "Rather, well, nn ..how can I put it? That's.. as you see, well, it's not that .."
```

---

[3] The function of the particle "ne" will be discussed later.

[4] There seems to be a subtle difference in pronouncing these types of "soo desu ne." The agreement type has a short "ne" in the end, where as the filler type has a little longer "ne(:)" Also they often seem to have different prosodic features: while the former has a stronger stress on the place of "so:" and "ne" does not have a strong sound, in the latter a stronger stress is on "ne".

```
30   N:                                 huhhhu
31   K:   kochira no hito o hiteesuru toka sooyuuno wa ISsai
32        nain desu yo kochirano hito o chanto kooteetekini
33   T:                    un
34   K:   kangaerun desu kedo (.) yappri (.) saigo no
35   T:                                              un
36   K:   bimyoona kotoba no mondai toka yappari nijyuunannenkan
37   T:                              un
38   K:   [toka ikitekita dojyoono chigai de
```
"I have nothing against women here (in the US), you know, I do think about
women here positively, but, as you know, because in the end (there are) problems
regarding the subtle language differences , and because the environment in
which I grew up for over twenty years is different (from theirs) ,..."
```
39   T:   [u:n
40   N/T: un
41   K:   yappari [chigauka na:
```
"as you see, I think/wonder if(American women are) different..."

In this instance, it seems that K does not have his answer ready immediately after T asks him a question. This is evidenced by his long s-sound
"ssss::::" in line 25-26 before he finally utters "soo desu ne" in line 26. Also,
even after he starts speaking, K exhibits a lot of pauses between words and
phrases. (line 28-29) Therefore, this "soo desu ne" in line 26 seems to function
as a filler[5]; he needs more time for organizing his thoughts and deciding what to
say. This "soo desu ne," therefore, can be interpreted as an equivalent of "well,
let me think" in English. Interestingly, however, this does not mean that the
"soo desu ne" in line 26 does not function as an agreement marker. Notice that T
replies to K's "soo desu ne" by saying "yappri ne" (as (I) thought) in line 27.
Prior to this section, T, N, K talked about how Japanese men seem to prefer
Japanese women due to their (excessive) feminine appeal. In fact, T and N, who
are both Japanese women, seem to hold a rather negative view on the kind of
women who assert the feminine side and try to flatter. Then N says "demo dan-
see kara shitara ... sooyuu hito no hoo ga ii no kana" (but I wonder if those
women (who flatter) are preferable from a man's point of view) in line 8, 12, and
14. T comments in a rather sarcastic way ," ma sorede kawaigatte moraeru kara
tanoshiin janai no" (well, but they(those women who flatter) probably enjoy

---

[5] Mori (1999) suggests that, sometimes "soo desu ne" represents the speaker's strong agreement
while some other times "soo desu ne" is used to show a rather weak agreement. In the former case,
the phrase is immediately replied, and the speaker often continues to provide elaborate statements
that confirm his/her agreement. The latter type of "soo desu ne", on the other hand, is not usually
provided immediately as a reply. It often comes after some pause, or as a delayed reply. In this
particular case, the phrase is probably the latter case of "soo desu ne" (the one that shows only a
weak agreement).

themselves because they are liked (by men) by doing so (flattering)). Therefore, T's comment on "yappari ne" (as (I) thought) in line 27 to K's "soo desu ne" in line 26 must be interpreted that "as I thought, you too (as those majority of men do) prefer Japanese women because of their feminine behavior." T must have interpreted K's "soo desu ne" in line 26 as an agreement marker.

Probably noticing T's interpretation, K continues and says "to yuuka" in line 28 after T's "yappari ne." "To yuuka" is usually used to rephrase something uttered previously, so K seems to try to show that it is not because of the reason that T and N might think. This again shows that K used "soo desu ne" in line 26 as a filler rather than as an agreement marker, although it was taken as an agreement marker by T. This "soo desu ne" can be viewed as functioning both as a reply of agreement, and at the same time, as a filler. In either way, the form is desu/masu form; either way, this utterance is directly addressed to T.

Also, if we look at K's utterance in line 66, we see K's second use of "soo desu ne."

```
62   N: =amerikano otokono hito wa iiwayo ne: mattaku.
         "American men are good, aren't they, really?"
63   K:                                        un
64      [zen a ippantekini. =
         ".. generally speaking"
65   K: [(are?)
66-> K: =soo desu [ne.
         "That's right"
67   N:           [ma ippanron wa (.) ikenai to omou kedo.=
         "Well, (I) think generalization isn't good, but..."
68   K: =SS:: ma: ooooni shite (.) [ne?
         "Yeah... Well... (it is)often so,.. right?"
```

Even if K says in line 66 "soo desu ne," which is a reply to N's remark in line 62 and 64 where she says "America men are good, really, aren't they. Generally speaking," we again see that K is not completely agreeing with N. It becomes clear when we look at K's comment in line 68 where he says "ma: oooo ni shite " (well, (it is) often (so)), in other words, it is not always the case. Therefore, this "soo desu ne" seems to indicate K's at least partial agreement. It is addressed to N, and has desu/masu form.

Let us look at K's short reply other than "soodesu ne."

```
92   T: un tatoeba doa motteru toka sa: nanaka
         "yeah, for example, (they) hold the door or something.."
93   K: AAh [soo ne
         "Oh, that's so..."
```

```
94    T:  [sorede nihon ni kaeruto
```
"then, when (I) go back to Japan"
```
95    K:  Batan
```
"Slam!"
```
96      T: ne: depaato toka itte batan toka doa [me no mae de
97         shimerarechauto sonna toka omou kedo
```
"Right? When (I) go to the department store or something and if the door is shut
right in front of me, (I) feel 'oh, no'..."
```
98-> K:                                         [Arewa Arewa
99->    ii shuukan desu yo ne, tashikani
```
"That's.. that's a good custom, indeed"
```
100   T: u:n maa: sooyuu shuukan ga nai kara shikatanai kedo=
```
"uh-huh, well, it can't be helped since (we) don't have that kind of custom"
```
101   K: =to yuuka ma: tada nihon de wa angai jidoodoa ga ooi to
102      yuu
```
"Yeah, but, well, (there is a fact that) there are a lot more automatic doors than we
think..."

When K agrees with T's comment on the custom that American men hold the
door for women (line 92), K says "Are wa Are wa ii syuukan desu yo ne, tashi-
kani" (that is, that is, indeed, a good custom) in line 98-99. Again we see K uses
desu/masu form when commenting on the previous remark made by other participants.

The examples given so far are all the instances of either the reply functioning as a filler and/or showing K's (at least partial) agreement with other
participants. K also uses short replies in desu/masu form even when he does not
quite agree with T or N. In line 116 and 118, we see his repeated "soo desu ka" .

```
109   T: tatoeba mono o sa: [nanka tatoeba onnanoko ga mono o
110   K:                    [un
111   T: mottete sa: kaisha (.) toka dattara mata chotto
112   K:              un
113   T: chigatteru kamoshirenai kedo sa: (.) boku ga motteyaruyo
114   K:                                              un
115      tte anmari nai (.) nainjya nai=
```
"for example, like,... for example if a girl is carrying something, -- in the case of business
situations maybe things are different but -- there aren't many instances where (a man)
would say 'I'll carry it for you' , are there?"
```
116->K: =soo desu ka
```
"Is that so?"
```
117   T: =u:n=
```
"yeah"
```
118->K: =SOo desu ka?
```
"Is that SO? (Really?)"

```
119  K: [(Shiranai)
```
        ("I don't know")
```
120  T: [Kimurakun wa [yasashii kara::
121  N:              [yasashii kara::
```
        "You (Kimura-kun) ARE kind, so..."
```
122  K: iyaiya
```
        "no, no"

Here, he questions T's opinion (line 109-115) that there are not many Japanese
men who would offer help and say "I'll help you" if a girl was carrying something (heavy), by saying "soodesu ka" (Is that so?) twice in line 116 and 118 in a
relatively louder voice. The fact that K repeats the same phrase ("soo desu ka"
(Is that so?)) twice in louder voice appears to display K's strong disagreement
with T's claim. Despite his strong disagreement, however, the form of his
speech remains desu/masu form. And, instead of directly disagreeing with T
(e.g., saying "soojya nai to omoimasu yo" (I don't think so)), K uses a linguistic
form of an interrogative sentence that shows his strong doubt regarding the
validity of T's statement. Consequently K indicates that he does not quite agree
with the previous statement.

From these observations, one can see that even when the reply is used
in part as a filler, or a tool to show K's agreement or disagreement to the previous remark made by T and/or N, K never fails to use desu/masu form when he
comments on another participant's remarks.

3-2. Plain form in presenting opinion

Let us look at an example where K uses plain form in his presentation.

```
96   T: ne: depaato toka itte batan toka doa [me no mae de
97       shimerarechauto sonna toka omou kedo
```
         "Right? When (I) go to the department store or something and if the door is shut
         right in front of me, (I) feel 'oh, no'..."
```
98   K:                                      [Arewa Arewa
99       ii shuukan desu yo ne, tashikani
```
         "That's.. that's a good custom, indeed"
```
100  T: u:n maa: sooyuu shuukan ga nai kara shikatanai kedo=
```
         "uh-huh, well, it can't be helped since (we) don't have that kind of custom"
```
101  K: =to yuuka ma: tada nihon de wa angai jidoodoa ga ooi to
102      yuu
```
         "Yeah, but, well, (there is a fact that) there are a lot more automatic doors than we
         think..."
```
103  T: (ma: ne:)
```
         "Well, right"
```
104      (laughter)
```

```
105->K: dakara aayuukoto yaranakutemo ii koto ga ooi kara, kizui
106->    amari (.) kocchikite -zui kara hajimete kizuita.
         "That's why, because we don't have to do such a thing (holding a door) often; I
         noticed it for the first time when I came here. "
107      (3.0)
```

Here, we see his initial response in the form of desu/masu in line 98-99. ("Are wa Are wa ii syuukan desu yo ne.") However, when he adds something on this remark in line 101-102 and 105-106, (i.e., the reason Japanese men do not hold the door for women is that there are more automatic doors than we think in Japan so that he never thought of holding a door for other people; he noticed it for the first time after he came here (to the US)), he never uses desu/masu form. In these, K uses quotative form in line 102, plain form "ooi" (many) in the subordinate clause in line 105, and ends his statement with a plain form predicate "kizuita" (noticed) in line 106.

Let us look at another instance where K initially makes a reply in desu/masu form but then switches to plain form as he elaborates on his argument.

```
69  N:                         [yasa- yasashii desu
70      [yo ne:: karera. hhhh
        "They are kind, aren't they?"
71  T: [u::n
       "uh huh"
72  K: (tsch!)
73  K: Yasashisa no mondai tteiu no wa demo (.) iroiro aru
74      [desho
        "But, regarding yasashisa(kindness), there are various types, aren't there?"
75  N: [iroiro aru[yo ne
        "(There are) various types, yeah"
76  K:              [nihonshiki no yasashisa wa sakki no niu- ano
77                                                            un
78-> tanakasan mitainja nai kedo jigyoo de (.) wakaru hito
79      tte iwaretemo te o agenai gurai de
        "The Japanese style of kindness is -- it's not like Ms Tanaka talked about a few
        minutes ago but -- it's like no one raises their hand even when (the teacher asks) 'who
        knows the answer?' in a classroom situation."
80 T/N: [un
81  K: [DE otagai no futari toka no kominyukeeshon demo
82      ichiichi aishiteru dano nandano tte [kuchinidasu no ga
83  T:                                       [u:n
84  K: (2.0) tte jyanakute nanka=
        "And, in the communication between two, it's not like saying something like 'I love
        you' out loud all the time, but..."
```

```
85   T:  =ma: syuukan dakara ne=
         "Well, that's their habit I suppose.."
86   K:  =un moo ai kontaku- kondakuto to iuka moo (.5)
87 T/N:                      un
88-> K:  wakattereba iijanaika mitaina tokoro ga aru kara (2.0)
89       ma: dakara (.) chotto (.) ne? yasashisa no honshitsu ga
90   T:                      un
91-> K:  chigattarimo suru kedo
         "Yeah, it's like eye-contact or something like that, we feel it's okay as long
           as we understand each other's feelings, so,.. (it's) a bit (different), (it's) like the
           quality of kindness is different, but..."
```

As we discussed, K's initial reply to N's remark in line 69-70 has desu/masu form; his first statement in line 73-74 says "Yasashisa no mondai tte iuno wa demo (.) iroiro aru deshoo." (Regarding "kindness," there are various types of kindness.) Then K elaborates on his opinion on what is "yasashisa" (kindness, care), especially focusing on the Japanese style "yasashisa" (kindness) over line 76-91. In this elaboration of his argument, no desu/masu form appears in the rest of his statement. Instead, we observe his use of plain form. For example, he says "tanakasan mitainjya nai kedo," (not as the case of Ms Tanaka) in line 78, and "aru kara" (there is) in line 88.[6]

Let us look at one more example where K responds to T and/or N by means of a reply with desu/masu form, but then he uses plain form as he expands his argument.

```
191  N:  =koyoo no seido toka mo [zen zen chigau shi ne:
         "As for the system of employment, it is totally different, isn't it?"
192  K:          nn              [soo desu ne: moo hakkiri
193->    yuukoto ga (.) bitoku: tte iu toko aru kara nihon wa
194  T:          u:n                         u:n
195  K:  shikkari kakaete morau kawari ni amari kuchi ni wa
196  T:                      un
197->K:  waruikoto dasanai tte tokoro ga aru kara (.) kocchi wa
198  T:                      un
199  K:  betsuni (.) yameru kakugode tsugi yu- sugu
200      mitsuketeyaru kara tte kakugo de iitai koto iiau tte
201  T:                      un
202->K:  kanji aru kara,
```

---

[6] There may be a tendency for people to use plain form in certain subordinate clauses such as in -*kara, -kedo* clauses. However, the use of plain form is still optional and in our data, K does use desu/masu form in the subordinate clause in line 34 where he says " --kangaerun desu kedo(.) ..." Therefore, the use of K's plain form here constitute a valid data as his choice of plain form.

```
203  T:      un
```
"That's right. (Here) it is considered to be a virtue to say things directly; in Japan, we don't
say bad things, and in exchange for that, the company provides us with protection, but
here, it seems that (they) say anything they like to because they are ready to quit and find
a new job at any time..."

Here again we see his initial response in desu/masu form (line 192 "soo desu
ne:") but after that, as he presents a more detailed explanation on the different
employment system in Japan, he consistently uses plain form in line 193, 197,
202.

From these examples, there seems to be a pattern in K's speech in terms
of his switching between desu/masu form and plain form. Namely, he makes an
initial response in a relatively short form (such as "soo desu ne") using
desu/masu form. Then as he develops his arguments, he switches to plain form.

3-3. desu/masu form used in seeking an agreement

An example of desu/masu form used by K other than in short replies is seen in
line 242. From line 238 to 242, K presents his opinion just like the ones discussed above, using plain form. But this time, he ends it with desu/masu form.

```
236  N:   = saa moo otonanandakara tte iu kotoba tte nai[mon
237       ne::
```
"There is no such phrase like 'well, you are already adult,' is there?"
```
238                                              [ahh nee
239  K:   hajimekkara moo (1.0) ne heya wa [ataerareru shi
```
"Oh, right. They are given (their own) rooms from the beginning, and..."
```
240  N:                                   [(....) dashi
241       sore ni kurabetara maa nihon wa oya ni kakaeareteru
242->     uchiwa hontoni kodomo desu yo ne
```
".. compared to that, well, in Japan while they are protected by their parents, they are
still kids, aren't they?"
```
243  N:   un
```
"uh huh"

The difference between the environment of this particular ending and
the other ending where he used plain form is that, in line 242, he seems to be
seeking an agreement from the other participants, T and N. This is observed
from his use of sentence final particle "ne" after "desu yo" in line 243.

Cook (1992) talks about the function of "ne" and proposes that " the
particle *ne* directly indexes affective common ground between the speaker and
the addressee, that is, agreement in feeling between the speaker and the addressee. ... also *ne* indirectly indexes social acts such as requesting confirmation." (510) Therefore, in the instance of K's use of "ne" in line 242 indications
are that while he is presenting his opinion, "nihon wa oayni kakaerareteru

uchiwa hontoni kodomo desu yo" (in Japan, while (they are) supported by their parents, they are like kids) he is seeking agreement from T and N by the use of the sentence final particle "ne". In fact, N does provide an agreement reply to K, "un" (yeah/yes), in line 243.

If we compare this to the other places where K elaborates on his opinion, there are no other instances where he seeks an agreement from T and/or N. For example, in line 106, K completes his explanation on why Japanese men are usually unaware of the need to hold a door for other people, with his own experience that he himself was unaware of it until he came to the US. In line 167, he ends his statement with "omou" ((I) think) where he simply provides his impression on the ways his roommate deals with his parents. Therefore, he is not seeking by T or N's reply in these instances.

Thus, there is a pattern in K's speech styles. He responds to other participants with desu/masu form, often in the form of a short reply, which is usually a comment on their opinion. Then as he develops more explanation on the topic, he switches to plain form. But if he asks T or N's opinion directly, he then switches back to desu/masu form.

4. Summary and Conclusion

From the data analyzed, it is confirmed that social factors (e.g., *senpai/koohai* relationship, *uchi/soto* grouping, age, etc.) play an important role in their overall choice of desu/masu versus plain forms. We saw that T and N, who are in higher status than K, have no hesitation in constantly using plain form in the conversation. On the other hand, K, who is in lower status, switches back and forth between desu/masu form and plain form. The alternation between these forms does not seem to be arbitrary. Although there are some exceptional cases[7], the speaker in lower status tends to use desu/masu form constantly when initially replying to other participants. Then, as he develops or elaborates on his opinion extensively, he uses plain form. If the speaker wants to receive some feedback from other participants, then again desu/masu form is used.

This study focused on the observation of the alternation between honorific and non-honorific speech styles using the methodology of conversation analysis. In this respect, I believe this paper offers a unique perspective and I hope it serves as a starting point for the future analysis of a wider range of data, and a deeper examination of the reasons behind the phenomenon.

---

[7] See Megumi (1999) for further discussion of these exceptional cases.

Appendix:

Table 1. The number (and %) of desu/masu form vs. plain form used

	desu/masu form	plain form
T	0/28 (0%)	28/28 (100%)
N	1/20 (5%)	19/20 (95%)
K	20/36 (55.56%)	16/36 (44.44%)

The predicates used in the following environments are excluded from the number above because of the reasons provided below.

1) V/Adj + *(t)te* : a form called *te*-form is required
2) V/Adj + *to* (quotative use of *to*), *to iu* : a quote of someone's phrase/thoughts
3) V/Adj + *tte* (quotative use of *–tte*), *tte iu* : a quote of someone's phrase/thoughts
4) V/Adj + *toka* : very strong tendency that plain form precedes *toka*
5) V/Adj modifying a Noun : plain form is required before the Noun

On the other hand, the predicates used in subordinate clauses (such as in – *kara*, - *kedo*, - *shi* clauses) are counted since there are instances of desu/masu form preceding these conjunctions as well as plain form. For their mode of casualty, contraction forms (such as –*chau*) are counted as a plain form in this data.

The treatment of "deshoo"

I have excluded the number of instances where the form "deshoo" is used by female speakers from Table 1, because there seems to be a problem as to whether "deshoo" should be counted as an instance of the use of desu/masu form or as an instance of plain form. According to Makino, (1989: 100) "deshoo" is considered to be a formal version of "daroo," an auxiliary verb indicating "the speaker's conjecture which is not based on any particular information or evidence." From this perspective, "deshoo" should be categorized as desu/masu form, and the form of "deshoo" is, obviously, desu/masu form. However, there is some difference in the use of "deshoo" depending on whether the form is used by a male speaker of a female speaker.

It has been pointed out by various scholars (Maynard, Niyekawa, among others) that there are some differences between male and female speakers' speech style. As Mizutani and Mizutani (1978: 75) states," *deshoo* becomes *daroo* in men's speech, while *deshoo* is used in women's speech." Because of this difference, it does not seem to be adequate to count the use of "deshoo" by a female speaker as an instance of the use of desu/masu form. For this reason, although T actually uses "deshoo" once in line 14, it is counted neither as a plain form or as a polite form.

References

Brown, P. and Levinson, S. C. 1987. *Politeness: Some universals in language usage*. Cambridge University Press. Cambridge.

Cook, H. M. 1992. Japanese Language Socialization: Indexing the Modes of Self. In *Discourse Processes 22*. pp171-197.

Cook, H. M. 1996. Meanings of non-referential indexes: A case study of the Japanese sentence-final particle *ne*. In *Text 12 (4)*. pp507-539.

Hinds, J. 1976. *Aspect of Japanese Discourse Structure*. Tokyo: Kaitakusha.

Ide, S. 1989. Formal forms and discernment: two neglected aspects of universals of linguistic politeness. In *Multilingua 8-2/3*. pp223-248.

Ikuta, S. 1983. Speech level shift and conversational strategy in Japanese discourse. In *Language Sciences 5*. pp37-53.

Makino, S. and Tsutsui, M. 1989. *A Dictionary of Basic Japanese Grammar*. The Japan Times. Tokyo.

Matsumoto, Y. 1988. Reexamination of the universality of face: politeness phenomena in Japanese. In *Journal of Pragmatics 12*. pp403-426.

Matsumoto, Y. 1989. Politeness and conversational universals – observation from Japanese. In *Multilingua 8-2/3*. pp207-221.

Maynard, K S. 1991a. Discourse and Interactional Functions of the Japanese Modal Adverbs *Yahari/Yappari* In *Language Sciences 13*. pp 39-57.

Maynard, K S. 1991b. Pragmatics of discourse modality: A case of da and desu/masu forms in Japanese. In *Journal of Pragmatics 24*. pp381-392.

Maynard, K S. 1993. *Discourse Modality: Subjectivity, emotion and voice in the Japanese Language*. Amsterdam: Benjamins.

Megumi, M. 1999. The switching between desu/masu form and plain form: A pattern observed in a conversation in Japanese. Unpublished manuscript. The University of Iowa.

Mizutani, O and Mizutani, N. 1987. *How to be polite in Japanese*. The Japan Times. Tokyo.

Mori, J. 1999. Negotiating Agreement and Disagreement: Connective Expressions and Turn Construction. Amsterdam: John Benjamins.

Niyekawa, A. M. 1991. *Minimum essential politeness: A guide to the Japanese Honorific Language*. Koodansha International. Tokyo.

Okamoto, S. 1999. Situated politeness: manipulating honorific and non-honorific expressions in Japanese conversation. In *Pragmatics 9*. pp51-74.

Reichman, R. 1978. Conversational Coherence. In *Cognitive Science 2.4*. pp283-327.

Stance Marking in the Collaborative Completion of Sentences: Final Particles as Epistemic Markers in Japanese[1]

EMI MORITA

University of California, Los Angeles

1. Introduction

Over the past few decades, a considerable number of studies have been conducted on collaborative production of a single syntactic unit by multiple speakers (e.g. Goodwin & Goodwin 1987; Lerner 1991; Sacks 1992). This phenomenon has also been examined in Japanese discourse (e.g. Ono & Suzuki 1996; Hayashi & Mori 1998; Lerner & Takagi 1999, Hayashi 2000). For, as Sacks (1992) pointed out early on, more may be going on in collaborative completion than simply one speaker filling in the syntactic blanks of another speaker's utterances. Such collaboration, for example, has often been interpreted as displaying congruent understanding - i.e.,

---

[1] I would like to thank Charles Goodwin and Emmanuel Schegloff for their helpful advice on the early versions of this paper. In addition, I am grateful to Marianne Celce-Murcia, Haruko Cook and Shoichi Iwasaki for their thoughtful comments and support. Finally, I wish to offer special thanks to Makoto Hayashi and Don Favareau, whose careful readings of my later drafts greatly helped me clarify my thoughts.

participants' alignment with each other (Goodwin & Goodwin 1987) and as a device which allows 'private territory' to be negotiated (Hayashi & Mori, 1998).

Similarly, in reviewing my Japanese data, I find that there are cases in which utterance completion includes attitudinal markers (in particular, final particles), which indicate that second speakers are not merely "voicing" propositions attributable to the first speaker, but are, in fact, themselves "selecting the sentiments that are being expressed and the words in which they are encoded" - Goffman's definition of *authorship* (1981, 144).

In these cases, the second speaker is contributing some content of their own to the utterance rather than merely filling in syntactic blanks. The purpose of this study is to investigate how Japanese speakers use the final particles, *yo*, *ne* and *yone* as stance markers to mark relative degrees of *authorship* and, as I attempt to show in this paper, relative degrees of *authority* with which they collaboratively complete a given utterance.

Traditional views of the final particles *yo* and *ne* usually describe these particles in terms of speakers' "access to information," or in terms of a proposed "sharedness" of information or of feeling (Kamio 1990; Cook 1990, 1992). I would like to propose in this paper, however, that such concepts as differential "access to information" and "sharedness of information or feeling" presuppose a degree of omniscience (or mind-reading) on the part of one or both participants that can never be reliably established.

Instead, I propose here a view of final particles based on interaction. According to this perspective, final particles do not mark the content of the proposition, but mark the speaker's stance - i.e., the interactional position that a speaker wants to set up *with another speaker* in relation to a given utterance.

1.2 Goffman's Notion of "Authorship" and Beyond

Goffman (1981) shows how a change in alignment between participants in a conversation (both towards each other and towards the utterances of the talk itself) is a naturally occurring feature of talk-in-interaction. As a result, he proposes that dyadic, "speaker-hearer" models of communication fail to adequately account for the various "statuses" and "alignments" in a conversation between which the participants continually "jump back and forth" (156).

For instance, Goffman notes that the traditional idea of a "speaker" can include at least three possible *production formats*: these he delineates as *animator* (simply: "the sounding box"), *principal* (someone whose position of responsibility is "represented" by an utterance), and – the status which we are most concerned with here – *author* (which Goffman has defined as the participant who has "selected the [current] sentiments that are being expressed and the words in which they are encoded") (144).

A change in production formats constitutes what Goffman calls a change in *footing* – which is defined by Goffman as: "a change in the alignment we take up to ourselves and the others present as expressed in the way we manage the production or reception of an utterance" (128). Using a similar perspective in examining English data, Antaki, Díaz, and Collins (1996) have argued that collaborative completion, "to be successfully accepted, must maintain the footing on which the original utterance was made, and it is the original speaker, in the third turn of the sequence, who makes that decision" (153).

Yet this third-turn response often is more than just the first speaker's "evaluation" of the second speaker's performance of the job of 'footing keeper' as Antaki et al. (1996) claim. Rather, interactional statuses of the interlocutors may change due to the nature of the second speaker's contribution and subsequent interactional sequences may change as a result. For example, in much collaborative completion, the second speakers may be merely displaying their understanding of the entire sentence before it is completed (filling in syntactic and semantic blanks), and in these cases the degree of the second speaker's "authorship" is minimal or not at all.

However, if the second speaker is expressing his/her own stance towards the proposition and using this completion opportunity to make his/her own claim, the first speaker may, in turn, respond to that stance display. Therefore, to determine whether a collaborative completion is being used to 'change' or merely to 'continue' the flow of a conversation, we need to examine which interactional stances are being taken by each of the participants regarding the mutual alignment.

Hayashi (2000) has shown that in Japanese discourse, participants collaboratively complete utterances and in so doing not only display their agreement with the other, but also achieve a variety of social actions, such as claiming independent understanding of a situation and negotiating shared perspectives through assertion of their own stances. Hayashi shows several types of clusters of utterance-final elements such as *yo ne/na, mon ne/na* or tag-question-like elements as devices for such interactional achievement; each marks a speaker's own assertion as well as elicits agreement or confirmation from the interlocutor.

One aspect of epistemic stance that is particularly salient in Japanese discourse involves speakers' claim about their own experiential access to a particular piece of information. These stances are marked differently in different languages. In English such stances may be marked by clauses such as "As you say," "I'm not sure, but..." "I heard that..." "Is it true that..?" etc., which are canonically positioned sentence initial (though in collaborative completion of sentences, such clauses usually do not appear). In Japanese, on the other hand, such displays of epistemic stance can be marked at utterance final position by particles such as *yo* and *ne* to indicate the speaker's stance in the collaborative completion of sentences as well. Thus inclusion of various utterance final particles suggests that collaborative completion and other attitudinal markers are helpful linguistic resources with which to analyze speakers' dynamic change of alignment during interaction.

This is why Goffman's notion of authorship may be insufficient for explaining what is going on in collaborative completion, since Goffman treats the role of "speaker" (or *author* or "produc[er]…of an utterance") as a role that is fulfilled by one person at a time.[2] Looking at my Japanese data, I find that many times authorship cannot be either claimed by nor guaranteed to any one speaker alone. For "authorship" of an utterance can rarely, if ever, be attributed as the product of a single interlocutor, but rather, reflects a joint achievement that "emerges from, and is situated in, the talk of others, to which it is inextricably linked" (Goodwin, 1995; p. 234).

Moreover, even in the collaborative achievement of establishing joint authorship, the alignment of both speakers is not always symmetrical. Thus, we need to expand upon Goffman's notion of authorship (as regards relationship between a speaker and a proposition of an utterance) and incorporate into our explanations as well the notion of *authority* - i.e., the relationship between the speakers regarding the relative degree of autonomy (or dependency) with which one advances a given utterance.

Focusing on the use of final particles in collaborative completion, I find that Japanese speakers claim different stances toward an utterance in their "displaying congruent understanding" and "alignment." I call such positions marked "stances of authority." *Authority* is a stance that has to do, not so much with access to information *per se*, but with the *relations* that speakers want to put themselves in *with each other* in regard to the utterances they are exchanging.

It is important not to think of this new term as referring to power relations, in terms of shared knowledge, or as completely determining participants' roles in interaction. Rather, by *authority*, I mean something closer to an acknowledgement that there is nothing that one can "say" without invoking at least tacit participation of one's interlocutor. In this sense, authority is the obligatory denotation that one's relations are indeed social -i.e., just as one can only claim degrees of social autonomy and never perfect independence or autonomy, so too is this true of one's utterances. One cannot say, "Here is my utterance. You must take it and do what I want you to do with it." Rather, all one can do is to take a stance toward one's utterance hoping that by doing so, one can attach to it some "persuasive

---

[2] This is not to say that one person does not adopt multiple roles simultaneously (such as author, principal and animator as Goffman clearly states). Rather, my point is that one role can be adopted simultaneously by multiple speakers.

force", "warrant for action", or "commanding influence" (all definitions of *authority* according to Webster's College Dictionary).

Likewise, autonomy and dependency here are not being thought of in a social or psychological sense, but strictly as regards ongoing interaction - how much response (if any) on the part of one's interlocutor is needed to *pragmatically* (not just syntactically) "complete" the utterance.

In other words, although authorship is negotiable, there are concerns - at least in Japanese discourse - as to what degree of interactional sovereignty speakers are claiming in proposing their various alignments -- to put it the other way around, how much "reliance" second speakers are extending to first speakers in the negotiation of such claims.[3]

In this paper I expand upon Goffman's notions of *production formats* and *authorsihp* to examine the various types of *stance* that each speaker in a collaborative completion takes. In particular, I will examine the specific type of epistemic stance that indicates speakers' *authority* in situating the claim they are advancing. For, although "authorship" attempts to establish ownership of a given utterance, "authority"- in considering the dialogic nature of discourse - attempts to mark the interactional nature of a speech action for any given utterance in relation to the interlocutors.

I want to propose that Japanese, unlike English, overtly distinguishes degrees of authority in collaboratively completed sentences, and does so by the use of final particles *ne*, *yo* and *yone* to mark epistemic stance. These displays of various degrees of authority result in different uptake of the first speaker- i.e., different interactional consequences appear in the third position after the collaborative completion, since such a marking of stance towards an utterance elicits different actions from the other party.

In the section that follows, several types of collaborative completion are identified based on stances marked in the utterances of the second speaker.

2. Data

The data for this study was videotaped in 1994 by Shoichi Iwasaki for the 'Northridge Earthquake Conversation Project' (JEQ) and consists of face-to-face conversations between Japanese native speakers. These speakers were previously unknown to each other, although they all had experienced the earthquake in Los Angeles in 1994.

3. Analysis

Japanese has various final particles, and of those, the particle *ne* appears most frequently. The particle *yo* appears less frequently and both are studied as a pair since they were thought to be complementarily distributed (Kamio

---

[3] See also discussions on "pragmatic constraints" in collaborative completion by Ono & Yoshida 1996 and Hayashi & Mori 1998.

1990, Maynard 1997, Katagiri 1995; but see Kinsui 1993 for a semantic point of view). I discuss the final particles *ne*, *yo*, and the combined form *yo-ne* in an attempt to show that the ways in which final particles function in collaborative completion are part of their larger function as an interactional resource in Japanese discourse.[4] This resource is the marking of epistemic stance. In other words, by manipulating the final particles, a speaker can show their own stance toward their utterance *in respect to the other interlocutor*. These interlocutors, in turn, actively negotiate with the speaker regarding the degrees of authority that are being advanced.

3.1 *ne*

Example (1) is a conversation between A (female) and T (male). Both are graduate students who experienced the Northridge earthquake. Here, A asks T whether Japanese boys of his generation would attempt to disguise their fear in a crisis situation like an earthquake. T confirms that is so, and offers two contrasting hypothetical instances of how he and Japanese boys of his generation might behave in such a situation:

```
(1) (JEQ1:10)
1   T:  ma     onnanoko to   sh<   onnanoko to    ne:?
        EMPH   girls     with        girls     with  FP
        'Say, with girls, with girls..'

2   A:  n:n.
        mm
3       ...

4   T:  nanka nanka futari kkiri dattari shitara ne:?
        SOF   SOF   two    just  CP-REP  do-COND FP
        'if (I am) somehow alone (with a girl), you know?'

5       (1.0)

6       nn. nanka nanka henna koto  kangae tari,
        nn  SOF   SOF   weird thing think  REP

7       soo  yuu u u,
        such say

8   A:  [nain].
```

---

[4] Tanaka (to appear) demonstrates how the final particle *ne* functions differently in turn-taking operations, depending upon its various positions within a turn (turn-initial, turn-internal, turn-final, and occupying an entire turn). Because of space limitations in this paper, I am focusing on *ne* in its turn-final position only, though my view of *ne* as a stance-marker is consistent across occurrences of *ne* in all other positions as well.

```
9   T:  [yatara]kowagatta furi demo suru kamoshinnnaikedo.
        unduly scared-AUX show SOF do    MOD         CONN
```

   'I may think something weird or maybe pretend to be ridiculously
   scared but...'

```
10  A:  nnnnn.
```

```
11⇒T:  nnn. soojanai toki wa otoko to issho   dattarito..
        so CP-NEG case TOP boy with together CP REP
```

```
12      dattari shitara [ne]?
        CP REP   do COND  FP
```
   'Otherwise, if, for example, (I were) with boys...'

```
13⇒A:  [muda] desu mon [[ne: kowagatte misete]] mo ne:.
        no.use CP   thing FP scared-AUX show       HP FP
```
   '...it is no use, right? even if you pretend to be scared, right?'

```
14  T:                  [[yappari xxxxxx]
                        as.expected
```
                        'as you expect....'

Previous studies of *ne* have treated this particle as an evidential marker
of speakers' or hearers' access or relevance to information (Kamio 1990,
Okamoto 1993, Maynard 1997). Cook (1988, 1990, 1992) has argued that
from the standpoint of psychological motivation *ne* is an indexical which
carries social meaning - i.e., "affective common ground." However, Tanaka
(to appear) objects to such views and, from the standpoint of conversation
analysis, proposes *ne* as a turn-management device.

   My view of the function of *ne* is that it advances a stance of "weak" or
"incomplete" authority in relation to the other speaker. This is the type of
stance that requires participatory uptake by the other speaker. My view is
that it is important to distinguish that such stances are being taken by the
speaker not toward the information itself but *toward the other speaker*.

   For example, in line 13, A's use of *mon* before *ne* marks her assertion
that she can emotionally relate to T in his hypothetical situation.
Nonetheless, she requests validation for her claim using *ne* to mitigate the
force of asserting something only her interlocutor truly has the authority to
claim. Thus A's use of *ne* situates her stance as a "limited authority"
regarding the issue being discussed (A convergent view of the function of
mon ne appears in Hayashi 2000).

Thus, although A can assert her independent understanding of such hypothetical situation as a human being, and as someone who understands male-female relations, because A is not a male, and because she cannot speak with authority about the inner thoughts of T, she can not claim symmetrical authority with T. Therefore, the degree of authority which A is claiming for herself is one which *invites validation by her interlocutor*. This I feel is the epistemic function of *ne*.

In the next example, the speaker displays his/her stance as an authority whose claims do not require such validation or mitigation.

3.2 *yo*

Final particles have also been studied from psychological and cognitive perspectives. Some researchers claim that *yo* indicates a speaker's strong conviction or assertion (Makino and Tsutui 1986) or that it indicates that certain information is more accessible to the speaker than to the hearer, and hence *yo* and *ne* are complementarily distributed (Kamio 1990, Maynard 1997).

My claim is that *yo* marks an epistemic stance of authority on the part of the speaker that is not open to negotiation on the part of the hearer. *Yo* does not require any approval or confirmation from the hearer, and hence marks a stance of "strong" authority on the part of the speaker. Since this stance is essentially one of non-collaboration, it is not surprising that *yo* very rarely is found at the end of a second speaker's collaborative contribution.

Note that in the example below, *yo* does not occur in the second speaker's (H's) completion. Rather, it occurs in the first speaker's (A's) utterance in the third turn, the place where H's contribution can be evaluated.

(2) (JEQ2:1)
```
1  H:  demo haashii hooru tte  kekkoo huru soo
       but  Hershey Hall  QUO  pretty old  looks

2         ...hurui desho are?
             old   MOD   that

       'But Hershey Hall looks pretty old, it's old, isn't it?'

3⇒ A:  are hurui-n desu kedo are  wa<
       that old     CP   but  that TOP
       'That is old but that is..'

4⇒ H:  taishin    koozoo<
       aseismatic structure
       'Aseismatic structure- '
```

```
5⇒ A:  nn shiteru-n desu yo.
       mm do-ASP-SE CP    FP

6      chanto shiteru kara:.  anmari,
       well   do-ASP  because not.so.much

7      ...nanka betsuni       huan  wa   nakatta
          SOF   particularly  worry TOP  not.exist:PAST

8      tte iu  ka, [kichinto shiteru tte].
       QUO say or   well     do-ASP  QUO
```

'Mm, (it) has (aseismatic structure). Since it has (aseismatic structure), not so much... I would say I didn't worry so much. I heard it's well (built).'

Thus, in my functional analysis, the final particle *yo* is a marker which indicates autonomy in a given speech action. This view is demonstrated by the above example, where one speaker's attempt at joint alignment towards the utterance is preemptively evaluated to be correct in a way that makes further negotiation impossible. For it is important to remember that the function of these final particles as stance markers is forward-looking. That is, they set the ground for subsequent interactions (as we have seen above in the case of *ne*). Thus the use of the final particle *yo* does not invite negotiation and by so doing advances a stance of "strong authority" towards one's interlocutor.

3.3 *yo-ne*

As Takubo and Kinsui (1997) have pointed out, it is problematic to think of *yo* and *ne* as markers of "sharedness" since the existence of the compound final particle *yo-ne* would imply that the information that it refers to is simultaneously "shared" and "not shared". But if we consider *yo* and *ne* as stance markers for *relative degrees of authority* - and not "sharedness" of "feeling" or "information" - we can see how in the combination of *yo* and *ne*, these two final particles do not necessarily contradict each other.

In the above two examples, we have seen how the particle *yo* marks a stance of strong authority and the particle *ne* marks a stance of relatively weak authority. Not surprisingly, compound particle *yo-ne* partakes of *both* stances simultaneously, mitigating the force of assertions which may otherwise be considered too direct.

In example (3), a male student H and a female student A are discussing how the American service sector coped with the earthquake, concluding that in general, the Americans provided good service. In the following segment, they talk about the service sector in Europe, since both H and A had been in England for a while:

(3) (JEQ#2:14)

```
1    H:   Yooroppa nanka sugai @@@
          Europe    SOF   terrible
          'Such as Europe is terrible, hahaha'

2    A:   @@@

3    H:   saabisu seeshin    mo,
          service mentality  also
          '(their) service mentality also...'

4⇒ A:    zero desu yo ne?
          zero CP   FP FP
          'does not exist.'

5⇒ H:    zero desu yo ne?
          zero CP   FP FP
          'does not exist'

6    A:   kaitai-n        dat-tara kae     yo tte kanji.
          want.to.buy-SE  CP-COND  buy-IMP FP QUO like
          'It's like "if you want to buy, just buy!" '

7    H:   nnn
          nnn
```

H starts his turn by stating his opinion about service in general in Europe. A comes in and collaboratively finishes H's sentence in line 4 using the final particle *yo*. A presents her utterance not only as her understanding of what H is going to say, but also as assertion of her independent understanding of the issue discussed here. Her marking of this statement with *yo* here indicates that she can state her opinion independently, but at the same time, A also marks her speech action with *ne*, indicating this action needs an uptake from H, possibly as a politeness strategy.

Thus A displays weak authority in this statement, eliciting H's confirmation by adding *ne*. At line 5, H validates A's contribution by repeating the exact phrase that A has contributed in line 4. Thus, authority toward the claim advanced is confirmed mutually by both speakers, and hence joint authorship is taking place, exactly as the same alignment is established interactively.

In this case, both speakers are claiming authority toward the utterance, though not necessarily "against" the claims of the other. Rather, they co-construct equal authority in sequentially organized interaction. In the Japanese language, final particles, as I have shown in this section, play an important role in enabling such perspectival co-construction.

Note here, too, how my notion of authoritative stance taking is convergent with Hayashi's (2000) notion of the co-construction of a shared perspective - i.e., "by soliciting confirmation and agreement from the first speaker [with *ne*], the second speaker proposes his/her utterance as a collaborative (rather than an individual) assertion of a shared perspective, for which the first speaker's validation is indispensable" (158).

With this concept in mind, let's examine how even "bare" forms of collaborative completion use a "zero marker" to mark stance. This stance will be a stance of neither greater *nor* lesser authority – but of *symmetrical* authority and authorship. That is, the stance being advanced will be one in which both speakers are "exactly on the same wavelength" and one in which the marking of "authority" is not a relevant issue.

3.4 Bare Form

While I have shown that Japanese speakers mark stances of authority toward the on-going speech action by using final particles such as *ne* and *yo*, I want to further claim that *not* marking an utterance with any such final particle (shown here as ∅) is also a display of particular type of stance. This is a stance of authoritative symmetry - i.e., "I am taking the stance that the alignment between us is so complete, that questions of who has more "authority" are not even an issue." Let us consider the next example:

(6) (JEQ6, p.11)
```
1   A:  rikuchi ga kooyatte...zure tari nanka.. shite (.)
        land    SUB like.this  slide REP SOF      do-TE

2       shindoo sureba(.)[sono bun<  sono .. shindoo ga:
        quake   do-COND   that amount that   quake   SUB

        'If the land slides or something and quakes, to that extent, the
        quake...'

3   B:                          [mm mh.

4⇒B:    ..tsutawa [tte:∅,
          be.conveyed:TE
          '... is conveyed.'

5⇒A:              [tsutawatte    umi  ni tsutawatte      de
                  be.conveyed:TE ocean to be.conveyed:TE then
                  '...is conveyed, is conveyed to the ocean, then...'

6       [[tsunami ga (.)
          Tsunami SUB
```

```
7    naru   kanoosee   mo   aru  to  omou-n desu kedo.
     become possibility also exist QUO think-SE CP but
     'I think there is also a possibility of it becoming a Tsunami, but...'

8  B: [[ee.
      'uh huh.'
```

The lack of fluency in line 2 of A's speech and the pause in line 4 suggest that A is having trouble finding words for the forthcoming segment. In line 4, B offers an anticipated predicate for A's sentence. This is accepted by A who repeats that segment when he resumes his speech at line 5. My view of the stance marking function of final particles reveals that even their absence in collaborative completion marks a stance. Here, no confirmation or validation is asked for and no claims need to be mitigated, because the stance that is being marked is one of perfect alignment of symmetry. Here no one speaker is claiming more authority than the other. Thus we find that the bare form marks an active orientation toward symmetry that may go far beyond merely filling in syntactic blanks.

4. Conclusion

As Cook reminds us (1992), capturing non-propositional aspects of language (such as attitude or feeling towards the content of speech, epistemic stance, etc) offers a key to understanding participants' actions in conversation. Likewise, here I propose that in Japanese, relations that speakers want to put themselves in with each other in regard to any given proposition are marked in talk-in-interaction by the speaker's stance.

I have argued that it is important to distinguish that such stances are being taken on the part of the speaker not toward the information itself but toward the other speaker. In other words, speakers position themselves in different degrees of authority, situating themselves as candidates for collaboration to various degrees.

Considering final particles as markers of epistemic stance, we can see how a second speaker can claim different degrees of authority by deploying this structural resource. Also, not marking the utterance with any stance marker indicates the speaker's attitude of "no attitude" toward the claim. I also found that consequences of marking different stances appear as different uptake by the first speaker. *Interactional stance-taking* is critical to this interpretation. Because under this perspective, final particles mark the speaker's stance regarding the *relations* that the speaker wants to set up *with another speaker* in relation to a given utterance.

It does NOT mark the relation of that speaker to "what the other speaker knows" or to "what quantity of (or access to) information" either of them has. These last two things are not the type of thing that could ever be known between participants, much less marked. Interaction is something that happens between two human beings - not between propositions or the accessibility of information that one guesses is in the other speaker's mind.

The finding of this paper, therefore, is a suggestion about the ways in which speakers of Japanese display their ongoing relations of authority to each other using final particles. This in turn provides a new interactional perspective to interpreting Japanese final particles, i.e., how participants of a conversation situate their authority towards their utterances - and, by extension, towards each other - in moment-to-moment interaction.

Appendix 1: Transcript conventions

[The point where overlapping talk starts
(0.0)   length of silence in tenths of a second
::   lengthened syllable
?/./,   rising/falling/continuing intonation respectively
( )   unintelligible stretch
@   laughter

Appendix 2: Symbols used in the interlinear gloss

AUX	auxiliary	CP	various forms of copula verb be
CONN	connective	EMPH	emphasis marker
FP	final particle	HP	highlighting
IMP	imperative form	MOD	modal
N	nominalizer	NEG	negative
QUO	quotative marker	REP	representative
SOF	softening word	SE	sentence extender
SUB	subject	TE	-te(conjunctive) form

References

Antaki, Charles; Diaz, Felix, and Collins, Alan F. 1996. Keeping your footing: Conversational completion in three-part sequences. *Journal of Pragmatics*. 25:151-171.

Cook, H. M. 1988. Sentential particles in Japanese conversation: a study of indexicality. Ph.D. Dissertation. University of Southern California.

Cook, H. M. 1990. The sentence-final particle *ne* as a tool for cooperation in Japanese conversation. In H. Hoji. Ed. *Japanese/Korean Linguistics* 29-44.

Cook, H. M. 1992. Meanings of non-referential indexes: A case study of the Japanese sentence-final particle *ne*. *Text,* 12 (4) 507-539.

Costello, R. et al. (Eds.). 1991. *Random House Webster's college dictionary.* New York: Random House.

Goffman, E. 1981. *Forms of Talk.* Philadelphia; University of Pennsylvania Press.

Goodwin, C. 1995. Co-constructing meaning in conversations with an aphasic man. *Research on Language and Social Interaction* 28:233-60.

Goodwin, C. & M. H. Goodwin. 1987. Concurrent operations on talk: Notes on the interactive organization of assessments. *IPRA Papers in Pragmatics* 1.1-54.

Hayashi, M. 2000. Practices in joint utterance construction in Japanese conversation. Doctral dissertation.

Hayashi, M. & J, Mori 1998. Co-construction in Japanese revisited. In N. Akatsuka, H. Hoji, S. Iwaaki, Sung-Ock, Sohn, & S. Strauss eds., *Japanese/Korean Linguistics* Vol. 7, 77-93. Stanford: CSLI.

Kamio, A. 1990. *Joohoo no nawabari riron* [The theory of territory of Information]. Tokyo: Taishukanshoten.

Katagiri, Y. 1995. Shuujoshi ni yoru taiwa choosei [Dialogue coordination by Japanese sentence-final particles]. *Gengo* 24: 38-45.

Kinsui, S. 1993. Shuujoshi yo, ne [Final particles *yo* and *ne*]. *Gengo* 22: 118-121.

Lerner, G. H. 1991. On the syntax of sentences-in-progress. *Language in Society, 20*, 441-458.

Lerner, G. H., & T. Takagi. 1999. On the place of linguistic resources in the organization of talk-in-interaction: A co-investigation of English and Japanese grammatical practices. *Journal of Pragmatics,* 31:49-75.

Makino, S. & M. Tsutui. 1986. *A dictionary of basic Japanese grammar.* The Japan Times.

Maynard, S. K. 1997. *Japanese communication: language and thought in context.* Honolulu: University of Hawai'i Press.

Ono, T. & E. Yoshida. 1996. A study of co-construction in Japanese: We don't "finish each other's sentences", in N. Akatsuka, S. Iwasaki, & S. Strauss eds., *Japanese/Korean Linguistics* Vol. 5, 115-130. Stanford: CSLI.

Sacks, H. 1992. Lectures on Conversation. 2 volumes. Ed. by G. Jefferson, with Introductions by E. A. Schegloff. Oxford: Blackwell.

Takubo, Y. & S. Kinsui. 1997. Discourse management in terms of mental spaces. *Journal of Pragmatics,* 28: 741-758.

Texts: 1994 Los Angeles earthquake data collected by Shoichi Iwasaki

Part III

Historical Linguistics and Grammaticalization

A Dispersion Account on Middle Korean Vowel Shifts[*]

Sᴀɴɢ-Cʜᴇᴏʟ Aʜɴ

Kyung Hee University

1. Optimality and Dispersion

Optimality Theory (OT henceforth, McCarthy & Prince 1995) is a model of constraints and constraint interactions, whereas the standard generative theory is a model of rules and derivations. In OT, we allow all possible candidate outputs and then evaluate them with a set of constraints. As the main analytical proposal is that constraints are ranked in a hierarchy of relevance. an optimal output can minimally violate certain low-ranked constraints.

In Dispersion Theory, on the other hand, there are constraints on the well-formedness of phonological contrasts and the selection of phonological contrasts is subject to the three functional goals shown in (1) (Flemming 1995, 1996). The possibility of incorporating these principles into OT emerges from the fact that the functional goals in (1) are in conflict with each other. The figures in (2) illustrate the relations among the requirements.

---

[*] This work was supported by the Brain Korea 21 Project in 2000. I am grateful to Gregory Iverson for his helpful comments.

(1) a. Maximize the number of contrasts.
   b. Maximize the distinctiveness of contrasts.
   c. Minimize articulatory effort.

(2) a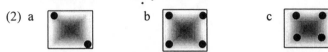

First, (2a) shows an inventory with only one contrast, but the contrast is maximally distinct. (2b) shows the case in which we fit more sounds into the same auditory space. Therefore, the goals of maximizing the number of contrast and maximizing the distinctiveness of contrast conflict. Moreover, the third constraint for ease of articulation also conflicts with the constraint maximizing distinctiveness. As the sounds in the periphery of the space requires more effort than those located in the less peripheral regions, it is necessary to restrict sounds to a reduced area as in (2c) (Flemming 1996).

The basics of Dispersion Theory can be incorporated in OT in that the requirements on contrast conflict and the selection of an inventory of contrast involves achieving a balance between them. Within OT, this paper shows how the historical chain shifts are justified in terms of the phonetic naturalness and the functional role of the distinctiveness of contrasts. As the well-formedness of the vowel system cannot be evaluated in isolation, the overall result is obtained by the pattern evaluation of the adjacent vowels.

2. The Vowel Shift in Middle Korean
2.1. The Chain Shift Hypothesis

In Korean phonology, we have recognized the so-called chain shift hypothesis proposed by K.-M. Lee (1961, 1972), stating that there were massive vowel shifts before the 15th century Late Middle Korean.

(3) Old Korean   >   Early Middle Korean   >   Late Middle Korean
      (before 13c)   (13c)   (15c)

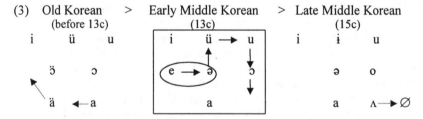

K.-M. Lee claims that the vowel shift between Old Korean and Early Middle Korean was a "drag chain" since the low central vowel [ä] was raised to the mid front [e] to fill the gap in the front region. Then, [a] was centralized, forming the Early Middle Korean vowel system more symmetric than the earlier one. On the other hand, as shown in the box, the vowel shifts of

Early Middle Korean were initiated by the [e] >[ə] change shown in the circle followed by [ə] > [ü] and [ü] > [u]. Unlike the earlier change, however, the Middle Korean chain shift shows a "push chain" in that the [e] >[ə] change triggered the subsequent vowel movements [ə] > [ɨ], [ü] > [u], [u] > [o], and the lowering of [ɔ].

Various sorts of evidence have been proposed to support this hypothesis (W.-J. Kim 1963, 1978, C-W. Kim 1978, S.-O. Lee 1984, Ahn 1998, etc.). Moreover, K.-M. Lee (1972: 107) claims that [u] and [o] in early Chinese loanwords were orthographically represented as {o} "ㅗ" and {u} "ㅜ" respectively in the 15th century Korean texts. (I will use curly brackets to show orthographic representations.) This observation implies that there were [ü] > [u] and [u] > [o] changes.

2.2. Possible Problems of the Chain-Shifts

There are, however, several possible problems on this chain shift hypothesis. First, due to the weak textual evidence, it is difficult to recognize the [e] > [ə] change as the trigger of the chain shift. Thus, as argued in Oh (1998), it is difficult to find phonetic evidence supporting Lee's claim that the [e]>[ə] change triggered the chain shift destroying the symmetrical vowel system.

Second, contrary to the assumed shift [ə] > [ü] shown in a broken circle, we can think of an alternative change, such as [i] > [ü] as shown in a solid circle below. Thus, we have to explain why the slot vacated by [ü] is filled by the upward movement of [ə], not by the rightward movement of [i]. Oh (1998) also regards [ə] > [ü] (later [ɨ]) as unnatural as it disobeys the general principle of Natural Phonology (Stampe 1973).[1]

(4)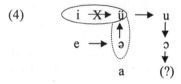

Third, we also need to explain the cause of the rightward movement of [ü] destroying the symmetry of the vowel system. Thus, we may ask what kind of motivation forced this process.

Fourth, we need to explain why [i] and [a] were exempt from such changes like [i] > [e], ([i] > [ü],) and [a] > [ə]. In other words, we may

---

[1] In Natural Phonology, every regular sound change is the result of the operation of one or more of a set of natural phonological processes. Thus every regular sound change is explained in terms of its phonetic motivation since natural phonological processes are the natural or automatic responses of the speakers to articulatory and perceptual difficulties.

raise a question why the slots filled in by the universally basic vowels [i, a, u] are not to be emptied, while the original slot for [u] was newly filled in by the rightward movement of [ü].

Fifth, observe that being pushed by the downward movement of [u], the mid round vowel [ɔ] moved downwards to the lowest corner of the back region before it disappeared after the Late Middle Korean period. Thus, we need to explain the reason of the disappearance.

Finally, Oh (1998) claims that Lee's proposal conflicts with Labov (1994)'s general principle of sound change: back vowels move to the front in chain shifts.[2]

3. A New Look at the Chain Shift: A Dispersion Account

Given the various problems on the chain shift hypothesis, I argue that it is quite natural to recognize the Middle Korean vowel shifts since they are not only phonetically natural but also inevitable from a functional viewpoint. For this, I will first point out the trigger of the whole process from a phonetic viewpoint, where we do not have to appeal to any specific theory since the triggering factor can be found in common phonetic ground. I will then explain how the subsequent changes followed the initial movement. I will employ several phonetic constraints based on universal facts on vowel distribution (Lass 1976, Clark & Yallop 1992, Ladefoged 1993, etc). Moreover, for the overall pattern of the change, I will also employ the basic notions of Dispersion Theory (Flemming 1995) in conjuction with OT.

3.1. Constraints and the Trigger

First of all, I propose the [ü] > [u] move as the trigger for the overall chain shift. Consider that Lee's proposal on the [e] > [ə] trigger not only phonetically unnatural but also shows no concrete textual evidence for the trigger of the chain shift. However, our new proposal for [ü] > [u] move as the trigger can be supported by a universal constraint suppressing front/central round vowels because, among the five possiblities, this is the only plausible and natural process from phonetic viewpoints.

(5)

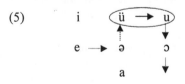

---

[2] Oh thus denies the existence of the Korean vowel shifts since the alleged chain shifts conflict with the expected changes in Natural Phonology, e.g., [ə] > [a], [o] > [u], [ɒ] > [o], or [ɔ] > [ɒ].

Consider that, due to the ease of ariticulatory movement, most round vowels are tend to be located in the back region of the mouth. The answer for this may be found in acoustics since rounding has the effect of suppressing the second formant (F2), which accentuates a key characteristic of back vowels relative to front vowels having high F1. Thus, it is much more common to observe back round vowels in most languages, rather than front round vowels. Considering this, we propose the following universal constraint accounting for the [ü] > [u] move triggering the subsequent changes.

(6) *[+round, -back] → Round vowels are located in the back region.

This argument can be supported even by Natural Phonology since this process changing a labial vowel to a nonpalatal one is a natural process in this theory (Oh 1998: 459).[3] We can get further support from textual data on Mongolian loanwords showing the (bold-faced) [ü] > [u] move between Early Middle Korean and Late Middle Korean (K.-M. Lee 1961, 1972): e.g., *küreng > kurəŋ (məl)* 'chestnut colored horse', *šülen > sjura* 'soup', etc.

Second, the subsequent upward movement of [ə] should be regarded as a functional attempt to fill the gap vacated by the intial [ü] > [u] change. There, however, arises one question why the gap of [ü] is not filled in by the rightward movement of [i] instead. We, thus, need a constaint banning any gap for the three (universally) basic vowels /i, u, a/ as shown in various literatures (Lass 1976, Clark & Yallop 1992, Ladefoged & Maddieson 1996, etc.).[4]

(7) Keep /i, a, u/
     Any vowel pattern lacking any of the three basic vowels is prohibited.

Note that /i/ and /a/ have not undergone any change, while the position for /u/ was newly filled by the rightward movement of /ü/, forcing the downward movements of /o/ and /ɔ/. Unless filled in by other vowels like [e], therefore, the slot for [i] cannot be left empty due to this constraint.

The universal constraint Keep /i, a, u/ also takes a crucial function in the [e] > [ə] change. Being vacated by the upward movement of [ə], the empty slot for a mid central vowel was filled by the [e] > [ə] change, rather than by

---

[3] In Natural Phonology, it is a fortition process which is context-free.. A fortition process optimizes (or intensifies) individual segments and limits the possible segment inventory (Oh 1998).

[4] In Clark & Yallop (1992: 103), for example, those languages with only three vowels show /i, a, u/, while those with five vowels (e.g., Spanish, Russian, Japanese) show /i, e, a, o, u/. Moreover, the mid round vowel /ɔ/ is found only in those languages with more than five phonemic vowels such as Italian.

the alternative [a] > [ə] change. The alternative change fatally violates the "Keep /i, a, u/" constraint and is, thus, eliminated.

(8) 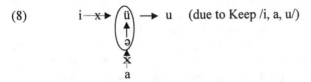 (due to Keep /i, a, u/)

As there is no possibility to fill the new gap for the mid central vowel by the upward movement of [a], the other alternative of [e] > [ə] change follows the upward movement of [ə] filling the gap for the high central (or high nonround back) vowel. In other words, this process is to be regarded as a subsequent change following two preceding changes, [ü] > [u] and [ə] > [ü], rather than as the trigger of the whole shift as claimed in K.-M. Lee.

(9)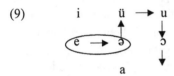

Recognizing those two processes as phonetically natural or functionally inevitable, we can easily explain the rest of the movements, i.e., the downward movements of [u] and [ɔ]. First, the downward movement of [u] is a result of the [ü] > [u] push movement. In other words, being pushed by the rightward movement of [ü], [u] has no other option but to move downward since we allow only one slot for the high back round vowel. This is a very general constraint reflecting the effort to maintain the underlying contrast between two phonemes (Flemming 1996). Thus, we posit the following constraint.[5]

(10)   Maintain Contrast
The contrast between phonemes is to be maintained during chain shifts.

Finally, the forced downward movement pushes the vowel [ɔ] to the lowest corner of the auditory vowel space, which completed the whole chain

---

[5] Note that this contrast accounts for many well-known chain shifts in which the original phonemic contrasts of an earlier historical stage have been maintained in a later stage. For example, by being realized as [aj] and [ī], the phonemic contrast between [ī] and [ē] have been maintained in the Great Vowel Shift of English (e.g., *divine* vs. *serene*) since there is only one slot for the high front vowel.

shift. Consequently, [ɔ] being pushed to the most peripheral region of the vowel space disappeared after existing as [ʌ] for a short while (Lee 1972).

(11)　　　i　　ɨ　　u

　　　　　　　ə　　o

　　　　　　　a　　(ʌ/ɔ)[6]

3.2. Identity Violation

In the vowel system of the 15th century Middle Korean, however, we also observe that the phonetic value of a moved vowel was not always realized as the one before the movement. For example, the upward movement of [ə] ended up with [ɨ], rather than [ü], and the downward movement of [u] produced [o] rather than [ɔ] since [o] is preferred to [ɔ] as the optimal mid back vowel (Clark & Yallop 1992: 103). Thus, we need evaluate the degrees of phonological stability in those positions. For the [ə] > [ɨ] change, we state that it is highly marked to have [ü] in the high central slot since round vowels are preferred in the back region as we already observed above in the [ü] > [u] change. We, thus, get a more stable [ɨ], rather than [ü], in this location, even though it violates a faithfulness constraint Ident-IO.

(12)　Identity Input-Output (Ident-IO)
　　　Correspondent segments are identical in feature F.

For the selection of the more stable vowel, this constraint should be dominated by *[+round, -back] already posited above. Thus, we may get the following tableau for the distribution of high vowels.

(13)	Input: i ü u	*(+round -back)	Keep /i, a, u/	Maintain Contrast	Ident-IO
a.	i ü u	*!			
b.	i ɨ ü		*!		**
c.	i ü ü	*!	*!	*!	*
d. ☞	i ɨ u				*

---

[6] As for the vowel quality of the back low vowel, however, we still have to consider the other possibility. As shown in Oh (1998: 461), for example, it could have been the round [ɔ], rather than the unround [ʌ]. Consider that (the most conservative) Cheju dialect seems to retain this vowel (at least orthographically) being realized as [o] by most speakers of the dialect: e.g., cʰɔm [cʰom] 'genuine, true', hɔta [hoda] 'to be', kɔtɨk [kodik], etc. Without any textual or other evidence, therefore, the possibility for [ɔ] looks more plausible than the other option.

The input segments remain intact in (13a) but this output pattern violates the high-ranking constraint *[+round, -back] due to the existence of [ü] in the central region. (13b) violates Keep /i, a, u/ since the high back vowel slot is filled in by [ü] replacing [u]. This candidate also violates Ident-IO twice in that the output segments [ɨ] and [ü] do not correspond to the input segments [ü] and [u]. (13c) is the worst candidate in that it violates all the constraints. Thus, the last candidate violating Ident-IO is selected as the optimal pattern.

As for the [u] > [o] change, we state that that [o] is more natural than [ɔ] in the mid back slot, observing that [ɔ] is more marked than [o]. This statement can also be supported by the distributional pattern of the languages shown in Lass (1976) and Clark & Yallop (1992) showing [o] has less marked distribution.

The consequence of the chain shift resulted in the system shown in (11). This system looks somewhat symmetrical and, thus, stable. Consider, however, that [ɔ] pushed to the most peripheral corner of the auditory space eventually disappeared from the phonemic inventory. This disappearance violates the faithfulness constraint Max requiring every segment of the input have a correspondent in the output. Nevertheless, there is good phonetic reason for the disappearance, which can be formulated as follows.

(14) *[+round, +low] → Round vowels are suppressed in the low region.

As shown in numerous languages, it is quite rare (if not nonexistent) to have a low round vowel universally. Being subject to this constraint, [ɔ] in the low region was expected to disappear. Thus, this constraint dominates the faithfulness constraint Max and [ɔ] is, therefore, discouraged.[7]

3.3. Pattern Evaluation

Employing all the constraints introduced above, we show how to select the optimal vowel shift in the following tableau illustrating pattern evaluation. This tableau shows that the optimal selection of the natural chain shift requires pattern evaluation in which every vowel involved in the chain shift should be evaluated in conjunction with the adjacent vowels. (Input segments violating high ranking constraints are shown in parentheses.) Here we evaluate the overall vowel pattern, rather than each individual vowel since the optimal balance of the vowel inventories is achieved between maximizing the number of contrasts and maximizing the distinctiveness of the contrasts.

---

[7] When we recognize Oh's claim denying any chain shift in Middle Korean, there is no way to explain this final change. Therefore, Oh (1998)'s claim against any vowel shift is falsified here.

(15)

Input: i ü u / e ə ɔ / a	*[+rnd, -back]	*[+rnd, +low]	Keep /i, a, u/	Maintain Contrast	Max	Ident-IO
a. i ü u e ə ɔ a	*! (/ü/)					
b. i ɨ u ↑ e ə ɔ ↑ ø		*! (/a/)			* (/a/)	** (/ü, a/)
c. i ü → ü ↑ ↓ → ə o ↓ a ɔ		*! (/ɔ/)	*! (/u/)	*! (/ü/)	* (/e/)	** (/e, u/)
d. i ɨ → u ↑ ↓ → ə o ↓ a ɔ		*! (/ɔ/)			* (/e/)	*** (/e, ü, ɔ/)
e. ☞ i ɨ → u ↑ ↓ → ə o ↓ a ø					* (/e, ɔ/)	*** (/e, ü, ɔ/)

First, having no change, (15a) is identical to the input satisfying Ident-IO. However, it violates the high-ranking constraint *[+round, -back] due to the existence of [ü]. Second, (15b) lacks the basic vowel [a] which has been moved upwards and realized as [ə]. Thus, it violates Keep-/i, a, u/ and Max. Moreover, due to the input-output mismatches, i.e., [ü]/[ɨ] and [a]/ø, it also violates Ident-IO twice. Third, (15c) shows no contrast between two [ü]s violating Maintain Contrast. It also violates Keep /i, a, u/ due to the lack of [u], and Ident-IO is violated twice as well. The rightward movement of [e] is allowed in (16d) but the existence of [ɔ]violates another high-ranking constraint *[+round, +low]. Moreover, (15d) violates Ident-IO in [e, ü, ɔ] since their input correspondents show mismatches. Consequently, the final candidate (15e) is selected as the optimal vowel pattern in spite of the violation of the two faithfulness constraints, Max and Ident-IO. Note that this pattern reflects the one appearing after the completion of the chain shift.

4. On Possible Conflicts with Other Principles of Sound Change

As already introduced above, the general pattern of the Middle Korean vowel shift seems to be in conflict with the principles of Natural Phonology or with those proposed by Labov (1994).

First, Oh (1998) argues that every regular sound change is the result of the operation of a set of natural phonological processes in Natural Phonology. According to Oh (1998), however, only the two changes in K.-M Lee's proposal complies with the general principles of Natural Phonology.[8]

(16)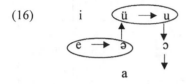

According to the principles of Natural Phonology, a labial must be nonpalatal (i.e., [ü] > [u]) and a nonhigh palatal must be achromatic (i.e., [e] > [ə]). (As achromatic vowel are neither palatal nor labial, [i, ə, a] belong to this category.) Therefore, according to Oh, the other three changes in (16), i.e., [ə] raising, [u] lowering, [ɔ] lowering, are not natural. Oh (1998: 460) claims that the expected natural processes are the ones shown below.

(17) a. An achromatic vowel must be lowered to increase sonority:
        e.g., [ə] > [a] lowering
      b. A labial vowel must get raised to increase its color:
        e.g., [o] > [u] raising, [ɔ] raising
      c. A labial vowel must get lowered to increase sonority:
        e.g., [u]> [o] lowering, [ɔ] lowering

Here we observe a paradox between (17b) and (17c), showing that either process can be regarded as natural. Employing the OT framework, however, this paradox can be reinterpreted that two constraints are (inherently) in conflict but the constraint (17c) dominates (17b), which enables us to get the [u] and [ɔ] lowering processes. Therefore, assuming all the principles as phonetically tenable constraints, there is only one constraint (17a) disobeyed in Middle Korean chain shift. As all universally natural constraints can be incorporated in OT, we state that the principle (17a) being formulated as a constraint like *achromatic-raising is dominated by the other constraint requiring [ə] raising filling the gap vacated by the leftward movement of [ü]. This aspect confirms the crucial role of pattern evaluation of the adjacent vowels in Dispersion Theory since the well-formedness of the vowel system

---

[8] These two changes are depalatalization processes described as "bleaching" in Natural Phonology. Oh (1998) also recognizes the two changes in Old Korean as natural: i.e., [ä] > [e] and [ɒ] > [a]. (Oh uses the [ɒ], for [ɑ].)

cannot be evaluated in isolation. In other words, constraints for pattern evaluation dominate other constraints for individual vowel shifts, producing "constraints for pattern evaluation >> constraints for individual vowel shift". Moreover, first thing in analyzing chain shift is to locate a trigger. Thus, we may get the following universal constraint ranking.

(18)   constraints for trigger >> constraints for pattern evaluation
       >> constraints for individual vowel shift

This universal ranking also accounts for the other argument by Oh (1998) claiming that Labov (1994)'s universal principles for sound change are not compatible with the chain shift in K.-M Lee (1961). Labov (1994: 138) states that Korean does not have long/short vowel contrasts, so the single series of vowel would be expected to follow Principles II and III, moving up and to the front, but in the development of Early Middle Korean to Late Middle Korean we see extended shifts to the back and downward.

(19)   Principle I: In chain shifts, long vowels rise.
       Principle II: In chain shifts, short vowels fall.
       Principle III: In chain shifts, back vowels move to the front.

However, we first argue that due to the lack of short/long contrast in Korean, the Korean vowel shift is not subject to Principles I and II.[9] Then we can reformulate Principle III as a general constraint but rank it below other constraints, appealing to the universal dominance hierarchy (18).[10]

5. Textual Evidence

One of the biggest problems in Korean historical phonology is the lack of enough textual evidence, and the case of Middle Korean vowel shift is no exception. For example, there seems to be no clear texual evidence in K.-M. Lee (1961, 1972) showing which movement triggerered the whole chain shift, i.e., we cannot find texts showing [e] >[ə] change occurred before other changes. Nevertheless, Lee's textual data can provide a clue to my hypothesis that [ü] > [u] could be the trigger of the whole chain shift.

According to Lee, the vowel system of Early Middle Korean can be construed from the textual study of Mongolian loanwords. The data for Mongolian loanwords are based on the orthographic representation of

---

[9] Or, we can also state that these principles, being reformulated as general constraints, are dominated by other constraints in Korean Phonology lacking short/long vowel contrast.

[10] Principles I and II may play crucial roles in those cases where no outright trigger is found: e.g., Great Vowel Shift in English. However, as shown here, they do not play much role if there exists an apparent trigger. For this issue, refer to Ahn (200) on French nasal vowel lowering.

Hangul made in the 15-16th century. The following table shows how Mongolian vowels are represented in the loanwords around the 15th century.

(20)	Mongolian (13c)	a	o	u	e	ö	ü	i
	Loanwords appeared in Late Middle Korean (15-16c, Orthography)	{a} ㅏ	{o} ㅗ		{ə} ㅓ	{wə} ㅟ	{u} ㅜ	{i} ㅣ

According to Lee (1961: 98), this table shows several facts. First, the [o, u]-{o} "ㅗ" correspondence indicates that there was only one high round vowel in the 13th century when Old Korean borrowed Mongolian loanwords since the orthographic representation {o} in Late Middle Korean corresponds to two phonetic values [o, u] in the 13th century Middle Mongolian.[11]

(21) olaŋ   > olaŋ   'belt'
      qula   > kora (mɔl) '(dark) yellow horse'
      baɣudal > baodal   'camp'

Here we should ask why this merge had to occur in a stage of the historical changes. For investigating the cause of the merge, therefore, we need to observe the Mongolian vowels and the corresponding Korean orthographic representations very carefully.

(22)   i ㅣ   (ü)ㅜ ----▶(u)ㅗ

      e ㅓ   ö ㅟ   (o)ㅗ

            a ㅏ

Here we observe that the high round vowel [u] merged with the mid vowel [o] by being lowered. And the cause of the lowering must have been the rightward movement of [ü] motivated by the phonetic reason discouraging a round vowel in nonback positions, i.e., *[+round, -back]. This interpretation enables us to consider [ü] > [u] movement as the trigger of the whole vowel shift. In other words, the initial [ü] > [u] change pushed [u] downwards. Thus, the two vowels [u] and [o] were merged in a certain period.

   Lee further states that the [ü]-{u} correspondence indicates that the phonetic value for "ㅜ" {u} was presumably [ü] in the 13th century Korean. Moreover, the [e]-{ə} pair shows that {ə} had the value of [e] in the 13th

---

[11] This account is also further supported by various documents showing [ü] and [u] often neutralized in Mongolian loanwords (Lee 1961).

century. (Finally, the [ö]-{wə}correspondence indicates that there was no monophthong equivalent to [ö] in Korean (K.-M. Lee 1961: 98).) In order to verify this hypothesis, we can cite some of the examples in K.-M. Lee (1961: 100-101), showing the systematic correspondence relations of between Middle Mongolian words and the Mongolian loanwords transcribed in the 15ᵗʰ century Korean.

(23) a. ažirɣa   > acilge (mɔl)   'baby horse'
         qarciɣai   > kalcige   'yellow hawk'
    b. ǯe'erde   > cjəlda (mɔl)   'red horse'
         qula   > kora (mɔl)   '(dark) yellow horse'
         küreng   > kurəŋ (mɔl)   'chestnut colored horse'
         ba'atur   > patʰol   'warrior'

Here we observe another important fact that only [a] and [i] were exempt from the chain shift. This observation supports the validity of the constraint (i.e., Keep /i, a, u/) requiring us keep three basic vowels. Consequently, Lee's loanword data indicates not only the trigger of the whole chain shift but the validity of the constraints employed in the previous section.

6. Conclusion

Our dispersion account, in conjunction with OT, not only shows the naturalness of Middle Korean chain shift but also the uniformity of the explanation. I first introduced the so-called the chain shift hypothesis on Middle Korean vowel shift and pointed out various problems with this hypothesis. Then, within Dispersion Theory, I argued that there is enough phonetic grounding in the chain shift. For this, I proposed to locate the trigger of the chain shift based on phonetic grounding. I argued that several phonetic constraints are responsible for the subsequent changes. I also showed that these constraints are not only phonetically natural but well fit in the frameworks of OT and Dispersion Theory. Specifically, pattern evaluation of the whole vowel system is inevitable to select the optimal chain shift and vowel system. Finally, I showed that some textual evidence supports the current dispersion account.

As a consequence, this account is claimed not to be limited to any specific theoretical framework. Therefore, our functional approach is a unified account incorporating not only the major constraints in Dispersion Theory but also the general principles of Natural Phonology or Labov's proposal in the framework of Optimality Theory.

References

Ahn, S.-C. 1998. *An Introduction to Korean Phonology.* Seoul: Hanshin Publishing.

----------. 2000. Lowering of nasal vowels in French. *Proceedings of the 8ᵗʰ National Conference on Speech Sciences,* 113-120. Korean Association of Speech Sciences.

Aoki, H. 1968. Toward a typology of vowel harmony. *International Journal of American Linguistics* 34, 142-145.

Clark, J. and C. Yallop. 1995. *An Introduction to Phonetics and Phonology.* Cambridge, MA: Blackwell.

Flemming, E. 1995. *Auditory Representations in Phonology.* Doctoral dissertation, UCLA.

Flemming, E. 1996. Evidence for constraints on contrast: the dispersion theory of contrast. *UCLA Working Papers in Phonology* 1, 86-106.

Huh, W. 1965. *Kwuke Umwunhak* (Korean Phonology). Seoul: Cengumsa.

Kim, C.-W.. 1978. Diagonal vowel harmony?: some implications for historical phonology. *Kwukehak (Journal of Korean Linguistics)* 7, 23-45.

Kim, W.-J.. 1963. Kwuke mowum chekeyuy sinkochal (A new look at Korean vowel system). *Cintanhakpo* 24.

----------. 1978. Moum chekyeywa moum cohwaey tayhan panseng (Reflections on the vowel system and vowel harmony). *Language Research* 14.2, 127-139.

Kim, Y.-J.. 1990. Moum chekey (Vowel system). *Kwuke yenkwu etikkaci wassna (Current Status of the Studies on the Korean Language),* 55-67. Department of Korean, Seoul National University.

Labov, W. 1994. *Principles of Linguistic Change.* Cambridge, MA: Blackwell.

Ladefoged, P. 1993. *A Course in Phonetics.* New York: Harcourt Brace.

Ladefoged, P. and I. Maddieson. 1996. *The Sounds of the World's Languages.* Oxford, UK: Blackwell.

Lass, R. 1976. *English Phonology and Phonological Theory.* London: Cambridge University Press.

Lee, K.-M. 1961. *Kwukesa Kaysel (An Outline of the History of Korean).* Seoul: Tower Press.

----------. 1972. *Kwuke Umwunsa Yenkwu (A Study of Korean Historical Phonology).* Seoul: Tower Press.

Lee, S.-O. 1984. An overview of issues in the vowel system and vowel harmony of Korean. *Language Research* 20.4, 417-451.

Lindblom, B. 1986. Phonetic universals in vowel systems. In J. Ohala and J. Jeager (Eds.) *Experimental Phonology.* Orlando: Academic Press.

McCarthy, J. and A. Prince. 1995. Faithfulness and reduplicative identity. *University of Massachusetts Occasional Papers 18: Papers in Optimality Theory,* 249-384.

Oh, S.-s. 1998. The Korean vowel shift revisited. *Language Research* 34.2, 445-463.

Stampe, D. 1973. *A Dissertation on Natural Phonology.* Doctoral dissertation, University of Chicago.

Genitive *tu* in OJ and Historical Changes of Genitive Particles

Yu Hirata
The Ohio State University

1. Introduction[1]

This paper examines historical changes of genitive (GEN) particles in Japanese, with a special focus on GEN *tu* in Old Japanese (OJ).[2] As shown in (1), there are three genitive particles in OJ, namely *ga, no,* and *tu*:

(1)   a.   *imo*   *ga*   *ipye*
           beloved GEN house   'beloved's house'

        b.   *opokimi no*   *mikoto*
           lord   GEN words   'words of the lord'

        c.   *ama*   *tu*   *kami*
           heaven GEN god   'a god in the heaven'

While undergoing various historical changes, *ga* and *no* have been very productive all the way into standard modern Japanese (Std-ModJ), and the differences between the two particles have inevitably attracted the interest of

---

[1] I would like to thank Charles Quinn, James M. Unger, and Brian Joseph for their valuable comments. I also benefited from discussions with the audience at the 10th J/K conference, especially with Shoichi Iwasaki, Masayoshi Shibatani, and Satoshi Kinsui.

[2] OJ refers to a variety of Japanese spoken around the capital in Nara in the eighth century.

many scholars. In contrast, GEN *tu* has been studied less, perhaps because it was not very productive in OJ and occurs only in fossilized compounds in Std-ModJ, such as *oto-tu-i* (< *woto-tu-pi* [far.place-GEN-day]) 'the day before yesterday' and *ma-tu-ge* [eye-GEN-hair] 'eyelash'. The most common practice in past studies has been to seek a specific function of *tu* by generalizing from attested examples (e.g. Ôno S. et al. 1974; Ôno T. 1978), and *tu* is regarded as a locative-genitive by many scholars (e.g. Murayama 1957; Miller 1971).

A general point I would like to make in this paper is that what we observe in OJ documents represents only part of the language uses practiced in Japan at the time. As for GEN *tu*, particularly, we should recognize its importance for our studies of OJ, pre-OJ, and the Korean connection. For this purpose, I will first examine dialectal variations in particle use in ModJ. Second, I will present findings about GEN *tu* in Man'yôshû (ca. 759). Lastly, I will suggest a relationship of GEN *tu* with Korean.

This study concerns the following functional morphemes, which are indicated by underlines in the examples:

(2) a. GEN: *Taro <u>no</u> hon*
Taro GEN book   'Taro's book'

  b. Pro-GEN: *watasi <u>no</u>*
I   GEN.one   'mine'

  c. Bd-Pro: *akai <u>no</u>*
red one   'the/a red one'

  d. NMZ: *Taberu <u>no</u> ni ii*
eat NMZ for good 'For eating, (it's) good.'

  e. SFP: *Tabe-nai <u>no</u>?*
eat-NEG SFP   'Don't (you) eat (it)?'

GEN *no* in (2a) connects two nouns. I call the particle *no* in (2b) pronominal genitive (Pro-GEN), because it combines the function of genitive and a general pronominal, as in *watasi no* [I GEN.one] 'mine'. The next *no* in (2c), *akai no* [red one] 'a red one', is called bound pronominal (Bd-Pro), since it cannot occur alone, just like the pronominal *one* in English. While Bd-Pro has a concrete referent as a pronominal, NMZ (nominalizer) *no* does not have a referent on its own. As in (2d), it nominalizes the preceding clause, and the whole phrase *taberu no* refers to an act of eating, but NMZ *no* itself does not have any concrete referent. Lastly, SFP (sentence final particle) *no* in (2e) has various functions with different intonations. For example, by *Tabe-nai no?*, we understand that it is a question about a certain situation. As for the distributions of these particles, while GEN and Pro-

GEN occur only after nouns, the others, i.e. Bd-Pro, NMZ, and SFP, do no occur after nouns. NMZ occurs sentence-medially without any significant effect from intonation, while SFP occurs sentence-finally with particular intonation patterns which change its connotations.

There are four specific claims in this paper:

(3)   a. GEN *no* in Std-ModJ, GEN *to/tu* in Fukuoka, and GEN *ga* in Toyama took the same developmental path, i.e.

GEN > Pro-GEN > Bd-Pro > NMZ > SFP;

b. GEN *tu* was more widely used as a general genitive in pre-OJ than in OJ;

c. Bd-Pro *tu* had already developed in pre-OJ long before *ga* and *no* developed into Bd-Pros in Middle Japanese (MJ);[3]

d. GEN *tu* in OJ and GEN *s* in Middle Korean (MK) are very likely to be cognates, and to have taken similar developmental paths;[4]

The dialect study, combined with two other pieces of evidence, namely functional/semantic developments and historical evidence, leads to the claim in (3a). The study of Man'yôshû data leads to the claims concerning GEN *tu* in (3b) and (3c). The claim in (3d) is deduced from phonological similarity, the development of GEN *to/tu* in Fukuoka, and the development of GEN *s* in MK.

2. Dialect Variations

As noted above, I compare GEN, Pro-GEN, Bd-Pro, NMZ, and SFP.[5] Relevant data are taken from Kokuritsu Kokugo Kenkyûsho (1989), Hirayama (1997-98), and Martin (1975), as well as from my own informants. In this paper, I present only the most revealing three variations, i.e. those in Std-ModJ, Fukuoka dialects, and Toyama dialects.

2.1 Genitive (GEN)

In both Fukuoka and Toyama dialects, *no* is the productive genitive particle,

---

[3] MJ refers to a variety of Japanese approximately from the ninth century.

[4] MK refers to a variety of Korean after the Hankul characters were invented, i.e. the second half of the fifteenth century.

[5] It is generally agreed that GEN *ga* has developed into NOM(inative) *ga* in Std-ModJ, but we can also observe NOM *no* in some dialects, such as Fukuoka dialects. The development of nominative from genitive is a separate independent change from the changes of genitives discussed in this paper, and thus I do not discuss it any further this time.

just as in Std-ModJ; there are no peculiarities. GEN *ga* is observable in some places, but only with the first person pronoun *ore* 'I'.

2.2 Pronominal Genitive (Pro-GEN)

The data in (4) shows the correspondence for a Pro-GEN expression 'mine'. The morphemes that are targets of comparison are underlined:

(4) Variations in Pro-GEN expression 'mine'

Std-ModJ:	*ore no*	[I GEN.one]	'mine'
Fukuoka:	*ore n to*	[I GEN one]	(north)
	ore ga tu	[I GEN one]	(south)
Toyama:	*ore n ga*	[I GEN one]	

In Fukuoka, we observe *ore n to* in the north, and *ore ga tu* in the south. Toyama has *ore n ga*. Unlike Std-ModJ, Fukuoka and Toyama do not have a single morpheme for Pro-GEN [GEN.one]. Instead, they exhibit the combination of GEN *n/ga/n* with Bd-Pro *to/tu/ga* 'one' as separate morphemes.

2.3 Bound Pronominal (Bd-Pro)

Two sets of correspondences for Bd-Pro are presented in (5). One is after a verb, *aru* 'exist', and the other is after an adjective, *nagai* 'long':[6]

(5) Variations in Bd-Pro

a. Std-ModJ: *Koko ni aru no wa   nani ka*
here at exist one TOP what Q
'What is the one that exists here?'

Fukuoka: *Koko ni   at-to wa   nan ka*
(*at-ta tu wa* [exist-PERF one TOP], possible in PERF.)

Toyama: *Koko ni   aru ga wa   nan ka*

b. Std-ModJ: *nagai   no*   [long one] 'the/a long one'

Fukuoka: *nagai   to*   (or *nanka tu* in the south)

Toyama: *nagai   ga*

Again, Fukuoka dialects exhibit the *to/tu* variation. In the north, we observe Bd-Pro *to*, as in *at-to* 'the one that exists' in (5a), and *nagai to* 'a long one' in (5b). In the south, *tu* can be used after the perfective *-ta* suf-

---

[6] Glosses are not given when they parallel the first gloss line.

fixed to verbs, as in *at-ta tu* 'the one that existed' in (5a), and after the *ka*-type adjective endings, as in *nanka tu* 'a long one' in (5b). Toyama uses *ga* as Bd-Pro, as in *aru ga* in (5a) and *nagai ga* in (5b).

2.4 Nominalizer (NMZ)

Let us look at the correspondence for NMZ in (6) below:

(6) Variations in NMZ

Std-ModJ: *Iku <u>no</u> ni benri-da.*
go   NMZ for convenience-COP
'For going, (it) is convenient.'

Fukuoka: *Iku <u>to</u> ni benri n   yoka.*
NOM good

(cf. S-Fukuoka: *It-ta   <u>tu</u>   no   bare-ta*
go-PERF NMZ NOM   come.out-PERF
'That (I) went (there) came out')

Toyama: *Iku <u>ga</u>   ni benri-da.*

Again, NMZ *to/tu* in Fukuoka and NMZ *ga* in Toyama correspond to the standard *no*. Just as with Bd-Pro, dialects in southern Fukuoka use NMZ *tu* when the preceding verb is in perfective.

2.5 Sentence Final Particle (SFP)

Lastly, SFP *no* is involved in determining various moods, such as assertion, order, question, explanation, and surprise, functioning together with particular intonation patterns and contexts. I only present two types of uses in (7) below, but we can observe the *no/to/ga* correspondences across most functions:

(7) Variations in SFP

a. Std-ModJ: *Sonna   ni hayaku tabe-nai <u>no</u>.* (Order)
that.way   in fast   eat-NEG SFP
'Don't eat quickly like that.'

Fukuoka: *Sogen   hayo   tabe-n   <u>to</u>.*

Toyama: *Sonna   ni   hayaku tabe-n   <u>ga</u>.*

b. Std-ModJ: *Doo si-ta   <u>no</u>?* (Question)
how do-PERF SFP

'What happened?'

Fukuoka:	*Dogen si-ta*	*to?*
Toyama:	*Doo si-ta*	*ga?*

Again, *to* in Fukuoka and *ga* in Toyama correspond to *no* in Std-ModJ. It is interesting to note that, by my own intuition as a Fukuoka native, Fukuoka dialects do not exhibit the *to/tu* variation in SFP. While SFP *to* is very common in all Fukuoka dialects, the use of *tu* at the very end of the sentence is rather awkward even in the south, where we usually find *tu*-variations. For example, *Dogen sita tu ne* [how did *tu* SFP], with a falling intonation, means 'What happened?' and is perfectly acceptable, but *Dogen sita tu?* is awkward.

2.6 Developmental Sequence

Up to this point, I have presented the nearly perfect correspondences among *no* in Std-ModJ, *to/tu* in Fukuoka, and *ga* in Toyama across a variety of functions. Now, I would like to consider their developmental path.

Pro-GEN appears to have started out by omitting the noun after the genitive particle, in contexts where its referent would be easily understood. Examples from Man'yôshû are provided in (8):

(8) a. *sipwi* <u>*no*</u> *(omina)* *ga* *sipwi-gatari* (M 236)
    Shihi GEN (old.lady) GEN insisting-talk
    'the insistent talk of (the old lady) of the Shihi clan'

   b. *sumyera-mikoto sipwi no omina ni tamapu opomi-uta*
    emperor   Shihi GEN old.lady to give   song
    'a song the Emperor gives to the old lady of the Shihi'

   c. *sena* <u>*no*</u> *(kimi/mikoto)* *ga* *swode* *mo*
    husband GEN (lord/honorable.person) GEN sleeve even
    saya-ni pura-si-tu. (M 3402)
    clearly wave-Honorific-PERF
    'My (lord/honorable) husband clearly waved a sleeve.'

   d. *wa ga* *se* <u>*no*</u> *kimi*
    I GEN husband GEN lord
    'my admirable husband'

   e. *imo/papa/titi* <u>*no*</u> *mikoto*
    beloved/mother/father GEN honorable.person
    'honorable beloved/mother/father'

In (8a), *omina* 'old lady' is omitted after GEN *no*. This *omina* can be recovered from the preface note to the song, as shown in (8b). Example (8c) is a case of omitting *kimi* 'lord' or *mikoto* 'honorable person' after GEN *no*, based on common set phrases in (8d) and (8e). In these cases, GEN *no* became Pro-GEN by gaining the function of a general pronominal, because it can contextually imply various kinds of omitted nouns. Later, the genitive function was bleached out, and the particle *no* came to be used as Bd-Pro, as in *akai no* 'a red one' in Std-ModJ. The result is the underlined portion of the development in (9):

(9)   GEN > Pro-GEN > Bd-Pro > NMZ > SFP

This development is also crosslinguistically supported. For example, the genitive suffix *-s* in English functions not only as Pro-GEN, as in *This is Tom's*, but also as Bd-Pro, as in *your-s* 'your thing'. Similarly, GEN *de* in modern Mandarin Chinese functions as Pro-GEN and Bd-Pro, e.g. *wǒ de shū* [I GEN book] 'my book'; *wǒ de* [I GEN.one] 'mine'; and *hóng de* [red one] 'a red one'.

Given the developmental path in (9), if we go back to the Pro-GEN expressions in Fukuoka and Toyama in (4), it is most likely that Bd-Pro *to/tu* in Fukuoka, as in *ore n to* or *ore ga tu* 'mine', came from GEN *tu* in OJ. Likewise, Bd-Pro *ga* in Toyama, as in *ore n ga* 'mine', came from GEN *ga*. These possessive expressions seem to be a sort of 'reverse formation'. That is, once Bd-Pro was established by bleaching the genitive function of Pro-GEN, the possessor *ore* 'I' and Bd-Pro *to/tu/ga* 'one' were connected again by the genitive appropriate at the time, and thus *ore n to, ore ga tu*, and *ore n ga* 'mine' resulted. We may regard these as 'double genitive derivative constructions'.

Martin (1975, 1990) speculates that Bd-Pro *no* in Std-ModJ came from shortening of *mono* 'thing'. If so, however, the correspondence among Bd-Pro *no/to/tu/ga* in these dialects is left a remarkable coincidence that does not have any explanation. Therefore, the various Bd-Pros are most likely to be genitive derivatives.

Now let us look at the development from Bd-Pro to NMZ. As shown in (10), Bd-Pro and NMZ may occur in the same environment:

(10)   a.   *Nedan ga takai no wa kawa-nai.*
               prices NOM high one TOP buy-NEG
               '(lit.) (I) don't buy ones whose price is high.'

          b.   *Nedan ga takai no ga mondai da.*
               prices NOM high NMZ NOM problem COP
               '(lit.) That prices are high is the problem.'

In (10a) and (10b), *Nedan ga takai no* is the same. In (10a), however, *no* denotes a general but concrete thing, whereas in (10b), *no* itself does not have a referent, but the whole nominalized clause refers to a certain situation. Thus, the function of Bd-Pro *no* in (10a) is more concrete, and that of NMZ *no* in (10b) is more abstract. Therefore, the nominalizing function seems to be a natural extension from Bd-Pro, as indicated in (11) below:

(11)   GEN > Pro-GEN > <u>Bd-Pro > NMZ</u> > SFP

Next, why does the same SFP *no*, *to*, or *ga* have the various connotations? If we look at other lexical items *koto* 'fact' and *mono* 'thing', we notice that they are often used as NMZs, but they can also be used as sentence-final elements with various connotations, as shown in (12):

(12)   a. NMZ *koto*

Uwaki o sita <u>koto</u> de   kenka ni natta.
affair ACC did fact due.to quarrel to became
   'Due to (the fact that I) had an affair, (we) resulted in a quarrel.'

b. Sentence-Final *koto*   (surprise)

Uwaki-mono desu <u>koto</u>.   (female speech)
fickle.person COP fact
   'What a fickle person!'

c. Sentence-Final *koto*   (order)

Yuu koto   o   yoku   kiku <u>koto</u>.
say thing ACC carefully listen thing
   'Listen to me.'

d. NMZ *mono*

Ano koro wa yoku turi   ni itta <u>mono</u> desu.
that time TOP often fishing to went thing COP
   'I used to go fishing often at that time.'

e. Sentence-Final *mono*   (explanation)

Gakusei desu <u>mono</u>.   (female speech)
student COP thing
   'The thing is that (it is because) (someone) is a student.'

All of these functions seem to have stemmed from nominalization. That is, nominalization promoted various contextual connotations by making sentences referential. Therefore, SFPs *no/to/ga* in various dialects seem to have come from NMZs. As in (13), this is the last step in the development:

(13) GEN > Pro-GEN > Bd-Pro > <u>NMZ > SFP</u>

From (8) to (13), I have discussed functional/semantic developmental processes. This developmental path is also supported by historical evidence.
As shown in (8), Pro-GEN is observable in Man'yôshû in the eighth century. We do not find Bd-Pro until the tenth century, in Sotanshû. As for
NMZ *no*, according to Yoshikawa (1977), it can be confirmed in written
language only since the eighteenth century. SFP *no* became recognizable
only in the nineteenth century.

In the history of Japanese, the emergence and spread of NMZ *no*
came after so-called *rentaikei* (adnominal forms) took over the functions of
shûshikei (conclusive forms). In other words, NMZ *no* developed after
adnominal forms lost their distinctiveness as such. This makes sense since
adnominal forms in OJ and MJ had functioned as nominalizations when used
without following nouns. Thus, it can be said that in Japanese NMZ *no*
replaced nominalization by the use of adnominal forms. However, the loss
of distinctiveness of adnominal forms is not a necessary condition for the
development from Bd-Pro to NMZ, since this change is also observable in
Mandarin Chinese and Middle Korean (Hirata 2000), the former of which
does not have any verb morphology, and the latter maintained distinctive
adnominal forms, substantive (i.e. nominal) forms, and assertive forms.

Given the three kinds of evidence, i.e. the dialectal correspondences,
functional/semantic developments, and the historical evidence, I claim that
GEN *no* in Std-ModJ, GEN *to/tu* in Fukuoka, and GEN *ga* in Toyama took
the same developmental path, as shown in (13). Neither GEN *to/tu* nor
GEN *ga* is productive in modern Fukuoka dialects or Toyama dialects.
However, this development suggests that at least for some time in the past,
in the competition among the three genitive particles, GEN *to/tu* was more
commonly used in Fukuoka, as was GEN *ga* in Toyama.

3. GEN *tu* in Man'yôshû

Let us shift our discussion to GEN *tu* in Man'yôshû. Ôno S. et al. (1974)
explain that GEN *tu* in OJ was used in many cases with nouns which
express location or basic positions. However, this is a simplistic generalization based on limited examples.

First, despite the locational or positional nouns in (14a) below, the
data in (14b) show us that GEN *tu* is not a mere locative:

(14) Nouns Marked by GEN *tu* in Man'yôshû

    a. Locations, Positions

ama 'heaven, sky'; *ipye* 'house'; *umi* 'sea'; *oki* 'offing'; *oku* 'inner part'; *kami* 'upper part'; *kuni* 'earth; state'; *Kuni* 'Kuni (proper N)'; *saki* 'ahead'; *sima* 'island'; *simo* 'lower part'; *toki* 'time'; *two* 'outside'; *naka* 'middle'; *nipa* 'yard'; *nwo* 'field'; *pye* 'beach'; *muka* 'far side'; *yama* 'mountain'; *wata* 'sea'; *woto* 'far place'

    b. Other Kinds of Nouns

ipo '500'; *siko* 'fool'; *tanabata* 'loom'; *tama* 'gem'; *toko* 'eternity, eternal (root)'; *topo* 'far (root)'; *pana* 'flower'; *po* 'jut, tip'; *mi-ke* 'food'; *mi-wo* 'water stream'; *moto* 'root, base, past'; *momo* 'hundred'; *yu* 'holy thing'

Secondly, the examples in (15) show that GEN *tu* and GEN *no* may mark the same nouns or bound nominals; there is no reason to regard GEN *tu* as a different kind of genitive:

(15) Overlaps between GEN *tu* and GEN *no*

    a. *ama tu sirusi* [sky GEN mark] 'Milky Way' (M 2007)
       ama no gapa [sky GEN river] 'Milky Way' (M 3658)

    b. *kuni tu kamwi* [earth GEN god] 'God of the earth' (M 904)
       kuni no kami [state GEN head] 'governor' (M 3098)

    c. *siko tu okina* [fool GEN old.man] 'stupid old man' (M 4011)
       siko no mi-tate [... shield] 'my humble shield' (M 4373)

    d. *topo tu kuni* [far(root) GEN country] 'the other world' (M 1804)
       topo no kuni   'far country (i.e. Korea)' (M 3688)

Lastly, GEN *tu* can be used to connect two nouns in very complex semantic relationships, as seen in (16) below:

(16) Advanced Uses of GEN *tu*

    a. *pana tu duma* [flower GEN wife] 'flower-like wife' (M 3370)

    cf. *tuyu no inoti* [dew GEN life] 'dew-like life' (M 3933);
       waka-kusa no tuma [young-grass GEN wife] (M 4331)

    b. *ama tu swora nari* [heaven GEN sky COP] 'be empty' (M 2887)

    cf. *uwa no sora* [upper.part GEN sky] 'empty minded' in ModJ;
       ya-tuka po no ikasi po [eight-grip ear.of.grain GEN vigorous ear]
       (appositive use) (Norito)

c. *mi-ke tu kuni*   [Prefix-food GEN country]
   'countries offering food (tribute)' (M 933)

d. *tanabata-tu-mye* [loom-GEN-woman]
   'female weaver; Orihime'(M 2027)

(16a) is a metaphorical use. (16b) is appositive. These are also similar to some of the uses of GEN *no*. The other two, (16c) and (16d), do not express a prototypical genitive relationship, either, such as possession, belonging, or location.

If we assume that GEN *no* and *tu* were derived from content words, these complex uses suggest that semantic meanings of these genitives were already well-bleached out in OJ. Or, even if we assume that these genitives started out from a very basic genitive function, such as possession or location, still we have to say that GEN *tu* and *no* were at an advanced stage of their development as genitives in OJ.

Given these observations, it can be claimed that *tu* was in all likelihood more widely used as a general genitive in pre-OJ than in OJ. In OJ, the use of GEN *tu* was limited, and it became unproductive in MJ. In fact, there is no possessive expression in the attested examples of *tu*. Was GEN *tu* ever used to express possession? I suspect it was, for three reasons. First, possessive is one of the most basic functions of genitive markers, and it is likely to precede the more complex uses of (16). Second, as seen above, Fukuoka dialects have developed various functions out of GEN *tu*. Among them, Bd-Pro *to/tu* is observable in possessive expressions. And third, as we will see shortly, Middle Korean has so-called *sai sios* (medial *s*), which was used to express possession or belonging as one of the basic genitive functions.

Therefore, sometime prior to the OJ period, the three genitives, *tu*, *ga*, and *no*, came into competition, and for some reason, the possessive function of GEN *tu* was completely swept out by GEN *ga* and *no* in OJ. Or, another possible scenario would be that GEN *tu* was the primary genitive in a dialect in northern Kyushu in the pre-OJ period, and some of its uses got into the dialect in Nara, but not the possessive use, because of the preexisting GEN *ga* and *no*. GEN *tu* in OJ may appear to be a locative, simply because we do not observe its possessive use in OJ documents.

4. GEN *tu* and Numeral Expressions

In relation to GEN *tu*, numeral pronominals are intriguing. As shown in (17a) below, the numeral series with *tu*, e.g. *pito-tu* 'one' and *puta-tu* 'two', can occur alone as pronominals. In contrast, as in (17b), the numeral series without *tu*, e.g. *pito-* 'one' and *puta-* 'two', cannot be used by themselves:

(17)   a. Numeral Pronominals

pito-tu [one-*tu*] (e.g. *wa ga mwi pito-tu pa* [I GEN body one TOP] 'myself (TOP)', M 2691); *puta-tu* [two-*tu*] (e.g. *puta-tu nasi* [two lacking] 'It is the only one,' M 412); *mi-tu* [three-*tu*]; *yo-tu* [four-*tu*]; *itu-tu* [five-*tu*]; *mu-tu* [six-*tu*]; *nana-tu* [seven-*tu*]; *ya-tu* [eight-*tu*]; *kokono-tu* [nine-*tu*]

b. Bound Numeral Nouns

pito- 'one' (e.g. *pito-pye* 'one layer' M 2520); *puta-* 'two' (e.g. *puta-yo* 'two lives' M 1410); *mi-* 'three' (e.g. *mi-tose* 'three years' M 1740); *yo-* 'four'; *i-/itu-* 'five'; *mu-* 'six'; *nana-* 'seven'; *ya-* 'eight'; *kokono-* 'nine'

Martin (1987: 367) explains that this *tu* is a specialized use of GEN *tu*, but he is rather vague. To be specific, this *tu* in numeral pronominals is Bd-Pro *tu*, as in *akaka tu* 'a red one' in southern Fukuoka, or equivalent to *no* in *akai no* in Std-ModJ. Thus, *puta-tu* is literally 'two things'.

It seems plausible that Bd-Pro *tu* developed in numeral expressions, because, as seen in (18) below, the use of GEN *tu* is observable in some numeral expressions in OJ:

(18) Numeral-GEN-

i-tu-tu [5-GEN-one] 'five things' (cf. *i-po-* [5-100-]; *i-so-* [5-10-]) (cf. double GEN: *ore ga tu* [I GEN one]; *your-s* [you(GEN)-one]) *ipo-tu tori* [500-GEN bird] 'many birds' (M 4011); *ipo-tu tudwopi* [500-GEN beads] 'many beads' (M 4105); *ipo-tu tuna* [500-GEN rope] 'many ropes' (M 4274); *momo-tu sima* [100-GEN island] 'many island' (M 3364); cf. *momo-na pito* [100-GEN person] 'many people'
                                                        (Nihonshoki, Poem 2)

Perhaps, the use and the non-use of GEN *tu* in numeral expressions co-existed in pre-OJ, and GEN *tu* developed into Bd-Pro *tu* by omitting the following noun.

An interesting example to note is *itutu* 'five', which has double *tu*. In fact, the morpheme *i-* meant by itself 'five', as in *i-po* '500' attested in OJ and *i-so* '50' attested in MJ. Thus, *i-tu-tu* seems to be what I have called the double genitive derivative construction. That is, the first *tu* is genitive, and the second Bd-Pro, similar to *ore ga tu* [I GEN one] 'mine' in southern Fukuoka.

Given these observations, I claim that Bd-Pro *tu* had already developed in pre-OJ, long before *ga* and *no* developed into Bd-Pros in MJ.

5. Korean Relationship

Lastly, I suggest a strong possibility that GEN *tu* in Japanese and *sai sios* (GEN *s*) in MK are cognates. Although this view is not totally new (e.g. Yamada 1913; Hashimoto 1969; and Martin 1990), the following set of observations combined together strengthens the hypothesis:

(19) MK GEN *s* (> *t* before *s*- or *c*-) and OJ GEN *tu*
  a. Korean Place Names recorded in Nihonshoki (720 A.D.)
                             (Yamada 1913; Hashimoto 1969)
       Oko-si-tari 'upper Tari'   (cf. *Kami-tu-Ke'nwo* 'upper Keno')
       Aru-si-tari 'lower Tari'   (cf. *Shimo-tu-Ke'nwo* 'lower Keno')

  b. MK GEN *s/t* (Martin 1992)
       e.g. *pwuthye s 'na.h* 'Buddha's age'   (Sakpo sangcel: 1447)

  c. MK Nominalizer *s/t* 'the fact that ... ' (Martin 1992)
       e.g. ... *'s oy* [NMZ LOC] (cf. *no ni*);
           ... *'s ol* [NMZ ACC] (cf. *no o*)
       Extended Predicate: ... *'s i-* [NMZ COP] 'It is that ... ' (cf. *no da*)

  d. ??MK Emotive -*'s(o)-/-'t(o)*- or modulated -*'swo-/-'two*- (ibid.)
       e.g. -*two-ta; (i)la-s-ta; -ta-s-ta* (cf. SFP *no/ga/tu*)

  e. Korean Numerals (not all numbers) (Martin 1990)
       Pronominal: *sey-s* 'three'; *ney-s* 'four' (cf. *puta-tu* 'two')
       Bound Nominal: *sey-* 'three'; *ney-* 'four' (cf. *puta-* 'two')

If based on the Nihonshoki data, GEN *s* in Korean seems to date back at least to the eighth century. It is also interesting to note that Fukuoka, where GEN *tu* developed into various functions, is the closest prefecture to Korea. The Korean/Japanese relationship certainly needs further study, but it is very likely that GEN *tu* in OJ and GEN *s* in MK are cognates, and took similar developmental paths.

6. Conclusion

Based on the dialect data, functional/semantic developmental processes, and the historical evidence, I have claimed that GEN *no* in Std-ModJ, GEN *to/tu* in Fukuoka, and GEN *ga* in Toyama took the same developmental path, i.e. GEN > Pro-GEN > Bd-Pro > NMZ > SFP. By examining all the uses of

GEN *tu* and numeral expressions in Man'yôshû, I have also claimed that GEN *tu* was more widely used as a general genitive in pre-OJ than in OJ, and that Bd-Pro *tu* had already developed in pre-OJ long before *ga* and *no* developed into Bd-Pros in MJ. Taking all these observations together, GEN *tu* in OJ and GEN *s* in MK are very likely to be cognates, and to have taken similar developmental paths. It is my hope that this paper has shed new light on the historical changes of genitive particles in Japanese, as well as on the importance of GEN *tu* in our understanding of OJ, pre-OJ, and probably proto-Korean/Japanese, and that it will promote further studies.

References

Hashimoto, S. 1969. *Joshi/jodôshi no kenkyû*. Tokyo: Iwanami.

Hirata, Y. 2000. Historical changes of genitive morphemes in Japanese and other languages. Ms. The Ohio State University.

Hirayama, T. ed. 1997-98. *Nihon no kotoba sirîzu* V. 1-48. Tokyo: Meiji shoin.

Kokuritsu Kokugo Kenkyûsho. 1989. *Hôgen bunpô zenkoku chizu*, V.1. Tokyo: Ôkurashô.

Martin, S. E. 1975. *A Reference grammar of Japanese*. New Haven: Yale University Press.

Martin, S. E. 1987. *The Japanese language through time*. New Haven: Yale University Press.

Martin, S. E. 1990. Morphological clues to the relationships of Japanese and Korean. *Linguistic change and reconstruction methodology; Trends in linguistics: Studies and monographs* 45, ed. P. Baldi, 483-509. Berlin: Mouton de Gruyter.

Martin, S. E. 1992. *A reference grammar of Korean*. Rutland, Vermont: Charles E. Tuttle Company.

Miller, R. A. 1971. *Japanese and the other Altaic languages*. Chicago: University of Chicago Press.

Murayama, S. 1957. Vergleichende Betrachtung der Kasus-Suffixe in Altjapanischen. *Studia Altaica*. 126-31.

Ôno, S. et al. eds. 1974. *Iwanami kogo jiten*. Tokyo: Iwanami.

Ôno, T. 1978. *Nihongo no sogen-teki kenkyû*. Tokyo: Takayama honten.

Yamada, Y. 1913. *Nara-chô bunpô-shi*. Tokyo: Hôbunkan. (1954 reprint)

Yoshikawa, Y. 1977. Keishiki meishi 'no' no seiritsu. *Kindaigo-shi*, Y. Yoshikawa, 252-266. Tokyo: Kadokawa.

On the Emergence of Korean Concessive *myense*: Focusing on the Grammaticalization of *se**

Minju Kim

University of California, Los Angeles

1. Introduction

The Korean clausal connective *myense* has both simultaneous and concessive meanings, as with the English 'while' and the Japanese *nagara* and *tsutsu*. Based on cross-linguistic evidence, many linguists have shown that the more complicated concept, concessivity, developed from simultaneity. This seemingly clean mapping, however, poses one problem in the case of Korean where both *myense* and its cognate *mye* have simultaneous meanings. Between the two simultaneous markers, why did *myense* and not *mye* engender concessivity? Or, more precisely, what affects the choice of *myense* over *mye* as a concessive marker? This study will attempt to answer this question by investigating the complex grammaticalization of the Korean morpheme *se*.

In this paper, I will first show that *myense* is composed of *mye* and *se*. Second, provided that the added meaning of *se* affects the choice of *myense* over *mye*, I will map out the grammaticalizational paths of *se* in the history of Korean. Finally, I will show that, indeed, due to the

* I deeply thank Sung-Ock Sohn, Shoichi Iwasaki, Noriko Akatsuka at UCLA and Ross King at UBC for their helpful comments and suggestions on an earlier version of this paper. The abbreviations used in this paper are Acc (Accusative), Conn (Connective), Cop (Copular), Dec (Declarative), Dn (Dependent noun), Gen (Genitive), Nom (Nominative), Prog (Progressive), Pst (Past), Retro (Retrospective), Rl (Relativizer), and Top (Topic).

grammaticalized meaning of *se*, *myense* is preferred over *mye* as a concessive marker.

2. Can *myense* be thought of as the combination of *mye* and *se*?

The first evidence supporting this proposition derives from a phonological trace. Middle Korean (hereafter MidK) documents demonstrate that the erstwhile form of *myense* is *myesye*, which can be considered as *mye* plus *sye*, the old form of *se*.

\<simultaneous: *myesye* => *myense*>
(1) [*penyek sohak* 1517, 8:2]   [adapted from Yu 1964]
    sum-e sal-myesye epezi lul hyoyanghA-teni
    hide-Conn live-myense parents-Acc support-Retro
    "While living in hiding, (Master Hyowu) supported his parents..."

\<concessive: *myesye* => *myense*>
(2) [*nungemkyeng enhay* 1462, 6:102)   [adapted from An 1985]
    congcong ep-ul cizu-myesye ta pulpep-ila nilu-ko
various business-Acc do-myense all Buddha's teaching-Cop say-and
"While doing various businesses, they (thieves) call them Buddha's teaching..."
(note: Buddha taught that begging is the right way of living)

Then how did the MidK *myesye* end up as the Present Day Korean (hereafter PDK) *myense*? The change from the diphthong *sye* into the simple vowel *se* is a common trend as seen in (3).

(3) *eysye* 'at' > *eyse*;   *syeta* 'stand' > *seta*;   *syepang* 'husband' > *sepang*

Next, the insertion of *n* is explained as an effort to make the pronunciation easier. Yu (1975) explains that, as in example (4), *n* can be inserted between the vowel and the palatal (*c*, *ch*), and the vowel and the alveo-dental sound (*s*, *z*).[1]

(4) Insertion of *n*   [from Yu 1975:109-111]
a.   Vow + Palatal (*c*, *ch*)
: *te ci ta* 'throw' > *ten ci ta*; *ma chi* 'amount' > *man chi*; *i cey* 'now' > *in cey*
b.   Vow + Alveo-dental (*s*, *z*)
: *mye sye* 'while'> *myen sye*; *hA o za* 'alone' > *hA on za*

---

[1] In his analysis, Yu (1975) states that the insertion of *n* occurred "within the morpheme boundary" and all examples he cited fall under this category. His analysis does not contradict our proposition of *myense* as *mye* plus *se*. The addition of *n* in *myesye* started only in the 18th century, as demonstrated in the mixed use of *myensye* (in *chengku youngen* 1728) and *myesye* (in *songkang kasa* 1747). Considering that *myesye* was already observed in the earliest Korean documents in the 15th century, we can safely reason that the Korean speakers of the 18th century perceived *myesye* as one morpheme rather than a combination of two morphemes, *mye* and *se*.

As a result, the transformation of *myense* over time is documented as follows.

(5) *myesye* (15th C) > *myensye* (18th C) > *myense*

Based on this account, the suggestion by some linguists such as Martin (1992) and Strauss (1997) that *myense* is the combination of the conditional *myen* and *se* cannot be supported. *Myen* and *myesye* were both documented in 15th C. texts. In order for *myense* to be the combination of *myen* and *se*, *myensye* and not *myesye* should have been documented in the 15th C. texts.

The second piece of evidence is found by comparing a number of grammatical forms that contain *se*, such as *ese*, *eyse*, *melise*, and *etise*. These forms of *se* were once considered inseparable. However, research on MidK (S.N. Yi 1976, T.Y. Yi 1988 on *eyse* and *ese*) and evidence in early documents reveal that they are in fact added morphemes grammaticalized from a common source *isye*, a connective form of the existential verb *isi-ta* (*isi* + suffix *e* => *isye*).[2]

(6) *e/a isye* < *e/a se* 'sequential connective'
icey o-a isye conponghAzAv-om-Al estey nwuki-lio
now come-Conn isye respectfully serve-Nom-Acc how neglect-End
"Having come this far, how can I neglect serving (the King Sejong)?"
[*welin sekpo* 1459, preface:13b]

(7) *ey isye* < *ey se* 'source and dynamic locative particle'
nay cip-uy isye syangnyey hwanto mye maktahi lAl twuluko isy-eto twulip-teni
I house at isye always sword and stick Acc carry-Prog-although fear-Retro
"Although I always carried a sword and a stick at home, I was in fear..."
[*welin sekpo* 1459, 7:5b]

(8) *meli isye* < *meli se* 'from a distance' [*welinsekpo* 1459, 7:55b]
meli isye-n pozAp-ko
distant isye-Top see-and
"From a distance, you can see (the shadow of Buddha)..."

(9) *eti isye* < *eti se* 'where' [*nokeltay enhae* 1670, 2:14]
ney etuy isye sal-mye
you where isye live-and   "Where do you live and...?"

The third piece of evidence is that *mye* and *myense* share many semantic similarities that cannot be considered coincidental. As clausal

---

[2] As the origin of *se*, Ramstedt (1939) suggested *isi-ta*, Huh (1975) *is-ta/isi-ta*, S.N. Yi (1976) *si-ta*, and T.Y. Yi (1988) *(i)si-ta*. The core meaning of them is the same, existence, and they appear to have been phonologically conditioned variants (see Huh 1975 and T.Y. Yi 1988). In this paper, *isi-ta* will be considered as the origin of *se*.

connectives, both of them have simultaneous meanings. As sentence-final particles, both function to request confirmation of the information that the speaker has heard earlier, as in example (10) (cf. Sohn 1995).

(10) "I heard that John and Jane got married, isn't it true?"
   John i Jane hako kyelhonha-ss-ta-mye (=*myense*) ?
   John Nom Jane with marry-Pst-Dec-mye (=myense)

The only prominent difference between them is that, besides the above meanings, as clausal connectives, *myense* expresses concessivity while *mye* expresses juxtaposition.

   Finally, *mye* dates back much earlier than *myense* in the history of Korean. Unlike *myense*, *mye* has been in use since before the Korean alphabet, in the form of *itu* (Kang 1998, Yu 1964). This historical fact is in accordance with our proposition that the coining of *myense* was affected by *mye*.

   Evidence listed so far attests to the proposition that *myense* is composed of *mye* plus *se*. In spite of the strong evidence, no study has really analyzed the relationship between *mye* and *myense*. The difficulty seems to lie in explaining the concessive meaning of *myense,* which is not present in *mye*. This paper will focus on this aspect in the context of the grammaticalization of *se*.

3. Previous studies on *se*

   Probing the meaning of *se* is crucial to answering our question at hand. Hence, before moving on to the grammaticalization of *se*, I will briefly touch on some previous studies of *se*. As mentioned earlier, *se* has not been widely recognized as having its own independent meaning. This is understandable, considering the wide range of grammatical constructions to which *se* is attached and the irregularities in the behaviors of *se*.[3] These factors defy any unified account of the morpheme *se*. Nevertheless, a number of researchers have attempted to describe how *se* functions. The first serious attempt to study the meaning of *se* was made by S.N. Yi (1976). By investigating the historical development of *se*, Yi showed that *se* in particles and *se* in the connective *ese* in fact share the same lexical origin of an existential verb. Furthermore, he suggested the primary meaning of *se* in *ese* as adding durative aspect, and this view is shared by other major studies on *se* such as Huh (1975) and T.Y. Yi (1988).

---

[3] For example, the attachment of *se* to one grammatical form appears optional while its addition to another form is mandatory. Also, some particles with *se* function as subject markers while others function as locative particles.

Besides the above diachronic studies, there are also other studies that approach the meaning of *se* from a more synchronic viewpoint. These studies generally seem to agree on attributing the meaning of *se* to its original lexical meaning, existence (Sung 1979, I.T. Kim 1984) or something related to it, such as the claim of existence (C.M. Suh 1984), the precedence of existence (T.S. Kim 1986), or the completion of existence (T.L. Suh 1988). The studies mentioned so far perceptively acknowledged the independent meaning of *se*. Nevertheless, they had their share of common drawbacks. That is, almost all of the studies failed to consider the full range of grammatical constructions to which *se* is attached. While most of them focused on *se* in locative particles, *myense* was seldom discussed.

There are a few studies that deserve closer attention. First, An (1985) is distinguished from others in that he first attempted to encompass the full range of uses for *se*. However, the arguments for *se* as 'presupposition' seem to need further development in order to more appropriately explain the functions of *se* in clausal connectives. Next, T.Y. Yi (1988) provided a detailed analysis on the historical change of *se* in the subject marker *ise* and in locative particles. Although his historical evidence is extremely convincing, his discussion does not go beyond particles and the connective *ese*. Third, Strauss (1997) is remarkable for its coverage of the full range of uses of *se* and for its insightful analysis. She defined *se* as the marker of inclusiveness and realis. And under this definition, she proposed that *se* has a function of linking clauses as well. Strauss (1997) is also pioneering in that it has brought this interesting morpheme to the attention of the mainstream linguists.

In line with these pioneering works, I will continue to probe the meaning of *se* in this paper. Instead of trying to encompass the various functions of *se* under one definition, I will map out the historical development of *se* in each grammatical domain where *se* occurs. By doing so, I will show that the diverse meanings of *se* resulted from its long history of grammaticalization, where *se* interacted with a number of different grammatical constructions at different stages in its development.

4. Grammaticalization of *se* in particles

The grammaticalization of the Korean morpheme *se* takes at least two separate paths, particles and connectives. Research on MidK showed that the grammaticalization of *se* in particles preceded the grammaticalization of *se* in connectives. This study will address particles first. For a detailed analysis of the grammaticalization of *se* in particles, please refer to works by S.N. Yi (1976), T.Y. Yi (1988), and Sohn and Strauss (1998).

As can be seen in example (11), when *se* is attached to particles, the meanings which *se* conveys are more or less the same, that is, the 'source.'[4]

(11)   <*Se* in particles: 'source'>
ey   'to' [inanimate]   *eyse*   'from' [inanimate]
          'at' stative locative   'at' dynamic locative
(u)lo   'to' [inanimate]   *(u)lose*   'from' [inanimate] (obsolete)
eyke   'to' [animate]   *eykese*   'from' [animate]
hanthey 'to' [animate]   *hantheyse* 'from' [animate]

Among these particles, the original site of the grammaticalization of *se* is *eyse*. In PDK, the division between *ey*, a goal and static locative, and *eyse*, a source and dynamic locative, is clear. However, in the past, *ey* was used to cover the functions of both *ey* and *eyse*. The separation of the source and dynamic locative meanings from *ey* started only after the grammaticalization of *eyse* (T.Y. Yi 1988). The grammaticalizational path of *eyse* from '*ey isi-e*' appears in (12).

(12)   -*ey isi-e*> -*ey isye* > -*eyisye* > -*eysye* > -*eyse*
        'at be-Connective'   >   'at', 'from' [Sohn and Strauss 1998]

Through this process, *eyse* took over the dynamic locative and source meanings from *ey*. More importantly, with the grammaticalization of *eyse*, *se* came to take on the meaning of 'source' since, with the addition of *se*, the source meaning became separated from *ey*. Once *se* obtained the source meaning, it began to be attached to other particles. As seen in (13), particles, such as *lo* and *eykey*, which expressed both the goal and source meanings like *ey* followed the same path as *ey* and *eyse* (T.Y. Yi 1988).

(13)   *lo* (goal, source)   ⇨   *lo* (goal), *lose* (source)
        eykey (goal, source)   ⇨   *eykey* (goal), *eykeyse* (source)

5. Grammaticalization of *se* in clausal connectives
So far we have reviewed the grammaticalization of *se* in particles. Now, we will see that a parallel pattern is also observed in the grammaticalization of *se* in clausal connectives. There are three connectives to which *se* is attached: *ese* (along with its phonological variant, *ase*), *myense*, and *kose* as seen in (14).[5] Among these, the original site of the grammaticalization of *se* in connectives is the sequential and

---

[4] Exceptions to this are *ise* and *kkeyse* (subject markers), and *lose* ('having the role/position as'). Details of each form will be discussed in a later study.

[5] As seen in (14), the phonological variation of connective -*e* is -*a*.

causal connective *ese*. The following section discusses the grammaticalization of *ese*.

(14)   <clausal connectives with *se*>
e/a   sequential, causal   *ese/ase*   sequential, causal
mye   juxtaposition, simultaneous   *myense*   simultaneous, concessive
ko   juxtaposition, sequential   *kose*   sequential

5.1. Grammaticalization of *ese*

Connective *ese* originated from a MidK periphrastic construction composed of a verb with a connective suffix *e*, followed by the existential verb *isi-ta*. Although most of the literature agrees that this V-*e isi-ta* construction is the erstwhile form of the PDK resultative (V-*e* + the existential verb, *iss-ta*), it expressed broader meanings in the 15th C. As one example, unlike the PDK resultative, the MidK V-*e isi-ta* could occur with more diverse types of verbs, including descriptive verbs, which cannot denote resultative state (re-quoted from H.S. Lee 1991). Based on this evidence, H.S. Lee (1991) insightfully pointed out that the meaning of this construction in the 15th C. should be extracted compositionally. That is, "the combination of a completion of a situation, expressed by the main verb, and its duration expressed by the existential verb" (ibid. p. 254). Starting from its compositional meaning (rather than the resultative meaning) also allows us to find a way to explain how this so-called MidK resultative form was grammaticalized into the clausal connective *ese*.

(15)   *V-e/a isi* + *e* (connective suffix *e*) = *V-e/a isye* > *V-e/asye*> *V-e/ase*

Following the example of *ey* + *isye* > *eyse*, the same structural analogy seems to have been applied to V-*e* + *isye*. It results in the clausal connective V-*ese*.

Then, what is the meaning of *se* in the connective *ese*? Among a number of previous studies, the most compelling conclusion is by Huh (1975), S.Y. Yi (1976), and T.Y. Yi (1988). Drawing on its lexical origin, they proposed the meaning of *se* as durative aspect. I agree with this only in part. In the following, I will address why the meaning of *se* is more than just duration.

When discussing the connective *ese*, it is essential to note that without *se*, the connective *e* can convey more or less similar sequential and causal meanings.

(16)
a.   *na-nun hakkyo-ey ka-a(se) kongpwuha-ss-ta* [Sequential]
      I Top school to go-a(se) study-Past-End
      "I went to school and studied there"

b. *na-nun ap-a(se) hakkyo-ey kaci anh-ass-ta*   [Causal]
    I Top <u>sick-a(se)</u> school Loc go Neg-Past-End
    "Since I was sick I did not go to school"

In (16a) and (16b), with or without *se* the same content can be delivered. Based on this, many linguists, including S.C. Song (1988), K.S. Nahm (1993), and H.M. Sohn (1999) proposed that *ese* is the basic form with *se* optionally deletable. However, MidK documents demonstrate that it is the other way around. The predominant form in MidK was simple *e* without *se*. Only over time is *se* added more and more frequently to the connective *e*, as exemplified in Chinese *nokeltay* translations in (17).

(17) <Chinese *nokeltay* translations>

	year	# of tokens		year	# of tokens
penyek nokeltay	(c. 1517):	*ese* 18	*nokeltay enhae* (1670):	*ese* 18	
chenge nokeltay	(1765):	*ese* 63	*monge nokeltay* (1790):	*ese* 38	

e.g.,   "Buy cotton and silk and bring them to Kaykyeng and..."
(c. 1517)   *soom kwa kip tAl ketwuw-e <u>s-a</u> wangkyeng uy kaceyk-a*
(1670)   *soom kwa kip ul ketwuw-e <u>s-a</u> wangkyeng uy kaceyk-a*
(1765)   *soom kwa kip ul ketwu-e <u>s-asye</u> wangkyeng ey tolak-a*
(1790)   *soom kwa kip ul ketwu-e <u>s-asye</u> wangkyeng ey kaceyk-a*
            cotton and silk Acc gather-Conn <u>buy-a (sye)</u> Kaykyeng to bring-Conn

It should then be asked just what triggered the addition of *se* to *e*, when without it, more or less the same meaning can be conveyed. This question could be answered by looking at the early examples.

Previously, we discussed that the MidK V-*e isi-ta* construction expressed the compositional meaning of the duration after a completion of an action. In MidK, among others, position verbs such as 'sit', 'stand', and 'lie' frequently collocated with the -*e isi-ta* construction and these frequent collocations appear to have been the local context for the grammaticalization of the connective *ese*. For example, in the 1517 *nokeltay* text when the grammaticalization of *ese* was still at its onset, the distribution of *ese* was heavily skewed to the position verbs as follows:
(26)
# of clausal connective *ese* / # of clausal connective *e* -depending on verb types-

'sit' 4/1	'stand' 2/0	'go' 1/72	'come' 2/17	'buy' 0/19
total ratio 86:14		total ratio 3:97		

The *nokeltay* texts depict the merchants' travel. Hence, 'go', 'come', and 'buy' are the most frequently used verbs and they are selected for comparison here. During the 16th C., the use of connective *ese* was still limited as shown in (17). The ratio between *ese* and *e* from verbs, 'go', 'come', and 'buy' rightfully reflects this fact. However, as seen in (26), with 'sit' and 'stand', which are the two position verbs observed in the text, the ratio becomes 86:14 attesting to the point under discussion.

When those verbs that collocated with *-e isi-ta* construction appeared in 'a subordinate clause followed by a main clause', in this specific position, the added existential verb brought on effects other than the simple addition of duration. For example,

(18) *cwasen-un anc-a-isye kiphun toli sAlanghA-lssila* [*welin sekpo* 1459, 1:5b]
sitting-in-meditation-Top sit-a-isye deep right way think-End
"Sitting-in-meditation is to sit and think the profound right ways."

In example (18), *anc(sit)-a(connective)-isy-e(be-connective)* was used, and this is the original form of *anc-ase*. The addition of *isye*, which is an infinitive form of the existential verb *isi-ta* (*isi-e > isye*) added duration to the verb. While doing so, since *isye* was located at the nexus of two clauses, it could emphasize that the result of the action attached by *isye* remained until the second/main clause. In turn, the first clause could express a stronger bearing on the second clause, and the first clause could be more clearly marked as ground/preparation for the second clause. In other words, the addition of *isye* clarified or emphasized the ground-event relationship between the two clauses. Due to this, the *e isye* (also *esye* or *ese*) construction rather than the simple *e* was frequently adopted in 'possible trouble areas'. Namely, in combining two clauses, if there were conceptual, physical, or temporal distances between the two involved clauses, *e isye* rather than the simple *e* was utilized for their connection. Finally, the use of *e isye* resulted in the emergence of a new connective *ese*.

The next examples nicely illustrate this point. Examples (19) and (20) are also from the 1517 *nokeltay* text. The same verb *selupota* 'meet' is followed by connective *e* in (19) and by *ese* in (20).

(19) [penyek nokeltay 2:6]
onAli paspu-ni lAyzil tasi selu pow-a swuw-ul meketo nusti ani-kheni-stAna
today busy-Conn:cause tomorrow again meet-a drink-Acc eat-Conces late Neg-Conj-End
"Since today I am busy, it would not be late even if we meet tomorrow again and drink."

(20) [penyek nokeltay 1:41]
soin-tAlh-i kwakulun nAchAy selu pow-asye khun hyengnim-i
we-Pl-Nom unacquainted face (first time) meet-asye big brother-Nom
ili twyunghAn ptutulo chapan cwue meki-si-keni esti oyoneki-l-ko
this generous will-with food with feed-SHon-Conn:cause how blame-mood-Q
"Having met for the first time (i.e., Being unrelated strangers), you big brother (host) fed us with food generously. Then, how would we blame you?"

In example (19), in reply to an invitation to a drink, the speaker suggests postponing to the next day. In his talk, the sequential connection of 'meet' and 'drink' is close enough not to require the use of *ese*. In accordance, the connective *e* is employed. In example (20), a group of travelers visited a stranger's house on the way and asked for food. While granting their request, the host asked the travelers' pardon for the humble food. To this, the travelers reply by saying that "when/although we met for the first time, you offered food. Then how could we blame you for the humble food?" Here, the connection between the two clauses, "we met for the first time (i.e., we are strangers)" and "you offered food" is marked as a sequential one with *ese*. Nevertheless, the actual reading in this context is almost equivalent to a concessive one, which expresses the incompatibility or the twist of expectation. Accordingly, clausal connective *ese*, instead of *e*, is employed here. We can find similar distributional difference in MidK documents, which illustrates the different pragmatic force between *e* and *ese*.

Based on the above account, I will now argue that through the grammaticalization of *ese*, *se* gained its own function as an emphatic marker. More specifically, it functioned as a relevance augmentation marker that tightened the relationship between the two combined clauses. Once having obtained the new function, *se* began to be attached to other clausal connectives, such as *ko* and *mye*.

5.2. Grammaticalized function of se in clausal connectives

We have already seen that the evolution of meaning for *se* in particles started as existence and moved on to source. I propose that the same pattern occurred with connectives. What started as duration extended to a relevance augmentation marker.

Understanding *se* as a relevance augmentation marker rather than as an added duration also can better account for the function of *se* in *myense* and *kose*. For example, when *se* is combined with other connectives, these connectives with *se* cannot express simple juxtaposition, as seen in (21).

(21)

mye	juxtaposition, <u>simultaneous</u>	*myense*	<u>simultaneous</u>, concessive
ko	juxtaposition, <u>sequential</u>	*kose*	<u>sequential</u>

Mye denotes, first, juxtaposition of states or actions and, second, simultaneity of actions. However, when *mye* is combined with *se*, *myense* can no longer convey simple juxtaposition and the meaning changes exclusively to simultaneity. Similarly, when connective *ko* is combined with *se*, *kose* cannot carry the meaning of juxtaposition.

From the case of *ese* and *e*, we have seen that the addition of emphatic *se* functioned 1) to more clearly mark the ground-event relationship between the conjoined clauses and 2) to eventually make a connective stronger. However, juxtaposition, which combines two listings, does not need to emphasize the ground-event relationship between the two. Furthermore, juxtaposition is one of the loosest kinds of clause-combining. Accordingly, it does not require the use of a stronger connecting force. In short, the addition of *se* was not needed for the juxtaposing connection.

6. Preference of *myense* over *mye* as a concessive marker

In the above, I proposed that the grammaticalized meaning of *se* is relevance augmentation. Based on that account, this paper will now focus on *mye* and *myense*.

The examples of *myense* in the earliest Korean documents are rare. However, when *myense* was used for simultaneous meaning, it appears to have been distinguished from *mye*, in a similar way as *ese* was distinguished from *e*. The most revealing example is (22).

(22) *malhA-mye wuzwum wuzu-myesye cwukyu-mul haynghA-ni*
　　 talk-mye laughter laugh-myense murder-Acc commit-Conn
　　 "While talking and laughing, (soldiers) commited murder..."
　　　　　　　　　　　　　　　　　　　　 [*twusi enhay* 1481, 6:39]

This text describes an atrocity of war where people were casually murdered. Here, both *mye* and *myense* are used to express three simultaneous actions: talking, laughing, and killing. Depending on the compatibility of the described actions, *mye* and *myense* appear in complementary distribution. That is, to connect talking and laughing, *mye* is used; and to connect talking and laughing with the incompatible action of killing, the stronger connective, *myense*, is used. In other early examples, a similar distribution occurs. In examples (23) and (24), to highlight extreme filial sacrifice, two incompatible actions are listed together and they are tightened up using *myense*.

(23) *sumesal-myesye epezi lul hyoyanghA-teni*　 [*penyek sohak 1517, 8:2*]
　　 hide-live-myense parents-Acc support-Retro
　　 "While living in hiding, (Master Hyowu) supported his parents..."

(24) *pang mwun paskuy os pasti anihA-ko ca-myesye anpwu-lul mwut-tela*
　　 room door outside clothes take-off Neg-and sleep-myense wellbeing-
　　 Acc inquire-Retro
　　 "While sleeping outside of the door of their room without taking his clothes off, he inquired after his parents' health."　 [*penyek sohak 1517, 9:75*]

In contrast, in examples (25) and (26), the two combined clauses do not have this incompatibility problem. Hence, *mye* is utilized for their connection.

(25) *onkacilo wul-mye olmtAnni-nAn koskoli-nAn kencangkwung-ey*
     in hundred ways sing-mye move-around-Rl nightingale-Top palace-Loc
     kAtAkhA-ays-tota
     fill-Perf-End
"The nightingales, which move around while singing in hundred different ways,
have filled the palace."   [*twusi enhay* 1481, 6:3b]

(26) *Kasep i Anan Ay meli mAni-mye nilo-tAy*   [*sekpo sangcel* 1447, 24:3a]
     Kasep Nom Anan Gen head pat-mye say-Conn
     "While patting Anan's head, Kasep said (to Anan)..."

Such differences between *mye* and *myense* -triggered by the
addition of *se-* directly relates to the question of why *myense* was
preferred over *mye* as a concessive marker. There are extensive studies on
the emergence of concessivity, especially by König and Traugott.

(27)   [from König 1985, 1988, and 1991]
Eng. nevertheless, while, regardless, *Germ.* dennoch, (meanwhile), zugleich (at
the same time, nevertheless), bei all (by all), *Sp.* con todo (with all) *Hung.* megis
(still-too), *Turk.* iken (while). *Tagalog* pa...na (already...still) *Hawaiian* oiai
(while), *Port.* contudo (with everything), *Rum.* cu toate ca (with all that), etc.

Based on cross-linguistic evidence listed in (28), König (1985,
1988, and 1991) suggests "expressions asserting remarkable co-
occurrence or co-existence" as one of the five major sources for
concessivity. As Traugott and König (1991) explain, this
grammaticalization process is a type of metonymy, "the
conventionalization of conversational inferences." In a simultaneous
sentence, through conversational inference, "the subordinate clause
served not only as the temporal reference but also as ground for the event
in the main clause." Next, when a simultaneous marker was frequently
used to connect less compatible actions as with *myense*, another inference
intervened, namely, a "surprise concerning the overlap in time or the
relations between the event and the ground." When this conversational
inference became conventionalized, it resulted in the concessive meaning.
     In this regard, König (1985, 1988, and 1991) also points out that,
in the making of a concessive marker due to this incompatibility between
the two conjoined clauses, the use of 'emphatic elements', such as 'all',
'already', and 'still' is very common. The 'emphatic element' asserts that,
in spite of any incompatibility with the speakers' norms or knowledge,
the two involved clauses are indeed related. Clearly, the addition of the
emphatic element is not required. Nevertheless, we can presume that
considering the incompatibility inherent in concessive clauses, the
addition of the emphatic element is still preferred.

Finally, based on this framework, we can understand why *myense* was favored over *mye* as a concessive carrier. I suggest that with the grammaticalized function of relevance augmentation, *se* worked as an emphatic element in the connective *myense*. Between *myense* and *mye*, *myense* was assigned for the patching up of less compatible simultaneous actions, as demonstrated in examples (22) through (26). With the addition of *se*, *myense* could assert more strongly the relatedness between the conjoined simultaneous clauses. In the same way, with this capacity, *myense* was better equipped than *mye* for overriding the inherent contradiction in concessivity. Namely, although the two conjoined clauses express irreconcilable events, the second clause should be interpreted on the grounds of the first. At last, in light of the above, it seems only natural that *myense* was preferred over *mye* as a concessive marker.

7. Final Notes

The final discussion regards the current status of *se*. Bleaching ('semantic erosion with overuse') is a common process that old grammatical forms undergo. The grammaticalization of *se* is observed in the earliest Korean documents from the 15th C. Hence, it is not surprising to find that the bleaching phenomenon also occurred with *se*. Most prominently, in PDK *se* does not function as an emphatic morpheme any longer. Rather, its addition is routinized. For one example, in the early MidK texts, the primary simultaneous marker was *mye* with rare tokens of *myense* observed for the combining of less compatible actions. Now in PDK, *myense* has completely taken over the simultaneous function from *mye*. Regardless of the compatibility, for simultaneous marking *myense* is employed, and the use of *mye* is restricted to formal, written registers. In the case of *ese* as well, in MidK connective *e* was predominantly used and connective *ese* emerged to add pragmatic force to the connective *e*. Now the use of *ese* is widespread and routinized. In PDK, connective *ese* is predominantly employed in combining clauses. The use of connective *e* for clause combining sounds literate and archaic.

In this study, we have seen a rather sketchy review of the history of morpheme *se*. This morpheme has made an extensive impact on the current shape of the Korean language. This study showed only one fraction of it with *myense*. More discussions in this line on *ese*, *kose*, and other particles with *se* will be followed in later studies.

References

An, M.C. 1985. *Poco cosa se uy uymi*. *Kwukehak*. vol. 14.
Hopper, P. and Traugott, E. 1993. *Grammaticalization*. Cambridge: CUP.
Huh, W. 1975. *Wuli yeysmal pon* (Studies on Middle Korean) Seoul: Sam.
Kang, Y. 1998. *Taymyenglyulcikhay itu uy emal emi yenkwu* (Studies on

Taymyenglyulcikhay itu) Seoul: kwuke calyowen
Kim, I.T. 1984. Towum thossi se ey tay han yenkwu, (Studies on the particle *se*). *Kwuke kwukmwunhak* vol. 22.
Kim, T.S. 1986. Hyengtay se wa apse issum. (Morpheme *se* and precedence). *Hanname Mwunhak* vol. 12.
König, E. 1985. On the History of Concessive in English, Diachronic and Synchronic Evidence. *Lingua* 66:363-381.
_____ 1986. Conditionals, Concessive Conditionals and Concessives: Areas of Contrast, Overlap and Neutralization. *On Conditionals*, eds. E. Traugott et al. Cambridge: CUP.
_____ 1988. Concessive Connectives and Concessive Sentences: Cross-linguistic Regularities and Pragmatic Principles. *Explaining Language Universals*, ed. J. Hawkins. Oxford: Blackwell.
_____ 1991. Concessive Relations as the Dual of Causal Relations. *Semantic Universals and Universal Semantics*, ed. D. Zaefferer. Berlin:Foris.
Kuno, S. 1973. *The Structure of the Japanese Language*. Cambridge, MA: Harvard Univ. Press.
Lee, H.S. 1991. *Tense, Aspect, and Modality: a Discourse-Pragmatic Analysis of Verbal Affixes in Korean from a Typological Perspective*. UCLA dissertation.
Martin, S. 1992. *A Reference Grammar of Korean*. Rutland:Charles E. Tuttle.
Nahm, K.S. 1993. *Kwuke yenkey emi ui ssuim* (The functions of Korean clausal connectives). Seoul:Sekwang.
Ramstedt. G.J. 1939. *A Korean grammar*. Helsinki.
Rhee, S.H. 1996. *Semantics of Verbs and Grammaticalization: The Development in Korean from a Cross-Linguistic Perspective*. Seoul:Hankuk.
Sohn, H.M. 1999. *The Korean Language*. Cambridge:CUP.
Sohn, S.O. 1995. On the development of sentence-final particles in Korean. *Japanese/Korean Linguistics*. vol. 5 eds. N.Akatsuka, S. Iwasaki, and S. Strauss. 219-234. Stanford:CSLI.
Sohn, S.O. and Strauss, S. 1998. The Intersection of Diachronic Syntax and Current Morphology: An Analysis of -ey and -eyse in Korean. *Proceedings from the 11th ICKL*. University of Hawaii.
Song, S.C. 1988. *Explorations in Korean Syntax and Semantics*. Berkeley: Berkeley Center for Korean Studies.
Suh, C.M. 1984. pwuchisa se uy uymiey tayhaye, (On the particle *se*) *Ene*. 9:1.
Suh. T.L. 1988. Kwuke hwalyong emi uy hyengtay wa uymi, (Forms and meanings of Korean predicates). Seoul:Tap.
Sung, K.S. 1979. *Kwuke cosa uy yenkwu*, (Studies on Korean particles). Seoul: Hyungsel.
Strauss, S. 1997. A cognitive Account of the Korean Morpheme -se: A Marker of Inclusiveness. *Japanese/Korean Linguistics*. vol. 6. eds. H.M. Sohn and J. Haig. Stanford: CSLI.
Yi, S.N. 1976. 15th C kwuke ui pyenhyenge ista sita ui paltal ey tayhaye (On the development of the 15th C. verbs *ista* and *sita*). *Kwukehak* vol. 4.
Yi, T.Y. 1988. *Kwuke tongsaui mwunpephwa yenkwu*, (Studies on the grammaticalization of Korean verbs). Seoul:Hanshin.
Yu, C.T. 1975. *Ico Kwukesa yenkwu*, (Studies on Middle Korean). Seoul:Iwu.

From Relativization to Clause-linkage: A Constructional Account of Japanese Internally Headed Relativization*

KYOKO HIROSE OHARA

Keio University

1. Introduction

So-called internally headed relativization (IHR) in Modern Japanese has been discussed in recent years. Researchers have noted that the external marking on internally headed relative clauses (IHRCs) is typically the nominative or the accusative and that IHRCs are generally restricted in occurrence (e.g. Hirose and Ohori 1992). These facts, however, have not been fully accounted for. Moreover, researchers disagree as to the nature of the relation between the sentences exemplifying the IHR construction such as (1) and concessive bi-clausal sentences such as (2) (e.g. Kuroda 1999, Martin 1975, Mihara 1994).

(1) IHR sentence
   a.   [[ringo ga   teeburu no ue ni atta]$_{S1}$ **no]   ga**
         apple NOM table   GEN above LOC existed NMLZ NOM
         otita.
         fell
         i.   '[That there was an apple on the table] fell.'
         ii.   *Lit.* 'There was an apple on the table, and (it) fell.'

I am grateful to Jim McCawley for encouraging me to work on Japanese IHRCs when I was first a graduate student at UC Berkeley. My special thanks also go to Kaoru Horie, Satoshi Kinsui, Shige-Yuki Kuroda, Yo Matsumoto, Masayoshi Shibatani, and Charles De Wolf for their helpful comments on the present paper. Any remaining errors are my own. This research project was partially supported by a grant from Koizumi Foundation at Keio University.

279

b.   [[<u>ringo</u> ga   teeburu no ue   ni   atta]$_{S1}$ **no**]   o
          apple   NOM table   GEN above LOC existed   NMLZ ACC
          midori wa totta.
          Midori TOP took
          i.   'Midori picked up [that there was an apple on the table].'
          ii.   *Lit.* 'There was an apple on the table, and Midori picked (it) up.'

(2) Concessive bi-clausal sentence[1]

a.   [rei-nen da to   asa-yuu   sukooru ga   aru]
          every-year COP CONJ morning-evening squall   NOM exist
          no ga, kotosi wa   hotondo ame ga   huranai.
          this-year TOP   scarcely   rain NOM fall-NEG
          'Whereas every year we have a squall in the morning and in the evening, this year it has scarcely rained.'
                                              [Asahi Newspaper]

b.   kare wa [kesseki sita hoo ga ii] **no o** muri o sita.
          he   TOP absent   had.better.be   pushed.oneself.too.hard
          'Whereas he should have stayed home, he pushed himself too hard.'
                                            (Lê 1988:86, (66))

This paper discusses a possible reason for the restricted occurrence of IHRCs, by specifically investigating the relation between IHR sentences and the concessive bi-clausal sentences. On the basis of its syntactic and semantic properties, it will be argued that the concessive clause-linking construction should indeed be recognized separately from the IHR construction. It will be proposed, however, that the IHR construction in Modern Japanese is being reanalyzed as the concessive clause-linking construction, which may account for the restricted occurrence of IHR sentences in present-day Japanese.

The claim presented here that both the IHR construction and the concessive clause-linking construction should be recognized is similar to that of Kuroda (1999). The paper gives a new set of arguments for the claim employing an approach which is different from the one that Kuroda assumes. It emphasizes the need to regard a form-meaning pair as a grammatical construction (Kay and Fillmore 1999, Goldberg 1995, Lambrecht 1994, Fillmore, Kay, and O'Connor 1988). The paper also examines the syntactic, semantic, and pragmatic properties of the concessive bi-clausal sentences,

---

[1] I have purposely left out the glosses for *no ga* and *no o* for the time being.

which have not been fully investigated in the literature. Furthermore, although it has been established that the conjunctive particles *ga, wo,* and *ni* in Classical Japanese represent extended developments of the case particles *ga, wo,* and *ni* (Ishigaki 1955, Kitayama 1951, Kuroda 1974), the development of clausal conjunctions *no ga* and *no o* in Modern Japanese has not been extensively discussed in the literature. The paper gives an account of the mechanism through which these have come to be used.

The organization of the paper is as follows. Section 2 discusses whether the concessive sentences and IHR sentences should be analyzed as instances of the same grammatical construction. Section 3 compares the structural, semantic, and pragmatic properties of the IHR construction and the concessive clause-linking construction. In Section 4, it is hypothesized that the IHR construction in present-day Japanese is being reanalyzed as the concessive clause-linking construction and arguments for the hypothesis are presented.

2. The need to posit two distinct grammatical constructions

Before examining the relation of concessive bi-clausal sentences to IHR sentences, let us briefly look at the IHR construction first.

2.1. The internally headed relativization (IHR) construction

IHR sentences such as (1)a and (1)b have structures that suggest literal translations in (1)a.i and (1)b.i respectively, but in fact have the meanings shown in (1)a.ii and (1)b.ii.

The morpheme *no,* which follows S1 in the sentences above, can be used as a sentence nominalizer, hence the pseudotranslations in (1)a.i and (1)b.i.[2] The subject argument referent of the main predicate in (1)a must be an entity and not a proposition. The same is true for the direct object argument referent in (1)b. Hence, the meanings shown in (1)a.ii and (1)b.ii.

There is NP coreferentiality between the two clauses in the sentences above. The coreferenced NP *ringo* 'apple' is shown by underlinings. Also, the case marking on the nominalized clause (S1 plus *no*) coincides with the one required by the main predicate for the role of the coreferenced NP: In (1)a it is the nominative *ga* and in (1)b it is the accusative *o,* as indicated by the bold type.

These two properties, namely, NP conferentiality between the two clauses and the 'case-matching' phenomenon between the actual case-marking on the nominalized S1 and the one required by the main predicate for the role of the coreferenced NP, have led researchers to characterize

---

[2] Throughout this paper I will call the 'subordinate' clause S1 and the 'main' clause S2, based on the order of the predicates.

these types of sentences as involving IHRCs (Kuroda 1992 (1974-77), Itô 1986, inter alia).

2.2. The concessive clause-linking construction

In Modern Japanese, there are sentences which closely resemble IHR sentences. The sentences in (2) and (3) are taken from a newspaper article, a work of nonfiction, and a work of fiction. Just like S1 in typical IHR sentences, S1 in these sentences is followed by the sequence *no ga* or *no o*, as indicated by the bold type.

(3)   [saisyo wa noriko ga   syutai deatta]   **no o,**
        first   TOP Noriko NOM leader COP-PAST
        itunoma ni ka tatuo to   gyaku   no   iti   ni   natta.
        eventually   Tatsuo   opposite   GEN place   became
        'At first Noriko was the leader, but eventually (she) got the opposite place from Tatsuo.'

                                                        (Lê 1988:85, (59))

If these sentences were to be analyzed as IHR sentences, then they should exhibit the two defining properties of the IHR construction, namely, NP coreferentiality between the two clauses and 'case-matching' between the actual marking on the *no*-nominalized S1 and the one required by the verb of S2 (hereafter V2) for the target NP. These sentences, however, do not exhibit the 'case-matching' phenomenon. Example (2)a lacks both NP coreferentiality and 'case-matching'. Here, the only valence requirement of V2 is satisfied within S2 by the nominative-marked NP *ame* 'rain (noun)', and there is thus no NP coreferentiality between the two clauses. Consequently, there is no 'case-matching'. In (3), there is NP coreferentiality between the clauses but no 'case-matching' is observed. *Noriko* inside S1 is construed as the subject of V2, but the external marking on S1 is *o*, not the expected nominative *ga*. I will call these types of sentences which do not exhibit the 'case-matching' phenomenon CONCESSIVE SENTENCES, due to the adversative semantic relation between the situations described in the two clauses.

Are concessive sentences still considered instances of the same grammatical construction as IHR sentences, in spite of the fact they do not exhibit the 'case-matching' phenomenon? Some have proposed that the answer is indeed 'yes' (cf. Lê 1988, e.g. Mihara 1994). Here I will argue against such a view.

First, unlike IHR sentences, concessive sentences allow *wa* to be attached to two phrases, which are made foci of contrast. In the concessive sentences below, *wa* is attached to two phrases, one in each clause, making the phrases foci of contrast. In (4)a, the two *wa*-marked adverbials, *mukasi* 'old days' in S1 and *ima* 'now' in S2, are the foci of contrast. In (4)b, *wa* is attached to the locative of S1 *amerika de* 'in America' and to the grammatical subject of S2 *watasi* 'I', making them the foci of contrast. The writer is thus contrasting the different ways in which the book was designed: in America and in Japan.

(4) Concessive

a. [**mukasi wa** iti-nen o hatuka de kurasu
old.days TOP one-year ACC twenty-days work
yoi otoko datta] no ga, **ima wa** iti-nen
happy guys COP-PAST now TOP one-year
roku-basyo dearu.
six-tournaments COP
'Whereas in the old days they [sumo wrestlers] were happy fellows working 20 days a year, nowadays there are 6 tournaments a year.'
[Asahi Newspaper]

b. kono hon wa [**amerika de wa** e-hon
this book TOP America LOC TOP picture-book
no ookisa de syuppansareta] no o,
GEN size COP publish-PASS-PAST
watasi wa itumo beddo saido ni
I TOP always bed side LOC
okareru hon ni natte hosii to omotta.
put-PASS book become want CMPL thought
'Whereas in America the book had been published in the size of a picture book, I thought I wanted it to be a book which would always be kept by the bed.'
[Asahi Newspaper]

Attaching *wa* to the two phrases in S1 and S2 of IHR sentences, on the other hand, results in unacceptable sentences, as shown by (5)a' and (5)b'.

(5) IHR

a. [[**kinoo** ringo o okutte kudasatta] no] ga
yesterday apple ACC sent NMLZ NOM
kyoo tukimasita.
today arrived
'(You) sent me apples yesterday, and I received (them).'

a'. *[[**kinoo wa** ringo o okutte kudasatta] no] ga
TOP   NMLZ NOM
kyoo wa tukimasita.
TOP

b. taroo wa [[**kinoo** ringo o katte kita] no] o
Taro TOP   apple ACC bought NMLZ ACC
kyoo   tabeta.
today   ate
'Taro bought an apple yesterday, and he ate (it) today.'

b'. *taroo wa [[**kinoo wa** ringo o katte kita] no] o
TOP   NMLZ ACC
Kyoo wa tabeta.
TOP

I have argued elsewhere that IHR sentences function to advance a narrative within a sentence (Ohara 1996, inter alia). The unacceptability of the contrastive *wa* in IHR sentences suggests that the discourse function of IHR sentences may not be compatible with the discourse function of emphasizing a contrast in propositions. On the other hand, the concessivity expressed by concessive sentences seems congruent with an emphasis on a contrast between propositions (See also Section 3.2).

Furthermore, the concessive meaning is CONVENTIONALIZED in these types of sentences. The fact that the contrastive *wa* is allowed in concessive sentences by itself does not entail that the meaning of concessivity is conventionalized in these types of sentences. It may be argued that the concessivity found in them is just a CONVERSATIONAL implicature and that the contrastive *wa*, when it is used, strengthens such a reading. The examples below, however, show that the concessive relation is not cancellable and thus is indeed conventionalized in concessive sentences:

(6) a. [rei-nen da to asa-yuu   sukooru ga aru]
every-year COP CONJ morning-evening squall   NOM exist
no ga, kotosi wa hotondo ame ga   huranai.
this-year TOP   scarcely rain NOM   fall-NEG

#rei-nen sukooru ga aru kara   kotosi   hotondo ame ga
because
huranakute   toozen   dakedo.
follows   but
'Whereas every year we have a squall in the morning and in the evening, this year it has scarcely rained.
#From the fact that we have squall every year it follows that it has scarcely rained this year, but.'

b.   kare wa [kesseki sita hoo ga ii] no o, muri o siteita.
     he   TOP   absent   had.better.be   pushed.oneself.too.hard

#kesseki sita hoo ga iikoto   to muri o suru koto wa
                       COMPL and   TOP
muzyunsinai   kedo.
conflict-NEG   but

'Whereas he should have stayed home, he pushed himself too hard.

#Being in a condition such that one should stay home and pushing oneself too hard do not conflict with each other, but.'

It thus follows that if we regard a form-meaning pair as a grammatical construction, then the concessive clause-linkage must be recognized as a grammatical construction separately from the IHR construction. In the concessive clause-linking construction, the sequences *no ga* and *no o* are used as the devices for connecting two clauses, which are not fully lexicalized into clausal conjunctions yet, as can be seen from the fact that dictionaries do not list them (See also Horie 1993, 1998). I do not know at this moment whether there exist any semantic or pragmatic differences between concessive sentences with *no ga* and those with *no o*. I therefore treat them as instances of the same grammatical construction. The concessive clause-linking construction is thus schematized as follows[3]:

(7)   The concessive clause-linking construction

$$S1 \quad \begin{Bmatrix} no - ga \\ no - o \end{Bmatrix} \quad S2$$

no-ga, no-o: clausal conjunctions (CONJ)

3. IHR *vs.* concessive clause-linkage

Let us now compare the structural, semantic, and pragmatic properties of the IHR construction and the concessive clause-linking construction.

3.1. Structural comparison

Based on the traditional coordination-subordination distinction, IHRCs are categorized as [+dependent, +embedded] (cf. Van Valin 1993). IHRCs can-

---

[3] Hereafter, the clausal conjunctions *no-ga* and *no-o* will be indicated using a hyphen. Cf. Section 4.1.

not be used on their own to refer and must be used in combination with another clause (Ohara 1996). In this sense, IHRCs are distributionally dependent. Moreover, the *no*-nominalized S1 fills a syntactic valence requirement of V2 and is thus embedded within S2.

The syntactic relation between S1 and S2 of the concessive clause-linking construction, on the other hand, can be described as [+dependent, −embedded]. First, S1 of concessive sentences is distributionally dependent. It cannot stand alone, even though it does not depend on S2 for operators. S1 of concessive sentences is not, however, embedded in S2: S1 is not a syntactic argument of V2 and there is no 'case-matching' between the two clauses. The concessive clause-linking construction is therefore more 'coordination-like' than the IHR construction, which is categorized as [+embedded]. IHRCs, even though they are [+embedded] in that they externally function as NPs, structurally behave like coordinated clauses with respect to *ga-no* conversion and *wh*-questions (Ohara 1996: 71-73). S1 of concessive sentences exhibits the same 'coordination-like' behavior with respect to the two syntactic processes. Its behavior with respect to *wh*-questions is illustrated:

(8) *wh*-Question

    a.   EHRC

        [[**dare ga**   katte kita]   ringo] o
            who   NOM buy-ASP-PAST apple   ACC
        hanako ga   tabemasita ka?
        Hanako   NOM eat-POLITE-PAST-Q
        'Who bought the apple and Hanako ate?'

    b.   S1 of coordinated sentence

        *[**dare ga** ringo o katte kita] ga   hanako ga
            NOM   CONJ   NOM
        tabemasitaka?
        Intended: 'Who bought the apple, and Hanako ate it?'

    c.   IHRC

        *[[**dare ga**   ringo o katte kita]   no]   o
                NOM   NMLZ ACC
        hanako ga   tabemasitaka?
        Hanako   NOM
        Intended: 'Who bought the apple, and Hanako ate (it)?'

d.   S1 of concessive sentence
     *[mukasi wa **dare ga** ringo o katte ita]   no-ga,
       old.days TOP   used.to.buy
     ima   de wa hanako no yakume desuka?
       nowadays   TOP   GEN duty   COP-POLITE-Q
     Intended: 'Whereas in the old days who used to buy apples, nowdays it is Hanako's duty?'

3.2. Semantic comparison

In terms of referential structure, the IHR construction is characterized by NP coreferentiality between the two clauses: The target NP inside S1 not only fills a semantic valence requirement of the verb in S1 (hereafter V1) but also of V2. This NP coreferentiality translates itself in discourse-structure terms as participant continuity. The IHR construction advances a narrative by reporting two events which share a participant and the target NP referent corresponds to the participant shared by the two events.

In concessive sentences NP coreferentiality between the two clauses is not obligatory but can be present. We noted that in (3), *Noriko* satisfies a semantic valence requirement of not only V1 but also V2, and both S1 and S2 are thus construed as about *Noriko*.

Even when there is no NP coreferentiality between the two clauses, concessive sentences may contain a grammatical-topic NP, i.e. a *wa*-marked topic NP, whose scope is both S1 and S2. In (4)b, the sentence-initial NP *kono hon* 'this book', marked by *wa*, serves as the topic of the entire sentence. The whole sentence is construed as about 'this book' and it is indeed translatable in the form 'this book is such that ...'.

It is also possible to identify a discourse topic shared by the two clauses of concessive sentences, even if it is not explicitly realized as a grammatical-topic NP. In (4)a, for example, both of the clauses are about sumo wrestlers.

The concessive clause-linking construction is thus always characterized by topic continuity. The IHR construction, on the other hand, is characterized by participant continuity.

I have argued elsewhere that a temporal sequence is often expressed by IHR sentences (Ohara 1996, inter alia). It is typically observed in concessive sentences as well. Example (2)a may not seem to involve a temporal sequence at first glance. Nonetheless, the sentence may still be said to involve a temporal sequence, since it is about two situations, one typically observed until this year and another taking place in the current year. Furthermore, in concessive sentences, the contrastive *wa* often attaches to a time adverbial in each of the two clauses, emphasizing a contrast in the situations holding at the two different time frames, as in (4)a. Although the contrastive *wa* does not attach to time adverbials in (4)b, the sentence still has to do with two different time frames. Concessive sentences therefore do not express just any kind of contrast in propositions. Rather, they specifically present a contrast involving two different time frames on a temporal axis.

3.3. Pragmatic comparison

Even though IHRCs are embedded inside S2, its structural behavior with respect to *ga-no* conversion and *wh*-questions argues for the view that V1 of IHRCs makes an assertion, just like that of coordinated clauses and main clauses (Ohara 1996: Chapter 4). Since S1 of the concessive clause-linking construction is not embedded inside S2, V1 of concessive sentences can also be construed as making an assertion.

4. From relativization to clause-linkage

Now we are ready to discuss why IHRCs are restricted in occurrence. I suggest that IHR sentences in Modern Japanese are being reanalyzed by some speakers as concessive sentences.

4.1. The reanalysis hypothesis

My proposal concerning the reanalysis of the IHR construction involves the following two features. First, the sequence the nominalizer *no* plus a case marker in IHR sentence is reanalyzed as the clause-linking device in concessive sentences. As for the nominative-marked IHRCs, the nominalizer *no* plus the nonconjunctive nominative *ga* is reanalyzed as a clausal conjunction, *no-ga*. Similarly, in the case of the accusative-marked IHRCs, the nominalizer plus the accusative *o* is reanalyzed as a clausal conjunction, *no-o*. Second, S1 of IHR sentences undergoes a change from an embedded clause to a non-embedded clause and all the constituents up to *no-ga* or *no-o* are reanalyzed as belonging to S1 of concessive sentences. At the same time, S2 undergoes a boundary addition, in that all the constituents occurring after the nominalizer plus a case marker in an IHR sentence are reanalyzed as comprising the S2 of a concessive sentence. The hypothesized processes can thus be schematized as follows. NP_i within S1 in (9)a and (9)b represents the target in the IHR construction.

$$(9) \quad a. \quad [\,[\,[... NP_i ... \quad V1\,]_{S1}\,no]\quad ga \quad ... \quad V2\,]_{S2}$$
$$\phantom{(9) \quad a. \quad [\,[\,[... NP_i ... \quad V1\,]_{S1}\,}\text{NMLZ} \quad \text{NOM}$$

$$\rightarrow \quad [\quad ... \quad ... V1\,]_{S1}\, no\text{-}ga \qquad [... \quad V2\,]_{S2}$$
$$\phantom{\rightarrow \quad [\quad ... \quad ... V1\,]_{S1}\,}\text{CONJ}$$

b. $[... [[... NP_i ... V1]_{S1} \quad no] \quad o \quad V2]_{S2}$

                                   NMLZ   ACC

$\rightarrow$ $[... \qquad ... \qquad V1]_{S1} \quad no\text{-}o \qquad [V2]_{S2}$

                                      CONJ

4.2. Arguments for the reanalysis hypothesis

I will give morphological, syntactic, and semantic grounds in favor of the reanalysis hypothesis.

4.2.1. Analogy to other clausal conjunctions

In what follows I discuss the polyfunctionality of particles *ga* and *o* and the existence of other two-part clausal conjunctions in Modern Japanese, which support the reanalysis hypothesis.

Ga and *o* after nominalized clauses are polyfunctional in Modern Japanese. In addition to being used as case markers, the particles *ga* and *o* may be used as conjunctive particles, connecting a nominalized clause to another clause.[4] The conjunctive particles *ga* and *o* appear in combination with certain nominalizers such as *tokoro* − literally 'place', or *mono* − literally 'thing', in effect forming two-part clausal conjunctions.

The nominalizer *no* can be the first part of such a two-part clausal conjunction. I have in mind the concessive clausal conjunction *noni* 'although', which is generally believed to derive from the nominalizer *no* plus a clausal conjunction *ni* (Konoshima 1966, *Nihon Kokugo Daijiten*). *Noni* started out as a two-part clausal conjunction and later lexicalized into a clausal conjunction through the mechanism of boundary loss. It is now listed as a lexeme in dictionaries.

It thus seems possible to hypothesize that *no-ga* and *no-o* are being reanalyzed as two-part clausal conjunctions perhaps by analogy (See also Horie 1993, 1998).

---

[4] *Ga* and *o* became polyfunctional in Middle Japanese (1192-1602) (Ishigaki 1955, Konoshima 1966, Nishida 1977, Saeki 1966). Japanese grammarians generally believe that the nominative *ga* and the accusative *wo* gave rise to the concessive conjunctive particles *ga* and *wo*. By the time of Late Old Japanese (794-1191), *ga* and *o* came to attach to NPs as case particles. It was also possible for them to follow the nominalized form of a predicate. In Japanese, which has been an OV (verb-final)/postpositional language throughout its history, clause-linking devices appear clause-finally. The position of the case particles, i.e. after a nominalized clause, thus made it possible for them to be reinterpreted as conjunctive particles which link two clauses. Genetti (1986, 1991) discusses developments from case markers to clausal conjunctions in various Bodic languages of Tibeto-Burman. The developments from the nominative and accusative case markers to clausal conjunctions, however, seem to be rare cross-linguistically (Ohori 1991).

4.2.2. Constructional simplicity

If it is possible to suppose that such a reanalysis is taking place, what are the motivations for it? It has been suggested in the literature that languages will tend to change so as to maximize optimality. Although tendencies toward various types of optimality will often conflict with one another, others may be regarded as tendencies in the direction of greater simplicity (Hopper and Traugott 1993:63-67, Langacker 1977:102). Langacker (ibid.:107) proposes constructional simplicity as one such type of language optimality. According to him, there is a tendency for marked constructions to give way to more commonplace ones and for the intrinsic complexity to be reduced.

Two kinds of discrepancies between form and meaning exist in the IHR construction. First, syntactically the entire *no*-nominalized S1 satisfies one of the syntactic requirements of V2, as can be seen by the fact that the case marking on the nominalized S1 correspond to the case marking required for a valence requirement of V2. Semantically, however, a NP inside S1 corresponds to a valence requirement of V2. In other words, there is a syntax-semantics 'mismatch' in the IHR construction (Ohara 1992).

Second, although structurally the *no*-nominalized S1 is embedded within S2, S1 is functionally 'coordination-like' in that, like main clauses, it makes an assertion. There is thus a discrepancy between structure and function. Because of these discrepancies between form and meaning, the IHR construction can be regarded as a marked construction. Reanalysis as the concessive clause-linking construction reduces the complexity.

4.2.3. The directionality of semantic change

The proposed reanalysis is accompanied by a semantic change. Whereas the IHR construction advances a narrative within a sentence, the concessive clause-linking construction expresses a contrast between two propositions. In other words, while the meaning of the IHR construction has to do with the temporal domain, the meaning of the concessive clause-linking construction crucially involves the logical domain. This kind of semantic change is commonly observed in grammaticalization (Sweetser 1990, inter alia).

It was also observed in Section 3.2 that even though concessivity is conventionalized in the concessive clause-linking construction, a temporal sequence relation typically obtains between its two clauses. When a form undergoes grammaticalization, some traces of its original meanings tend to adhere to it ('persistence'). The persistence of temporal sequence relation observed in the concessive clause-linking construction is compatible with the hypothesis that the IHR construction is being grammaticalized into the concessive construction.

5. Conclusion

I have argued in this paper that the concessive clause-linking construction should be recognized separately from the IHR construction, due to its lack of the 'case-matching' phenomenon and its conventionalized meaning of concessivity. After examining the syntactic, semantic, and pragmatic properties of the concessive-clause linking construction, I have proposed that the IHR construction in Modern Japanese may be being reanalyzed as the concessive clause-linking construction, which may account for the restricted occurrence of IHRCs in present-day Japanese. Although the hypothesis presented in this paper needs to be tested against diachronic corpora, I hope to have shown the need to take the grammaticalization process into account when analyzing and explaining grammatical constructions in Modern Japanese.

References

Fillmore, C. J.; P. Kay; and M. C. O'Connor. 1988. Regularity and Idiomaticity in Grammatical Constructions: The case of *Let Alone*. Language 64.501-538.

Genetti, C. 1986. The Development of Subordinators from Postpositions in Bodic Languages. *Berkeley Linguistics Society* 12.387-400.

Genetti, C. 1991. From Postposition to Subordinator in Newari. *Approaches to grammaticalization*. ed. Elizabeth Closs Traugott and Bernd Heine, vol. 2. 227-255. Amsterdam/Philadelphia: John Benjamins Publishing Company.

Goldberg, A. E. 1995. *Constructions: a constructional grammar approach to argument structure*. Chicago and London: The University of Chicago Press.

Hirose, K., and T. Ohori. 1992. Japanese internally headed relative clauses revisited. Paper presented at the annual meeting of the Linguistic Society of America, Philadelphia.

Hopper, P. J., and E. C. Traugott. 1993. *Grammaticalization*. Cambridge: Cambridge University Press.

Horie, K. 1993. From zero to overt nominalizer no: a syntactic change in Japanese. *Japanese/Korean Linguistics* 3. ed. Choi Soonja, 305-321. Stanford, California, CSLI Publications.

Horie, K. 1998. Functional Duality of Case-marking Particles in Japanese and Its Implications for Grammaticalization: A Constrastive Study with Korean. *Japanese/Korean Linguistics* 8. ed. D. J. Silva; 147-159. Stanford, California, CSLI Publications.

Ishigaki, K. 1955. *Joshi no rekishiteki kenkyû* (A historical study of auxiliaries). Tokyo: Iwanami Shoten.

Itô, J. 1986. Head-Movement at LF and PF: The Syntax of Head-Internal Relatives in Japanese. *University of Massachusetts Occasional Papers in Linguistics* 11: 109-138.

Kay, P., and C. J. Fillmore. 1994. Grammatical Constructions and Linguistic Generalizations: the *What's X doing Y?* Construction. *Language*, 75 (1), 1-33.

Kitayama, K. 1951. *Genji Monogatari no Goho* (The Usages and Expressions of *the Tale of Genji*). Tokyo, Tokoshoin.

Konoshima, M. 1966. *Kokugo joshi no kenkyuu - joshi shi no sobyo* (A study of particles). Tokyo: Ohusha.

Kuroda, S.-Y. 1992. *Japanese syntax and semantics: collected papers.* Dordrecht: Kluwer Academic Publishers.

Kuroda, S.-Y. 1992 (1974-77). Pivot-independent relativization in Japanese. *Japanese syntax and semantics: collected papers.*114-174. Dordrecht: Kluwer Academic Publishers.

Kuroda, S.-Y. 1999. Shubu Naizai Kankei Setsu (Internally headed relative clauses). *Kotoba no Kaku to Shuhen: Nihongo to Eigo no Aida* (Language, its core and periphery: Explorations in English and Japanese). ed. S.-Y. Kuroda and M. Nakamura. Tokyo, Kuroshio Shuppan: 27-103.

Lambrecht, K. 1994. *Information structure and sentence form.* Cambridge: Cambridge University Press.

Langacker, R. W. 1977. Syntactic Reanalysis. *Mechanisms of Syntactic Change.* ed. Charles N. Li 57-139. Austin: University of Texas Press.

Lê, V. C. 1988. *'NO' ni yoru bun umekomi no koozoo to hyoogen no kinoo* (The Structure and function of sentence embedded by *no*). Tokyo: Kuroshio Shuppan.

Martin, S. 1975. *A Reference Grammar of Japanese.* New Haven: Yale University.

Mihara, K. 1994. Iwayuru shuyôbu naizaigata kankeisetsu ni suite (On so-called internally headed relative clauses). *Nihongogaku* .7.80-92.

Nihon Kokugo Daijiten (Unabridged Dictionary of Japanese). 1974. Tokyo: Shogakukan.

Nishida, N. 1977. Joshi (Auxiliaries) 1. *Bunpo* (Grammar) II. Tokyo: Iwanami Shoten.

Ohara, K. H. 1992. On Japanese Internally Headed Relative Clauses. *Berkeley Linguistic Society*18: 100-108.

Ohara, K. H. 1996. *A constructional approach to Japanese internally headed relativization.* University of California, Berkeley. Ph.D. dissertation.

Ohori, T. 1991. Case Markers and Clause Linkage: Toward a Semantic Typology. Paper presented at the Second International Cognitive Linguistics Association Conference (ICLA) at Santa Cruz, California.

Oono, S. 1993. *Kakari musubi no kenkyuu* (A study of bound ending). Tokyo: Iwanami Shoten.

Saeki, B. 1966. *Joodai Kokugohoo Kenkyuu* (A study of Old Japanese). Tokyo: Daito Bunka Daigaku Tokyo Kenkyusho.

Sweetser, E. 1990. *From Etymology to Pragmatics: Metaphorical and Cultural Aspects of Semantic Structure.* Cambridge, Cambridge University Press.

Van Valin, R. D., Jr., (ed.) 1993. *Advances in Role and Reference Grammar.* Amsterdam/Philadelphia: John Benjamins Publishing Company.

Kakarimusubi and Focus Structure

KAORU OHTA

University of Washington

1. Introduction

This paper deals with the Old Japanese Focus construction often referred to as Kakarimusubi (hereafter, KM for short) and proposes an analysis for how the Focus interpretation of KM is derived. In particular, I argue that the pseudocleft like interpretation of KM sentences is derived by mapping the Presupposition and the Focus portions of KM sentences onto a representation where the Topic and Focus are annotated. In this analysis, the morpho-syntactic requirement that the predicate of KM be the adnominal form stems from the need to represent the Presuppositional portion of the sentence onto the Topic position. In addition, I will show that both the Presupposition and Focus are mapped onto the A'-positions and that both Old and Modern Japanese Focus constructions have the same Focus position.

2. The Kakarimusubi Rule

Let me begin the discussion by outlining the structure of KM sentences. As illustrated in (1), the rule of KM under discussion has two components: i) there is a constituent marked with a Kakari-particle (K-particle for short) (originally, Yamada 1908) (for convenience, I will refer to a phrase marked by a K-particle as a K-phrase) and ii) The predicate of a KM sentence generally takes the 'adnominal' form.

(1)   [... [K-phrase-*zo/namu/ya/ka*] ... V$^{\text{adnominal form}}$]

Relevant examples are given in (2): The K-phrase is underlined and the adnominal form is in bold face.

(2) a.   ozora-no   tsuki no   hikari-si kiyoke-reba <u>kage   misi</u>
         broad:sky-gen. moon-gen. light-Pt. bright-if   image see

   <u>midu-zo</u> madu kohori-**ker-u**
   water-ZO first   freeze-aux(recollective)-adn.   (KKS 316)[1]

   'Last night the moonlight in the broad skies was so bright that the waters that reflected it have frozen to translucence first of all.'

   b.   Itunomani kouyou   si-nu-ran   yamazakura
        unnoticed turning:yellow do-aux.-aux:adn. mountain:cherry

   <u>kinoo-ka</u>   hana-no   tir-u-wo.
   yesterday-KA flower-nom. fall-adn.-acc.

   osimi-**si**
   lament-aux(past):adn. (SKS 523)[2]

   'Unnoticed, leaves of cherry turned yellow; was it yesterday that we lamented that the flower fell?'

   c.   Ofotome-no Dainagon-wa   <u>tatu no   kubi-no tama-ya</u>
        Otomo-gen. Councillor-top. dragon-gen. head-gen. ball-YA

   tori-te. owas-i-**tar-u**   (TM)
   take-TE come:honorific-cont.-aux(perfect/result).-adn.

   'Did Otomo-no Dainagon get the eyes of the dragon's head?'

In Older Japanese, the adnominal form of certain classes of verbals is morphologically distinguished from the conclusive form. For instance, in

---

[1] In this paper, I use the abbreviations listed below for the titles of the work from which the examples are cited:

KKS	<	*Kokinsyuu*
SKS	<	*Shin-Kokinsyuu*
TM	<	*Taketori-monogatari*
MYS	<	*Manyoushuu*
MS	<	*Makura-no Soushi*

[2] The auxiliary *-si* is the adnominal form of the past auxiliary *-ku*.

(3), the form of the verb *in-* 'to go' is morphologically distinguished depending on where it occurs: When it occurs in the sentence-ending (conclusive) position, the suffix *-u* follows it. In contrast, it is suffixed with *-uru* when in the adnominal position.

(3) a. Sikibu-kyoo-no miya-no   Minamoto-tyuuzyou,
            -lord-gen. palace-gen.   -middle:captain
         mui-domo -nado,   ari-ker-u-wa   **in-u.**(MYS: 132)
         sixth-chamberlain -so:on exist-aux.-adn.-top. go-concl.

   'Those who were there, likes of the Middle Captain Minamoto, the (second son of) Lord Shikibu, and the Sixth Rank Chamberlain, all went.

   b. Ayasi-ku **in-uru** mono-domo-kana. (MYS: 132)
       oddly-adv. go-adn. people-pl.-SP

   'How oddly those who went behaved.'

What is peculiar about this type of KM sentence is that the sentence-ending predicate takes the adnominal form, instead of the conclusive form. For convenience, in the discussion that follows I will refer to the clause containing the adnominal form as the A-clause.

Semantically, by using KM, the speaker of the sentence highlights the information in the K-phrase, drawing the hearer's attention. This function is generally on a par with the notion 'Focus' as defined by Erteschik-Shir 1997. She defines the notion of Focus as in (4) (Ertschik-Shir 1997:11):

(4) The Focus of a sentence S = the (intention of a) constituent c of S which the speaker intends to direct the attention of his/her hearer(s) to, by uttering S.

The choice of a K-particle affects how the Focus phrase is interpreted. For instance, when the particle *-ka* or *-ya* marks the Focus, the Focus phrase is generally interpreted as the Focus of a question. On the other hand, with the particle *-zo*, the Focus phrase is interpreted as representing an emphatic, assertive information. To see how KM works, let me reexamine example (1c), which is repeated in (5) with the surrounding context.

(5) Sekai-no hitono   ih-i-ke-ru-wa   "<u>Ohotomo-no</u>
    worldly-gen. person say-cont.-aux.-adn.-top.   -gen.

    <u>dainagon-wa tatu-no kubi-no   tama-**ya** tori-te</u>
      -top.dragon-gen.head-gen. ball-YA take-TE

    <u>ohasi-ta-ru</u>."   "Ina, sa-mo ara-z-u.   Mimanako
    come:honorific-aux.-adn. No so-even be:irrealis-neg.-concl. eyeball.

    hutatu-ni sumomo-no yau-nar-u   mono-wo-zo sohe-te
    two-at   plum-gen.   appearance-be-adn thing-acc.-ZO accompany-TE

    imasi-tar-u"-to   ihi-kere-ba, ...
    exist:polite-aux.-adn. -quot. say-aux:realis-if

    'What the worldly person says is "<u>is it the eyes of the dragon that
    Otomo-no Dainagon came back with?</u>" "No, that's not so," the other
    person replies, "he (Dainagon) supplied the one with something like
    two plums in the location of (dragon's) eyes..."'

The context clearly shows that in (1c) (the underlined part in (5)), the K-phrase, *tatu-no kubi-no tama-ya* 'eyes of a dragon head+YA' is what the speaker wants to draw the hearer's attention to. With the particle *-ya*, the KM sentence in (1c) is interpreted as a confirmatory question. The response to this question (1c) (*Ina, sa-mo ara-z-u. Mimanako hutatu-ni sumomo-no yau-nar-u mono-wo-zo sohe-te imasi-tar-u.* 'No, that's not so. He supplied the one with something like two plums in the location of (dragon's) eyes.') states that what Otomo-no Dainagon brought back is something resembling a plum, not eyes of a dragon. This illustrates that the Focus of the question (1c) is the item that K-phrase refers to (i.e. eyes of a dragon). Apparently, the speaker knows that Ohotomo-no dainagon brought something back and this portion is represented by the A-clause. Hence, it is reasonable to assume that in (1c), the K-phrase (*tatu-no kubi-no tama-ya* 'eyes of a dragon head') constitutes the Focus and the A-clause portion (*tori-te ohasi-ta-ru* 'took and came back') presents what is already understood.

3. Issues

In analyzing the KM phenomenon, the two questions in (6) are often asked.

(6) a.   What is the role of the A-clause?

     b.   How is the Focus interpretation given to the K-phrase?

From observing the KM sentence in (5), the answer to the question in (6a) is readily available. Iwasaki 1997, for instance, argues that OJ A-clauses in general represent what is presupposed (or in Iwasaki's terminology, 'suppressed assertions'). Presupposed information creates the background against which the Focus is highlighted (or foregrounded). In plain terms, the A-clause portion describes the information that is assumed to be known (or not at issue) in the speaker's utterance.

Syntactically, OJ A-clauses are 'nominalized' clauses as evidenced by the fact that they can occur in argument positions as shown in (7).

(7) a. niwakani [[[wazurah-u] hito-no   ar-u]-ni...   (MS 26)
         suddenly   get:sick-adn. person-nom. exist-adn.-at

         'Suddenly, (at the sight of) a person who is sick...'

    b. Fuzi-no   hana-wa   [sinahi   nagaku, iro koku
        wisteria-gen. flower-top. dangling:blossoms long   color deep

        saki-tar-u]   ito   medetas-i. (MS 35)
        bloom-aux.-adn.extremely be:auspicious-concl.

        'As for wisteria flowers, their long dangling blossoms which bloom in deep color are extremely auspicious.'

The A-clause in (7a) is marked with the particle -*ni* and the one in (7b) occurs as the subject of the predicate *ito medetasi* 'be extremely auspicious'. In this sense, OJ A-clauses correspond to the Modern Japanese nominalized clause headed by -*no*. In MJ, *no*-nominalization allows the predicate to occur in any argument position. In fact, it has been pointed out that OJ A-clauses correspond to MJ *no*-nominalization clauses (Horie 1997, Kaplan and Whitman 1995, among others). The MJ translation of (7) is given in (8).

(8) a. totuzen [[[byooki-no] hito]-ga   i-ru-no]-ni...
         suddenly   sick-be:adn. person-nom. exist-pres.-<u>NO</u>-at

    b. Fuzi-no   hana-wa   [hanbusa-ga   nagaku,
        wisteria-gen. flower-top. dangling:blossoms-nom. long

        iro-ga   koku sai-te i-ru-no]-ga   taisoo
        color-nom.   deep:adv.bloom-TE exist-pres.-<u>NO</u>-nom. extremely

        kekkou-da.
        wonderful-be:pres.

Another correspondence between OJ A-clauses and MJ *no*-nominalization clauses is observed in the MJ pseudocleft sentence given in (9). In this construction, the *no*-nominalization clause represents the Presupposition and what appears in precopula position constitutes the Focus of the sentence.

(9) Taroo-ga   hanasi-te i-ru-no-wa   Suwahirigo-da.
       -nom. speak-TE exist-pres.-NO-top. Swahili-copula:pres.
    'What Taro is speaking is Swahili.'

    Presupposition: [Taroo-ga hanasi-te i-ru-no]
    Focus: [Suwahirigo]

Both KM and MJ pseudocleft constructions are Focus constructions and in these constructions, the A-clause and the *no*-nominalization clause function to represent the Presupposition. Semantically, these two constructions are comparable to each other.

4. Licensing Focus Construction

At this point, let me briefly discuss the word order of MJ pseudocleft. The word order of the MJ pseudocleft is quite different from that of its non-pseudocleft counterpart. For instance, the non-pseudocleft sentence corresponding to (9) should look like (10).

(10) Taroo-wa/ga   Suwahirigo-o hanasi-te i-ru.
       -top./nom. Swahili-acc.   speak-TE exist-pres.

    'Taro is speaking Swahili.'

As comparing (9) and (10) reveals, one peculiar feature of the pseudocleft is that the Presupposition and Focus portions are related with the copula.

This is exactly what Rochemont 1986 observes for cleft constructions. Rochemont points out that a cleft-like relation is (syntactically) established by means of the copula. Via the copula, the Presupposition and the Focus hold an identificational relationship. Given this analysis, even though KM apparently does not require a syntactic representation of this sort, it is plausible that KM is represented as the pseudocleft in order to yield a pseudocleft-like interpretation. In this representation, KM sentences are mapped onto the copulative structure where the Presupposition and the Focus are annotated. I assume that this mapping looks like the one in (11b) and that this mapping renders a pseudocleft like interpretation to KM sentences.

(11) a.   KM: [$_{\text{A-clause}}$··· [K-phrase] ...]

    b.   Focus Representation:
        [$_{\text{Presupposition}}$ A-clause](-wa) [$_{\text{Focus}}$ K-phrase](-da)

Given this analysis, the A-clause requirement of KM is considered to stem from the condition of mapping the A-clause and the K-phrase onto the Focus representation. In order for the predicate to be mapped onto the Presupposition position in (11b), it must be nominalized. Being nominalized, the predicate becomes an NP and functions as the semantic 'Subject' of the identificational sentence.

This is in principle identical to the 'type-shifting' operation that Ogihara 1987 proposes for the Modern Japanese 'obligatory Focus' construction as in (12).

(12) Taroo-ga   okubyoo-da.
     -nom. timid-be:pres.

    'It is Taro who is timid.'

Ogihara argues that in the MJ obligatory Focus construction, two type-shifting operations are involved: One is 'type-shifting' of a VP to an NP through which the denotation of a VP is shifted to that of an NP. As a result, the VP is interpreted as the semantic 'subject.' Secondly, the NP is 'type-shifted' to a VP and is interpreted as the semantic 'predicate.' Through this operation, (12) is interpreted as denoting that there is a singlton set of entity which is timid and it is identified as Taro. In the end, (12) is interpreted as equivalent to a pseudocleft sentence such as (13).

(13) [Okubyoo-na-no]-wa   Taroo-da.
     timid-be:adn.-NO-top.   -be:pres.

    'The one who is timid is Taro.'

Nominalization involved in this construction is assumed to turn the property into an individual having this property (Ogihara 1987, p. 218).

If this analysis is on the right track, the nominalized nature of the A-clause is viewed as a morpho-syntactic type-shifting operation and enables its mapping onto the Presupposition position.

5. Consequences

Given this analysis, the KM sentence in (1c) is mapped onto the representation in (14).

(14) (=(1c))
[Topic Ohotomo-no dainagon-wa tori-te ohasi-ta-ru]= [Focus tatu-no kubi-no tama-ya]

This representation should be translated into MJ as (15), which takes the form of the pseudocleft construction.

(15) Ohotomo-no dainagon-ga   totte irasyat-ta-no-wa
                            -nom. take come:honorific-past-NO-top.

tatu-no   kubi-no   tame   desu-ka?
dragon-gen. head-gen. crystal be:polite-KA

'Is it eyes of a dragon that Ootomo-no Dainagon brought back?'

In regards to the Focus position, syntactic evidence suggests that the position of Focus NP in both OJ and MJ is the outside of the maximal projection of a clause. Ikawa 1993 observes that the K-phrase is generally preposed in the position preceding the subject NP, citing the examples in (16).

(16) a.   ... ta-ga   tamoto-wo-ka wa-ga makuraka-m-u   (MYS 439)
          who-gen. sleeve-acc.-KA I-nom. have:as:a:pillow-aux.-adn.

     '...whose sleeve should I have as my pillow?'

     b.   ... tawakoto-ka   hito-no   ihi-tu-ru.   (MYS 3333)
          nonsense-KA people-nom. say-aux.-adn.

     'Is it idle talk that people are telling?'

     c.   Katayori-ni ito-wo-zo   wa-ga yor-u...   (MYS 1987)
          singly-adv. thread-acc.-ZO I-nom. twist-adn.

     'I twist the thread to one side only...'

     d.   ...nageki-zo wa-ga   su-ru.   (MYS 714)
          crying-ZO I-nom. do-adn.

     '... I can but lament.'

In the KM sentences in (16), the object K-phrases are preposed in front of the subject NPs (marked either with -*ga* or *no*). Based on this observation, Ikawa goes on to argue that the syntactic position of the K-phrase can be outside the maximal projection of a clause.

In MJ, Mihara 1990 argues that the Focus NP-*ga* in the multiple nominative construction appears outside of the sentential node, proposing that the multiple nominative construction should look like the 'split-S' structure shown in (17). The position of NP-ga_1 in (17) is assumed to be the position of the Focus NP-*ga*.

(17)

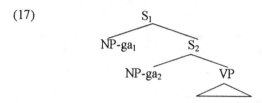

Mihara shows that NP-ga_1 in (17) yields a different quantifier scope interpretation from the NP-ga_2. In order to see his point, let's first consider the sentences in (18).

(18) a. Dare-mo-ga   konpyuutaa-o mot-te   i-ru.
         who-even-nom. computer-acc. own-TE exist-pres.

         'Everyone owns a computer.'

    b. [dare-mo-ga   tukat-te i-ru]   konpyuutaa-ga koware-te
        who-even-nom. use-TE exist-pres. computer-nom.break-TE

        simat-ta.
        end:up-past

        'The computer that everyone uses broke down.'

(18a) is ambiguous between the following two readings:

(18a') $\exists x$, x=a computer, everyone has x (computer > everyone)
(18a") $\forall x$, x=person, x has a computer (everyone > computer)

Under the reading illustrated in (18a'), there is a single computer that everyone owns (the number of computers is, therefore, one). I will refer this reading as the single-computer reading. This reading arises because the universal quantifier (*daremo* 'everyone' in this case) is within the scope of the existential quantifier (*konpuutaa* 'a computer'). In contrast, under the reading represented in (18a"), each individual owns his/her own computer (i.e. there are multiple number of computers; hereafter the multiple-computer reading). This is because the universal quantifier takes its scope over the existential quantifier.

The sentence in (18b), on the other hand, is not ambiguous. This sentence has only the single-computer reading. This is because the universal quantifier is syntactically located inside the embedded clause and therefore, the existential quantifier takes wide scope over the universal quantifier. The contrast in quantifier scope in (18) suggests that the scope of a quantifier inside a lower clause does not extend over a clause boundary.

With this in mind, let us consider the example in (19).[3] In (19), the first NP-*ga subete-no daigakuinsei-ga* 'all the graduate students' yields the Focus interpretation.

(19) Subete-no daigakuinsei-ga   [[e tukat-te i-ru]   konpyuutaa-
     all-gen.   graduate:student-nom.   use-TE exist-pres. computer-

     ga koware-te simat-ta].
     nom. break-TE end:up-past

     '(lit.)All the graduate students, a computer (that they are using) broke down.'

The quantifier interpretation of (19) is unambiguous. The only possible reading is the multiple computer reading. This means that the universal quantifier takes wide scope over the existential quantifier (everyone > computer). The wide scope reading of the existential quantifier, i.e. the single-computer reading (*computer > everyone) is excluded.

This fact is accounted for by assuming that there is a clause boundary between NP-*ga*$_1$ and NP-*ga*$_2$ as in (17). Since NP-*ga*$_1$ yields the Focus interpretation, Mihara goes on to argue that the Focus NP-*ga* is projected as an adjunct to a maximal projection of a clause (which I simply mark as S). Mihara also argues that NP-*ga* in (20) is base-generated in this adjunct Focus NP position and is interpreted as Focus.

---

[3] It is worth to pointing out that there should be a slight pause between *subete-no daigakuinsei-ga* 'all the graduate students-nom.' and *tukat-te i-ru* 'is using' in (19). Without a pause, this sentence is likely to be interpreted as the universal quantifier being the subject of the relative clause (thus, it occupies the position of [e]). The interpretation of the sentence would be reversed, as predicted, if the universal quantifier is in the embedded subject position.

(20) a.   Taroo-ga tensai-da.
                -nom. genious-be:pres.   'Taro is genious.'

     a'.   [Taroo-ga [$_S$ tensai-da]]

     b.   Hanako-ga kawai-i.
                -nom. be:pretty-pres.   'Hanako is pretty.'

     b'.   [Hanako-ga [$_S$ kawai-i]]

Given these observations, it is plausible to assume that the Focus phrase is outside of the maximal projection of a clause. Following Rizzi 1997, I assume that the Topic and the Focus phrases in (11b) are projected as adjuncts in A'-positions as shown in (21).

(21) [$_{Topic}$] [$_{Focus}$] [$_{clause(=IP/VP)}$]

In the Topic position, the Presupposition portion of the sentence is mapped. There are a few options by which this mapping is carried out: One option is to nominalize the clause as observed in KM and MJ pseudocleft, where the predicate takes the nominalized form. The other option is, as Ogihara 1987 proposes, to somehow 'type-shift' the VP and the Focus NP so that the VP becomes the semantic subject and the Focus NP becomes the semantic predicate. Even though this analysis is somewhat speculative at this moment, examples such as the one in (22) suggest that this analysis is on the right track. In MJ, a response to a wh-question generally takes the form of a copulative sentence as shown in (22).

(22) Q: Dare-ga   ki-ta-no/   ki-masi-ta-ka?
           who-nom. come-past-NO/come-polite-past-KA   'Who came?'

     A: Tanaka-san (da-yo/desu).
                (be:pres.-YO/be:polite:pres.)   'It is Tanaka-san.'

In the exchange in (22), the response to the question, *dare-ga ki-ta-no?* 'who came?' simply consists of the information sought by the wh-phrase. It is possible to add the copula as the predicate. Since the wh-phrase typically represents the Focus of the (wh-) question as Rochemont 1986 and Erteschik-Shir 1997 show, it is reasonable to assume that the way the response to the question in (22) is formed is a result of mapping the Presupposition and the Focus of the question onto the Topic and Focus positions, respectively. In the question sentence in (22), the speaker presupposes 'someone came' and draws the hearer's attention by posing a

wh-phrase *dare-ga* 'who-nom.' as the Focus of the sentence. The
Presupposition and the Focus of this question sentence can be represented
as in (23).

(23) [Topic ki-ta-no]   [Focus dare-ga]
      come-past-NO   who-nom

The answer in the exchange in (22) indicates that the hearer identifies the
Topic and Focus of the sentence and composes a response only with the
information corresponding to the Focus.

6. Summary

To summarize, in this presentation, I have shown that in both OJ and MJ
Focus constructions, the Presupposition and Focus constituents are subject
to mapping onto the A'-positions of Topic and Focus Phrases. In OJ, the A-
clause requirement of KM is attributed to the requirement that the
Presupposition portion of the sentence be mapped onto the Topic Phrase. In
MJ, there are more options to carry out this mapping. Finally, I have shown
that a typical response observed to a wh-question in MJ is reasonably
analyzed as the result of Presupposition and Focus mapping.

References

Erteschik-Shir, N. 1997. *The Dynamics of Focus Structure*. Cambridge, UK:
Cambridge Univ. Press.

Ikawa, H. 1993. On Kakarimusubi in Old Japanese: A Possibility under a
Generative Grammatical Perspective. unpublished ms. UC Irvine.

Iwasaki, S. 1997. Suppressed Assertion and the Functions of the Final-Attributive
in Prose and Poetry of Heian Japanese. (to appear) *Textual Parameters in Older
Languages* eds. S. Herring et al. Amsterdam: John Benjamin.

Kaplan, T. and J. B. Whitman. 1995. The Category of Relative Clauses in
Japanese, with Reference to Korean. *Journal of East Asian Linguistics* 4:29-58.

Kuroda, S.-Y. 1992. Judgement Forms and Sentence Forms. *Japanese Syntax and
Semantics: Collected Papers* ed. S.-Y. Kuroda. 13-77. Dordrecht: Kluwer
Academic Publishers.

Matsuda, Y. 1997. Representation of Focus and Presupposition in Japanese.
Doctoral dissertation. University of Southern California.

Mihara, K. 1990. Tajuu-Shukaku-Koubun-o Megutte (Issues on the Multiple-
Subject Construction). *Nihongogaku 9:8*:66-76.

Niita, Y. 1984. Kakari-musubi-ni Tsuite (On Kakari-musubi). *Kenkyuu-shiryoo
Nihon Bunpou 5: Jojihen 1: Joshi.* eds. K. Suzuki and O. Hayashi, 101-135.
Tokyo: Meiji Shoin.

Ogihara, T. 1987. 'Obligatory Focus' in Japanese and Type-Shifting Principles. *Proceedings of the West Coast Conference on Formal Linguistics 6*, ed. M. Growhurst, 213-227. Stanford: The Stanford Linguistics Association.

Ohno, S. 1993. *Kakari-musubi-no Kenkyuu (Studies on Kakari-musubi)*. Tokyo: Iwanami Shoten.

Quinn, C. 1987. *A Functional Grammar of Predication in Classical Japanese*. Doctoral dissertation. University of Michigan.

Rizzi, L. 1997. The Fine Structure of the Left Periphery. *Elements of Grammar Handbook in Generative Syntax*. ed L. Hageman, Dordrecht: Kluwer.

Rochemont, M. 1986. *Focus in Generative Grammar*. Amsterdam: John Benjamins.

Shibatani, M and C. Cotton. 1976-7. Remarks on Double Nominative Sentences. *Papers in Japanese Linguistics 5*, 261-277.

Whitman, J. B. 1997. Kakarimusubi from a Comparative Perspective. *Japanese/Korean Linguistics 6*, eds. H.-M. Sohn and J. Haig, 161-178. Stanford: CSLI Publications.

Yamada, Y. 1908. Nippon Bunpouron. Tokyo: Houbunkan.

Yanagida, S. 1985. *Muroachi-jidai-no Kokugo*. Tokyo: Tokyodou Shuppan.

Discourse, Grammaticalization, & Intonation: An Analysis of *-ketun* in Korean

MEE-JEONG PARK & SUNG-OCK S. SOHN
University of California, Los Angeles

1. Introduction[1]

Recent work on grammaticalization phenomena indicate that there are two types of grammaticalization: sentence-based and discourse-based (cf. Brinton 1996, Ramat & Hopper 1998). While traditional approaches to grammaticalization have mainly focused on the diachronic process of grammatical markers, evidence suggests that grammaticalization is also motivated by strategic interaction in the flow of communication (cf. Hopper & Traugott 1993, Traugott 2000). The purpose of this study is to investigate the role of discourse and intonation in grammaticalization by examining the linguistic evolution of the Korean sentence ender *-ketun(yo)* which functions as an interactional marker, meaning 'you see?', 'the fact is ...' (Park 1998). The data for this study consist of historical data as well as naturally occurring conversations. Historical data reveal that the *-ketun* form has undergone a

---

[1] We would like to thank Noriko Akatsuka, Marjorie H. Goodwin, Sun-Ah Jun, Chungmin Lee, Hyo-Sang Lee, Emanuel Schegloff, Ho-min Sohn, and Hongyin Tao for their helpful comments. Any errors, however, are our own.

functional shift from a clause connective suffix 'if, when, since' to an utterance final marker, as illustrated in example (1) and (2) below.[2]

(1)   *uysimtapin kot-i   is-kekun molomay nepi mwulwum-al puthe*
        doubtful thing-NOM be-if certainly widely question-ACC attach
        '<u>If</u> there are things you are not sure of, then you should raise
        questions, and ...' [*welinsekpo* 1459]

(2)   S: *owel samsipil-i Memorial Day-i-ntey*
           May 30-NOM Memorial Day-be-and
   →   *welyoil-i   ketun-yo.*
           Monday-be KETUN-POL
           kunkkanun ku ttay-ka yenhyu-ka com   kin seym-i-kwu
           so   that time-NOM long weekend-NOM a bit long case-be-and
           '(<u>You see</u>) May 30th is Memorial Day and it falls on Monday.
           So it is rather a long weekend, and ...'

In example (1) taken from middle Korean, -*ketun* is used as a conditional marker. The same form -*ketun* is used as a sentence ender in modern Korean, as illustrated in (2). As a sentence-ender, -*ketun* can be used for various interactional purposes such as justification, clarification, or tightening up an argument better (Park 1998).

In this paper, we suggest that -*ketun* has undergone a historical process of grammaticalization from a textual function to an interpersonal marker which highlights the speaker's epistemic stance.[3] We attempt to demonstrate that the new interactional function of -*ketun* as an utterance-final particle has developed from its erstwhile meaning of conditional. It will be shown that the boundary tones of -*ketun* and discourse contexts play a crucial role in the process of grammaticalization.

2. The development of -*ketun*

Middle Korean data suggest that all occurrences of -*ketun* are limited to a single clausal connective position. Table 1 indicates all tokens of -*ketun* in four different versions of the same text [*nokeltay*], which is a highly conversational style, are used as clause connectives.

---

[2] The following abbreviations are used on this paper: ACC: Accusative; COMP: Complementizer; DEF: Deferential; GEN: Genitive; MD: Modal; NM: Nominalizer; NOM: Nominative; POL: Polite; Q: Question; REL: Relativizer; SH: Subject honorific; TOP: Topic

[3] The term 'epistemic' is used here to indicate degrees of commitment by the speaker to what he says (cf. Palmer 1986:51).

Table 1. The use of -*ketun* as a clause connective

Text	Year	# of tokens
penyek nokeltay	1517	83
nokeltay enhay	1670	76
chenge nokeltay	1765	39
monge nekeltay	1790	38

When used as a clause connective, -*ketun* functions to express conditional, concessive, temporal, or causal relationship between two events. While the use of -*ketun* as conditional is most commonly observed in historical texts, a concessive meaning appears after 16[th]C, as illustrated in (3).[4]

(3)   <u>Concessive</u>   [*penyek nokeltay* (1517)]
       amwuna han mal-ul mwul-<u>etun</u>   sto taytapti mos hA-myen
       anyone one word-ACC ask-KETUN also answer not do-if
       talAn salam-i   wuli-lultaka musum   salAm-ul   poli-o
       other people-NOM we-ACC   what   person-ACC see-Q
       'If we are unable to answer even one word anyone asks, what would they think of us?'

-*ketun* is also used to signal a BACKGROUND for the proposition made in the main clause. In (4), for example, the -*ketun* clause functions to provide the background information for the main clause event.

(4)   <u>Backgrounding</u> (scene-setting)   [*welinsekpo* (1459) 1:29]
       soy seng-s   kaontAy kolAn pul-i-<u>etun</u>[5]
       iron castle-GEN middle all   fire-be-KETUN
       kuey tuli-ketun wulunAn-la
       there enter-if   cry out-DEC
       'There is all fire inside the iron castle, <u>and</u> if people enter there, they cry out.'

In (5) below, -*ketun* is used to provide the ground for the speaker's desire to travel together. Note that the -*myen* conditional is unacceptable in (5).[6]

---

[4] Crosslinguistic evidence suggests that conditionals are the source of concessive (Hopper and Traugott (1993:180).

[5] -*etun* is an allomorph of -*ketun*.

[6] Note that in an earlier version, *penyek nokeltay* (1517), instead of -*ketun*, connective -*keni* whose main function is to express reason or background information, is used.

(5)   <u>Reason</u> 'since' 'because'   [*nokelytay enhay* (1670)]
       *ney imi   mal   phA-lla ka-<u>ketun</u>/*myen*
       you already horse sell-in order to go-KETUN
       wuli pes cie   ka-m-i   machi tyotho-ta
       we friend make go-NM-Nom just be good-DEC
       'Since you already plan to go and sell horses, it will be good to go
       together as friends.'

(6)   *nay-ka say-*ketun/lamyen melli nallaka-ko   siph-ta.*
       I-NOM bird-be- if   far fly-want-COMP want-DEC
       'If I were a bird, I want to fly far away.'

       While all occurrences of -*ketun* in historical data are limited to a
clause connective, our conversational data as well as written narratives in
modern Korean reveal that -*ketun* is used predominantly at a sentence-final
position. What is the motivating force in the grammaticalization from a
conditional connective to a sentence ender which highlights the speaker's
epistemic stance? This paper will demonstrate that the diachronic functional
shift of -*ketun* is the result of the interplay of grammar and discourse by
examining strategic interactions and intonational contours encoded in -*ketun*.

3. -*ketun* with high boundary tone H%

Our conversation data reveal that a vast majority of -*ketun* (45 tokens of out
of total 56 occurrences) at the sentence-final position carry a high boundary
tone H%. In this section, we will examine the pragmatic aspect of -*ketun*
which triggers the frequent use of high boundary tone when used in natural
discourse. Among many different clause connectives which are also used as
sentence endings, such as -*nuntey*, -*nikka*, etc., only -*ketun* takes H% with
such a high frequency. This seems to emphasize the unique aspect that makes
-*ketun* different from other similar clause connectives.

3.1 Data

The data consist of 240 minutes of naturally occurring audio taped
conversations during a small group bible study. The group consists of eight
Korean speakers studying abroad in Los Angeles. Scicon's Pitch Works
speech analysis software was used to determine the exact type of boundary
tone for each occurrence of -*ketun* from spoken data. From the 240 minutes
of conversations, a total of 72 tokens were found. Among them, only 56
tokens had recognizable pitch tracks due to background noise, overlapping,
creaky voice, etc. The remaining 16 tokens were not taken into consideration

in this study. The analysis reveals that 80.4% of the occurrences of -*ketun* carry the high boundary tone H%, and 19.6% of L%, HL% or LHL%.

Table 2. Tone types and tokens of -*ketun*

Tone type	Total #
H%	45
L%	6
HL%	4
LHL%	1
Total	**56**

3.2 Structure of Korean prosody

Jun (1998) provides two tonally marked prosodic levels in Korean: Accentual Phrase (AP) and Intonational Phrase (IP). In utterances, one or more syllables constitute an AP, and one or more AP constitute a higher prosodic level unit called Intonational Phrase (IP) which Pierrehumbert & Hirschberg (1990) considers as the primary unit of meaning analysis. The final syllable of an IP is marked with a big juncture and associated with a special tone assigned to the last syllable of the IP called boundary tone. In Korean, there are 9 boundary tones L%, H%, LH%, HL%, LHL%, LHLH%, HLHL%, and LHLHL% (Jun 2000) marking the end of Intonational Phrase (IP) which does not necessarily coincide with the syntactic sentence endings.

The use of boundary tone in conjunction with the sentence ending not only manifests the speaker's stance, but also intensifies the meaning of the utterance and at the same time ratifies the particular stance of the interactional relationship between the speaker and the interlocutor(s).

3.3 Analysis

In this section, we analyze the speaker's stance and discourse organization constructed through the boundary tones associated with the sentence ending -*ketun*. The data analysis supports that H% used with -*ketun* has two main functions--to elicit the other's response and for hierarchical signaling. In Korean, as well as in most other languages, yes-no questions always take H% (Jun & Oh 1996) to signal 'other-directed' utterances which elicit a response or reaction from the hearer. According to Pierrehumbert & Hirschberg (1990), H% in English may also be signaling a hierarchical relationship between intentions underlying the current utterance and a subsequent one. That is, the clause that contains -*ketun* H% functions as a bridge connecting the preceding and/or the following utterance, or even two larger discourse segments.[7]

---

[7] Out of the 56 tokens of -*ketun*, there was no single case where the speaker initiated a new topic

We will delineate two types of environments in which the sentence ending -*ketun* is associated with H%: a) between two sentences within the same turn by the same speaker, and b) at an utterance-final position triggering a turn change resulting in sequence expansion.[8] Out of the 56 tokens of -*ketun* found from our data, 50 of them correspond to the first case, i.e., expansion of the turn by the same speaker. The remaining 6 cases out of the 56 tokens correspond to the second case, i.e., an expansion of the turn between two or more speakers. In some instances, there are 'other initiated repairs' in forms of post expansion or insert expansion.[9] However, -*ketun* still functions as a bridge connecting the preceding and the following segments separated by a big chunk of expanded turns between them.

3.3.1 -*ketun* -H% within the same turn

In the following excerpt, four Korean speakers talk about a guy the speaker M1 met at the bible class offered by the church they attend. Speaker M1 is amazed at this guy who has an incredible memory.

(7)   **[Excerpt #1: Bible quiz]**

1	M1:	*ku pwun-i seymilhan pwupwun-ey tayhayse* **A**
		that person-NOM detailed part -at regarding
2		*kieklyek-i cohun ke kathay-yo.*
		memory-NOM good COMP seem-POL
		'I think his memory about small details is very good.'

3	M2:	*a::*
		'Oh'

4	M1:	*kulenikka kukey wuli-ka mayil* **B**
		thus that we-NOM everyday
5 -->		*sengkyeng sihem-ul po-**ketun**-yo* **[H%]** *maycwu* **[H%]**

---

with -*ketun*. At least, certain context was implied beforehand.

[8] Sequence Expansions are additional participation by the speech act participants through additional turns over and above the two which compose the minimal version of the sequence, minimal adjacency pair (Schegloff 1995).

[9] Expansions occur in the three possible places; before the first pair part (pre-expansions), between the first and the projected second pair part (insert expansions), and after the second pair part (post-expansions).

bible   test-ACC take-KETUN-POL   every week
'That is, we always take the bible exam-**KETUN**, every week'

6   *kuntey uyoylo   mwuncey isanghan ke manha-yo*
       but   unexpectedly question weird   thing a lot-POL
       'but there are many weird questions.'

(omitted)

10   M 1:   *oa::: cengmal ceyil elyewun mwuncey mak ceyil*   **C**
              Wow really   most difficult question very most
              heyskalli-nun mwuncey
              confuse-REL question
              'Wow. Even the most difficult question, the most tricky question,

11   *ceyil ttaci-nun   mwuncey ku pwun-i   kunyang*
              most intrigue-REL question that person-NOM just
              ta maca-yo
              all be correct-POL
              the most intriguing question, he gets them all right.'

12   *ettehkey kulehkey toinun-ci molukeysse-yo*
              how   so become-COMP not know-POL
              'I don't know how he does that.'

In this excerpt, M1 talks mostly in a narrative style. In segment A, the speaker M1 describes how this guy in his bible class has such a good memory. In order to justify that this is not just speculation, but reliable information, M1 explains how he got acquainted with the man in segments B and C. To elaborate his point, M1 provides background information: 'They have bible quiz every week-*ketun*-H%'. H% used with -*ketun* cues the upcoming details, i.e., 'The guy gets all the weird and difficult questions right' which support the speaker's earlier claim about the guy's good memory.

In the above excerpt, M1 provides information about the guy, the bible quiz, the weird and difficult questions, etc. There must be a reason why the speaker uses -*ketun* in line 5, 'we take bible test every week -*ketun* -H%' but not with the preceding and following sentences. The data analysis suggests that the -*ketun* marked information functions as background for the upcoming proposition, and at the same time, serves as a bridge connecting the claim and further justification.

Below is a diagram that illustrates the function of -*ketun* -H% in the above excerpt.

Figure 1. The usage of -*ketun* within the same turn

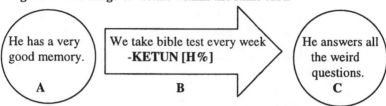

As the diagram illustrates, the utterance in segment A is further supported by segment B, which serves as background information to the segment C. In other words, the -*ketun* marked entity functions as a bridge between the two sets of discourse segments A and C. In this case, the underlying meaning 'because', 'you see?' conveyed in -*ketun* surfaces throughout the whole sentence in line 5-6, 'we take bible test every week -*ketun* -H%'. The use of -*ketun* in line 5 may be understood as an expanded version of the clause connective at a discourse level in that the -*ketun* marked information serves as a condition for the truth of the subsequent utterance.

3.3.2 -*ketun* -H% triggering sequence expansion

In the above section, -*ketun* -H% was used between sentences or discourse segments within the same turn of the same speaker. In contrast, the following excerpt illustrates the use of -*ketun* -H% triggering a sequence expansion. That is, the utterance final -*ketun* triggers the hearer to take the turn.

(8)   **[Excerpt #2: Do you have the jack?]**

1   M   *ike kulem ettek ha -si -llay -yo*
                this then how   do-SH -INT-POL
                'Then, what are you gonna do with this?'

2   F: *cikum*
                'now..'

3   M: | *cikum sipsa-pwun cengto hay -ss -nuntey*   A |
                | now   14 minutes approx. do-PST-CIRCUM |
                | 'Now it recorded around 14 minutes |

4 *ike nacwungey nokum hay tulil-kka*
  this later   record do give-INTR
  do you want me to record it back later,

5 *ettehkey ha-l-kka-yo*
  how do-PROSP-Q -POL
  Or what should I do?'

6 F: 'Uh..'

7 M: *kulem cayk issu-sey-yo*
       then jack have-SH -POL
       ike-lang yenkyel ha-nun ke -yo
       this-with connect do-REL thing-POL
       'Then, do you have a jack? The one that goes with this?'

8 --> F: *ani eps-**ketun**-yo* **[H%]**   **B**
       no not have -KETUN-POL
       'No, I don't-**KETUN**.'

9 M: *kulemyenun cwu-si-myenun cey-ka taum cwu-ey* **C**
       then   give-SH -if I-NOM next week-at
       'Then, if you give it to me, next week I could.'

10 F: *yey ike an toyn ccok-ey iccok-ey ha-si-myenun*
      yes this not become side-at this side-at do-SH-if
      toyl ke kathay-yo
      become seem-POL
      'Yeah. I think you have to record it in this side,
      the blank side.'

11 M: *ney al-keyss-supnita*
      yes know-MD -DEF
      'Yes. I will.'

12   *ku kamkye iss-ci anhun ccok-eyta ha-myen toynun keci-yo*
      that wind be-NEG side-at do-if be all right-POL
      'I have to use the unwound side, right?'

13 F: *ney.*
      'Yes.'

The speaker M(ale) records something for F(emale) in his own recorder. Once the recording is finished, M asks F in line 3-4 if she wants him to transfer the data in her own tape. When F hesitates in line 5 with 'uh:', M provides F with another option by asking if she has the jack to connect the two recording devices. F answers in line 7 with 'No, I don't-*ketun* -H%'. In line 8, M answers right back with the conjunction, *kulemyen* 'if so' (then) that he will do the transfer for her. It seems like F's utterance in line 7 with -*ketun* -H% triggers M's help offering. This use of -*ketun* functions to mitigate the illocutionary force of making a direct request. Namely, the speaker gives the other interlocutor the option of making the final decision on the basis of the -*ketun* marked information (H. Sohn 1999).

As discussed earlier, yes-no questions always take H% to signal 'other-directed' utterances which elicit a response from the hearer. -*ketun* used with H% within adjacency pair carries an interactional feature seeking for a response or reaction from the interlocutor triggering a sequence expansion.

Figure 2. The usage of -*ketun* triggering sequence expansion

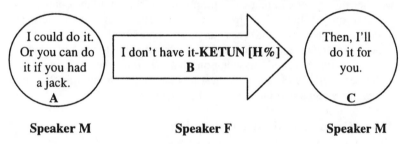

| **Speaker M** | **Speaker F** | **Speaker M** |

As the diagram above implies, the basic function of -*ketun* -H% is similar to that of the same speaker turn discussed earlier. The high boundary tone marked with -*ketun* may be understood as a turn or sequence expansion strategy.[10]

In our data -*ketun* with a low boundary tone L% does not trigger a turn expansion in a similar way as -*ketun* in the high boundary tone H%.[11] The utterance containing the [-*ketun* L%] is mainly used to express an

---

[10] There was one case in our data where the sentence containing -*ketun* was not preceded by the segment A to be connected to the following segment C. However, the segment A was implied by the context.

[11] The total number of L% used with -*ketun* was only 6 out of 56 tokens in our data. The speakers in the data were not close enough to drop the polite ending -*yo* except in a few instances where the speech act was not 'other-directed.'

answer/response to the preceding question. Two out of 56 tokens of -*ketun* were used without the polite sentence ending -*yo* suffixed to -*ketun,* and in these two cases L% was used. The L% used without the polite ending -*yo* is more conceivable than H% without the polite ending. The two cases of -*ketun* -L% without the polite ending -*yo* were used by the oldest man and woman of the group. In other data, where the speakers felt close enough to each other, there were many more instances of -*ketun* -H% without the polite ending. This proves that the H% used with -*ketun* is not triggered by the polite ending -*yo*, nor L% by the absence of the polite ending -*yo*.

Thus far, we have discussed two types of the H% marked -*ketun*. Within the same turn, -*ketun* functions to serve as a basis for further elaboration for the upcoming and/or the preceding utterance. Between two different speakers, -*ketun* is used to invite the other into the discourse. In both cases, the primary function of -*ketun* with H% is to signal a turn or sequence expansion.

Hirschberg & Ward (1995) claim that speakers use high-rise question in English to convey that the propositional content of the utterance is to be added to speaker and hearer's 'mutual beliefs', and to question whether the hearer can relate that propositional content to the contents of the hearer's own beliefs. The frequent use of H% with a non-interrogative sentence ender -*ketun* in Korean can be accounted for by the function of H% which highlights and enhances the interactional aspect of -*ketun* by projecting the speaker's assumption that the information is new to the addressee (Park 1998) and so it must be monitored. In this way, the speaker elicits the hearer's involvement into the discourse.

4. The Grammaticalization path of -*ketun*

The use of -*ketun* as a turn expansion strategy in an utterance-final position is viewed as an expansion of the clause connective -*ketun* whereby the sentence-bound conditional has been grammaticalized into a discourse level. As a conditional connective, the prepositional content of the -*ketun* clause is contingent upon the consequent clause, often implying some kind of causal relationship between the two clauses. In our conversational data, the primary function of -*ketun* with a high boundary tone H% is to signal a turn expansion either by the same speaker or by another participant. At the same time, -*ketun* indicates the speaker's epistemic stance toward the status of the information introduced in the clause ending with -*ketun*; the speaker is aware that -*ketun* marked information is new to the interlocutor and wants the interlocutor to accept the content of the utterance. This epistemic function of -*ketun* markers seems to derive from the speaker's certainty about the realizability of the antecedent clause. As discussed in section 2, the -*ketun* clause expresses the speaker's conviction about the actualization of the state of affairs expressed by the antecedent. The speaker's certainty about the propositional content of the conditional clause implies the reliability of the current utterance, and thus has the effect of persuading his/her interlocutor. This explains why -*ketun* in a sentence-final position is often used to elaborate arguments or to provide further justification. In other words, the epistemic function of -*ketun* is to assure the interlocutors of the truth of the current utterance.

Note further that there is a strong correlation between the backgrounding function of -*ketun* and its low transitivity (cf. Hopper and Thompson 1980). In our spoken data, nearly 80% (70 out of 88 tokens) of the clauses with -*ketun* in the utterance-final position contain intransitive verbs. The low transitivity of the -*ketun* clause signals its backgrounding function. By using the -*ketun* form, the speaker invokes or signals the truthfulness of the current or subsequent utterance. As discussed earlier, this function of -*ketun* reflects its erstwhile meaning as a conditional marker whereby the propositional content of the -*ketun* clause serves as a condition for endorsing the reliability of the current utterance. This argument is confirmed by the types of discourse conjunctions following -*ketun*. As shown in Table 3, 33 out of total 72 occurrences of -*ketun* in our conversational data are followed by discourse conjunctions that indicate a cause-effect relationship or a justification.

Table 3. Conjunctions following -*ketun(yo)* and # of tokens

Types of conjunction	Meaning	# of tokens
Kuntey	'by the way' 'however'	16
Kulayse	'so, thus'	3
Kulenikka	'so; thus'	9
kulay kaciko	'so; as a result'	2
Kulemyen	'then; if so'	2
Kulayssteni	'as a result'	1

(Total number of tokens = 33 out of total 72 occurrences of -*ketun(yo)*)

The development of the interpersonal meaning of -*ketun* from the conditional meaning can be seen as a result of a pragmatic inference and is a case of intersubjectification. From a conditional meaning implying the realizability of the antecedent comes an interactional strategy of soliciting the interlocutor's acceptance of the information conveyed by the speaker.

The grammaticalization path of -*ketun* is summarized in (9) below.

(9)   **Grammaticalization path of -*ketun***
        Stage I   Stage II   Stage III
        CONDITIONAL > CONCESSIVE >   JUSTIFICATIVE
        Clause connective ────────────→ Sentence ender

At stage I, -*ketun* is used as a sentence-bound conditional meaning 'if'. At stage II, it acquires a speaker-oriented concessive meaning 'even if'.[12] The semantic shift from conditional to concessive is viewed as a case of subjectification whereby the meaning has become to encode the speaker's own perspective and attitude (Traugott & Dasher 2001). At stage III, -*ketun* further develops into an interactional marker that expresses the speaker's justification for the current utterance.[13] The meaning shift at stage III is thus viewed as INTERSUBJECTIFICATION in that the new meaning becomes more centered on the addressee (Traugott & Dasher 2001). Note further that the linear order in (9) does not necessarily indicate that the interactive function of -*ketun* as a sentence ender develops out of its use as a CONCESSIVE. The grammaticalization path in (9) indicates that -*ketun* as a sentence ender is viewed as a later development, and that Stage II may be optional. At stage III, a phonological change such as -*keteng*, -*ketullang*, or -*kellang* is observed.[14]

5. Theoretical implication and conclusion

The use of -*ketun* in modern Korean illustrates a case of discourse-oriented grammaticalization in that a sentence-bound 'conditional' meaning of -*ketun* is extended to a higher level of discourse. The analysis of intonation in -*ketun* shows that the grammaticalization process is interactionally motivated. By employing high boundary tones, the speaker signals the speaker stance toward the ongoing discourse with respect to the information status and communicative needs.

Very little study has been done on the interplay of discourse and intonation. In particular, no previous studies on grammaticalization have discussed the role of intonation in language change. This study shows that language change is the result of strategic interaction among interlocutors within a speech community. A speaker chooses a particular tone to mark the speaker stance with respect to the discourse organization.

This study also sheds lights on the diachronic functional shift from clause connectives to sentence enders in Korean. Not only -*ketun*, but there is also a series of sentence enders such as -*nuntey*, -*myen*, *nikka*, -*ci*, -*(u)lkel*, etc. in Korean which developed from clause connectives (Sohn 1999). When used at a sentence-final position, they serve to indicate interactive communication such as backgrounding, hedging, surprise, etc. However, unlike other sentence enders, such as -*nuntey* which also indicate background

---

[12] The concessive meaning is viewed as a later development of conditional (cf. Hopper & Traugott 1993:180).

[13] Note that the JUSTIFICATIVE function of -*ketun* at Stage III is meant in a weak sense to refer to the speaker's solicitation of the interlocutor's positive response.

[14] The phonologically reduced form was also mentioned in Park (1998).

information, only -*ketun* carries H% with such a high frequency. Furthermore, while other sentence enders still function as clause connectives as well, -*ketun* is predominantly used as a sentence-ender in conversation. The high frequency of the H% associated with -*ketun* indicates that the primary function of -*ketun* in conversation is to signal a turn expansion either by a same speaker or by additional participation. The turn expansion strategy of the H% -*ketun* interacts with the speaker's epistemic stance whereby the speaker signals the reliability of the current utterance.

References

Akatsuka, Noriko. 1985. "Conditionals and the Epistemic Scale." Language. Vol. 61. No. 3: 625-639.

Brinton, Laurel J. 1996. Pragmatic Markers in English: Grammaticalization and Discourse Function. Berlin: Mouton de Gruyter.

Hirschberg, J. & Ward, G. (1995). "The Interpretation of the High-Rise Question Contour in English." Journal of Pragmatics, 1995, 24, 4, Oct, 407-412.

Hopper, Paul & Sandra Thompson. 1980. "Transitivity in grammar and discourse." Language. Vol. 56:2. 251-299.

_____ & Elizabeth Traugott. 1993. Grammaticalization. Cambridge, UK: Cambridge University Press.

Jun, Sun-Ah (1998) "The Accentual Phrase in the Korean prosodic hierarchy", Phonology. 15.2: 189-226

_____ & Mira Oh. 1996. "A prosodic analysis of three types of wh-phrases in Korean." Language and Speech. 39 (1). 37-61.

Palmer, F. R. 1986. Mood and Modality. Cambridge University Press.

Park, Yong-Yae. 1998. "A discourse analysis of the Korean connective *ketun* in conversation." In B. Park & J. Yoon (Eds.) Selected Papers from the 11th International Conference on Korean Linguistics. 861-870

Pierrehumbert, Janet & Julia Hirschberg. 1990. "The Meaning of intonational contours in the interpretation of discourse." In P. Cohen, J. Morgan, and M. Pollack (Eds.). Intentions in Communications. 271-311

Ramat, Anna Giacalone & Paul Hopper. (Eds.) 1998. The Limits of Grammaticalization. John Benjamins Publishing Co.

Schegloff, Emanuel A. 1995. Ms. "Sequence Organization." UCLA.

Sohn, Ho-min. 1999. The Korean Language. Cambridge University Press.

_____. 2000. ms. "Development of sentence enders in Korean with reference to Japanese." Paper presented at UCLA, March.

Traugott, Elizabeth. 2000. "From etymology to historical pragmatics." Paper presented at the SHEL (Studies in the History of the English Language) 1, UCLA. May

Traugott, Elizabeth & Richard Dasher. In press. Regularity in Semantic Change. Cambridge, UK: Cambridge University Press.

Kakari Musubi, *Noda* -constructions, and How Grammaticalization Theory Meets Formal Grammar

WOLFRAM SCHAFFAR

The National Language Research Institute, Tokyo

1.   Typology of focus marking constructions

It is a widely held opinion that the Kakari Musubi construction of Classical Japanese is a unique phenomenon in so far as it does not occur in the Modern Japanese or in other languages of the world (Whitman 1997 acknowledges that it occurs in Sinhala but argues that apart from that, it is an isolated phenomenon). In order to argue against this view I will start with a brief overview of focus marking phenomena in a typological and historical perspective.

I will start with a very rough definition of the term 'focus' and an overview of morphological focus marking strategies. Although the term focus is used in many different and sometimes contradictory ways, there is the general idea that 'focus' is the part of a sentence that contains new information. The complementary notion to 'focus' is 'background'. The background is that part of the sentence which comprises old and already known information or which specifies the set of alternatives in a contrastive focus construction.

1.1.   Marking of the focused constituent

There are languages that mark the focused constituent of a sentence. In Boni, a Sam language spoken in focus marking is optional (Sasse 1982). Example (1) is a sentence where no special constituent is focused. If on the other hand, a single constituent is focused, as a contradiction to the assumption made in the question in (2) or (3) the particle -*e* for nominal or *a*- for verbal constituents is used.

320

(1) aṇ   biyóo   ajɪk-a
     I   water   drink
     'I drink water.'

(2) A: 'Do you drink tee?'   B: aṇ [F biyóo-é]   ajɪk-a
                                  I   water-**FOC** drink
                                  'I drink WATER.'

(3) A: 'Do you boil water?' B: aṇ biyóo [F á-ajɪk-a]
                                  I water   **FOC**-drink
                                  'I DRINK water.'

In Rendille, a language closely related to Boni, however, focus marking is obligatory (Heine & Reh 1984). There is no unmarked case, but the sentence meaning 'the boy came' has to be expressed either as (4) or (5). I interpret the fact that the focus marker is obligatory as a sign that it partly lost its focus marking force. Thus (4) can express a neutral sentence without exposing the subject as a (contrastive) focus.

(4) inam-é   y-imí   (5) inam á-y-imí
     boy-**FOC** he-came   boy **FOC**-he came
     'THE BOY came.'   'The boy CAME.'

Note, that in Boni as well as in Rendille, the focus marking particles can be historically traced back to copula morphemes. In their study of focus morphology, Heine and Reh (1984) took Boni and Rendille as two stages of a development of focus constructions. Rendille with its obligatory focus marking is a later stage of development of a general grammaticalization path.

1.2. Marking of the background

In contrast to languages that mark the focus of a sentence there are languages that mark the background part of a focus construction. In Chin, a Tibeto-Burman language spoken in Burma (Osburn 1975), every verb has two stems, a so called primary stem and a secondary stem. The primary stem is used for the unmarked case of a main clauses predicate like in (6). The secondary stem of the verb in (7) or (8) is distinguished only by tone. This stem usually occurs in nominalizations or embedded contexts like in (7). If it occurs as the verb of a main clause, it marks a special focus reading as in (8). Here it is the object that is contrastively focused.

The verb itself, by contrast, is unfocused and constitutes backgrounded material. Since the marking strategy is not on the focused object but on the backgrounded verb, I call this strategy 'background marking'.

(6) qaársâ   kaqéey
    Chicken-meat   I-eat
    'I ate the chicken.'

(7) thiqsî   qaqěey   hnû (qaq), ...
    poison   he-eat   after at
    'After he took the poison, ...'

(8) A: Did you eat the fish?   B: [F qaársâ]   kaqěey
                                  Chicken-meat   I-eat
                                  'I ate the CHICKEN.'

The occurrence of embedded verb forms in main clauses as a means of focus marking is a common phenomenon among very different languages of the world, as pointed out by Schachter (1973) and Takizala (1974).

1.3. Cleft constructions as source for focus morphology

Most languages that show morphological focus marking, however, use both marking of the focus as well as marking of the background. The historical connection between focus particles and copula verbs together with the phenomenon that morphological background marking is done with embedded verb forms led to the analysis that focus morphology is derived from cleft sentences (Heine & Reh 1984, Saeed 1984).

Clefts are a metalinguistic means for focus-background partition that is available in every language. The backgrounded part is expressed by a embedded sentence where a gap and an operator creates an open proposition and the focused constituent is connected to this proposition by a copula verb as in (9) (Drubig 2000). There are, however, two different kinds of clefts to be distinguished. Whereas it-clefts as in (9) are the unmarked case of a cleft, pseudo-clefts as in (10) are constructed with a topicalised backgrounded part (Meinunger 1998, Drubig 2000) and can only be used in marked environments, as pointed out by Prince (1982).

(9) [PredP [NP] [Pred' copula [CP Opi [......ti.......]]]
           focus   background
    It is the children   that read the books.

(10) [$_{CP}$ Op$_i$ [......t$_i$......]]   copula   [NP]
         background   focus
      Who read the books   are   the children.

It-clefts, however, are subject to historical development. Consider the examples of Breton in (11) and (12) from Harris & Campbell (1995). (11) shows a historically older stage where an *it*-cleft has a bi-clausal structure corresponding to the structure given in (9). In a later stage, however, this structure developed into a construction as in (12) where the copula was deleted. The development yielded a mono-clausal construction in which the focus is moved directly to its syntactic position by an instance of operator movement - an analysis which has also been proposed for many other focus moving languages like Hungarian (Kiss 1986), Arabic (Ouhalla 1992) and others.

(11) Ar   vugale$_i$ eo [$_{S'}$ Op$_i$ [$_S$ a lenne t$_i$ al levrioù]]
      the   children Copula   that read   the books
      'It is the children that read the books. '

(12) Ar   vugale$_i$ [$_S$ a   lenne t$_i$ al   levrioù]
      the   children   that read   the   books
      'The CHILDREN read the books. '

2.   Focus in Japanese
2.1.   Modern Japanese *noda*-constructions

On the background of the typological data presented in the previous section, consider the following examples of Modern Japanese (taken from McGloin 1980 with slight modification). In an unmarked context, (13) can be used as neutral description of some fact. In this case the plain finite verb form is used.

(13) Boku wa   Kouichi   to   kon'yaku shita.
      I   TOP   Kouichi   with   engage do-PAST
      'I got engaged to Kouichi.'

If example (13) is used in a context like in (14), it is bad. Instead of the finite verb form, a construction like in (14b) is used, where the main verb is nominalized with *no*. I interpret this as a focus effect. In (14) the object is contrastively focused in order to contradict the assumption made by speaker A. From this perspective, the effect that in Japanese the *no*-nominalization is used for focus constructions corresponds neatly to the data in Chin, where the verb takes the secondary stem for background marking. The focus interpretation of (14b) can be made clear by the paraphrase (14c) where the focused object is isolated in a pseudo-cleft.

(14a) A: Katsuki to   kon`yaku shita   sou da ne.
          Katsuki with engage do PAST   hearsay Cop PRT
          'I heard you got engaged to Katsuki.'

(b)   B: Chigau. [B Boku wa [F Kouichi to] kon`yaku shita?(no) da).
          No   I TOP   engage PAST NO Cop
          'No, that`s wrong. It`s to Kouichi that I got engaged to.'

(c)   B: Chigau. [B Kon`yaku shita no] wa   [F Kouichi] da.
          no   engage do PAST NO TOP   Cop
          'No, that`s wrong. Who I got engaged to is Kouichi.'

2.1.2 Syntactic analysis of Modern Japanese focus constructions

The analysis of pseudo-clefts like (14c) is relatively uncontroversial. I will follow Hoji (1987), Murasugi (1990), and others in treating *no* as a complementizer and assume the structure in (15). Note that this structure in principle corresponds to the general analysis of pseudo-clefts as given in (10).

(15) [CP Op$_i$ [...t$_i$ ...V] [C^0 no]] wa NP$_i$ da

The analysis of *noda*-constructions as in (14b), however, is difficult. The function and interpretation of (14b) is that of an *it*-cleft in English. Parallelly to the distinction between moved *wh*-constructions and constructions with *wh* in situ, I assume that *noda*-sentences are in situ constructions of *it*-clefts. This assumption leads to the analysis in (16) which corresponds to the general structure of *it*-clefts, the only difference being that the focused nominal constituent inside the backgrounded part is identified with an empty element in the specifier position of the predication phrase. I will call these *noda*-constructions 'circumnominal clefts', suggesting a syntactic parallelism with circumnominal relative clauses.

(16) [PredP e$_i$ [CP Op$_i$ [...NP$_i$ ...V] [C^0 no]] da]

Syntactic ambiguities of *no*-constructions

As uncontroversial as the treatment of *no* as a complementizer might seem, it can be shown that most constructions with *no* are in fact syntactically ambiguous. Hoji (1987) and Murasugi (1991) showed that among pseudo-clefts, two types have to be distinguished. In one type *no* can be analyzed as a complementizer as in (17). In another type, however, *no* is a nominal head as in (18).

(17)   [CP Op$_i$ [IP ... t$_i$ ...] no$_i$] wa   NP$_i$ da.
(18)   [NP [CP ... pro$_i$ ...] no$_i$] wa   NP$_i$ da.

In the same way, Kuroda (1992), Kitagawa (1977), and Tsubomoto (1981) showed that within circumnominal relative clauses (internally headed relative clauses) we can distinguish between circumnominal relative clauses where *no* is a complementiser as in (19) and so called '*no*-introduced relative clauses' where *no* shows the characteristics of a nominal head as in (20). Both analyses are rather tentative. What is crucial is the syntactic ambiguity of *no*.

(19)   [NP [CP Op$_i$ [IP ... NP$_i$ ...] no] [NP e$_i$]]
(20)   [NP [CP Op$_i$ [IP ... NP$_i$ ...]] [NP no$_i$]]

Note that pseudo-clefts, circumnominal clefts and circumnominal relative constructions constitute one class of syntactic environments (cf. Tsubomoto 1981). In all three constructions a *no*-nominalization creates an open proposition in a predicative relation to a nominal constituent - focus or relative head. I assume that *noda*-constructions are syntactically ambiguous in the same way and I interpret this ambiguity of *no* as a sign of language change. *No* is in transition from an interpretation as a nominal head to an interpretation as a complementizer. This kind of grammaticalization is a rather common and well documented for a number of other languages (Ramson 1988).

2.2.   Classical Japanese Kakari Musubi constructions
In previous studies Classical Japanese Kakari Musubi constructions have been identified as focus constructions (Quinn 1987, Whitman 1997, Shinzato 1998). Example (21) with the verb in the finite form (Shushikei) is the unmarked case for main clause predications in neutral sentences. There are two main types of Kakari Musubi constructions. In (22), one nominal constituent is morphologically marked as focus with the Kakari particle *zo* and the main clause verb takes the adnominal verb form (Rentaikei) (The particles *ka*, *ga*, *ya*,and others follow the same pattern). In another construction as in (23) the focus is marked with *koso* and the verb takes the realis conditional (Izenkei) verb form.

(21)   Mukashi   otoko ari-keri.
       formerly   man   exist.-FACT^{SHÛSHI}
       'In the past, there was a man.' (Ise Monogatari)

(22)   [$_B$ [$_F$Hana zo]   mukashi noka ni   nioi-keru.]
       flower KAKARI formerly fragranceDAT   smell-FAKT^{RENTAI}
       'It is these blossoms that breathe the fragrance of times past.'
       (Kokin Wakashû 42, Quinn 1987)

(23)   [$_B$[$_F$ Aki no ashita koso]   kiyo-kere.]
          autumn morning KAKARI   bright-FAKT^{IZEN}
       'It's autumn morning that's bright.' (Lewin 1975:219)

On the background of our typological introduction, the Kakari Musubi construction appears as a very common case of morphological focus marking. The Kakari particle marks the focus and the corresponding Musubi verb form marks the background. Note that the most frequent background marking form, the adnominal form (Rentaikei) also occurs in Classical Japanese pseudo-clefts and circumnominal relative clauses just as the *no*-nominalization in Modern Japanese.

2.2.1 Syntactic analysis of Classical focus constructions

Some linguists have treated the Kakari Musubi construction as an agreement phenomenon along the lines of subject-verb agreement (Bedell 1968). Although since the work of Quinn (1987) it should be settled that the Kakari Musubi construction does not express a subject-predicate partition but a focus-background partition, and although Whitman (1997) showed that the Kakari Musubi construction resembles *it*-cleft constructions, it is worthwhile to consider the similarity between Kakari Musubi phenomena and agreement patterns.

First, the Kakari particles of Late Classical Japanese are specified for certain speech acts. As summarized in (24), *ka* marks a *wh*-word in a question, *ya* marks the focus of a yes-no question, and *zo, ga, koso* and other particles mark the focus of an assertive sentence. Furthermore, the correspondence between a certain focus particle and the background marking verb form is fixed. The particle *koso* demands for the realis conditional (Izenkei) and all the other particles demand for the adnominal form. However, there is no systematic or logical connection between the form of the particle, its speech act specification and its Musubi correspondence.

(24) ka - [wh, Q]   {ka, ga, zo, ya...} -> V-ru (Rentaikei)
      ya - [Q]   koso   -> V-re (Izenkei)
      ga, zo, koso - [F]

To account for the focus marking properties as well as for the agreement
properties, I analyze Kakari-Musubi sentences as a mono-clausal focus
constructions where the morphologically marked focus is moved into the
specifier position of a complentizer phrase as in (25). (25a) shows the in
situ variant of such a construction if the focus remains in its base position
and is bound by an empty operator. (25b) is an ex situ variant with the
focus overtly moved to its operator position.

(25a) [CP Op$_i$ [... NP$_i$-KAKARI ...V-]   [C0 -MUSUBI$_i$]]
(b)   [CP NP$_i$-KAKARI   [... t$_i$ ... V-]   [C0 -MUSUBI$_i$]]

Note that (25b) corresponds to the structure of grammaticalized cleft constructions of Modern Breton it-clefts cited in (12) and to the focus constructions of many other languages with overt focus movement. Unlike in
Breton, however, Classical Japanese shows signs of agreement which I
analyze as an agreement phenomenon in CP (cf. Rizzi 1997 for similar
phenomena in other languages).

2.3. Morphological correspondences
There are a number of morphological correspondences between Classical
Japanese Kakari Musubi constructions as in (26) and (27) and Modern
Japanese sentences as in (28) that are difficult to explain. It is well known
that the adnominal form (Rentaikei) of Classical Japanese that ended with
-ru in many verb classes as in (26) and (27) became the unmarked finite
form (Shushikei) of Modern Japanese as in (28). The Old Japanese finite
form, however, died out and many functions of the Old Japanese adnominal form are expressed by the no-nominalization in Modern Japanese.

(26) [B Ware wo ba   [F kimi ga]   omoi heda-tsuru.]
      I AKK TOP   you KAKARI   estrange-PERF^{RENTAI}
      'It is you who becomes estranged from me.' (Lewin 1975:78)

(27) Aga koromo   sureru ni wa ara-zu [F hagi no   sureru   so.]
      my robe   dye COP NEG   clover   dye^{RENTAI} KAKARI
      'It's not that my robes are relief dyed: It's that the bush clover
      rubbed against them' (Manyôshû 2101, Quinn 1997:84)

(28)   Taro **ga**   hashitte iru   **zo**.
       Taro NOM   run ASP   PRT
       'Taro is running.'

The development of the Kakari particles is connected to this development. Consider example (26) with the Kakari particle *ga*. Actually, treating *ga* as focus marking Kakari particle is not uncontroversial. Originally it was included among the number of Kakari particles in the treatise of Norinaga (1771). Later it was interpreted as an attributive or genitive particle and together with *no* it was excepted from the canonical number of Kakari particles. In (26), however, the interpretation suggests that *ga* indeed marks a focus. Given that *ga* used to be a focus marking Kakari particle, we have to account for the fact that it became a case particle of Modern Japanese as in (28).

Other Kakari particles show a very different development. In 2.2. I argued that *zo* marks the focus on a nominal constituent. In sentences like (27), however, the particle occurs at the end of a sentence and marks a focus reading on the whole sentence (cf. Delahunty 1996 and Schaffar 2000 for a analysis of these constructions). At the same position we find the particles *zo* and *ka* as sentence final particles in Modern Japanese as in (28).

3.   Putting all together: Four steps of grammaticalization

In order to account for the genesis of Kakari Musubi constructions and their development, as well as for the *noda*-construction of Modern Japanese, I will argue for a cyclic grammaticalization process that I describe as a four step development.

3.1.   Step I: Predication construction in Pre Nara Japanese

Unger (1975) reconstructs the verb forms of Classical Japanese as in (29). The finite verb form (Shushikei) is reconstructed as verbal root plus *-u*, the adnominal form (Rentaikei) as verbal root plus *-re* plus *-u* and the realis conditional (Izenkei) as verbal root plus *-re*.

(29)   Shushikei: $\sqrt{}$-(i)-u   Rentaikei: $\sqrt{}$-re-u   Izenkei: $\sqrt{}$-re

Unger argues that the morpheme *-re* corresponds to a complementizer like *que* in Romance languages. However, on the basis of cross-linguistic comparison we can trace back the different morphemes even further. I argue that - *re* in a stage of development in Pre-Nara Japanese was a nominal head. In the demonstrative paradigm of Old Japanese we find traces of this head in the difference between *ko* vs. *ko-re*. A number of Altaic languages still have a similar morpheme in their demonstrative paradigm like Manchu *e-re*, *te-re* 'this, that', Solon *ri* 'this'. I further reconstruct - *u* as a copula verb of Pre-Nara Japanese. We find traces of this independent use in the Old Japanese existential verb *wu*- 'to be, to exist', which also has many Altaic cognates leading to a reconstruction of Proto Altaic *bü*- 'to be, to exist' in Poppe (1960). The Kakari particles *so*, *ka*, *koso* can be reconstructed as demonstratives *ko-so-ka* (Quinn 1987, 1997).

With this morphological reconstruction and with the structure of modern Japanese *noda*-constructions in mind, I analyze the starting point of Kakari Musubi constructions as a predication construction shown in (30). I give this structure as an in situ variant in (30a), parallel to Modern Japanese *noda*-sentences or circumnominal relative clauses, and as an ex situ construction in (30b). In addition to these two structures we can also expect a structure like (30c) with the demonstrative attached to the nominalized verb. Note that the structure of (30b) is a formalized description of the reconstruction of Quinn (1997). According to Quinn, the focus is marked by attaching a demonstrative to it and the nominalized sentence is connected to this constituent in a afterthought or quasi copulative relation. In my reconstruction, however, the focus is connected to the re-nominalization by the optional copula -*u* which sets up a verbal predication relation.

(30a)   [$_{PredP}$ e$_i$ [$_{NP}$ [Op$_i$ ... NP$_i$-KAKARI ... V]   [$_{NP}$ -re$_i$]] -u/ø]

(b)   [$_{PredP}$ NP$_i$-KAKARI [$_{NP}$ [Op$_i$ .... t$_i$ .... V]   [$_{NP}$ -re$_i$]] -u/ø]

(c)   [$_{PredP}$ e$_i$ [$_{NP}$ [.........V]   [$_{NP}$ -re$_i$]] -u/ø] -KAKARI

3.2.   Step II: Bi-clausal cleft in Nara (Early Old) Japanese

In the history of the Japanese language, Nara Japanese (or Early Old Japanese) can be distinguished from Classical Heian Japanese (or Late Old Japanese) by a number of linguistic characteristics. Kakari Musubi constructions exhibit some crucial differences as well. In Nara Japanese the Kakari particles were neither specified for a certain speech act and nor for a specific Musubi verb form. As Quinn (1987) notices, there are a great number of exceptions of the canonical Kakari Musubi rule, like *wh*-words marked with *so* and Kakari particles other than *koso* in correlation with the realis conditional (Izenkei) instead of the adnominal form (Rentaikei).

Between the reconstructed forms of Pre Nara forms and Nara forms, however, there are a number of phonetic changes. By the time of Nara Japanese, the verb forms as reconstructed by Unger (1975) were already fused. The particle *so* was unstable and occurred as a voiceless variant alongside with a voiced variant *zo*.

To account for these characteristics, I analyze Early Old Japanese Kakari Musubi constructions as in (31). The morpheme *-re* lost its nominal features and was reanalyzed as a complementizer. The old copula verb *-u* also lost its independence and partly fused with *-re*. Thus by the time of the Nara period the Kakari Musubi construction developed into a bi-clausal cleft construction. (31a) is the in situ variant that is the predominant construction type of Japanese. (31b) is an ex situ variant, and (31c) is the variant with the Kakari particle attached to the end of the sentence. Note that (31a) corresponds to the Modern Japanese *no*-construction with *no* as a complementizer and (31b) to the construction of old Breton clefts (as well as to clefts in many other languages).

(31a)   [$_{PredP}$ e_i [$_{CP}$ Op$_i$ [... NP$_i$-KAKARI ... V]   [$_{C^0}$ -re$_i$]] -u/ø]]

(b)   [$_{PredP}$ NP$_i$-KAKARI [$_{CP}$ Op$_i$ [..........t$_i$ ...... V] [$_{C^0}$ -re$_i$]] -u/ø]]

(c)   [$_{PredP}$ e_i [$_{CP}$ [..........V]   [$_{C^0}$ -re$_i$]] -u/ø] -KAKARI

3.3. Step III: Mono-clausal focus constructions with operator movement in Heian Japanese

The transition from Nara to Heian Japanese is marked by the following development. The fusion of *-re* and *-u* was completed and yielded the morphologically opaque inflected verb forms Rentaikei and Izenkei. The voicing of particles like *so* -> *zo* was completed, and the particles became specified for certain speech acts. The agreement between a particle and a certain verb form was fixed and yielded the canonical Kakari Musubi pattern. In 2.2. I already argued that these characteristics can be accounted for in an analysis as in (32), which I give as an in situ variant, an ex situ variant and as a construction with the Kakari particle in a sentence final position. Note, that the step of development between Nara and Heian Japanese corresponds to the development that was described for clefts in Breton by Harris & Campbell (1995) as a common step of grammaticalization.

(32a)   [$_{CP}$ Op$_i$ [... NP$_i$-KAKARI ...V]   [$_{C^0}$ -ru$_i$/-re$_i$]]

(b)   [$_{CP}$ NP$_i$-KAKARI   [........... t$_i$ .... V]   [$_{C^0}$ -ru$_i$/-re$_i$]]

(c)   [$_{CP}$ [....................V]   [$_{C^0}$ -ru/-re]] -KAKARI

3.3.1 Renewal of *no* in a construction step I

Once the development proceeded to this point, the construction of step III can serve as input to a renewed construction as in (33). The Rentaikei, reanalyzed as an embedding verb form, can occur in a relative construction with *no* as a nominal head. Thus (33) is an example of a *no*-nominalization in the first step of the development, corresponding to the Pre Nara construction type. At this point the grammaticalization of clefts starts again and creates a cyclic development.

(33)   [NP [CP Op$_i$ [......V]   [C^0 -ru$_i$]] [NP no]

3.4.   Step IV: Mono-clausal construction with case movement in Modern Japanese

The transition between Heian Japanese and Modern Japanese is a complex process. The steps that are relevant for the development of Kakari Musubi constructions, are already summarized in 2.3.. The old adnominal form (Rentaikei) became the unmarked verb form for finite sentences. At the same time the Kakari particles developed into either nominal case particles (like *ga*) or into sentence final particles (like *ka* and *zo*). All these developments can be accounted for if we analyze the last step of the grammaticalization as in (34). The verb ending was reanalysed from a complemetiser head to an inflectional head. Kakari particles in the middle of the sentence which were in an agreement relation with the complementizer morpheme *-ru*, ended up in an agreement relation with the inflectional head *-ru*, which is the standard analysis for subject agreement or case checking in recent formalist grammatical theories. In this way *ga* became a nominal case particle. If a Kakari particle was grammticalized at a sentence final position, however, the last step of development yielded a sentence final particle that is attached to finite verbs.

(34a)   [IP   [...NP$_i$-KAKU...V] [I^0 -ru$_i$]]
(b)   [IP NP$_i$-KAKU   [........t$_i$...   .....V] [I^0 -ru$_i$]]
(c)   [IP   [...................V] [I^0 -ru]] -SHŪ

Note that the development from a marked embedded verb form to a un-marked finite verb form is not unique to Japanese. Poppe (1965) describes this tendency as a typical development in Altaic languages. Apart form this language family, the same step of development can be discovered as the dialectal variation between Boni and Rendille as shown in 1.1., as well as in many other languages where a historic cleft based focus construction became reanalyzed as the unmarked finite way to construct a sentence (cf. Somali as analyzed by Saeed 1984 and Schaffar 2000)

3.4.1 Renewal of *no* proceeds to step II

The final step of development is accompanied by a further step in the renewed structure with *no*. Once the verb form is reanalyzed as a finite verb form, the morpheme *no* can take over the function of the complementizer. This yields a construction like (35) which is found as one variety of *no*-construction in Modern Japanese as I showed in 2.1..

(35) [CP [IP   [......V]   [I⁰ -ru]] [CP no]

4. Summary

In this paper I have shown how Modern Japanese *noda*-sentences and Classical Japanese Kakari Musubi constructions can be analyzed as focus constructions in a unified way. In a historical perspective, both constructions appear as two stages of a cyclic grammaticalization development.

5. References

Bedell, G. 1969. *Kokugaku Grammatical Theory*. Doctoral Dissertation, MIT

Cole, P. 1987. The Structure of Internally Headed Relative Clauses. *Natural Language and Linguistic Theory* 5: 277-302.

Delahunty, G. P. 1995. The Inferential Construction. *Pragmatics* 5:3, 341-364.

Drubig, H. B. 2000. *Focus and Connectedness: Towards a Typology of Focus Constructions*. Manuscript, Universität Tübingen. (to appear in *Linguistics*)

Harris, A. & L. Campbell 1995. *Historical Syntax in Cross-Linguistic Perspective*. Cambridge: Cambridge University Press.

Heine, B. & M. Reh. 1984 *Grammaticalization and Reanalysis in African Languages*. Hamburg: Buske.

Hoji, H. 1987. Japanese Clefts and Reconstruction/Chain Binding Effects. *WCCFL* 6.

Kiss, K. É. 1986. *Configurationality in Hungarian*. Reidel, Dordrecht.

Kitagawa, C 1977. No-Introduced Relative Clauses. *The Journal of the Association of Teachers of Japanese* 12:2&3, 229-247.

Kuroda, S.-Y. 1992. *Japanese Syntax and Semantics*. Dordrecht: Kluwer.

Lewin, B. 1975². *Abriß der japanischen Grammatik auf der Grundlage der klassischen Schriftsprache*. Wiesbaden: Harrassowitz.

McGloin, N. H. 1980. Some Observations Concerning *NO DESU* Expressions. *Journal of the Association of Teachers of Japanese* 15:2, 117-149

Meinunger, A. 1998. A Monoclausal Approach to Cleft and Pseudo-Cleft Sentences. *NELS* 28.

Moto'ori Norinaga 1771. *Te-ni-wo-ha himo kagami*. Moto'ori Norinaga Zenshû Vol 5, Tôkyô: Chikuma Shobô.

Murasugi, K. 1991. *Noun Phrases in Japanese and English: A Study in Syntax, Learnability and Acquisition*. Doctoral Dissertation, University of Conneticut.

Osburne, A. G. 1975. *A Transformational Analysis of Tone in the Verb System of Zahao (Laizo) Chin*. Doctoral Dissertation, Cornell University.

Ouhalla, J. 1992. *Focus in Standard Arabic*. Manuscript., Queen Mary and Westfield College.

Poppe, N. 1960. *Vergleichende Grammatik der altaischen Sprachen, Teil 1, Vergleichende Lautlehre.* [=Porta linguiarum orientalum, neue Serie 4], Wiesbaden: Harrassowitz.

Poppe, N. 1965. *Introduction to Altaic linguistics*, [=Ural-altaische Bibliothek 14], Wiesbaden: Harrassowitz.

Prince, E. F. 1986. On the Syntactic Marking of Open Propositions. *Papers from the Parasession on Pragmatics and Grammatical Theory*, CLS 22:208-222.

Quinn, C. J. 1987. *A Functional Grammar of Predication in Classical Japanese*. Doctoral Dissertation, University of Michigan.

Quinn, C. J. 1997. On the origins of Japanese sentence particles ka and zo. *Japanese/Korean Linguistics* 6, ed. H. Sohn & J. Haig, 61-89, Stanford University.

Ransom, E. N. 1988. The Grammaticalization of Complementizers. *BLS* 14:364-374.

Rizzi, L. 1997. The Fine Structure of the Left Periphery. *Elements of Grammar: Handbook of Generative Syntax.* ed. L. Haegeman, 281-337, Dordrecht: Kluwer.

Saeed, I. J. 1984. *The Syntax of Focus & Topic in Somali.* Hamburg: Buske.

Schachter, P. 1973. Focus and Relativization. *Language* 49:19-46.

Schaffar, W. 2000. *Fokuskonstruktionen im japanischen Sprachraum. Eine synchrone, diachrone und typologische Analyse zirkumnominaler Spaltätze.* Doctoral Dissertation, Universität Tübingen.

Shinzato, R. 1998. *Kakari Musubi* Revisited: Its Function and Development. *Japanese/Korean Linguistics 8*, ed. D. J. Silva, Stanford: Center for the Study of Language and Information.

Takizala, A. 1972. Focus and Relativization: The Case of Kihung an. ed. J. Kimball, *Syntax and Semantics 2*, 123-148, Tokyo: Taishukan.

Tsubomoto, A. 1981. It's all *no*: Unifying Function of *no* in Japanese. *CLS* 17:393-403.

Unger, J. M. 1975. *Studies in Early Japanese Morphophonemics*. Doctoral Dissertation, Yale University.

Watanabe, A. 1992. Sujacency and S-Structure Movement of Wh-In-Situ. *Journal of East Asian Linguistics* 1:255-291.

Whitman, J. 1997. Kakari Musubi from a Comparative Perspective. *Japanese/Korean Linguistics*. ed. H. Sohn & J. Haig, 161-178, Stanford: Stanford University.

Part IV

Phonetics and Phonology

Rendaku

S.-Y. KURODA

University of California, San Diego

0. Prologue

I am very grateful to the organizers for inviting me to this conference, an occasion to commemorate Jim McCawley.[1]   Thirty five years ago, in 1965, Jim graduated from MIT with a PhD dissertation: *The Phonological Component of a Grammar of Japanese*. Jim, thus, laid down the foundations of generative phonology of Japanese. My interest in Japanese phonology also goes back to pre-MIT days. I have decided to dedicate my talk to the dear memory of the times I spent with Jim at MIT discussing topics of our common interest and to take up an idea Jim was familiar with at that time.

There also happened to be, not a divine, but a friendly intervention that made this possible. Early this year, when I had not yet had any idea about what I would talk today, Osamu Fujimura, an old mentor of mine, now at the Ohio State University, began sending me unsolicited copies of correspondence he had with some phonologists on Japanese phonetics/phonology. The correspondence concerned, not rendaku, today's topic, but geminate consonants, *soku-on*. Though perhaps not widely known, the last chapter of my dissertation was devoted to the problem of *soku-on*. So my interest was aroused, and when I visited Kobe in June I made a point of seeing Haruo Kubosono, to get his advice. Then, I also visited Matt Shibatani at his office. There, I happened to see a project report from Tsukuba on top of a pile of mess on his desk. I found there a short note by Itô & Mester, which is a response to Keren Rice's squib in LI. Rice's squib, in turn, is a comment on earlier papers by Itô and Mester, and Itô, Mester and Padgett. These papers are concerned with the problem of rendaku. Now, it also happens that the first term paper I wrote at MIT, in the fall semester of 92/93, was about rendaku. But since shortly after I left MIT, I stopped paying active attention to phonology, let alone Japanese

---

[1]I would like to express my special gratitude to my old mentor Osamu Fujimura and my teacher Morris Halle. The former recently awoke me from hibernation in phonology, which has led me to return to an old idea that I developed as a student in the latter's class of historical linguistics. I would also like to thank Noriko Akatsuka for her constant support and encouragements and for providing me with impetus to put this work out within a short period of time.

phonology. I was not familiar with Itô and Mester's work on rendaku. Were it not the case that Osamu's unsolicited email had raised my consciousness on phonology, I wouldn't have paid any attention to Itô and Mester's note I happened to see at Matt's office. But I did, and from there I was led to Rice's squib and the original Itô and Mester's work on rendaku. I was thus awaken from 30 years of hibernation in the Phonology Land.

I must confess that my phonology clock stopped in 1966. I am not familiar with technicalities of autosegmental or metrical phonology, lexical phonology, let alone optimality theory. I must look like a Neanderthal man in Phonology Land. But let us see what I could possibly have discussed with Jim in the barracks called Building 20.

There are two things I want to say on rendaku. One directly relates to the exchange between Itô and Mester on the one hand, and Rice on the other. Itô and Mester assume that rendaku is a process restricted in terms of Yamato stratum (that is, the native stratum) of vocabulary; the Sino-Japanese stratum is outside the domain of rendaku. Rice has raised a question about this claim and casts doubt on the relevance of vocabulary stratification for the process of rendaku. On this issue, I wish to support Rice and maintain that as far as formal mechanism of rendaku is concerned, the stratification of vocabulary into native and Sino-Japanese is orthogonal to rendaku. I have presented this claim at another conference this summer, and this is not the topic I wish to discuss today.[2]

1. Introduction

Another thing I want to say on rendaku, the topic of this paper, is this. Rendaku is usually understood as a process of voicing: If an internal component of a compound word begins with a voiceless obstruent, change it to the corresponding voiced obstruent, as illustrated below:

(1) sima-kuni   => sima-guni   'island country'
    maki-susi   => maki-zusi   'rolled sushi'
    oo-tanuki   => oo-danuki   'large badger'
    mura-hito   => mura-bito   'villager'[3]

This is what conventional wisdom says. I would like to turn conventional

---

[2]See Kuroda (2000). For rather complicated factual details concerning rendaku, the reader is referred to Martin (1952, 1987), Vance (1979, 1987) and the Japanese sources cited in these works.

[3]The surface /h/ in the non-foreign strata is underlyingly /p/.

wisdom inside out. That is, I would like to propose that the rendaku phenomenon is a consequence of the following process: devoice voiced obstruents at word-initial position.[4] This is an intentionally impressionistic, and hence somewhat misleading formulation, but it conveys an intuitive idea behind my proposal fairly well. With the same proviso, one could say that for a word that exhibits rendaku alternation, we take as an underlying representation the voiced alternant of the word which we see as an internal component of compounding, and derive the form we see as an independent word by devoicing the initial voiced obstruent. The voiced underlying form surfaces when the word is contained in a compound word as a noninitial component:

(2) guni   => kuni   'country'   sima-guni   'island country'
     zusi   => susi   'sushi'   maki-zusi   'rolled sushi'
     danuki => tanuki 'badger'   oo-danuki   'large badger'
     bito   => hito   'person'   mura-bito   'villager'

What do we buy by abandoning the conventional wisdom? Before going into this question, let me make a few preliminary remarks.

2. Preliminary remarks
2.1. Rendaku is unpredictable
First, rendaku is a process that is not phonologically or morphologically totally predictable. Martin (1952:49) presents an interesting pair to highlight the point:

(3) "Minimal pair" in Modern Japanese
     kata-kana   'the square style Japanese syllabary'
     hira-gana   'the cursive style Japanese syllabary'

One can speculate that rendaku was once a regular phonological and morphological process, but there is an indication that a total regularity was already lost in Old Japanese of the 7th or the 8th century, as one can surmise from a similar pair given by Motoori Norinaga (1790/1822; 1968:37), the greatest Japanese classical philologist of the 18th century:

(4) "Minimal pair" in Old Japanese
     miya-hito < miya-pito   'person serving at the court'
     sato-bito   'person of a village/person not serving at the court'

---

[4]First proposed in Kuroda (1963) as a rule of historical change.

One can find various types of subregularities; see, for example, Martin (1987), Haraguchi (1999). But I am not concerned with this aspect of the rendaku problem in this paper.

2.2. Lyman's Law

There is a well-known law understood by conventional wisdom as a constraint imposed on rendaku voicing, commonly known as Lyman's Law: if a word contains a voiced obstruent inside it, it cannot undergo rendaku voicing.[5]

(5) mati-kado   => *mati-gado   'street-corner'
     oo-suzume   => *oo-zuzume   'big sparrow'

Lyman's Law is a quite robust generalization; there are only a very few, well-known exceptions to the rule.

2.3. Rendaku immunity

There are, however, also words that do not violate Lyman's Law and still never undergo rendaku voicing. Let us call such words RENDAKU-IMMUNE.

Definition: A word (morpheme, stem, root) is **R(endaku)-immune** if it never undergoes rendaku voicing even though the voicing would not violate Lyman's Law.

The following examples are considered as R-immune by Martin (1987:114) and Vance (1979:69f):

saki	'tip, end'	sio	'tide' (but not 'salt')		
kase	'shackles'	kasu	'dregs',	kemuri	'smoke'
kita	'north'	tuya	'gloss'	tuti	'earth'

For some of R-immune words, we can speculate why they are rendaku-immune. For example, *kemuri* is historically derived from *keburi,* a form prohibited from undergoing rendaku voicing by Lyman's Law. Perhaps *kemuri* preserved this property even after it underwent a phonological change and got out of the bound of Lyman's Law. But in general, we cannot tell from the phonological or morphological properties of a word why it is

---

[5]Lyman (1894), referred to in Itô & Mester (1986:55). Lyman's Law is believed to have been known to Motoori: Motoori (1790/1822), referred to in Martin (1987:93).

rendaku-immune. Rendaku immunity is also phonologically unpredictable.

2.4. NIVO

Finally, we need to recall another well-known constraint in Japanese phonology. Original native Japanese words do not begin with a voiced obstruent, as far as in the mainstream dialects are concerned. Let me call this No Initial Voiced Obstruent Constraint:

NIVO: No words begin with a voiced obstruent.

In the present-day Japanese, we can find some native words with an initial voiced obstruent, such as *deru* 'go out', *gomi* 'trash' *zurui* 'sly' etc. and even in Man'yoshu there were some such words. But presumably they are later developments, additions or intrusions from dialects. The word-initial voiced obstruents were of course introduced massively with the Sino-Japanese vocabulary later in classical Japanese and became common in the language.

Now, conventional wisdom would conceive NIVO as a general constraint independent of rendaku; even if Japanese lacked NIVO, our understanding of the rendaku phenomenon would not be affected. In fact, Modern Japanese do not have NIVO; Sino-Japanese words with an initial voiced obstruent are common and there are also a number of native words with an initial voiced obstruent. But this fact is by conventional wisdom taken as orthogonal to our understanding of rendaku, a process of initial consonant voicing. In contrast, for the radical idea I am going to propose, NIVO , taken together with Lyman's Law, provides an integral body of evidence for a proper account of the rendaku phenomenon. In this view, the later introduction of initial voiced obstruents cannot be accounted for just by the removal of a distributional constraint (NIVO).

3. The radical idea

Let us know proceed to discuss the radical idea. Let me introduce some notational conventions:

K: voiceless obstruent   G: voiced obstruent   R: sonorant
A: vowel
Q: obstruent unspecified for voicing
γ: autosegmental feature to be explained below
QA: γ -linked mora with an obstruent onset

We adopt a standard markedness convention:
An unspecified obstruents are phonetically interpreted as unvoiced, unless otherwise instructed.

3.1.   Gedankenexperiments

Lyman's Law and the NIVO motivate the introduction of the radical idea.
To explain why so, let me first discuss an imaginary idealized Japanese for
a Gendankenexperiment. For the sake of argument we consider two mora
roots: CVCV, where C is restricted to obstruents. We assume that there are
no sonorants, that is, there are no voiced non-obstruent consonants.

System E. Let us assume that there are rendaku immune words, as in
Modern Japanese. Consider the possible patterns of distributions of surface
representations of words, as independent words and as internal components
of compound words, as shown below. K represents an unvoiced obstruent
and G a voiced obstruent.   Thanks to NIVO, we have no G initially in free
words; and thanks Lyman's Law, -GAGA is missing as a compound-word
internal form.

[a] Surface distribution patterns:

Free word form	KAKA	KAKA	KAGA	*KAGA
Compound-internal:	-KAKA	-GAKA	-KAGA	*-GAGA
Exemples	tuti	kaki	kagi	*
	'soil'	'persimmon'	'key'	
	kuro-tuti	huyu-gaki	ai-kagi	*.
	'black siol'	'fuyu-prsmmn'	'master key'	

Looking at this array of patterns, the distribution of K and G is skewed, on
the one hand, in favor of K, i.e., more K's than G's , and on the other in
favor of compound-internal forms, three, i.e., -KAKA, -GAKA, -KAGA, as
opposed to free word forms, two, i.e., KAKA and KAGA.

To account for the latter imbalance, it would be a standard technique of
derivational generative phonology to take the compound internal forms as
underlying representations and derive the free word forms by a word-initial
devoicing rule that merges two patterns into one. This assumption also
accounts for the predominance of K's over G's in the free word forms.

What is left unaccounted for is the imbalance in the underlying
representations: we do not have GAGA. This gap means that there can be at
most one voiced consonant. This suggests on the one hand that voicing is a
manifestation of an autosegmental/prosodic feature of an unknown character
and on the other the voicing can be left unspecified in the underlying
representation of an obstruent. Let us represent voice-wise unspecified
obstruents by Q. We introduce a prosodic feature γ , which is linked to at
most one obstruent. If Q is linked to γ, it realizes as a voiced obstruent,
and if it is not linked to γ it realizes as an unvoiced obstruent.

To sum up, we have underlying representations as given in [b]:

[b] Underlying representations:

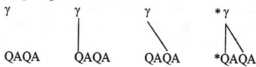

Word-initially, a γ-linked Q appears as an unvoiced obstruent. This means that there is a rule to delink γ at word-initial position:

γ-delinking: Delink γ at word-initial position.

[c] below displays distributional patterns of underlying and surface representations derived from them. Bold faced **QA** represents a γ-linked mora.

[c] Underlying representations and   word allomorph patterns

Underlying	Surface		Examples		R-immune
	W-initial	W-internal			
QAQA	KAKA	-KAKA	tuti	kuro-tuti	*kuro-duti
QA**QA**	KAKA	-GAKA	kaki	huyu-gaki	
QAQA	KAGA	-KAGA	kagi	ai-kagi	

γ–"atonic" words, i.e., words where γ are left unlinked in underlying representations, are rendaku-immune words. The column "R-immune" displays a nonexistent "rendaku" form thanks to R-immunity.
 Let us summarize. Obstruents Q are underlyingly unspecified. There is a prosodic feature γ linked to (at most) one mora headed by Q. γ is allowed to be left unlinked. There are two phonetic interpretation rules: a γ– linked **Q** is interpreted as voiced; a plain Q is interpreted as unvoiced (according to a standard markedness convention). Word-initial obstruents are devoiced. The devoicing rule can be replaced by de-linking rule: γ is delinked word-initially. Then, delinked Q is interpreted as unvoiced by the markedness convention. For now, a choice between these two options is immaterial, though for a proper description of Japanese, we must take the latter option.
 Notice that rendaku is accounted for without Lyman's Law. The constraint *-GAGA is a reflex of Lyman's Law in this language, but it is not a rule or constraint of the grammar. It is only an observational generalization, which can be deduced as a theorem from the premises of the system.

3.2. Towards a proper account of Japanese
An account of real Japanese is inevitably more complicated, for two reasons.

First, for Modern as well as Classical and Old Japanese, there are sonorants. Secondly, Sino-Japanese words can have an initial voiced obstruent, and there are also a limited number of native words with an initial voiced obstruent in Modern Japanese.

3.2.1. Accommodating the presence of sonorants

First of all, γ is a prosodic, autosegmental feature that actualizes as voicing of an obstruent in Modern Japanese. Can this prosodic feature γ get linked to a sonorant? Sonorants are inherently voiced and voicing cannot be imposed on it. There is no indication in Modern standard Japanese that γ can be linked with a sonorant.

It is well-known, however, that in some dialects voiced obstruents are accompanied by nasalization; they are (pre)nasalized. This tendency is also indicated in some older records of the language and it is widely believed that it was an earlier characteristic of the language. See, for example, Martin (1987:20ff). Thus, the way γ actualizes in phonetic form can undergo changes. It is conceivable that the physical manifestation of γ took a form that can be associated with sonorants at some earlier stage of the language, but I am not pursuing this possibility in this paper. We consider System I below where γ may be left unlinked but may not be linked to a sonorant.

System I is not an account of Modern Japanese, because it is simplified by disregarding the possibility of word initial voiced obstruent. Nonetheless, a language of System I manifests a rendaku phenomenon with the same formal characteristic as that which we have in Modern Japanese. In this sense, System I may be said to account for rendaku in Modern Japanese, and probably in Old Japanese, too, insomuch as it is likely that rendaku-immune words existed in Old Japanese.

System I
Underlying representations and word allomorph patterns

Underlying	Surface		Examples		R-immune
	W-initial	W-internal			(gloss)
QAQA	KAKA	-KAKA	tuti	kuro-tuti	*kuro-duti
QAQA	KAKA	-GAKA	kaki	huyu-gaki	
QA**QA**	KAGA	-KAGA	kagi	ai-kagi	
QARA	KARA	-KARA	tuya	iro-tuya	*iro-duya
QARA	KARA	-GARA	kame	ko-game	('turtle')
RAQA	RAKA	-RAKA	neko	ko-neko	('cat')
RAQA	RAGA	-RAGA	mado	ko-mado	('window')
RARA	RARA	-RARA	nami	ko-nami	('wave')

3.2.2. Languages without initial devoicing

System II exhibited below is underlyingly the same as System I. But this language lacks word-initial devoicing rule, or alternatively put, it lacks a word-initial delinking rule. It has no rendaku. The Standard Japanese word *hati < pati* 'bee' must be *bati* in this imagined language, a form only possible in a compound word like *o-bati* 'male bee' in Standard Japanese.[6] The word *gama* 'toad', which is considered to have an aberrant form in Standard Japanese, is a word of a common form in this dialect. Standard Japanese has presumably been "contaminated" by the intrusion of this word from a dialect that allowed initial voiced obstruents. Note that even though this language does not have rendaku, it attests a "residue" of Lyman's Law: there can be no words of the form such as *dago* or *gagi*. For such a word to exist, γ would have to be linked to two consonants, to produce a pattern **QAQA**. Indeed here with this language we can see the true nature of Lyman's Law better than with Standard Japanese: Lyman's Law essentially is not a constraint on rendaku voicing, but only a surface manifestation of the prosodic character of obstruent voicing that it can be linked to at most one obstruent. What is commonly understood as "Lyman's Law" is simply a way to describe this surface manifestation in a language like Standard Japanese. In reality, Lyman's Law can also affect a language that does not manifest rendaku voicing.

System II   Without an initial devoice rule
Underlying representations and word allomorph patterns

Underlying	Surface		Examples		
	W-initial	W-internal			
QAQA	KAKA	-KAKA	tuti	kuro-tuti	
QAQA	GAKA	-GAKA	bati	ko-bati	'bee'
QA**QA**	KAGA	-KAGA	kagi	ai-kagi	
QARA	KARA	-KARA	tuya	iro-tuya	
QARA	GARA	-GARA	gama	ko-gama	'toad'
RAQA	RAKA	-RAKA	neko	ko-neko	
RA**QA**	RAGA	-RAGA	mado	ko-mado	
RARA	RARA	-RARA	nami	ko-nami	

3.2.3.   Introduction of inherently voiced obstruents

Finally, with System III we have reached a real world of the speakers of Standard Japanese, or not quite, but almost. The borrowing of Sino-

---

[6]*Bati* 'bee' recorded as an independent word form in Fukushima dialect. [Martin 1987:29]

Japanese vocabulary and the intrusion from dialects that lacked an initial devoicing rule have introduced word-initial voiced obstruents into the language. So, we now have those voiced obstruents at word-initial position that alternate with their voiceless counterparts and those that do not, and we have to distinguish these two categories. Underlyingly, the former is represented as an obstruent unspecified with respect to voicing but linked to γ and actualizes as a voiced obstruent. The latter must be inherently marked as voiced in underlying representations. Let us represent this inherently voiced obstruent by underlined $\underline{G}$.

It it is important to note that the innovation of Language III is not an addition of free occurring inherently marked voiced obstruents. $\underline{G}$ must be restricted to word-initial position, as long as Lyman's Law, as an observational generalization, holds in the new language, as it does in Modern Japanese. For, if $\underline{G}$ were allowed word-internally, there would arise a word of the underlying form QA$\underline{G}$A, where QA is linked to γ. Such a word would exhibit the rendaku alternation KAGA/-GAGA, a violation of Lyman's Law.

System III [System I (+ System II)].
$\underline{G}$: underlyingly marked as [+voiced]

Underlying representations and word allomorph patterns

Underlying	Surface		Examples		R-immune
	W-initial	W-internal			(gloss)
QAQA	KAKA	-GAKA	kaki	huyu-gaki	
QAQA	KAGA	-KAGA	kagi	ai-kagi	
QAQA	KAKA	-KAKA	tuti	kuro-tuti	*kuro-duti
$\underline{G}$AQA	GAKA	-GAKA	bati		('drum stick')
$\underline{G}$AQA	$\underline{G}$AGA	-$\underline{G}$AGA	goza		('mat' a loan from II)
QARA	KARA	-GARA	kame	ko-game	
QARA	KARA	-KARA	tuya	iro-tuya	*iro-duya
$\underline{G}$ARA	GARA	-GARA	gama		('toad', a loan from II)
RAQA	RAGA	-RAGA	mado	ko-mado	
RAQA	RAKA	-RAKA	neko	ko-neko	
RARA	RARA	-RARA	nami	ko-nami	

Initial position constraint: $\underline{G}$ is restricted to initial position.

A language accounted for by System III can emerge when a language accounted for by System I absorbs vocabulary items from languages of System II. We may say that Language III has emerged by language I partially incorporating language II. This is a fair description of the development, as far as we are concerned with e-languages.

But as a matter of grammar, or i-languages, the change is not a simple merger. Language I and language II are underlyingly very similar. In both languages, all voiced obstruents are surface manifestations of unspecified obstruents linked to γ. Not any more in language III. Word initial voiced obstruents of language III are now inherently marked as voiced.

Note that words with two obstruents are possible in this language: **GA**QA is a possible underlying form: *goza*. 'mat', *hana-goza* 'flower-mat', *ganbari* 'persistence' *oo-ganbari* 'strong persistence'.

Initial position constraint means that when language I is exposed to language II, it does not reinterpret words of type QAQA as QA**GA**, even though such an reinterpretation would not affect phonetic forms of such words. We get *kagi* 'key', *ai-kagi* 'master-key' either from QA**QA** or QA**GA**. Instead, it adds Initial position constraint for newly introduced **GA** and keep the effect of Layman's Law intact. This leads to our assumption that language III assigns underlying representation type **GAQA** to new loans like *goza*, instead of **GAGA**, though we cannot have any phonetic evidence to distinguish between **GAQA** and nonexistent **GAGA**.

System III (the introduction of **G** with the initial position constraint) is also sufficient to account for the borrowing of the Sino-Japanese vocabulary. In fact, no Sino-Japanese morpheme has a voiced medial: we have daku as in /ren-daku/, but no morpheme of the form */dadu/ or */tadu/. Hence, the introduction of **G** is required to accommodate Sino-Japanese morphemes, but it can be done with the initial position constraint. Furthermore, the linkage of γ to an obstruent would not be needed. However, some Sino-Japanese morphemes with an initial voiceless obstruents were re-interpreted as linked to γ. This reinterpretation caused the effect of accommodating the Sino-Japanese vocabulary into the native rendaku system.[7]

System III describes an IDEALIZED Japanese where rendaku is regular; in this language, if a word does not contain a voiced obstruent internally, thus not contradicting Lyman's Law, either it never undergoes rendaku (rendaku-immune or initially voiced) or it does undergo rendaku without exception. So, the language can have no pairs like *kata-kana* and *hira-gana,* but it can have only pairs like *kata-kana* and *hira-kana,* or *kata-gana* and *hira-gana.*

---

[7]Compare *koku-min* 'subject (of a state)' vs. *hon-goku* 'native-land'. I maintain that the native vs. Sino-Japanese stratification is irrelevant to rendaku, contrary to a widely held view. See Kuroda (2000) for details.

348 / S.-Y. KURODA

4. Summary and conclusion

We are now in a position to give a formal account of the relevant part of Japanese phonology.

Inventory of elements for underlying representations in the lexicon:
  Q: unspecified obstruents
  <u>G</u>: voiced obstruents
  γ: autosegmental feature. γ is linked to at most one Q.
Initial position constraint: <u>G</u> is restricted to initial position.[8]
Unpredictability of rendaku: Insert # to the left edge of a right branch where, though expected, rendaku voicing is missing.
LBC: Insert # at L-initial position.
Rules to interpret unspecified obstruents:
Rule 1. (γ Delinking) Delink γ after #
Rule 2. (Voicing)   Mark γ–linked **Q** as [+voice]
Rule 3. (Markedness convention for obstruents)   Interpret unmarked Q as [-voice]

Now that we have fully developed a formal account of the rendaku phenomenon we need to reflect on the implication of the account and to describe the significance of the account more adequately.

As mentioned earlier, voiced obstruents are believed to have been (pre)nasalized in earlier Japanese. Hence, "it is tempting to consider the structure N-ⁿN (compound-noun nigori [i.e., voiced--SYK]) as a reduction of N n[o] N when the first noun is subordinated to the second, and N n[i] N when it is coordinated, as in reduplications...." (Martin 1987:26) In this view, the historical origin of rendaku is nasal-spread from, or nasal harmony with, an inserted particle. The account by Itô and Mester (1986:57f.) has some structural similarity: an insertion of a [+voice] autosegment followed by voicing spread. The nasal spread or voicing spread is accompanied by a constraint, Lyman's Law.

In contrast, according to the view developed here, rendaku arises from the interaction of a prosodic feature, γ, inherent to lexical morphemes with

---

[8]There are however exceptions to this morpheme structure constraint: a few well-known counterexamples to Lyman's Law such as *hasigo* 'ladder' (cf. nawa-basigo 'rope-ladder'), *Syoo-Zaburoo* (< Syoo+Saburoo, a proper name). Another example often cited in this connection, hun-zibaru (< hun-sibaru, an emphatic form of sibaru 'tie') should probably not count as an exception to Lyman's Law and thus to the morpheme structure constraint in question, but I leave the matter without further comment for the moment. This morpheme structure constraint does not apply to the foreign (i.e., recent loan) stratum.

the ways underspecified obstruent segments are phonetically interpreted. There is no Lyman's Law in the generative grammar of the language; it is only an observational generalization on the distributional phenomenon inevitably resulting from the existence of this prosodic feature and the necessity of interpreting unspecified segments.

In the preceding exposition, I have so far characterized the radical idea in contrast with the conventional view in terms of devoicing of morpheme-initial obstruents at word-initial position. This is a necessary step for the expository strategy. However, the contrast between the allomorphic pair that characterizes rendaku, such as exhibited in (2), is, exactly speaking, not a product of devoicing. Rather, it is a consequence of the delinking of a voice-wise unspecified obstruent from γ.

There are two independent rules that phonetically interpret voice-wise unspecified obstruents and specify their voice feature. If unspecified obstruents are not γ-linked, a universal rule of phonology interprets them as unvoiced obstruents. If they are γ-linked, they are specified as voiced by a rule which is as a matter of course language specific.

It is important to distinguish these two sets of rules in Japanese phonology, one delinking γ and others specifying phonetic values of obstruents. The former is a rule deep-rooted in the phonology of Japanese, invariant through time and space. It embodies the genius of Japanese phonology. The latter are surface rules that determine the phonetic interpretation of obstruents and, as a matter of fact, can vary through time and dialects. This phonetic interpretation is quite plain in Standard Japanese; it follows the universal markedness convention for obstruents. In contrast to the phonetically straightforward interpretation in Modern Standard Japanese, in some dialects and at older stages of the language, γ-linked obstruents are interpreted as (pre)nasalized voiced obstruents. Furthermore, in some of such dialects, γ-unlinked obstruents are interpreted as unvoiced at word-initial position and voiced word-internally.

To sum up, according to conventional wisdom, rendaku is accounted for by rendaku voicing; the conventional account is a voicing account of rendaku. According to the radical idea developed here, the rendaku phenomenon is accounted for by means of γ-delinking; we have a γ-delinking account of rendaku. To call our account a devoicing account of rendaku is a kind of misnomer and could be misleading. Nonetheless we must recognize that this designation must serve as an expedient substitute in expository or nontechnical contexts.

Besides voiced obstruents that are word-internal phonetic realization of γ-linked obstruents, there are also obstruents that are marked as voiced in the lexicon, symbolized as G above. They are common in the Sino-Japanese stratum but fairly limited in the native stratum.

Finally, let us note that no reference is made to the distinction between the native and the Sino-Japanese stratum of vocabulary in the formal account of the part of Japanese phonology we have been concerned with here, the part of phonology that accounts for the rendaku phenomenon.

References

Haraguchi, Shosuke (2000). Shin-'rendaku'-ron no kokoromi. Kazuko Inoue ed. *Researching and Verifying an Advanced Theory of Human Language*. Kanda University of International Studies. 715-732.

Itô, Junko & Armin Mester (1986). "The phonology of voicing in Japanese: Theoretical Consequences for morphological accessibility," *Linguistic Inquiry* 17.49-73.

Itô, Junko & Armin Mester (1995). "Japanese phonology," John Goldsmith ed. *Handbook of Phonological Theory*, 817-838. Oxford: Blackwell.

Itô, Junko, Armin Mester & Jaye Padgett (1995). "Licensing and underspecification in optimality theory." *Linguistic Inquiry* 26.571-613.

Kokugogakkai (1955). *Kokugojiten*. Tokyo:Tokyo-Do.

Kuroda, S.-Y. (1963). "A historical remark on 'rendaku,' a phenomenon in Japanese morphology." ms., MIT.

Kuroda, S.-Y. (1965). *Generative Grammatical Studies in the Japanese Language*. MIT Dissertation. Published from Garland Press, New York, 1979.

Kuroda, S.-Y. (2000). Rendaku and vocabulary stratification. A talk presented at LP2000, Prague. (To appear in Proceedings LP2000)

Lyman, B. S. (1894) "Change from surd to sonant in Japanese compounds" *Oriental Studies of the Oriental club of Philadelphia*, 1-7.

McCawley, James D. (1968) *The Phonological component of a Grammar of Japanese*. The Hague: Mouton.

Martin, Samuel (1952). Morphophonemics of Standard Colloquial Japanese. *Language, Supplement. Language Dissertation* No. 47.

Martin, Samuel (1987) *Japanese Language through Time*. New Haven: Yale University Press.

Motoori, Norinaga (1790/1822). *Kojikiden*. Nagoya: Eirakuya. 2nd ed.(1844) reprinted in *Motoori Norinaga Zenshu*, vol. 9. 1968. Tokyo:Iwanami Shoten.Ono, Toru (1962) *Man'yoogana no Kenkyu*. Tokyo:Meiji-shoin.

Rice, Keren (1997) "Japanese NC clusters and the redundancy of postnasal voicing," *Linguistic Inquiry* 28.541-551.

Vance, Timothy (1979). *Nonsense-word Experiments in Phonology and their Application to* rendaku *in Japanese*. Dissertation, The University of Chicago.

Vance, Timothy (1987). *An Introduction to Japanese Phonology*. Albany: State University of New York Press.

Vance, Timothy (1996). "Sequential voicing in Sino-Japanese," *Journal of the Association of Teachers of Japanese*, 30.22-43.

Supporting Korean and Japanese on the Internet: Web Standards, Unicode and National Character Encodings[1]

KATSUHIKO MOMOI

Netscape Communications Corp.

1. Introduction:

In recent years, internationalization of the Internet has been accelerating. Organizations such as World Wide Web Consortium (W3C) and The Internet Engineering Task Force (IETF) have published various standards documents to deal with languages that require non-ASCII writing script support.

Supporting East Asian scripts such as Chinese, Korean and Japanese is a complex affair requiring cooperation of web site developers, server software and client software that access such non-ASCII web sites. Standards are not binding laws but rather a set of guidelines most legitimate software developers agree to use in order to achieve inter-operability among the parties involved. The alternative is chaos and poor usability. Thus widely accepted standards have strong binding power.

With this trend towards standardization as a backdrop, this paper focuses on some of the major issues in supporting Korean and Japanese writing scripts on the Internet. The topics include such standards-related issues as 1) what are the prevailing and upcoming national characters set standards in Korea and Japan, 2) what national encodings are used to support these character set standards, 3) what is the role of Unicode encoding in supporting these language scripts, 4) what problems/issues need to be addressed to improve support for these 2 languages, etc.

In developing network client software such as browsers and mail programs, attention must be paid to issues such as 1) how to ensure that a program is properly internationalized for eventual localization, 2) what it means to localize a program for specific language and locale, 3) how to achieve browser's inter-operability with web pages and servers, 4) how to make your mail program inter-operate properly with other mail programs, 5) which standard protocols in addition to HTML need to be supported, 6) the role of standard mail charset and emerging UTF-8 as mail charset, etc.

Studying these concrete issues should help us paint a picture of the processes and issues involved in contemporary global software internationalization and localization. I will also talk about the role users of software can play in improving the software quality in the context of Open Source development.

---

[1] To the memory of Jim McCawley as a small token of my appreciation for what he has taught me about language, linguistics and what it means to be a teacher.

2. Terminologies:

Let me begin by defining key concepts in electronic handling of writing scripts.

Character:

A character is an abstract entity somewhat like phoneme or morphome in linguistics. A character represents a set of variants that may differ in shape but still belong to the same abstract unit of a writing script.

Glyph:

A glyph is a specific instantiation of a character. A character may have more than one glyphs to represent itself. Several glyphs may all be classified as variants of the same character. A typical example is a glyph difference between 2 or more typefaces such as Mincho and Gothic typefaces. There are also some borderline cases where it may not be clear whether two glyphs belong to the same or different characters. A glyph then is similar to allophone or allomorph in linguistics.

Character Set:

A character set is a group of characters. While this definition will qualify any set of characters as a character set, the ones we are interested in are usually those promulgated by an official agency or a standards body such as JSA (Japanese Standards Association). As such, we might call it a character set standard. Character set standards for particular languages promulgated by official standards organization are also called national character sets. A character set standard is usually not used directly for electronic purposes. Rather it defines a standard set of characters for use within a specific writing system. Well-known characters set standards usually have names with prefixes that indicate their origins. For example, JIS X 0208-1997 is a character set standard published by JSA, while KS X 1001:1992 is a standard published by Korean Industrial Standards Association.

A character set can be coded or non-coded. A non-coded character set is not designed for electronic purposes. For example, Japanese character sets such as Gakushu Kanji (学習漢字 1006 Kanji for Education), Joyo Kanji (常用漢字 1945 Kanji for everyday use), or Korean Sangyong Hanja (상용한자/常用漢字 1800 Hanja for every day use to be learned by the end of High School) and Middle School Hanja (the first 900 of the Sangyong Hanja to be learned by the end of Middle School). These character sets do not follow organizing principles optimized for computerization.

In contrast to a non-coded character set, a coded character set is designed from the outset to be used in electronic transmission and storage. Such character sets are usually arranged in grids or matrices. JIS character sets use 94 by 94 grids and thus characters can be referenced by its grid position. This method is called Row-Cell notation (KUTEN code in Japanese). For example, the notation

04-02 in the JIS X 0208:1997 character set points to the Hiragana 'a' あ, while
24-22 in the KS X 1001:1992 character set refers to the Hangul syllable 'ma' 마.

While this type of grid coding method is convenient for classifying members in a character set, it is actually not directly used in computerizing characters.

Encoding (Method):
An encoding is a way to assign code points to characters in a character set standard. An encoding method can use one or more bytes to code a character. If an encoding method requires only 1 byte to code target characters, such a method is sometimes called a single-byte encoding method and a character represented by such a method, a single-byte character. If a method requires 2 bytes to encode each character, then such a method is called a double-byte encoding method, etc. If an encoding method mixes one or more bytes in representing characters, e.g. some characters with a 1-byte sequence while others with a 2-byte or more sequence, it is called a multi-byte encoding method.

Most language scripts of the world can be encoded using a 1-byte method. Notable exceptions are East Asian languages like Chinese, Japanese, and Korean, all of which use multi-byte or 2-byte encoding methods.

Well-known 1-byte encoding methods include ISO-8859-1 (Latin 1) and other ISO-8859-x series. In many of these encoding methods, the names used are also the names of the character sets they are en-coding. Some encodings such as ISO-8859-1 and ISO-8859-2 (Latin 2) are used to represent more than 1 language scripts. For example, ISO-8859-1 covers practically all Romance and Germanic languages, while ISO-8859-2 is for most of the East European languages which use Latin-derived scripts, e.g. Polish, Czech, Romanian, etc.

Unlike these pan-European encoding methods, many Asian encodings are specific to each language and country and in that sense can be called national, locale-specific, or native encoding methods. Examples of East Asian locale-specific encodings include Shift_JIS (Japanese), Johab (Korean), GB2312 (Simplified Chinese) and Big5 (Traditional Chinese). There are also encodings with names like ISO-2022-xx and EUC-xx. These encodings are actually locale independent encoding methods but can be applied to particular character sets.

Since the late 1980's, the Unicode Consortium has been mounting a steadily successful campaign to create, maintain, and improve on a universal encoding method whose goal is to uniquely encode every known character in world's known language scripts including archaic ones no longer used in living languages. In national or locale-specific encoding methods, a character in one language can be encoded with exactly the same byte sequence as a totally different character in another language. Unicode, on the other hand, does not suffer from this type of ambiguity. Every character is assigned a uniquely different code point of a fixed 2-byte sequence. Thus, if 2 characters share the same code point, then, by definition, they must be the same character in Unicode.

Font:
A font is a collection of character glyphs drawn from specific character sets.
There are two major types of fonts distinguished by technologies used to create
them. They are Bitmap fonts (e.g. BDF, HBF) and Outline fonts (e.g. PostScript,
True Type, Open Type). For our purpose, it is sufficient to note that each font
must explicitly (or implicitly if it is not specified explicitly) include encoding
information, i.e. what coding point under what encoding method corresponds to
each character glyph in the font. Most contemporary Asian language fonts
utilized under popular operating systems such as Windows and Macintosh also
provide information on multiple encoding methods. In such fonts, in addition to
locale-specific encoding information, Unicode mapping information is also provided in a file known as a CMap file.

This then means that a software program can refer to a specific character
glyph via either its locale-specific encoding or Unicode code point.

Language and Locale:
These 2 terms are sometime synonymously used. Strictly speaking, Locale is a
broader term than Language and it includes not only a language, but also associated linguistic and cultural conventions of that language. For example,
consideration for date & time formats, currency symbols, collation/sorting
methods, etc. would be part of the coverage for a locale. It has become more or
less conventional in software development to designate a locale by a schema
[Language-Region], e.g. en-US, en-GB, ja-JP, ko-KO, zh-CN, zh-TW, etc. zh-
CN points to Chinese in China while zh-TW points to Chinese in Taiwan. In
software development, full support for a language X normally requires full support for a locale of that language X.

A byte: (8 bits)
1 byte (8 bits) can distinguish 256 characters -- 2 to the power of 8. A byte can
be represented in any number of ways (see below) but in computing it is usually
represented in a hexadecimal notation.

Binary	Decimal	Hexadecimal
00000000	0	0x00
11111111	255	0xFF

Table 1

Unicode and native/national encodings:
Here is an illustration of differences between Unicode and local/national encoding methods. In Table 2, a byte sequence 0xB5 0xA4 corresponds to 2 characters, µ¤, if you are using the ISO-8859-1 encoding, to 1 character 気 if you're

using Japanese EUC-JP encoding and to 1 Hangul character, 덮 if you're using Korean EUC-KR encoding. That is, all three representations bear the exact same byte sequence and their glyph representations cannot be made properly without knowing what the encoding is. Under Unicode, the 3 characters bear different encoding points and thus there is no overlap.

Native Byte sequence (0xB5 0xA4)	Character	Unicode
ISO-8859-1	µ¤	00B5 00A4
EUC-JP	気	6C17
EUC-KR	덮	B36E

Table 2

3. Requirements for Global Internet Software Development

In this discussion, I will assume that software development targets the global market. It is possible and even desirable in some cases to limit the target to a single language, but in today's global software business, this is usually both impractical and ultimately will prove to be more costly. Thus, from the beginning, most major software development firms design a program to be capable of handling many different language scripts and targets the world marketplace.

What does it take then to support Korean and Japanese in an Internet software program such as a browser or an integrated network tool? I will first present a laundry list of support items and then pick out some of them for further discussion. Here's one such list of items:

(1) Unicode, (2) National/Native character set standards and National/Native encoding methods for browsing and mail, (3) Auto-detection among Japanese (ISO-2022-JP, Shift_JIS, EUC-JP) and Korean (EUC-KR, ISO-2022-KR) encodings, (4) Font display of the scripts, (5) Input Method Editor (IME) support: platform specific implementations -- Windows, Macintosh, Unix. Also Global IME support for Win95/98/ME/NT4. (Win 2000 ships with own IMEs). This is available for Windows only, (6) Line-breaking rules (禁則処理), (7) Support for general Internet-related standards such as HTML4, XML, RDF, ECMA (JavaScript), CSS, mail standards for different languages, (8) CSS1/CSS2 List styles -- cjk ideographic, hiragana, katakana, hiraga-iroha, katakana-iroha, etc., (9) Printing – Various printing technologies for Windows, Mac and Unix platforms, (10) Mixed Latin & non-Latin baseline adjustment: ex. "This is 日本語 meaning "Japanese Language" in Japanese." – is the baseline for Japanese aligned level as the Latin characters? (11) Character spacing, (12) Collation and date support, (13) Ruby, (14) Vertical.

4. Unicode support

Unicode support is essential in today's global development. There are a number of reasons to recommend it:

(1) For internal processing of data, Unicode makes the process simpler since there is no need to carry around locale-encoding information. (Note the ambiguity of code points in native encodings as discussed above.)

Input (Native Charset data) → Internal Processing (Unicode) → Output (Native Charset data)

In this model of processing, all internal processing is performed in Unicode and native encodings are used only at perimeter of processing, i.e. for handling input data and for outputting data.

(2) All new Internet related protocols now list Unicode (e.g. UTF-8) as the default charset if no explicit charset is specified. E.g. HTML 4, XML, RDF, etc.

(3) Unicode can simplify file exchange transactions. No need to ask what locale encoding is used for a specific file.

(4) Unicode can support multilingual documents easily.

(5) Unicode can simplify process of localization considerably for global software.

(6) Unicode is fully supported on all major platforms: Windows NT4/2000 (partial support on Windows 98/ME), Macintosh (starting w/ 8.0), most Unix vendors offers Unicode locales.

(7) Unicode incorporates the characters of all the major government standards for ideographic characters from Japan, Korea, China, and Taiwan, and more. Sources for CJK ideographs in Unicode Version 3.0 include:

China/Hong Kong/Singapore: GB2312-80, GB12345-90, GB7589-87, GB7590-87, General Purpose Hanzi List for Modern Chinese Language, and General List of Simplified Hanzi, Singapore Characters, GB8565-88, and GB16500-95.

Taiwan: CNS 11643-1992, Planes 1-7 & 15.

Japan: JIS X 0208-1990, JIS X 0212, and Unified Japanese IT Vendors Contemporary Ideographs

Korea: KS C 5601-1987 (unique ideographs), KS C 5657-1991, PKS C 5700-1 1994, and PKS C 5700-2 1994.

Vietnam: TCVN 5773:1993, and TCVN 6056:1995

Others: KS C 5601-1987 (duplicate ideographs), ANSI Z39.64-1989 (EACC), Big-5 (Taiwan), CCCII: level 1, GB 12052-89 (Korean), JEF (Fujitsu), PRC Telegraph Code, Taiwan Telegraph Code, Xerox Chinese, Han Character Shapes Permitted for Personal Names (Japan), IBM Selected Japanese and Korean Ideographs.

(8) While not perfect, Unicode uses 3-dimensional conceptual model to identify characters culled from many different sources. The 3 primary attributes for identification are:

Semantic (X) – are meaning and function same or different?
Abstract Shape (Y) – are general forms same or different?
Actual Shape (Z) – are the differences merely due to typeface differences?

(9) Unification of various CJK ideographs were carried out with 3 primary criteria:

A. Source Separation Rule: If two ideographs are distinct in a primary source standard, then they are not unified. E.g. 剣, 劍, 劒 (JIS X 0208-1990)

B. Non-cognate Rule: If two ideographs are unrelated in historical derivation (non-cognate characters), then they are not unified. E.g. 土, 士

C. Any two ideographs that possess the same abstract shape are unified provided that either the Source Separation Rule or the Non-Cognate Rule does not disallow their unification.

(10) The Unicode Standard, Version 3.0 (published 2/2000) lists almost 28,000 CJK ideographic characters. Total assigned characters: 49194. Total assigned code points: 57709. Unassigned: 7827. Unicode is fully compatible with the international standard ISO/IEC 10646 Character set.

5. National Character Set standards:

Which national character set standards should be supported? The answer depends on a variety of factors such as development time allocated, customer/user requirements, types of software to be developed, etc. For an Internet program like a browser, it may not be necessary initially to support character sets that contain rarely used characters. On the other hand, database software used by local governments may need to support all officially approved character sets as official documents often include rare family or personal names, which can be accommodated only with latest character set standards.

Propagation of a new character set often takes some time and if support for it is mandatory to conduct official business, it is customary for governments to allow a reasonable period, e.g. several years, for implementation. Sometimes officials are quite impatient and come down with a requirement that must be met within a very short period of time. Such requirements are generally met with a chorus of disapproval from software developers.

Below are 2 tables summarizing major character set standards for Japanese and Korean in Lunde (1999) with my update.

Japanese:

Character Set standard	What it defines
JIS X 201-1997	Hankaku Katakana + JIS-Roman (overline, yen)
JIS X 208: 1997	JIS level 1 (2965), JIS level 2 (3384), Extra Kanji (6), Symbols (524) = 6879 characters.
JIS X 0212-1990	5801 Kanji + 266 symbols = 6067 characters -- not supportable by Shift_JIS encoding.
JIX X 0213: 2000	JIS level 3 (about 2000), JIS level 4 (about 2400)

Table 3

Korean:

Character Set standard	What it defines
KS X 1003: 1993	KS-Roman (overline, won). Formerly KS C 5646-1993.
KS X 1001: 1992	4,888 Hanja (268 duplicates) + 2,350 (pre-composed) Hangul (Wansung 완성/完成) + 986 Symbols. Standard plane (formerly KS C 56011992.)
KS X 1001: 1992	Alternate plane. 11,172 (all possible modern Hangul syllables: 조합/組合 Johab): 19 initial Jamo, 21 medial Jamo, and 27 final Jamo. Includes many non-existing syllables.
KS X 1002:1991	Extended character set (3,605 Hangul + 2,856 Hanja + 1,188 others). Hangul set is already part of Johab set. Formerly KS C 5657-1991.
KPS 9566-97	North Korea. Similar to KS X 1001. (2,679 Hangul + 4,653 Hanja (no duplicates) + 927 others.). 김일성 (Kim Il Sung) and 김정일 (Kim Jong Il) are listed separately and duplicates syllable entries are found elsewhere.

	Includes some Hangul syllables not found in KS X 1001: 1992 standard plane. E.g. 咄 (ddom).
GB 12051-89	China. Defines 5,297 Hangul + 682 other characters for use of Koreans in China.

(Note: Until 1997, Korean character sets bore a prefix **KS C**.)

Table 4

As can be imagined from the sheer number of character sets, there are currently few fonts that can include all the characters defined in them. A question arises as to why a single character set standard cannot be established for a language rather than several ones. Some of them even overlap with each other. The answer is that these standards developed over a period of time and were reflective of what was needed and known at that given time. It is also not easy to abolish a standard once it is established since many software programs use it. Thus older standards need to be often preserved for backward compatibility. It is clearly desirable to agree on a fewer standards which can address all the language needs but this is not always easy to do since new characters are discovered and added from time to time.

For Internet software development, the following core character sets are probably sufficient at present though additional sets will probably be needed in the near future.

For Japanese, JIS X 0201 is essential for Hankaku and JIS-Roman characters. JIS X 0208's Level 1 Kanji characters are needed to cover Joyo Kanji. Support for JIS X 0212, which includes additional rare Kanji characters, is probably optional.

For Korean, KS X 1003:1993 is essential to cover the KS-Roman characters. The standard plane of KS X 1001:1992 constitutes the core set of modern Korean characters. There is one problem, however, with KS X 1001:1992. Precomposed Hangul syllables are lacking some characters used in modern Korean. E.g. 咄 (ddom). This problem can be solved when the alternate plane of KS X 1001 is used. But this requires a Johab encoding or an equivalent. (This issue will be discussed below under encoding support.)

6. Encoding methods requirements:

What encodings to support are closely tied to the question of character sets. Some character sets are not supportable by certain encodings. Below are major encodings in use for Japanese and Korean and the ones that would be required for Unicode.

Japanese Encoding	Character set(s) it supports
ISO-2022-JP	JIS X 201, JIS X 0208. Used in Mail, News, web pages.
Shift_JIS	JIS X 201, JIS X 0208. *Cannot support JIS X 0212. Used in web pages.
EUC-JP	JIS X 201, JIS X 0208, JIS X 0212, JIS X 0213. Used in web pages.
ISO-2022-JP-1	Adds JIS X 0212 (RFC 2237) to ISO-2022-JP
ISO-2022-JP-2	JIS X 0212 & other character sets (GB 2312-80, KS X 1001:1992, ISO-8859-1, and ISO-8859-2).

Table 5

Korean Encoding	Character set(s) it supports
ISO-2022-KR	KS 1003:1993, KS X 1001:1992. No longer used in Mail but is required for legacy documents.
EUC-KR	KS 1003:1993, KS X 1001:1992-standard plane only. (Used for Mail, News, web pages)
Johab	KS 1001: 1992-alternate plane. 11,172 Hangul pre-composed syllables. Forward compatible with Unicode.
UHC	KS 1001: 1992-alternate plane. Backward compatible with EUC-JP and Forward compatible with Unicode. Unified Hangul Code.

Table 6

Unicode	Character set(s) it supports
UCS-2, UTF-16, UTF-8, UTF-7	JIS X 201, JIS X 208, JIS X 0212, KS X 1001 (standard & alternate planes), KS X 1002, KS X 1003.

Table 7

Of the 3 Japanese encodings, ISO-2022-JP uses 7-bit encoding method and is used as the standard Mail and News encoding in addition to some web pages. Both Shift_JIS and EUC-JP are 8-bit encoding methods and are used for web pages and text documents primarily. Shift_JIS was developed for Microsoft Windows and Apple Macintosh, while EUC-JP is a specific instantiation of EUC method developed for Unix platforms.

For current Japanese needs on the Internet, these 3 encodings would be sufficient. For the future, much will depend on how JIS X 0212 and JIS X 0213 are promoted. If they are to be regarded as important, then either ISO-2022-JP-1 or ISO-2022-JP-2 would become necessary.

For Korean, EUC-KR is the main encoding needed at present. ISO-2022-KR used to be the standard mail encoding until a few years ago but now EUC-KR is the sole standard encoding used for both Mail and News in Korean. But because there are legacy documents in ISO-2022-KR, its support would be still important. It is not clear if support for Johab or UHC would be needed. Clearly there is strong need to support more Hangul syllables and some of KS X 1001 alternate plane characters are needed. However, these can be supported under Unicode as it includes all the Johab encoding set of KS X 1001:1992.

For Unicode, UCS-2 and UTF-16 are primarily needed for internal processing. The difference between the 2 is that the latter can encode "surrogate" area characters of UCS-4. UCS-2 is a fixed 2-byte length encoding method. UTF-16 is a variable-byte encoding method using up to 4-bytes sequence depending on what character it is encoding. When the term Unicode is used by itself, normally UCS-2 is the intended meaning. In addition to these, it is also customary to use transfer-safe encoding methods called UTF-8 and UTF-7. When saving files into Unicode or sending Unicode data over the Internet, the UTF-8 encoding is usually employed. UTF-7 was once promoted as the standard Mail/News encoding due to the use of its 7-bit encoding scheme but has never gained ground. Instead UTF-8 is now the encoding used as the default encoding of the Internet protocols in general. A slightly modified form of UTF-7 is used today in a mail server protocol called IMAP in writing non-ASCII mail folder names.

7. Line Breaking Rules (禁則処理)

Japanese does not use a space to break a word. You can fold a line at any character except that the following set of rules must be observed:

- Characters which should not begin a line
  、。,.：；？！’”）]｝＞≫」』】々ーあいうえおやゆ
  よわアイウエオツヤユヨワカケ"°ヽヾゝゞ—-'"℃°
  Ｆ¢％‰
- Characters which should not end a line
  "（〔［｛〈《「『【¥＄£＠§〒♯

Korean unlike Japanese uses a space as a word break. Thus presumably the rules such as the above do not have to apply except to Hanja portion of Korean texts. This type of line-breaking rules is an essential part of supporting these languages.

8. IME support

East Asian operating systems usually come with an Input Method Editor (IME) specific to that locale, i.e. native IMEs. The idea that an IME must be tied to a specific locale is a common one but it is not quite accurate. Macintosh, for example, has for some time allowed users to input CJK characters under English and other non-CJK operating systems with the aid of language kits. Windows operating systems until a few years ago only had native IMEs and it was not possible to input CJK characters unless an operating system matching a particular CJK language was used.

This deficiency was corrected by the appearance of Global IMEs on Windows 95/98/ME/NT4. Global IMEs are not as good as native IMEs but provide adequate support for occasional users of IMEs. They were meant to be part of a bridging plan until a truly multilingual operating system became available. Windows 2000 is such an operating system. On Windows 2000, all internal processing takes place in Unicode, and any language input can be accepted easily. On older operating systems such as Windows 95 that does not process in Unicode, this seemingly simple task is much harder to do.

On Unix, it is possible to input Japanese or Korean under non-Asian locales with appropriate font and locale support files but this is not as transparent as it would be on Macintosh or Windows and requires more than cursory knowledge of the operating systems. Availability of such IMEs on Unix varies from platform to platform and users must be generally enterprising to get CJK input to work.

9. Other support issues

I will take up some remaining items in this section.

The issue of font availability has long been a problem. This issue is also tied to that of IME availability. Just as locale and IME have been de-coupled by the appearance of Language Kits and Global IMEs, font should go the same way. There is no logical reason why Japanese fonts should not be available on operating systems of any language. Fonts should not be something application program developers have to be concerned about. In recent years, operating systems such as Windows 2000 and Macintosh 8.5 (and later) have begun the trend of providing fonts for major languages of the world free. This trend is likely to accelerate.

As to detecting encoding and language, newer Internet browsing software programs come with the so-called auto-detection modules. These are built-in program routines to sniff out the encoding of the incoming data based on byte-pattern detection mechanisms. When the target is relatively small, i.e. the incoming data are either Japanese or Korean, it is not so difficult to determine what encoding the data are in based on a relatively small amount of data. These days it is also trendy to offer a so-called universal auto-detection, which claims to detect any encoding. Such a detection technology is not yet highly reliable. For Japanese and Korean, language specific auto-detection modules are essential at present. A universal encoding/language detector is not.

10. Conclusion and residual issues:

As mentioned above, there is a gradual shift toward the use of Unicode on the Internet. This trend is accelerated by various Internet-related standards and internal requirement of software. On the other hand, there is enormous amount of data encoded in various national/local encodings and they and Unicode should continue to co-exist for some time to come. Eventually it is hoped that in a manner transparent to the user, software can unify on the use of Unicode. From a user point of view, there should be nothing remarkable when such a shift occurs. But from a software development point of view, it would represent tremendous advances.

I will address below some of the common problems in Internet software development in the context of current and future Internet trends.

(1) Inter-operability problems: These are problems caused by incompatibility of one or more programs. For example, in Internet documents and mail messages, it is required to designate a charset for them. One program may label a document with a non-standard charset name and thus causes a problem in other programs. They key in such a case would be to agree to use a preferred charset name.

(2) Failure of auto-detection: This problem is encountered particularly when incoming data is too small for detection routines. A related question to ask is if auto-detection will be really necessary at all in the future. There are some trends converging on this issue. First, more and more, web site developers label web documents with a correct charset label. Second, web servers can send charset/encoding information in a Content-Type header.

Third, if/when more web documents are converted into Unicode, no labeling may be necessary since in future all un-labeled documents can be assumed to be in UTF-8.

(3) The round-trip problem: Software usually converts from a native encoding into Unicode for internal processing and then back to native encoding when an output is required. What if the same character maps to a different Unicode point depending on a platform? The result is a chaos. Problems of this type exist in both Japanese and Korean. These operating system differences are not easy to resolve in a short amount of time.

(4) 8-bit unsafe: Today's microprocessors are capable of processing 32, 64 and even 128 bits all at once. Thus, it would seem quaint to talk about whether

or not servers are 8-bit safe. Yet, this continues to be a problem even today. I still hear from people complaining that mail software mangles accented character like "é" into "i". This occurs because a server that is transmitting the data strips off the 8th bit of a byte. Thus, a binary sequence "11101001" (0xE9 = é) turns into "1101001" (0x69 = i).

There are a couple of major factors that will help alleviate many of these problems. One is an economic factor, which drives web site development. Having to deal with individual differences of browsing software by creating extra ways to accommodate non-standard behavior is costly adding more time to web development. Thus more and more web developers are demanding that standards be strictly adhered to.

Another factor is a form of development gaining favor these days called Open Source. This form of development has been around for some time – for example, GNU, Perl, and more recently, Linux (OS) and Mozilla (Browser) projects. Under Open Source development, software's source code is made available publicly to anyone who wants to download and take a look. It also accepts coding contributions from anyone who can show that changes proposed are sound and good. Typically, contributors are scattered all over the world and communication for development takes place by either mail or community chats. It would be virtually impossible to do development without standardization in this type of environment. Open Source software is a common property. Contributing to it helps anyone who will be using that software. It is no surprise that the Internet is breathing new fire into this form of development. The promise of the Internet has always been its openness and shared benefits. Supporting complex writing scripts such as Japanese and Korean is no easy affair and contributions from average users in the form of comments, bug reports, requests, and bug fixes have been and will continue to be vital to such a development process.

11. References

Communicator/Netscape 6 International Users Page : http://home.netscape.com/eng/intl
Daniels, Peter T. & William Bright, editors. 1996. *The World's Writing Systems*. Oxford University Press.
JIS standards (Japanese Standards Association): http://www.jsa.or.jp/
Kano, Nadine. 1995. *Developing International Software for Windows 95 and NT*. Microsoft Press.
Lunde, Ken. 1999. *CJKV Information Processing*. O'Reilly.
Mozilla.org : http://www.mozilla.org/
Mozilla Internationalization : http://www.mozilla.org/projects/intl
Multilingual Computing & Technology Magazine: A quarterly.
RFC (Internet Requests for Comments): http://www.cis.ohio-state.edu/hypertext/information/rfc.html
Unicode Consortium. 2000. *Unicode Standard 3.0*. Addison-Wesley. http://www.unicode.org/

Semantic Bifurcation in Japanese Compound Verbs

TIMOTHY J. VANCE

University of Arizona

1. Compound Verbs

Japanese is rich in verbs that can be analyzed as containing two verb roots.[1]
For example, *kak-i+tor-u* 'write down' contains the roots of *kak-u* 'write'
and *tor-u* 'take'.[2] The first component verb in such a compound is invariable;
it must appear in its STEM form (*reNyookei*). The second component verb
bears whatever inflectional ending is required for the compound as a whole.
The examples in (1) illustrate with *hik-i+das-u* 'pull out' (cf. *hik-u* 'pull'
and *das-u* 'put out').

(1) *hik-i+das-u*   nonpast indicative   *hik-i+das-eba* conditional
    hik-i+dashi-ta past indicative   *hik-i+das-oo*   volitional

The citation (dictionary) form of any Japanese verb, compound or not, is the
nonpast indicative (*shuushikei*).

---

[1] These verbs are such an important segment of the vocabulary that manuals exist for nonnative learners. The two I know of are Tagashira and Hoff 1986 and Niimi, Yamaura, and Utsuno 1987.

[2] I use hyphens to separate roots from inflectional endings and plus signs for other morphological divisions. I am not committed to the analysis that these conventions reflect. I cite Japanese examples in a modified Hepburn romanization which uses double letters for long vowels, *N* for the mora nasal /N/, and *Q* for the mora obstruent /Q/. For an introductory discussion of Japanese mora consonants, see Vance 1987, Chapter 5.

The role of such compound verbs in Japanese is similar to the role of verb-particle combinations in English, and as with both examples in (1), an English verb-particle combination is often a serviceable translation for a Japanese compound verb.[3] Each language's pattern is productive; new combinations can be coined and may catch on. It stands to reason, however, that the possibilities are richer in Japanese, since there are far more Japanese verbs than there are English particles.

Japanese compound verbs vary widely along a scale of semantic transparency. The four examples in (2) range from quite transparent to quite opaque.

(2) *nigir-i+tsubus-u* 'grasp'+'squash' = 'grasp and squash'
    tach-i+mawar-u 'stand up'+'go around' = 'conduct oneself'
    moch-i+awase-ru 'hold'+'put together' = 'happen to have on hand'
    och-i+tsuk-u 'fall'+'reach' = 'settle down'

I will not restrict the class of items I consider here on the basis of transparency. I use the label 'compound verb' for any item that can be analyzed as such morphologically, no matter how semantically opaque it may be.[4] Needless to say, like any compound, even the most transparent Japanese compound verb will have an exact literal meaning and conventional figurative uses that are not entirely predictable from the meanings of its two roots. For example, *nigir-i+tsubus-u* 'grasp and squash' has the conventional metaphorical meaning 'prevent action from being taken' when the direct object is some kind of plan or proposal.[5]

2. (C)V ~ /Q/ Alternations

In many Japanese compound verbs, the first component verb appears with the mora obstruent /Q/ in place of the last mora of its stem form. The examples in (3) illustrate.

---

[3] Most introductory linguistics textbooks written in English at least mention English verb-particle combinations, although terminology varies. See, for example, O'Grady, Dobrovolsky, and Aronoff 1989:144–145, Fromkin and Rodman 1998:152–153, and Hudson 2000:302–303.

[4] Tagashira and Hoff (1986:8–9) propose categorizing nontransparent examples as 'idiomatic', 'fused', or 'simple', but they admit that these distinctions are not clear-cut.

[5] There is nothing new or original in this background discussion, but it was all new to me when Jim McCawley covered it in a course called Comparative Japanese and English Vocabulary. I was only an auditor, but it was an unforgettable experience that makes the topic of this paper particularly appropriate for my contribution to a conference dedicated to Jim's memory.

(3) a. *buQ+toos-u* 'push on without a break'
      cf. *buts-u* 'smack' (stem *buch-i*); *toos-u* 'put through'

   b. *hiQ+kakar-u* 'get stuck'
      cf. *hik-u* 'pull' (stem *hik-i*); *kakar-u* 'become attached'

   c. *noQ+tor-u* 'hijack'
      cf. *nor-u* 'board' (stem *nor-i*); *tor-u* 'take'

   d. *saQ+pik-u* 'deduct'
      cf. *sas-u* 'hand' (stem *sash-i*); *hik-u* 'pull'

   e. *yoQ+para-u* 'get drunk'
      cf. *yo-u* 'get drunk' (stem *yo-i*); *hara-u* 'clear away'

This kind of mora obstruent appears only if the second component verb begins with a voiceless obstruent, as in *toos-u* (3a), *kakar-u* (3b), *tor-u* (3c), *hik-u* (3d), and *hara-u* (3e). When the second component verb begins with /h/ or /f/ in other environments, it begins with /p/ after /Q/, as in *saQ+pik-u* (3d) and *yoQ+para-u* (3e).[6] Also, this kind of mora obstruent appears only if the first component verb belongs to the larger of the two regular inflectional classes (*godan-katsuyoo*). For convenience, I will refer to the verbs in this class as CONSONANT VERBS.[7]

The set of alternations just described for compound verbs overlaps with, but is not identical to, two other sets of alternations. One is the set found in inflectional forms of consonant verbs; an example is given in (4a). The other is the set found in Sino-Japanese BINOMS; an example is given in (4b).[8]

(4) a. *mach-i ~ maQ*
      mach-i 'waiting'
      maQ-ta 'waited'

   b. *nichi ~ niQ*
      nichi·botsu 'sunset'
      niQ·koo 'sunlight'

---

[6] In modern Japanese, /f/ (pronounced [ɸ]) and /h/ do not occur immmediately following /Q/ except in mimetic words and recent borrowings. Modern /f/ and /h/ in native Japanese words are both descended from a phoneme that was once pronounced [p]. For discussion, see Okumura 1972:126–130, Kiyose 1985, and Shibatani 1990:167. I will not offer any analysis of the synchronic /p/~/f/ and /p/~/h/ alternations here.

[7] This terminology is Bloch's (1946:100). A consonant verb has at least some inflectional forms containing what can be analyzed as a consonant-final allomorph of the root. If the citation form ends V-*u*, as in *yo-u* (3e), the negative suffix *-azu* will be preceded by *w*, as in *yow-azu*. For details, see Vance 1987, Chapter 12, or a good textbook treatment such as Jorden and Noda 1987:222–226.

[8] A binom is a Sino-Japanese word written with two Chinese characters, and I use a dot to separate the portions represented by each character. Sino-Japanese binoms pose well-known challenges for morphemic analysis that I will not go into here.

Table 1 shows all the alternations in each of the three sets.

COMPOUND VERBS	SINO-JAPANESE BINOMS	CONSONANT-VERB INFLECTION
$ch\text{-}i \sim Q$ ··········	$chi \sim Q$ ··········	$ch\text{-}i \sim Q$
	$tsu \sim Q$	
$k\text{-}i \sim Q$ ···········	$ki \sim Q$	
	$ku \sim Q$	
$r\text{-}i \sim Q$ ·····························		$r\text{-}i \sim Q$
$sh\text{-}i \sim Q$		
$\text{-}i \sim Q$ ·······························		$\text{-}i \sim Q$

Table 1: Alternations in Compound Verbs, Sino-Japanese Binoms, and
Inflectional Forms of Consonant Verbs

The dotted lines in Table 1 show the matches between the alternations in
each set.

All the attested examples of /Q/ in place of (C)V in compound verbs
involve the second mora of a two-mora stem. Longer stems, such as those in
(5), never appear with a final /Q/ as the first component verb in a compound
verb.

(5) *kakar-i* — never *kakaQ*   (*kakar-u* 'become attached')
   hanash-i — never *hanaQ*   (*hanas-u* 'speak')
   tsuka-i — never *tsukaQ*   (*tsuka-u* 'use')
   hatarak-i — never *hataraQ*   (*hatarak-u* 'work')

Even when all the conditions mentioned above are met, this kind of /Q/
in compound verbs is attested only for the thirteen stems listed in (6) — a
very small subset of all the relevant two-mora stems.

(6) *buch-i ~ buQ* 'smack'   *nor-i ~ noQ* 'board'   *tsuk-i ~ cuQ* 'thrust'
   fuk-i ~ fuQ 'blow'   *o-i ~ oQ* 'pursue'   *yo-i ~ yoQ* 'get drunk'[9]
   hik-i ~ hiQ 'pull'   *osh-i ~ oQ* 'push'   *yor-i ~ yoQ* 'approach'
   kak-i ~ kaQ 'scratch'   *sash-i ~ saQ* 'hand'
   kir-i ~ kiQ 'cut'   *tor-i ~ toQ* 'take'

---

[9] It is often difficult to determine whether the second vowel in a sequence of two nonidentical
vowels is in a single long syllable together with the first vowel or in a separate syllable (see
Vance 1987:73–76), but the stems *o-i* and *yo-i* have two moras each, regardless of how many
syllables they have.

Furthermore, the /Q/-final allomorphs of these thirteen stems appear only sporadically, not in every compound verb whose second component verb begins with a voiceless obstruent.

3. Coexistence

When the first component in a compound verb is one of the thirteen alternating two-mora stems listed in (6), a dictionary will often have two entries, one with the first component ending in (C)V (i.e., its regular stem form) and the other with the first component ending in /Q/. For example, every Japanese dictionary I have checked lists *hik-i+kom-u* and *hiQ+kom-u* as separate headwords. The main concern of this paper is how the members of such pairs differ in meaning.

Needless to say, a dictionary listing is no guarantee that a word is part of an actual native speaker's lexicon. To keep the investigation on track, I asked ten native speakers of Japanese to fill out a questionnaire designed to elicit judgments about existence.[10] An English translation of the instructions for this questionnaire appears in (7).

(7) Are the words given below used in the common language? Even colloquial language is fine. For each word, please select one of the five choices ('is used', 'maybe is used', etc.) and circle it. If you have any comments, please feel free to add them.

The five choices for each item were: (1) *is used*; (2) *probably is used*; (3) *cannot decide*; (4) *probably is not used*; (5) *is not used*.[11] The questionnaire contained a total of 147 items, of which 134 were 67 pairs of compound verbs of the relevant type, i.e., one with the first component ending in (C)V and the other with the first component ending in /Q/. The two members of each pair were widely separated. For 27 of these 67 pairs, both members are listed in *Daijirin* (Matsumura 1988), a widely used dictionary put out by one of Japan's major publishers. For the remaining 40 pairs, only one member (the form with (C)V or the form with /Q/) is listed in *Daijirin*. Some examples are given in (8).

---

[10] I would like to thank Yoshi Ono and Tomoe Nakamura for their help in designing and administering both of the questionnaires reported in this paper. I am also very grateful to all the native speakers who responded so generously.

[11] These are translations of: (1) *tsukawarete iru*; (2) *tabun tsukawarete iru*; (3) *handan dekinai*; (4) *tabun tsukawarete inai*; (5) *tsukawarete inai*.

(8)   listed: *kak-i+kir-u* 'cut off'
         listed: *kaQ+kir-u* 'id.'
              cf. *kak-u* 'scratch'; *kir-u* 'cut'

         listed: *tor-i+kes-u* 'cancel'
     not listed: *toQ+kes-u*
              cf. *tor-u* 'take'; *kes-u* 'extinguish'

     not listed: *tsuki-i+har-u*
         listed: *tsuQ+par-u* 'prop up'
              cf. *tsuk-u* 'thrust'; *har-u* 'stretch'

When the ten respondents gave both members of a pair an average rating under 2.0 (i.e., in the range from *is used* to *maybe is used*), that pair was included on a second questionnaire designed to elicit semantic judgments. This second questionnaire is described below in §4. A total of 13 pairs satisfied the criterion. For 12 of these 13, both members are listed in the *Daijirin* dictionary. For the remaining pair, only the form with (C)V is listed: *buch-i+kowas-u* 'hit and smash' (cf. *buts-u* 'smack' and *kowas-u* 'break'). However, *buQ+kowas-u* is listed in other dictionaries. For a list of all 26 words, their dictionary definitions, and their earliest citations, see the Appendix.

In some cases, even when both members of a pair are listed in dictionaries, one or the other is probably not a 'real' word for most native speakers. Consider the examples in (9), all four of which are listed in *Daijirin*.

(9) average rating 3.8: *hik-i+kos-u* 'change residence'
     average rating 1.0: *hiQ+kos-u* 'id.'
          cf. *hik-u* 'pull'; *kos-u* 'go over'

     average rating 1.0: *nor-i+kir-u* 'ride out'
     average rating 4.0: *noQ+kir-u* 'id.'
          cf. *nor-u* 'board'; *kir-u* 'cut'

There was a great deal of variation among participants in the responses, and regional differences were confounded with individual differences. Nonetheless, this first questionnaire succeeded in limiting the domain of further investigation to a manageable set of items about which there should be minimum disagreement regarding existence.

4. Semantic Bifurcation

To the best of my knowledge, the term 'bifurcation' is original with Dwight

Bolinger.[12] The explanation in his introductory textbook (Bolinger 1968:110) reads as follows:

> There comes a moment in every phonetic change when some speakers are using the older form and some the newer. This is the potential source of bifurcation. If I use *burned* as the past of the verb *burn* and you happen to prefer *burnt*, and our conversation turns on the subject of something charred and you refer to it as burnt, I may suspect that you are in possession of a formula that I lack, whereby a thing that gets burned ends up burnt. It is as if I said to myself, "He is using a different form; it must mean something different." Perhaps my impression is supported by the length of the words — *burned* takes longer to say, it sounds like something going on, while *burnt* is short, like something finished. No more than this may be needed to balance our calculations in favor of a shift in meaning, if we start with the suspicion that any difference in form must be intentional. Our mental calculators immediately go to work to assess the slightest difference in context or association, to interpret what the difference is.

The other side of the coin is that one of two similar-sounding items can drive out the other, even if they are not actually homophonous (Bolinger 1968:113):

> Though reinterpretation usually has the effect of diversifying meanings — this is bifurcation — sometimes it deflects them toward each other. In the resulting competition a word may go down.

A well-known example of such reinterpretation in modern American English is *flaunt* threatening to drive out *flout*, as in *flaunt the speed limit* in reference to a person who drives 100 miles an hour.

Returning to Japanese compound verbs, it seems clear that the forms with the mora obstruent /Q/ originated as colloquial spoken forms, and the phonological change involved is nothing especially remarkable. The oldest citations for the mora-obstruent compounds I have looked up in *Nihon kokugo daijiten* (Nihon Daijiten Kankôkai 1972–76) are from a spoken genre, namely, *yookyoku*. These are Japanese Noh drama songs that date from the 14th century (see Appendix).

I suspect that in many cases the mora-obstruent compound never became sufficiently well established to compete with the regular-stem compound and simply died out. Perhaps this is what happened to *noQ+kir-u* (see (9) above). And, of course, there may have been many mora-obstruent compounds that were so ephemeral that they were never recorded in dictionaries. In

---

[12] I first came across the term in a more recent introductory textbook by Grover Hudson (2000:262–263), who pointed me to the Bolinger reference when I asked him about its origin.

other cases, the mora-obstruent compound has driven out the regular-stem compound. For example, *hiQ+kos-u* seems to have ousted *hik-i+kos-u* (see (9) above).[13]

The examples I want to focus on here, however, are the 13 pairs for which, according to the questionnaire responses described in §3, both members coexist in the lexicons of many speakers. These pairs show a bewildering array of semantic divergences. The data reported below was gathered from eight native speakers of Japanese using a second questionnaire. An English translation of the instructions for this questionnaire appears in (10).

(10) Two words are given on each of the following pages. In each case, please answer the questions.

An English translation of the questions on each page is given in (11).

(11) Do you know the following words? Please choose one of the three responses and circle it.

WORD 1   WORD 2

    1. I know both.
    2. I only know one.
    3. I don't know either.

If you chose 1, please answer the following questions. If you chose 2 or 3, please go to the next page.

• Is there any difference in the meaning or use of these two words? If so, please explain.

• Do you think there are sentences in which only one of these words can be used? If so, please write them.

On each page, **WORD 1** and **WORD 2** were the two members of one of the 13 selected pairs. Both words were written with *hiragana* glosses (*furigana*) above each *kanji*. For example, the pair on the last page (*tor-i+hara-u* and *toQ+para-u*) appeared as in (12).

(12) 　と　　はら　　　　と　　ばら
　　取り払う　取っ払う

It comes as no surprise, of course, that the judgments from this second

---

[13] According to the entries in *Nihon kokugo daijiten* (Nihon Daijiten Kankôkai 1972–76), the earliest citation for *hik-i+kos-u* is from about 800, but the earliest citation for the meaning 'change residence' is from 1902. The earliest citation for *hiQ-kos-u* is from 1821–24, and 'change residence' is the only meaning given.

questionnaire deviate in a variety of ways from the dictionary definitiions in the Appendix. I used the judgment data to sort the 13 pairs into four crude categories. Those in Category 1 have nearly identical meanings, but the word containing the mora obstruent is more colloquial and more emphatic. The pair that seems to fit best in this category is *o-i+cuk-u* – *oQ+cuk-u* 'catch up'.

The pairs in Category 2 are like those in Category 1 semantically, but they show specialization of particular forms. A pair that seems to fit in this category is *tor-i+kum-u* – *toQ+kum-u* 'grapple'. Several respondents said that the citation form of the mora-obstruent verb *toQ+kum-u* is not used, although other forms are, including the gerund *toQ+kuN-de* and the derived adverb *toQ+kum-i+nagara* 'while grappling'. In addition, only the stem *toQ+kum-i* can appear in the longer compound *toQ+kum-i+a-i* 'grappling with each other', but only the stem *tor-i+kum-i* can be used as a noun denoting a sumo bout.[14]

The pairs in Category 3 show overlapping but divergent meanings. A pair that seems to belong in this category, at least for some speakers, is *tsuk-i+kaes-u* – *tsuQ+kaes-u* 'push back; return'. Some respondents said that *tsuk-i+kaes-u* can mean either 'push back' or 'return', whereas *tsuQ+kaes-u* can only mean 'return' and not 'push back'.

The pairs in Category 4 have completely divergent meanings. One pair that seems to fit into this category is *hik-i+kom-u* – *hiQ+kom-u*. Almost all the respondents said that *hik-i+kom-u* is transitive and that *hiQ+kom-u* is intransitive. The meanings offered for *hik-i+kom-u* were 'pull in' and 'entice into', and those offered for *hiQ+kom-u* were 'retire', 'hide', 'go inside', and 'become sunken'.

Another pair that seems to belong in Category 4 is *osh-i+hirak-u* – *oQ+pirak-u*. Most respondents said that *osh-i+hirak-u* means 'push and open' and that *oQ+pirak-u* means 'open wide; open boldly'. These intuitions are reflected in the fact that the *oQ* in *oQ+pirak-u* is ordinarily written entirely in *hiragana* (おっ) rather than with the *kanji* used to write *osh-i* (押し). This orthographic practice suggests that *oQ* and *osh-i* are not identified with each other synchronically.[15]

---

[14] Compare the specialization of *burned* and *burnt* in the English of many Americans. For me, only *burned* is possible as a preterite or a past partciple, but *burnt* often sounds fine as an attributive adjective, and in some collocations, such as the color name *burnt orange*, only *burnt* is possible.

[15] The *buQ* in *buQ+koros-u* and *buQ+kowas-u* (see Appendix) is also usually written entirely in hiragana. In fact, the *Daijirin* dictionary (Matsumura 1988) lists both *oQ* and *buQ* as a headwords and describes them as intensifying prefixes.

5. Conclusion

The judgments reported in §4 are only a small sampling of what I collected, and there is little doubt that what I collected is only the tip of the iceberg. Needless to say, such judgments cannot plausibly be considered direct reflections of actual usage, but it is hard to imagine how more reliable data could be collected in any reasonable amount of time. One of the people who filled out the second questionnaire is a linguist colleague, and during an informal presentation of the results he told me that the more he thinks about each pair, the more differences he notices. In fact, I got the distinct impression in the course of the presentation that he and other speakers were not just passively noticing differences but actively imposing them to some extent. In other words, the activity they were engaged in may have been akin to semantic bifurcation in action.

Finally, it is well known that adding a mora obstruent is a common way of giving a word an emphatic and colloquial flavor, as in *toQtemo* versus *totemo* for 'very'. Sound symbolism is presumably at work here, but notice that compound verbs with /Q/ do not involve this kind of addition. The mora obstruent in a compound verb appears IN PLACE OF a (C)V mora and thereby leaves the total mora count unchanged.[16] Nonetheless, the dictionary definitions in the Appendix and the speaker judgments I collected both show a consistent tendency for the mora-obstruent member of a pair to be regarded as more colloquial and more emphatic than its regular-stem partner. This colloquial, emphatic flavor is something of a mystery, since it contrasts so starkly with the lack of any such flavor in superficially comparable words. As noted in §2, many verb roots and many Sino-Japanese morphemes also exhibit (C)V~/Q/ alternations that maintain mora count. But words like *maQ-ta* 'waited' (4a) and *niQ·koo* 'sunlight' (4b) are no more emphatic or colloquial than, for example, *tabe-ta* 'ate' and *deN·koo* 'electric light'. Perhaps the difference is just a matter of potential contrast. No alternative pronunciation without the mora obstruent is possible for words like *maQ-ta* and *niQ·koo*.

Appendix

The 26 verbs (13 pairs) on the semantic judgment questionnaire are listed below. For each the 24 that have citations in *Nihon kokugo daijiten* (Nihon Daijiten Kankôkai, 1972–76), the date of the earliest citation is given in braces. In some cases, this date is only approximate. For each of the 25 that

---

[16]There are some compound verbs that do show mora-obstruent addition. An example is *de+Q+par-u* 'stick out', which combines *de-ru* 'go out' and *har-u* 'stretch'. In contrast to all the first component verbs in the compounds under consideration in this paper, *de-ru* is not a consonant verb (see note 7); its stem is identical to its root: *de-*.

are listed in the *Daijirin* dictionary (Matsumura 1988), English translations
are provided for all the *Daijirin* definitions identified as modern.

o-i+cuk-u {900–950} ① go after from behind and pull even with a person who
was ahead ② an ability or a skill reaches the same level as a goal or as
something excellent ③ satisfy a necessity or insufficiency; compensate

oQ+cuk-u {14th c. (?)} a changed form of *oitsuku* [see above]

o-i+hara-u {712} go after and send away something bothersome; *opparau* [see
below]

oQ+para-u {14th c. (?)} a word that expresses *oiharau* [see above] emphatically

osh-i+hirak-u {800–850} ① push and open ② a word that expresses *hiraku*
['open'] emphatically

oQ+pirak-u {1792} an emphatic, slang word meaning *hiraku* ['open']

osh-i+hiroge-ru {1603} ① extend and spread; enlarge ② spread widely and
affect something else

oQ+piroge-ru {20th c.} an emphatic, slang word meaning *hirogeru* ['spread']

sash-i+hik-u {1603} ① take a certain quantity away from another quantity;
sappiku [see below] ② the tide rises and ebbs

saQ+pik-u {20th c.} a changed form of *sashihiku* [see above]

tsuk-i+kaes-u {712} ① push and return to the original place; push back in
response to a pushing adversary ② refuse to accept and return coldly something
someone else has presented

tsuQ+kaes-u {20th c.} (a changed form of *tsukikaesu* [see above]) a somewhat
slangy expression for *tsukikaesu* [see above]

tor-i+kakar-u {950–1000} begin to do; set about

toQ+kakar-u {no citation in *Nihon kokugo daijiten*} a changed form of *torikakaru*
[see above]; begin to do; set about

tor-i+kum-u {1177–81} ① grapple with each other ② compete with as an
opponent, especially in sumo ③ deal with ardently

toQ+kum-u {1772} (a changed form of *torikumu* [see above]) ① grapple with an
opponent ② do something earnestly

tor-i+tsuk-u {800–850} ① grab onto another person tightly and not let go; cling
② begin doing something; set about; start ③ make up one's mind to climb
over; begin climbing up

toQ+tsuk-u {1783–86} (a changed form of *toritsuku* [see above]) ① cling to a
person or thing ② begin doing something ③ an illness or spirit possesses
one ④ become close to a person; usually used in the forms *tottsuki-yasui*
['easy to get to know'] and *tottsuki-nikui* ['hard to get to know']

tor-i+hara-u {971} remove completely; *topparau* [see below] *toQ+para-u* {not listed in *Nihon kokugo daijiten*} a changed form of *toriharau* [see above]

hik-i+kom-u {1350–1400} ① pull and put inside; pull in ② attract a person's heart or soul ③ make the flow of a river or a straight object branch off and extend in one's own direction ④ invite a person to join in; invite into; entice into ⑤ catch a real cold ⑥ stay at home; *hikkomu* [see below] ⑦ become sunken; *hikkomu* [see below]

hiQ+kom-u {1477} (a changed form of *hikikomu* [see above]) ① something that was protruding returns to its original condition; also, sink farther in than the original surface; become sunken ② a person who was out in public goes inside a building and avoids notice; also, an actor on the stage in a play leaves the stage ③ go into a more interior area that is hard to see from in front ④ retreat from a public place or position and stay in an inconspicuous place

buch-i+koros-u {1705} a word that expresses *korosu* ['kill'] emphatically; *buk-korosu* [see below]

buQ+koros-u {1869} (a changed form of *buchikorosu* [see above]) a word that expresses *korosu* ['kill'] emphatically

buch-i+kowas-u {1715–80} ① hit and break; break to bits ② obstruct a plan or idea that looks as if it will go well; ruin something that is set up

buQ+kowas-u {1867} not listed in *Daijirin*

References

Bloch, Bernard. 1946. Studies in Colloquial Japanese I: Inflection. *Journal of the American Oriental Society* 66:97–109.

Bolinger, Dwight. 1968. *Aspects of Language*. New York: Harcourt, Brace & World.

Fromkin, Victoria, and Robert Rodman. 1998. *An Introduction to Language*, 6th ed. Fort Worth: Harcourt Brace.

Hudson, Grover. 2000. *Essential Introductory Linguistics*. Oxford: Blackwell.

Jorden, Eleanor Harz, and Mari Noda. 1987. *Japanese: The Spoken Language*, Part 1. New Haven: Yale University Press.

Kiyose, Gisaburô N. 1985. Heianchô hagyô-shiin p-onron. *Onsei no kenkyû* 21.73–87.

Matsumura, Akira, ed. 1988. *Daijirin*. Tokyo: Sanseidô.

Nihon Daijiten Kankôkai, ed. 1972–76. *Nihon kokugo daijiten*. Tokyo: Shôgakukan.

Niimi, Kazuaki, Yôichi Yamaura, and Tokuko Utsuno. 1987. *Fukugô-dôshi*. Tokyo: Aratake.

O'Grady, William, Michael Dobrovolsky, and Mark Aronoff. 1989. *Contemporary Linguistics: An Introduction*. New York: St. Martin's.

Okumura, Mitsuo. 1972. Kodai no on'in. *Kôza kokugoshi 2: on'inshi, mojishi*, ed. by Norio Nakata, 63–171. Tokyo: Taishûkan.

Shibatani, Masayoshi. 1990. *The Languages of Japan.* Cambridge: Cambridge University Press.

Tagashira, Yoshiko, and Jean Hoff. 1986. *Handbook of Japanese Compound Verbs.* Tokyo: Hokuseidô.

Vance, Timothy J. 1987. *An Introduction to Japanese Phonology.* Albany: SUNY Press.

Moraic Structure and Segment Duration in Korean*

EMILY CURTIS

University of Washington

1. Introduction

Two phonological units are claimed to affect the *phonetic* realization of segments: the mora and the syllable. Several studies have asserted a correlation of moraic structure and segment duration in Japanese and other languages (Sato 1993, Port, Dalby, and O'Dell 1987, Homma 1981, Port, Al-Ani, and Maeda 1980), but are the correlations reliable and similar cross-linguistically? Likewise, the *syllable* is said to be a universal construct which may affect segment durations. Maddieson (1985) asserts that phonetic closed syllable vowel shortening (CSVS) is a universal tendency. Notably, Japanese is one of few exceptions to Maddieson's CSVS *as well as* a main source of support for the correlation of moraic structure and segment duration. What is the status, then, of the correlation of segment durations to syllable versus moraic structure cross-linguistically? The two approaches, critically, make contradictory predictions for syllables closed with a moraic coda. After presenting the research on which the contradictory predictions are based, this study specifically examines durational patterning in Korean with respect to syllable versus moraic structure, including a production study and the implications of its results.

---

* This paper is based on my University of Washington master's thesis, Curtis (2000). I wish to acknowledge my adviser, Sharon Hargus, and committee members, Richard Wright and Ellen Kaisse, as well as Soohee Kim for help with both papers: errors are my own.

2. Theoretical Background

It has been suggested that the syllable and the mora each may have an influence on temporal aspects of segments. Claims have been made separately for the two units and contradictions arise on closer at the predictions of the models that have been proposed.

2.1 The Syllable and Phonetics

The syllable has been implicated as a factor influencing the acoustic properties of segments, especially in terms of duration and the timing of articulatory gestures that make up segments. Researchers such as Byrd (1994), Keating (1990) and Fowler (1980), argue that the syllable is a domain for articulatory gestural overlap between segments, which could effect what was previously considered the duration of the segment as a whole.

Maddieson (1985) presents data from 16 languages found to exhibit a tendency toward shorter vowels in closed syllables (before geminates) than in open syllables and he suggests that the tendency is universal.

Maddieson, furthermore, presents data from several languages where vowels are found to be shorter in closed syllables than in open syllables "in general" – presumably monosyllabic words or where phonological data shows that the following consonant is clearly a coda, though not the first half of a geminate. Specific data cited for Korean (the subject language of this study) is from Han (1964): 29 words elicited from 4 speakers revealed that vowels in CV structures averaged 266 milliseconds and vowels in CVC structures averaged 127 milliseconds. Maddieson (1985) dismisses several potential counter-examples to the tendency for closed syllable vowel shortening, including Japanese; an important point for this study.

The overall conclusion is that the universal tendency toward phonetic closed syllable vowel shortening is well-supported in phonetic studies of the phenomenon and in data at large in the phonetics literature. Maddieson's study, then, suggests that the syllable is an organizing unit in *phonetics*. Vowels are reliably shorter in closed syllables compared to open syllables, so that we can attribute the shortening to syllable shape and therefore conclude that syllable shape and the syllable affiliation of segments affect the phonetic duration of those segments.

2.2 The Mora and Duration

Another phonological unit which might be expected to have a temporal manifestation is the mora. Recent studies have posited durational correlates to the moraicity of segments and to the mora-count of syllables and words, suggesting that the mora organizes the phonetic duration of segments as well as marking phonological syllable weight and segmental length.

One extension of the role of the mora in marking *phonological* length distinctions are findings that moraic segments have longer *durations* than non-moraic segments (Sato 1993). Other studies link the number of moras in a given domain with differences in duration for that domain; Sato (1993) and Duanmu (1994) find that *syllable* durations reflect mora-count (c.f. Gordon 1998). In Port et al. (1987) and Homma (1981) segment durations varied to effect a *word-level* correlation of mora-count and duration.

Of particular interest is the finding of Homma (1981) where the ratio of durations of bimoraic CVCV words to trimoraic CVGemV words with the same segmental make-up (except for the geminate versus singleton in C2) was 2: 2.9, almost exactly the ratio of mora counts (2:3). Also, Port et al. (1987) find that the durations of CVVCV forms was nearly equal to that of CVGemV forms on average despite findings that a consonant that bears a mora is not as long as a vowel that bears a mora: the isochrony between these forms was obtained by a *lengthening* of the vowel preceding the geminate. This last finding directly contradicts the findings in Maddieson (1985).

It is also of note that most of these studies finding correlations of moraic structure and duration draw on data from *Japanese*, an exception to the proposed universal tendency toward closed syllable vowel shortening as per Maddieson (1985). This point adds interest to both approaches.

Meanwhile, an intriguing upshot of some phonetic studies is a model of moraic structure where the mora is said to dominate more than one segment, thereby affecting the duration of (i.e. shortening) the segments that share the mora. This model is suggested by Kubozono (1995), Homma (1981), and Port et al. (1980) for Japanese onset-nucleus CV pairs to account for mutual compensation for inherent segment duration differences (as shown in (1)a.). A similar model is applied in the rhyme by Maddieson (1993) and Hubbard (1995) to account for a certain compensatory lengthening of vowels in Bantu languages; when a nasal moves from coda to form a prenasalized stop in the following syllable onset, vowel lengthening derives a vowel approximately 1.5 times as long as a short vowel, while long vowels are 2 times as long as short vowels on average (see (1)b.)

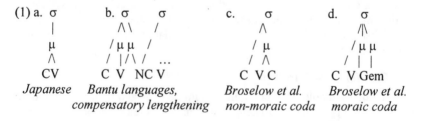

(1) a. σ   b. σ   σ   c. σ   d. σ

CV   C V NC V   C V C   C V Gem

Japanese   *Bantu languages,*   *Broselow et al.*   *Broselow et al.*
       compensatory lengthening   *non-moraic coda*   *moraic coda*

Broselow et al. (1997) raise this mora-sharing model to theoretical status with data from four languages with differing weight-by-position parameters and therefore different mora-sharing structures. They suggest, recalling Hyman (1985) and Hayes (1989), that coda consonants that do not bear their own mora share the mora of the preceding vowel as in (1)c., compared to (1)d. with a geminate in coda bearing its own mora. According to their data and predictions, a segment has a shorter duration when sharing a mora as in (1)c. than when bearing its own mora as in (1)d.

The mora-sharing model predicts that vowels will be *shorter* before non-moraic codas than before moraic codas or in open syllables and that vowels preceding geminates should have durations similar to vowels in open syllables because they independently bear a mora. These predictions based on moraic structure directly contradict the predictions of Maddieson (1985) for syllables closed by a geminate (moraic) consonant. According to CSVS, there should be shortening, but according to the mora-sharing approach, there should be no shortening with respect to open syllables. Furthermore, as mentioned above, Port et al. (1987) found that vowels before geminates in Japanese were in fact *lengthened.* This study hopes to shed light on the issue, specifically:

> Will vowels shorten in syllables closed with a moraic consonant as well as in syllables closed by a non-moraic consonant [due to syllable closure], or will there be no vowel shortening before moraic consonants [because the moraic coda (and nuclear vowel each) bears its own mora]?

3. Production Experiment

To test for the effects on vowel duration of various syllable and moraic configurations while maximizing control for irrelevant factors, it would be ideal to use a single subject language that exhibited the pertinent configurations. According to recent assessments of its phonology, Korean is appropriate for the study; allowing comparison of syllables closed by moraic and non-moraic codas.

3.1 Subject language: Korean

It is generally accepted that codas do not contribute to syllable weight[1], however, the language allows both underlying and derived geminates which are moraic in coda position. Within the same language, then, it is possible to compare vowel durations preceding moraic as well as non-moraic codas, even of the same place and manner of articulation and phonation.

Speakers employed for the production study had a seven-vowel system with no length distinction, which has been lost in younger generations of Seoul dialect speakers (Cho and Iverson 1997). Most remarkable in the phoneme inventory is the three-way laryngeal contrast on obstruents, which are underlyingly voiceless; lenis, heavily aspirated and fortis.[2] The maximal syllable for Korean is CGVC, or CVGC in the case of the diphthong /ij/.

---

[1] Discussion continues on this topic for mimetics, which may be a separate lexical strata (with different moraic structures) from non-mimetic vocabulary which is at hand in the present study.

[2] The fortis consonants are transcribed using capital letters herein (instead of apostrophes, because they are not ejective).

Interesting for our purposes is that geminate nasals and liquids occur in mono-morphemic native words as shown in (2), indicating an underlying consonant length distinction for consonantal sonorants except for /ŋ/ which cannot occur in syllable-initial position[3]. The length distinction is accounted for if the geminates are said to bear a mora underlyingly.

(2) *Monomorphemic native Korean words illustrating underlying geminates*

/ɤmma/	*mom*	/nolla-/	*to be surprised*
/manna-/	*to meet*	/tilli-/	*to visit*
/ɤnni/	*older sister*	/Pallaŋ/	*jingle*
	(of a female)	/kɤllɛ/	*rag*

All consonants except /ŋ/ and the fricatives can occur as derived geminates; e.g. /ka-S-ne/ → (regressive nasal assimilation) [kanne] (*[kane]) *went, I see.* Derived geminates likewise bear a mora in coda position, marking them as long segments, and as distinct from singleton ambisyllabic or resyllabified consonants that might arise from some sort of fusion process.

It is generally accepted that other non-geminate codas in Korean are non-moraic (Ongmi Kang (p.c.), Kim 1996, Suh 1993, Kang 1992 (except [-cont]), cf. Jun 1994 (only for mimetic forms). However, Davis (1999) shows that while umlaut is allowed across singleton intervocalic consonants and heterosyllabic clusters as in (3)a. and b., it does not occur across geminates or in syllables with historical long vowels as in (3)c. and d. (All but italicized data are from Davis (1999), Davis and Lee (1996).)

(3) a. *Umlaut in open syllables CV*

/aKi-/	[aKi] ~	[ɛKi]	*to hold dear (verb root)*
/son-tʃapi/	[sontʃabi]	[sondʒɛbi]	*handle*

  b. *Closed syllables (CVC)*

/nampi/	[nambiɾ]	[nɛmbi]	*kettle*
/ɤŋki-/	[ɤŋgiɾ]	[eŋgi]	*to be curdled (verb root)*

  c. *Syllables closed by geminates (CVG$_{em}$)*

/ak-ki/	[akKi]	*[ɛkKi]	*instrument (Sino-Korean)*
/ɤnni/	[ɤnni]	*[ɛnni]	*sister*
/Palli-/	*[Palli]*	*[Pɛlli]*	*quickly (verb stem + suffix)*

  d. *historical long vowels CVV*

/saːlm-ki/	[saːmgi]	*[sɛːːmgi]	*to be boiled*
/pɤːli/	[pɤːɾi]	*[peːɾi]	*earning*

---

[3] It would likely be impossible to distinguish underlying *obstruent* geminates from fortis consonants due to the Post-Obstruent tensing rule and resyllabification rules.

These latter two syllables types are precisely the bimoraic syllables, as geminates bear a mora while singleton consonants do not. It appears that Korean phonology diagnoses syllables closed by a geminate as heavy, i.e. *different* from syllables closed by a singleton consonant.

3.2 Data and Methods

Korean phonology thus allows for the following data set, ignoring the mora-affiliation of onsets, which is not presently relevant, and applying a mora-sharing model for weightless coda consonants:

(4)

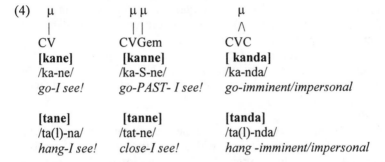

CV	CVGem	CVC
[kane]	**[kanne]**	**[kanda]**
/ka-ne/	/ka-S-ne/	/ka-nda/
go-I see!	*go-PAST- I see!*	*go-imminent/impersonal*
[tane]	**[tanne]**	**[tanda]**
/ta(l)-na/	/tat-ne/	/ta(l)-nda/
hang-I see!	*close-I see!*	*hang -imminent/impersonal*

The target words were based on the verbs /ka-ta/ *to go*, /tal-ta/ *to hang (intransitive)* and /tat-a/ *to close (transitive)*. Several phonological rules derive the surface pronunciations: inter-sonorant voicing of lenis stops, regressive nasal assimilation, and /l/-deletion before certain suffixes. Data with obstruents following V1 were also included for imperfect comparison;[4] no non-geminate coda obstruent was possible.

Target words were placed in the carrier phrase in (5) and randomized with an equal number of sentences containing distractor words of various forms so that the focus of the experiment was not obvious. Each sentence was repeated five times in sequence. The reading list was presented in Han'gul orthography.

(5) [kɨ yɤdʒa-ga _____ ɾago SɤSɤjo]
    the woman-NOM _____ CONJ write-PAST-POLITE
    The woman wrote "[target word]."

Speakers were three female and three male native speakers of Seoul Korean between the ages of 21 and 34, and they had been in the US for

---

[4] Those data were [kada] /ka-ta/ *go-dictionary form*, [katTa] /ka-S-ta/ *go-PAST-dictionary form*, [tada] /tat-a/ *close-plain present*, and [tatTa] /tat-ta/ *close-dictionary form*. For discussion of the data set and statistical analysis including the [following obstruent] data, see Curtis 2000.

three months to three years except for one female (seven years) and one male (nine years).

To test the hypothesis of vowel shortening in closed syllables versus the hypothesis of vowel shortening before only non-moraic codas, I measured the duration of the first vowel (V1) [a] in all forms. Measurements were made from a waveform with the spectrogram as a guide using Kay Lab's MultiSpeech (11025 Hz sampling rate). VOT was included in the vowel measurement so that /k/- and /t/- onset data could be combined.

A series of two-way Factorial Analysis of Variance (ANOVA) was performed to test for effects of independent variables such as speaker, gender, repetition and syllable and moraic configuration on the dependent variable, vowel length. The Fisher PLSD, a post-hoc test for statistical significance of effects of a variable, was also performed.

Due to the confounding factor [speaker] – i.e. speaker variation in speech rate – normalized data[5] was used for ANOVA as well as raw data, and all ANOVA were run as two-factor ANOVA with [speaker] as a factor.

3.3 Results

Results of the ANOVA showed that the main factor affecting vowel durations was indeed syllable closure, with a p-value of $p<.0001$. Vowels are reliably and statistically significantly shorter in closed syllables [kanda], [kanne], [tanda] and [tanne] than in open syllables [kane], [tane]. The average duration difference between vowels in open- versus closed-syllables was 32 milliseconds.

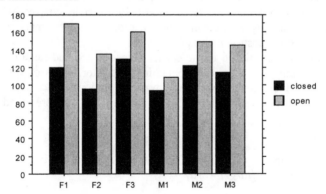

Figure 1. Speakers' average V1 durations (in milliseconds) for closed versus open syllables.

---

[5] Normalized score = raw V1 duration (for Speaker a) divided by the mean V1 duration for Speaker a. , i.e. a ratio expressing how long V1 was compared to the speaker's average. Statistics using normalized scores were similar to those using raw scores, so only the latter are included here.

For the factor [mora-sharing], the model of Broselow et al. (1997) predicts that vowels in syllables closed by geminates should not be shortened with respect to vowels in open syllables, because in each case the vowel (and geminate in coda) bears its own non-shared mora. However, the effects of syllable closure (shortening) were so robust that a strict interpretation of the model is untenable. It is clear that there was significant vowel shortening preceding geminates. In a weak interpretation of the model, there may be syllable closure effects *in addition to* moraic structure effects; to assess this possibility, open-syllable data should be excluded lest the effect of the moraicity of the coda be eclipsed by syllable closure effects.

A two-way factorial ANOVA for [speaker] by [mora-sharing] performed on only the data [kanda, kanne, tanda, tanne] showed no significant effect for mora-sharing: vowel durations before geminate (non-shared) and non-geminate (shared) codas were not significantly different. It is clear that in Korean the main factor affecting vowel duration is syllable closure, and the moraicity of the coda, for nasals, does not correlate with vowel shortening.

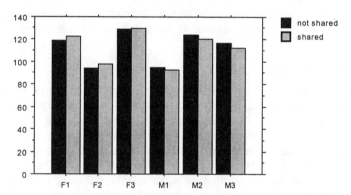

Figure 2. Speakers' average V1 durations (in milliseconds) in closed syllables with non-shared-mora versus shared-mora configurations.

One final [speaker] by [mora-sharing] ANOVA was run on the data [kanda vs. kanne, katTa; tanda vs. tanne, tatTa]. In this case, mora-sharing was found to have a significant effect on vowel duration (*p=.03* for normalized and for raw scores alike), but *in the opposite direction* than was predicted by moraic models. Vowels in this comparison were *shorter* preceding geminates than preceding singleton consonants. This finding is in accord with the Maddieson (1985) survey where vowels were shorter preceding geminates than in open syllables, but adds the factor of moraicity. Here, vowels were shorter preceding geminates than preceding *other, non-moraic codas*. It should be noted, of course, that there was no [following obstruent] data that involved mora-sharing – no non-moraic obstruent dafa was available following the disyllabic pattern of the data set, such that the comparison was [kanne, katTa, tanne, tatTa] versus [kanda, tanda] without [*katCV, *tatCV]. Preceding nasals only, there was evidence of greater shortening before geminates, but it was not statistically significant.

4. Implications

Despite the many prior findings concerning the mora as a unit of acoustic timing, the current study finds no significant effect for the moraicity of codas in a controlled context in Korean. The data does not provide phonetic support for the mora-sharing hypothesis of Broselow et al. (1997), Maddieson (1993), and Hubbard (1995) where segments are expected to shorten when dominated by a mora that dominates another segment. The effect of syllable closure is obvious and robust in the present data, and adds one more to the list of languages that demonstrate the tendency Maddieson (1985) suggests is universal.

Given these findings, what is the role of the mora in Korean, and what phonological models can we justly propose based on this phonetic evidence? What can account for the findings correlating moraic structure and temporal patterns in Japanese as well as the lack of correlation in this Korean data?

4.1 Methodological Differences

One potential account of the differences between the current study and other mora-sharing studies is that the methodologies of the experiments differ. In fact, some studies do not elaborate on their experimental methods. Broselow et al. (1997), for example, do not discuss recording methods or measurement heuristics. In Homma (1981), what *we* consider an essential measurement, vowel duration before geminates, was not included in the study. The current study controlled for vowel quality, following consonant, and other potential confounding factors, but investigation into moraic effects in other contexts may be desirable.

4.2 Mora effects at various levels

Another potential confounding factor is the prosodic level at which effects for moraic structure are sought. Prior studies cited in Section 2 associated moraic structure with temporal aspects of words, syllables, moraic units and segments. Does moraic structure affect durations at all these levels? If so, how might the effects interact? To what extent might syllable closure or local effects (of the voicing or length of the coda nasal, for example) have overpowered potential moraic structural effects in the current data?

The current study controlled for higher-prosodic-level effects such as phrase, word, and syllable shapes as well as lower level segmental make-up of the target vowel's context, but did not, therefore, *investigate* the effects of the moraic structure on temporal aspects at the various levels. A third experiment reported in Port et al. (1987), for example, found that in CVCV words, where C2 was varied, compensation for inherent C2 durational differences affected the preceding (*hetero-syllabic, hetero-moraic*) vowel (V1). In the current data on Korean, there may be temporal changes in the second syllable of the target word, reflecting a word-level effect of first syllable coda-moraicity or word-level mora-count, for example.

4.3 Linguistic variation

Finding the studies on Japanese mora-timing to be reliable at any given level does not entail that the correlations of mora and duration should hold cross-linguistically. There may be linguistic variation. Instead of the question 'is CSVS universal or does moraic structure alter its effects?' a more correct question may be 'does Korean *pattern with* Japanese with respect to moraic structure and durational correlates or with languages that show CSVS?'

As mentioned above, many studies that found correlations of the mora and duration employed only Japanese data. It should be emphasized that the mora has an especially salient role in Japanese phonology and is a consciously recognized unit in Japanese education, poetry, and writing systems. The mora plays a role in many phonological rules in Japanese, such as vowel length and geminate-singleton consonant distinctions, hypocoristic formation (Poser 1990), loanword truncations, compound abbreviations, minimality constraints (Ito and Mester 1990), language games (Tateishi 1989 and others), and so on. In addition, there are two Japanese syllabaries taught in elementary schools and applied in all registers of writing, which are based, in fact, on the V or CV *mora*, with coda nasal /N/ and gemination marked by (moraic) symbols of their own. Kubozono (1995) and anecdotal evidence also shows that Japanese speakers are aware of the mora and moraic organization, to the exclusion of the syllable and rhyme.

The mora seems to have a different and more *salient* role in the phonology *and/or the phonetics* of Japanese than it has in some other languages. Not only is Korean an exception to mora-duration findings, supporting Maddieson's CSVS hypothesis instead, but, analogously, Japanese was an exception to closed syllable vowel shortening.

The *syllable* also appears not to have the same role in the two phonologies. Note that the while the Japanese writing system is based on the mora, the Korean writing system is a segmental alphabet which is arranged more or less into syllables (which also abide by morphemic boundaries). The syllable is also brought to the level of awareness (that the mora has in Japanese, perhaps) in traditional Chil-o Jo (7-5 rhythm) and Shi Jo syllable-counting poetry in Korean. Factors such as these, which are sometimes ignored by linguists, may in fact indicate or underscore a difference in the salience of phonological units such as the syllable and the mora in different languages.

4.4 The Mora in Korean

Moraic representations of Korean are in fact rare and sometimes controversial. It is generally accepted, though, that codas are not moraic in Korean, and that cross-linguistically geminates are moraic. Also it should be noted that *if* all the codas in the study, geminates as well as singletons, were moraic, the results would be even more troublesome for the mora-sharing models of Broselow et al. (1997), Hubbard (1995), Maddieson (1993), Hyman (1985), and Hayes (1989). If the codas are all moraic, they bear their own mora and should not correlate with vowel shortening, according to the mora-sharing model, when, in fact, vowels are significantly shorter before the codas in this study. It is possible that the role of the syllable is greater than the role of moraicity in determining segmental durations, but with such extreme syllable closure results, it is unlikely that we can determine any mora effects at all, even if all codas were moraic. If, on the other hand, all codas including geminates are assumed to be non-moraic (Tranel 1991 for other languages), some means of representing the geminates, especially the underlying geminates, and the data of Davis (1999) must be offered. In either case, Korean shows a large, obvious and statistically significant effect of closed syllable vowel shortening, which may be seen as underscoring the salience of the *syllable* in Korean phonology, leaving open the question of the mora in Korean phonology.

Several researchers (e.g. Hyman 1985 and Hayes 1989) indicate that moraic theory need not apply equally to all languages. Hayes (1989), in fact, lists three linguistic structures that must be present for moraic structure to be manifest in underlying representations in a language:

> If (a) the distribution of high vowels and glides is predictable, (b) there is no vowel length contrast and (c) there are no geminates, then underlying forms may consist simply of segmental strings, with all moras inserted by rule. (page 257)

Korean satisfies Hayes's (a) and (b) since vowel length has been lost, but the geminates are recognized in Korean phonology underlyingly and in phonological rules (e.g. umlaut). Geminates require representation in the larger structures, and a moraic representation is appropriate for Korean geminate codas unless there is evidence for a phonological diagnosis of segmental length as different from syllable weight, as Hume, Muller, and van Engelenhoven (1997) argue to be the case for Leti onset geminates.

That is, does the existence of geminates entail syllable weight? Hayes (1989) suggests it does not in the following passage.

Languages that exhibit a syllable weight distinction typically also have a vowel length distinction, and vice versa. This is to be expected in a moraic theory, since the same formal configuration, bimoraic syllables, is used to represent both. We would not expect the correlation to be absolute, however: a few languages allow heavy syllables but do not permit a vowel to occupy two moras (see below); and a language could in principle have long vowels but happen to *lack phonological rules that diagnose a syllable weight distinction.* (page 255, italics added)

Hayes's comment suggests that it is possible for a language to give no role to heavy syllables in its phonology and, by extension, no role to the mora as a phonological unit at all, or perhaps no role other than its role in distinguishing between long and short segments. That is, the mora may be more or less *inert* in the phonology of one language, but salient in another language where weight and length are intricately linked. If Korean has lost vowel length, is it possible that the mora is losing any phonological salience that it may have (or may not have) had? Is it possible that geminates are moraic but that syllable weight is sparsely diagnosed by the phonology? Is there any reason to propose à la Hume et al. that segmental weight and syllable weight are distinguished by the phonology? Syllable weight in Korean is a topic justly to be pursued. Meanwhile, geminates must be represented as different from singleton consonants since they occur underlyingly (sonorants) and because they are diagnosed by the phonological rule of umlaut.

Can a segmental approach can be applied to distinguish the geminates from singletons as Hume et al. 1997) might suggest. What if a geminate was simply a segment matrix linked to more than one skeletal slot? In this case, singleton and geminate codas should equally cause vowel shortening if vowel shortening is based in the number of skeletal slots in the rhyme. There would also be means to distinguish the two in phonological rules that can be said to diagnose *segmental length*. Is it reasonable to assume, then, that umlaut is blocked by long segments as opposed to heavy syllables? And if so, how does assimilation, which derives a geminate consonant as in /ka-S-ne/, for example, also derive a long segment, or, a single segment associated with two skeletal slots? This may be a model to consider for Korean data.

Questions such as these merit further research into the phonetics and phonology of Modern Korean, in order to establish an accepted representation of geminates, syllables and prosodic structure in general that is based on modern data.

5. Conclusion

The results of this experiment reveal a strong effect of vowel shortening in closed syllables in Korean and a slight durational effect *opposite* that predicted by the proposed mora-sharing configurations of coda consonants. That is, vowels were slightly shorter before geminates than before non-moraic codas, and vowels in closed syllables were much shorter than vowels in open syllables. These durational effects could be attributed to a number of factors, including the possibility that the mora has different phonological roles and different acoustic properties cross-linguistically – if it has any acoustic effect at all.

The data at hand cannot be said to disprove any phonological analysis proposed for Korean that is accurately based on modern Korean phonological data. It is not reasonable to deduce from the current study that geminates are not moraic in Korean or that all nasals and geminates are moraic simply because all the closed syllables in the study patterned similarly with respect to vowel shortening. It is important to remember that phonological units represent abstract patterning and that their correlation with phonetic output is still being examined.

The current study compared the contradictory predictions arising in the literature concerning the shortening effects of coda consonants in different syllable configurations. The predictions of one, closed syllable vowel shortening, a syllable-based prediction, were borne out, and the predictions of the other, the mora-sharing hypothesis (that weightless codas share vocalic mora thereby shortening both segments), were not supported by the Korean data at hand. The search for explanation of the findings, begun in the preceding discussion, is by no means completed.

As is common, the data raise many questions when considered in the context of the current theoretical and acoustic literature. Perhaps most significantly, the current study raises the question of what role the mora has in different languages when syllable effects on segmental durations, such as closed syllable vowel shortening, are expected.

References

Beckman, Mary E. 1982. Segment Duration and the 'mora' in Japanese. *Phonetica* 39:113-135.

Broselow, Ellen, Su-I Chen, and Marie Huffman. 1997. Syllable Weight: Convergence of phonology and phonetics. *Phonology* 14: 47-82.

Byrd, Dani. 1994. Articulatory Timing in English Consonant Sequences. *UCLA Working Papers in Linguistics* 86.

Cho, Young-mee Yu, and Gregory K. Iverson. 1997. Korean Phonology in the Late Twentieth Century. *Language Research* 33 (4):687-735.

Davis, Stuart. 1999. On the moraic representation of underlying geminates: evidence from Prosodic Morphology. In *The Prosody-Morphology Interface*, edited by R. Kager, H. v. d. Hulst and W. Zonnefeld: Cambridge University Press.

Davis, Stuart, and J.-S. Lee. 1996. Korean partial reduplication reconsidered. *Lingua* 99:85-105.

Duanmu, San. 1994. Syllabic weight and syllabic duration: a correlation between phonology and phonetics. *Phonology* 11:1-24.

Fowler, C. 1980. Coarticulation and theories of extrinsic timing. *Journal of Phonetics* 8:113-133.

Gordon, Matthew. 1998. A phonetically-driven account of syllable weight. (ms.), University of California, Los Angeles, Los Angeles.

Hayes, Bruce. 1989. Compensatory Lengthening in Moraic Phonology. *Linguistic Inquiry* 20 (2):253-303.

Homma, Yayoi. 1981. Durational relationship between Japanese stops and vowels. *Journal of Phonetics* 9:273-281.

Hubbard, Kathleen. 1995. 'Prenasalised consonants' and syllable timing: evidence from Runyambo and Luganda. *Phonology* 12:235-256.

Hume, Elizabeth, Jennifer Muller, and Aone van Engelenhoven. 1997. Non-moraic geminates in Leti. *Phonology* 14:371-402.

Hyman, Larry M. 1985. *A Theory of Phonological Weight*. Dordrecht: Foris Publications.

Ito, Junko, and R. Armin Mester. 1990. Prosodic Minimality of Japanese. *CLI* 26 (2):215-239.

Jun, Jongho. 1994. Metrical Weight Consistency in Korean partial reduplication. *Phonology* 11:69-88.

Kang, Seok Keun. 1992. A Moraic Study of Some Phonological Phenomena in English and Korean. Dissertation, University of Illinois at Urbana-Champaign.

Keating, Patricia. 1990. The window model of coarticulation: Articulatory evidence. In *Papers in Laboratory Phonology I*, edited by J. Kinston and M. Beckman: Cambridge University Press.

Kim, Soohee. 1996. Emergence of the Unmarked: Korean Partial Reduplication. Paper presented at the CLS meeting.

Kubozono, Haruo. 1995. Perceptual evidence for the mora in Japanese. In *Papers in Laboratory Phonology IV: Phonology and phonetic evidence*, edited by B. Connell and A. Arvaniti: Cambridge University Press.

Maddieson, Ian. 1985. Phonetic Cues to Syllabification. In *Phonetic Linguistics: essays in honor of Peter Ladefoged*, edited by V. A. Fromkin. San Diego: Academic Press, Inc.

———. 1993. Splitting the mora. *UCLA Working Papers in Linguistics* 83:9-18.

Port, Robert F., Salman Al-Ani, and Shosaku Maeda. 1980. Temporal Compensation and Universal Phonetics. *Phonetica* 37:235-252.

Port, Robert F., Jonathan Dalby, and Michael O'Dell. 1987. Evidence for mora timing in Japanese. *Journal of the Acoustical Society of America (JASA)* 81:1574-1585.

Poser, William. 1990. Evidence for foot structure in Japanese. *Language Research* 66 (1):78-105.

Sato, Yumiko. 1993. The Durations of Syllable-Final Nasals and the Mora Hypothesis in Japanese. *Phonetica* 50:44-67.

Tateishi, Koichi. 1989. Theoretical Implications of the Japanese Musician's Language. *WCCFL* 8:384-398.

Tranel, Bernard. 1991. CVC light syllables, geminates and Moraic Theory. *Phonology* 8 (2):291-302.

Mora Augmentation in Shizuoka Japanese

STUART DAVIS & ISAO UEDA

Indiana University & Osaka University of Foreign Studies

1. Introduction

In this paper, we will consider the rather complex pattern of mora augmentation found with adjectival emphasis in the Shizuoka dialect of Japanese. We have two goals in this paper. First is the descriptive goal of presenting a mora augmentation phenomenon that is not generally known to phonologists nor to many working on Japanese linguistics. The second is a theoretical goal of showing how the various instantiations of mora augmentation can be accounted for in a unified manner under an optimality-theoretic approach.

2. Data and Description

In Shizuoka Japanese, adjectives are emphasized by augmenting the first syllable by one mora. How this augmented mora gets realized depends on the phonemic content of the adjective. Consider the representative data in (1)-(3) illustrating the different ways that the mora can be realized. The data on Shizuoka Japanese are based on Hino (1977) and Yamaguchi (1987) as well as consultant work carried out by the second author. The pattern we describe is found among older speakers in a fairly large area of central Shizuoka prefecture.

(1) Mora augmentation by gemination

	Adjective	Emphatic Form	Gloss
a.	katai	kattai	hard
b.	osoi	ossoi	slow
c.	takai	takkai	high
d.	atsui	attsui	hot
e.	kitanai	kittanai	dirty
f.	kusai	kussai	stinky
g.	ikai	ikkai	big
h.	kanasi	kannasi	sad
i.	amai	ammai	sweet

(2) Mora augmentation by nasal insertion

	Adjective	Emphatic Form	Gloss
a.	hade	hande	showy
b.	ozoi	onzoi	terrible
c.	yowai	yonwai	weak
d.	hayai	hanyai	fast
e.	karai	kanrai	spicy
f.	nagai	naŋgai	long

(3) Mora augmentation by vowel lengthening

	Adjective	Emphatic Form	Gloss
a.	zonzai	zoonzai	impolite
b.	kandarui	kaandarui	languid
c.	onzokutai	oonzokutai	ugly
d.	suppai	suuppai	sour
e.	okkanai	ookkanai	scary

In describing how the emphatic adjective is formed from its nonemphatic base, we observe that the first syllable is augmented by one mora. The manner in which mora augmentation is realized varies depending on the nature of the first syllable of the base adjective and what the (first) postvocalic consonant is. It can be described as follows: If the first syllable of the base adjective is closed (ends in a consonant), then mora augmentation occurs by vowel lengthening as in (3); if the initial syllable of the base adjective is light and the (first) postvocalic consonant of the base is a voiced obstruent or glide (w, y, r), then augmentation occurs by the insertion of a nasal consonant in the coda of the first syllable as in (2). Otherwise, mora augmentation occurs by the gemination of the (first) postvocalic consonant as in (1). (It should be noted that that the data in (1h-i) are ambiguous as to whether there is nasal insertion or nasal gemination. We assume that they reflect gemination. See Rose 2000 for relevant discussion.) The location of the augmented mora in (1)-(3) is always after the first vowel. The Shizuoka pattern is different from standard Japanese where adjectives are typically emphasized by lengthening the accented vowel. This is seen in (4) below where the accented vowel of the second syllable is lengthened.

(4) Comparison with standard Japanese -- lengthen the accented vowel

	Adjective	Emphatic Form	Gloss
a.	katai	kataai	hard

In terms of the analysis of the Shizuoka pattern of adjectival emphasis, one can ask how the emphatic morpheme is represented. We suggest that it is represented as in (5), with a floating mora.

(5) Representation of the emphatic morpheme as a floating mora
     μ_e (μ_e = emphatic mora)

The floating emphatic mora is realized toward the left edge (beginning) of the adjective because of the alignment constraint given in (6).

(6) Align-L(μ_e, Wd) -- Align the emphatic mora with the beginning (left edge) of the word.

We assume that this alignment constraint is calculated with respect to the syllable. For example, an augmented mora that surfaces in the first syllable of the adjective respects Align-L, while an augmented mora that surfaces in the second syllable would have one violation of Align-L. (This is not a crucial assumption, but it simplifies our analysis.) Consequently, what we view as the input to the emphatic adjective is exemplified in (7). The input includes the prosodified base adjective plus the floating mora. The emphatic adjective is thus in an output-output relation with its nonemphatic counterpart.

(7) Input of the Emphatic Adjective (example from 1a)

μ_e μ μ μ
     | | |
     k a t a i   output = [kattai] 'hard (emphatic)'

Given this, we are now in position to develop an optimality-theoretic analysis that can account for the different means by which the floating emphatic mora can be realized.

3. An Optimality-theoretic Analysis

In developing an optimality-theoretic analysis of the mora augmentation data in (1)-(3) it is useful to consider an adjective, such as <u>katai</u> 'hard' in (1a) and examine the many different means that the additional mora can be realized. Some potential candidates are shown in (8) for the word <u>katai</u>. (The failed candidates are indicated by the asterisk.)

(8) Possible candidates for the augmentation of [katai] 'hard' (1a)
   a. *kkatai   b. *kaatai   c. kattai   d. *kantai
   e. *kataai   f. *kataii

Except for the form in (8a) with an initial geminate, all the other forms are phonotactically permissible in Japanese. The question then arises as to why the form in (8c) with gemination is preferred to the other candidates with vowel lengthening or nasal insertion. From the optimality theoretic perspective it reflects a ranking relation between the three constraints shown in (9).

(9) a. *LongVowel -- Long vowels are not permitted.
    b. *Gem -- Geminate consonants are not permitted.
    c. Dep-Nasal -- Nasal segments should not be inserted.

The preference for (8c) must mean that the constraint militating against geminate consonants (*Gem) is lower-ranked than either the constraint militating against long vowels (*LongVowel) or the insertion of nasals (Dep-Nasal). This, thus, establishes the ranking shown in (10) where *Gem is the lowest ranked of the three constraints.

(10) *LongVowel, Dep-Nasal >> *Gem

With respect to the ranking relation between *LongVowel and Dep-Nasal, the data in (2) is quite relevant. The comparison between (1) and (2) shows that not any consonant can be geminated in Japanese. Only voiceless consonants and nasals can be geminated. Let us consider the three output candidates in (11) for the emphatic form of the adjective in (2b).

(11) Possible candidates for the augmentation of [ozoi] 'terrible' (2b)
    a. *ozzoi   b. *oozoi   c. onzoi

Because of a ban on geminate voiced obstruents in Japanese, stated by the constraint in (12), the candidate in (11a) is not possible.

(12) *GemVoicedObstruent --- Geminate Voiced Obstruents are not permitted.

The choice then is between (11b) with a long vowel or (11c) with an inserted nasal consonant. The preference for (11c) establishes the ranking of *LongVowel over Dep-N shown in (13). If the ranking were reverse (11b) would be preferred.

(13) *LongVowel >> Dep-Nasal

In (14) we put together the rankings from (13) and (10) which expresses the priority of preference for the means of mora augmentation.

(14) *LongVowel >> Dep-Nasal >> *Gem

Let us now consider the data in (3) focussing on (3c). Some relevant output candidates for this data item are shown in (15).

(15) Possible candidates for the augmentation of [onzokutai] 'ugly' (3c)
    a. oonzokutai   b. *onnzokutai   c. *onzokkutai

The comparison of the three forms in (15) is interesting. The actual form that surfaces, (15a), has the additional mora realized through the lengthening of the first vowel. The alternative in (15b) realizes the additional mora by the gemination of the nasal after the first vowel; the alternative form in (15c) realizes the additional mora by the gemination of a voiceless consonant, but here, the gemination is later in the word, after the second vowel. First, in considering why (15b) fails to surface, we note that if mora augmentation is realized through the gemination of the nasal, the output would have impermissible syllabification. The first two syllables of (15b) would either include a complex coda ([onn.zo]) or a complex onset ([on.nzo]), thus constituting a fatal violation of the *Complex constraint given in (16) which is normally respected in Japanese.

(16) *Complex - Neither complex onsets or complex codas are allowed.

On the other hand, the output in (15c) with gemination of the /k/ after the second vowel is phonotactically fine. It should be the actual output given the ranking established in (10) where *LongVowel outranks *Gem. Consequently, for (15a) to be the winning candidate there must be some other constraint that outranks *LongVowel which (15c) fares worse on. The constraint that (15c) fares worse on in comparison with (15a) is the Align-L(μ_e,Wd) constraint given in (6). That is, the candidate in (15a) with a long vowel in the initial syllable better respects Align-L(μ_e,Wd) as compared to (15c). This is because the augmented mora is realized in the first syllable in (15a), but is realized in the second syllable of (15c) and so violates Align-L. That (15a) is the winning candidate establishes the ranking in (17a) where Align-L(μ_e,Wd) outranks *LongVowel. The fuller ranking in (17b) combines (17a) with (14).

(17) a. Align-L(μ_e,Wd) >> *LongVowel
      b. Align-L(μ_e,Wd) >> *LongVowel >> Dep-Nasal >> *Gem

In (18) we compile the constraints discussed so far as convenience to the reader, adding a constraint militating against word-initial geminate consonants (*Gem-Initial) and a constraint against geminate glides (*Gem-G). We assume the Japanese /r/ to be a glide along with /y/ and /w/. (After each constraint in (18) we provide in parentheses the abbreviation to be used in the tableaux.)

(18) Constraints
a. Align-L(μ_e,Wd) -- Align the emphatic mora with the beginning (left edge) of the word. (Align-L)
b. *LongVowel -- Long vowels are not permitted. (*LV)
c. *Gem -- Geminate consonants are not permitted. (*Gem)
d. Dep-Nasal -- Nasal segments should not be inserted. (Dep-N)
e. *GeminateVoicedObstruent -- Geminate voiced obstruents are not permitted. (*GVO)
f. *Complex -- Neither complex onsets nor complex codas are allowed. (*Comp)
g. *Gem-Initial -- Word-initial geminate consonants are not permitted. (*Gem-In)
h. *Gem-Glide -- Geminate glides are not permitted (*Gem-G)

In (19), we present the tableau for the emphatic form of the word [katai] from (1a) in order to show the formalization of the constraint rankings discussed above.

(19) /μₑ + katai/ --- [kattai] 'hard (emphatic)' (2a)

μₑ μ μμ
  | | |
  k a t a i
	*Gem-In
	*GVO
	*Gem-G
		*Comp	Align-
			L
				*LV	Dep-
					N
						*Gem

a. kkatai	*! (Gem- In)	(*)				*
μₑ μ μ μ V | | b. k a t a i [kaa.tai]				*!		
μμₑ μ μ V || c. k a t a i [kaa.tai]				*!		
μ μₑ μμ || || ☞ d. ka t ai [kat.tai]						*
μ μₑ μ μ || || e. ka n t a i [kan.tai]					*!	
μ μₑ μ μ | \/ | f. kat a i [ka.taai]			*!	*		

In order to make clear how some of the constraint violations are being determined in (19), it is useful to go over each of the candidates. First, (19a) is eliminated because it violates the undominated constraint against initial geminates. With respect to *Complex, we have indicated a violation in parentheses. This signifies an uncertainty as to whether an initial geminate would comprise a complex moraic onset or have an extrasyllabic mora. Since this issue is not crucial in determining the status of (19a) we do not take a position on it (but see Hume et al. 1997 and Davis 1999 for relevant discussion). Candidates (19b) and (19c) are phonetically identical. In candidate (19b) the emphatic mora is realized on the first part of the long vowel which would be the first mora of the word while in candidate (19c) the emphatic mora is realized as the second mora of the long vowel. Both (19b) and (19c) are identical with (19d) except that (19b) and (19c) violate *LV while (19d) violates *Gem. These two constraints are in direct conflict. The fact that (19d) is the winner constitutes a ranking argument for *LV being higher ranked than *Gem, as discussed earlier. Similarly, candidate (19f) violates *LV in addition to violating the Align-L constraint and so would be eliminated. The final comparison then is between (19d) and (19e) where the only difference between them is that (19e) violates Dep-N while (19d) violates *Gem. Again, that (19d) is the winner constitutes a ranking argument for *Dep-N being higher ranked than *Gem, as discussed earlier.

In (20), we provide the tableau for the emphatic form in (2b) with nasal insertion.

(20) /μ_e + ozoi/ --- [onzoi] 'terrible (emphatic)' (3b)

$\mu_e\ \mu\quad \mu\,\mu$ | | | o z o i	*Gem-In *GVO *Gem-G	*Comp	Align-L	*LV	Dep-N	*Gem
$\mu\mu_e\ \mu\,\mu$ V | | a. o z o i [oozoi]				*!		
$\mu\mu_e\mu\,\mu$ || || ☞ b. onz o i [onzoi]					*	
$\mu\ \mu_e\,\mu\,\mu$ || || c. o z o i [ozzoi]	*! (*GVO)					*

In (20c), we see that mora augmentation cannot be realized through gemination because of the violation of the undominated *GVO constraint. If we compare the two realistic competitors, (20a) with a long initial vowel and (20b) with an inserted nasal consonant, we notice that their evaluation is the same except that (20a) violates *LV while (20b) violates Dep-N. The fact that (20b) is the actual winner provides an argument for the ranking of *LV over Dep-N as discussed earlier.

In (21) we provide the tableau for the emphatic form of (3c) with vowel lengthening. (To accommodate the margins, some constraints that are not violated by the given candidates will not be shown.)

(21) /μ_e + onzokutai/ --- [oonzokutai] 'ugly (emphatic)' (3c)

μ_e μ μ μ μ μ μ | || | || o nzokut a i	*Gem-In *GVO *Gem-G	*Comp	Align-L	*LV	*Gem
μμ_e μ μ μ μμ V || | || ☞ a. o nzoku ta i [oon.zo.kutai]				*	
μ μ μ_e μ μ μμ | | | | | || b. o n zo kut a i [onz.zo.kutai]	*! (*GVO)	*			*
μ μ μ μ_eμ μ μ || V | || c. o n z o kut a i [on.zoo.kutai]			*!	*	
μ μ μμ_e μμμ || || ||| d. o nzok uta i [on.zok.kutai]			*!		*

The interesting comparison in (21) is between (21d) with gemination of the voiceless consonant after the second vowel and (21a) with lengthening of the initial vowel. This comparison makes clear the role of Align-L. Given the tableau in (21) and the previous discussion we know that gemination is the preferred means of mora augmentation. However, it is not preferred if gemination occurs later in the word (i.e. beyond the second vowel). As shown by the comparison of (21a) with (21d), candidate (21a) wins out over (21d) because it better satisfies the Align-L constraint.

The discussion and the analysis of mora augmentation presented here as shown by the tableaux in (19), (20), and (21) formally accounts for the various means of mora augmentation in Japanese. We see that the most preferred way is by gemination. This is reflected in (19) in which consonant gemination, vowel lengthening, and nasal insertion all result in phonotactically permissible outputs. In such cases, mora augmentation is by gemination. When gemination of the consonant is not possible then the preferred way of mora augmentation is by nasal insertion as reflected by the tableau in (20); when neither these means are phonotactically possible then mora augmentation is achieved through vowel lengthening as in (21). Always these preferences are controlled by the Align-L constraint so that for example a gemination later in the word (beyond the second vowel) would be dispreferred to vowel lengthening of the initial vowel as illustrated by the tableau in (21).

Given our analysis, we now consider two types of cases that have not been formally discussed. First we consider the case where the first syllable of the (base) adjective has a long vowel and then we consider the case where the first two vowels of the (base) adjective are in hiatus. For each case we need to refer to constraints not previously introduced in order to account for the emphatic forms. The first case involving a long vowel in the initial syllable is illustrated by (22a-b). An example involving hiatus is shown in (22c). (The period in the emphatic form indicates a syllable break.)

(22)	Adjective	Emphatic Form	Gloss
a.	kii.roi	kiin.roi	yellow
b.	tootoi	toot.toi	respectable
c.	o.i.sii	oo.i.sii	delicious

First, consider the first type of case in (22a-b) involving an adjective whose initial vowel is long. The constraints and rankings that we have established so far readily predict the correct output for this case. This is shown in the tableau in (24) for the emphatic form of [kii.roi] 'yellow'. In (23) we add a high-ranking constraint militating against the occurrence of trimoraic vowels which plays a role in the evaluation.

(23) *VVV -- Trimoraic vowels are not allowed.

(24) /μ$_e$ + kii.roi/ -- [kiinroi] 'yellow (emphatic)' (22a)

μ$_e$ μ μ μμ \/ ‖ k i r o i	*Gem-In *GVO *Gem-G	*V$_{μμμ}$	*LV	Dep- N	*Gem
μ μ$_e$ μ μ μ \\/ ‖ a. k i r o i [kiiiroi]		*!	*		
μ μμ$_e$ μμ ∨ | ‖ ☞b. ki n r o i [kiinroi]			*	*	
μ μμ$_e$ μ μ ∨ | | | c. k i r o i [kiirroi]	*! (*Gem-G)		*		*

Now let us consider the formal analysis of the emphatic form of [o.i.si] 'delicious' in (22c). We will only consider the two candidates given in (25) since other potential candidates such as [o.ii.si] or [o.is.si] would violate Align-L

(25) Possible candidates for the augmentation of [o.i.si]
    a. [oo.i.si]   b. [on.ni.si]

Candidate (25a) is the actual augmented adjectival form of [o.i.si]. However, as shown by the tableau in (26), the constraints and ranking established so far picks out (25b) as the winning candidate.

(26) /μ_e + o.i.sii/ -- [oo.i.sii] 'delicious (emphatic)' (22c)

μ_e μ μ $\mu\mu$ | | V o i s i	*Gem-In *GVO *Gem-G	Align- L	*LV	Dep- N	*Gem
μ μ_e μ μ μ \/ | \/ a. o i s i [oo.i.sii]			*!		
μ $\mu_e\mu$ $\mu\mu$ | | | V b. o n i s i [on.ni.sii]				*	*

The comparison of the two candidates in (26) is quite interesting. The candidates both respect the Align-L constraint. (26a) fares worse on the *LV constraint because of its initial long vowel, but it respects both Dep-N and *Gem. On the other hand, (26b) respects *LV but it has a violation of both Dep-N and *Gem. Because *LV is higher-ranked than either Dep-N or *Gem candidate (26a) should be eliminated; however (26a) is the winning candidate, not [on.ni.sii] in (26b).

In order to account for the fact that [on.ni.sii] in (26b) is not the correct emphatic form of [o.i.sii] we make reference to constraint conjunction which has been developed in works such as Smolensky (1995), Ito & Mester (1999), and Baertsch (1998) among others. The idea behind constraint conjunction is that two lower ranking constraints may be combined as a single conjoined constraint with a ranking that is higher than either of the two lower ranking constraints. For the analysis of the augmented adjectives as reflected in (26) we propose that Dep-N and *Gem are conjoined and ranked higher than *LV. This is shown in the tableau in (27).

(27) $/\mu_e$ + o.i.s´ii/ -- [oo.i.s´ii] 'delicious (emphatic)' (22c)

$\mu_e\,\mu\,\mu\,\mu\mu$ | | V o is i	*Gem-In *GVO *Gem-G	Dep-N & *Gem	*LV	Dep- N	*Gem
$\mu\,\mu_e\,\mu\,\mu\,\mu$ \/ | \/ ☞ a. o isi [oo.i.sii]			*		
$\mu\,\mu_e\mu\,\mu\mu$ | | | V b. on isi [on.ni.sii]		*!		*	*

Here the conjoined constraint eliminates (27b) with an inserted geminate nasal from consideration. Thus, (27a) with the lengthened vowel
is correctly predicted to be the emphatic adjective for [oisii].

We would maintain that the use of constraint conjunction in
this particular case captures something fundamental about the mora
augmentation process. As shown by the data in (1)-(3), mora augmentation is either realized by means of gemination, nasal insertion (into
the coda), or vowel lengthening; it is not realized by a combination of
these. Thus, candidate (27a) has the augmented mora being realized
through the single process of vowel lengthening. (27b), though, realizes
mora augmentation by means of both nasal insertion and gemination.
Mora augmentation can only be realized by a single process. The conjoined constraint Dep-N & *Gem in (27) neatly captures this. Thus we
do not view the use of constraint conjunction here as an analytical trick
but as something that is fundamental in accounting for the mora augmentation process.

In summary, we have presented a detailed optimality-theoretic
analysis of the formation of emphatic adjectives through mora augmentation in the Shizuoka dialect of Japanese. What clearly emerges
from the analysis is the prioritization of the means of mora augmentation. The preferred way of mora augmentation is by gemination, if
gemination is not possible then nasal insertion, and if that is not possible then vowel lengthening. Mora augmentation always occurs toward
the left edge of the word so that augmentation by lengthening the first
vowel is preferred to geminating a consonant after the second vowel as
was shown by the discussion of (15c). Finally, mora augmentation is
realized by means a single process and not by a combination of processes as shown by the discussion of (25)-(27).

Acknowledgement

We wish to thank Karen Baertsch, Masa Deguchi, Matthew Gordon, and Natsuko Tsujimura for helpful comments related to this paper. We also acknowledge our Shizuoka dialect consultants Kaneko Aoshima, Sachiko Aoshima, and Tamotsu Koizumi.

References

Baertsch, K. 1998. Onset Sonority Distance Constraints through Local Conjunction, *CLS* 34.2:1-15

Davis, S. 1999. On the Representation of Initial Geminates. *Phonology* 16:93-104.

Hino, S. 1977. Shizuoka-ken no hogen (The Dialect of Shizuoka). In *Furusato Hyakuwa* 20 (A Hundred Stories of our Native Place 20), 11-80, Shizuoka Newspaper Company.

Hume, E., J. Muller & A. van Engelenhoven. 1997. Non-moraic Geminates in Leti. *Phonology* 14:371-402.

Ito, J. & A. Mester. 1999 On the Sources of Opacity in OT: Coda Process in German. To appear in *The Syllable in Optimality Theory*, C. Féry and R. van de Vijver. Cambridge: Cambridge University Press.

Rose, S. 2000. Rethinking Geminates, Long Distance Geminates, and the OCP. *Linguistic Inquiry* 31:85-122.

Smolensky, P. 1995. On the Internal Structure of the Constraint Component Con of UG. Handout of a talk given at UCLA, April 7, 1995. (ROA-86)

Yamaguchi, K. 1987. *Shizuoka-ken no Hogen* (The Dialect of Shizuoka). Shizuoka Newspaper Co.

Phonetic Duration of English /s/ and its borrowing in Korean*

SOOHEE KIM & EMILY CURTIS
University of Washington

1. Introduction

This paper examines loan word adaptation with a special focus on the alveolar voiceless fricative /s/. Based on a production and a perception experiment, we propose that speakers of Korean heed a sub-phonemic length contrast in English in a categorical fashion, leading to split borrowing of the English phoneme /s/ to two Korean phonemes, lenis /s/ and fortis /s*/.

. The organization of this paper is as follows. In Section 2, following borrowing patterns of English words with /s/ to Korean, loan word phonology and a summary of the acoustic characteristics of Korean /s/'s are presented. This section also proposes hypotheses for fricative borrowing: i) there exists a consistent duration difference between single-onset and cluster-onset *s*'s in English, and ii) native Korean speakers make use of a length difference found in English /s/'s as a category-judging cue. In Section 3, a production experiment is conducted to measure the duration of singleton and cluster /s/'s in English. In section 4, a perception experiment is conducted to show how the length difference in English /s/ affects Koreans' perception. Section 5 discusses the theoretical implications of the experimental findings, and section 6 closes the paper with suggestions for future research.

---

*
Many thanks to Sharon Hargus, Richard Wright, Ellen Kaisse, Alicia Wassink, Donca Steriade, Taehong Cho, Charles Ulrich, William Boltz, Zev Handel, and the audience at the University of Washington Colloquium for their comments, questions, and interest.

2. Background

2.1 Patterns of borrowing English /s/ into Korean

The single English /s/ phoneme is borrowed as either fortis /s*/ or lenis /s/ into Korean. Examples in (a) and (b) below are cases of initial /s/ borrowing, and (c) and (d) are those of final /s/.

(1) *English words borrowed to Korean*   *Initial Korean phonemes*
a) slump, smog, snack, spar, skate, etc.   /s/
b) ceramic, single, size, solo, etc.   /s*/
c) test, toast, postcard, disk, mask, etc.   /s/
d) gas, bus, peace, news, juice, DOS, etc.   /s*/

Words in (a) are invariably borrowed with the lenis /s/ while words in (b) are borrowed with the fortis /s*/. Thus the word *slump* is borrowed as [silʏmpʰi], and the word *solo* is borrowed as [s*olo][1]. The same generalization can be made for the data containing final /s/'s in (c) and (d).

The split borrowing of English /s/ seems to be based on the English syllable structure. English initial /s/ occurring in a cluster is mapped onto the Korean lenis /s/, and English singleton /s/ is mapped onto the Korean fortis /s*/. What would be an appropriate phonological model of borrowing for this case?

2.2 Loan word phonology

Paradis, *et al* (1995) propose that target language phoneme selection is based on feature matching between the phoneme of the source language and that of the target language. According to their Theory of Constraints and Repair Strategies, illegal foreign phonemes are adapted to native phonemes and phoneme sequences based on universal constraints.

Problematic for Paradis, *et al*, Korean borrows *some* English [s]'s as fortis /s*/ and *others* as lenis /s/, splitting the source phoneme into two target language phonemes. That is, a distinction is made in borrowing *one phoneme* in the absence of any feature(s) to 'repair'. English /s/ is not *illegal* in Korean; it is *'incomplete'*, and the Paradis, *et al* model cannot account for its borrowing.

Silverman's (1992) multi-scansion model, on the other hand, formally incorporates the phonetic information perceived by *listeners* of the borrowing language, into a phonological theory. In his model, foreign word bor-

---

[1]Words in (b) optionally allow the lenis fricative /s/ onset in spelling, but 10 native speakers we consulted insisted that it is only an orthographic convention.

rowing consists of two ordered scanning processes, one perceptual and the other phonological. We agree that recognizing the phonetic component is necessary; however, we believe the *scansion* of phonetics and phonology is simultaneous.

We mentioned that English syllable structure might be relevant to the split borrowing. If, however, what constrains the borrowing process were the phonological instantiation of English syllable structure, the phoneme selection might as well be reversed. Singleton /s/ in English might as well be borrowed as the lenis fricative in Korean, and cluster /s/ in English as the fortis fricative in Korean. But the phoneme selection is fixed, and syllable structure gives no motivation for the mapping.

The explanation for the split borrowing may be found where the phonetics of English meets the phonetics and phonology of Korean. The following section explores possible phonetic motivations for the split borrowing.

2.3 Phonetic characteristics of Korean /s/ and /s*/

While studies on Korean *s*'s are lacking, phonetic studies of Korean stops and affricates in the literature include C. W. Kim (1965), Hardcastle (1973), Hirose, *et al* (1974), Kagaya (1974), Silva (1992), J. I. Han (1996), M. R. Oh and Johnson (1996), J. Y. Shin (1998), M. R. Kim (1994), and Iverson (1983). The main findings of the previous phonetic research on Korean obstruents are that vowels following fortis obstruents have a sharper onset as well as a higher F_0 than those following lenis obstruents and that fortis stops and affricates have a longer closure duration than lenis obstruents.

Kagaya (1974) found that /s*/ and /s/ demonstrate the same characteristics observed in other obstruents in terms of the quality of the post-consonantal vowel. The fortis fricative is distinctly marked by characteristics of the following vowel; the vowel onset shows more distinct high formants (F_3 and/or F_4) and the F_0 is usually 10 to 15 Hz higher than that of vowels following the lenis fricative. When we looked at Korean *s*'s, the most characteristic acoustic feature distinguishing fortis and lenis fricatives was indeed the post-fricative vowel, or transition into the vowels. When the vowel portions of [sa] and [s*a] were digitally swapped, the opposite pair [s*a] and [sa] was perceived.

It is important to point out, however, that cues from the post-fricative vowel are not available in English. Auditory and visual examinations revealed that there is no discernible F_0 difference in vowels following English [s] based on syllable structure. Also, English [sV] sequences seem inherently fortified; the English [sV] sequences with the majority of the frication taken out sound something comparable to Korean [tʃ*V] (not lenis [tʃV]) to the Korean ear. Eliminating all frication and aspiration noise before the vowel results in something similar to Korean [t*V] (not lenis [tV]). In sum, the quality of the post-fricative *vowels* contribute to distinguishing the fortis fricative from the lenis fricative in *Korean*, but English does not provide such a cue. Thus, we conclude that the cue that Koreans use in split mapping must come from English [s] itself.

Cues from the post-fricative vowels excluded, we hypothesize that Korean *s*'s may be differentiated in two different ways. If fricative *duration* is comparable to stop closure, fortis /s*/ should be longer than lenis /s/. If intensity of frication is comparable to intensity of stop burst, the fortis /s*/ aspiration intensity should be greater than lenis /s/ (due to different degrees of narrowing of the vocal folds giving rise to higher air pressure than lenis /s/). Either of these may be cues in the phonemes themselves.

A pilot study revealed that the fortis fricative /s*/ tends to have longer frication than the lenis fricative /s/ in Korean. Also, the fortis fricative /s*/ showed no word-medial shortening, whereas the lenis /s/ was significantly shorter in the medial position than in the initial position, comparable to other Korean fortis-lenis obstruent pairs in the language. Spectrograms in other researchers' studies also show longer frication period for fortis /s*/ than for lenis /s/ (e.g. Kagaya 1974, p. 171). It is interesting to note that the Korean lenis /s/, but never the fortis /s*/, sounds more like English [ts] to the native speaker of English; this supports the claim that the duration of /s/ is shorter than that of /s*/ in Korean.

The intensity of frication did not differ noticeably for /s/ and /s*/ according to visual observation of the spectrograms and random aural examination.

To conclude, the lenis fricative /s/ in Korean is differentiated from the fortis fricative /s*/ mainly by the characteristics of the following vowels. As for the fricatives themselves, the fricative duration of fortis /s*/ is in general longer than that of lenis /s/, mirroring the typical fortis-lenis closure durations of other obstruents in the language.

Acoustic duration in the shape of closure duration plays an important role in the distinction of fortis stops or affricates, and the duration of frication does so in fricatives. The length distinction is exploited in the medial position, and some researchers take it further to posit that fortis obstruents are geminates in Korean (e.g. J. I. Han 1996, J. M. Kim 1986). It is plausible, then, that a longer duration in English segments is somehow associated with the *duration* of fortis consonants in the minds of the Korean speaker, which in turn affects the speaker's interpretation of the English signal.

We propose that native speakers of Korean have internalized a *fortis = long* relationship and that they use this association in mapping English /s/ to Korean fricatives. This proposal suggests i) that syllable type in English has a phonetic correlate in terms of /s/ duration: more explicitly, there exists a consistent duration difference between single-onset and cluster-onset *s*'s in English, and ii) that native Korean speakers make use of the length difference found in English *s*'s as a cue to mapping English /s/ to Korean /s/ or /s*/.

3. Production Experiment

The first experiment examined English speakers' production of /s/ in initial singleton vs. cluster to assess the hypothesized duration differences.

3.1. Methods

Stimuli consisted of English words with initial and final /s/ or /sC/ followed by 8 different vowels i, ɪ, æ, ɑ, ʌ, o, ʊ, and u (e.g. seek, sick, sack, soak, etc). The consonant following the *s* in the cluster was restricted to /t/ for /sC/ words (e.g. stick, stack, stuck).

Eight subjects read the stimuli three times each in the carrier phrase 'I'm going to say ___ again' (8 subjects x 3 repetitions x 8 /s/ words + 8 /sC/ words).

Recording took place in a sound-treated booth in the Phonetics Lab at the University of Washington. Subjects read the stimuli off the word list into a standing cardioid microphone (Electro Voice RE 20 with a frequency response of 45-18,000 Hz), which was placed 3 inches from one side of the speaker's mouth. The sound source was amplified by a stereo mixer (Shure FP 32) and was fed to an analog recorder (TASCAM 122 MK III).

Recording samples were digitized on a CSL speech analysis system (Kay 4300 B) with a sampling rate of 22,050 Hz to capture the high frequencies of [s]. For measurements, the Multi-Speech Signal Analysis Workstation (Model 3700, version 2.01) was used with a 0.8 built-in pre-emphasis. Measurements were taken by identifying the fricative portion in the waveform signal and spectrogram display. The figure 4-1 below shows the portion [isæ] in one of the subjects' utterance 'I'm going to say _sa_ck again'.

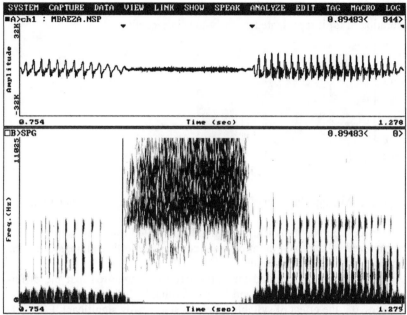

Figure 1. Waveform and spectrogram of the utterance [isæ] generated by Multispeech. The vertical lines mark the onset and the offset of the frication.

In addition to absolute [s] duration, we also measured a normalized [s] duration to control for varying speech rates between subjects, dividing the duration of [s] by a reference duration for the utterance of the individual [s] measured.

3.2 Results

The measurements revealed that the absolute duration of [s] was longer for the [s] type than for the [sC] type both word-initially and word-finally. The average duration of initial [s] was 170 milliseconds and that of initial [sC] was 133 milliseconds across speakers. The average duration of final [sC] was about 145 milliseconds and that of final [sC] was 100 milliseconds across speakers. The minimum and the maximum duration of [s] (initial and final together) was 76 milliseconds and 380 milliseconds, respectively, with standard deviation (SD) of 57 milliseconds. The minimum and the maximum duration of [sC] was 56 milliseconds and 294 milliseconds, respectively, with the SD of 50 milliseconds. There was also duration difference between initial vs. final /s/'s.

The following figure displays a summary of the results. In the figure, duration of [s] is represented on the y-axis in seconds.

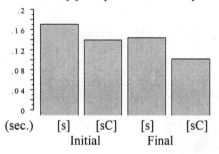

Figure 2. Average duration of [s] and [sC] by syllable type and position.

A descriptive statistical analysis also revealed that the findings using normalized [s] and [sC] duration were comparable to the findings using the absolute [s] and [sC] duration.

The results of repeated measures ANOVA suggested that the difference in duration between [s] and [sC] was reliably different. With an alpha level of .05, the effect of syllable type was statistically significant, $F(1, 381)$ = 78.348, $p < .0001$. The duration of [s] was significantly longer than that of [sC].

Effect of syllable position was also found to be significant. With an alpha level of .05, the effect of syllable position was statistically significant, $F(1, 381)$ = 171.899, $p < .0001$. The duration of [s] and [sC] in the initial position was significantly longer than that of [s] and [sC] in the final position.

Overall, syllable type (cluster vs. singleton) was found to affect the duration of /s/. Measurements of the data showed that the duration of /s/ was longer when it appeared alone than in a cluster. This durational difference was statistically significant, indicating that the difference in duration between [s] and [sC] in English is persistent and may not be attributed to chance. The difference in duration between [s] and [sC] was found in both word-initial and word-final positions, confirming that the difference is systematic.

4. Perception Experiment

The second part of our hypothesis is that native Korean speakers perceive English /s/ categorically, based on its segment duration, which was found to differ between /s/ and /sC/. Korean speakers are expected to interpret English singleton /s/ with long frication as the Korean fortis fricative

/s*/, biased by their internalized association of segment duration and fortis obstruents.

4.1 Methods

A control stimulus was made by digitally editing the word 'sock' said by a native English speaker. The control stimulus was created including 140 milliseconds of [s] frication + 50 milliseconds of vowel [a]. We chose 140 milliseconds as the fricative duration of the control stimuli, as it was an approximate average of our production data, also close to the average English /s/ duration found in Haggard's study (1972). Stimuli were then made by altering frication duration. The shortest frication duration in the stimuli was 60 milliseconds, and the longest fricative duration was 300 milliseconds. There were 7 stimuli, and each stimulus was repeated 5 times. The sound files were randomized by computer, with 3 second intervals between each file.

Sixteen native Korean speakers (6 male and 10 female) listened to the stimuli binaurally in a quiet room, at a comfortable listening level. For the listening task, ATH-M40fs Precision Studio headphones with 5-28,000 Hz frequency response were used. Subjects were instructed to give a forced choice judgment of what they perceived each stimulus to be by circling either *sa* or *s*a* written in the Korean orthography. Subjects were *not* told that the stimuli were English [sa].

4.2 Results

The results of the experiment confirmed that Korean listeners were sensitive to the durational changes in the stimuli. Table 5-1 below shows the number of responses that subjects gave for each stimulus at each frication duration.

Table 1. Total number of responses for /sa/ and /s*a/ to English stimuli [sa]

Duration of [s]	Response		Total
	/sa/	/s*a/	
60ms	63	17	80
80ms	54	26	80
110ms	44	36	80
140ms	30	50	80
170ms	15	65	80
230ms	5	75	80
300ms	4	76	80
Total	**215**	**345**	**560**

For the shortest [s] duration (60 milliseconds), 78% (63 out of 80) of the response was for lenis [s]. For the longest [s] (300 milliseconds), 95% of the response was for fortis /s*/.

The number of responses for lenis /s/ decreased by 10-15 as the duration of the frication increased. The following figure summarizes the results. The vertical axis represents the total number of responses for either /s/ at the bottom or /s*/ from the top of each bar.

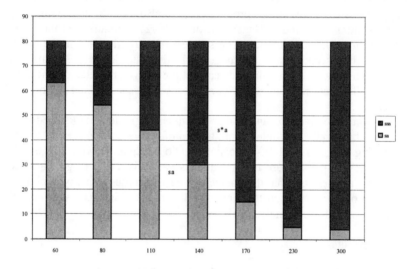

Figure 3. Bar chart showing the number of /s/ and /s*/ responses on the vertical axis, based on the duration of [s] frication (in milliseconds)

Starting with the shortest stimuli, the number of responses for lenis /s// continues to decrease until it meets a cross-over point where the preferred interpretation for fortis /s*/ and lenis /s/ switches. This point is somewhere between 110 milliseconds and 140 milliseconds of [s] frication. Interestingly, the cross-over point is what researchers consider an average English [s] frication duration when it occurs in isolation.

It should be mentioned that all 16 subjects found the stimuli to be very difficult to judge, suggesting that duration alone is usually *not* the only attribute that is used to distinguish the fortis from lenis phonemes in fricatives. Also note that the response for lenis /s/ decreased *gradually* as the opposite response increased accordingly. There is no *one point* beyond which speakers unanimously choose either /s/ or /s*/.

In stark contrast to the previous experiment, Korean speakers showed almost unchanged response for English [sa] stimuli when the intensity was manipulated. The following figure shows results of a control experiment, in which amplitude (e.g. intensity) of the stimuli was decreased or increased.

Effect of amplitude on perception of
/s/ vs. /s*/ by Korean listeners

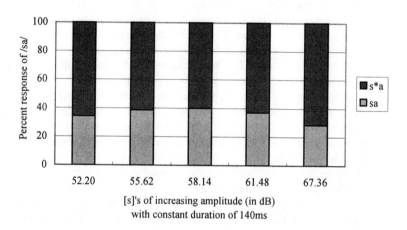

Figure 4. Bar chart showing the number of /s/ and /s*/ responses on the vertical axis, based on the intensity of [s] frication.

Unlike the results from the duration experiment, subjects did not respond to amplitude differences in the stimuli, assuring that the results we obtained in the previous experiment are important; Korean listeners heed the *duration* of the frication when they hear English [s].

5. Discussion

The two experiments reported in this paper show that there is a systematic sub-phonemic duration difference in English /s/, and that Korean listeners categorically respond to the durational difference in English /s/'s. This is presumably because the Korean language makes use of segmental duration, though as a secondary cue, to differentiate fortis from lenis phonemes.

This study has significant theoretical implications for both loan word phonology and the phonology-phonetics interface. In many cases of borrowing, the target language has fewer phonemes and stricter constraints such that the borrowed word involves simplification with respect to the input source language form. While cases of this many-to-few borrowing may easily be explained by feature mapping, neither feature mapping nor the idea of simplification applies to few-to-many borrowing situations; that is, cases where the phoneme inventory of the target language is richer than the source language, as we have seen in the case of Korean and English.

This study emphasizes the importance of the phonetics of the source language and the perception of the target language in one case of few-to-many borrowing. Theories of loan words must be expanded to account for both many-to-few and few-to-many borrowing. Manipulation of abstract features alone is inadequate. This study underscores the role of the listener and crucially the role of phonetics in loan word phonology.

Furthermore, this study suggests a role for loan word phonology in research on the phonetics-phonology interface as well as in theoretical phonetics. When we look closely at the phonetics of the source language, we make discoveries about the phonetics of the language and about how those phonetic facts fit into theoretical phonetics and phonology. For example, this study found a systematic sub-phonemic duration difference in English /s/. At first glance, this duration differences in /s/ might not seem of any interest because they are subphonemic. However, they suggest that syllable structure has an effect on segment durations, that fricative duration can vary, perhaps to different degrees in different languages, and that duration is interpreted differently in different languages. This kind of cross-linguistic phonetic (perceptual/production) study can bring focus to something never before considered.

Moreover, duration is not a main cue for distinguishing fortis from lenis obstruents in Korean (while pitch of the following vowel probably is, as discussed in section 3), and no feature [+long] distinguishes fortis vs. lenis in Korean phonology. The feature [+long] is not relevant to the subphonemic /s/ duration difference in English, either. Then how do we characterize the subphonemic differences? The feature [voice] does not make a phonemic distinction in Korean, but subphonemic [t] and [d] differ by the feature [voice] and are recognized as allophones. Are English [s]'s not allophones because there is no feature to distinguish them... in Western phonologies? Do we want the definition of *allophone* to be 'subphonemic variation characterized by a feature we have discovered to be distinctive in some language'? In a parallel case, how do we characterize the duration distinction in English vowels preceding voiced vs. voiceless codas? We leave the questions to future research and consideration.

6. Future Research

In closing, we would like to point out that this study may be taken up in interesting further studies.

In our statistical analysis, we saw effects of syllable position in English, where syllable-initial singleton /s/ was the longest, and the syllable-final cluster /s/ was the shortest, but the durations of syllable-initial cluster /s/ and that of syllable-final singleton /s/ were comparable. These findings are interesting in the psycho-perceptual analysis of syllable positions and in syllable theories as well as in characterizing the aforementioned subphonemic frication duration differences.

Crystal and House (1988) found the duration of /s/ in English to be longer phrase-finally. In this study we controlled for phrasal position and stress. However, it would be interesting to see how stress and higher prosodic constituency may interact with the duration of /s/ and other segments in a variety of languages.

Furthermore, note that the perception study we conducted only involved *initial* /s/'s fearing it might be a confounding factor that Korean does not allow [+continuant] codas. It may be worthwhile to replicate the present perception experiment with /s/-final English words to further analyze Koreans' perception of English /s/ vs. /s*/. This may help to pinpoint a cut-off duration in their categorical perception, which we found to be about 140 milliseconds in the initial position. Unlike /s/ in the initial position, the amplitude of the /s/ frication might also be relevant in the coda position.

Finally, it may be possible to replicate portions of this study with final /s/ and /sC/ English forms. Words like *bo_x_*, *dance* and *chance* have been borrowed with the fortis /s*/. It is possible that *box* has been subject to the Korean post-obstruent tensing rule, but this does not account for words like *dance* and *chance*. Maybe we need a loan word phonology rule to account for these forms, where post-obstruent tensing is postlexical but post-sonorant tensing is (loan word) stratum-specific. More likely, there may be differences in the phonetic output of these words--for example, excrescent *t*-insertion in words like *dance* --that are cues for Korean listeners. In any case clusters clearly do not prevent English /s/ from being borrowed as fortis /s*/ in Korean. Maybe /s/ being the very last segment in the syllable allows more frication time. More detailed analysis of local effects like these as well as prosodic-based differences are left to further research.

References

Behrens, Susan J. and Sheila E. Blumstein 1988. Acoustic characteristics of English voiceless fricatives: a descriptive analysis. *Journal of Phonetics, 16*, 295-298.

Crystal, Thomas H. & Arthur S. House 1988. A note on the durations of fricatives in American English. *Journal of Acoustical Society of America, 84*, No.5.

Haggard, Mark 1972. Abbreviation of consonants in English pre-post-vocalic clusters. *Journal of Phonetics, 3,* 7-24.

Han, J.I. 1992. On the Korean Fortis Consonants and Tensification. *CLS 28.*

Han, J. I. 1996a. Perception of Korean Fortis and Lenis Consonants: Evidence for a Geminate Analysis of Fortis Consonants IN *Japanese/Korean Linguistics 5.* Iwasaki & Strauss eds.. CSLI Publications and SLA, Akatsuka.

Han, J. I. 1996b. The Phonetics and Phonology of "Fortis" and "Plain" Consonants in Korean. Doctoral dissertation. Cornell University.

Han, M. S. & R. S. Weitzman 1970. Acoustic features of Korean /P, T, K/, /p,t,k/, and /ph, th, kh/. *Phonetica, 22,* 112-128.

Hardcastle, W.J. 1973. Some observations on the *fortis-lax* distinction in initial stops in Korean. *Journal of Phonetics, 1,* 263-272

Heinz and Stevens 1961. On the Properties of Voiceless Fricative Consonants *Journal of the Acoustical Society of America, 33,* No. 5, 589-596.

Hirose H., Lee C., and T. Ushijima 1973. Laryngeal control in Korean stop production, *Journal of Phonetics, 2,* 145-152.

Hyman, Larry M. 1970. The role of Borrowing in the Justification of Phonological Grammars. *Studies in African Linguistics, 1 ,* 1-48.

Ingram, John C.L. and See-Gyoon Park 1998 Language, context, and speaker effects in the identification and discrimination of English /r/ and /l/ by Japanese and Korean listeners. *Journal of the Acoustical Society of America, 103,* No. 2.

Iverson, Greg 1983. Korean *s. Journal of Phonetics 11,* 191-200.

Johnson, Keith and M. Oh 1995. Intervocalic consonant sequences in Korean, Papers from the Linguistics Laboratory. *OSU Working Papers in Linguistics No. 45.* Stefanie Jannedy ed. The Ohio State University, Columbus, OH.

Jongman, Allard 1989. Duration of frication noise required for identification of English fricatives. *Journal of Acoustical Society of America, 84,* No. 4, 1718-1725.

Jun, S. 1994. The domains of laryngeal feature lenition effects in Chonnam Korean. *Papers from the Linguistics Laboratory Working Papers in Linguistics, 43* Edited by Sook-hyang Lee, Sun-Ah Jun. The Ohio State University, Columbus, OH.

Kagaya, Ryohei 1974. A fiberscopic and acoustic study of the Korean stops, affricates and fricatives. *Journal of Phonetics 2,* 161-180.

Kaye, Jonathan & Barbara Nykiel 1979. Loan words and abstract phonotactic constraints. *Canadian Journal of Linguistics,* 24, No. 2, 71-93.

Keating, Patricia , T. Cho, Cecile Fougeron, and C.S. Hsu 1998. Domain-initial articulatory strengthening in four languages, *draft* for *Papers in Laboratory Phonology 6.*

Kim, C.W. 1988. On the Autonomy of the Tensity Feature in Stop Classification with special reference to Korean stops. *Sojourns in Language II; Collected papers by Chin-W. Kim.* Tower Press. Also 1965 ***Word,*** *21,* 339-359.

Kim, C.W. 1988 A Theory of Aspiration. *Sojourns in Language II; Collected papers by Chin-W. Kim.* Tower Press, 73-82.

Kim M. R. 1994 Acoustic characteristics of Korean stops and perception of English stop consonants. Doctoral dissertation. University of Wisconsin, Madison. UMI Order number 9419368. Ann Arbor, MI.

Lee, K. 1998, Korean Fortis Consonants and Tensification. handout from NWLC at Simon Fraser University.

Lisker, L. & Abramson, A. S. 1964. A cross-language study of voicing in initial stops: acousticsl measurements. *Word, 20,* 384-422.

Oh, Mira and Keith Johnson 1996. Intervocalic Consonant Sequences in Korean. *Working Papers in Linguistics, 45,* 85-97. Columbus, OH.

Oh, M. 1997 Aspiration in Korean Phonology, *Japanese/Korean Linguistics 6,* Ho-min Sohn and John Haig eds.. CSLI Publications and SLA, 319-331.

Oh, M. 1998. The Prosodic Analysis of Intervocalic Fortis Consonant Lengthening in Korean 317. *Japanese/Korean Linguistics 8.* James Silva ed. CSLI Publications and SLA.

Ohala, John 1990. There Is No Interface between Phonology and Phonetics: A Personal View. *Journal of Phonetics, 18,* 153-71.

Paradis, Carole, Caroline Lebel, and Darlene LaCharite 1995. Saving and cost in loanword adaptation: predictions of the TCRS-phonological model. ms.

Paradis, Carole 1988. Towards a Theory of Constraint Violations. *McGill Working Papers in Linguistics. 5,* No. 1, 1-43., Montreal, PQ, Canada.

Ramsey, Robert 1977. S-clusters and Reinforced Consonants. *Papers in Korean Linguistics,* Chin-W. Kim ed., 59-66.

Rhee, S. 1997. Constraints on Post-Obstruent Tensification in Korean. *Japanese/Korean Linguistics 6.* Ho-min Sohn and John Haig eds.. CSLI Publications and SLA, 253-274.

Shadle, Christine H. and Celia Scully 1995. An articulatory-acoustic-aerodynamic analysis of [s] in VCV sequences. *Journal of Phonetics 23,* 53-66.

Shin, J.Y. 1998. 한국어 ㄷ, ㄸ, ㅌ, ㅈ, ㅉ, ㅊ 의 조음적 특성에 관한 연구 [Study on the articulatory characteristics of Korean t, t', th, c, c', ch]. 국어학 [Korean Linguistics] 31, 53-80.

Silva, James 1992. The phonetics and phonology of stop lenition in Korean. Doctoral dissertation. Cornell University, Annarbor, MI. UMI order number 9300771.

Silva, James 1993. A Phonetically Based Analysis of [Voice] and [Fortis] in Korean, *Japanese/Korean Linguistics 2,* Patricia Clancy ed.. Stanford: SLI. 164-174.

Silverman, Daniel 1992. Multiple scansions in loanword phonology: evidence from Cantonese. *Phonology,* 9, 289-328.

Sohn, H. 1977 Tensification in Compound Boundaries in Korean, *Papers in Korean Linguistics,* Chin-W. Kim ed., 113-117.

Stevens, P. 1960. Spectra of Fricative Noise in Human Speech. *Language and Speech,* 332-49.

Takagi, Naoyuki and Virginia Mann 1994. A perceptual basis for the systematice phonological correspondences between Japanese load words and their English source words [sic]. *Journal of Phonetics, 22,* 343-356.

Treiman, Rebecca, Jennifer Gross and Annemarie Cwikiel-Glavin 1992. The syllabification of /s/ clusters in English. *Journal of Phonetics 20,* 383-402.

Walsh, Thomas and Frank Parker 1983. The duration of morphemic and non-morphemic /s/ in English. *Journal of Phonetics 11,* 201-206.

Yip, Moira 1993. Cantonese Loanword Phonology and Optimality Theory Journal of Phonetics. *Journal of Phonetics, 3.*

Local and Global Patterns of Temporal Compensations in Korean*

BYUNG-JIN LIM

Indiana University

1. Introduction

This paper presents experimental evidence concerning how temporal compensation for aspiration, tension and voicing occurs under V(C)CV environments, and how such compensation interacts with syllable structure in Korean. The main questions raised in this study are 1) whether different syllable structures affect how segmental material contributes to the durational patterns of neighboring segments, and if so, 2) how to characterize cross-syllabic durational effects. This paper also examines whether spoken syllabic structure is isomorphic with orthographic syllabic structure.

1.1 Compensation

It is our main concern to investigate dynamic patterns of temporal compensations around features (or contrasts) such as aspiration, tension, and voicing with respect to syllable structure. In a broad-sense, we use the term *'compensation'* when there is any trade-off observed in adjacent (or even

---

*
This paper has benefited from discussions with and comments from Ken de Jong, Stuart Davis, Minkyung Lee, Kwang-Chul Park, and Taehong Cho.

rather distant) segmental make-ups within a word. For example, intervocalic voicing of lax stops makes preceding vowel longer, which is compensated by following shorter stop closure duration. Figure 1 shows an illustration of this temporal modulation.

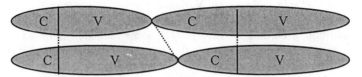

[Figure 1] A schematic illustration of compensation

Since the current study is concerned with how temporal compensation
for features (or contrasts) such as aspiration, voicing, and tension occurs in
V(C)CV environments, a comparison to CV prosodic positions is reasonable in the following subsection for further arguments.

1.2 Positional variants

It is quite a well-known fact that Korean has a three-way distinction in
stops, lax, tense and aspirated. It has been well documented that this three-
way contrast varies by prosodic positions impressionistically, acoustically,
and articulatorily. Impressionistic descriptions on positional variants of
Korean stops can be summarized as voicing-occurrence for lax stops and
some reductions in stops in VCV environments as shown in Table 1 (Martin, 1974; Kim-Renaud, 1974).

Stops	#CV	..VCV..
Lax	Small aspiration	Voiced
Tense	Long, emphatically pronounced	Reduction in tension
Aspirated	Heavily aspirated	Considerable reduction in aspiration

[Table 1] Positional variants: *Impression*

Previous durational studies of Korean stops have shown us a similar picture in general. For the duration of aspiration, Lisker and Abramson (1964)
report that there is a slight reduction for lax stops while tense stops show no
difference in aspiration between CV and VCV positions. For aspirated
stops, there is a significant reduction in aspiration as shown in Table 2.

Stops	#CV	..VCV..
Lax	32ms	26ms
Tense	13ms	13ms
Aspirated	105ms	82ms

[Table 2] Positional Variants: *Aspiration duration*

In addition, according to Silva (1992), some reduction is found in stop closure duration for lax stops while there seems to be no observable differences between CV and VCV for tense and aspirated stops as shown in Table 3[1].

Stops	#CV	..VCV..
Lax	66ms	48ms
Tense	104ms	103ms
Aspirated	85ms	84ms

[Table 3] Positional Variants: *Stop closure duration*

Finally, Kagaya (1974) reports that there are some differences in the glottal opening around stops between CV and VCV environments as shown in Table 4.

Stops	#CV	..VCV..
Lax	+	-
Tense	-	-
Aspirated	++	++

(+: open glottis, ++: larger opening than '+', -: closed glottis)
[Table 4] Positional variants: *Glottal width*

In sum, previous studies have shown a variation in how Korean stop contrasts are expressed, in terms of durational patterns of relevant articulators as well as acoustic parameters. In this paper, we will examine how these temporal differences affect surrounding segments.

1.3 What we are going to do
Previously, we have shown that only lax stops can be categorized as shortened and voiced intervocalically, which has been formalized as an intervo-

---

[1] Under a two-timing units analysis for tense stops in VCV environments (Silva, 1992; Han, 1996), there could be a significant reduction in stop closure for tense stops. Alternatively, if we follow 'domain-initial strengthening' (Fougeron & Keating, 1996), there could be rather a lengthening in stop closure under #CV environments compared to VCV environments. However, testing these two arguments is beyond the purpose of this paper.

calic voicing rule. This phonological rule is restricted in its application since it applies only to lax stops and only under VCV environments. In addition, the VCV environments also show various durational patterns in stop closure and aspiration for different stops. This paper investigates the dynamic modulation patterns in VCV environments of features (or contrasts) such as 'voicing', 'aspiration, and 'tension'. We also examine syllable structure. Intervocalic environments may have two possible syllable structures in Korean; 1) VCV and 2) VCCV. In the latter case, the addition of a second consonant also causes durational modulation, which will be called 'coda compensation' in this paper. The main questions addressed in this study are 1) whether different syllable structures affect how segmental material contributes to the durational patterns of neighboring segments, and if so, 2) how to characterize cross-syllabic durational effects. This study also questions whether spoken syllabic structure is isomorphic with orthographic syllabic structure in order to determine the fitness of boundary division imposed by traditional approaches.

2. Methods

In doing so, an experiment was carried out wherein 396 tokens of two-syllable non-sense words in various combinations of syllable types were produced by two native speakers of Standard Korean. To examine the temporal compensation of segments over a syllable boundary, the initial consonants of the second syllable were lax, tensed, and aspirated stops.

2.1 Recordings

Two native speakers (one male and one female) of Standard Korean were recorded in the Indiana University Phonetics Lab. Speakers were presented with a list of randomized 'words' to be produced. Prior to recordings, a practice session was given to familiarize each speaker with the task.

2.2 Stimuli

For stimuli, we used two-syllable nonce words varying in syllable structure with lax, tense, and aspirated stops as the initial consonant of the second syllable as shown in Table 5.

	Syllable structures	Some examples
Set 1	CV.CVC	na.ton na.t'on na.t^{h}on
Set 2	CVC.CVC	nan.ton nan.t'on nan.t^{h}on

[Table 5] Stimuli

2.3 Measurements

The timing of various points was obtained using *SoundScope* implemented on a Power Mac in the Indiana University Phonetics Lab. The duration of each segment was measured using broad band spectrogram and waveform displays. Syllables were divided into four intervals: closure duration, VOT, vowel duration, and a remaining portion. Figure 2 illustrates each measurement.

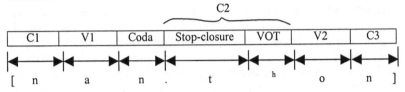

[Figure 2] Measurements

2.4 Hypotheses

With respect to segmental modulations next to a syllable boundary, there are three different compensatory patterns one might find. There are three possibilities illustrated in Figure 3. It could occur on the previous syllable or on the following syllable. Or it could occur on both syllables.

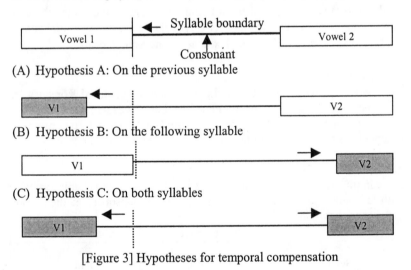

[Figure 3] Hypotheses for temporal compensation

These patterns in Figure 3 can be visualized in terms of segment durations, as plotted in Figure 4. Here, for example in (A), an increase in duration (filled bar) can be compensated by a decrease in previous (or following) segment durations.

(A) Uni-directionality

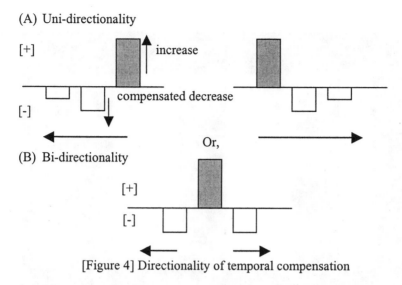

[Figure 4] Directionality of temporal compensation

3. Results

Figures 5(a-b) are proportional cumulative stack bars for speaker 1. Here durations are plotted as proportions of the word duration, starting from the bottom and reading upward.

(a)

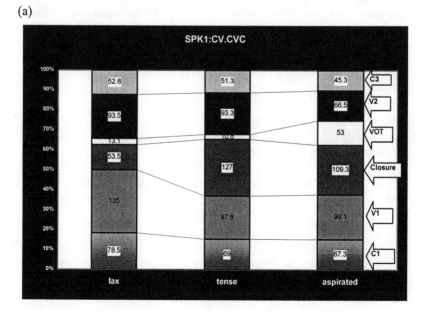

(b)

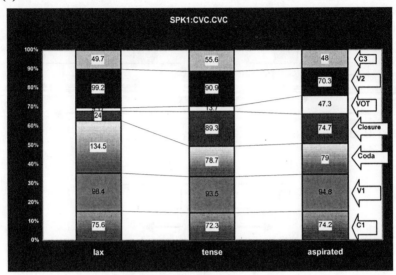

[Figure 5] Proportional durations for speaker 1

As shown in 5(a), the vowel duration (V1) before lax stops (left column) is significantly longer than before other stops. For stop closure duration, tense stops show the highest value, which is followed by aspirated stops, in turn, followed by lax stops. Aspirated stops show longer VOT durations than others. Of interest, the vowel duration after aspirated stops (V2) is noticeably shorter. These durational patterns are also shown in 5(b) except that V1s are the same before all stops. Here, the added coda segments vary by stop type instead.

3.1 Patterns of temporal compensation
Figure 6 plots mean differences in segment duration from regression analyses where segment durations were regressed against voicing. Here, like Figure 4, these figures plot the durational effect of putting a lax stop instead of a tense or aspirated stop. We separate syllable structures in 6(a) and 6(b).

(a) CV.CVC

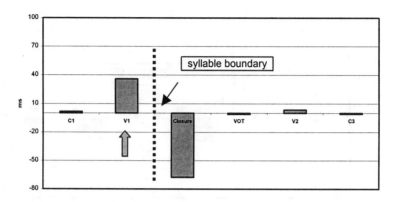

(b) CVC.CVC

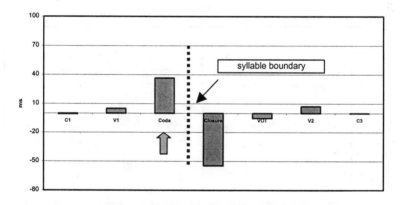

[Figure 6] Voicing compensation

As shown in 6(a), compensations are made cross-syllabic boundary; that is, there is an increase in V1 with a trade-off in the following stop closure duration. The same pattern is shown in 6(b) as well except that additional coda duration replaces the increase in V1 since they are closer to the syllable boundary.

In Figures 7(a-b), mean differences in segment duration were regressed against aspiration. As shown below, temporal modulation is made within the second syllable. Increased VOT indicates the presence of an aspirated stop. It is compensated by preceding stop closure and following vowel durations, both of which are in the same syllable as the increased VOT.

(a) CV.CVC

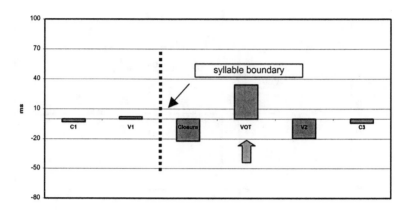

(b) CVC.CVC

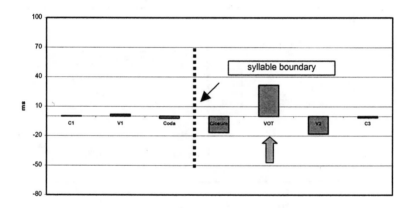

[Figure 7] Aspiration compensation

Let us turn to the compensational patterns for 'tension' as in Figure 8. Interestingly, the temporal compensation for tension is made both across and within syllables. Longer stop closures are compensated by shorter pre-ceding vowel duration (V1) in the previous syllable and shorter VOT in the same syllable.

(a) CV.CVC

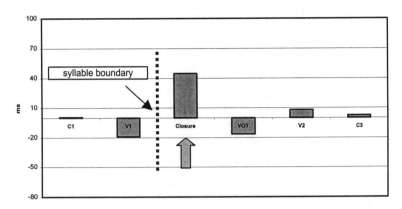

(b) CVC.CVC

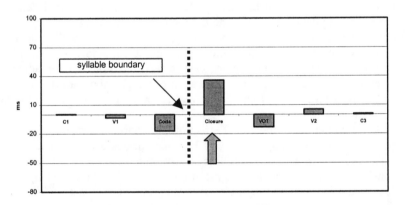

[Figure 8] Tension compensation

Finally, Figure 9 shows temporal compensation made for the addition of coda consonants, which is realized on the preceding syllable as well as on the following syllable. As shown in Figure 9, additional coda duration is compensated by neighboring segments: It is compensated by shorter preceding vowel duration (V1) and shorter stop closure duration.

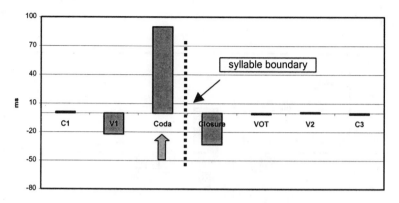

[Figure 9] Coda compensation

3.2 A consistency of segment timing

Results so far do not indicate any role for higher level prosody in durational patterning. Syllable boundaries do not seem to govern compensatory direction. Also, all temporal compensation appears to involve local compensation between neighboring segments. There are no cases in which introduction of temporal modulation in one place affects duration in a non-adjacent location. However, there is another way in which global organization might be involved in durational patterning, that is, in the results of the temporal changes.

If we intend to see the global effect of these various compensations, we should examine composite intervals between various events in successive syllables. If compensation produces constant intervals, one would expect a consistent ratio of a certain interval to a word to be unaffected by local segmental modification. Figure 10 shows a group of intervals one of which could be considered as an ideal candidate for projecting a consistency of segmental timing effects.

F: Word duration

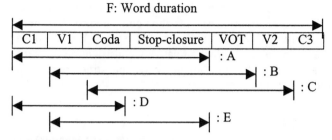

A: C1 onset to consonant release
B: V1 onset to V2 onset
C: V1 offset to V2 offset
D: Traditional (i.e., orthographic) syllable division
E: Consonant release to consonant release

[Figure 10] Candidates for a consistency of segmental timing

If local compensation contributes to global consistency in timing of one of the intervals shown above, we could expect that average interval would be the same under different conditions. One would also expect a relatively small amount of variation in the duration of this interval across the corpus.

(a)   (b)

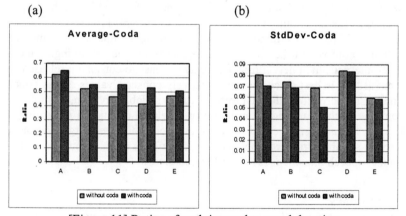

[Figure 11] Ratios of each interval to word duration

Figure 11(a) shows ratios of the intervals in Figure 10 to the total word duration. Intervals A, B, and E show pretty consistent ratios between words without codas and with codas.

Among these, interval E also exhibits less variation, as evident in a lower standard deviation in both word types as in 11(b). Orthographic interval (D) exhibits a lot of variation with a higher standard deviation, which indicates that the interval is strongly affected by addition of codas. On the other hand, interval E shows a relatively lower variation compared to other intervals. The whole picture in Figure 11 indicates that interval E (i.e., consonant release to consonant release) shows a relatively consistent ratio regardless of segmental addition, and that orthographic syllabic structure may not appropriate for projecting spoken syllabic structure.

4. Discussion

In this study, a connection is examined between contrasts (or features) and durational modulation in V(C)CV environments in Korean. Especially, voicing as contrast (Keating, 1984; Steriade, 1999 among others) shows complicated but dynamic temporal patterns in Korean. Systematic temporal adjustments around this contrast are realized cross-syllabically. It is alleged that a phonological intervocalic voicing rule for lax stops indicates categorical perception for this contrast. However, when we put this contrast into consideration observable only under the environments VCV which are redundant reservoirs in terms of perceptional cue recoverability (Wright, 1996), it is highly likely that a dynamic phonetic compromise is going on between the contrast and temporal compensation (Flemming, 1995). That is, there is a connection between a compromise of functional goals (*Maximization of the number of contrasts, Maximization of distinctiveness, and Minimization of articulatory effort*: Flemming, 1995) and hierarchy in perceptual cue recoverability (VCV >> CV>>VC: Wright, 1996).

In an effort to examine the global temporal compensation, intervals within a word were tested for consistency across segmental timing. Among other intervals, the interval from consonant release to consonant release (the interval 'E') is best since it shows relatively constant values across conditions. Compared to traditional (orthographic) syllabic division, this interval could be further pursued as an indicator of global durational patterning in Korean. This interval could be a testing ground for (re-) organization of internal syllable structure when we consider effects of paralinguistic factors such as speech rate changes (cf. de Jong, in press)

5. Summary

The present study confirms the previous studies in that vowel duration before tense and aspirated stops is shorter than before lax stops (Zhi, 1982; Choe & Jun, 1998). In addition, vowel duration tends to be shorter after aspirated stops (Zhi, 1982). There is also an inverse relationship in duration between VOT and following vowels (Roberts & Lee, 1997).

Results from the present study indicate local and global patterns of temporal compensation in Korean. That is, the current study shows local temporal compensation over a syllable boundary: e.g., if a preceding syllable is heavy (CVC), 1) the preceding vowel duration and 2) the closure duration of following stops are significantly shortened compared to where a light syllable (CV) precedes. It also shows global temporal compensation within a word: vowel duration of heavy syllable seems to be shorter than that of light syllable due to the Closed Syllable Vowel Shortening (Maddieson, 1985). However, this shortening does not affect the portion of the word and between the two consonantal releases.

References

Choe, S. W. and J. H. Jun. 1998. Are Korean Tense and Aspirated stops Geminates?: Based on Closed Syllable Vowel Shortening (written in Korean). *Ohakyongu* 34. Vol. 3: 521-546.

Flemming, E. S. 1995. *Auditory Representation in Phonology.* Doctoral dissertation, UCLA.

de Jong, K. J. in press. Effects of Syllable Affiliation and Consonant Voicing on Temporal Adjustments in a Repetitive Speech Production Task. *Papers in Laboratory Phonology VI*. Cambridge: Cambridge Univ. Press.

Fougeron, C. and P. A. Keating. 1996. Variations in Velic and Lingual Articulation Depending on Prosodic Position: Results for Two French Speakers. *UCLA Working Papers in Phonetics* 92: 88-96.

Han, J. I. 1996. *The Phonetics and Phonology of "Tense" and "Plain" Consonants in Korean.* Doctoral dissertation, Cornell University

Kagaya, R. 1974. A Fiberscopic and Acoustic Study of the Korean Stops, Affricates, and Fricatives. *Journal of Phonetics* 2: 161-180.

Keating, P. A. 1984. Phonetic and Phonological Representatioins of Stop Consonants. *Language* 60: 286-319.

Lisker, L. and A. S. Abramson. 1964. A Cross-Linguistic Study of Voicing in Initial Stops: Acoustical Measurements. *Word* 20: 384-422.

Maddieson, I. 1985. Phonetic Cues to Syllabification. *Phonetic linguistics: Essays in honor of Peter Ladefoged*, edited by V. Fromkin, 203-21. Orlando: Academic Press.

Martin, S. E. 1974. Korean Reference Grammar. Unpublished manuscript, Yale University.

Kim-Renaud, Y. K. 1974. *Korean Consonantal Phonology.* Doctoral dissertation, University of Hawaii.

Roberts, E. W. and K. J. Lee. 1997. VOT in Korean with Particular Reference to CV Transition and Phonological Segmentation. *SICOL '97*: 256-265.

Silva, D. J. 1992. *The Phonetics and Phonology of Stop Lenition in Korean.* Doctoral dissertation, Cornell University.

Steriade, D. 1999. Paradigm Uniformity and the Phonetics-Phonology Boundary. In M. Broe and J. B. Pierrehumbert (eds.), *Papers in Laboratory Phonology V:* 313-334. Cambridge: Cambridge Univ. Press.

Wright, R. A. 1996. *Consonant Clusters and Cue Preservation in Tsou.* Doctoral dissertation, UCLA.

Zhi, M. J. 1982. Studies on the Phonetics of Korean Obstruents. *Essay* 10, Dept. of Phonetics. Umea University.

Prosody and Information Structure in Japanese: A Case Study of Topic Marker *wa*[1]

Kimiko Nakanishi
University of Pennsylvania

1. Introduction

Languages have various ways of expressing the information structure. It is generally assumed that there are mainly three means, i.e., phonological, syntactic, and morphological (de Sward and de Hoop 1995). In Japanese, it is well known that various syntactic and morphological means can be used to convey different information (Kuno 1973, Shibatani 1990, among others). It is not clear, however, to what extent phonological means alone can express information structure in Japanese. There are some previous studies which suggest that Japanese uses phonology for this purpose. For example, Pierrehumbert and Beckman (1988) have shown that, in Japanese, 'pitch range can be expanded on individual lexically specified pitch accents to convey focus or emphasis effects similar to those conveyed by postlexical pitch accents in languages like English' (cited in Ladd 1998:195). However, it seems that Japanese uses fewer phonological means than other languages because of its rich syntactic and morphological means. In other words, the

[1] I would like to thank Mark Liberman, Kazuaki Maeda, John Bell, and Eon-Suk Ko for valuable discussions and their insights. Thanks are also due to Gene Buckley, Rolf Noyer, Ellen Prince, and Chulwoo Park for their helpful comments.

morphological and syntactic means of Japanese are so rich that conveying information structure by phonological means might not be as effective as in other languages. Although there are many cases where phonological effects seem to change the information structure, they may be merely a side-effect of morphological or syntactic means, given that these means are used at the same time in most cases. For example, in a language with free word order such as Japanese, different information can be conveyed by different word orders without using phonological means *per se*, although prosodic change is likely to be observed along with the word order change. On the other hand, in English, for example, phonological means are more likely to be used given that the word order is relatively rigid.[2]

In this paper, I address the question of whether the information structure in Japanese is influenced by phonology in significant way. I conduct experiments and a corpus study of the prosodic pattern of the topic marker *wa*, which is claimed to have two discourse functions: thematic and contrastive. Although syntactic and morphological means cannot distinguish these functions, I show that the two functions are realized by different prosodic patterns. Based on this finding, I conclude that Japanese crucially uses phonological means, specifically prosody, to express information structure independently of syntax and morphology.

The structure of the paper is as follows: in section 2, I summarize two functions of *wa*, namely, thematic *wa* and contrastive *wa*, proposed by Kuno (1972, 1973). In section 3, I briefly describe the phonology and phonetics of Japanese. In section 4, I give the methodology and results of the two kinds of experiments I conducted and also a corpus study. Section 5 is the conclusion.

2. Two Functions of *wa*: Thematic and Contrastive *wa*

It is well known that Japanese uses morphological markers to encode information structure. In particular, the topic marker *wa* plays a crucial role to convey pragmatically different information. The most widely accepted view of the functions of *wa* is presented in Kuno (1972,1973):

(1) *Wa* marks either the theme or the contrasted element of the sentence. The theme must be either anaphoric (i.e. previously mentioned) or generic, while there is no such constraint for the contrasted element. (Kuno 1972:270)

---

[2] For various languages which use phonological means to convey information structure, see Bolinger (1965), Halliday (1967), Jackendoff (1972), Lambrecht (1994), Hirst and Di Cristo (1998), and Ladd (1998).

The two functions of *wa* are defined as follows:[3,4]

(2) a. *wa* for the theme of a sentence: "Speaking of ..., talking about ..."
    John-wa   gakusei desu.
    John-TOP student is
       'Speaking of John, he is a student.'
  b. *wa* for contrasts: "X ... , but ... , as for X ..."
    John-wa sono hon-o   yon-da   ga Mary-wa yoma-nakat-ta.
    John-TOP that book-ACC read-PAST but Mary-TOP read-NEG-PAST
       'John read the book, but Mary didn't.'   (Kuno 1973)

The theme must be either generic or anaphoric:

(3) a. *Generic NP*
    Kuzira-wa honyuudoobutu-desu.
    whale-TOP mammal-be
       'Speaking of whales, they are mammals.' 'A whale is a mammal.'
  b. *Anaphoric NP*[5]
    Futari-wa party-ni kimasi-ta.
    two-TOP party-to come-PAST
       'Speaking of the two persons (under discussion), they came to
       the party.'   (Kuno 1973:ex.17)

The contrastive *wa*, as opposed to the thematic *wa*, has no such restriction: it can be generic, anaphoric, or neither.

(4) a. *Generic NP*
    Kuzira-wa honyuudoobutu-desu ga, sake-wa   chigai-masu.
    whale-TOP mammal-be   but salmon-TOP different-be
       'A whale is a mammal, but a salmon is not.'

---

[3] In this paper, the following abbreviations are used: ACC=accusative, GEN=genitive, NEG=negation, NOM=nominative, PAST=past tense, PROG=progressive, Q=question, TOP=topic marker.

[4] If the topic marker is attached to a non-subject element, there is a strong preference for the contrastive reading (cf. Choi 1996). This is probably because a non-subject element is usually not a theme of a sentence. The subject, on the other hand, is naturally understood as a theme, and neither the thematic or contrastive reading is preferred. For this reason, I consider only the cases in which the topic marker is attached to the subject.

[5] An anaphoric NP, for Kuno (1972, 1973), simply means that the relevant NP was previously mentioned.

b. *Anaphoric NP*
Futari-wa party-ni kimasi-ta   ga Tim-wa   kimas-en-desita.
two-TOP party-to come-PAST but Tim-TOP come-NEG-PAST
'Two persons (under discussion) came to the party, but Tim didn't.'
c. *Non-generic, Non-anaphoric NP*   (Kuno 1973:ex.21)
Oozei-no   hito-wa   paatii-ni kimasi-ta   ga
many-GEN people-TOP party-to come-PAST but
omosiroi hito-wa   hitori   mo   imas-en-desita.
interesting people-TOP one-person even be-NEG-PAST
'Many people came to the party indeed, but there was none
who was interesting.'

As we can see in (3a-b) and (4a-b), if the subject is generic or anaphoric
NP, the sentence can be ambiguous among thematic and contrastive readings. The subject in (3a-b) is most naturally interpreted as theme, whereas
the subject in (4a-b) is interpreted as contrast. Note that the two functions of
the topic marker are identical in surface. In other words, morphology and
syntax cannot distinguish these two functions.[6]

3. Phonology and Phonetics of Japanese

The word level prosody of Japanese is known to have a pitch-accent system.
In this system, some words can be distinguished only by accent. The location of the accent corresponds to the mora before the pitch drop, i.e., the
accent is on the H immediately before L (Haraguchi 1999). Accents of
words are partly determined by rules of word-level phonology (McCawley
1968, Haraguchi 1977, Poser 1984).[7]

(5)   ⌐   ⌐⌐   ⌐
    a. kaki-ga   b. kaki-ga   c. kaki-ga
       oyster-NOM   fence-NOM   persimmon-NOM

Furthermore, Japanese shows Downstep: 'a change in pitch register
which is manifested as a marked lowering in the stretch of an utterance following an accented syllable' (Selkirk and Tateishi 1991:519).[8]

---

[6] By claiming that syntax cannot distinguish the two functions of *wa*, I simply mean that there
are no overt syntactic differences, such as word order difference, used to distinguish the two
functions. In other words, I do *not* mean that the underlying syntactic structures are necessarily
the same. For this issue, see Nakanishi (in prep).

[7] '⌐' marks a low-high sequence of pitch, and '⌐' marks a high-low sequence of pitch.

[8] See Poser 1984, Pierrehumbert and Beckman 1988, and Kubozono 1993 for a detailed discussion of Downstep.

Poser (1984) claims that 'the topic phrase (marked by the particle *wa*) is generally set off from the rest of the sentence by a major phrase boundary,[9] as indicated by the fact that it seems to have no effect on the following material' (1984:101).

However, no prosodic distinctions are made between thematic *wa* and contrastive *wa*.[10,11] Thus the question is whether the prosodic patterns of thematic *wa* and of contrastive *wa* are the same, which I explore at the rest of the paper.

4. Experiments and Corpus Study

4.1. Methods

Two experiments and a corpus study were conducted to examine the prosodic patterns of thematic and contrastive *wa*. For this purpose, I used the Fundamental Frequency (F_0) contour. F_0 is 'the number of times per second that the vocal folds complete a cycle of vibration' (Clark and Yallop 1995:332). Specifically, I measured the value of the F_0 peak immediately before and after *wa*. P1 is the value of F_0 peak immediately before *wa*, and P2 is the value of F_0 peak immediately after *wa*.

---

[9] 'Major phrase' is the phonological domain over which Downstep applies. For how to determine Major Phrases, see Selkirk and Tateishi (1991).

[10] Although the interpretation of Poser's (1984) analysis is oversimplified, suffice it to say here that he does not make any distinction between thematic *wa* and contrastive *wa*. See Poser (1984) for a comprehensive discussion.

[11] Finn (1984) did experimental studies on the prosody of the thematic *wa* and contrastive *wa*, and showed that these two types were differentiated by pauses as well as fundamental frequency (F_0). Her claim is based on experimental studies in which she measured the peak of F_0 contours before *wa* and the valley F_0 of *wa*, and also the pause between *wa* and the following word. Her experimental methods, however, are problematic; unfortunately, I do not have space to discuss them here.

4.2. Experiments

4.2.1. First Experiment: without Context

For these experiments, constructed examples were used. The structure of the examples is 'Subject-*wa* Predicate', with an anaphoric subject allowing ambiguity between thematic and contrastive readings. The subject and the verb are three or more moras, accented, and nasals or glides in accented positions.[12] Following are the examples used for the first experiment:

(6) *Thematic*

    a. Naoya-wa   nonbiri-site-imasu.[13]
       Naoya-TOP relax-do-PROG
        'Naoya is relaxing.'

    b. Maria-wa   nonbiri-site-imas-en.
       Maria-TOP relax-do-PROG-NEG
        'Maria is not relaxing.'

(7) *Contrastive*

    a. Naoya-wa   nonbiri-site-imasu ga Maria-wa nonbiri-site-imas-en.
       Naoya-TOP relax-do-PROG   but Maria-TOP relax-do-PROG-NEG
        'Naoya is relaxing, but Maria is not relaxing.'

    b. Maria-wa nonbiri-site-imas-en ga Naoya-wa nonbiri-site-imasu.
       Maria-TOP relax-do-PROG-NEG but Naoya-TOP relax-do-PROG
        'Maria is not relaxing, but Naoya is relaxing.'

Two native speakers of Japanese, Subjects KM (male) and RN (female), were Subjects in the first experiment. Four cards on each of which one sentence in (6) and (7) was written were provided to the Subjects. The Subjects were asked to read sentences on each card aloud five times with an interval of a few seconds between each sentence. They are also asked to read sentences in a natural speed without any pause inside of each sentence.

First, let us examine the difference in F_0 contour. Data 1 are the F_0 contour of the thematic and the contrastive *wa* taken from Subject KM (male).

---

[12] Nasals and glides exhibit smoother F_0 contours than other consonants or voiced segments, without being disturbed much by segmental effects.

[13] The predicate *nonbiri-site-iru* can describe either the current state or the permanent state. For example, (7a) is ambiguous between 'Naoya is currently taking a rest' and 'Naoya is a laid-back person'. In this study, only the first meaning is considered.

Data 1. F_0 Contour of Thematic *wa* and Contrastive *wa*[14]
Above: Thematic *wa*: Subject KM (male)
Below: Contrastive *wa*: Subject KM (male)

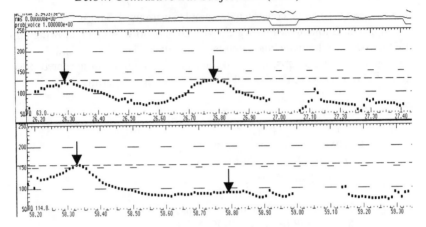

When *wa* is contrastive, P2 is much lower than P1 (P1: 159.7, P2: 91.0 in Data 1). When *wa* is thematic, on the other hand, P2 is slightly higher than P1 (P1: 127.7, P2: 129.9 in Data 1), or may be slightly lower than P1 (P1: 124.5, P2: 123.6, for example). A similar result is obtained from Subject RN (female). The distribution of the thematic and the contrastive cases are given in Chart 1:

Chart 1. Distribution of Thematic *wa* and Contrastive *wa*[15]
a. Subject KM (male)   b. Subject RN (female)

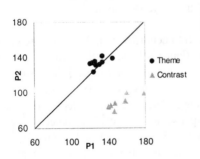
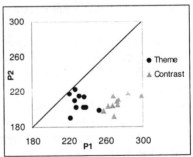

---

[14] The first and second arrows in the F_0 contour indicate P1 and P2, respectively.
[15] In the following charts, the line expresses 'x=y'.

In sum, when *wa* is contrastive, P2 is much lower than P1. When *wa* is thematic, on the other hand, P2 is only slightly lower than P1, or may even be higher than P1.

4.2.2. Second Experiment: with Context

There is a potential problem in the first experiment: without a context, each speaker may understand the information status of the subject and the verb differently (cf. Prince 1981, 1992) and it may influence the prosodic pattern. To avoid this problem, in the second experiment, examples were constructed along with a context. Specifically, I constructed a question sentence for each test sentence, such that the test sentence is an appropriate answer to the question. In this way, the information status of the subject and the verb can be controlled. The subject of the test sentence always appears in the question, i.e., the subject is always anaphoric. The verb is either anaphoric (i.e., mentioned in the question), or non-anaphoric (not mentioned in the question). The answer sentences are the same as the sentences used in the first experiment.

(8) *Thematic 1*
   a. Naoya-wa   heya-de nani-o   site-imasu-ka?
      Naoya-TOP room-in what-ACC do-PROG-Q
      'What is Naoya doing in the room?'

   ⌐‾   ⌐‾ ⌐‾
   b. Naoya-wa   nonbiri-site-imasu.
      Naoya-TOP relax-do-PROG
      'Naoya is relaxing.'

(9) *Thematic 2*
   a. Naoya-wa   heya-de nonbiri-site-imasu-ka?
      Naoya-TOP room-in relax-do-PROG-Q
      'Is Naoya relaxing in the room?'

   ⌐‾ ⌐‾   ⌐‾ ⌐‾
   b. Hai, Naoya-wa   nonbiri-site-imasu.
      yes Naoya-TOP relax-do-PROG
      'Yes, Naoya is relaxing.'

(10) *Thematic 3*
   a. Maria-wa   heya-de nonbiri-site-imasu-ka?
      Maria-TOP room-in relax-do-PROG-Q
      'Is Maria relaxing in the room?'

   ⌐‾   ⌐‾ ⌐
   b. Iie, Maria-wa   nonbiri-site-imas-en.
      no   Maria-TOP relax-PROG-NEG
      'No, Maria is not relaxing.'

(11) *Contrastive 1*

    a. Naoya-to   Maria-wa   heya-de nani-o   site-imasu-ka?
       Naoya-and Maria-TOP room-in what-ACC do-PROG-Q
       'What are Naoya and Maria doing in the room?'

    b. Naoya-wa   nonbiri-site-imasu ga Maria-wa nonbiri-site-imas-en.
       Naoya-TOP relax-do-PROG   but Maria-TOP relax-do-PROG-NEG
       'Naoya is relaxing, but Maria is not relaxing.'

(12) *Contrastive 2*

    a. Naoya-to   Maria-wa   heya-de nonbiri-site-imasu-ka?
       Naoya-and Maria-TOP room-in relax-do-PROG-Q
       'Are Naoya and Maria relaxing in the room?'

    b. Naoya-wa   nonbiri-site-imasu ga Maria-wa nonbiri-site-imas-en.
       Naoya-TOP relax-do-PROG but Maria-TOP relax-do-PROG-NEG
       'Naoya is relaxing, but Maria is not relaxing.'

The second experiment involved eight native speakers of Japanese: Subjects KI (male), KO (male), TM (male), YG (male), SN (female), NO (female), YU (female), MA (female). Five cards on which each question-answer pair in (8-12) was written were provided to the Subjects. The Subjects were asked to read both question and answer on each card aloud twice with an interval of a few seconds between sentences. The Subjects were also asked to read sentences in a natural speed without any pause inside of each sentence. There were three sessions per Subject.

Let us examine the F_0 contours taken from Subject SN (female):

Data 2. F_0 Contour of Thematic *wa* and Contrastive *wa* with Context
      Above: Thematic *wa*: Subject SN (female)
      Below: Contrastive *wa*: Subject SN (female)

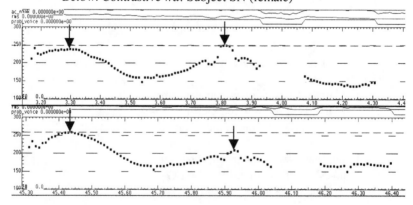

In the thematic case, P2 is higher than P1 (P1: 238.4, P2: 249.6 in Data 2). In some cases, P1 is higher than P2 (P1: 235.5, P2: 230.5, for example). In the contrastive case, P1 is again higher than P2 (P1: 259.4, P2: 209.4 in Data 2), but the difference is much larger than the thematic example. Other Subjects show the same tendency.

The distributions of the thematic and the contrastive *wa* are given below. When *wa* is contrastive, P2 is significantly lower than P1. When *wa* is thematic, on the other hand, P2 ranges between slightly lower than P1 to higher than P1.

Chart 2. Distribution of Thematic *wa* and Contrastive *wa* with Context[16]

a. Male Total (left: Thematic *wa*, right: Contrastive *wa*)

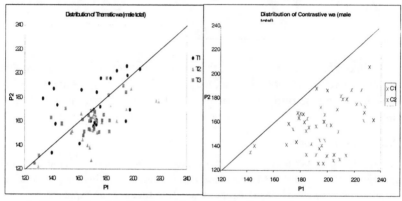

b. Female Total (left: Thematic *wa*, right: Contrastive *wa*)

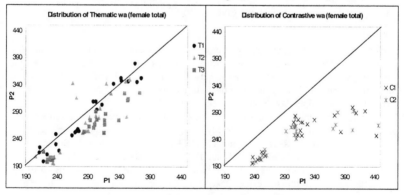

[16] T1, T2, T3, C1, and C2, in the charts mean Thematic 1, Thematic 2, Thematic 3, Contrastive 1, and Contrastive 2 in examples (8)-(12).

c. Total

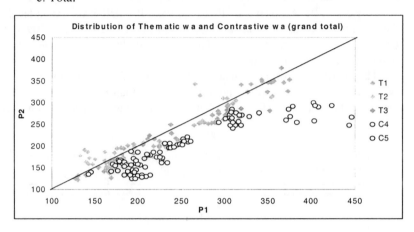

Although, for some speakers, the prosodic patterns of thematic *wa* and of contrastive *wa* are not clear-cut, the results here show the same tendency overall: in the case of the thematic *wa*, the difference between P1 and P2 is not as large as the difference in the case of the contrastive *wa*.[17]

4.3. Corpus Study

As follow-up, I examined a speech corpus called 'Callhome Japanese' and its transcripts available at Linguistic Data Consortium. This corpus consists of telephone conversations between two native speakers of Japanese.[18]

Ten examples (five thematic, five contrastive) are taken from two female speakers.[19] Examples are given below:

---

[17] Each Subject seems to show different prosodic patterns among Thematic 1, 2, and 3 and also among Contrastive 1 and 2. However, when the results of all Subjects are combined, there is no straightforward pattern to distinguish between Thematic 1, 2, and 3, and also between Contrastive 1 and 2. I leave this issue for the further study.

[18] The detailed description of the corpus is cited below:

The CallHome Japanese corpus of telephone speech was collected and transcribed by the Linguistic Data Consortium primarily in support of the project on Large Vocabulary Conversational Speech Recognition (LVCSR), sponsored by the U.S. Department of Defense. This release of the CallHome Japanese corpus consists of 120 unscripted telephone conversations between native speakers of Japanese. The transcripts cover a contiguous 5 or 10 minute segment taken from a recorded conversation lasting up to 30 minutes. All speakers were aware that they were being recorded. They were given no guidelines concerning what they should talk about. Once a caller was recruited to participate, he/she was given a free choice of whom to call. Most participants called family members or close friends overseas. All calls originated in North America.

(cited from http://www.ldc.upenn.edu/ldc/about/chjapanese.html)

[19] The two speakers have similar pitch levels.

(13) *Thematic*

[Speakers A and B are complaining about the bad manners of the taxi driver, with whom B talked the other day.]

            ⌐ ⌐   ⌐   ⌐
Speaker A: Mukoo-wa   syoobai-desyo ...
          the other party-TOP business-be
          'For him, it's his job ...'

(14) *Contrastive*

[Speaker B recently went back to Japan. B says that nothing is particularly exciting to be back.]

        ⌐   ⌐ ⌐
Speaker B: Gohan-toka-wa oishii-kedo ...
          food-etc.-TOP good-although ...
          'Although food etc. is good ...'

The results from the corpus study agree with the findings in the experiments. As can be seen in Data 3, in the thematic case, P1 and P2 are about the same value (P1: 213.4, P2: 200.9 in Data 3). In the contrastive case, P1 is much higher than P2 (P1: 290.6, P2: 157.8 in Data 3).

Data 3. F_0 Contour of Thematic *wa* and Contrastive *wa*
        Above: Thematic *wa*: Speaker B (female)
        Below: Contrastive *wa*: Speaker B (female)

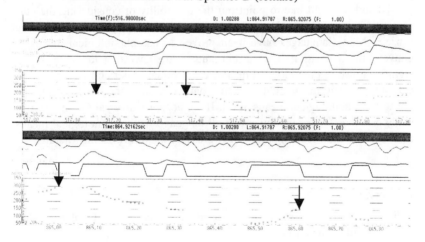

Chart 3. Distribution of Thematic *wa* and Contrastive *wa* in Corpus

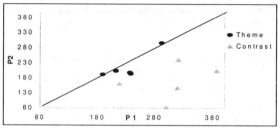

5. Discussion

In this paper, I examined the F_0 contour of thematic *wa* and contrastive *wa* by conducting two experiments and a corpus study. I found that these two cases of *wa* are realized differently with respect to prosody: when *wa* marks theme, the highest value of F_0 contour after *wa* (P2) is as high as or even higher than the highest value before *wa* (P1). When *wa* marks contrast, on the other hand, P2 is much lower than P1. Thus, in the case of contrastive *wa*, there is a dramatic drop of F_0 contour, which makes prominent the element to which *wa* is attached. Given that syntax or morphology cannot distinguish two functions of *wa*, prosody alone significantly expresses the information structure. In other words, the present study has shown that Japanese makes crucial use phonological means as well as syntactic and morphological means to convey the information structure.

To end, I would like to point out the possibility of considering the current findings as a contribution to language universality in the following sense.[20] Many languages have been proved to use phonological means to convey the information. The current study had shown that Japanese makes significant use of phonological means, even though it is rich in morphological and syntactic means. On the other hand, no language has been proved not to use phonological means at all. If we accept Universal Grammar, this study provides further evidence that all languages have phonological means as one of the significant methods of expressing the information structure.

References

Bolinger, D. 1965. *Forms of English: Accent, Morpheme, Order*. Cambridge: Harvard University Press.

Choi, H.-W. 1996. Topic and focus in Korean: The information partition by phrase structure and morphology. Japanese/Korean Linguistics 6, 545-561.

---

[20] I thank Rolf Noyer for discussion on Universal Grammar.

Clark, J., and C. Yallop. 1995. *An Introduction to Phonetics and Phonology.* Cambridge: Blackwell.

Finn, A.N. 1984. Intonational accompaniments of Japanese morphemes *wa* and *ga*. *Language and Speech* 27:1, 47-57.

Halliday, M.A.K. 1967. Notes on transitivity and theme in English, part II. *Journal of Linguistics* 3, 199-244.

Haraguchi, S. 1977. *The Tone Pattern of Japanese: An Autosegmental Theory of Tonology.* Tokyo: Kaitakusha.

Haraguchi, S. 1999. Accent. In N. Tsujimura ed., *An Introduction to Japanese Linguistics*, 1-61. Cambridge: Blackwell.

Hirst, D., and A. Di Cristo. 1998. *Intonation Systems: A Survey of Twenty Languages.* Cambridge: Cambridge University Press.

Jackendoff, R. 1972. *Semantic Interpretation in Generative Grammar.* Cambridge: MIT Press.

Kubozono, H. 1993. *The Organization of Japanese Prosody.* Tokyo: Kuroshio.

Kuno, S. 1972. Functional sentence perspective -- a case study from Japanese and English. *Linguistic Inquiry* 3, 269-320.

Kuno, S. 1973. *The Structure of the Japanese Language.* Cambridge: MIT Press.

Ladd, R. 1996. *Intonational Phonology.* Cambridge: Cambridge University Press.

Lambrecht, K. 1994. *Information Structure and Sentence Form: Topic, Focus and the Mental Representations of Discourse Referents.* Cambridge: Cambridge University Press.

McCawley, J. 1968. *The Phonological Component of a Grammar of Japanese.* Hague: Mouton.

Nakanishi, K. in prep. Prosodic patterns of the Topic Marker *wa* in Japanese and its Implication for the Syntactic Structure. Ms. University of Pennsylvania.

Poser, W. 1984. The Phonetics and phonology of tone and intonation in Japanese. Ph.D. dissertation, MIT.

Pierrehumbert, J., and M. Beckman. 1988. *Japanese Tone Structure.* Cambridge: MIT Press.

Prince, E. 1981. Toward a taxonomy of given/new information. In P. Cole ed., *Radical Pragmatics*, 223-254. NY: Academic Press.

Prince, E. 1992. The ZPG letter: subjects, definiteness, and information-status. In W. Mann and S. Thompson eds., *Discourse Description: Diverse Linguistic Analyses of a Fund-raiding Text*, 295-325. Philadelphia: John Benjamins.

Selkirk, E., and K. Tateishi. 1991. Syntax and downstep in Japanese. In C. Georgopoulos and R. Ishihaha eds., *Interdisciplinary Approaches to Language: Essays in Honor of S.-Y. Kuroda*, 519-543. Dordrecht: Kluwer.

Shibatani, M. 1990. *The Languages of Japan.* Cambridge: Cambridge University Press.

de Swart, H. and H. de Hoop 1995. Topic and focus. *GLOT International* 1:7, 3-7.

Part V

Syntax and Semantics

Information Unpackaging: A Constraint-based Unified Grammar Approach to Topic-Focus Articulation

SUK-JIN CHANG
Seoul National University

1. Introduction

The process of information unpackaging starts with its antithesis, information packaging, which is traditionlly referred to as topic-focus articulation (TFA, hereafter), a discourse-functional notion of the Prague School.* Taking the process of TFA as given (or generated), information unpackaging, as conceived of and concerned with here, proceeds to (i) the structural description of the interface between TFA and stress and (ii) dialog analysis from the perspective of TFA. The two-step process of information unpackaging is carried out in the framework of Constraint-based Unified Grammar of Korean (CUG/K) (Chang 1994, 1999, Chang and Choe 1993). A four-level stress system for spoken Korean, interacting with the discourse-functional structure of TFA and contrastiveness, is presented as a default constraint on the prosody-pragmatics interface.

CUG(/K) is an outgrowth of HPSG, and as such, it is (i) sign-theoretic, (ii) type-hierarchical, (iii) feature-structured, and (iv) lexicon-oriented; furthermore, it is discourse-interpretive. It is conceived of as

---
*I would like to thank the following for their helpful comments and suggestions: Choe Jae-woong, Kim Jong-Hyun, Lee Chungmin, Lee Hyunoo, Lee Ik-hwan, Lee Kiyong, Park Byung Soo, Ryu Byong-Rae, Yoo Eun-Jung.

a set of constraints on signs, the realizations of form and meaning in the Saussurean sense. Signs are formalized as typed feature structures and organized hierarchically with overridable default constraints. CUG starts out at the lexicon, ending up with discourse and its analysis. It encompasses prosody and pragmatics—two peripheral and grey areas of grammar.

After an overview of the feature structures of prosody and pragmatics (Section 2), their interface is disclosed and specified in the form of AVM (attribute-value matrix) (Section 3), and two short dialog exchanges are unpacked and analyzed (Section 4). Prospects for CUG are listed in the closing remarks (Section 5) and some conventions and principles of CUG/K are attached as an appendix.

2. Prosody and Pragmatics: Feature Structures

A sign has two immediate subtypes: lexical sign and phrase. The lexical sign is further subdivided into two types, lexeme and word (Sag and Wasow 1999:359). The two topmost attributes of a sign are PPM and SSP. According to the convention of type hierarchy inheritance with default constraints (Carpenter 1992, Lascarides and Copestake 1998) words and phrases inherit the feature structure of their supertype *sign*.[1]

(1) Type *sign*:

$$
\begin{bmatrix}
sign \\
\text{PPM} \begin{bmatrix} ppm \\ \text{PROS} & pros \\ \text{PHON} & \text{list}(phon\text{-}form) \\ \text{MORPH} & morph \end{bmatrix} \\
\text{SSP} \begin{bmatrix} ssp \\ \text{SYN} & syn \\ \text{SEM} & sem \\ \text{PRA} & pra \end{bmatrix}
\end{bmatrix}
$$

---

[1] Abbreviations: PPM=phonology-prosody-morphology, SSP=syntax-semantics-pragmatics, PROS=prosody, PHON=phonology, MORPH=morphology, SYN=syntax, SEM=semantics, PRA=pragmatics. Names of types are written in italics.

Pragmatics, a subtype of *ssp*, is posited to have the feature structure consisting of three attributes, SA, DF and BKG. TFA, along with POV and CTR, is an attribute of DF.

(2) Pragmatics[2]

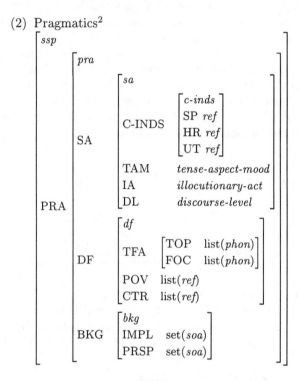

Prosody is assumed to have two features, TC (terminal contour) and STR (stress), their values ranging over as indicated in (3).

(3) Prosody

$$
\begin{bmatrix}
ppm \\
PROS \begin{bmatrix} pros \\ TC & \langle \searrow, \rightarrow, \nearrow \rangle \\ STR & \langle 0,1,2,3 \rangle \end{bmatrix}
\end{bmatrix}
$$

---

[2]SA=Speech-Act, C-INDS=Contextual-Indices, SP=Speaker, HR=Hearer, UT=Utterance-Time, TAM=Tense-Aspect-Mood, IA=Illocutionary-Act, DL=Discourse-Level, DF=Discourse-Function, POV=Point-Of-View, CTR-Center, BKG=Background, PRSP=Presupposition, IMPL=Implicature, ref=referent, soa=state-of-affairs

TC's value is based on the research reported in Chung et al. (1998), in which nine IP (intonational phrase) boundary tones are presented as basic. Their three tones, HL%, H% and LH%, represented respectively as ↘, →, ↗ in (3), are selected as distinctive in CUG/K.

Setting up a four-level stress system is based on the experiments by Chung and Kenstowicz (1997) and Lee and Kim (1997). Following Chung and Kenstowicz (1997:102), I assume stress to be the phonological correlates of focus. And their measures of fundamental frequencies (F_0) of the two APs (accentual phrases)[3] <Unhi-ka> (narrow focus) and <Unhi-nun> (contrastive focus) indicate that the amount of F_0 increase from the initial L to the peak in the latter is saliently greater than that in the former, as shown in the following figure.

(4) Narrow Focus vs. Contrastive Focus

    a. *Unhi-ka* (Narrow Focus)   b. *Unhi-nun* (Contrastive Focus)

Both APs belong to the so-called B-type (LH) accent of English (Jackendoff 1972, Pierrehumbert and Hirschberg 1990), which means they cannot be distinguished in terms of the A- or B-accent. In CUG/K, these two APs are kept apart by distinct values of the feature stress [4]

3.   Prosody-Pragmatics Interface

The four-level stress – <0, 1, 2, 3 > – is interfaced with TFA in the following way: Stress-0 is correlated to zero topic, Stress-1 to thematic topic, Stress-2 to narrow focus and Stress-3 to contrastive topic or contrastive focus. They are default constraints and overridable, depending on discourse situations.

---

[3] AP is the basic tonal unit and its basic pattern is LH in spoken Korean (Jun 1993). The syntactic counterpart of the prosodic unit of AP is NP (e.g. <Mia-ka/lul/nun> (Mia-Subj/Obj/Top-marker), or PP <Mia-eykey/lopwuthe> ('Mia-to/from')).

[4] Correlates: Stress - TFA - F_0

STRESS	0	1	2	3
TFA	Zero Topic	Topic	Narrow Focus	Contrastive Focus/Topic
(Abbr.)	(t_0)	(t)	(f)	(f_c/t_c)
F_0(Hz)		297	314	335

The F_0 values are those averaged over from the findings in Chung and Kenstowicz (1997).

Contrastiveness is a speaker-oriented notion. It arises from the speaker's choice of some constituent(s) out of a contrast set he has explicitly or implicitly in mind. Topics are inherently contrastive but foci may as well. In CUG, the speaker's contrastive response to the hearer's inactivated knowledge base at the time of his inquiry, is interpreted as focal; his contrastive response to the hearer's activated knowledge base as topical.[5]

(5) a. Topic and Stress

    i. Zero Topic (t_0)

$$\begin{bmatrix} \text{STR} & \langle 0 \rangle \\ \text{PHON} & \langle \boxed{1} \rangle \\ \text{TFA} & \begin{bmatrix} \text{TOP} \langle \boxed{1} \rangle \end{bmatrix} \end{bmatrix}$$

    ii. (Themaitc) Topic (t)

$$\begin{bmatrix} \text{STR} & \langle 1 \rangle \\ \text{PHON} & \langle \boxed{1} \rangle \\ \text{TFA} & \begin{bmatrix} \text{TOP} \langle \boxed{1} \rangle \end{bmatrix} \end{bmatrix}$$

    iii. Contrastive Topic (t_c)

$$\begin{bmatrix} \text{STR} & \langle 3 \rangle \\ \text{PHON} & \langle \boxed{1} \rangle \\ \text{TFA} & \begin{bmatrix} \text{TOP} \langle \boxed{1} \rangle \end{bmatrix} \end{bmatrix}$$

b. Focus and Stress

    i. (Narrow) Focus (f)

$$\begin{bmatrix} \text{STR} & \langle 2 \rangle \\ \text{PHON} & \langle \boxed{1} \rangle \\ \text{TFA} & \begin{bmatrix} \text{FOC} \langle \boxed{1} \rangle \end{bmatrix} \end{bmatrix}$$

    ii. Contrastive Focus (f_c)

$$\begin{bmatrix} \text{STR} & \langle 3 \rangle \\ \text{PHON} & \langle \boxed{1} \rangle \\ \text{TFA} & \begin{bmatrix} \text{FOC} \langle \boxed{1} \rangle \end{bmatrix} \end{bmatrix}$$

I will now briefly introduce Engdahl and Vallduví's (1996) design of information structure. Their INFO-STRUCT, corresponding to our TFA, has two features: ground and focus. Ground is divided into link and tail. Focus and link are correlated with two accent types, Accent A and Accent B, respectively. In addition, they have an underspecified value 'u'. They have feature ACCENT in place of CUG's STRESS. The feature structure of their focus is shown in (6).

(6) Engdahl and Vallduví (1996): Focus

---

[5]There has been a split in the use of the terms: Bolinger (1961), Chafe (1978) and Hajičova (1994) use 'contrastive topic'; Gundel(1995) and many phoneticians, including Chung and Kenstowicz (1997) use 'contrasitve focus'. For discussion of contrastiveness, see C. Lee (1999).

$$
\boxed{1} \begin{bmatrix} word \\ \text{PHON} & \begin{bmatrix} \text{ACCENT:} & \text{A} \end{bmatrix} \\ \text{INFO-STRUCT} & \begin{bmatrix} \text{FOCUS:} & \boxed{1} \end{bmatrix} \end{bmatrix}
$$

Note that the value of focus is the sign itself (tagged $\boxed{1}$). It incurs indeterminacy, due to the cyclicity of the sign.

4. Dialog Analysis

With TFA and prosody interfacing in the AVM structures as described in Section 3, we will now unpack the information structures in two question-answer dialogs below. Each analysis consists of two representations plus comments: (i) Linear Surface Representation (LSR) and (ii) AVM Representation.

LSR is a phonological representation aligned in parallel with TFA information marked with t's, f's, t_c's, f_c's, t/f's).[6] To facilitate the understanding of the information package, the phonological string is represented with different typefaces: boldface plus upper cap for contrastive stress and boldface for focus. The IP boundary is marked with a percent sign %. The segment enclosed in IP boundaries is an utterance unit (U). For AVM representations, only those immediately relevant features are entered; syntax, semantics and other pragmatic components are altogether left out for the space limit and also for ease of exposition.

The illustrations center around the two uses of NUN-phrases, thematic and contrastive; the latter is either topical or focal. Furthermore, by presenting the Japanese renditions in parallel, which bear close syntactic and lexical affinities with the Korean source, it is intended to demonstrate that the information structure of the two languages can be easily unpacked in the same vein and to suggest that a constraint-based unified grammar of Japanese (CUG/J) be designed and developed along with CUG/K.[7]

---

[6]t, f, and t/f are also used by Hajičová et al.(1995); instead of 't/f', we may as well use 'u'.

[7]The Japanese topic marker 'wa' also has two functions, thematic and contrastive (Nakanishi (2000), this volume); the latter may be divided into two sorts, based-generated 'true' topic and fronted 'stylistic' topic with mild emphasis (Shibatani 1990). This classification may well be applied to the Korean 'nun'. The contrastive WA-phrase with prominent intonation is considered focal (Fry and Kaufmann (1998). The WA-phrase, whether thematic or contrastive, appears to be of HL($\searrow$) tone (Nakanishi 2000), in contrast to the LH ($\nearrow$) tone of the NUN-phrase as shown in (4).

(7) Dialog-1

    Q: K: Aytul   kongpwu calhani?
         J: Kodomodati benkyoo yokuyatteiru?
         'Are the kids doing well?'
    A: K: Swuhak-un Mia-nun calhaciman, Yuna-nun moshay.
         J: Suugaku-wa Mia-wa yokudekiruga, Yuna-wa dekinai.
         'Math, Mia does well, but Yuna doesn't.'

         K: Yenge-nun Yuna-nun calhaciman, Mia-nun moshay.
         J: Eigo-wa   Yuna-wa yokudekiruga, Mia-wa dekinai.
         'English, Yuna does well, but Mia doesn't.'

(8) Linear Surface Representation (7A)

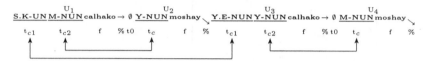

Comments: In the dialog, Q provides the thematic background—
a set of subject matters {math, English} and a set of children {Mia,
Yuna}, which are active in Q's knowledge base. Accordingly, 'math'
and 'English' are topics and contrastive; likewise, 'Mia' and 'Yuna' are
contrasted, following the primary topics of 'math' and 'English'. The
first segment of U_1 is contrasted with the first segment of U_3. In each
utterance unit, topicality is stronger in the initial element than in the
others. In U_2, even the zero topic is stronger than the contrastive
one.[8] These observations may lead to posiiting the following kind of
topicality scale: Topicality, whether contrastive or not, increases along
the linear surface of an utterance unit: the more leftward, the stronger
the topicality.

(9) Topicality Scale

        a. $<t_{(c)1} \cdots t_{(c)n} >$ b. $t_{(c)1} > \cdots > t_{(c)n}$

The utterance units (U_1-U_4) of Dialog-1 (7A) are each shown in
AVM representations.

---

[8] In terms of Centering theory, Cb (backward-looking center) is realized twice
(in U_2 and U_4) in the form of zero topic. CTR, which is an attribute of DF with
the list value of Cfs (forward-looking centers) of the preceding utterance. In this
respect, CTR, unlike TFA, is a global feature, functioning across utterance and
speaker boundaries.

(10) AVM (8A)

U₁:

$$
\begin{bmatrix}
\text{TC} & \rightarrow \\
\text{STR} & \langle 3, 3, 2 \rangle \\
\text{PHON} & \langle \boxed{1}\text{swuhak.un}, \boxed{2}\text{mia.nun}, \boxed{3}\text{calhako} \rangle \\
\text{TFA} & \begin{bmatrix} \text{TOP} & \langle \boxed{1},\boxed{2}, \rangle \\ \text{FOC} & \langle \boxed{3} \rangle \end{bmatrix}
\end{bmatrix}
$$

U₂:

$$
\begin{bmatrix}
\text{TC} & \searrow \\
\text{STR} & \langle 0, 3, 2 \rangle \\
\text{PHON} & \langle \boxed{1}\emptyset, \boxed{2}\text{yuna.nun}, \boxed{3}\text{moshay} \rangle \\
\text{GAP} & \langle \boxed{1} \rangle \\
\text{TFA} & \begin{bmatrix} \text{TOP} & \langle \boxed{1},\boxed{2} \rangle \\ \text{FOC} & \langle \boxed{3} \rangle \end{bmatrix}
\end{bmatrix}
$$

U₃:

$$
\begin{bmatrix}
\text{TC} & \rightarrow \\
\text{STR} & \langle 3, 3, 2 \rangle \\
\text{PHON} & \langle \boxed{1}\text{yenge.nun}, \boxed{2}\text{yuna.mun}, \boxed{3}\text{calhako} \rangle \\
\text{TFA} & \begin{bmatrix} \text{TOP} & \langle \boxed{1}, \boxed{2} \rangle \\ \text{FOC} & \langle \boxed{3} \rangle \end{bmatrix}
\end{bmatrix}
$$

U₄:

$$
\begin{bmatrix}
\text{TC} & \searrow \\
\text{STR} & \langle 0, 3, 2 \rangle \\
\text{PHON} & \langle \boxed{1}\emptyset, \boxed{2}\text{mia.nun}, \boxed{3}\text{moshay} \rangle \\
\text{TFA} & \begin{bmatrix} \text{TOP} & \langle \boxed{1}, \boxed{2} \rangle \\ \text{FOC} & \langle \boxed{3} \rangle \end{bmatrix}
\end{bmatrix}
$$

Comments: In each AVM, only immediately relevant attributes of PPM and SSP are represented as a phrasal sign, satisfying the constraints on a headed phrase, such as the Head Feature Principle and the Valence Principle (Sag and Wasow 1999) on top of those discourse interpretive conventions of CUG/K, including Stress Inheritance and TFA Inheritance (see Appendix)[9]

---

[9]The attribute GAP has a list value, containing coindexed constituents even

Let us take up another question-answer exchange in (11). For the proper unpacking of the information contained in the dialog, it is essential that the interpreter, as well as the dialog participants, should have shared knowledge about the identities of the Three Kims, referring to DJ, YS, and JP and these initials standing for Kim Dae-Jung, Kim Young-Sam and Kim Jong-Pil, respectively.

(11) Dislog-2

> Q: K: Nwuka sam Kim-i cohuni?
> J: Dare-ga san Kim-ga suki?
> 'Who likes Three Kims?'
>
> A: K: Mia-ka DJ-lul cohahay. Yuna-to. YS-nun silhthay.
> J: Mia-ga DJ-ga suki. Yuna-mo. YS-wa iyadatte.
> 'Mia likes DJ. Yuna, too. She dislikes JP, she says.'

(12) Linear Surface Representation(11A)

U_1	U_2	U_3
Mia-ka DJ.를 cohahay $\searrow$	**Yuna-to** $\emptyset$ $\emptyset$ $\searrow$ $\emptyset$	**YS-NUN silhehay** $\searrow$
f t_1 t_2 %	f t_1 t_2 % t t_{c2}	f %

Comments: 'cohta' (J: 'sukida'), rather than 'cohahata' (J: 'sukigaru') is more appropriate when the speaker 'empathizes' the third-person referent (in the sense of Kuno (1976)'s empathy or CUG's POV); otherwise, the other way around in both languages. 'Yuna-to' in U_2 and 'YS-nun' in U_3 are syntactically ambiguous between the two interpretations given in (13) and (14), respectively. The TO- ('also', 'even') phrase (i.e. x-*to*) can be said 'contrastive' as well, by arguing that the implicature in the TO-phrase (namely, 'there is someone other than x' is the meaning *contrasted to* x. Then, the 'contrastive' meaning of the NUN-phrase, which may be interpreted as 'only concerned'[10] or 'exclusively chosen', is also an implicature. Instead of treating the implicational meaning of the TO-phrase as contrastive, it is entered in PRA|IMPL in CUG.[11] In (13) and (14), the b-readings are irrelevant, violating the Relevance-theoretic Construal. Yuna is not one of the Three Kims. YS is one of them but he is not one of 'who's' in question, although factually it may be true that YS doesn't like DJ.

---

from the preceding utterances. In this respect, it is different from that in Sag and Wasow (1999), whose value is a list of fillers, satisfying the constraint on a head-filler phrase.

[10]This is the asserted meaning of the delimiter NUN, explored by Yang In-Seok nearly thirty years ago in his seminal work on Korean delimiters (Yang 1973); his passing away last spring is a great loss to us, Korean linguists.

[11]Implicature of <Yuna-to>:

(13) (cf. (12-U$_2$))
    a. Yuna-to ∅ ∅.   'Yuna (likes DJ), too.'
    b. # ∅ Yuna-to ∅   '(She likes) Yuna, too.'

(14) (cf. (12-U$_3$))
    a. ∅ YS-nun silhehantay.
        'She (=Mia/Yuna) doesn't like YS, she says.'
    b. # YS-nun ∅ ∅
        '(YS) doesn't like DJ, she says.'

The zero topic in (14a) can stand for either Mia or Yuna but the Recency-Preference Construal of CUG dictates that 'Yuna' is the preferred referent.

5. Concluding Remarks

Interactions of prosody and pragmatics—one is physical, the other mental—are not one-to-one but many-to-many relations. What is proposed here concerning the interactions of TFA with different levels of stress is the first approximation for the default constraints on TFA and stress. The interface of prosody and pragmatics remains as a major area of linguistic exploration by those interested in the sound and meaning of language.

In addition to this interative study on prosody and pragmatics, CUG, which is eclectic and ever in the growing, has prospects for the following areas of linguistic enterprise: (i) morpholexical theory (such as Koenig 1999)—for developing feature-structured morphology; (ii) constraint-based syntax (such as Sag and Wasow 1999)—for deepening and broadening sign-theoretic phrase structure grammar; (iii) MRS (Minimal Recursion Semantics) (such as Copestake et al. 1996)—for constructing flat semantics for discourse analysis; (iv) OT (optimality theory) (such as Barbosa et al. 1998)—for ranking and overriding default constraints, and for grading Gricean maxims.

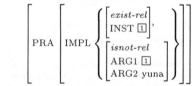

The implicature is interpreted as 'there is someone, who is not Yuna':
   ∃x(human(x) ∧ x ≠ *yuna*)

A   Conventions and Principles

Abbreviations: hd-ph=headed phrase, HD-DTR=head daughter, NHD-DTRS=non-head daughters

1. Stress Inheritance

$$\textit{hd-ph:} \begin{bmatrix} \text{STR} & \left\langle \boxed{str-1}, \ldots, \boxed{str-m}, \oplus \boxed{str-n} \right\rangle \\ \text{HD-DTR} & \left[\text{STR } \boxed{str-n} \right] \\ \text{NHD-DTRS} & \left\langle \left[\text{STR } \boxed{str-1}, \ldots, \boxed{str-m} \right] \right\rangle \end{bmatrix}$$

2. TFA Inheritance

$$\textit{hd-ph:} \begin{bmatrix} \text{PRA} \left[\text{DF} \left[\text{TFA} \begin{bmatrix} \text{TOP} \left\langle \boxed{t-1}, \ldots, \boxed{t-m} \right\rangle \oplus \boxed{t-n} \\ \text{FOC} \left\langle \boxed{f-1}, \ldots, \boxed{f-m} \right\rangle \oplus \boxed{f-n} \end{bmatrix} \right] \right] \\ \text{HD-DTR} \left[\text{PRA} \left[\text{DF} \left[\text{TFA} \begin{bmatrix} \text{TOP} \left\langle \boxed{t-n} \right\rangle \\ \text{FOC} \left\langle \boxed{f-n} \right\rangle \end{bmatrix} \right] \right] \right] \\ \text{NHD-DTRS} \left\langle \left[\text{PRA} \left[\text{DF} \begin{bmatrix} \text{TOP} \left\langle \boxed{t-1}, \ldots, \boxed{t-m} \right\rangle \\ \text{FOC} \left\langle \boxed{f-1}, \ldots, \boxed{f-m} \right\rangle \end{bmatrix} \right] \right] \right\rangle \end{bmatrix}$$

3. POV Inheritance

$$\textit{hd-ph:} \begin{bmatrix} \text{PRA} \left[\text{DF} \left[\text{POV} \left\langle \boxed{v-1}, \ldots, \boxed{v-n} \right\rangle \right] \right] \\ \text{NHD-DTRS} \left[\text{PRA} \left[\text{DF} \left[\text{POV} \left\langle \boxed{v-1}, \ldots, \boxed{v-n} \right\rangle \right] \right] \right] \end{bmatrix}$$

4. Speech-Act Inheritance

$$hd\text{-}ph: \begin{bmatrix} \text{SSP} & \begin{bmatrix} \text{PRA} \begin{bmatrix} \text{SA} \boxed{sa-1} \end{bmatrix} \end{bmatrix} \\ \text{HD-DTR} & \begin{bmatrix} \text{SSP} \begin{bmatrix} \text{PRA} \begin{bmatrix} \text{SA} \boxed{sa-1} \end{bmatrix} \end{bmatrix} \end{bmatrix} \end{bmatrix}$$

5. Head Feature Principle (cf. Sag and Wasow 1999)

$$hd\text{-}ph: \begin{bmatrix} \text{SYN} & \begin{bmatrix} \text{HEAD} \boxed{h-1} \end{bmatrix} \\ \text{HD-DTR} & \begin{bmatrix} \text{SYN} \begin{bmatrix} \text{HEAD} \boxed{h-1} \end{bmatrix} \end{bmatrix} \end{bmatrix}$$

6. Valence Principle (cf. Sag and Wasow 1999)

$$hd\text{-}ph: \begin{bmatrix} \text{SYN} & \begin{bmatrix} \text{COMPS} & \boxed{c-1} \\ \text{SPR} & \boxed{sp-1} \end{bmatrix} \\ \text{HD-DTR} & \begin{bmatrix} \text{SYN} \begin{bmatrix} \text{COMPS} & \boxed{c-1} \\ \text{SPR} & \boxed{sp-1} \end{bmatrix} \end{bmatrix} \end{bmatrix}$$

References

Barbosa, Pilar, Danny Fox, Paul Hagstrom, Martha McGinnis, and David Pesetsky. 1998. *Is the Best Good Enough?* Cambridge, MA: MIT Press.

Bolinger, Dwight L. 1961. 'Contrastive Accent and Contrastive Stress,' *Language* 37:83-96.

Carpenter, Bob. 1992. *The Logic of Typed Feature Structures*. Cambridge: Cambridge University Press.

Chafe, Wallace L. 1976. 'Givenness, Contrastiveness, Definiteness, Subjects, Topics, and Point of View,' in C. N. Li, ed. *Subject and Topic* (New York: Academic Press), 27-56.

Chang, Suk-Jin. 1994. *Thonghap Munpeplon [Unified Grammar Theory]*. Seoul: Seoul National Univerity Press.

Chang, Suk-Jin. 1999a. 'Where Grammar Meets Pragmatics,' A Constraint-based Approach to Korean Discourse,' Paper presented at LSA Korean Linguistics Conference (University of Illinois at Urbana-Champaign, 1999).

Chang, Suk-Jin and Jae-woong Choe. 1993. 'Toward Understanding Discourse Structure: Flow of Contextual Information in Spoken Korean,' in C. Lee and B. Kang, eds. *Language, Information and Computation* (Seoul: Taehaksa), 1-13.

Chung, Kook et al. 1998. *A Study of Korean Prosody and Discourse for the Development of Speech Synthesis/Recogniton System.* Center for Artificial Intelligence Research, KAIST.

Chung, Soo-Jin and Michael Kenstowicz. 1997. 'Focus Expression in Seoul Korean,' *Harvard Studies in Korean Linguistics* 7:93-105.

Copestake, Ann, Dan Flickinger, Robert Malouf, Susanne Riehemann, and Ivan A. Sag. 1995. 'Translation using Minimal Recursion Semantics,' Proceedings of the Sixth International Conference on Theoretical and Methodological Issues in Machine Translation, Leuven.

Engdahl, Elisabet and Enric Vallduví. 1996. 'Information Packaging in HPSG,' in *Edinburgh Working Papers in Cognitive Science. Vol 12: Studies in HPSG*, Chapter 1, 1-32. Centre for Cognitive Science, University of Edinburgh.

Fry, John and Stefan Kaufmann. 1998. 'Information Packaging in Japanese,' in the Proceedings of FHCG-98, 55-65.

Hajičová, Eva, Petr Sgall and Hana Skoumalov. 1995. 'An Automatic Procedure for Topic-Focus Identification,' *Computational Linguistics* 21:1.81-94.

Jackendoff, Ray S. 1972. *Semantic Interpretation in Generative Grammar.* Cambridge, MA: MIT Press.

Koenig, Jean-Pierre. 1999. *Lexical Relations.* Stanford: CSLI Publications.

Kuno, Susumu. 1976. 'Subject, Theme, and the Speaker's Empathy: A Reexamination of Relativization Phenomena,' in C. N. Li, ed., *Subject and Topic* (New York: Academy Press), 417-44.

Kuboň, Petr. 1998. 'Information Repackaging,' in the Proceedings of FHCG-98, 36-46.

Lascarides, Alex and Ann Copestake. 1998. 'Default Representation in Constraint-Based Frameworks. *Computational Linguistics* 7.1-7:1-54.

Lee, Chungmin. 1999. 'Contrastive Topic: A Locus of the Interface Evidence from Korean and English,' K. Turner, ed. *Current Research in the Semantics/Pragmatics Interface* Vol. 1, 317-42.

Lee, Hyuck-Joon and Hee-Sun Kim. 1997. 'Phonetic Realization of

Seoul Korean Accentual Phrase.' *Harvard Studies in Korean Linguistics* 7:153-166.

Lee, Ik-Hwan and Minhaeng Lee. 1998. 'Cisicek Pyohyenkwa Cengpokwucouy Haysekul wihan Incicek Mohyeng' [A Cognitive Model for the Interpretation of the Referential Expressions and Information Structure], *Korean Journal of Linguistics* 23.1:65-85.

Nakanishi, Kimiko. 2000. 'Prosody and Information Structure in Japanese: A Case Study of Topic Marker *wa*. (this volume)

Pierrehumbert, Janet and J. Hirschberg. 1990. 'The Meaning of Intonational Contours in the Interpretation of Discourse,' in P. Cohen, J. Morgan, and M. Pollack, eds. *Intentions in Communication.* Cambridge, MA: MIT Press, 271-311.

Pollard, Carl and Ivan A. Sag. 1987. *Information-based Syntax and Semantics.* Stanford: CSLI, Stanford University.

Pollard, Carl and Ivan A. Sag. 1994. *Head-driven Phrase Structure Grammar.* Stanford, CA. CSLI, Stanford University.

Sag, Ivan A. and Thomas A. Wasow. 1999. *Syntactic Theory: A Formal Introduction.* Stanford, CA: CSLI Press.

Shibatani, Masayoshi. 1990. *The Languages of Japan.* Cambridge: Cambridge University Press.

Vallduví, Enric and Elisabet Engdahl. 1996. 'The Linguistic Realization of Information Packaging,' *Linguistics* 34:459-519.

Yang, In-Seok. 1973. 'The Semantics of Delimiters,' *Language Research* 9.2:84-121.

NPI Licensing, *O/Ga* Alternation, Verb Raising and Scrambling

SUSUMU KUNO

Harvard University

1. Introduction

It has been generally held that potential and experiential constructions such as (1a) and (2a) below start out with the bi-clausal underlying structures shown in (1b) and (2b) and undergo verb raising, which adjoins the embedded verb to the matrix verb and triggers tree-pruning, yielding the mono-clausal structures shown in (1c) and (2c):

(1) a. Taroo wa kankokugo o hanas-u   koto ga deki-ru.
             Korean Acc speak-Pres   to Nom can-Pres
         'Taro can speak Korean.'
     b. Underlying Structure
         [Taroo [$_{VP}$ [$_{S}$ PRO kankokugo hanas-u] koto deki-ru]]
     c   After Verb Raising
         [Taro [$_{VP}$ kankokugo [$_{V}$ hanas-u-koto-ga-deki-ru]]
(2) a   Taroo wa yooroppa ni it-ta   koto   ga ar-u.
             Europe   to go-Past experience Nom have-Pres
         'Taro has the experience of having been to Europe.'
     b. Underlying Structure
         [Taroo [$_{VP}$ [$_{S}$ PRO yooroppa ni it-ta] koto ar-u]]
     c. After Verb Raising
         [Taroo [$_{VP}$ yooroppa ni [$_{V}$ it-ta-koto-ga-ar-u]]]

The proponents of the verb raising analysis (e.g., Muraki 1975) have used negative polarity items in support of their claim that the derived structures of these sentences are mono-clausal. Observe first the following simple sentences that contain negative polarity items:

(3) a   Taroo wa nihongo **sika** hanas-**ana**-i.
                Japanese only speak-Neg-Pres
            'Taro doesn't speak any language other than Japanese.'
     b.   *Taro wa nihongo **sika** hanas-u.
                Japanese only speak-Pres
            '(Intended Meaning) Taro speaks only Japanese.'
(4) a   Taro wa **nanimo** hanas-**ana**-i.
                anything speak-Neg-Pres
            'Taro doesn't talk about anything.'
     b.   *Taro wa **nanimo** hanas-u.
                anything speak-Pres
            '(Intended Meaning) Taro doesn't talk about anything.'

Sika 'only' in (3) and *nanimo* 'anything' in (4) are negative polarity items, and as such, they require a negative morpheme -*(a)na*- that licenses them, as witnessed by the fact that (3b) and (4b) are unacceptable. The following sentences establish that the negative morpheme that licenses a negative polarity item must be its clausemate:

(5) a.   Hanako wa [s Taroo ga nihongo **sika** hanas-**ana**-i]   to it-ta.
                        Japanese only speak-Neg-Pres that say-Past
            'Hanako said that Taroo speaks only Japanese.'
     b.   Hanako **sika** [s Taroo ga nihogo o hanas-u]   to iw-**anakat**-ta.
                only   Japanese speak-Neg-Pres that say-Neg-Past
            'Only Hanako said that Taroo speaks Japanese.'
     c.   *Hanako wa [s Taroo ga nihongo **sika** hanas-u]   to iw-**anakat**-ta.
                        Japanese only speak-Pres that say-Neg-Past
            '(Intended Meaning) Hanako didn't say that Taroo speaks only Japanese.'
     d.   *Hanako **sika** [s Taroo ga nihogo o hanas-**ana**-i]   to it-ta.
                only   Japanese speak-Neg-Pres that say-Past
            '(Intended Meaning) Only Hanako said that Taroo speaks Japanese.'

In (5a), the NPI and the Neg are clausemates in the embedded clause, and in (5b), they are clausemates in the main clause. These sentences are acceptable. In contrast, in (1c) the NPI is in the embedded clause, while the Neg is in the main clause. Likewise, in (1d), the NPI is in the main clause, while the Neg is in the embedded clause. These two sentences are unacceptable because they violate the constraint that an NPI and the Neg that licenses it should be clausemates. I will refer to this constraint as 'the NPI Clausemate Constraint.'

Returning to the potential and experiential constructions, we observe that the following sentences are acceptable:

(6) a   Taroo wa nihongo **sika** hanas-u   koto ga deki-**na**-i.
               Japanese only speak-Pres to   can-Neg-Pres
               'Taro cannot speak any language other than Japanese.'
    b.   Taroo wa eigo-no syukudai **sika** su-ru   koto ga deki-**na**-i
               English homework only do-Pres to can-Neg-Pres
               'Taro can do only English homework.'
    c.   Taroo wa **nanimo** hanas-ita koto ga   **na**-i.
               anything speak-Past experience have=Neg-Pres
               'Taro hasn't ever talked about anything.'[1]

The proponents of the verb raising analysis argue that since these sentences are acceptable, *nihongo sika* 'only Japanese' and *nanimo* 'anything' must be clausemates of the main clause Neg. They attribute this clausemate relationship to verb raising, which, together with the resultant application of tree-pruning, turns the underlying bi-clausal structure to a mono-clausal structure.

In Kuno (1995, 1999), I have attributed the acceptability of sentences such as (6a-c) not to verb raising (and subsequent mono-clausalization), but to the leftward scrambling of the NPIs from inside the embedded structure to the main clause. Namely, I have assumed that (6a), for example, is derived as shown in (7):

(7) a.   Underlying Structure
      [Taroo [$_S$ PRO nihongo **sika** hanas-u]   koto deki-**na**-i]
                 Japanese only speak-Pres to can-Neg-Pres
      N.B. the NPI Clausemate Constraint violated
    b.   After Scrambling
      [Taroo nihongo **sika** [$_S$ PRO e hanas-u] koto deki-**na**-i]
               |_____|
      N.B. the NPI Clausemate Constraint observed

The acceptability of (6a) shows that sentences whose underlying structures violate the NPI Clausemate Constraint become acceptable if scrambling yields a structure that satisfies the constraint. The following example makes the same point.

---

[1] The Neg in (6a) is an affix that follows the stem form of a verb, while the Neg in (6b) is a suppletive form of **ar-ana-* 'have + Neg'. The fact that there are two morphemes involved in *na-* in (6c) is confirmed by the fact that its polite form is *ar-imas-en* 'have + Polite + Neg'.

(8) a.   Kanzya wa mizu **sika** nom-i-ta-i   to iw-**anakat**-ta.
          patient   water only drink-ing-want-Pres that say-Neg-Past
          'It was only water that the patient said that he wanted to drink.'
     b.   Before Scrambling
          [Kanzya [PRO mizu **sika** nom-i-ta-i] to iw-**anakat**-ta.
          N.B. the NPI Clausemate Constraint violated
     c.   After Scrambling
          [Kanzya mizu **sika** [PRO e nom-i-ta-i] to iw-**anakat**-ta.
                      |_____|
          N.B. the NPI Clausemate Constraint observed

I have also noted, following Kato (1991), that sentences that satisfy the NPI Clausemate Constraint at the pre-scrambling stage remain acceptable even if scrambling extracts the NPI out of the clause that contains the licensing Neg. Observe, for example the following sentence and its derivation:

(9) a.   Hanako ni **sika**, boku wa a-i-ta-ku-**na**-i   to omot-te i-ru.
                    to only I see-ing-want-ing-Neg-Pres that think-ing be-Pres
          'I feel that I don't want to see anyone other than Hanako.'
     b.   Before Scrambling
          [Boku [PRO Hanako ni **sika** a-i-ta-ku-**na**-i] to omot-te i-ru.
          N.B. the NPI Clausemate Constraint observed
     c.   After Scrambling
          [Hanako ni **sika** boku [PRO e a-i-ta-ku-**na**-i] to omot-te i-ru]
                       |_____|
          N.B. the NPI Clause Mate Constraint violated

The acceptability of (9a) shows that scrambling must be allowed to front NPIs in embedded clauses. If so, the same scrambling rule should also be allowed to apply to NPIs in the potential and experiential constructions such as (6a-c), thus making the NPI licensing a nonargument for verb raising.

I have further noted that sentences whose underlying structures observe the NPI Clausemate Constraint become unacceptable if their surface structures immediately before the application of scrambling violate the constraint. I have based this hypothesis on NPIs in subject-raising sentences. Observe first the following sentences:

(10) a.   Karera wa *mina* [Hanako **ga** syooziki da] to sinzi-te   i-ru.
          they   all   honest is that believe-ing be-Pres
          'They all believe that Hanako is honest.'
     b.   *Karera wa [Hanako **ga** *mina* syooziki da] to sinzi-te   i-ru.
          they   all   honest is that believe-ing be-Pres
          '*(Lit.) They believe that Hanako all is honest.'

The acceptability of (10a) and the unacceptability of (10b) show that a main-clause quantifier cannot be floated into an embedded clause. Observe, next, the following sentences:

(11) a.   Karera wa *mina* Hanako **o** syooziki da to sinzi-te   i-ru.
          they   all   Acc honest is that believe-ing be-Pres
          'They all believe Hanako to be honest.'
     b.   Karera wa Hanako **o** *mina* syooziki da to sinzi-te i-ru.

In Kuno (1976), I proposed that (11a) is derived by raising the embedded clause subject to the object position of the main clause verb. Note that (11b), in which the main clause quantifier *mina* 'all' appears after *Hanako o*, is acceptable, indicating that *Hanako o* is a main clause constituent.

Now let us embed a negative polarity item in the subject position of (10a) and see how it behaves after Subject Raising:

(12) a.   Underlying Structure
          Karera wa *mina* [Hanako **sika** syooziki de **na**-i] to sinzi-te
          they   all   only honest Neg-Pres that believe-ing
          i-ru.
          be-Pres
          N.B. the NPI Clausemate Constraint observed.
     b.   Subject Raising
          *Karera wa Hanako **sika** *mina* [e syooziki de **na**-i] to
          sinzi-te   i-ru. |_____|
          believe-ing be-Pres
          N.B. the NPI Clausemate Constraint violated

(12b) is unacceptable in spite of the fact that its underlying structure (12a) observes the NPI Clausemate Constraint.

The above observations lead to the following constraint on NPIs:

(13) *NPI Clausemate Constraint*:
     A sentence that contains an NPI in Japanese must have a clausemate
     (i.e., S-mate) Neg at surface structure either immediately before or
     immediately after the application of scrambling.

As summarized above, we now have two alternative explanations for the acceptability of (6a-c). The verb raising analysis claims that *hanas-u koto-ga* and *hanas-ita koto-ga* have been raised and adjoined to the main-clause verbs *deki-ru* and *ar-u*, yielding mono-clausal structures in which the negative polarity item and the negative morpheme are clausemates. In contrast, the scrambling analysis claims that there is no verb raising for the *potential koto-*

ga dekiru and the experiential *koto-ga aru* constructions, but rather, scrambling raises negative polarity items out of the embedded clause into the main clause. In Sections 2 and 3, I will present new arguments for the scrambling analysis, and against the verb raising analysis.

2. Negative Polarity Items in the Experiential Construction

The experiential construction *koto ga aru* is interesting in that it can have negative embedded clauses, which the potential pattern *koto-ga dekiru* cannot. Observe the following sentences:

(14) *Taroo wa 3-punkan iki o   si-**na**-i   koto ga deki-ru.
          minutes breathing do-Neg-Pres to   can-Pres
    '(Lit.) Taro can not-breathe for 3 minutes.'

(15) a.   Taroo wa issyuukan syokuzi o si-**nakat**-ta   koto ga   ar-u.
                    one-week meals   take-Neg-Past experience have-Pres
          'Taro has the experience of not having eaten for a week.'

  b.   Taroo wa ikkagetukan kazoku to renraku wo tor-**anakat**-ta
                    one-month family with contact   take-Neg-Past
       koto-ga   ar-u.
       experience have-Pres
       'Taro has the experience of not having contacted his family for a
       month.'

The fact that a negative element can appear in the embedded clause of the *koto ga aru* construction presents a challenge to the proponents of the verb raising analysis for NPI licensing. Observe first the following sentences:

(16) a.   Taroo **sika**, yuusyoku ni peanut butter sandwich o tabe-ta
                 only dinner   for   eat-Past
       koto-ga   **na**-i.
       experience have=Neg-Pres
       'Only Taro has the experience of having had peanut butter
       sandwiches for dinner.'
       N.B. V complex after verb raising = tabe-ta-koto-ga-**na**-
       [**V-final Neg**]

  b.   *Taroo **sika**, [yuusyoku ni peanut butter sandwich o
                 only   dinner for
       tabe-**nakat**-ta] koto-ga   ar-u.
       eat-Neg-Past experience have-Pres
       '(Intended Meaning) Only Taro has the experience of having
       eaten peanut butter sandwiches for dinner.'
       N.B. V complex after verb raising = tabe-**nakat**-ta-koto-ga-ar-
       [**V-internal Neg**]

The unacceptability of (16b) suggests that in the framework of the verb raising analysis, a V-internal Neg cannot license an NPI.[2]

But the above constraint runs into difficulty explaining the acceptability of the following sentence:

(17) Taroo wa tyuusyoku ni peanut butter sandwich **sika** tabe-**naka**t-ta
            lunch   for   only eat-Neg-Past
      koto-ga   ar-u.
      experience have-Pres
      'Taro has the experience of not having eaten anything other than peanut
      butter sandwiches for lunch.'
      N.B. V Complex = tabe-**naka**t-ta-koto-ga-ar-   **[V-internal Neg]**

The acceptability of (17) will be unaccounted for if the V-internal Neg   -
nakat- is blocked from licensing *peanut butter sandwich sika.*

The proponents of the verb raising analysis are most likely to claim that NPI licensing takes place at two stages: once before verb raising, and the second time after verb raising, and that a sentence containing an NPI is acceptable if the NPI is successfully licensed either before or after verb raising. According to this analysis, (17) is acceptable because the NPI licensing was successful before verb raising, but (16b) is unacceptable because the NPI licensing is successful neither before nor after verb raising.

---

[2] It is felt that the *ga*-marked NPs in the following sentences are within the *koto-*clauses:

(i) a. [Ame ga 3kagetukan hur-anakat-ta] koto ga ar-u.
          rain 3-month-for fall-Neg-Past occasion exist-Pres
          'Once there was a time when it didn't rain for three months.'
     b. [Akanboo ga hitoban-zyuu nak-i-tuduke-ta]   koto ga ar-u.
          baby   night-through cry-continue-Past occasion exist-Pres
          'There were times when the baby continued to cry all through
          the night.'

Likewise, (16b) is acceptable if *Taroo sika* is pronounced as the subject of the embedded clause:

(ii). [Taroo **sika** yuusyoku ni peanut butter sandwich o tabe-**naka**t-ta]
            only dinner   for   eat-Neg-Past
       koto-ga   ar-u.
       occasion exist-Pres
       'It once happened that only Taro ate a peanut butter sandwich for
       dinner.'

On the above interpretation, *Taroo sika* and Neg are clausemates.

Now, observe the following sentences:

(18) a.   Taroo wa syuumatu ni nonbirito hanniti **sika** benkyoosi-**nakat**-ta
             weekend on leisurely half-a-day only study-Neg-Past

       koto ga   ar-u.
       experience have-Pres
       'Taro has the experience of having leisurely studied only half a
       day on weekends.'

       b.   Taroo wa syuumatu ni   hanniti **sika** benkyoosi-ta koto ga
             weekend on half-a-day only study-Past experience

       na-i.
       have=Neg-Pres
       'Taro hasn't ever studied any more than half a day on weekends.'

       c.   *Taro wa syuumatu ni nonbirito hanniti   **sika** benkyoosi-ta
             weekend on leisurely half-a-day only study-Past

       koto-ga   **na**-i.
       experience have=Neg-Pres
       '(Intended Meaning) Taro has the experience of having leisurely
       studied only half a day on weekends.'

(19) a.   Hanako wa kogoe   de hai to **sika** i-e-**nakat**-ta   koto ga
             whisper with yes only say-can-Neg-Past experience

       ar-u.
       have-Pres
       'Hanako has the experience of having been able to say only yes
       whisperingly.'

       b.   Hanako wa hai to **sika** i-e-ta   koto ga   **na**-i.
             yes   only say-can-Past experience have=Neg-Pres
       'Hanako hasn't ever been able to say anything other than yes.'

       c.   *Hanako wa kogoe de hai to **sika** i-e-ta   koto ga
             whisper with yes   only say-can-Past experience

       na-i.
       have=Neg-Pres
       '(Intended Meaning) Hanako hasn't ever been able to say
       whisperingly anything other than yes.'

In the verb-raising framework under discussion, the acceptability of (18a) and
(19a) is accounted for because NPI licensing is successful before verb raising:
at that stage, *hanniti sika* 'only half a day' / *hai to sika* 'only yes' and Neg are
clausemates in the embedded clause. Likewise, the acceptability of (18b) and
(19b) is accounted for because *hanniti sika* / *hai to sika* and the V-final Neg
have become clausemates after verb raising. But how can the unacceptability
(and the nearly unparsable nature) of (18c) and (19c) be accounted for in that
framework? If verb raising applies to (18b) and (19b), it should also apply to
(18c) and (19c), and the subsequent mono-clausalization should take place,

making the V-final Neg and the NPI clausemates. Thus, the unacceptability of (18c) and (19c) is unaccounted for in the framework of the verb raising analysis for NPI licensing.

In contrast, the scrambling analysis of NPIs can account for the difference between (18b, 19b) and (18c, 19c) without any difficulty. In that framework, the acceptability of (18b, 19b) can be attributed to the scrambling of *hanniti sika* 'only half a day' and *hai to sika* 'only yes' out of the embedded clause to the main clause. As claimed in Kuno (1995, 1999), this process is very much like the scrambling of topic-marked elements out of the embedded clause to the main clause:

(20) a.   *Taroo wa [kankokugo **wa** hanas-u] koto ga deki-ru
                    Korean   speak-Pres to   can-Pres
     b.   Taroo wa [kankokugo **wa**] [hanas-u koto ga deki-ru]
                    Korean   speak-Pres to   can-Pres
          'As for Korean, Taro can speak it.'

There is a general rule in Japanese that *wa*-marked NPs cannot show up in embedded clauses (except for quotative clauses) unless they are used contrastively, with the contrasted elements overtly present. For example,

(21) *Watakusi wa [Taroo **wa** ki-ta] koto o sit-te i-ta.
      I   come-Past that know-ing be-Past
     'I knew that Taro came.'

In the same way, (20a), with *kankokugo wa hanas-u* 'speak Korean' pronounced as a constituent, is unacceptable because that pronunciation makes *kankokugo wa* 'as for Korean' a constituent of the embedded clause. On the other hand, with a long pause after *kankokugo wa* as shown in (20b), the sentence is acceptable. This fact is explainable only by assuming that the *wa*-marked element in (20b) has been scrambled out of the embedded clause into the main clause. I am claiming here that the same or similar scrambling process is responsible for extracting NPIs in (6) out of the embedded clauses.

Returning to the contrast between (18b, 19b) and (18c, 19c), *hanniti sika* 'only half a day' in (18c) and *hai to sika* 'only yes' in (19c) can be licensed by the main-clause Neg only if they can be scrambled out of the embedded clause, as has been assumed for (18b, 19b). But in order for this scrambling to take place, embedded-clause manner adverbials *nonbirito* 'leisurely' and *kogoe de* 'whisperingly' must first be scrambled out of the embedded clause. But this scrambling is next to impossible because there is nothing topical about these manner adverbials. The adverbials are thus interpreted as belonging to the embedded clause, and this prevents the NPIs from being interpreted as main-clause constituents. Therefore the NPIs cannot be licensed by the main clause Neg, and hence the unacceptability of (18c, 19c).

In order for the verb raising analysis to replicate the above effect, it would have to claim that verb raising is blocked when there is a nontopical adverbial to the left of an NPI in the embedded clause. The ad-hocness of such a constraint makes clear that the verb raising analysis fails to capture the real factors that affect NPI licensing.

3. *O/Ga* Alternation

It is well known that the objects of stative verbs, adjectives and nominal-adjectives are nominatively case-marked in Japanese as illustrated in the following examples:

(22) a.. Boku wa kankokugo **ga** wakar-u.
          I   Korean   Nom understand-Pes
          'I understand Korean.'
     b.   Boku wa okane **ga** hosi-i.
          I   money Nom want-Pres
          'I want money.'
     c.   Boku wa Hanako **ga** suki   da.
          I   Nom fond-of is
          'I am fond of Hanako.'

It is also well known that the objects of verbs embedded in potential and desiderative sentences can "optionally" be in the nominative case:

(23) a.   Taroo wa kankokugo **o/ga**   hanas-(r)e-ru.
                   Korean Acc/Nom speak-can-Pres
          'Taro can speak Korean.'
     b.   Boku wa kimi no ronbun **o/ga**   yom-i-ta-i.
          I   your   paper Acc/Nom read-want-Pres
          'I want to read your paper.'

In Kuno (1999), I have followed Dubinsky (1992) and attributed the *o/ga* alternation in these sentences to the absence or presence of verb raising. If *kankokugo hanas-* 'speak Korean' and *kimi no ronbun yom-* 'read your paper' remain as constituents, accusative case marking takes place because the nonstative verbs *hanas-* 'speak' and *yom-* 'read' are involved. On the other hand, if *hanas-* and *yom-* are raised and adjoined to the main clause verbs, then nominative case marking takes place because the stativity of the main clause verbals *-(r)e-* 'can' and *-ta-* 'want' percolates to the V complexes *hanas-(r)e-* 'can speak' and *yom-i-ta-* 'want to read'. [3]

---

[3] There is no contradiction beween the claim here that verb raising can take place in the potential *–(r)e-* and desiderative *–ta-* constructions and the claim made in §1 and §2 that there is no verb raising in the potential *koto-ga dekiru* and experiential *koto-ga*

(24) a.

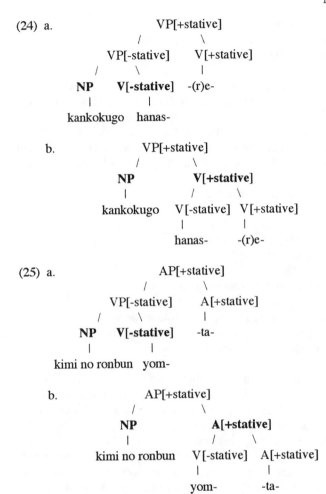

b.

(25) a.

b.

Note in (24b) that the stativity of the matrix verb *-(r)e-* is percolated onto the V complex *hanas-(r)e-*. Note also that in (25b), the stativity of the matrix adjective *-ta-* is percolated onto the AP *yom-(i)-ta-*.

The percolation of the stativity of the matrix verbs and adjectives is not blocked even when the embedded verb is in the continuative *-te* form. Observe the following sentences:

---

constructions. In the *–(r)e-* and *–ta-* constructions, embedded verbs are tenseless, while in the *koto-ga dekiru* and *koto-ga aru* constructions, they are tense-marked, and followed by a *ga*-marked complementizer.

(26) Boku wa nanika   **o/ga**   si-te   mi-ta-i.
     I   something Acc/Nom do-Cont see-want-Pres
     'I want to (try to) do something.

I am using here the indefinite noun *nanika* 'something' to exclude the exhaustive listing reading of the underlying object of *su-* 'do' The nominative marking of *nanika* 'something' in (26) can be explained only by assuming that the stativity of *-ta-* 'want' has percolated upward onto the V complex *si-te-mi-ta-* 'want to try to do'. The acceptabilty of this sentence shows that the stativity percolation is not blocked when the verb complex contains continuative morpheme *-te*.

Now, observe the following sentences:

(27) a.   Taroo wa nanika   **ga**   deki-ru.
              something Nom can-Pres
          'Taro can do something.
     b.   Taroo wa nanika   **o/ga**   tukur-(r)e-ru.
              something Acc/Nom make-can-Pres
          'Taroo can make something.'
     c.   Taroo wa nanika   **o/*ga**   su-ru   koto ga deki-ru.
              something Acc/Nom do-Pres to Nom can-Pres
          'Taro is capable of doing something.'

In my and many other speakers' idiolects, the nominative-case marking of the underlying object of *su-* 'do' in (27c) yields unacceptability. I account for this by assuming that *deki-* 'can', unlike *-(r)e* 'can' in (27b) and *-ta-* 'want' in *-te-mi-ta-* 'want to try to do' in (26), does not allow the raising of the embedded verb. Therefore, *nanika* 'something' remains the object of the nonstative verb *su-* 'do'. In contrast, the proponents of the verb raising analysis must assume that *su-ru koto ga deki-* 'can do' has become a V complex, because this is the assumption that they have had to make in order to account for the acceptability of the NPI sentence (6c). Therefore, they will have to attribute the unacceptability of (27c) with the nominative case marking to the blocking effect of *koto-ga* on stativity percolation. That is, they will have to claim that the sentence is unacceptable because the stativity percolation is blocked when a V complex contains the complementizer *koto (ga)*. This would be an ill-motivated constraint, to say the least, because there is no doubt that *su-ru koto ga deki-* 'can do' is a stative predicate.

Furthermore, the above constraint in the framework of the verb raising analysis would have a hard time accounting for the following contrast:

(28) a. ?/*Taroo wa kankokugo **ga** hanas-u koto ga deki-ru.
               Korean Nom speak-Pres to can-Pres
               'Taro can speak Korean.'

    b. ?/*Taroo wa kankokugo **ga** hanas-u koto ga deki-na-i.
               Korean   speak-Pres to   can-Neg-Pres
               'Taro cannot speak Korean.'

(29) a. ok/? Taroo wa kankokugo **ga**, yom-u koto mo hanas-u koto mo
                   Korean Nom read-Pres to also speak-Pres to also
    deki-ru.
    can-Pres
    'Taro can both read and speak Korean.'

    b. ok/? Taroo wa kankokugo **ga**, yom-u koto mo hanas-u koto mo
                   Korean Nom read-Pres to also speak-Pres to also
    deki-na-i.
    can-Neg-Pres
    'Taro cannot either read or speak Korean.'

The acceptability judgments of (28a, b) vary from speaker to speaker. The sentences are unacceptable unless *kankokugo ga* is stressed with a long pause after it, in which case the sentences are acceptable, awkward or marginal depending upon the speaker. In my and many other speakers' idiolects, (29a, b) are considerably better than (28a, b). In these sentences, *kankokugo ga* is the shared object of *yom-u koto mo hanas-u koto mo deki-ru* 'can both read and speak'. This *ga*-marked NP can receive an exhaustive listing interpretation, but it doesn't have to.

    There is a readily available explanation for the contrast between (28) and (29) in the scrambling (and non-verb-raising) analysis. In (29), *kankokugo* 'Korean' undergoes left-node raising, and gets extracted out of the conjoined embedded clauses. *Deki-(na-)* 'can' undergoes right-node raising, and gets extracted out of the conjoined clauses. These two processes, after tree-pruning, yield the structure shown below:

(30) a. Underlying Structure
    [Taroo [[kankokugo hanas-u] koto mo deki-ru]] AND
    [Taroo [[kankokugo yom-u] koto mo deki-ru]]

    b. After application of Left-node Raising and Right-node Raising
    [Taro kankokugo [$_{VP}$ [$_{NP}$ *e* hanas-u koto mo *e* yom-u koto mo]
    [$_V$ deki-(na)-Pres]]]

Now, *kankokugo* 'Korean' has become the left sibling of the VP *hanas-u koto mo yom-u koto mo deki-* 'can both speak and read.' Let us assume that the complementizer *koto* does not block the percolation of the stativity of *deki-* 'can' onto the VP node. Then, *kankokugo* 'Korean' is the object of the stative VP, and hence it is nominatively case-marked. On the other hand, in (28a, b), since neither left-node raising nor right-node raising applies to the structure, *kankokugo* 'Korean' remains in the object position of the nonstative verb *hanas-* 'speak'. Hence the impossibility of marking it with a nominative case marker.

In the above, I have tried to account for the acceptability of (29a, b) on the basis of left-node raising and right-node raising. The following examples, however, suggest that this raising process is not dependent upon the presence of syntactically conjoined *koto ga deki-ru* structures:

(31) a. ok/? Taroo wa kankokugo **ga**, hanas-u koto sae deki-ru.
              Korean   Nom speak-Pres to even can-Pres
         'Taro can even speak Korean.'

   b. ok/? Taroo wa kankokugo **ga**, hanas-u koto mo deki-ru.
              Korean   Nom speak-Pres to also can-Pres
         'Taro can also speak Korean.

The presence of *sae* 'even' in (31a) and *mo* 'also' in (31b) implies that Taro can understand spoken Korean, can read written Korean, and can write Korean. That is, semantically speaking, (31a) and (31b) have structures similar to that of (30a). It seems that this allows *kankokugo* to be raised *from [[kankokugo hanas-u] koto ga deki-ru],* and become a sibling of the stative *[e hanas-u koto ga deki-ru].*

It is interesting to note that the way that (31a), for example, is pronounced is very different from the way that its accusative-case marked counterpart is pronounced. Observe the following:

(32) a. Taroo wa [kankokugo o hanas-u] koto sae deki-ru.
   b. *Taroo wa [kankokugo ga hanas-u] koto sae deki-ru.
   c. ok/?Taroo wa [kankokugo ga] [hanas-u koto sae deki-ru]

While *kankokugo o hanas-u* 'speak Korean' can be pronounced as a constituent as shown in (32a), *kankokugo ga hanas-u* cannot be, as witnessed by the total unacceptability of (32b). The unacceptability of (32b) parallels that of sentences that contain *wa*-marked elements in embedded non-quotative clauses, as discussed in Section 2 of this paper.

Let us assume that there is a process similar to topic raising that extracts a focus element out of an embedded clause and makes it a main clause element. This process, which I will refer to as "focus raising," must be responsible for the fact that (33a, b) are acceptable, awkward, or marginal on the exhaustive listing interpretation of the *ga*-marked embedded object.

(33) a.   ok/?Taroo wa [kankokugo **ga**] // [hanas-u koto ga deki-ru]
                    Korean Nom   speak-Pres to   can-Pres
            'It is Korean that Taro can speak.'

    b.   ok/?Taroo wa [kankokugo **ga**] // [hanas-u koto ga deki-na-i.
                    Korean   speak-Pres to   can-Neg-Pres
            'It is Korean that Taro can't speak.'

We can attribute the idiolectal variations in the acceptability judgments of these sentences to the idiolectal variations in the status of the focus raising rule. For some speakers, there is no penalty in the application of this rule, while for other speakers, there are varying degrees of penalty.

    In the above, I have identified two ways that an underlying object of the embedded verb in the potential construction can become a main clause constituent - via the application of left-/right-node raising, and via focus raising. (27c) with a nominative case marker is unacceptable because neither the former not the latter process could have applied to it. The sentence does not involve either syntactic or semantic coordination. Likewise, *nanika* 'something' is semantically too nonspecific to qualify for focus raising. (28a, b) are unacceptable on the non-focus interpretation of the *ga*-marked underlying embedded object because left-/right-node raising could not have applied to them; but they are acceptable, nearly acceptable, or marginal, depending on the speaker, on the focus interpretation of the *ga*-marked NP because *kankokugo* 'Korean' is specific enough to undergo focus raising. (29a, b) are acceptable on both nonfocus and focus interpretations of the *ga*-marked underlying embedded object NP, because the underlying coordinated structure can undergo left-/right-node raising, and because the extracted underlying object is specific enough to undergo focus raising. There are also two derivations of (31a, b), but the focus interpretation of the *ga*-marked NP is pragmatically less likely because contexts in which one can say "It is Korean that Taro can even/also speak" are not readily available.

    Finally, observe the following contrast:

(34) a.   Taroo wa kankokugo **o** ryuutyooni hanas-u koto ga deki-ru.
                    Korean   fluently   speak-Pres to can-Pres
            'Taro can speak Korean fluently.'

    b.   ok/?Taroo wa kankokugo **ga**, ryuutyooni hanas-u koto ga deki-ru.
            [acceptable only on the exhaustive listing interpretation of
            kankokugo ga]

(35) a.   Taroo wa ryuutyooni kankokugo **o** hanas-u koto ga deki-ru.
                    fluently   Korean   speak-Pres to can-Pres
            'Taro can speak Korean fluently.'

    b.   ??/*Taroo wa ryuutyooni kankokugo **ga**, hanas-u koto ga deki-ru.

While (34a) and (35a) are equally acceptable, (35b) is considerably worse than (34b). This can be attributed to the presence of *ryuutyooni* 'fluently' to the left of the *ga*-marked object. This adverb, since it is a nontopical, nonfocus adverb, cannot be easily scrambled out of the embedded clause, and is interpreted as an embedded clause constituent, and thus blocks the interpretation of the underlying embedded object as a main clause constituent.

The task for the proponents of the verb raising analysis is to account for the above facts without resorting to left-/right-node raising, or to scrambling processes such as topic and focus raising. I predict that it will be impossible to do so without making verb raising dependent upon those factors that trigger or block such processes. These factors can readily be motivated for NP extraction, but cannot be for verb raising. Furthermore, if the proponents of the verb raising analysis opt to claim that the stativity of *deki-* 'can' is percolated up onto the VP node dominating *V-ru koto-ga deki-*, with the unacceptability of (27c) to be accounted for by some other means, they will get into a rule-ordering paradox. In order to obtain the *ga*-marking of *koto* as in *hanasu koto-ga deki-*, nominative case marking must take place before verb raising. On the other hand, in order to obtain the nominative case marking of the embedded object as in (29a, b), nominative case making must apply after verb raising. I have to conclude that the *ga*-marking of the underlying object in the potential *koto-ga dekiru* construction favors the scrambling analysis, and disfavors the verb raising analysis. This, coupled with the conclusion in Section 2 that the scrambling analysis can, but the verb raising analysis cannot, account for certain NPI licensing facts, seems to firmly establish that it is not possible to justify the claim that the potential *koto-ga dekiru* and the experiential *koto-ga aru* constructions involve the raising of "V + Tense + *koto ga*" to the main clause verbs *deki-* 'can' and *ar-* 'have'.

References

Dubinsky, S. 1992. Case Assignment to VP-adjoined Positions: Nominative Objects in Japanese. *Linguistics* 30: 873-910.

Kato, Y. 1991. Negative Polarity in Japanese and the Levels of Representation. *The Tsuda Review* 36:151-179.

Kuno, S. 1976. Subject Raising. *Japanese Generative Grammar*. Ed. M. Shibatani. 17-49. New York: Academic Press.

Kuno, S. 1995. Negative Polarity Items in Japanese and English. *Harvard Working Papers in Linguistics*. 5:165-197. ed. S. Epstein et al. Department of Linguistics, Harvard University.

Kuno, S. 1999. The Syntax and Semantics of the *Dake* and *Sika* Constructions. *Harvard Working Papers in Linguistics*. 7:144-172. ed. B. Vaux et al. Department of Linguistics, Harvard University.

Muraki, M. 1975. The *Sika Nai* Construction. *Problems in Japanese Syntax and Semantics*. ed. J. Hinds and I. Howard. 155-177. Tokyo:Kaitakusha.

Negative Polarity in Korean and Japanese

CHUNGMIN LEE

Seoul National University

1. Introduction

Monotone-decreasingness (Ladusaw 1979) and non-veridicality (Zwarts 1995) are nice function types to characterize the licensing contexts of NPIs and Free Choice Items (FCIs) but the former fails to account for weak NPIs and the latter for emotive factive predicates (*lucky*, etc.)(C. Lee 1999).[1]

Here we propose a unified solution by concession. The majority of languages such as Japanese (J), Korean (K), Chinese, Mongolian, Hindi, Zapotec and Basque form NPIs and FCIs by combining *wh*-based (otherwise, [*any*]-like) indefinites and concessives ("even"). In all languages, the lowest indefinite natural number "one"/a minimizer with a concessive also forms an

[1] I benefited from co-work with Ed Keenan, Daeho Chung and Seungho Nam for my NPI project supported by KRF (1998-2000 Grant) through the Institute for Cognitive Science of SNU and also from discussion with UCLA and UCI people (including Harkema and Fukui). I owe Y. Takasu and Y. Miura among others for consultation in Japanese. Thanks go to Noriko Akatsuka for the memorable J/K 10 and to the guests and audience for discussion.

NPI. For the *wh*-based type, which is qualitative, concession is made by arbitrary choice. A *wh*-Q is a set of alternative answers as (true) propositions (Hamblin 1973) and the set of individuals that correspond to the *wh*-information focus is a "*wh*-domain."

2. Types and Distribution

Consider Zwarts' (1995) definition of veridicality: (1) a. *Op* is veridical iff *Op* (*p*) → *p* is logically valid. Otherwise, *Op* is nonveridical. b. A nonveridical *Op* is averidical iff *Op* (*p*) → ¬ *p* is logically valid. An averidical operator makes its proposition always false, strongly negative. A nonveridical though not averidical is weakly negative and does not always license NPIs. A veridical context is episodically assertive. Contexts in K are:

(2) (a) averidical contexts (antimorphic [overt negation]; anti-additive): negated S, *eps-ta/moru-ta* 'not-exist'/'know' S, *cen-ey* 'before' clause, (strongly negative predicates)
(b) nonveridical contexts: [weak NPIs] conditionals, generic/ universal modifiers, questions, *kikkethaeya* 'at most', emotive factive predicates, negative predicates; [FCIs] modals, imperatives, future, comparatives (strong form *–to*), generics, etc. Cf. A similar pattern in Greek (Giannakidou 1998).

Consider the strong and weak polarity types as well as the *-i-na* type:

Types \\ Contexts	*Amwu*(*etten*) N-*to*	*Amwu*(*etten*) N-*i-ra-to*	*amwu*(*etten*) N-*i-na*
1. Negative S	√	*	*(?)
2. *eps-/molu-*'not-exist'/'not-know'	√	*	*
3. '*before*'-clauses	√	√(?)	?
4. Negative Predicates	√(?)	√?	?
5. Modals	*	√	√
6. Imperatives	*	√	√
7. Future tense	*	√	√
8. Generics	*	√	√
9. *kikkethayya* 'at most'	*	√	*
10. Rhetorical Q	*	√	√
11. Questions	*	√(?)	?
12. Conditionals	*	√	?
13. Comparatives/Prefer	√/*	*/√?	*/√
14. Habituals	*	√?	*

15. Generic Quantifier	*	√	√
16. Affirmative S	*	*	√

Table 1. The distribution of *amwu-N-to/-i-rato/-i-na* in various contexts

The *wh*-based ones and the *amu* N-*to* and *amwu*-N-*i-ra-to* occur in the same contexts. The FC *nwukwu-ra-to* in modal contexts and the FCIs such as *nwukwu*-pota-*to* 'than whoever else' in comparatives are perfect.

Turn to the types and distribution in J. J does not have the series of items corresponding to the non-*wh*-based *amu* N-*to* or *amu* N-*i-ra-to* in K or *any* in English. J only has the *wh*-based polarity items. Observe:

Types Contexts	A DaRE-MO DoNNA N-MO NaNI-MO	B DAre-mo(ga) Donna N-mo NAni-mo(ga)	C DaRE-DEMO DoNNA N-DEMO NaN-DEMO	D DAre-demo DOnna N-demo NAn-demo
1. Negative S	√	√	*	*?
2. 'before'-Cls	*/√	*	*?	*?
3. Neg Preds	√(?)	√	√	√
4. Modals	*	√	√	√
5. Imperatives	*/√	*/√	√	√
6. Future tense	*	√	√	√
7. Generics	*/√	*/√	√	√
8. 'at most'	*	*	√?	√?
9. Rhetorical Q	√	√	√(?)	√(?)
10. Questions	*	*	√?	√?
11. Condit'nals	*	*	√?	√
12. Compr'tves	√	*	√	√
13. Habituals	*	*	*	*
14. Generic Qntfr	*	*	√	√
15. Affrmt'v S	*	√ ?(o)	√(o) ?(s)	√(o) ?(s)

Table 3. The distribution of *donna* N-*mo/-de-mo* in various contexts

Note the typological and distributional affinities between the strong type in K (*amu/etten* N-*to*) and that in J (*donna* N-*mo*, (A)). The strong type occurs in 'before' clauses rather felicitously in K and defectively in J. The strong and weak types are mutually exclusive in licensing contexts and may be common in their semantic nature. NPIs are variable-like CNC INDs.

The third type in K (*amwu(etten)* N-*i-na*) became different from the other types. Likewise, the B type of J became universal and different from A.

Ss with strongly 'negative predicates' such as *kecel-ha-ta* 'refuse' in J/K license strong NPIs, although negation in them is not overt and it makes their Ss a little unstable in K but quite tolerable in J, licensing between the strong and the weak. These are not included in Zwarts' (1993) licensor types.

Although averidical entails nonveridical, it does not follow that a strong NPI form in J/K can also be used in affective or modal contexts.

3. How Concession Works

3.1 Quantitative Scale
When the particle –*to/–mo* is attached to a definite NP, it either is additive, or is concessive (C. Lee 1993). Even in the concessive sense, a definite + –*to/–mo* can occur with either a positive or negated predicate. But –*to/–mo* attached to an indefinite such as a numeral/minimizer (and IND-*wh*- including *amu*- (and *any* (Lee and Horn 1994))) can only be concessive:

> (3) a. sacang –to   w-ass-e/an w-ass-e
>   b. shatyoo-mo   kitta/ko-nakatta
>   president-also/CNC came/didn't come
>   'The president also/Even the president came/didn't come.'
> (4) a. han saram –to   an w-ass-ta
>   one person-CNC not come-PAST-DEC
>   b. hitori   -mo   ko-nakatta (a, b) 'One person-CNC didn't come.'
> (5) a. han saram –i[NOM]   an w-ass-ta (NOM=Nominative)
>   b. hitori (-ga)   ko-nakatta (a, b) 'One person didn't come.'
> (6) a. *han saram –to w-ass-ta
>   b. *hitori -mo   kita   (a, b) 'One person-CNC came.'

In (4), *han saram* 'one person' is indefinite, nonspecific and not a partition, if followed by a CNC, as shown. If it is followed by a NOM, as in (5), it must be either specific or a partition, though not definite, taking wide scope over the negation in the S. So, 'more didn't come' is not scalarly entailed by (5). Attributing polarity simply to focus, as done by Rooth (1985), Krifka (1994) and Lahiri (1998) or to simple scalar implicatures as proposed by Chierchia (2000) is not adequate enough. [2] Further, the simple focus-induced alternatives to *sacang* 'president' followed by a focus NOM may be

---

[2]Chierchia's approach simply lacks an ultimate motivation behind polarity. Concession triggers an adversative scale and suspends scalar implicatures. So, contrary to his expectation, an implicature of 'not both' is suspended in the following S because of the concessive 'even' without any negative predicate such as 'doubt': *Even Kim or Lee will show up* ('Both will show up' is OK). With *even*, it is suspended.

{president, professor, secretary, ---}. Rooth's focus alternatives are not scalar and his simple extension to *even* for likelihood implicatures lacks explanation. The motivation of scalar alternatives lies in concession. When you make concession you go down the scale of alternative adverse steps. So, the weakest bound must be negatively rendered. Thus total negation of the maximization of the relevant *wh*-domain is possible. The emphatic concessive adversity reaches maximization reversely. (4) has the original assertion part (7) and the likelihood hierarchy implicature part (8):

(7) $\neg \exists x[\mathbf{one}(x) \wedge \text{person}(x) \wedge x \text{ came}]$ (assuming that **one** is true of any entity that contains at least one atomic part)

(8) For every cardinality natural numeral predicate U, U' such that
$\forall x[\mathbf{U}(x) \to \mathbf{U'}(x)]$,
likelihood $(\widehat{\ }\neg \exists x[\mathbf{U}(x) \wedge \text{person}(x) \wedge x \text{ came})])$
$>$likelihood $(\widehat{\ }\neg \exists x[\mathbf{U'}(x) \wedge \text{person}(x) \wedge x \text{ came})])$

Positive scalarity is reversed to negative scalarity in (8). Lahiri's (1998) formalization along with Rooth's (1985) about simple alternatives as opposed to **one** fails to show any scalarity based on concession, unlike the above formalization. The maximality of U above is that of the relevant *wh*-domain, which can hardly be definite, and the minimality of U' is **one**.

Why are the Ss of (6) above 'ill-formed'? Up to the point of *han saram - to, hitori -mo* 'one person + CNC,' because of concession marked by CNC and its foreseen negativity/adversity, a proposition involving a stronger predicate (larger number) is likelier than the one involving a weaker one in an expected negative context. But, if it turns out to be combined with a positive predicate like *w-ass-ta/kita* 'came,' because of $\forall x[\mathbf{U}(x) \to \mathbf{U'}(x)]$, likelihood is reversed, contradicting (8) to cause unacceptability, as (9):

(9) likelihood $(\widehat{\ }\neg \exists x[\mathbf{U}(x) \wedge \text{person}(x) \wedge x \text{ came}])$
$<$likelihood $(\widehat{\ }\neg \exists x[\mathbf{U'}(x) \wedge \text{person}(x) \wedge x \text{ came})])$

The process of conflict itself except scalarity was well captured in Lahiri (1998). Lack of scalarity in Rooth and Lahiri, however, leads to the failure of distinguishing between contrastive focus and concession. Contrastive focus induces simple alternatives, which may cause difficulty treating this:

(10) sey saram -to   an   w   -ass   -ta
     three person-CNC not   come-PAST-DEC
(11) SAN NIn -MO   KO -nakat -ta
     three person-CNC   come-NEG-PAST
     (a, b) 'Not even three persons came.' ('Less than three came.')

Simple alternatives to 'three' include not only numbers higher than 'three' but also numbers lower than 'three,' whereas concession requires 'three' with

CNC as a lower bound on the quantitative scale from the least as expected in the discourse, denying propositions with higher numbers scalarly.

If CNC is attached to a universal quantifier, it becomes ill-formed; CNC requires a lower bound. A universal quantifier is a maximality operator.

(12) a. *motu -to (an) w -ass -ta
      all   -CNC not come-PAST-DEC
    b. *minna -mo ko -nakat-ta/kita (a, b) 'Even all didn't come/came.'

How about a definite NP plus CNC in (2)? It does not require a negative context, unlike an indefinite (except a kind-referring common noun). The affirmative S of (3) in the concessive sense is still the least likely thing to happen and there is only one concession denoting marker -to/-mo or particle *even* in favor of Wilkinson's (1996) one *even* thesis over Rooth's two *evens*.

The stressed *hana* 'one'/minimizer plus a classifier (and CNC) function as a strong NPI. The combination even without a classifier is used as an adverbial NPI not only for the countable but also for mass/abstract in K:

(13) ku-nun yangsim -i   hana-to/cokum-to/cenhye eps-ta
    he-TOP conscience-NOM one-CNC/a little-CNC/at all not exist
    'He has no conscience at all.'

In (13), *cenhye* 'at all'(K) (*cencen* 'at all'(J)) originate from universals and that is why they cannot be followed by -to/-mo but because they occur only with negation for total negation with negation narrow scope ($\forall\neg$) they tend to mean the same as the minimizing NPIs ($\neg\exists$). English *ever* also originated from a universal and may still be used with emphasis on it like *not Ever* but more often it is used in its IND plus CNC sense of *even one time* in affective contexts (Heim 1984, Lee 1999). They acquired concessive meaning indirectly as soon as they become polarity-sensitive and equivalent to weak quantitatives in wide negative scope. However, because they come from the universal, they cannot occur with CT, as in **cenhye'*ever'-*nun*(CT), **jenjen'*ever'-*wa*(CT)(J), unlike minimizers, as in *han pen-un* and *cokum-un* (C. Lee 2000). In J/K even those lowest cardinal numeral/minimizer NPIs have the strong vs. weak forms. The weak form is licensed in the anti-additive context of a modifier of a generic in J/K (*ichi-do-de-mo* 'ever' J): *cungkuk-ey han pen-i-ra-to ka po-n saram -un son tul -e-ra* 'Those who have ever been to China, raise your hands!'

The quantitative NPIs are also based on *wh*-domains; they can serve as answers to Qs such as **'How many/much** students/water came/leaked?' Then, the answer set of is the contextually determined set of propositions with 'students' or amount of 'water' --- *wh*-domains. The *wh*-domain for Q cannot be 'definite,' though approximated to definite, contra Kawashima (1994). If a cardinal with a positive matrix predicate is given as an answer, e.g., 'Seven students came,' then it is a maximal number that came to be informative enough. But if it appears with a monotone-decreasing predicate such as 'sufficient', it is **minimal** and any higher number is also sufficient (cf. Beck and Rullmann 1999). It has a hidden sense of permission deontic modality, which is inherently concessive. It turned out that quantitative scalar NPIs are also basically *wh*-based, though restricted to quantity.

3.2 Qualitative Scale

C. Lee (1996) showed how concession calls for arbitrariness in treating qualitative NPIs including *amu/etten- - (-ra) -to* and *any*, which are underlyingly based on IND-*wh*-. Any number of modifiers can modify a head noun as adjectives/restrictive relative clauses. If something is n times modified, an n number of subsets arise. The more modified, the stronger it becomes in information. If modification decreases, the head nominal gets more general and weaker in information and the weakest possible is a headless *what*. It may stand for a totality in ontology but can be restricted in contexts.

Concession is made by going down the scale of different layers of characterization of the head N or even no head denotation in affective contexts. The headless *what* and its equivalents can refer to anything in the world for an answer (*wh*-domain) and its indefinite form can be just the same form *what* in many languages, as in J/K (*muet*-K, *nani*-J). Reduplicated IND-*wh*-forms easily function as FCIs in many languages such as Latin (*quid-quid* 'whatever'). In still many other languages, the IND-*what* is a combination of *what/quelque* and *thing/chose*, equivalent to an abstract nonspecific nonpartition SOMETHING. This is the weakest predicate we can think of on the scale of quality. Then, by concession with its expression *-to/-mo/even*, we go down level by level of properties from the most specific, say restricted by n modifications, to the n-1 modifications, to the lowest possible/weakest predicate, by increasing the degree of concession and thus the degree of arbitrariness proportionally. So, the expression [n modifications + *etten/amu/donna*(J)-N-(*i-ra-*)*to/-*(*de*) *-mo*(J)] denotes an *arbitrary* N-denotation with n properties. If there are no modifications, then the levels of arbitrariness increase because the *wh*-domain widens accordingly. This arbitrary choice is done by 'blind' choice in its game-theoretic sense and is conceptually different from the pure quantitative scale. However, it is tested by going down the scale of arbitrariness degree (for the most likely/easy thing) to turn it to the most adverse/unlikely thing because of concession. If the context is strongly negative, universal negation is meant; if affective, 'begging' for an early existential satisfaction is meant; and if modal, free choice of approximation to universal is meant by means of 'betting' in the choice with a permission functor plus disjunctive arguments along the scale (C. Lee 1997). Speakers intensify this degree of arbitrariness with the prosodic feature of stress. Fine (1985) independently discussed a related notion of 'arbitrariness,' interpreted as possessing all and only properties characteristic of a class. Tovena and Jayez (1997) nicely applied it to *any*.

3.3 Where Does It Come From and Where Does It Go?

In argumentation, concession is typically made by the speaker's admitting the other party's or a hypothesized given assertion adversely and projecting one's own assertive position. A concessive construction is "*pi-ka w-a-to---,*" (*ame-ga hutte-mo --- J*) 'Even if it rains, ---.' We will go on a picnic even if it is cloudy, less adverse than raining (cf. Koenig 1988, no scalarity). The concessive clause ends with the same *–to/-mo*, just as *even* in English *even if*. It presupposes a conditional 'If it rains, (people/I) don't go on a picnic.' The concessive and the consequent are not compatible, unlike in the conditional. When a concessive has a hypothetical, not factual adversative, sense ('concessive conditional'), its main clause tends to be modal/generic/future.

All these intensional predicates anchor an extended modal base (Kratzer 1977) of P = set of propositions in W(P), a set of worlds to which the propositions in their scope are anchored and become true. A general concessive situation would be 'Whatever the weather looks like (*etteh-hae-to*), ---.' If we extend the level of concession to the most adverse situation possible, this steps in: *nani-/donna koto-ga atte-mo pikunikku-ni iku* 'Whatever happens, (we) (will) go on a picnic.' The most arbtrary event is expressed with the free relative *whatever* in English and a stressed INDwh + N----to (CNC) in K, showing an *irrealis* concessive situation. Some abstract postulate such as 'EVEN IF + stressed INDwh-' corresponds to 'whatever,' with the stressed INDwh- applying to a *wh*-domain of events, with IF/'in case' applying to the set of worlds where the relevant propositions are anchored or become true. A concessive clause started as an adjunct and then became an argument NP clause and then a non-clausal NP (*I can do **whatever***). Then, what is the difference between [*amu* --- CNC] and [INDwh- --- CNC] in K, when the former is not present in J? The two are almost interchangeable. But the former gives a sweeping generalization in arbitrariness like English *any*, whereas the latter gives more attention to individuals/events one by one more specifically in checking. The former, because of its sweepingness, becomes more dominant than the latter in most situations, the latter becoming slightly unstable in various contexts in K.

Now, where do they go? In K, the [*amu*/INDwh- N-*i-na*(DISJunctive)] series became near-universal quantifiers because of its predominent indiscriminacy (more in *amu* --- than in INDwh-), occurring in even episodic contexts, although they still favor modal contexts. In J, the series INDwh- - - *mo*(*-ga*) became (near-)universals, via FCIs, occurring in episodic contexts. A concessive construction develops into an FCI (and further it can become a universal) and an FCI into an NPI in negatively narrowed-down contexts.

The derogatory *amu-i-na*, which occurs in underlyingly quality-wise per-mission/selection-oriented contexts, and the weaker form *amu-ra-to* cannot occur in overtly negative contexts just like *dare-de-mo* in J and *just any*:

(17) a. ?*amu-i-na[just anyone]/ *amui-ra-to an[not] w-ass-e[came]
    b. *daRE-DE-MO KO-nakatta
    (a, b) Lit: 'Just anyone didn't come.'
(18) a. *Just anyone* can't/didn't do it.
    b. *Not *anyone* came/can do it.
    c. Not *just anyone* can do it/came.

In a very limited denial context with a slight rising tone on *–na* and a com-pensatory pause after it, (17a-*amu-na*) can be barely acceptable. They are quality- but not quantity-based derogatoriness-denial understatements. Such degree adverbs as *póthong* (from 'commonly') and *yégan* (from 'relatively'), with stress on their first syllables, function as wide scope negation/modality-taking NPIs as norm-denying upward understatements. This is somewhat contrary to Cho and Lee (2001).[3] Similarly, *cóm* with stress (from *com* 'a little') is a weak NPI that typically occurs in a rhetorical Q and certainty-incredulity modality. These have up-ward assertive force and thus do not occur in a sincere Q, which has Q force seeking information on the degree.

In J/K, [INDnum CL CNC] constitutes an NPI, as shown in (10) and (11). But when the numeral gets stress on itself like [SAN-nin-mo] with the same marker *–mo*, the expression is no longer an NPI, and gets the meaning of 'as many as' in J, whereas the same expression is realized as [SEY saram-*i-na*] with the COP-DISJ marker *-i-na* in K. These in J/k can occur either in posi-tive or negative contexts, out of the scope of negation as PPIs (see 23 b, c):

(19) a. *SEY* saram *–i-na* (an) w-ass-ta (K)
    b. *SAN*-nin-*mo* ki-ta/ko-nakat-ta (J)
    'As many as three persons came/didn't come.'
(20) a. *SAN*-nin-*mo* ki-ta ato (-de) watashi-wa dekaket-ta (J)
          came after   I –TOP departed
    'After as many as three persons came, I left.'

---

[3] These are frozen with stress, being distinct from unstressed counterparts that are not NPIs. They can occur with incredulity modality in local domain with no long in such Ss as:
    ku   chinku póthong/yégan kananhae-ya-ji!/kemanhae-ya-ji/ton-i eps-e-ya-ji/ani-ya
    that friend commonly/relatively poor -not
    'That friend is unusually poor/vain/poor/not common, unbelievably.'
A rhetorical Q with *yekan* cannot be answered with *ani* 'no,' contrary to Cho and Lee. They treat *yégan* with interesting observations but their lexically-bound way misses semantically principle-based generalizations applicable to all the related items. Understatements are rooted in concession, avoiding a threatened face as a by-product strategy (Horn's (1984) QR).

b. ?*SAN-nin-mo kuru mae-ni [before] watashi-wa dekaket-ta (J)
c. ?*SEY saram –i-na o-ki   cen-ey   na-nun ttena-ss-ta (K)
(b, c) Lit. 'Before as many as three persons came, I left.'(bad)

The positive Ss in (19) are appropriate for a positive Q and the negative Ss for a negative Q both with focus on the information part corresponding to the wh-questions "How many". The negative Ss of (19) entail the Ss of the relative scope [three --- [NOT]], whereas (10) and (11) entail the Ss of [NOT[three---]] (Chung et al 2000). The Ss in (19) have A accent with H*LL%, whereas the Ss in (10) and (11) have some intonation pattern of [LL+H]$_{AP}$ L* L% in K. The Ss in (19) show a surprise at the higher turnout than expected (concessively 'not even two were expected'), with assertive force. So, the direction of attention is upward, although the denotation of the numeral is discrete. The same morpheme –mo in J is used, though with a different intonation pattern, for this direction-reversed situation.

4. The wh- Origin: Concessive Clause with INDwh-

In J, a wh-form associated with –mo is invariably called a wh- word from Kuroda (1965) to Shimoyama (1999). But (21) no Q marker to license it:

(21) [[**Dono** gakusei-ga   syootaisita] sensei]-mo kita. (J)
     INDwh- student-Nom   invited teacher-MO came
     (Lit.) 'The teacher(s) that whichever student invited came.'

The counterpart in K is not quite acceptable because of the episodic predicate; a negated predicate is required for a negative polarity complex NP in K. In a modal context in K, it would be a free choice complex NP with the weaker form –i-ra-to after the head noun.

If a stressed INDwh- occurs in an adjunct clause with the concessive operator –to, it must be followed by a modally context for universal force.

(22) a. Yumi-nun [**nuku**-rul manna-to]   son-ul huntu-n-ta
        -TOP INDwho-ACC meet-CNC hand-ACC waves
        'Yumi waves at whoever she meets.'
     b. [[**nu**-ka w-a-to] coh-ta] (K)'[Whoever may come] is OK.'
     c. [[**nuku**-i-ra-to]   coh-ta] (K) '[Whoever it may be] is OK.'

Then, the concessive clauses of (22) come to have FC reading. Even if a stressed definite NP such as [Sumi]$_F$ replaces the stressed INDwho **nuku** in (25a), the embedded S remains concessive, Sumi being the least likely person to wave at. This holds for J, contrary to Shimoyama's (1999) claim that only additive sense is available. Even if it occurs with a past predicate, it is a habitual past. The concessive INDwh- and –to cannot be factually past in K: *[**nuku**-rul manna-ss-nun-tey-to]--- cf. [nuku-rul---] ('someone'). The Ss of (22) can be changed into Qs by replacing the CNC operator –to by the conditional –myen 'if' and the DEC marker –ta by the Q ending –ni. In Slavic languages, a wh- n-word clause is analogously a concessive FC clause. The clause form '**nuku-i-ra-to**' functioning as a nominal in negative contexts changed to the shorter stronger **nuku-to**. The typical NPIs amu-i-ra-to and amu-to occur in similar contexts and are underlyingly analogous.

5. The So-called N-Words and Intervention Effect

The so-called n-words in n-concord languages such as Slavic, Modern Greek, Hungarian and Romance are NPIs with the same mechanism of concession. Because I argue that NPIs are underlyingly INDwh-based, we find similarities between wh-dependencies and n-concord (Higginbothom et al 1981). Multi-n-concord reflects multi-wh-questions and particularly wh-in-situ. Multi-NPIs in J/K are also n-concord. Observe:

(23) a. amu/nuku-to   amu/etten chaek-to   ilk-ci anh-ass-ta
         any/INDwh-CNC any/INDwh- book-CNC read-CNC not-did
     b. ??amu/etten chaek-to amu/nuku-to ilk-ci anh-ass-ta
        'No one read any books.'
(24) dare-mo nani-mo tabe-nakat-ta Cf. ??nani-mo dare-mo tabe-nakat-ta
     'No one ate anything.'

One sentential negation per clause (Klima 1964) applies to any number of NPIs and so does one modal to any number of weak form FCIs in J/K. There is no inherently negative feature in NPIs in J/K and most n-concord n-words. N-words as NPIs are inherently concessive indefinites triggering scales of arbitrariness. In J/K the underlying order of SOV is preferred by multi-NPIs.

Turn to intervention/blocking effects between wh-words and NPIs:

(25) ?*amu/nuku-to   mues-ul   mek-ci anh-ass-ni? (K)
         amu-INDwh-CNC what-ACC eat-CI not-PAST-Q
     'What did no one eat?'
(25') ?*dare-mo nani-o tabe-nakatta-no? (J)
(26) mues-ul   amu/nuku-to   mek-ci anh-ass-ni? (K)
(26') nani-o dare-mo tabe-nakatta-no? (J) 'What did no one eat?'

The NPI>wh-phrase order as in (25) and (25') is hardly acceptable whereas the scrambled order wh-phrase>NPI is quite all right. My initial claim (C. Lee 1999) was that there is a hierarchy of focality strength among different *wh*-based expressions: *wh*-phrase>IND*wh- -to/amu- -to* (NPI)>*wh*-IND in that order. Sh. Kim (2001) also made it clear that the above effect is due to a focality effect, modifying Beck and Kim's (1996) claim that it is blocking an intervening "quantifier." K. Lee and S. Tomoika (2001) extended the discussion to facts in embedded Ss and attributed the constraint to topicality:

(27) (?) ne-nun [amu/nuku-to mues-ul ilk-ci anhassta]-ko saengkakhani?
'What do you think that no one read?'
(27') (?) kimi-wa [dare-mo nani-o yom-ana-katta]-to omotteiru-no?
(28) ?ne-nun [amu/etten kes-to nu-ka ilk-ci anhassta]-ko saengkakhani?
'Who do you think didn't read anything?'

TOP is not marked for subjects in embedded Ss in general, but it is not marked in Q Ss in K except for the 2nd person pronoun, either. This is an embedding effect of Q Ss in K unlike in J. A non-contrastive TOP *–nun* often gets neutralized (never focused) NOM *–ka* marking when it competes with a following CT *–nun* even in a matrix S. There is a tendency of neutralization of information structure in embedded Ss. Even in a matrix S, when NPIs (with no case) of the same degree of focaltity (or bare nominals) occur, the reading in the order S-O-V wins, as in (26), (27) and in *amu-to amu-to sarang-ha-ci an-h-nun-ta* 'No one loves anyone.'

Note Ae. Kim's (2001) short-/long-form negation and my further data:

(29) a. *amu-to computer-man[only] an [not] sa-ss-ta [bought]
b. computer-man amu-to an sa-ss-ta [only>not]
(a-b) 'It is only the computer that nobody bought.'
(30) amu-to computer-man[only] sa-ci -nun[CT] anh-ass-ta
'It was not the case that anyone bought only the computer.'
[only(comp)<not, only(comp(buy))<not]
(31) a. amu-to computer-man-un sa-ci anh-ass-ta/an sa-ss-ta
b. computer-man-un[CT] amu-to sa-ci anh-ass-ta/an sa-ss-ta
(a,b) 'It was only the computer among alternatives that no one bought.' [among alternatives-only(comp)>not]

The focus-marked S-initial phrase *computer-man* has wide scope in (29b), whereas negation has wide scope in (30) and positing a higher structural position for the long NEG such as IP/vP seems plausible. Then, there occurs an embedding effect and the order NPI>Focus in (30) is explained away. However, with CT *–nun* a short NEG is also possible in (31a), unlike in (29a). In (31), scrambling of NPI and Focus is free with no meaning change. (29a) is not improved in an embedded situation and its uninterpretability is more serious than others. Another point Sh. Kim and K. S. Lee et al miss is that a focused NP associated with a CT (as partly observed by Sohn 1996) behaves differently from the *wh*-Focus-Phrase>NPI constraint. The order of NPI>CT-associated focused Phrase is OK but not the other way around:

(32) a. amu-to [computer-rul^F] sa –ci –***nun*** anh-ass-ta
     'Nobody bought a computer (but someone - some thing else).'
  b. *[computer-rul^F] amu-to sa –ci –***nun*** anh-ass-ta
     'Nobody bought a computer (but - - something else.' (Intended)
  c. amu-kes-to [Yumi-ka^F] sa –ci –***nun*** anh-ass-ta
     'Yumi bought nothing but someone other than Yumi - something.'
  d. *[Yumi-ka^F] amu-kes-to sa –ci –***nun*** anh-ass-ta
     'Yumi bought nothing but someone else - something.' (Intended)

Multi-NPIs in a row, in (32a) with *eti-ese-to* ---'- anywhere -,' is OK, but not multiple CT-associated phrases, as in *amu-kes-to [Yumi-ka^F][Sears-ese^F] sa-ci–nun anh-ass-ta* (cf. (32c)) 'Someone other than Yumi didn't buy anything at some place other than Sears.' As in (32e), a CT-marked NP can scramble before an NPI with its topical feature. We discussed its focal feature as well. This kind of partial "Link", which is also focal in a sense, is not easy to treat in terms of Vallduvi's (1998) Link and Tail. The notion of Tail is not clear and NPIs in J/K cannot take TOP because of their morphological constraint (*-mo/-to* originally an adverbializer) and their emphatic/focal nature associated with the negative focus. In Chinese, different degrees of Focus are shown by the additive *ye*, concessive *lian* N *ye*, *zhiyou* 'only', NPI *shei ye* 'IND*who* +CNC', with unacceptability getting more serious in that order when followed by a *wh*-phrase (Sh. Kim 2001), which holds true for K.

An S-initial *wh*-phrase or a high-pitched focus is followed by a downstepping or dephrasing effect (Jun 1993) but a wide scope Topic phrase (forming an AP in K) or a similar stuff may precede it. There is indeed a close interplay between Topic/Focus and intonation. A high-pitched CT is not felicitous in ?*nu-ka khong-unH mek-ess-ni? Cf. b. *khong-un nu-ka*--- 'Who ate the beans-CT?' The mid-sentential *–un* must become low in pitch and it may be interpreted as a Topic (or low-pitched CT) here.

If we follow the claim that surface reflects (hierarchical) structure a la Kayne (1994), we can attribute the above-mentioned constraints to structure-dependent interpretive dependencies as well as interfaces.

6. Concluding Remarks

We have examined the distribution of the strong type NPIs vs. the weak type in K and J in a unified account of NPIs and FCIs. We found core similarities.

We have proposed concession and arbitrariness. An indefinite from *what* is the weakest property predicate, from which choosing a member is most arbitrary. The form *amu* 'any' has the same basis.

We also tried to show how negative polarity developed from a concessive clause, via free choice. Adverbial NPIs such as stressed *pothong* and *yekan* are understatements, with a hidden sense of concession.

The n-words are NPIs with concession, underlyingly IND*wh*-based. We reviewed the intervention effect of ?*NPI>*wh*-/other Focus and related issues that call for interpretive dependencies as well as interfaces between structure, Topic-Focus information structure and prosody.

References

Beck, S. and Kim, Sh. 1997. On *Wh*- and Operator-Scope in K. *JEAL* 6, 339-384.

Chierchia, G. 2000 Scalar Implicatures and Polarity Items, UCLA Talk Abstract.

Cho, Seyun and Hangyu Lee. 2001. In N. Akatsuka et al (eds.) *Japanese and Korean Linguistics* 10. Stanford: CSLI.

Chung, Daeho, Chungmin Lee, Seungho Nam. 2001. On *amu-ra-to/amu-na*. (In Korean) Ms. Seoul Nat'l U.

Giannakidou, A. 1996 *The Landscape of Polarity Items*, U of Groningen Dissert'n.

Hamblin, C. L. 1973. Quest's in Montague English, *FL*. 10: 41-53.

Haspelmath, M. 1993 *A Typological Study of Indef Prons*. Free U of Berlin Diss't'n.

Heim, I. 1984 A Note on Negative Polarity and Downward Entailingness. *NELS* 14.

Horn, L. R. 1984. Toward a New Taxonomy for Pragmatic Inference: Q-based and R-based Implicature. In *Meaning, Form and Use in Context: Linguistic Applications* (Georgetown University Roundtable 1984), ed. D. Schiffrin. 11-42.

Israel, M. Polarity Sensitivity as Lexical Semantics. *L and P*. 19: 619-66.

Jun, Sun-Ah 1993. *The Phonetics and Phonology of K Prosody*. Dissertation, OSU.

Kato, Yasuhiko 1985 *Negative Ss in Japanese, Sophia Linguistica*. No.19.

Kawashima, R. 1994 *The Structure of Noun Phrases and the Interpretation of Quantificational NPs in Japanese*. Cornell University Dissertation.

Kim, Shin-Sook 2001 Interv'n Effects are Focus Effects. Akatsuka et al *J/K* 10.

Koenig, E. (1988) Concessive Connectives and Concessive Ss: In J. Hawkins (ed.) *Explaining Language Universals*.

Krifka, M. (1995) The Sem'tics and Prag's of Polarity Items. *Linguistic Analysis* 25.

Kuroda, S.-Y. 1965. Generative Grammatical Studies in the Japanese Language. Doctoral dissertation, MIT, Cambridge, Mass.

Lahiri, U. (1998) Focus and Negative Polarity in Hindi. *NLS*. 6. 57-123.

Lee, Chungmin 1993 Frozen Express's and Semantic Represent'ns. *Lg Res* 29:3.

_____ 1996. Negative Polarity Items in English and Korean. *Language Sciences* 18.

_____ 1999. Types of NPIs & Nonveridicality. *UCLA WPLing* 3, *Syntax at Sunset*.

_____ 1999. Cntr' Topic: A Locus of the Int'rfc-Evidence from K and Other Lgs. In K. Turner (ed.) *The Sem's/Prag'cs Int'rfc from Diff'nt Points of View*, Elsevier.

_____ 2000. Contrastive Predicates and Conventional Scales, *CLS* 36.

Lee, Kisuk and Satoshi Tomoika (2001) LF Blocking Effects are Topic Effects: *Wh*-Questions in J/K. In Akatsuka et al (eds.) *Japanese/Korean Linguistics* 10. CSLI.

Lee, Youngsuk, and L. Horn (1994) *Any* as Indefinite plus *Even*. Ms. Yale U.

Shimoyama, Junko. 1999. Complex NPs and Wh-Quantification in J. *NELS* 29.

Sohn, Keun-won 1996. Neg Polarity Items and Rigidity of Scope. *J/K L* 5, 353-368.

Vallduvi, E. 1998. *The Information Component*. Doctoral Dissertation, Upenn.

Zwarts, F. 1995. Nonveridical Contexts. *Linguistic Analysis* 25.

Incorporation vs. Modification in Deverbal Compounds[*]

YOKO SUGIOKA

Keio University

1. Introduction

Deverbal compounds (VCs for short) in Japanese consist of the non-head followed by V-infinitive (ren'yoo-kei), which is formed by verb stem + *i*. As the examples in (1) show, they can have various denotations.

(1) a. Act / Event   booru-nage 'ball throwing'   ame-huri 'rain fall' haya-gui 'fast eating'   pen-gaki '(with) pen-write'

    b. Agent / Instrument   hana-uri 'flower vendor'   syakkin-tori 'loan collector'   tume-kiri 'nail cutter' nezumi-tori 'mouse-catcher'

    c. Property / Result   mono-siri 'thing-know (knowledgeable)' usu-giri 'thin-sliced' kuro-koge 'burned black' isi-zukuri 'stone-built'

            (Kageyama 1982, 1993. Sugioka 1984, 1996, 1997.)

In contrast to English synthetic compounds which employ different suffixes such as *-ing* and *–er* to mark different referents, Japanese VCs all end with the same form. Furthermore, it is well known that in English synthetic compounds the internal argument must be realized within the compound, as shown by the unacceptability of (2a) below. In contrast, as shown by (2b) Japanese VCs can take the internal argument of the base verb outside.

(2) a. *fast-devouring of pasta,   *tree-eater of pasta

    b. pasuta no haya-gui   'fast eating of pasta'
     pasta GEN fast eat

---

[*]   I would like to thank the audience at the 10th J/K Lingsuitics Conference for their comments. This study was supported by the Grant-in-Aid for Scientific Research 08CE1001 from the Japanese Ministry of Education.

Because of these seemingly idiosyncratic and noncompositional characteristics, Japanese VCs have not been given systematic analyses on a par with
English synthetic compounds. In this paper I will propose to classify them
into two distinct types, depending on whether the non-head element is the
direct argument of the base verb or not.

2. Direct argument VCs vs. Adjunct VCs

First, those VCs whose non-head element corresponds to the direct argument of the base verb is a noun [+N, -V], as can be shown by their taking
the full verb –*suru* (3a) rather than the light verb –*suru*(3b).

(3) a. tegami-kaki o suru. 'do letter-writing'
    letter-write ACC do

   b. ??tegami-kaki suru[1]

Direct arguments mostly bear the Theme role, as shown in (4a) below,
but the noun with the Goal role (case-marked with *ni*) is also included, if it is
the sole internal argument of the verb as in (4b).

(4) a. Theme :   gomi-atume 'garbage collecting', yuki-kaki 'snow plowing'
             gake-kuzure 'landslide' ,   gasu-more 'gas leak'

   b. Goal :   Amerika-iki 'America going' hikooki-nori 'plane-rider (pilot)'

In forming a Direct argument VC, a noun is incorporated to a verb by
head movement under V', which is nominalized by conversion, as follows.[2]

(5)   Direct argument VC:

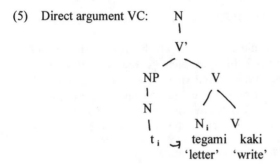

---

[1]   (3b) is OK as an instance of case-marker drop.
[2]   This movement is presumably motivated by the licensing of N; if a nominal is not properly
case-marked by a particle, it must be incorporated by the verb. The details of the derived
structure in (5) must be left for further study.

This structure reflects the semantics of these VCs; a certain action or event such as 'writing a letter' is given a name by turning it into a noun. Note that in this structure the verb is the head of the V', but it is not the head of the top N. In other words, (5) represents an exocentric structure, so the categorial features including the argument structure cannot percolate up to the top N node. Since it is a [-V] nominal, it cannot occur with the light verb as we saw in (3).

Furthermore, since the process of combining a direct argument and V to form V' is productive as long as the verb's selectional restrictions are met, it follows that Direct argument VCs are extremely productive. As exemplified in (6), a similar type of V-N compounds denoting agent or instrument is extensively found in Romance languages, and are assigned a similarly exocentric structure in Disciullo and Williams (1987).

(6) Romance compounds

French:	essui-glace (wipe window)	'window-wiper'
Italian:	apri-porta (open door)	'door opener'
Spanish:	lanza-cohetes (launch rocket)	'rocket launcher'
Portuguese:	afia-lápis (sharpen pencil)	'pencil sharpener'

In Japanese, as shown in (7), Direct argument VCs often denote act or event, but can be lexicalized to denote agent, instrument, property, as we have already seen in (1), as well as location and time.

(7) N: act / event → agent (1b) ; instrument (1b); property (1c *mono-siri*);
  location (*mizu-tamari* 'water-collect, puddle') ;
  time (*yo-ake* 'night-break, dawn')

In contrast to these, the VCs involving adjuncts are [+V] verbal nouns denoting predicates of some sort, so they appear with the light verb –*suru* and take the internal argument outside:

(8) a. Tegami o pen-gaki / hashiri-gaki suru.
  letter ACC pen-write / run-write do
  'to pen-write / quickly-write a letter'

 b. Tokei o siti-ire suru.   'to sell a watch to a pawn shop'
  watch ACC pawn-put do

These facts can be captured by assuming the structure of (9). Adjuncts are adjoined to the VN head whose category feature and argument structure percolate to the whole compound. A wide range of adjuncts can be found in this type of VCs, as exemplified in (10).

(9)

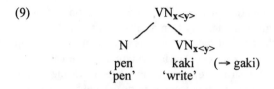

$VN_{x<y>}$

N $VN_{x<y>}$

pen   kaki   ($\rightarrow$ gaki)
'pen'   'write'

(10) **Instrument**: te-gaki 'hand write'   kikai-ami 'machine-knit'
    Cause: sigoto-zukare 'work tired'   huna-yoi 'boat sick'
    Manner: niwaka-zukuri 'fast building'   waka-zini 'young dyeing'
    Locative: soto-asobi 'outside playing'   **Time**: hiru-ne 'day-nap'
    Goal: syako-ire 'garage-put'   **Source**: kura-dasi 'storage-take out

Although the VCs in (10) are verbal nouns, certain types of adjuncts as shown in (11) form a stative predicate incompatible with the light verb *–suru*. We will return to this problem in Section 4.

(11) -da / *-suru :
    Result: kata-yude 'hard-boiled'   bisyo-nure 'wet
    Material: mohea-ami 'mohair wool-knit'   renga-zukuri 'brick-built'

In Section 3 we will look at some phonological evidence which support the different structures (5) and (9) for the two types of VCs.

3. Different Phonology of Argument VC vs Adjunct VC

3.1. Accent Patterns

The two types of VCs exhibit different accent patterns. The basic accent pattern of Direct argument VCs when the head consists of 2-mora is that the second element is preaccented (12a), while that of Adjunct VCs is that the whole compound is deaccented (12b).[3]

(12) a. Direct argument VC: hoN-YOmi 'book reading'
    b. Adjunct VC: boo-yomi 'flat reading'

This is puzzling in view of the following accent rules of Japanese (see McCawley 1977), since the (12a) and (12b) share the same head, *yomi*.

---

[3] The upper case characters represent the segments in high pitch. Since I cannot go into the complex details of the accent patterns of Japanese compounds here, I will only discuss the VCs with 2-mora heads.

(13) a. In a noun compound X#Y, the accent of Y predominates.

    b. If Y is short and final-accented, deaccent the whole compound.

We should note, however, that the infinitive form (*ren'yoo-kei*) in Japanese has two functions in a way comparable to English gerunds as shown in (14): one as a verb to appear in infinitival constructions such as (14a), and the other as a deverbal nominal (14b). And crucially, the infinitive *YOmi* is preaccented, while the deverbal nominal *yoMI* is final-accented.

(14)   YOm-u 'read' / KEr-u 'kick':

    a. Infinitive: initial accent

        YOmi / KEri ni iku   'go to read / kick'
        read   kick to go

    b. Noun :   final accent

        yoMI ga asai   'reading (interpretation) is shallow'
        reading NOM shallow

        keRI o ireru   'give a kick'
        kick ACC put

If our assumption in (5) that Direct argument VCs have a verb infinitive as its second element, while Adjunct VCs have a deverbal nominal, the accent rules of (13) give the correct predictions; namely in the former the initial accent of the head would predominate, while the latter would be deaccented. These predictions are borne out, as shown below.

(15) a. Direct arg.VC: HOn + YOmi   →   hoN-YOmi   'book reading
                     iSI + KEri   →   iSI-KEri   'pebble kicking'
                     kuSA + TOri   →   kuSA-TOri   'weed picking'

    b. Adjunct VC: boo + yoMI   → boo-yomi   'flat reading'
                     hiza + keRI   →   hiza-geri   'knee kick'
                     yoko + toRI   →   yoko-dori   'taking from side'

For some verbs infinitives forms and nominal forms are both final-accented, and VCs based on them are unaccented in both types, as predicted.

(16) a. Direct arg VC: usi+ kaI   →   usi-kai   'cattle herder'
        Adjunct VC: maTOME + kaI →   matome-gai 'collective buying'
    b. Direct arg VC: kane + kaSI   →   kane-kasi   'money lending/-er'
        Adjunct VC: zikan + kaSI   →   zikan-gasi   'lending by the hour'

These data show that the different accent patterns of the two types of VCs support the different categorial features of the righthand element we postulated for Direct argument VCs as opposed to adjunct VCs.

3.2. Rendaku

The second phonological difference is Rendaku, voicing of the initial consonant of the second element in a compound (17a). It is extremely common in Japanese compounds, but it cannot apply to apposition compounds (17b), which suggests that it is applicable only to the head of the compound.

(17) a. ame 'candy' + tama 'ball' → ame-**d**ama 'candy ball'
    b. oya-ko / *-go 'parent-child' kusa-ki / *-gi 'grass and tree'

This 'head' condition, applied to the different structures of the VCs yield the following contrast. As shown in (18), Direct argument VCs do not show Rendaku, because the verb is not the head of the whole compound N, this being an exocentric structure; the verb is the head of V', but Rendaku cannot apply above word-level. In contrast, the adjunct VCs show Rendaku because the verbal noun is the head of the compound.

(18)a. Direct argument VC   b. Adjunct VC

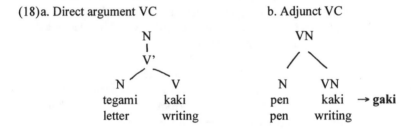

This contrast is quite pervasive, as exemplified in (19).

(19) a. te-huki 'hand wiper' / te-buki 'wipe with hand' kara-buki 'dry-wipe'
    b.tegami-kaki 'letter writing' manga-kaki 'comic writer' e-kaki 'painter'
        / pen-gaki 'pen-write' hasiri-gaki 'hastily written' sita-gaki 'draft'
    c. pan-kiri 'bread cutting' hara-kiri 'belly cutting' kan-kiri 'can opener'
        / usu -giri 'thin-sliced' yotu-giri 'cut into four'
    d. imo-hori'potato digging' ana-hori 'hole digging
        / roten-bori open air digging' kikai-bori 'digging by machine'
    e. musi-tori 'insect catching'/ yoko-dori 'side catch' ike-dori' catch alive'

Although this pattern is very pervasive, there are some Direct argument VCs that show Rendaku, such as *kome-zukuri* 'rice growing' and *hito-goroshi* 'man killing'. However, these can be analyzed as cases of reanalysis from the exocentric struture of (18a) to the endocentric (18b), which is more canonical as a word structure. On the other hand, as far as I can tell, there is no adjunct VC which should show Rendaku but does not.

Furthermnore, judging from the examples in (19) it might seem that the unaccented pattern of the adjunct VCs is responsible for Rendaku. Note, however, that in (16) Direct argument VC *usi-kai* is also unaccented, but does NOT show Rendaku. So the two phonological differences we find between the two types of VCs are at least partially independent.

4. Adjunct VC Formation and Predicate Decomposition

4.1. Selection of Adjuncts by Decomposed Predicates

In contrast to Direct argument VCs which limit the non-head element to be the subcategorized argument, Adjunct VCs can contain all sorts of adjuncts or adverbial modifiers of the base verb, as we saw in Section 2. This may lead one to think that the semantic association between the head and the adjuncts are random and subject only to pragmatics, as is the case with root compounds . However, I would like to argue that the adjuncts do not modify the verb per se, but rather they relate to the decomposed predicates at the level of LCS. As we will see in this section, looking at them this way can explain their behaviors in a systematic way.

(20) represents the basic LCS schemata for accomplishment verbs, which contains all the basic predicates.

(20)
```
                Event
             /  |  \   effect
         ACT  x  (y)        Event
                           /  \
                    BECOME  (y)  State
                                /  |  \
                              BE   y   AT-Z
```

Propositions are either Event (headed by ACT or BECOME) or State (headed by BE), and 'x' and 'y' represent the argument positions that are projected to the external and the internal argument positions, respectively, in syntax.

I will assume here that each basic predicate selects for different types of adjuncts or modifiers as shown in boldface below.

(21)   a. $_{Event}$ [ACT   (x)   y   **Manner   Instrument**]

   b. $_{Event}$ [BECOME   y   **Cause   Manner** $_{State}$ [BE   y   AT-Z]]

   c. $_{State}$[BE   y   AT - **Result** / OF - **Material**]

If adjuncts combine with these basic predicates in forming adjunct VCs, it follows that when ACT heads an Adjunct VC it takes either Manner or Instrument adjunct as its non-head element, while BECOME combines with Cause or Manner adjuncts, and BE with Result or Material.   We will now see how we can account for the various restrictions on adjunct VCs using this LCS scheme.

4.2. Argument Projection by Adjunct VCs

Let us first look at the class of act or contact verbs, which can form VCs with Manner and Instrument adjuncts, as shown in (22).[4]   As we saw in Section 2, these VCs are [+V] and take the light verb *–suru*.

(22) $_{Event}$ [ACT   x   (y)   **Manner   Instrument**]

Manner + ACT$_N$: haya-aruki 'fast walking'   oo-naki 'big crying'
                   metta-uti 'repeatedly hitting'   tada-mi 'free viewing'

Instrument+ACT$_N$: mizu-arai 'water washing' wakkusu-buki 'wax polish'
                   hirate-uti   'hand hitting'

Note, as shown in (23), that in this VC formation, the argument positions x and y are projected as open positions to syntax and can be realized as argument NPs.

(23)[yomi $_{ACT}$ x   y   (tati $_{Manner}$)]   →   [tati-yomi$_{ACT}$ x   y   ]

   a. Kodomo ga manga-o tati-yomi suru. 'A child browses a comic book.'
      child NOM comic book ACC stand-reading do

   b. Manga no tati-yomi   'Stand-reading of comic books'
      comics GEN stand-reading

---

[4]   The LCSs of verbs are simplified for the expository purpose, and show only the basic predicates along with the relevant adjuncts.

This way the 'argument inheritance' property of adjunct VCs can be captured on the level of LCS. Note that Japanese VCs based on LCS differ in this respect from English VCs which are regulated by the argument structure of the verb, and so cannot permit VCs consisting of an adjunct and a transitive verb; e.g. *fast devouring.

4.3 Event vs. State and [V] Feature

Verbs that denote some change, whose LCS corresponds to the Event clause headed by BECOME, select Cause and Manner (depictive) adjuncts to form VCs
as shown below.

(24) $_{Event}$[BECOME   y   **Cause   Manner** $_{State}$[BE   y   AT-Z]]

Cause + BECOME$_N$: hi-yake 'sun-burning'   ue-zini 'starve-dying'
Manner + BECOME$_N$: waka-zini 'young-dying' tati-gare' stand-wilting'

These VCs based on change verbs can occur with the light verb -suru, just like the VCs based on act verbs we saw in (22) and (23a).

(25)a. Hada ga hi-yake suru.   'My skin gets sun-burned.'
         skin NOM sun-burning do

   b. Kare wa waka-zini si-ta.   'He died young.'
      he TOP young-dying do-PAST

This fact might at first seem counter-intuitive because change and act are aspectually different, and while act is something you 'do' (suru), change is not.   Note also that the English counterparts often include participle as the head (e.g. sun-burned).   This is, however, consistent with the LCS postulated here, since both ACT and BECOME are the heads of the Event clause.   It then follows that nominalized event predicate retains the [+V] feature, and so licenses the light verb.

In the LCS of change verbs, there is another adjunct/modifier position, as shown in (26), namely the result state position under BE.   Result and BE form VCs as shown in (26).

(26) $_{Event}$[BECOME   y $_{State}$[BE   y   AT-**Result**]   ]

Result + BE$_N$:   kuro-koge 'black-burned',   bisyo-nure 'wet-soaked'

These VCs, in contrast with the ones in (24) (see (25)), cannot appear with the light verb suru.

(27)a. *kuro-koge suru / ^{OK}kuro-koge da
   black-burning do / black-burning be

   (cf. kuro-bikari suru 'black-shining'--Manner + ACT_N)

   b. *bisyo-nure suru / ^{OK}bisyo-nure da
   wet-soaking do / wet-soaking be

This contrast follows from the LCS schemata of adjunct selection in (21); namely, VCs with a Result modifier is based on the State clause, hence it is a predicate nominal requiring a copula rather than the light verb –*suru*.

4.4. Polysemy of Deverbal Nominals

Let us now see more verbs with such multi-layered LCS structures. The third class of verbs is the most complex one, act + change verbs. This class includes verbs of creation (caused existence) and verbs of caused change. (28) shows the LCS for verbs of creation.

(28) [ACT   x   **Instr. Manner**   Effect[BECOME [BE y OF-**Material**]]]

This LCS describes the event in which x act in such a way for there to be y from material of some kind. Although this Material adjunct does not always surface in the sentence containing creation verbs, it is an integral part of the creation verb. For instance, Pustejovsky (1995) includes Material elements as default argument and cites as evidence the alternation in (29).

(29) a. Mary carved the doll out of wood.
    b. Mary carved the wood into a doll.   (Pustejovsky 1995)

Since (28) contains multiple basic predicates, it is predicted that it can be the base for different types of adjunct VCs. (30) exemplifies VCs based on ACT.

(30)**Instrument**: pen-gaki' pen write' waapuro-gaki 'word-processor write'
          te-zukuri 'hand making'   kikai-bori 'machine carving'

 Manner : hasiri-gaki 'run(hastily) writing' niwaka-zukuri 'quick making'

Now contrast these with the VCs of (31), which include Material adjunct.

(31) [ACT   x $_{Effect}$[BECOME [<u>BE</u> y   OF-**Material**]]

Material: isi-zukuri   'stone made'   ki-bori   'wood carve',
keito-ami   'wool knit'   ke-ori   'wool woven'

Because Material adjunct is selected by BE, these VCs are [-V] predicate nominals as expected, and appear with the copula *da*, not the light verb *suru*. Consequently, VCs of (30) and (31), though based on the same verbs of creation, behave differently due to the different LCS predicates they are based on, as recapitulated in (32):

(32) a. Yoohuku o <u>te-zukuri</u> suru. (Instr. + ACT$_N$)   '(I) hand-make a dress.'
dress ACC hand-make do

b. *Ie o <u>ki-zukuri</u> suru.   (Material + BE$_N$)   ' (I) wood-make a house.'
house ACC wood-make do

cf. <u>ki-zukuri</u> da 'is wood-made'   <u>ki-zukuri</u> no ie   'wood-made house'

Similarly, the caused change verbs yield two types of VCs based on different predicates in the verb's LCS. They differ from the creation verbs in that the embedded BE selects Result state and not Material.

(33) [ACT   x   y   **Instr. Manner** $_{Effect}$[BECOME y [BE y AT-**Result**]]
Instrument: oobun-yaki   'oven-baking'   abura-itame   'oil-frying'
Manner :   musi-yaki   'steam(v.)-baking'   nido-nuri   'twice-painting'
Result: yotu-wari 'four-pieces cut'   usu-giri   'thin cut',
wa-giri   'circle cut'   siro-nuri   'white painted'

As expected, the VCs with Instrument or Material adjuncts (34) take *-suru* and allow the base verb's internal argument to be projected , while those with Result (35) do not.[5]

---

[5]   Actually, VCs based on ACT in the LCS of the verbs of creation or caused change can also be used as predicate nominals with *da* or as prenominal modifiers:
(i)   Kono doresu wa te-zukuri da.   'This dress is hand-made.'
this dress   TOP   hand -making be
(ii) oobun-yaki no sakana   'oven-baked fish'
oven -baking GEN fish
These examples can be accounted for by postulating the following Result Focus Rule:

[ACT x, y (Instrument) (Manner) $_{Effect}$[BECOME [BE   y   AT-z(Result)]]
→ [BE   y   AT-z(Result)   by [ACT-ON   x,   y   (Instrument) (Manner)]]

This rule reverses the cause-effect relationship, and the result state is made the main clause and

(34) a. Sakana o <u>oobun-yaki</u> suru.'(I) oven-bake the fish.'
     fish ACC oven-bake do

   b. Kabe o <u>nido-nuri</u> suru. '(I) twice-paint the wall.'
     wall ACC twice-paint do

(35) a. *Tamago o <u>atu-yaki</u> suru. '(I) thick-bake eggs.'
     egg ACC thick-bake do

   b.*Ringo o <u>yotu-wari</u> / <u>usu-giri</u> suru. '(I) four-cut / thinly slice apples.'
     apple ACC four-cut / thin-slice do

   cf. <u>atu-yaki</u> / <u>yotu-wari</u> ni suru.   'make (it) thick-baked / four-cut'
     thick-bake / four-cut be do(=make)

5. Concluding Remarks

In the preceding section we have seen some evidence showing that Adjunct VC formation in Japanese takes place at the level of LCS, and creates a deverbal nominal with [+V] or [-V] feature depending on the type of the basic predicate it is based on. In other words, Adjunct VC formation is a kind of complex predicate formation, by which a certain adjunct/modifier is combined with a verb to specify some semantic dimension of the head verb. In the studies on Japanese verb-verb compounds it has been pointed out (Kageyama 1993, Matsumoto 1996) that Japanese employs morphological compounding extensively in the lexicalization of various semantic elements into a verb, in the sense of Talmy (1985). Although Adjunct VC formation creates a nominal compound with a deverbal nominal head, it can be captured as basically the same process of predicate formation.

In this connection it is significant that some Adjunct VCs in Japanese find their English parallels not in compounds but in denominal verbs, as exemplified below.

(36) a. to pen the reply   (Clark & Clark 1973)
     cf. *to pen-write the reply

   b. henzi-o pen-gaki suru
     reply ACC pen-write do

   c. [ACT   x   y   with-PEN]

---

hence BE can combine with Instrument or Manner adjunct in the lower position. Kinsui (1993) discusses a similar type of result focus phenomenon observed with the tense suffix –ta. See Sugioka (1997) for the details of this LCS operation and its implications for further differences between English and Japanese VCs.

(36a) and (36b) are similar in two points: an adjunct (Instrument) is incorporated into the verb's meaning and the derived complex predicate projects the internal argument. If we assume, following Kageyama (1997), that English denominal verb formation is a type of complex predicate formation with the nominal filling the adjunct slot of the verb's LCS as illustrated in (36c), this parallelism follows naturally.

We have seen in this study that VC formation in Japanese takes place on different levels, under V' and in LCS. Rather than treating Direct argument VCs and Adjunct VCs as completely distinct objects, we can say that while VC formation itself is a uniform word formation process, the type of the non-head determines the level in which it takes place, and from different levels follow the various phonological and semantic differences between Direct argument VCs and Adjunct VCs. Namely, if the adjunct is compounded with the deverbal nominal in the semantic structure, i.e. LCS, it is a complex predicate formation, which retains the argument structure and the [V] feature of the head predicate. This process is only semi-productive because it is restricted by the selection of adjuncts by the relevant predicate type in LCS as we have seen in Section 4. On the other hand, argument incorporation is regulated by argument structure in syntax, where the internal argument is incorporated to the verb by head movement. The extreme productivity of Direct argument VC stems from that of the process whereby N and V are combined to form V' to denote an act or event. As long as it is a name-worthy act or event, VC can be created; there is no restriction that stems from lexicalization patterns of verbs as we have seen for Adjunct VCs. However, the interpretation of Direct argument VCs, whether it can denote an agent, property, location, and so on, is subject to the idiosyncracy of naming.

The two types of Japanese VCs in comparison with their English counterparts can be summarized as below.

(39)

	Argument structure	LCS
Japanese:	Direct argument VC	Adjunct VC
	tegami-kaki 'letter-writing'	*pen-gak i* 'pen-writing'
English :	Synthetic compound	Denominal verb
	letter-writing	*to pen (a letter)*

If our contention that Japanese VC formation is uniform but argument incorporation and adjunct incorporation takes place on different levels is on the right track, it suggests that the compounding process can take place in different components of grammar, which corroborates the modular theory of word formation (Kageyama 1993) and Borer (1988)'s Parallel Morphology model.

References

Borer, H. 1988. *Parallel Morphology.* Foris.

Clark, E.V. & H.H. Clark. 1979. When Nouns Surface as Verbs. *Language* 55: 767-811.

Di Sciullo, A.-M. and E. Williams. 1987. *On the Definition of Word.* MIT Press.

Grimshaw, J. 1990. *Argument Structure.* MIT Press.

Jackendoff, R. 1990. *Semantic Structures.* MIT Press.

Kageyama, T. 1982. Word Formation in Japanese. *Lingua* 57: 215-258.

Kageyama, T. 1993. *Bunpoo to Gokeisei* (Grammar and Word Formation). Hituzi.

Kageyama, T. 1997. Denominal Verbs and Relative Salience in Lexical Conceptual Structure. *Verb Semantics and Syntactic* Structure, ed. T. Kageyama, 45-96. Kurosio.

Kawakami, S. 1973. Doosi kara no Tensei Meisi no Akusento (Accentuation of De verbal Nouns). *Imaizumi Hakase Koki Kinen Kokugogaku Ronsoo,* 55-70.

Kinsui, S. 1993. Rentai-Syuusyoku no *ta* ni Tuite (On adnominal modifier *ta.* *Nihongo no Meisi-syuusyoku,* ed. Y. Takubo, 29-65. Kurosio.

Levin, B. & M. Rappaport. 1995. *Unaccusativity.* MIT Press.

Lieber, R. 1983. Argument Linking and Compounds in English. *Linguistic Inquiry* 14: 251-285.

McCawley, J. 1977. Accent in Japanese. *Studies in Stress and Accent,* ed. L. Hyman, 261-302. USC.

Roeper, T. and M.Siegel. 1978. A Lexical Transformation for Verbal Compounds. *Linguistic Inquiry* 9: 199-260.

Sato, H. 1988. Hukugoogo ni okeru Akusento Kisoku to Rendaku Kisoku (Accent Rule and Rendaku in Compounds). *Nihongo no Onsei to Onin:* 233-265. Meiji Shoin,.

Selkirk, E. 1982. *The Syntax of Words.* MIT Press.

Sugioka, Y. 1984. *Interaction of Derivational Morphology and Syntax in Japanese and English.* Ph.D. dissertation, U. Chicago. (Reprinted: Garland, 1986.)

Sugioka, Y. 1996. Regularity in Inflection and Derivation: Rule and Analogy in Japanese Deverbal Compound Formation. *Acta Linguistica* 45: 231-253.

Sugioka, Y. 1997. Projection of Arguments and Adjuncts in Compounds. *Grant-in-Aid for COE Research Report (1):* 185-220. Kanda U. of International Studies.

Talmy, L. 1985. Lexicalization Patterns: Semantic Structure in Lexical Forms. *Language Typology and Syntactic Description 2, ed. T.* Shopen, 57-149. Cambridge UP.

e-mail: sugioka@sfc.keio.ac.jp

Syntactic and Pragmatic Properties of the NPI *Yekan* in Korean

SAE-YOUN CHO & HAN-GYU LEE
Honam University & Kyung Hee University

1. Introduction

This paper presents a syntactic and pragmatic description of the Negative Polarity Item (NPI) *yekan* 'commonly' in Korean. There has been considerable discussion regarding various constructions containing NPIs in Korean. Much of the literature related to the discussion has focused mainly on NPIs' licensing environments. To account for their licensing environments, the pure syntactic approach including Sohn (1995) has claimed that all NPIs should co-occur with a negative predicate or an overt negation at the overt syntax. On the other hand, some semantic or pragmatic works on Korean NPIs including Nam (1994) have proposed a fine-grained NPI typology to explain their licensing environments. As illustrated in (1), sentence (1a), where the NPI *cenhye* 'at all' occurs with the inherent negative predicate *eps-* 'not exist', is grammatical whereas sentence (1b), where the NPI occurs alone, is ungrammatical. Under the previous approach, this grammatical difference can be explained either by specifying the NPI's type or by postulating a Clause Mate Constraint as the syntactic rule.

(1) a. Mary-ka   ton-i   **cenhye**   eps-ta.
        M-Nom   money-Nom   at all   not.exist-Decl
        'Mary does not have money at all.'

    b. *Mary-ka   ton-i   **cenhye**   iss-ta.
                                                          exist-Decl

       (Lit.) 'Mary has money at all.'

However, the NPI *yekan* exhibits various properties different from other NPIs such as *cenhye,* which would be hard to account for under the previous approach. For example, unlike declarative sentences containing *cenhye*, sentence (2a) is ungrammatical, where the NPI *yekan* occurs with the inherent negative predicate, while sentence (2b), where it occurs with the long-form negation '-*ci anh-*', is grammatical.

(2) a. *Mary-ka   ton-i   **yekan**   eps-ta.
          M-Nom   money-Nom   commonly   not.exist-Decl

b.   Mary-ka   ton-i   **yekan**   **eps-ci anh-ta.**
      M-Nom   money-Nom   commonly   not.exist-Decl   not-Decl
      'Mary has little money'

In the previous analyses, the difference in acceptability would be a puzzle. To avoid such difficulties, we argue that the assumption by the previous analyses that inherent negative predicates such as *eps-* have the same negative force as overt negation in Korean NPI licensability is false. Furthermore, we claim that the distributional behavior of each NPI should be explicitly specified in the lexicon and that sentences containing the NPI *yekan* can be fully understood by discerning the pragmatic role of *yekan*.

To provide an appropriate account for *yekan*, first of all, we show what kind of properties the NPI *yekan* exhibits in section 2. In section 3, we propose a constraint-based lexical analysis to explain the distributional behavior of *yekan* in various constructions. In section 4, we suggest a pragmatic account of semantic and pragmatic properties for *yekan*. We conclude this paper with a discussion of theoretical implications.

2. Properties of the NPI *Yekan*
2.1. *Yekan* in Declarative Sentences

The NPI *yekan* is an adverb functioning as a degree modifier. It is well-known that like the NPI *cenhye* 'at all', it cannot occur with positive predicates in a declarative sentence. As illustrated in (3) and (4), sentence (3a), where the NPI *cenhye* and the negation *anh-* co-occur, is grammatical while sentence (3b), where *cenhye* occurs alone, is ungrammatical. Similarly, when *yekan* co-occurs with *anh-* as in (4a), it is grammatical, but when *yekan* occurs alone as in (4b), it is ungrammatical.

(3) a.   Mary-ka   **cenhye**   yeyppuci   **anh**-ta.
          M-Nom   at all   pretty   not-Decl
     b.   *Mary-ka   **cenhye**   yeyppu-ta.
          M-Nom   at all   pretty-Decl
          'Mary is not pretty at all.'
(4) a.   Mary-ka   **yekan**   yeyppuci   **anh**-ta.
          M-Nom   commonly   pretty   not-Decl
     b.   *Mary-ka   **yekan**   yeyppu-ta.
          M-Nom   commonly   pretty-Decl
          'Mary is quite pretty.'

Though *yekan* cannot occur with positive predicates like other NPIs such as *cenhye*, there seems to be a difference in selecting their negative

forms. There are two overt negative forms in Korean: the Long-form Negation (LN) *anh-* and the Short-form Negation (SN) *mos* or *an*. Specifically,
the sentence containing *yekan* can be grammatical only when the negative
form is the LN *anh-*. Otherwise, it is unnatural and ungrammatical. When
cenhye occurs either with the LN or with the SN as in (5), it is acceptable.
By contrast, when *yekan* and the LN co-occur as in (6a), it is grammatical.
But when *yekan* and the SN co-occur as in (6b), it is ungrammatical.[1]

(5) a. Mary-ka   **cenhye**   ttwici   **anh**nun-ta.
         M-Nom   at all   run   LN-Decl
     b. Mary-ka   **cenhye**   **an/mos**   ttwin-ta.
         M-Nom   at all   SN   run-Decl
         'Mary does (can) not run at all.'
(6) a. Mary-ka   **yekan**   cal   ttwici   **anh**nun-ta.
         M-Nom   commonly   well   run   LN-Decl
     b. Mary-ka   **yekan**   cal   ??**an/*mos** ttwin-ta.
         M-Nom   at all   well   SN   run-Decl
         'Mary does(can) run quite well.'

Moreover, unlike *cenhye*, *yekan* cannot co-occur with inherent negative
forms such as *eps-* 'not exist/have' and *moru-* 'not know'. Sentence (7a),
where *cenhye* occurs with the inherent negative form *eps-*, is grammatical
while (7b), where *yekan* and the inherent negative form co-occur, is ungrammatical.

(7) a. Mary-ka   ton-i   **cenhye**   **eps-ta**.
         M-Nom   money-Nom   at all   not.exist-Decl
         'Mary does not have money at all.'
     b. *Mary-ka   ton-i   **yekan**   **eps-ta**.
         M-Nom   money-Nom   commonly   not.exist-Decl
         (Lit.) 'Mary has little money.'

This grammatical difference points to the fact that the assumption by the
previous analyses that inherent negative predicates such as *eps-* have the
same negative force as overt negation in Korean NPI licensability is false.
Furthermore, the overt negations such as the LN and the SN should also be
dealt with differently in Korean NPI licensability.

---

[1] The grammaticality of sentence (6b), where *yekan* and the SN *an* co-occur, is controversial in that only a few native speakers regard it as grammatical. Moreover, most of them interpret it not as "Mary runs quite well" but as "Mary does not run well". Since this is not an
NPI reading for *yekan*, we, hence, treat this sentence as ungrammatical in this paper.

512 / SAE-YOUN CHO & HAN-GYU LEE

2.2. *Yekan* in Questions

The NPI *yekan* behaves differently from other NPIs in interrogative sentences. When *yekan* occurs in a sincere question regardless of the existence
of a negation, the sentence is unacceptable. But the sincere question containing *cenhye* is acceptable as long as it occurs with an appropriate negation. Question (8), where *cenhye* and *anh-* co-occur, is acceptable but (9),
where *yekan* and *anh-* co-occur, is unacceptable.

(8)   Mary-ka   **cenhye**   pap-ul   mekci   **anh**-a?
      M-Nom   at all   rice-Acc   eat   LN-Ques
      ' Doesn't Mary eat rice at all?'
(9)   *Mary-ka   **yekan**   pap-ul cal   mekci   **anh**-a?
      M-Nom   commonly   rice-Acc well eat   LN-Ques
      ' Does Mary eat rice quite well?'

On the other hand, when *cenhye* occurs in a Rhetorical Question (RQ)
without a negation, the sentence is unacceptable. But the RQ containing
yekan is acceptable as long as there is no negation. As illustrated in (10),
cenhye cannot appear in a RQ without a negation. By contrast, the NPI
yekan can occur without any overt negation in an ARQ (Affirmative Rhetorical Question) as in (11a). If *yekan* and the LN co-occur in a RQ, the sentence seems to be rather unnatural as in (11b).

(10)   *Mary-ka   **cenhye**   ttwi-nya?
         M-Nom   at all   run-Ques
         (Lit.) 'Does Mary run at all?'
(11) a. Mary-ka   **yekan**   cal   ttwi-nya?
         M-Nom   commonly   well   run-Ques
         (Lit.) 'Does Mary run quite well?'
     b. *Mary-ka   **yekan**   cal   ttwi-ci   **anh**-nya?
         M-Nom   commonly   well   run   LN-Ques
         (Lit.) 'Does Mary run quite well?'

To be an adequate theory of Korean NPIs, the theory must provide an explanation for these idiosyncratic behaviors of the NPI *yekan* in interrogative
constructions.

2.3. Semantic or Pragmatic Properties of *Yekan*

The NPI *yekan* either combining with the LN in declarative sentences or
without any overt negation in a RQ is construed not negatively but posi-

tively. Unlike other NPIs such as *cenhye, yekan* combining with the LN is construed positively so that the sentence in (12) is interpreted not as "Mary does not run well" but as "Mary runs quite well".

(12) Mary-ka   **yekan**   cal   ttwici   **anh**nun-ta.
      M-Nom   commonly   well   run   LN-Decl
      'Mary does run quite well.'

Similarly, the NPI *yekan* without any overt negation in (13) is also construed positively so that the ARQ is interpreted as "Mary runs quite well".

(13) Mary-ka   **yekan** cal   ttwi-nya?
      M-Nom   commonly well   run-ARM
      (Lit.) 'Does Mary run quite well?'

So far, we have examined various syntactic, semantic, and pragmatic properties of the NPI *yekan*. As for syntactic properties, it is observed that *yekan* co-occurs only with the LN in a declarative sentence, unlike other NPIs, and that *yekan* cannot occur in a sincere question whereas it can appear without an overt negation in a RQ. As for semantic or pragmatic properties, it has been shown that *yekan* with the LN in a declarative sentence or without a negation in a RQ is construed positively. To be an adequate theory of Korean NPIs including *yekan*, the theory must answer the following questions: (i) What is an appropriate constraint to account for the co-occurrence restrictions in declarative sentences and interrogative sentences?; (ii) Why does *yekan* get a positive reading differently from other NPIs? To answer for the syntactic properties, we propose a constraint-based lexical analysis in the next section. Section 4 provides a pragmatic account of *yekan* to answer questions such as why *yekan* is construed positively and why *yekan* cannot be used in a sincere question.

3. A Proposal: Syntactic Account

As discussed above, the NPI *yekan* selects its negative form as the LN against the assumption by the previous approach that inherent negative predicates such as *eps-* 'not exist' have the same negative force as overt negation in NPI licensability. Furthermore, the LN should be dealt with differently from the SN when we analyze sentences containing *yekan*. Second, *yekan* and *cenhye* behave differently with respect to the Sentence Type (S-TYPE) to which each NPI belongs.

Specifically, the NPI *cenhye* selects various negative forms such as inherent negative predicates, the LN, or the SN in any S-TYPE. On the other hand, *yekan* selects the LN as overt negation in a declarative sentence (DECL), while it must occur alone in an ARQ. To accommodate this co-occurrence restriction, we specify which NPI selects which negation with respect to the S-TYPE in the lexicon as follows:

(14) *yekan*: (a) [MOD[verb [+AUX, +NEG, S-TYPE DECL]]]
                      OR
              (b) [MOD[verb [-AUX, -NEG, S-TYPE ARQ]]]
(15) *cenhye*:   [MOD[verb[+NEG, S-TYPE (DECL or NRQ)]]]

In (14), the lexical entry *yekan* in the lexicon bears the information that the word is an adverb modifying a VP containing a negative auxiliary verb (i.e. the LN) whose S-TYPE is DECL or that the word is an adverb modifying a VP without any negation whose S-TYPE is ARQ. Similarly, the lexical entry *cenhye* in (15) specifies the information that the word is an adverb modifying a VP containing any overt negation or negative predicates whose S-TYPE is either DECL or NRQ (Negative Rhetorical Question).

   This enables us to correctly predict the grammaticality of various sentences containing NPIs. For comprehensibility, we demonstrate how the feature system in the lexicon based on Pollard and Sag (1994) works for sentences with *cenhye* and *yekan*. First of all, the sentence (5a) with *cenhye* can be represented as in (16):

(5) a.   Mary-ka   **cenhye**   ttwici   **anhnun-ta.**
          M-Nom   at all   run   LN-Decl
          'Mary does not run at all.'
(16)   S

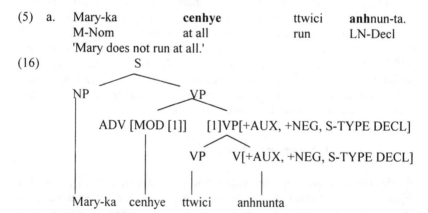

```
                           S
              _____/ _____
            NP                          VP
            |               _____/  _____
            |        ADV [MOD [1]]    [1]VP[+AUX, +NEG, S-TYPE DECL]
            |              |           ____/  \____
            |              |         VP       V[+AUX, +NEG, S-TYPE DECL]
            |              |         |            |
         Mary-ka        cenhye     ttwici      anhnunta
```

The lexical requirement of the NPI *cenhye* in (15) is satisfied because the [1]VP in (16) shares the same information with *cenhye*. By the same reasoning, (6a) is predicted to be grammatical. But (6b) is considered to be ungrammatical because *yekan* in that sentence bears no LN auxiliary verb.[2]

_____

   [2] Following Cho (1999), we regard the LN as an auxiliary verb with [+NEG] and treat the

Sentence (6b) can be represented as in (17a). As illustrated in (17a), there is a conflict in the AUX value between the lexical information of *yekan* in (14a) and the information of *yekan* in the tree diagram; so the lexical requirement of *yekan* cannot be satisfied. Therefore, (6b) is ungrammatical.

(6) a.   Mary-ka   **yekan**   cal   ttwici   **anhnun-ta.**
          M-Nom   commonly   well   run   LN-Decl
     b.   Mary-ka   **yekan**   cal   ??**an/*mos**   ttwin-ta.
          M-Nom   at all   well   SN   run-Decl
     'Mary runs quite well.'

(17a)

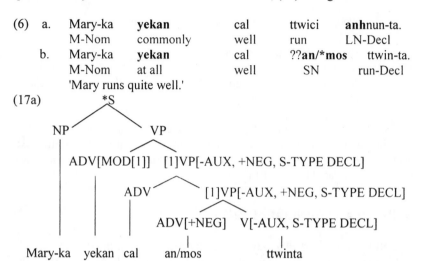

But as in (17b) representing (6a), the values of the [1]VP in the tree satisfies the lexical requirement of *yekan*. So (6a) is predicted to be grammatical.

(17b)

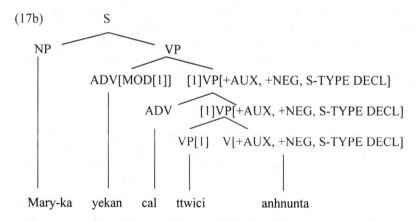

Similarly, the fact that the ARQ containing *cenhye* is not possible when there is no negative form within the sentence, just follows under this analy-

---

SN as an adverb with [+NEG].

sis. Because the NPI *cenhye* requires [+NEG] in the lexicon, the RQ in (10) has no negative forms so that it is predicted to be ungrammatical. By contrast, it is possible for *yekan* to occur alone in an ARQ as in (11a) because the NPI requires [-NEG] in a RQ.

(10)   *Mary-ka   **cenhye**   ttwi-nya?
              M-Nom   at all   run-Ques
              (Lit.) 'Does Mary run at all?'

(11) a.   Mary-ka   **yekan**   cal   ttwi-nya?
              M-Nom   commonly   well   run-Ques
              (Lit.) 'Does Mary run quite well?'

We have proposed a constraint-based lexical analysis to account for the distributional behavior of NPIs and demonstrated how it works. In the next section, we provide a pragmatic account to explain the semantic or pragmatic issues related to the NPI *yekan*.

4. Pragmatic Account of *Yekan*

The NPI *yekan* is a degree adverb literally denoting that the degree about a state or action is around the middle of the degree scale. It should occur only in a long-negated sentence to deliver the meaning that the degree about a state or action is quite high. In this section, we will demonstrate that the grammatical NPI use of *yekan* resulted from the conventionalization of its implicature which was inferred from long-negated sentences containing it. In addition, we will discuss why the NPI *yekan* occurs only with the long-negator, but not the short-negator, and how it can occur without the long-negator in an assertive-rhetorical question. Before discussing them, we are going to describe the pragmatic uses of the NPI *yekan*.

4.1. The Pragmatic Uses of the NPI *Yekan*

The NPI *yekan* is used to represent the speaker's expectation about the extent or degree of a state or action that he is describing with his utterance; that is, against his expectation, the degree or extent of the state or action is found to be quite high, not around the middle of the degree scale.[3] For in-

---

[3] Here we do not mean that the speaker's expectation is assumed to be the degree denoted by *yekan*, that is, around the middle of the degree scale. *Yekan* can be used even when the speaker expected the degree or extent about a state or action to be below the middle of the scale. However, *yekan* is usually used when the speaker who has no previous information about a state or action, guesses its degree or extent; in this case, the degree denoted by *yekan* is usually considered as the speaker's expectation. In this sense, the speaker's expec-

stance, by saying (18), the speaker intends to mean that he did not expect Semi to be fairly pretty, but he has found out that she is.

(18) (Semi-ka)   yekan   yeppu-ci   anh-a.
       S-Nom   commonly   pretty   LN-Decl
       'Semi is very pretty.'

Because the speaker uses *yekan* to express his expectation, he does not use it in a sincere question as seen in (19). We ask a sincere question to get some necessary information from the addressee. So, *yekan* in a sincere question like (19) means that the speaker is asking the addressee about his (=the speaker's) own expectation. This is quite a strange situation because it is the speaker, not the addressee who knows his expectation. That is why (19) sounds odd.

(19) *(Semi-ka)   yekan   yeppu-ci   anh-a?
       S-Nom   pretty   LN-Decl
       'Isn't Semi very pretty?"

The use of *yekan* to express the speaker's expectation is closely related to its politeness use. Instead of saying directly that the degree about a state or action is quite high, the speaker takes a strategy to make his utterance sound less assertive by using the NPI *yekan*. Making a strong assertion means that the addressee has no alternative but to accept the speaker's claim so that the former's opinion is disregarded and his face can be threatened. However, using the NPI *yekan* implies that, because the speaker delivers his opinion based on his expectation, it can be different from that of the addressee. So the utterance containing the NPI *yekan* sounds less assertive than the one containing emphatic intensifiers such as *acwu* 'very, fairly.' For example, (18) and (20) have the same interpretation that Semi is very pretty. However, they show the different attitudes of the speaker. In (20) the speaker represents Semi's beauty in a direct way by emphasizing it by using *acwu*, while in (18) he does it in an indirect way by understating it by using the NPI *yekan*. For this reason, (18) sounds less assertive than (20).

(20) (Semi-ka)   acwu   yepp-e.
       S-Nom   very   pretty-Decl
       'Semi is very pretty.'

Because the polite function of the NPI *yekan* is inferred from the speaker's less assertive attitude toward his intended meaning, he does not

---

tation is context-bound.

tend to use *yekan* in his utterance when he talks about the addressee's merits or virtues. By using *yekan*, he can threaten the addressee's face because he makes the impression that he is hesitating to be strongly assertive about her merits or virtues. In this situation, he needs to praise them in a direct way in order to maintain her face. For example, in the situation where the speaker is praising the addressee's beauty, (21a) sounds more polite than (21b). Even though they have the same interpretation, the speaker of (21a) makes a strong assertion about the addressee's excellent beauty, while the speaker of (21b) is not strongly assertive about it, which can threaten her face. This is why (21b) containing *yekan* is not used in this situation.

(21) a.   Cengmal   alumtawu-si-eyo.
        Truly   beautiful-HON-Decl
    b.   Yekan   alumtap-ci   anh-usi-eyo.
                    beautiful-   LN-HON-Decl
        'You are very beautiful.'

4.2. The Conventionalization of the NPI *Yekan*

We will demonstrate here how the degree adverb *yekan* has been used as an NPI to deliver the interpretation that the degree about a state or event is fairly high. Our claims are that *yekan* as a degree adverb was not an NPI and that it was used in long-negated sentences to get a scalar implicature which is the interpretation that the present NPI use of *yekan* produces, and that the use of *yekan* in a long-negated sentence to get this implicature has been conventionalized and that the other uses of *yekan* have disappeared. These claims are motivated by the fact that the NPI *yekan* lacks the property other degree adverbs display. In a negated sentence, all degree adverbs have two scalar implicatures, that is, upward and downward implicaures, but *yekan* as an NPI has only an upward implicature.

     When a speaker uses a certain degree adverb in a negated sentence, he intends it to implicate either a stronger degree (upward implicature) or a weaker one (downward implicature) than the degree it denotes. The downward implicature is linguistically inferable because the denial of a certain degree means that the intended degree is less than that. The upward implicature can be derived when there are some situations that allow the addressee to recognize that the speaker denies a certain degree because his intended degree is more than that. For example, by negating the degree adverb *manhi* 'much' in (22), the speaker can imply that he has some money, not much money (downward implicature). In addition, he can also expect the addressee to recognize that he spent not much money, but more than much, that is, all or almost all of the money (upward implicature).

(22)   Ton-ul   manhi   ssu-ci   anh-ass-e.
        money-Acc   much   spend   not-past-Decl
        'I did not spend much money.'

The upward implicature is derived from the speaker's understatement, and it is exploited for some nonlinguistic reasons, that is, social or cultural. For example, to represent the speaker's desire to mitigate face threatening acts which his utterance might induce. When the speaker of (22) believes that his use of a stronger form *ta* 'all' might threaten the face of the addressee, who had ordered him not to use all the money, he can intentionally choose the weaker form *manhi* 'much'.

The degree adverb *ecikanhi* is used to define the literal meaning of *yekan* in Korean dictionaries (Shin & Shin 1983). In a negated sentence, this adverb also produces both downward and upward implicatures. For example, by saying (23), the speaker can intend the downward implicature that the degree of Semi's beauty is low, not around the middle. Its upward implicature is that, because the degree of Semi's beauty is not around the middle, it is higher than that; that is, Semi is quite pretty.

(23)   (Semi-ka)   ecikanhi   yeppu-ci   anh-a.
                                        pretty   LN-Decl

However, unlike *ecikanhi* (and other degree adverbs as observed above), *yekan* does not allow the downward implicature, but only the upward implicature that the degree of a state or action is fairly high. In addition, the upward implicature from *ecikanhi* is cancelable, while the one for *yekan* is not. We cannot deny the interpretation that the degree of a state or action is fairly high without involving ourselves in a contradiction. So, for *ecikanhi* and other degree adverbs, the upward implicature is conversationally inferred; but for *yekan*, it can be grasped intuitively without considering the literal meaning, so that it is conventional. These differences between *yekan* and *ecikanhi* allow us to guess that *yekan* as a degree adverb would behave the same as *ecikanhi* and other degree adverbs; that is, it would produce the downward and upward implicatures inferred from its literal meaning and occur in a positive sentence. However, for some pragmatic motivations including the ones described as the pragmatic uses of the NPI *yekan*, using *yekan* in negated sentences to imply the upward interpretation would begin to grow more frequently. The more frequently *yekan* would be used this way, the less frequently it would be used for other purposes. Finally, *yekan* occurs only in a negated sentence to mean the upward implicature that the degree of a state or action is very high; therefore, it functions as an NPI. If we do not consider the conventionalization in this way, it will not be possible to explain the unbalanced properties of the degree adverbs *yekan* and *ecikanhi* in Korean.

4.3. Why Does the NPI *Yekan* Occur Only with the Long Negator?

In a sentence with the short-negator *an*, a degree adverb does not produce the upward implicature. For example, (24) has the downward implicature that the degree of Semi's beautify is low. However, as in (23), the degree adverb used with the LN induces the upward implicature as well as the downward one. Because *yekan* as an NPI needs to deliver the upward implicature, it occurs only with the LN, but not with the SN.

(24) (Semi-ka) ecikanhi an yepp-e.
                 very   SN pretty-Decl
      'Semi is very ugly.'

4.4 Why Is *Yekan* Used in an ARQ?

Rhetorical questions are a type of indirect speech in which the speaker insincerely asks for information so as to deliver his obvious opinion. So the speaker uses a rhetorical question when he believes that the addressee recognizes that its answer is already fixed by the context. For example, uttering (25) as a rhetorical question, the speaker intends to mean that Semi is quite busy, even though there is no negator to go with the NPI *yekan*.

(25)   Semi-ka yekan pappu-ni?
          S-Nom   busy-Ques
(26) a.   *Kuay,   yekan papp-a.
          yes   busy-D
     b.   Ani,   yekan pappu-ci anh-a.
          no   busy   LN-Decl

Because *yekan* as an NPI occurs with the LN, the affirmative answer (26a) is ungrammatical, while its negative answer (26b) is grammatical; the addressee has no choice but to say (26b) as an answer to question (25). Therefore, question (25) cannot be a sincere one, but a rhetorical one which always requires the answer to be negative. The case is that the speaker, by addressing the rhetorical question (25), has a definite idea about the answer (26b). This is why the NPI *yekan* can occur in an ARQ like (25).

5. Conclusion

Much of the literature regarding NPIs has focused on their licensing environment, which assumes that inherent negative predicates have the same negative force as overt negation in NPI licensability. To account for their licensing environment, the previous analyses have suggested either some syntactic or semantic/pragmatic generalizations. The generalizations on NPIs would be desirable only if they cover all empirical data. However, unless various properties of each NPI can be predicted by these generalizations, such generalizations would be worthless. *Yekan* challenges these generalizations since it exhibits a number of idiosyncratic properties different from other NPIs.

Specifically, *yekan* occurs only with the LN in a declarative sentence while other NPIs freely co-occur with negative predicates or overt negations. This points to the fact that the assumption that there is no difference in negative force among negative words is false. Furthermore, this suggests that the distributional behavior of each NPI should be accounted for in the grammar. Therefore, we have proposed that the syntactic properties can be explained by specifying the relevant information in each lexical item. This enables us to correctly predict the grammaticality of various sentences containing an NPI. We also have proposed a pragmatic account of the NPI *yekan* to answer the questions about its pragmatic role, and why it cannot be used in a sincere question, but it can be used in an ARQ. Rather than making a generalization for NPIs, we have attempted to account for the distributional behavior of the NPIs in the lexicon and syntax, and to provide a pragmatic account for the semantic/pragmatic properties of *yekan*.

Making a full description of each NPI would be more essential, even though making a big generalization on NPIs is important. Hence, we believe that this approach is on the right track in this context where more empirical research is required.

References

Cho, S.-Y. 1999. Some Properties of Short-form Negators in Korean. *Linguistic Research, Vol 17.* 201-212. Center for the Study of Language at Kyung Hee University.

Nam, S.-H. 1994. Another Type of Negative Polarity Item. In M. Kanazawa and C. Pinon (eds.) *Dynamics, Polarity and Quantification.* Stanford: CSLI Publications.

Pollard, C. and I. Sag. 1994. *Head-Driven Phrase Structure Grammar.* Chicago, IL: University of Chicago Press and Stanford: CSLI Publications.

Shin K.-C. and Y.-C. Shin. 1993. *Sae Wulimalpon Khunsacen.* SamSung Pressing Co.

Sohn, K.-W. 1995. Focus Barrier Amwu-to. *Harvard Studies in Korean Linguistics* 387-401. Department of Linguistics, Harvard University.

The Interpretations of *Wh*-elements in Conjoined *Wh*-questions

SUNGEUN CHO AND XUAN ZHOU

MIT & SUNY at Stony Brook

1. Introduction

It is generally accepted that the fundamental difference between English type of languages and Japanese and Korean type of languages with respect to *wh*-question is the presence of obligatory overt movement of *wh*-elements in the former and the lack of it in the latter. For example, in English, *which person* has to move from its base position to Spec-CP (1a); otherwise the sentence is ungrammatical (1b).[1] By contrast, the Japanese and Korean counterparts of *which person* may remain in situ (2).

(1) a. [$_{CP}$ which person$_i$ [does John like t$_i$]]
   b. *John likes which person?

(2) a. John-ga   dono hito-o   aisiteiru-no?
       John-NOM which person-ACC love-Q?
       Which person does John love?

---

[1] We exclude the so-called "echo question" interpretation.

b. John-i   enu salam-ul   salangha-ni?
   John-NOM which person-ACC like-Q
   Which person does John love?

English and Japanese/Korean *wh*-questions exhibit an associated difference that has not been discussed (to our knowledge). Consider the interpretation of English conjoined *wh*-questions like (3), involving overt ATB-movement. (3a) is ambiguous. It has a preferred reading, on which it asks a single question about a single individual; this "single question reading" is represented in (4a). Alternatively, (3a) has a less-preferred reading, on which it asks a conjunction of questions; the "multiple question reading" is represented in (4b).[2]

(3)a. **Which person** does John love and Mary hate?
  b. Which persons does John invite and Mary invite?

(4)a. which person x, John loves x and Mary hates x ?
    (possible answer: "Maxine")
  b. which person x, John loves x and which person y, Mary hates y ?
    (possible answer: "John loves Maxine and Mary hates Alice")

Interestingly, the Japanese and Korean counterparts of (3a), with *wh* in-situ are not similarly ambiguous. While (5a,b) can be understood with the multiple question reading (6b), they cannot be understood with the single question reading (6a). In other words, the preferred reading of the English example is missing in these cases.

(5) a. John-ga **dono hito-o**   aisitei-te Mary-ga
    J.-NOM   which person-ACC love-and M.-NOM
    dono hito-o   nikundeiru-no
    which person-ACC hate-Q
  b. John-i **enu   salam-ul**   salangha-ko Mary-ka
    J.-NOM which person-ACC like-and   M.-NOM
    enu   salam-ul   miweha-ni?
    which person-ACC hate-Q

(6) a.*which person x, John loves x and Mary hates x

---

[2] We note some variation in speaker's ability to get the multiple question reading in English. When the verbs in two conjuncts contrast as in (3a), the single question reading is strongly favored. When the same verbs occur, the multiple question reading seems to be more accessible. The possible answers of (3b) is "John invited his friends but Mary invited her classmates".

b. which person x, John loves x and which person y, Mary hates y

Single question readings are not, however, simply absent in Japanese and Korean. In addition to in-situ forms like (5a,b), Japanese and Korean also have local fronting sentences which resemble (3a) in the position of question word (7a,b). Perhaps surprisingly, however, such sentences are not ambiguous like the English case. They allow only the single question reading (8a,b):

(7) a. **dono hito-o** John-ga aisitei-te Mary-ga nikundeiru-no?
Which person J.-NOM love-and Mary-NOM hate-Q

b. **Enu salam-ul** John-i salangha-ko Mary-ka
Which person-ACC John-NOM love-and Mary -NOM
miweha-ni?
hate-Q

(8) a. which person x, John loves x and Mary hates x
b. *which person x, John loves x and which person y, Mary hates y

Thus unlike English, where movement in conjoined questions is associated with two readings, movement in conjoined Japanese/Korean questions maps to only one interpretation. The second reading is apparently reserved for the non-movement structure.

The data presented in (3) - (8) raise some simple questions: What is the source of the interpretational differences between English and Japanese/Korean? Why are English movement structures ambiguous and the Japanese/Korean movement/non-movement structures unambiguous? And how is this tied (if at all) to the presence of obligatory *wh*-movement in English versus its absence in Japanese/Korean?

2. Interpreting *Wh*-conjoined Questions

We argue that these questions can be answered by taking Williams (1978) analysis of ATB movement together with the "Copy Theory of Movement" introduced by Chomsky (1995). Williams (1978) proposes that English sentences like (3a) are derived by applying movement Across-the-Board (ATB) to the structure in (9a). In an ATB derivation, a single application of *wh*-movement places *which* in Spec-CP and simultaneously deletes both initial tokens of *wh*, thus deriving (3a), as shown in (9b).

(9) a. $[_{CP}$ $[_{IP}$John loves **which person**] and $[_{IP}$ Mary hates **which person**]]?
b. $[_{CP}$ **which person**$_i$... does $[_{IP}$ John love t$_i$] and
$[_{IP}$ Mary hate t$_i$]]

Chomsky (1995) proposes that movement is copying so that whenever an element moves, it leaves a copy in its original position instead of the trace (*t*) assumed by earlier theories. Under this view, the derivation in (9b) is recast as (10), where copies of *which person* have been left in the source positions:

(10)　　[CP **which person**$_i$ does　　[IP John love*which person*$_i$] and
　　　　　　　　　　　　　　　　　　　[IP Mary hate　*which person*$_i$]]

Although the copies of the moved *wh*-phrases are silent at PF, they remain at LF. In order to interpret (10), the LF component must convert this representation to one containing licit operator-variable chains. *Wh*-phrases like *which person* are typically analyzed as consisting of a *wh*-operator of category D (*which*) and a nominal restrictor phrase of category NP (*person*) (11).

(11) [DP [D which] [NP person]]

　　Given this bifurcation of *wh*-phrases, and given that the operator portion (*wh*-) must head an operator-variable chain, there will be two ways in which the LF component may map a structure like (10) to a licit operator-variable structure. One possibility is for both the *wh* and the nominal restrictor to be in the operator position. This results in a single copy of the nominal at LF (12a). The other possibility is for the *wh* alone to stand in operator position, with the nominal restrictor occupying the copy position (12b). In an ATB question, this results in multiple copies of the nominal at LF since there are multiple source positions (12b):

(12) a. [**which person**] does John love [DP t] and Mary hate [DP t]
　　 b. [**which**] does John love [DP t **person**] and Mary hate
　　　　[DP t **person**]

　　We saw earlier that there are two interpretations available for an ATB *wh*-question: single question & multiple question. We have now seen that there are two structures available for an ATB question: single nominal & multiple nominal. We suggest that the two are correlated. Specifically, we suggest that an ATB *wh*-question with the single nominal structure receives the single question reading (13). And we suggest that an ATB *wh*-question with the multiple nominal structure receives the multiple question reading (14):

(13) a. Which person does John love and Mary hate?
   b. [which person] does John love [$_{DP}$ t] and Mary hate [$_{DP}$ t]
   c. which person x, John loves x and Mary hates x ?

(14) a. Which person does John love and Mary hate?
   b. [which] does John love [$_{DP}$ t person] and Mary hate
       [$_{DP}$ t person]
   c. which person x, John loves x and which person x, Mary hates x ?

In essence, then, the number of nominal copies in the structure determines the number of questions understood.

3. Japanese and Korean *Wh*-questions

We have seen that in languages such as Japanese and Korean, *wh*-phrases do not move before Spell-Out. Chomsky (1995) proposes that these *wh*-phrases are also immobile at subsequent levels. Both the Q-features and the *wh*-features in these languages are taken weak, and hence invisible at PF, although intelligible in situ at LF. Chomsky (1995) suggests that *wh*-phrases are interpreted through a process like unselective binding in the sense of Heim (1982) and Pesetsky (1987): Q binds the *wh*-phrases in both conjuncts simultaneously, forming an operator-variable structure. Hence (5a-b) repeated below have LF structures (15a-b), respectively.

(5) a. John-ga **dono hito-o**   aisitei-te Mary-ga **dono hito-o**
       J.-NOM which person-ACC love-and M.-NOM which person-ACC
       nikundeiru-no
       hate-Q
   b. John-i **enu salam-ul**   salangha-ko Mary-ka **enu   salam-ul**
       J.-NOM which person-ACC love-and   M.-NOM which person-ACC
       miweha-ni?
       hate-Q
       which person x, John loves x and which person y, Mary hates y
       *which person x, John loves x and Mary hates x

(15) a. [$_{CP}$ [John-ga **dono hito-o**$_i$ aistei-te][Maru-ga **dono
       hito-o**$_i$nikundeiru-no] Q_i]
   b. [$_{CP}$[John-i **enu salam-ul**$_i$ cohaha-ko][Mary-ka **enu
       salam-ul**$_i$ miweha-ni]Q_i]

If this is correct, then Japanese and Korean conjoined in-situ *wh*-questions like (5) will have only one possible LF structure: one in which both *wh* and the nominal restrictor remain in their base-generated positions and are bound by a Q element. Given our crucial assumption that the number of nominal elements at LF corresponds to the number of questions understood, we predict that Japanese and Korean conjoined in-situ *wh*-questions like (5a,b) will receive a multiple question interpretation, where the individual loved by John is distinct from the one hated by Mary. This prediction is correct as we have shown above.

3.1 Scrambling & *Wh*-scrambling

Let us turn now to the cases in (7). Superficially, these resemble the English example in (3a), where *wh*- has been raised to CP Spec from its base position.

(7) a. **dono hito-o** John-ga aisitei-te Mary-ga nikundeiru-no?
     which person John-NOM love-and Mary-NOM hate-Q

  b. **Enu salam-ul** John-i salangha-ko Mary-ka
     which person-ACC John-NOM love-and Mary -NOM
     miweha-ni?
     hate-Q

Despite the surface resemblance, however, we argue that the sentences in (7) are not the same as English conjoined *wh*-questions, and do not result from overt *wh*-raising to Spec CP driven by strong *wh*-features.

Japanese and Korean both contain scrambling and processes that can displace a DP to the front of the sentence (16a,b). Furthermore, both languages allow this process to occur ATB, as shown in (17a,b).

(16) a. Bill-o, John-ga aisiteiru
     Bill-ACC, John-NOM loves
     Bill, John loves

  b. Bill-ul, John-i salanghanta
     Bill-ACC John-NOM love
     Bill, John loves

(17) a. Bill-o John-ga aisitei-te Mary-ga nikundeiru
     Bill-ACC John-NOM loves-and Mary hates

  b. Bill-ul John-i salangha-ko Mary miwehanta
     Bill-ACC John-NOM like-and Mary hates
     Bill, John loves and Mary hates

This kind of scrambling in Japanese and Korean has the A-movement properties of scrambling found elsewhere in the world's languages. Thus, fronted phrases do not induce weak-crossover: there is no prohibition on the co-reference indicated in (18a,b).

(18) a. John-o$_i$ kare-no$_i$ hahaoya-ga   aisite-iru
          John-ACC$_i$ his-GEN$_i$ mother-NOM loves
      b. John-ul$_i$ ku-uy$_i$ emma-ka   salanghanta
          John-ACC$_i$ his$_i$ mother-NOM loves
          John$_i$ his$_i$ mother loves

We propose that examples (7a,b) are not the product of ATB *wh*-movement but rather ATB scrambling of a *wh*-phrase to a position we will simply designate as IP.

(19) a [$_{CP}$ [$_{IP}$ **dono hito-o** [$_{IP}$ John-ga *dono hito-o* aisitei-te
                                        Mary-ga *dono hito-o* nikundeiruno]]]
     b. [$_{CP}$[$_{TopP}$ **Enu salam-ul** [$_{IP}$ John-i *enu salam-ul* coahaha-ko
                                        Mary-ka *enu salam-ul* miweha-ni]]]

This analysis is supported by the fact that sentences such as (7a,b) do not show weak-crossover effects (20a,b), in parallel with (18):

(20) a. **dono hito-o$_i$ pro$_i$** titioya-ga   aisitei-te **pro$_i$** hahaoya-ga
          which person his-GEN father-NOM love-and his-GEN mother
          nikundeiru-no?
          hate-Q
      b. **Enu salam-ul$_i$ pro$_i$** appa-ka   coaha-ko **pro$_i$** emma-ka
          which person-ACC his father-NOM love-and his mother-NOM
          miweha-ni?
          hate-Q
          'Which person$_i$ does his$_i$ father love and his$_i$ mother hate?'

3.2 Interpreting *Wh*-scrambling

Supposing that (7a,b) are *wh*-scramblings, consider their structure. In order to interpret (19a,b), the LF component converts them into interpretable LF objects, namely A-chains. Since A-chains do not show reconstruction effects proposed by Chomsky (2000), Lasnik (1999), and Miyagawa (to appear, in press), they must presumably be converted in such a way that their in-situ copies are eliminated (21)[3]:

(21) a. [$_{CP}$ [$_{IP}$ **dono hito-o** [$_{IP}$ John-ga t aisitei-te Mary-ga t nikundeiru-no]]**Q**]

　　b. [$_{CP}$ [$_{IP}$ **Enu salam-ul** [$_{IP}$ John-i t salangha-ko Mary-ka t miweha-ni]] **Q**]

Unselective binding of the scrambled *wh*-phrase will now occur by a Q element in CP Spec:

(22) a. [$_{CP}$ [$_{IP}$ **dono hito-o$_i$** [$_{IP}$ John-ga t aisitei-te Mary-ga t nikundeiru-no]] **Q$_i$**]

　　b. [$_{CP}$ [$_{IP}$ **Enu salam-ul$_i$** [$_{IP}$ John-i t salangha-ko Mary-ka t miweha-ni]] **Q$_i$**]

Given our assumption that the number of questions understood should correspond to the number of the nominal elements in the *wh*-operator chain at LF, the LF structures in (22) correctly predict that Japanese and Korean sentences with scrambled *wh*-phrases such as (7) have only readings like (4a) where the person loved by John and the one hated by Mary are construed as the same individual.

4. English Conjoined Multiple *Wh*-Questions

English conjoined multiple *wh*-questions illustrate our proposals in an interesting way since they involve both overtly moved *wh*-phrases and in-situ *wh*-phrases:

(23) I wonder **which person** likes **who** and admires **who**.

In (23), the subject of embedded clause *which person* has presumably raised ATB to CP Spec, leaving behind a copy in each conjunct, while the objects of embedded clauses, *who,* remain in their base positions. (24a-b) are the two possible LF structures of the subordinate clause of (23).

---

[3] We emphasize that the exact account of scrambling as A-movement is largely irrelevant to our paper. The crucial point is simply that A-movement does not show reconstruction effects, and under the copy theory of movement, this entails that copies in the source positions of ATB movement will not be active. See Tada (1994) and Ueda (1986).

(24) a.   **[which person [Q** [t likes who] and [t admires who]]]
which person x, (which person y, x likes y) &
(which person z, x admires z)

b.   **[which [Q** [t **person** likes who] and [t **person** admires who]]]
(which person x, which person y, x likes y) &
(which person w, which person z, w admires z)

c.   *which person y (which person x, x likes y) & (which person z, z
admires y)

d.   *which person x, which person y, (x likes y) & (x admires y)

With respect to the moved *wh*-subject phrase (*which person*) there will be two interpretive options under our principles. If the nominal restrictor is construed with the operator, we predict an interpretation of (23) where I wonder for single individuals x, who are the people x likes and who are the people x admires (24a). If the nominal restrictor is construed in the conjuncts, then, we expect an interpretation of (23) where I wonder about the answers to conjoined multiple *wh*-questions. Although the judgment task is not an easy one, the relevant interpretations do in fact seem to be available. By contrast, consider the in-situ *wh*-object phrases (*who*). Under our principles these will have only one interpretive option. They should always be interpreted in their base-generated positions and denote two different individuals, like *wh*-phrases in Japanese and Korean sentences such as (5). Interpretations like (24c-d) should not be available with (23). Again although the judgment are complex, the facts do indeed seem to be correct.

References

Chomsky, Noam. 1995. *The minimalist program*. Cambridge, Mass.: MIT Press.

Chomsky, Noam. 2000. Minimalist Inquiries: the framework. In Roger Martin, David Michaels, and Juan Uriagereka (eds.) Step by Step: Essays in honor of Howard Lasnik. Cambridge, mass.: MIT press.

Heim, Irene. 1982. The semantics of definite and indefinite noun phrases. Doctoral dissertation, MIT, Cambridge, Mass.

Higginbotham and Robert May. 1981. Questions, quantifiers and crossing. *The LinguisticReview* 1: 41-79.

Koopman, Hilda and Dominique Sportiche. 1982. Variables and the bijection principle. *The Linguistic Review* 2: 139-160.

Lasnik, Howard. 1999. Chains of arguments. In Working Minimalism, ed. Samuel Epstein and Norbert Hornsrein. Cambridge, Mass.: MIT press.

Miyagawa, Shigeru. In press. The EPP, scrambling, and wh in-situ. In Ken Hale: A

Life in a language, ed. Michael kenstowicz. Cambridge, Mass.: MIT Press.

Miyagawa, Shigeru. To appear. A-movement scrambling and options without optionality. In *Word order and scrambling*, ed. Simin Karimi. Blackwell Publishers.

Pesetsky, David. 1987. *Wh* in situ: movement and unselective binding. In *Representation of (in)definiteness*, ed. Eric Reuland and Alice Ter Meulen, MIT Press, Cambridge.

Tada, Hiroaki. 1994. A/A-bar partion in derivation. Doctoral dissertation, MIT, Cambridge, Mass.

Ueda, Masanobu. 1986. On quantifier float in Japanese. In *University of Massachusetts Occasional Papers in Linguistics*, 263-310. GLSA. University of Massachusetts, Amherst.

Williams, Edwin. 1978. Across-the-board application of rules. *Linguistic Inquiry* 9:31-43

Complex Predicate Formation and Argument Structure of Japanese V-V Compounds

THOMAS GAMERSCHLAG

Heinrich-Heine-Universität Düsseldorf

1. Introduction[*]

Japanese allows two lexical verbs to combine into compounds of the form [V1 V2]$_V$. Two major classes of such V-V compounds (=VVCs) are attested, referred to as "syntactic" and "lexical compound verbs", respectively (Kageyama 1989, 1993, 1999, Matsumoto 1996a, 1998). These two classes can be distinguished by the relation that V1 bears to the morphological head V2: In syntactic compound verbs such as *narai-hazimeru* (learn-begin) 'begin to learn', *yomi-tuzukeru* (read-continue) 'go on reading', or *kai-wasureru* (buy-forget) 'forget to buy', V1 is a complement of the head V2. By contrast, lexical compound verbs such as *huki-kesu* (blow-extinguish) 'blow out', *hane-mawaru* (jump-move.around) 'jump around' or *nagare-otiru* (flow-fall) 'flow down' are characterized by the absence of a complement-functor relation between V1 and V2.

This paper is concerned with lexical compound verbs, which are problematic in several respects: First, there is no morphological indicator of the

---

[*] The analysis presented in this paper grew out of my work in a project on verb structures which is part of the Sonderforschungsbereich 282 'Theory of the Lexicon' and supported by the German Science Foundation (DFG). I would like to thank Anja Latrouite, Ingrid Kaufmann, Barbara Stiebels, and Dieter Wunderlich for discussion on the topic. I am also grateful to my informants Hiroyuki Miyashita, Kazuko Tsugane, and Yi-chun Yang.

semantic relation between V1 and V2. Various classifications of the semantic relations that hold between the two verbs are found in the literature (Hasselberg 1996, Matsumoto 1996a, 1998, Tagashira 1978, among others). Matsumoto (1996a), e.g., suggests four subclasses of lexical VVCs: (i) In "pair compounds" such as *naki-sakebu* (cry-shout) 'scream', two verbs of similar meaning are combined with an intensifying effect; (ii) in "cause compounds" such as *ni-tumaru* (boil-be.packed) 'be boiled down', V1 denotes the cause for bringing about the result state denoted by V2; (iii) in "means compounds" such as *osi-taosu* (push-topple) 'push down', V1 explicates the means by which the action denoted by V2 is executed; and (iv) in "manner compounds" such as *odori-mawaru* (dance-move.around) 'dance around', V1 specifies the manner accompanying the action denoted by V2.

Second[1], there is no straightforward generalization with respect to the argument structure of lexical compounds (Kageyama 1993, 1999, Matsumoto 1996a, 1998, Nishiyama 1998, among others). In the vast majority of compounds, either two intransitive or two transitive verbs are combined with obligatory argument sharing. The sentence in (1) is a typical example with the transitive-transitive VVC *osi-taosu* (push-topple) 'push down'. Here, the subject and object arguments of the two transitive verbs are identified, yielding a compound of the same valency.

(1) *Rikisi*   *ga*   *aite*   *o*   *zimen*   *ni osi-taosi-ta.*
    sumo.wrestler NOM opponent ACC ground to push-topple-PAST
    'The sumo wrestler pushed his opponent to the ground.'

In comparison to compounds made up of verbs which agree in the number of their NP arguments, combinations of a transitive and an intransitive verb are rare, and intransitive-transitive sequences such as *mai-ageru* (whirl-raise) 'whirl up' are hardly ever found. Transitive-intransitive compounds, however, are more frequent. They are peculiar in that they do not behave uniformly with respect to the argument structure of the resulting compound. In *tumi-agaru* (pile-go.up) 'be piled up' in (2), only the shared object argument of the transitive V1 *tumu* 'pile' is transferred to the compound, whereas the subject of V1 is blocked from realization. As a consequence, the argument structure of the VVC is identical to the argument structure of the head V2.

---

[1] A third point which is closely related to the two problems outlined above is the distribution of verb combinations, i.e., which verb types can be combined. For example, the head verb in Matsumoto's cause compounds is always an unaccusative verb as in *nomi-tubureru* (drink-collapse) 'drink oneself unconscious' or *uti-agaru* (hit-go.up) 'be hit up'. This topic cannot be addressed in the present paper. For an in-depth discussion of the combinatorial patterns found in lexical compound verbs see Matsumoto (1996a, 1998).

(2) *Isi   ga   takaku tumi-agat-ta.*
     stone NOM high   pile-rise-PAST
     'The stones were piled up high.'

In contrast to the pattern in (2), there are also compounds such as *sagasi-mawaru* (search-go.around) 'walk around searching', shown in (3). In VVCs of this type, the subject argument of V1 is shared with the intransitive V2, whereas the unshared object argument is inherited by the compound. As a result, the argument structure of the compound appears to be identical to the argument structure of V1.

(3) *Watasi wa   tegami o   nizikan   sagasi-mawat-ta.*
     I   TOP   letter   ACC for.two.hours search-go.around-PAST
     'I looked around for the letter for two hours.'

Compounds of the type in (3) clearly show that the argument structure of the compound is not always a copy of the argument structure of the head verb.

The compounds in (2) and (3) contrast not only in argument structure: Whereas compounds of the type illustrated in (2) exhibit a causal relation (V1 causes V2), compounds of the type illustrated in (3) refer to two simultaneous subevents which are not causally related. I will refer to the former semantic type as "resultative compounds" (a term already used by Li 1990, 1993) and to the latter type as "non-resultative compounds".

In this paper, I will focus on the contrast exhibited by transitive-intransitive VVCs. I will argue that the two semantic types, i.e., resultative vs. non-resultative compounds, can be derived from a general constraint on the semantic relations exhibited by complex verbs. I will present a lexical analysis in which the argument structure of the compounds is derived from the hierarchical ranking of the respective argument variables in Semantic Form, a minimal semantic representation (Bierwisch 1983, Wunderlich 1997a). The differences in semantic type, then, lead to different Semantic Forms and, consequently, to different argument structures. Finally, I will demonstrate how the analysis of transitive-intransitive VVCs can be extended to other sequences such as transitive-transitive compounds (*osi-taosu* (push-topple) 'push down').[2] Before going into the details of the analysis, I will first sketch the lexical framework adopted here in the next section.

2. Lexical Decomposition Grammar (LDG)

LDG (Wunderlich 1997a, 2000) is a lexical theory that provides a principled account of the formation of complex predicates and the morphosyntactic realization of arguments ("argument linking"). In this model, four

---

[2] For a more detailed analysis of the patterns shown by lexical VVCs see Gamerschlag (2000).

levels of representation are interrelated by a set of mapping principles. The representation of the ditransitive verb *ageru* 'give' in (4) illustrates this four-level architecture.

(4) representation of *ageru* 'give'

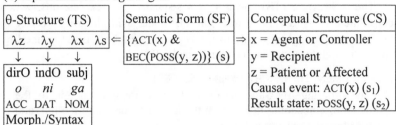

θ-Structure (TS)	Semantic Form (SF)	Conceptual Structure (CS)
λz λy λx λs ⇐	{ACT(x) & BEC(POSS(y, z))} (s) ⇒	x = Agent or Controller
↓ ↓ ↓		y = Recipient
dirO indO subj		z = Patient or Affected
o ni ga		Causal event: ACT(x) (s₁)
ACC DAT NOM		Result state: POSS(y, z) (s₂)
Morph./Syntax		

The central level of this model is the Semantic Form (SF). SF is a minimal semantic representation made up of decompositional predicates. The SF of *ageru*, e.g., consists of the activity predicate $ACT(x)$ and the change of state predicate $BEC(POSS(y,z))$. SF is considered a grammatical level which is hierarchically structured: The order of predicates determines the hierarchy of arguments from which the realization of the arguments at the level of Morphology/Syntax (MS) can be predicted (see below). The partial semantic representation at SF can be enriched by more elaborate information about thematic and event roles, implicit arguments, and temporal/causal relations at the level of Conceptual Structure (CS). The mapping between Conceptual Structure and Semantic Form is constrained by the two principles CONNEXION and COHERENCE (Kaufmann 1995, Kaufmann & Wunderlich 1998):

(5) CONNEXION
   In a decomposed SF structure each predicate must share at least one argument with another predicate, either explicitly or implicitly.

(6) COHERENCE
   Subevents encoded by the predicates of a decomposed SF structure must be contemporaneously or causally related to each other:
   A & B → A causes B or A is contemporaneous with B

COHERENCE, given in (6), allows only two interpretative options for a complex predicate: The partial predicates must be in a causal relation or in the relation of simultaneity. For *ageru*, this means that the unspecified agent predicate $ACT(x)$ is interpreted as an action which is causally related to the change of state expressed by $BEC(POSS(y,z))$. In the case of a causal relation, COHERENCE also restricts the order of predicates in SF: The predicate representing the cause has to precede the predicate representing the result. Thus, $ACT(x)$ has to precede $BEC(POSS(y,z))$. CONNEXION, given in

(5), requires some argument sharing between the partial predicates. For *ageru*, with the three distinct argument variables x, y, and z, this means that either y is interpreted as an implicit recipient of ACT(x) or z is interpreted as an implicit affected object of ACT(x).

The θ-Structure (TS) consists of a sequence of λ-expressions, which constitute θ-roles (argument roles) in this model, with the lowest θ-role to the left and the highest θ-role to the right. This ranking is determined by ARGUMENT HIERARCHY in (7), which relates SF and TS.

(7) ARGUMENT HIERARCHY (Bierwisch 1989)

The ordering of λ-abstractors in θ-Structure corresponds to the depth of embedding in SF, with the lowest argument to the left, and the highest argument to the right.

All the arguments of SF-predicates represented by θ-roles have to be realized in syntax or morphology, with the exception of the situation argument s, which is bound by tense and mood. In the canonical case, the projection of arguments is determined purely structurally by the hierarchy of arguments in θ-Structure: The lowest argument (=z) is mapped onto the direct object, the middle argument (=y) onto the indirect object, and the highest argument (=x) onto the subject.

If there is some lexical constraint that blocks a certain argument from being projected onto θ-Structure, this argument is preferably identified with another argument to be realized structurally. Only if such an identification is excluded for conceptual reasons, the respective argument variable is bound existentially. This is expressed by the constraint VISIBILITY in (8).

(8) VISIBILITY (OF ARGUMENTS)

a. Every SF-argument variable ξ is projected to θ-Structure unless this is blocked for independent reasons.

b. In such a case ξ is identified with another SF-argument variable unless this is blocked for independent reasons.

c. In such a case ξ is bound existentially (*last resort*).

3. Semantic type and composition

In contrast to syntactic compound verbs, the meaning of lexical compound verbs is not established via the complement-functor relation, i.e., V2 cannot be represented as a functor taking V1 as a (predicative) argument. In the present framework, the interpretation strategy which applies in such cases is formulated in form of the constraint COHERENCE (see (6) above). COHERENCE allows for two options: One option is to establish a causal relation between the two verbs. This is available in resultative compounds such as *tumi-agaru* (pile-go.up) 'be piled up', *ni-tumaru* (boil-be.packed) 'be boiled down', or *yaki-tuku* (burn-be.attached) 'be attached by burning', where V1 refers to an action affecting an argument and V2 specifies a transition. The other option is to merely unify the temporal structures of the single verbs so that the interpretation of simultaneity arises. This is the case in non-resultative compounds such as *sagasi-mawaru* (search-go.around) 'walk around searching', *uri-aruku* (sell-walk) 'walk around selling' or *hakobi-oriru* (carry-descend) 'carry downward'.[3]

With respect to the composition of VVCs, there are mainly two questions to be answered: (i) what determines the order of the two verbs in the compound? and (ii) what is the SF of the compounds from which the argument structure is derived and from which the asymmetry we have observed in transitive-intransitive compounds results?

Regarding the first question, it has already been stated by Li (1993) for resultative compounds that the order of verbs in syntax/morphology is determined iconically. (9) is a simplified version of Li's original formulation of his Temporal Iconicity Condition (TIC).

(9) TEMPORAL ICONICITY CONDITION (TIC, Li 1993, simplified):
The linear order of verbs corresponds to the temporal order of the events they refer to.

As a consequence of the TIC, event structure and morphological structure are mapped onto each other as shown in (10a) for resultative compounds.

(10) mapping morphology - event structure

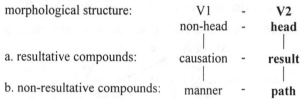

morphological structure:	V1	V2
	non-head	head
a. resultative compounds:	causation	result
b. non-resultative compounds:	manner	path

For resultative compounds the TIC has the effect that the verb denoting the cause precedes the verb denoting the result. This proposal can be extended to non-resultative compounds such as *sagasi-mawaru* (search-go.around) 'walk around searching' or *hakobi-oriru* (carry-descend) 'carry down', where V2 is a path verb and V1 specifies an accompanying manner (see (10b)). The manner and the motion along a path are two simultaneous actions, however, the path is only completed at the end of the motion event, thus, in a way manner (V1) is prior to path (V2). Alternatively, the order of verbs in non-resultative compounds may follow from the fact that Japanese

---

[3] In his analysis of lexical compounds, Matsumoto (1996a) has developed similar lexicalization constraints (DETERMINATIVE CAUSATION CONDITION, COEXTENSIVENESS CONDITION).

focuses on the path when referring to motion (Matsumoto 1996a,b; Wienold 1995). Therefore, it is more natural that the head V2 encodes the path, rather than the non-head V1.

We now turn to the second question, the formation of Semantic Form. In lexical compounds, neither of the two verbs can be represented as functor on the other. LDG treats complex predicates of this type by adding a position for a predicative argument via the lexical operation "Argument Extension" (ARG, Wunderlich 1997b). Such a predicative position allows the SF of another element to be incorporated. As a default, ARG applies to the respective head (=V2), see (11a). However, if this leads to a SF which is not well-formed with respect to COHERENCE, ARG can also be applied to the non-head (=V1), see (11b). P is a variable for a predicative argument of the type $<e, t>$, which is added to the SF of the base (represented by 'V1(...) (s)' and 'V2(...) (s)', respectively).

(11) ARGUMENT EXTENSION (ARG, Wunderlich 1997b)
    a.   ARG applied to the **head** (*default*):
        $...\lambda s$ V2(...) (s) $\rightarrow \lambda P_{<e, t>}...\lambda s$ [V2(...) (s) & P(s)]
    b.   ARG applied to the **non-head**:
        $...\lambda s$ V1(...) (s) $\rightarrow \lambda P_{<e, t>}...\lambda s$ [V1(...) (s) & P(s)]

In non-resultative compounds, the head V2 refers to the path according to (10b). Therefore, the default extension of the head verb leads to a SF in which the predicate referring to the path appears in the first position. This is exemplified by the lexical tree for the SF of *sagasi-mawaru* in (12).

(12) hierarchical SF of non-resultative *sagasi-mawaru* (search-go.around)
extension of the head:

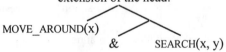

MOVE_AROUND(x)
                              &   SEARCH(x, y)

In (12), the predicates contributed by the single verbs refer to two simultaneous events. The predicate in the first (or highest) position introduces the concept of circular motion, and the second (or lowest) predicate specifies the accompanying manner. Since the events are not causally related, the ordering condition imposed by COHERENCE does not apply. The reverse order of predicates would be in line with COHERENCE as well, but since the SF in (12) results from the default extension of the head V2, the order in (12) is preferred. As will be seen in the next section, the availability of a representation with the transitive V1 in the lowest position yields an argument structure which allows the unshared object argument of V1 to be realized as the object of the compound.

In resultative compounds, the head V2 always refers to the result according to (10a). As a consequence, the default extension of the head would yield a SF where the result predicate is in the first position. However, if the second option provided by ARG is chosen and ARG is applied to the non-head V1, one arrives at a representation with the result predicate in the second position. For a compound such as *tumi-agaru* (pile-go.up) 'be piled up' the two options provided by ARG yield the two SFs in (13a) and (b) below.

(13) hierarchical SF of resultative *tumi-agaru* (pile-go.up)

a. *extension of the head: b. extension of the non-head:

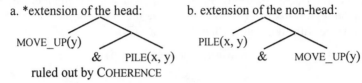

MOVE_UP(y)   PILE(x, y)

    & PILE(x, y)   & MOVE_UP(y)

ruled out by COHERENCE

Only the SF in (13b) is well-formed with respect to COHERENCE. (13a) is ruled out because in this SF the result predicate precedes the cause predicate, which is a violation of the ordering condition imposed on cause-result representations by COHERENCE. As already pointed out by Li (1993), the mapping of the result to the head V2 constitutes a syntax-semantics mismatch. This mismatch is reflected in the composition of SF: Only the non-default extension of the non-head V1 yields a well-formed SF. On the assumption that argument structure is derived from the order of predicates in SF, the demotion of the partial SF contributed by the head V2 leads to the highly restricted argument structure of resultative VVCs (see below).

4. Argument Structure of transitive-intransitive VVCs

Let us start with non-resultative compounds such as *sagasi-mawaru* 'walk around searching'. The composition and linking of the compound are demonstrated in (14).

(14) Composition and linking of *sagasi-mawaru* (search-go.around)

a. *mawaru*: $\lambda x\ \lambda s$ [MOVE_AROUND(x) (s)]

      $\to \lambda P\ \lambda x\ \lambda s$ [MOVE_AROUND(x) (s) & P(s)]

b. *sagasi-*: $\lambda v\ \lambda u\ \lambda s'$ [SEARCH(u, v) (s')]

c. *sagasi-mawaru*:

    $\lambda v\quad \lambda x\quad \lambda s$ [MOVE_AROUND(x_i)(s) & SEARCH(u_i, v)(s)]

  linking: dirO subj

     o ga

In (14a), the SF of V2 *mawaru* 'go around' is extended by a predicative position, into which the SF of V1 *sagasu* 'search' in (14b) is integrated by functional composition. (14c) shows the result of functional composition and subsequent λ-conversion. Due to CONNEXION, which requires sharing of at least one argument (see (5)), the single argument of V2 must be shared with V1 (indicated by coindexation). Since the argument that is shared must meet the sortal restrictions imposed by the verb, the single argument of V2 can only be identified with the subject argument of V1. As an effect of argument sharing, λu is removed in (14c), leaving only two arguments in the θ-Structure of the compound. Since the SF of the transitive V1 is integrated into the lowest position in the SF of the compound, the object argument of V1 (= v) becomes the lowest argument in the SF of the compound. Due to the depth of embedding, which is shown more explicitly in the lexical tree in (15), v is realized as the object of the compound in accordance with ARGUMENT HIERARCHY (see (7)).

(15) Lexical tree of *sagasi-mawaru* (search-go.around)

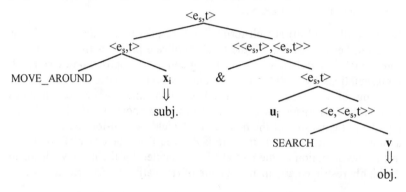

Turning to transitive-intransitive resultative compounds such as *tumi-agaru* (pile-go.up) 'be piled up', we see that the derivation of θ-Structure is slightly more complex. The composition of *tumi-agaru* is shown in (16). The tree in (17) shows the argument hierarchy. Functional composition and CONNEXION yield the representation in (16c), in which the object argument of V1 (=v) is identified with the single argument of V2 (=x). The θ-Structure in (16c), however, is that of a transitive verb with x realized as object and u realized as subject. What still needs to be explained is why u, the subject argument of the transitive V1 *tumu* 'pile', is blocked from realization.

(16) composition of *tumi-agaru* (pile-go.up)

a. *tumi-*: $\lambda v\ \lambda u\ \lambda s\ [\text{PILE}(u, v)\ (s)]$
   $\rightarrow \lambda P\ \lambda v\ \lambda u\ \lambda s\ [\text{PILE}(u, v)\ (s)\ \&\ P(s)]$

b. *agaru*: $\lambda x\ \lambda s'\ [\text{MOVE\_UP}\ (x)\ (s')]$

c. *tumi-agaru*: $\lambda x\ \lambda u\ \lambda s\ [\text{PILE}(u, v_i)\ (s)\ \&\ \text{MOVE\_UP}\ (x_i))\ (s)]$

(17) Lexical tree of *tumi-agaru* (pile-go.up)

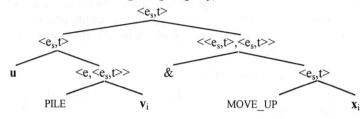

The importance of the position of the morphological head in the determination of argument structure has already been emphasized by Li (1993) in his contrastive analysis of Japanese and Chinese resultative compounds. In contrast to Japanese, head-initial Chinese transitive-intransitive compounds such as *qi-bing* (annoy-get.sick) 'annoy s.o. so much that s/he gets sick' in (18) do not require the subject of V1 to be blocked.

(18) *Lisi   qi-bing-le   Zhangsan.*
         annoy-get.sick-ASP
    'Lisi annoyed Zhangsan so much that Zhangsan got sick.'

The Chinese example in (18) shows that a general conceptual explanation for the blocking of the V1 subject in *tumi-agaru* can hardly be found. Therefore, I assume that the blocking of the subject in *tumi-agaru* should be explained by a structural property, namely the position of the head. To account for the contrast between Chinese and Japanese VVCs, I propose a constraint which requires that the highest argument (=subject) of the head verb remains the highest argument in the θ-Structure of the complex verb. This constraint, called the SUBJECT-HEAD CONDITION[4], is formulated in (19).

(19) SUBJECT-HEAD CONDITION
    The highest argument of the head verb is realized as the highest argument (=subject) of the complex verb.

The SUBJECT-HEAD CONDITION would be violated if the highest argument of V1 in *tumi-agaru* were realized structurally, so it has to be blocked. The realization of non-structural arguments is regulated by VISIBILITY, introduced in (8): If an argument cannot be realized structurally, it is preferably identified with a structural argument to remain visible. Since there is no

---

[4] This condition differs from the "principle of subject sharing" (Yumoto 1996), which was adopted by Matsumoto (1998) in his analysis of lexical compound verbs. In the present account the identification of the subject arguments is a result of the interaction between the SUBJECT-HEAD CONDITION, VISIBILITY, and CONNEXION. Since these principles do not require subject sharing in every case, compounds like *tumi-agaru*, which obviously violate the principle of subject sharing, do not pose a problem for the present analysis.

structural argument left with which the subject argument of V1 (=u in (17)) can be identified, the subject argument is bound existentially due to the last resort provided by VISIBILITY. Applying all the conditions introduced above to the representation of *tumi-agaru* yields the θ-Structure in (20) with only one argument left to be realized.

(20) linking of *tumi-agaru* (pile-go.up)

$\quad$ *tumi-agaru*: $\lambda x \quad \lambda s \, \exists u \, [\text{PILE}(u, v_i) \, (s) \, \& \, \text{MOVE\_UP} \, (x_i)) \, (s)]$

$\quad$ linking: $\quad$ subj

$\qquad\qquad\quad$ *ga*

5. Transitive-transitive VVCs

The analysis outlined above can also be extended to more frequent combinations such as transitive-transitive compounds, which were exemplified by *osi-taosu* (push-topple) 'push down' in (1) above (for the discussion of further patterns see Gamerschlag 2000). Both the composition and the linking properties of *osi-taosu* are illustrated in (21). *Osi-taosu* differs from transitive-intransitive resultative compounds such as *tumi-agaru* in that the causation and the result are not clearly distributed on V1 and V2. In compounds of this type (Matsumoto's "means compounds"), V2 is always a lexical causative and already comprises the result and some unspecified causing action, which is explicated by V1. It is V2, however, which contributes the result. As a consequence, COHERENCE requires that the SF of V1 precedes the SF of V2 in the representation of *osi-taosu* in (21). (21c) shows the result of functional composition, which yields a compound with four arguments. However, as can be seen in the tree structure in (22), both arguments of V1 (=u and v) are higher in the argument hierarchy than the subject argument of the head V2 (=x). To avoid violation of the SUBJECT-HEAD CONDITION, u and v cannot be realized structurally. In line with VISIBILITY they are identified with the conceptually adequate arguments of V2. As a consequence, we arrive at the representation in (21d), which predicts the correct realization of the arguments in syntax.

(21) Composition and linking of *osi-taosu* (push-topple) 'push down'

a. $\quad$ *osi-*: $\qquad\qquad \lambda v \, \lambda u \, \lambda s \, [\text{PUSH}(u, v) \, (s)]$

$\qquad\qquad\qquad\qquad \rightarrow \lambda P \, \lambda v \, \lambda u \, \lambda s \, [\text{PUSH}(u, v) \, (s) \, \& \, P(s)]$

b. $\quad$ *taosu*: $\qquad\quad \lambda y \, \lambda x \, \lambda s' \, [\{\text{ACT}(x) \, \& \, \text{FALL} \, (y)\} \, (s')]$

c. $\quad$ *osi-taosu*: $\lambda y \, \lambda x \, \lambda v \, \lambda u \, \lambda s \, [\text{PUSH}(u, v) \, (s) \, \& \, \{\text{ACT}(x) \, \& \, \text{FALL}(y)\} \, (s)]$

d. $\quad$ *osi-taosu*: $\lambda y \quad \lambda x \quad \lambda s \quad [\text{PUSH}(u_i, v_j) \, (s) \, \& \, \{\text{ACT}(x_i) \, \& \, \text{FALL}(y_j)\} \, (s)]$

$\qquad$ linking: $\quad$ dirO subj

$\qquad\qquad\qquad$ *o* $\qquad$ *ga*

(22) Lexical tree of *osi-taosu* (push-topple)

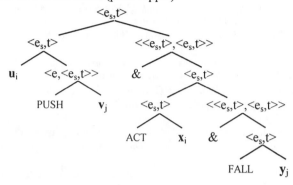

6. Conclusion

The results of the analysis can be summarized as follows. The possible semantic relations exhibited by lexical compounds follow from a general conceptual restriction on the Semantic Form of complex verbs (COHERENCE). Dependent on the semantic relation (causal vs. non-causal/simultaneous) two semantic types of lexical VVCs can be distinguished: "resultative compounds" and "non-resultative compounds". COHERENCE also restricts the order of predicates in the Semantic Form of the compound: The non-head V1 is in the lowest position in non-resultative compounds, whereas it is the head V2 which is in the lowest position in resultative compounds. As a consequence of this contrast in the underlying order of predicates, the unshared object argument of a transitive V1 is inherited by the compound in non-resultative compounds, while the unshared argument of a transitive V1 is blocked in resultative compounds. The latter follows from the SUBJECT-HEAD CONDITION, which requires the highest argument of the head to be realized as highest argument (=subject) of the compound.

References

Bierwisch, Manfred. 1983. Semantische und konzeptuelle Repräsentationen lexikalischer Einheiten. In *Untersuchungen zur Semantik.* Studia Grammatica, vol. 22, eds. R. Růžička and W. Motsch, 61-99. Berlin: Akademie-Verlag.

Bierwisch, Manfred. 1989. Thematische Rollen und Dekomposition. Seminar Papers. Third DGfS Summerschool, Hamburg.

Gamerschlag, Thomas. 2000. Deriving Argument Structure in Japanese V-V Compounds. *Working Papers of the SFB 'Theorie des Lexikons'* 114. University of Düsseldorf.

Hasselberg, Iris. 1996. *Verbalkomposita im Japanischen.* Hamburg: Buske.

Kageyama, Taro. 1989. The Place of Morphology in the Grammar: Verb-Verb Compounds in Japanese. In *Yearbook of Morphology* 2, eds. Geert Booij and Jaap van Marle, 73-94. Dordrecht: Foris.

Kageyama, Taro. 1993. *Bunpoo to Gokeisei* [Grammar and Word Formation]. Kasukabe: Hituzi Syobo.

Kageyama, Taro. 1999. Word Formation. In *Handbook of Japanese Linguistics*, ed. Natsuko Tsujimura, 297-325. Oxford: Blackwell.

Kaufmann, Ingrid. 1995. What Is an (Im)possible Verb? Restrictions on Semantic Form and Their Consequences for Argument Structure. *Folia Linguistica* 29, 67-103.

Kaufmann, Ingrid and Dieter Wunderlich. 1998. Cross-linguistic Patterns of Resultatives. *Working Papers of the SFB 'Theorie des Lexikons'* 109. University of Düsseldorf.

Li, Yafei. 1990. On V-V Compounds in Chinese. *Natural Language and Linguistic Theory* 8, 177-207.

Li, Yafei. 1993. Structural Head and Aspectuality. *Language* 69:3, 408-504.

Matsumoto, Yo. 1996a. *Complex Predicates in Japanese: A Syntactic and Semantic Study of the Notion 'Word'*. Stanford: CSLI Publications.

Matsumoto, Yo. 1996b. Subjective Motion and English and Japanese Verbs. *Cognitive Linguistics* 7-2, 183-226.

Matsumoto, Yo. 1998. Nihongo no Goiteki Hukugoodoosi ni okeru Doosi no Kumiawase [The Combinatory Possibilities in Japanese V-V Lexical Compounds]. *Gengo Kenkyu* 114, 37-83.

Nishiyama, Kunio. 1998. V-V Compounds as Serialization. *Journal of East Asian Linguistics* 7, 175-217.

Tagashira, Yoshiko. 1978. *Characterization of Japanese Compound Verbs*. Ph.D. Diss., University of Chicago.

Wienold, Götz. 1995. Lexical and Conceptual Structures in Expressions for Movement and Space. In *Lexical Knowledge in the Organization of Language*, eds. Urs Egli et al., 301-340. Amsterdam: Benjamins.

Wunderlich, Dieter. 1997a. Cause and the Structure of Verbs. *Linguistic Inquiry* 28, 27-68.

Wunderlich, Dieter. 1997b. Argument Extension by Lexical Adjunction. *Journal of Semantics* 14, 95-142.

Wunderlich, Dieter. 2000. Predicate Composition and Argument Extension as General Options - a Study in the Interface of Semantic and Conceptual Structure. In *Lexicon in Focus*, eds. Barbara Stiebels and Dieter Wunderlich, 247-270. Berlin: Akademie Verlag.

Yumoto, Yoko. 1996. Gokeisei to Goigainenkoozoo [Word Formation and Lexical Conceptual Structure]. *Gengo to Bunka no Syosoo*, Okuda Hiroyuki kyoozyu taikankinen ronbunsyuu kankookaihen, 105-118. Eihoosya.

Nominative-Genitive Conversion Revisited[*]

KEN HIRAIWA

Massachusetts Institute of Technology

1. Introduction

A long-standing analysis of Nominative-Genitive Conversion (NGC) in Japanese generative grammar and in Japanese linguistics has been to reduce the source of genitive Case to the presence of an external D head of relative clauses and nominal complements, which can check genitive Case (cf. Mikami 1953, Harada 1971, 1976, Bedell 1972, Saito 1982, Fukui and Nishigauchi 1992, Miyagawa 1993, Sakai 1994, and Ochi 1999 among many others; but cf. Watanabe 1996, Hiraiwa 2000a).

This article demonstrates that the generalization that NGC is dependent on the presence of an external D head is rejected on much empirical grounds. This immediately leads to a refutation of the ECM/Raising analysis of NGC (Miyagawa 1993, Ochi 1999), which is based on the generalization. Two further arguments against the ECM/Raising analysis are also presented. The main aim of this short article is to achieve a higher descriptive adequacy of NGC, restricting theoretical arguments to a minimum.[1]

---

[*] An earlier version of this article has been presented at the 10th Japanese/Korean Linguistics Conference at UCLA and various other opportunities. I would like to thank the audience. I am indebted to Cédric Boeckx, Noam Chomsky, Ken Hale, Satoshi Kinsui, Ken-ichi Mihara, Shigeru Miyagawa, David Pesetsky, Hiromu Sakai, Hiroyuki Ura, and Akira Watanabe for invaluable comments and discussions.

[1] Unfortunately, full discussions of theoretical issues are far beyond this short paper. Interested readers are referred to Hiraiwa (2000a).

2. Nominative-Genitive Conversion Revisited

2.1. A New Generalization of NGC in Japanese

NGC has the following six notable properties that call for explanation. This article focuses on (1a), (1d), (1e) and (1f) and provides principled accounts.[2]

(1)   a. A descriptive generalization. (Section 2.)
      b. Optionality.
      c. Lack of Accusative-Genitive conversion.
      d. Complementizer blocking effect. (Section 3.1.)
      e. Lack of defective intervention effects. (Section 3.2.)
      f. Transitivity restriction. (Section 3.3.)

(2) has been the descriptive generalization to NGC, which has almost never been called into question in the literature with only a few exceptions (cf. Saito 1982, Miyagawa 1993, Sakai 1994, Ochi 1999; cf. Watanabe 1996, Hiraiwa 2000a).

(2)   NGC is restricted to only relative clauses and nominal complements (i.e. structure with an external D-head).

As (3) and (4) show, NGC is possible only in relative clauses and nominal complements but not in main clauses.

(3)   Kinoo   John **ga/no**   katta   hon
      yesterday John-NOM/GEN buy-PST-ADN book
      'the book which John bought yesterday'

(4)   John wa   [$_{CP}$ kinoo   Mary-**ga/no**   kita   koto/no]
      John-TOP   yesterday Mary-NOM/GEN come-PST-ADN FN/C
      -wo   siranakatta
      -ACC   know-NEG-PST
      'John didn't know that Mary came yesterday.'

Miyagawa (1993), building on the generalization (2), argues that in NGC genitive Case on the subject DP is checked by an external D head at LF (hereafter *the ECM/Raising analysis*).
      However, very significantly, a close scrutiny reveals that the long-standing generalization in (2) is empirically quite inadequate. As shown in (5)-(11), NGC is allowed in the structures without any external D head.

---

[2]   Hiraiwa (2000a) shows that the properties (1a), (1c) and (1d) are cross-linguistically true in NGC. Explaining the properties (1b) and (1c) requires full development of theoretical discussions, which goes beyond the scope of this paper. See Hiraiwa (2000a) for a cross-linguistic study on NGC based on about twenty languages

(5) John wa [ame **ga/no** yamu made] office ni ita.
John-TOP rain-NOM/GEN stop-PRES-ADN until office-at be-PST
'John was at his office until the rain stopped.'

(6) [Boku **ga/no** omou ni] John wa Mary ga
I-NOM/GEN think-PRES-ADN -DAT John-TOP Mary-NOM
suki-ni-tigainai
like-must-PRES
'I think that John likes Mary.'

(7) [Sengetsu ikkai denwa **ga/no** atta kiri] John kara
last month once call-NOM/GEN be-PST-ADN since John-from
nanimo renraku ga nai.
any call-NOM be-not-PST
'There has been no call from John since he called me up once last
month.'

(8) Kono atari-wa [hi **ga/no** kureru ni tsure(te)]
around-here-TOP sun-NOM/GEN go-down-PRES-ADN as
hiekondekuru.
colder-get-PRES
'It gets chillier as the sun goes down around here.'

(9) John wa [toki **ga/no** tatsu to tomoni]
John-TOP time-NOM/GEN pass-PRES-ADN with as
Mary no koto wo wasurete-itta.
Mary-GEN FN-ACC forget-go-PST
'Mary slipped out of John's memory as times went by.'

(10) [John **ga/no** kuru to konai to]
John-NOM/GEN come-PRES-ADN and come-not-PRES-ADN and
de wa oochigai da.
-TOP great-difference CPL-PRES
'It makes a great difference whether John comes or not.'

(11) John wa [Mary **ga/no** yonda yori] takusan-no
John-TOP Mary-NOM/GEN read-PST-ADN than many-GEN
hon wo yonda
books-ACC read-PST
'John read more books than Mary did.'
(Watanabe 1996:396)

Very strikingly, in the examples above, NGC is allowed despite the fact that
no external D is involved. Furthermore, (12) confirms the lack of D in the
relevant embedded clauses in (5)-(11).

(12) a. *__sono__ *yori* / *__sono__ *made* / *__sono__ *ni* / *__sono__ *to* / *__sono__ kiri
      it(GEN)-than /it (GEN)-until / it(GEN)-DAT / it(GEN)-with /
      it(GEN)-since

    b. __sore__ *yori* / __sore__ *made* / __sore__ *ni* / __sore__ *to* / __sore__ kiri
      it-than / it-until / it-DAT / it-with / it-since

(12) demonstrates that none of the italicized P(reposition)-like elements that head CPs in (5)-(11) can select the genitive form of the pronoun '*sono*' but rather they take the full DP form '*sore*'. This explicitly excludes the possibility that these elements check inherent genitive Case or they function as an external D-head to check structural genitive Case. Thus the data (5)-(11) are crucial empirical counterevidence against the long-standing generalization of NGC (2).

    A further close examination, however, uncovers a very interesting new generalization that lies behind the distribution of NGC in Japanese. It should be noted that all the structures that allow NGC are headed by verbs with a special verbal inflection, predicate adnominal form (*P-A form*) (which has been termed *Rentai-kei* in the Traditional Japanese linguistics). This leads us to the following descriptive generalization.

(13) *A New Descriptive Generalization of NGC*
    NGC in Japanese is only licensed by the special verbal inflection
    (the predicate adnominal form; *the P-A form*).

It is sometimes difficult to demonstrate the validity of (13) in modern Japanese due to the well-known morphophonological merger of the verbal End form into the P-A form, which took place around the 13th century (see Kinsui 1995 among others). But fortunately, the so-called verbal adjective and copula, which still retain the relevant morphophonological distinction, confirm our claim. Note that the end form *da* is morphologically realized as *na* in relative clauses and nominal complements as illustrated in (14), whereas the end form *da* appears in the matrix clause.

(14) a. John ga   suki-__na__   ongaku wa   blues da
      John-NOM like-PRES-ADN music-TOP   blues be-PRES
      'The music that John likes is the Blues.'   cf. (3)

    b. John ga   Mary ga   suki-__na__   koto/no wa
      John-NOM Mary-NOM like-PRES-AND FN/C -TOP
      yuumei   da.
      well-known CPL-PRES
      'It is well-known that John likes Mary.'   cf. (4)

    c. John ga Mary ga suki-__da__
      John-NOM Mary-NOM like-PRES-END
      'John likes Mary.'

This diagnostic test reveals that the verbal inflection in (5)-(11) is the P-A form.

(15) a. John wa   ijou-**na**   *made* ni sinkeisitsu da
          John-TOP extraordinary-ADN   extent to nervous-PRES
          'John was extraordinarily nervous.'   cf. (5)

      b. John no   koto ga   simpai-**na**   *yori* mo
          John-GEN thing-NOM worried-PRES-ADN   than
          Mary ga   simpai da.
          Mary-NOM worried-PRES.
          'I am worried about Mary rather than about John.'   cf. (11)

This generalization is correctly borne out by the ungrammaticality of NGC in the clauses with other verbal inflectional forms. Consider the examples below.

(16) a. [Dare **ga/*no**   yon**de**-mo]   kamaimasen.
             whoever-NOM/*GEN read-COND-even care-NEG-PRES.
          'I don't care whoever will come.'

      b. [John **ga/*no**   ku**reba**]   minna   yorokobuyo
          John-NOM/*GEN   come-COND   everyone pleased-PRES
          'Everyone will be delighted if John comes.'

      c. Omae **ga/*no**   **koi**!
          you-NOM/*GEN   come-IMP
          '(You) Come here!'

      d. John ga   Mary **ga/*no**   **kita**   to/ka
          John-NOM Mary-NOM/*GEN come-PST-END C/Q
          itta/tazuneta
          say/ask-PST
          'John said/asked that/whether Mary came.'

Summarizing the discussions in this section, we have shown that the long-standing generalization of NGC (2) is empirically inadequate and demonstrated that NGC is crucially dependent on the presence of the P-A form, presenting the new generalization (13).

2.2. The Mechanism of NGC

Building on the new generalization in the previous section, I propose the following theory as a mechanism of NGC.

(17) A syntactic C-T-v-V head amalgamate, which is formed via
        AGREE, corresponds to the special verbal inflection (*the P-A form*).

This head amalgamate has a φ-feature that can check genitive Case as well as nominative Case.

(18) is the representation of the mechanism of NGC.

(18)

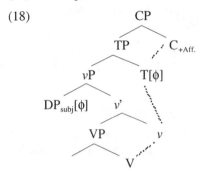

Adopting the insight of Kinsui (1995), I crucially propose that the P-A form in Japanese involves a zero C (cf. also Kaplan and Whitman 1995). It is further argued that this zero C is 'affixal' ([+Aff.]) and requires C-T-v-V head amalgamation ('head-movement') via AGREE (cf. Lasnik 1999).

In (18) each head AGREEs cyclicly; v AGREEs with V, which T AGREEs with. Now at the step of the derivation where $C_{+Aff.}$ is merged with the TP, $C_{+Aff.}$ requires AGREE with T-v-V, spelling out the special verbal inflection *the P-A form*. If there is no C-T-v-V head amalgamation due to the absence of $C_{+Aff.}$, the verb is realized as *the end form* as a result of T-v-V AGREE). The claim here is that this C-T-v-V head amalgamate has a φ-feature that can check structural genitive Case as well as nominative Case.[3] Crucially, note that under the proposed theory, there is no structural difference in nominative Case-checking and genitive Case-checking in NGC; the same single φ-feature is responsible for both nominative and genitive Case-checking in (18).[4]

Thus now the proposed mechanism of NGC (17) provides a natural explanation for our generalization (13).

---

[3] See Hiraiwa (2000a) for a precise theoretical implementation of the idea under the framework of Chomsky (2000) as well as much empirical justification, which space limitation disallows us to illustrate here.

[4] Interestingly, the proposed theory gives theoretical basis for claims in Traditional Japanese linguistics that in classical Japanese *no* and *ga* were both nominative and genitive (cf. Konoshima 1966, Nomura 1993 among many others).

3. Nominative-Genitive Conversion Elucidated

3.1. Defective Intervention Constraints: Against ECM/Raising

In this section I will demonstrate that data from locality/minimality in NGC presents crucial evidence against Miyagawa's (1993) and Ochi's (1999) ECM/Raising analysis.

Hiraiwa (2000b) shows that the ECM construction in Japanese the ECM construction gives empirical justification for Chomsky's (2000) *Defective Intervention Constraints*.

(19)   *Defective Intervention Constraints* (cf. Chomsky 2000:123)
$$\alpha > \beta > \gamma$$

(*AGREE (α, γ), α is a probe and β is a matching goal, and β is inactive due to a prior AGREE with some other probe)

(19) is a general locality condition on a syntactic operation which prohibits an establishment of checking relation between α and γ, in the presence of an intervening closer candidate β. Now let us consider the following ECM examples.

(20)   John ga   Mary **ga/wo**   totemo kawii   to omotta.
        John-NOM   Mary-NOM/ACC very   pretty-PRES C think-PST
        'John considered Mary to be very pretty.'

(21)   a. Mary ga   [John **ga**   me **ga**   warui   to] sinjiteiru
            Mary-NOM John-NOM eye-NOM bad-PRES C believe-PRES
            'Mary believes that John has a very bad eyesight.'

        b. Mary ga   [John **wo**   me **ga**   warui   to] sinjiteiru
            Mary-NOM John-ACC eye-NOM bad-PRES C believe-PRES

        c.*Mary ga   [John **ga**   me **wo**   warui   to] sinjiteiru
            Mary-NOM John-NOM eye-ACC bad-PRES C believe-PRES

(20) is a typical ECM construction in Japanese, which shows that ECM is possible across a CP clause boundary. In (21) a multiple nominative construction is embedded under an ECM verb. (21b) show that it is possible to ECM the higher nominative DP, assigning accusative Case. However, it should be noted that as (21c) shows, ECM/Raising of the lower nominative DP over the higher nominative DP yields ungrammaticality.

Hiraiwa (2000b) argues that the illicit derivation (21c) is excluded exactly by Defective Intervention Constraints, since the AGREE between the probe matrix v_ϕ and the goal ϕ-feature of the lower DP is blocked by the inactive goal ϕ-feature of the closer DP as a result of (19).

(22)

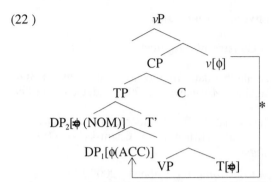

Now returning to NGC, if Miyagawa-Ochi's ECM/Raising analysis of NGC is correct, it should be predicted that the very same kind of locality effects emerge as represented in (23), on a par with the true ECM derivation (22).

(23)

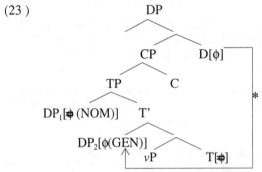

However, very importantly, this prediction is not borne out; NGC in a multiple nominative construction allows all the four logical possibilities that are illustrated in (24) (cf. also Miyagawa 1993 and Ochi 1999).

(24)   a. Totemo John **ga**   me **ga**   warui   riyuu
           very   John-NOM eye-NOM bad-PRES-ADN reason
           'the reason why John has a very bad eysight'   [NOM-NOM]

       b. Totemo John **no**   me **ga**   warui   riyuu
           very   John-GEN eye-NOM bad-PRES-ADN reason
                                                              [GEN-NOM]

       c. Totemo John **ga**   me **no**   warui   riyuu
           very   John-NOM eye-GEN bad-PRES-ADN reason
                                                              [NOM-GEN]

       d. Totemo John **no**   me **no**   warui   riyuu
           very   John-GEN eye-GEN bad-PRES-ADN reason
                                                              [GEN-GEN]

As shown in (24c), the lower DP can be ECMed and assigned genitive Case without any defective intervention effects, despite the presence of the closer nominative goal DP. This is totally unexpected, if NGC involves ECM/Raising by an external D. This strongly shows that NGC never has an ECM/raising structure, contra Miyagawa-Ochi's claim.

On the other hand, the proposed theory of NGC (17) correctly and naturally accounts for the absence of defective intervention effects in (24c); As (25) represents, the genitive Case is checked by the same single ϕ-feature on the C-T-V amalgamate, which can also check nominative Case. Recall that there is no structural difference between the probe for the genitive Case and the probe for the nominative Case and hence no defective intervention effects are triggered.

(25)

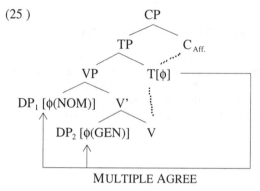

MULTIPLE AGREE

In other words, under the proposed analysis, (24d) is grammatical just as the multiple nominative derivation (24a) and the multiple genitive derivation (24d) are licit.

3.2. Complementizer Blocking Effects

The new descriptive generalization (13) and the proposed theory of NGC (17) also provide a straightforward explanation for the observation that NGC is blocked by a presence of an overt complementizer *toiu*, *to* and *ka* (cf. Inoue 1976, Ura 1993, Watanabe 1996, Hiraiwa 2000a). Consider (26) and (27) below.[5]

(26) a. [[syoorai   daijisin **ga/no**   okiru]
          in-the-future great-earthquake-NOM/GEN occur-PRES-ADN

---

[5] Hiraiwa (2000a) proposes that the so-called complementizer/nominalizer *'no'* (e.g. (4)) is not an overt C, but rather a morphophonological realization of genitive Case-checking on the head amalgamate, with far-reaching consequences for grammaticalization of Case particles as conjunction markers in Japanese (cf. Ishigaki 1955, Kinsui 1995, Kuroda 1999, Kondo 2000). Hence there is no blocking effect in the case of the complementizer *'no'*.

kanoosei]
possibility
'the possibility that a great earthquake will occur in the future'

b. [[syoorai   daijisin **ga/*no**   okiru
   in-the-future great-earthquake-NOM/*GEN occur-PRES-END
   toiu kanoosei]
   C   possibility
   'the possibility that a great earthquake will occur in the future'

(27)   [[House of Blues de   John **ga/*no**   ensoosuru   **to** no]
       House of Blues-at   John-NOM/*GEN play-PRES-END C-GEN
       joohou]
       information
       'the information that John will plat at the House of Blues'

As (26) indicates that the complementizer *toiu* is optional for the head noun *'kanoosei'*. The contrast between (26a) and (26b) as well as (27) show that NGC is disallowed when an overt complementizer appears in C.

Within the present theory, this phenomenon is explained quite straightforwardly. Consider the derivation (28) for the illicit sentence (26b) and (27).

(28)

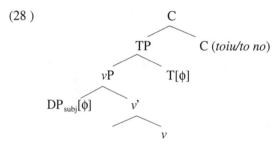

Recall that under the proposed theory, the C-T-*v*-V AGREE is a crucial pre-requisite for NGC. This is because the special verbal inflection P-A form is a realization of head amalgamation of C-T-*v*-V via AGREE. However, as (28) explicitly shows, the head amalgamate formation is syntactically blocked by the presence of the overt C, since an overt C, being non-affixal [-Aff.], bars the morphosyntactic head amalgamation and leaves the verb in the end form. This blocks genitive Case-checking, deriving surface com-plementizer blocking effects.

Note that under the ECM/Raising analysis, there is no good reason for NGC to be blocked by an overt C. Rather, as we have already seen in Section 3.1. above, Japanese does allow ECM/Raising despite the presence of an overt C in genuine ECM sentences. Thus complementizer blocking effect is another evidence against the ECM/Raising analysis of NGC.

3.3. Transitivity Restriction

Finally, I will briefly discuss Transitivity Restriction (TR) in NGC and propose a totally new perspective to the problem.

As it has been noted in the literature (Harada 1971, 1976, Watanabe 1996 among others), accusative objects are prohibited in NGC.

(29) Kinoo   John **ga/*no**   hon **wo**   katta   mise
      yesterday John-NOM/*GEN book-ACC buy-PST-ADN   store
      'the store where John bought books yesterday'

As Watanabe (1996) correctly points out, the restriction is lifted if the accusative object is wh-extracted.

(30) Kinoo   John **ga/no**   t$_i$ katta   hon$_i$
      yesterday John-NOM/-GEN   buy-PST-ADN book
      'the book which John bought yesterday'

Furthermore, interestingly, the suspension of TR is also observed in the case of *pro-drop* of the accusative object, which demonstrates that what is wrong is morphological accusative case.

(31) Kinoo   John **no**   (*hon-**wo**)   katta   mise
      yesteday John-GEN   book-ACC buy-AND-PST store
      'the store where John bought a book yesterday.'

Looking at the issue in a broader perspective, however, shows that this TR in NGC is an instance of a more general principle underlying the Japanese language. It should be noted that it is independently well-known that in Japanese, Dative Subject Construction (DSC) resists accusative Case-marking, allowing only the DAT-NOM Case pattern (Shibatani 1978, Ura 2000).

(32) John **ni**   nihongo **ga/*wo** hanas-eru   (koto)
      John-DAT Japanese-NOM   speak-can-PRES (that)
      'John can speak Japanese'

These facts suggest that in Japanese morphological accusative Case-marking is prohibited when the subject DP is in non-nominative Case. Thus I propose the following principle in Japanese (cf. Hiraiwa 2000a).

(33) Spell-out of morphological accusative case by v triggers nominative
      Case-checking on T in the next strong phase.

Putting aside the precise theoretical implementation for now, (33) captures an interdependence between morphological accusative case and abstract nominative Case-checking; more descriptively speaking,

As it is already obvious, the ungrammaticality of the NGC sentence (29) and the DSC sentence (32) is naturally expected under the single principle (33); in these examples, the spell-out of the accusative Case fails to trigger nominative Case checking on T. Instead, the subject is assigned structural genitive Case in (29) or inherent dative Case in (32) (cf. Ura 2000). Thus our principle (33) brings to light the significant nature underlying the Case system in Japanese, and gives a unified explanation for the ostensibly unrelated phenomena (TR in NGC and the ungrammaticality of the DAT-ACC case pattern in DSC).

The following data combining DSC and NGC shows the point more clearly.

(34) a. John **ga**   nihongo **ga/wo/no**   hanas-eru   koto
      John-NOM Japanese-NOM/ACC/GEN speak-can-PRES-ADN FN
      'the fact that John can speak Japanese.'

      b. John **no**   nihongo **ga/*wo/no**   hanas-eru   koto
      John-GEN Japanese-NOM/*ACC/GEN speak-can-PRES-ADNFN

      c. John **ni**   nihongo **ga/*wo/no**   hanas-eru   koto
      John-DAT Japanese-NOM/*ACC/GEN speak-can-PRES-ADNFN

(34) shows that among 9 possible Case patterns in Japanese, the two ungrammatical patterns are both with accusative case without nominative Case, conforming to the principle (33).

4. Concluding Remarks

In conclusion, in this paper, it has been shown that the new set of data presented above is a crucial empirical counterevidence against the longstanding generalization of NGC and hence the ECM/Raising analysis. A new descriptive generalization has been proposed that NGC is crucially licensed by the special verbal inflection (the P-A form) in Japanese and argued that genitive Case in NGC is checked via AGREE with the probe ϕ-feature on the C-T-v-V head amalgamate, which is realized as the P-A form. Two further arguments against the ECM/Raising analysis from defective intervention effects and complementizer blocking effects have been presented.[6] The end result is an achievement of higher descriptive adequacy with a principled explanatory mechanism.

Appendix: Apparent Counterexamples to the Generalization?

There are a small set of apparent counterexamples to our generalization (13); As Mikami (1953) already notes, NGC is prohibited in *'noda'* focus construction in *'node' (since)* and *'noni' (although)* conjunction construc-

---

[6] Miyagawa (1993) presents scope evidence for his ECM/Raising analysis. But see Hiraiwa (2000a) for arguments against it.

tions despite the apparent presence of the P-A verbal inflectional form preceding these elements

(35)   John **ga/*no**   genki-**na**   *noda/node/noni* ...
       John-NOM/*GEN healthy-PRES-ADN C-CPL/C-OBL/C-DAT

At first sight, (35) nullifies our proposed generalization (13) that NGC is licensed by the P-A inflection.

However, as it is obvious, these counterexamples forms a natural class: all of them are highly grammaticalized forms with a complementizer *no* combined with particles *de/ni/wo* or a copula *da* (cf. Ishigaki 1955, Kuroda 1999, Kondo 2000 and references therein).[7]
a mere morphological fossil. (see. Ishigaki 1955, Kuroda 1999, Kondo 2000).

In this respect, it is very interesting to note an interaction of NGC with the 'adverbial-type' head-internal relative clause (HIRC) (cf. Mihara 1994, Kuroda 1999). Consider (36)

(36)   John wa   gozentyuu wa hi **no**   tetteita   **no ga/?wo/**
       John-TOP morning-TOP sun-GEN shine-PST-ADN C NOM/ACC/
       *ni   gogo ni natte   ame ga   huridasite kara deteitta.
       DAT afternoon-DAT rain-NOM fall-begin-after go-out-PST
       'It was sunny in the morning and/but John went out after it began to rain in the afternoon.'   (cf. Kuroda 1999)

Notice that NGC is grammatical with *'noga'* type HIRC and marginally acceptable in *'nowo'* type HIRC, whereas in *'noni'* type HIRC, which is now fully grammaticalized into a concessive conjunction marker, NGC results in sever ungrammalicality. Thus generally, more grammaticalized, more difficult to apply NGC.

I just note here that the apparent counterexamples in (35) are not real problems for our generalization itself, but rather their ungrammaticality is closely related to a process of grammaticalization, leaving further theoretical investigation of this issue for future research.[89]

---

[7] This lexical contiguity of these expressions can be illustrated by the fact that focus particles such as *'dake (only)* cannot intervene.
(i)   John ga   genki-na   *no* ***dake** *da/de/ni* ...
      John-NOM healthy-PRES-ADN C   only   CPL/OBL/DAT

[8] In other words, NGC is allowed when a relevant CP clause headed by a verb in the P-A form is an argument/proposition; a 'phase' in Chomsky (2000). See also Hiraiwa (2000a).

[9] It is interesting to note that in an earlier stage where *noda* construction was not yet fully grammaticalized, it is possible to find an example with NGC in *noda* construction. The following is an example in the Edo era that Konoshima (1966) notes.
(i)   Hito no   mune **no**   warui   no da   to omotte ...
      person-GEN mind-GEN bad-PRES-ADN C CPL C think-CONT
      (Konoshima 1966: 53)

References

Bedell, G. 1972. On *No. UCLA papers in syntax 3.* 1-20. UCLA, California.

Chomsky, N. 2000. Minimalist inquiries: the framework: In *Step by step: Essays on minimalism in honor of Howard Lasnik.* (eds.) Roger Martin, David Michaels, and Juan Uriagereka. Cambridge, MA.: MIT Press.

Harada, S.-I. 1971. Ga-No conversion and idiolectal variations in Japanese. *Gengokenkyu* 60. 25-38.

Harada, S.-I. 1976. Ga-No conversion revisited. *Gengokenkyu* 70. 23-38.

Hiraiwa, K. 2000a. On nominative-genitive conversion. To appear in MITWPL#39.

Hiraiwa, K. 2000b. Multiple Agree and the defective intervention constraint in Japanese. To appear in *the Proceedings of the HUMIT 2000.* Cambridgdge, MA.: MITWPL&HWPiL

Ishigaki, K. 1955. *Josi no rekisiteki kenkyuu.* Tokyo: Iwanami Publishers

Kaplan, T. and J. Whitman. 1995. The category of relative clauses in Japanese, with reference to Korean. *Journal of East Asian Linguistics* 4, 29-58.

Kinsui, S. 1995 Iwayuru nihongo no N'-sakujo ni tsuite. In *The proceedings of 1994 Nanzan Symposium.*

Kondo, Y. 2000. *Nihongo kijutubunpoo no riron.* Tokyo: Kuroshio Publishers.

Konoshima, M. 1966. *Kokugojosi no kenkyuu: josi si sobyoo.* Ouhuusya.

Kuroda, S.-Y. 1974-77. Pivot-independent relativization in Japanese. In *Japanese syntax and semantics: collected papers.* 114-174. Dordrecht: Kluwer Academic Publishers. 1992.

Kuroda, S.-Y. 1999. Syubunaizai kankeisetsu. In *Gengo no naizai to gaizai.* (eds.) Masaru Nakamura et al.. Tokyo: Kuroshio Publishers.

Lasnik, H. 1999. Verbal morphology: *syntactic structures* meets the minimalist program. In *Minimalist analysis.* Oxford: Blackwell.

Mihara, K. 1994. *Nihongo no toogo kouzou.* Tokyo: Syoohakusya.

Mikami, A. 1953. *Gendai gohoo josetsu: syntax no kokoromi.* Tokyo: Kurosio Publishers.

Miyagawa, S. 1993. LF Case-checking and minimal link condition. In MITWPL#19 213-254. Cambridge, MA.:MITWPL.

Nomura, T. 1993. Joudai no 'no' to 'ga' ni tsuite. *Kokugo Kokubun* 62-2 & 62-3, 1-17 & 30-49.

Ochi, M. 1999. Move-F and ga/no conversion in Japanese. Ms., Uconn.

Saito, M. 1982. Case-marking in Japanese: A Preliminary Study. Ms., MIT.

Sakai, H. 1994. Complex NP constraint and Case-conversions in Japanese. In *Current topics in English and Japanese*, (ed.) Masaru Nakamura. Tokyo: Hitsuji Shobo 179-203.

Shibatani, M. 1978. *Nihongo no bunseki.* Tokyo: Taishuukan.

Ura, H. 2000. *Checking theory and grammatical functions in Universal Grammar.* Oxford: Oxford University Press.

Watanabe, A. 1996. Nominative-genitive conversion and agreement in Japanese: A cross-linguistic perspective. *Journal of East Asian Linguistics* 5 . 373-410.

hiraiwa@MIT.EDU
http://web.mit.edu/hiraiwa/www/home.html

A 'Removal' Type of Negative Predicates

JIEUN JOE & CHUNGMIN LEE
Seoul National University

1. Introduction[1]

This paper aims to introduce a new class of negative predicates, removal predicates, which have their own syntactic and semantic behavior, and to scrutinize their lexical properties and thus broaden the research of negative predicates. Interestingly, removal predicates and their lexical antonyms, generation predicates, have opposite characteristics in syntax and semantics. In this paper, we show that there are two kinds of removal predicates according to their negative force. One type of removal predicates, such as *absence of, devoid of, free from* and *sterile*, which we call absence-state predicates, is monotone decreasing and moreover anti-additive. And the other type of removal predicates, such as *disappear, turn off* and *destroy*, which we call removal-process predicates, is weaker in negativity, failing to be monotone-decreasing, than the absence-state predicates.

In Section 2, we propose the semantics of removal predicates in contrast with generation predicates. Removal predicates are universal and negative, whereas generation predicates are existential and positive. To show the universal nature of removal predicates we resort to

---
[1]We thank the NPI Project (KRF '99-'01grant) group including Daeho Chung, Seungho Nam and Ed Keenan for discussion and the audience of the 10th J/K Conference at UCLA including Ora Matushansky for comments and questions.

strong/weak readings in donkey anaphora. Our findings on the negative nature of removal predicates reveal: (a) monotone-decreasingness and anti-additivity of absence-state predicates; and (b) implicature suspension of removal-process predicates.

In Section 3, we discuss the syntax of removal predicates. We deal with the cases in which *any* is licensed by predicates such as *disappear* in preverbal position. Interestingly, *any* is not licensed by *didn't appear*, even though it seems more negative than *disappear*.

In Section 4, we discuss morphological characteristics of removal predicates. It is demonstrated that negative morphemes such as *indiscriminately* in English, *-peri-*'throw away; get through' in Korean and *-tesimau-* 'throw away; get through' in Japanese further support our claim that removal predicates are negative. Throughout the paper, we use the British National Corpus (henceforth BNC) to support our claim.

2. Semantics of Removal Predicates

2.1. Two Kinds of Removal Predicates

In this Section, we define a removal type of negative predicates on semantic grounds. Removal predicates are predicates whose meanings involve absence-state or removal-process. An absence-state predicate denotes a simple event and is not decomposable, whereas a removal-process predicate can be decomposed into a process subevent and a result-state subevent.

In the narrow sense of the term, *remove, eliminate* and *disappear* are removal predicates, but aspectual verbs such as *finish* and *end,* though broader in scope, may be included. Removal predicates are universal and negative. The lexical antonyms of these are generation predicates, whose meanings involve presence-state or the process of some entity's coming into being. In this paper, we divide removal predicates according to the observation (a) whether the predicate is monotone decreasing; (b) whether the predicate has implicature suspension; and (c) whether the predicate licenses *any*. (K stands for Korean examples and J for Japanese ones.) Observe:

(1) Absence-state predicates:
> absence of, clear of, be devoid of, free from, be freed of, independence from, be innocent of, regardless of, (up to here from Hoeksema and Klein 1995), sterile, barren of, arid, immune

(2) Removal-process predicates:
> a. Implicature suspension and licensing *any* in object/oblique position: remove, destroy, get rid of, cut off, blot out, erase, cancel, break down, annihilate, *ttey-*(K)/*hanare-*(J) 'remove', *chwuisoha-*(K)/*torike-*(J) 'cancel', *kkunh-*(K)/*tewoki-* 'cut', 'sever'(a relationship)(J), *agehana-* (the head) (J) 'cut off'

   b. Implicature suspension and licensing *any* in subject position: disappear, vanish, perish, *saraci-(*K*)/kie-*(J*)*'disappear'
   c. Implicature suspension and licensing *any* in both subject and object position: end, break (middle verbs)
   d. Implicature suspension and not licensing free choice *any* except in a sugtrigging context: turn off, *kku-*(K*)/ke-*(J*)*'turn off', *desalinize, dehydrate* (we adopt a unified theory of *any* (Lee 1999))

In the next section, we provide the semantics of two kinds of removal predicates: absence-state predicates and removal-process predicates.

2.2. Negative Nature of Removal Predicates

In this Section, we discuss negative nature of removal predicates. As mentioned in the previous section, absence-state predicates such as *be devoid of, sterile* and *barren* are monotone decreasing and anti-additive, based on Ladusaw (1996). And removal-process predicates such as *disappear* and *turn off* are neither monotone decreasing nor nonveridical in a strict sense. However, removal-process predicates are negative and thus necessarily yield implicature suspension and sometimes license *any*, while their antonyms, generation predicates, do not license it at all and do not yield implicature suspension.

2.2.1. Monotone Decreasingness and Anti-additivity: Absence-state predicates

Absence-state predicates given in (1) in the last section, are monotone decreasing and anti-additive. Consider the definition of monotone decreasingness and anti-additivity from Ladusaw (1996):

(3) a. If A and B are two Boolean algebras, the function f from A into B is polarity reversing/monotone decreasing iff any a1, a2 in A, if a1≤a2, then f(a2)≤f(a1)
   b. A functor f is *anti-additive* iff f (x∨y) = f (x)∧f y).

On this definition, absence-state predicates such as *be devoid of* are monotone decreasing. But removal-process predicates such as *destroy* and *eliminate* are not monotone decreasing. Compare (4) and (5):

(4) |a spelling error |≤|an error|
   a. John's term paper *is devoid of* an error.
   b. John's term paper *is devoid of* a spelling error.
(5) |a spelling error |≤|an error|
   a. John *eliminated* an error in the paper. --/-->
   b. John *eliminated* a spelling error in the paper.

(4a) entails (4b), whereas (5a) does not entail (5b). That is, if John's paper is devoid of an error, naturally it means there is no spelling error. However, if John eliminated an error, the error could be a spelling error, a citation error or another kind of error. Thus, *be devoid of* is monotone decreasing and *eliminate* is not monotone decreasing based on the definition (3).

However, Hoeksema and Klein (1995:153) treat these two predicates, *eliminate* and *be devoid of,* as monotone decreasing. Their claim is based on the fact that *eliminate* as well as *be devoid of* licenses *any* as shown in (6). In (6a) *any* is licensed by *be devoid of* and in (6b) it is licensed by *eliminate.* And in (6c,d) *any* is licensed by *destroy.* Still they are not monotone-decreasing. Observe:

(6) a. He *was devoid of* any of the normal human weaknesses such as fear or self-doubt. (from BNC)
   b. It is likely too that the priest tidied up and *eliminated* any traces there may have been distorted thinking or language, as he almost certainly corrected any theological mistakes, for his own safety. (from BNC)
   c. The death of Wordsworth's brother John in the spring of 1805 *destroyed* any remaining illusions. (from BNC)
   d. But the worsening weather conditions as we cycled *destroyed* any possibility of us seeing such stunning views. (from BNC)

Even though removal-process predicates such as *eliminate* and *destroy* license *any* as in (6b, c, d), their negative force is weaker than monotone decreasing, as demonstrated earlier. Consider (7).

(7) |a red-blocked house|$\leq$|a house|
   a. John *destroyed* a house.
   b. John *destroyed* a red-blocked house.

Example (7a) does not entail (7b). That is, in (7a) it is possible that John destroyed a white-blocked house or yellow-blocked house. Therefore, just like *eliminate* in (5), *destroy* (or even *remove*) is not monotone decreasing, although such verbs become more negative when they are used in their extended mental or abstract senses, as in (6d). It further shows that licensing *any* is not a sufficient condition but a necessary condition of monotone decreasingness.

Returning to absence-state predicates, whose negative force is stronger than monotone decreasing, the level of negativity differs. As shown in (3), anti-additivity is defined as follows:

(8) A functor f is *anti-additive* iff f $(x \lor y) = f(x) \land f(y)$.

Depending on this definition, absence-state predicates such as *be devoid of* is anti-additive. Consider (9):

(9) a. John's term paper *is devoid of* a spelling error or a citation error.
    b. John's term paper *is devoid of* a spelling error AND is devoid of citation error.

Examples like (9a) and (9b) above entail one another. That is, if it is true that John's term paper is devoid of a spelling error or a citation error, it is also true that John's term paper is devoid of a spelling error and is devoid of a citation error, and vice versa. Therefore, absence-state predicates are monotone decreasing and anti-additive. In the next section, we show the negative force of removal-process predicates.

2.2.2. Implicature Suspension: Removal-Process Predicates

Removal-process predicates given in (2) are neither monotone decreasing nor nonveridical. However, they yield implicature suspension, whereas their lexical antonyms do not have such a semantic characteristic. Observe the relevant examples on implicature suspension from Chierchia (2000):

(10) a. Every student who takes a written test or makes an oral presentation will pass.
     b. Expectation: a student that does both passes.
        (suspension of exclusion implicature.)

Chierchia (2000) points out that *any* licensing contexts as in (10a) can suspend implicature. That is, potential implicature 'not both A and B' is suspended as in (10b). And Horn (1989) indicates that the computation of scalar implicatures appears to be inhibited not only by negation but also generally in 'negation like' monotone decreasing contexts such as *doubt*. Our removal predicates can also suspend implicature 'not both A and B' and take a role as a 'negation-like' context, whereas generation predicates cannot suspend such an implicature. Consider the following Korean examples in (11) and Japanese examples in (12):

(11) a. Haksayng-tul-un ppippi-na handphone-ul *kke-t-ta*.
         Students-PL-TOP-beepers-or cellular phones-ACC turn off-PST-DEC
         'Students turned off beepers or cellular phones.'
      b. Haksayng-tul-un ppippi-na handphone-ul khy-e-tta.
         Students-PL-TOP-beepers-or cellular phones-ACC turn on-PST-DEC
         'Students turned on beepers or cellular phones.'
(12) a. Gakusei-tachi-wa pokeberu-ya keitaidenwa-no suichi-wo *kesi-ta*.
        Students-PL-TOP-pager-or cellular phones-POS-switch-ACC turn off-PST
        'Students turned off beepers or cellular phones.'

b.Gakusei-tachi-wa pokeberu-ya keitaidenwa-no suichi-wo ire-ta.
Students-PL-TOP-pager-or cellular phones-POS-switch-ACC turn on-PST
'Students turned on beepers or cellular phones.'

In (11a) and (12a), even if some students with both beepers and cellular phones turned off both of them, suspending the implicature 'not both,' the sentences are quite appropriate. However, in (11b) and (12b) even if some students with both beepers and cellular phones turned on only one kind of them, the sentences can be appropriate. Such an asymmetry occurs to all pairs of removal-process predicates and their lexical antonyms. The negative force of removal-process predicates is substantiated in the same line of Horn (1989), Chierchia (2000) and Chungmin Lee (2000). Consider (13), which also suspends implicature:

(13) a. Recently, the measles or chicken pox *disappeared* from the schools.
b. Recently, the measles or chicken pox appeared in the schools.

In (13a), if some schools did not have measles but had chicken pox, and the other schools did not have chicken pox but had measles, the sentence is not appropriate. In the same situation, however, (13b) is.

2.2.3. (Non)veridicality: Removal-Process Predicates

One of the interesting properties of removal-process predicates is that they are not nonveridical in its strict sense. In the previous section, we demonstrate that removal-process predicates are negative and suspend implicature, but are not monotone decreasing. Giannakidou (1998:116) notes that negative verbs in Greek such as *arnume* 'deny' and *apagorevo* 'forbid' are nonveridical. However, different from other negative predicates, removal-process predicates are not nonveridical. That is, if Jane denies that she saw Paul, this does not entail that she did not see Paul nor does it imply that she saw Paul, of course. Yet, in the case of removal-process predicates such as *disappear* and *destroy,* if any rumors about his past disappeared, this implies that there are no rumors about his past left. So, *disappear* is veridical in a sense, with no overt operator. Consider the following definition of (non)veridicality from Chungmin Lee (1999), originated from Zwarts (1995).

(14) Definition
Let O be a monadic sentential operator. O is said to be *veridical* just in case $Op\ p$ is logically valid. If O is not veridical, then O is *nonveridical*. E.g., 'it seems,' 'it is possible', 'Sue hopes.' Truth-functional connectives are likewise defined. E.g., in p *and* q, both the p- and q- positions are veridical; in p *or* q, and p *if* q, both the p-and q-positions are nonveridical.

Based on the definition, our removal-process predicates are weakly negative but are veridical. Consider:

(15) a. The death of Wordsworth's brother John in the spring of 1805 *destroyed* any remaining illusions. (from BNC)
    b. Any rumors/doubt about his past *disappeared*.

In (15a), if it is true that the death of Wordsworth's brother John destroyed any remaining illusions, then it is implied that there were no illusions left. In (15b), if it is true that any rumors/doubt about his past disappeared, then it is also implied that there remained no rumors or doubt.

2.2.4. Licensing *any* in object/oblique/subject positions

As shown in previous section, removal predicates are divided into two types: (a) absence-state predicates; and (b removal-process predicates. Absence-state predicates such as *be devoid of* and *immune* license *any* in object/oblique/subject position as in (16)l. Consider the examples in (16) from BNC:

(16) *Any* licensing in oblique position: Absence-state predicates
    a. His face *was devoid of* any warmth or humor.
    b. The rest of the room *was barren of* any furniture.
    c. A problem with making recordings direct from electronic instruments is that they are totally *free from* any natural reverberation.

In addition, some removal-process predicates such as *destroy, disappear* and *cut off* license *any* in object or subject positions. In most cases, if removal-process predicates license *any,* it denotes an abstract or psychological stuff such as *illusion* and *doubt*, with almost monotone decreasing force. However, other removal-process predicates such as *turn off* do not license *any* (except in a subtrigging context). Removal-process predicates such as *disappear, destroy* and *break* license *any* as in (17) but not their lexical antonyms, as shown in (17):

(17) *Any* licensing in subject/object position: Removal-process predicates
    a. Any rumors about his past *disappeared. (/*appeared.)*
    b. I urge the Minister to drop this idea and *cancel (/*make)* any tenders he may have called for the construction of such a cruel detention center. (from BNC)
    c. The Government buys very little from South Africa and should, in fact, have *ended (/*begun)* any purchase from that country long ago. (from BNC)
    d. The death of Wordsworth's brother John in the spring of 1805 *destroyed (/*built)* any remaining illusions. (from BNC)

However, generation predicates such as *appear* can license *any* in a subtrigging context, as in (18). In fact, almost every predicate can license *any* in a subtrigging context. (For a detailed discussion, see Section 3.)

(18) Any student who passed the entrance exam appeared (at the party).

Note that other removal-process predicates such as *turn off* as well as its lexical antonym *turn on* do not license *any* except in a subtrigging context, as in (19):

(19) a. *Jane *turned off* any lamps in the building.
      b. *Jane turned on any lamps in the building.
      c. Any lamps in the building were turned *off*/on.

Compared to absence-state predicates, removal-process predicates do not always license *any*. Additionally, the negative force of these removal-process predicates is weaker than absence-state predicates.

In Korean as well as in Japanese, removal-process predicates such as *saraci*-(K)/*kie*-(J) 'disappear' do not license strong NPIs such as *te isang* (K)/*koreijyo* (J) 'any more', as in (20), and predicates such as *phokiha*-(K)/*yame*-(J) 'give up' are anti-additive and thus license the strong NPI *te isang* (K)/*koreijyo*(J) 'any more', as in (21) below:

(20) a.* LA -ey-nun te isang kkamagui-tul-i *saracie-ssta*. (Korean)
         LA-in-TOP-any more-crow-PL-NOM-disappear-PST
     b.* LA-ni-wa koreijyo karasu-tachi-ga kie-tta. (Japanese)
         LA-in-TOP-any more-crow-PL-NOM-disappear-PST
         ' In LA any more crows disappeared.'
(21) a. Jane-un te isang nonmwun-ul sseki-rul phokihay-ssta (Korean)
         Jane-TOP-anymore-paper-ACC write-ACC-give up-PST
     b. Jane-wa koreijyo ronbun-wo kakukoto-wo yame-ta (Japanese)
         Jane-TOP-anymore-paper-ACC-write-ACC-give up-PST
         'Jane gave up writing paper anymore.'

Removal-process predicates in Korean license a weaker existential NPI form *etten- N-i-ra-to* 'any', as in (22):

(22) a. Etten toshi-i-ra-to   *pakoyhay-ss-ta*. (Korean)
         any city -be-DEC-C destroy-PST-DEC
         Lit. '(They) destroyed any city.'
     b.* Etten toshi-ra-to kenselhay-ss-ta.
         any city -be-DEC-C destroy-PST-DEC
         Lit. '(They) constructed any city '.

Etten- N -i-ra-to (K) 'any' is allowed to occur with removal predicates, but is awkward with generation predicates. In a clearer piece of evidence, removal predicates, as universal ones, are not likely to be combined with contrastive topic marker (heretofore CT-marker) *-nun*, whereas their lexical antonyms have no such problems. Consider (23):

(23) a. ?? *pakoy-/cwukiki-/saraciki*-NUN hay-ss-ta
destroy/kill / disappear   CT do-PST-DEC
' It (is) destroyed/killed/disappeared'
  b. kenselhaki-/kwucohaki-/natanaki-NUN hay-ss-ta
construct /rescue / appear   CT do-PST-DEC
'It (is) constructed/rescued/appeared'

In the next section, we show another semantic characteristics of removal predicates: universality.

2.3 Universal Nature of Removal Predicates

In this section, we discuss universal nature of removal predicates as well as existential nature of generation predicates. Krifka (1996) and Yoon (1996) introduce total/partial predicates to explain preferred strong/weak readings in a donkey sentence. We replace total by universal and partial by existential to generalize the phenomena. Consider the following examples from Krifka (1996:140):

(24) a. Every farmer who owned a donkey kept it healthy during the
rainy season.(strong reading)
  b. Every farmer who owned a donkey kept it sick during the rainy
season. (weak reading)

In the above examples, *healthy* is a total predicate and *sick* is a partial predicate. When the given predicate is total, the sentence is true if it involves almost all donkeys. However, when the predicate is partial, it is acceptable, even when the event involves 'some' of the donkeys with the anaphor *it*. The same judgment is valid for our removal and generation predicates. Removal predicates are total and, in our terms, universal, while generation ones are partial and existential. Consider:

(25) a. Every student who owned an error in his essay *obliterated* it.
  b. Every student who owned a reward added it to his resume.
(26) a. Every student who owned a lamp *turned* it *off.*
  b. Every student who owned a lamp turned it on.

As in (25a) and (26a), removal predicates such as *obliterate* and *turn off* show strong readings, while as in (25b) generation predicates such as *add* and *turn on* show weak readings. Thus, in the donkey sentence, if the main predicate is a removal predicate, the E-type pronoun *it* exhibits a strong reading, whereas if the main predicate is a generation predicate, the E-type pronoun *it* exhibits a weak reading. That is, in the situation of (25a), the sentence is expected to be true if every student obliterated any kind of errors in his paper, while in the situation of (25b) the sentence is expected to be true even if some students added only remarkable records, but not all of them. Interestingly, the following pair of aspectual predicates shares this strong/weak contrast:

(27) a. Every student who owned a comic book *finished* (reading) it.
     b. Every student who owned a comic book began (to read) it.

E-type pronoun *it* in (27a) has a strong reading as with removal predicates, whereas (27b) has a weak reading like generation predicates. Ter meulen (1995:32) tried to show that aspectual verbs such as *finish* and *end* are monotone decreasing, while the aspectual verbs such as *start* and *begin* are monotone increasing. However, in the strict sense of monotonicity, aspectual verbs such as *finish* and *end* are not monotone decreasing. Observe:

(28) |a spelling test |≤|a test|
     a. Jane ended a test. --/-->
     b. Jane ended a spelling test.

(28a) does not entail (28b).[2]

3. Syntax of Removal Predicates

    In this Section, we discuss the syntax of removal predicates. We analyze the cases in which *any* is licensed by removal predicates such as *disappear* in the preverbal position. Our analysis is based on the two theoretical assumptions: (a) *any* reconstruction at LF; (b) Unaccusative Hypothesis.

3.1. Asymmetries in NPI-licensing

Consider the following examples in (29):

(29) a. Any rumors/doubts about his past *disappeared.*
       (inherently negative predicate)
     b. *Any rumors/doubt about his past *appeared.* (positive predicate)
     c. *Any rumors/doubts about his past *didn't appear*
       (overtly negative predicate)

(29b) and (29c) are ungrammatical, whereas (29a) is grammatical. Examples in (29) raise the two problems as follows: (a) why *disappear*

---

[2] We owe Tim Stowell for his observation that *finish* does not seem to have any monotone-decreasingness effects.

licenses NPI *any*, whereas *appear*, the lexical antonyms of *disappear* does not license *any*; and (b) why *disappear* licenses NPI *any*, whereas seemingly more negative predicate *didn't appear* does not license it.

The asymmetry found in (29a, b) reflects the negative nature of *disappear* and further supports our claim that *disappear* is a negative predicate. However, the asymmetry found in (29b, c) is still problematic, as an overtly negative predicate does not license *any*, whereas an inherently negative predicate licenses *any*. In the next section, we propose a solution to this problem.

3.2. The Analysis

3.2.1. LF Approach to NPI licensing

From a syntactic point of view, there could be two approaches, based on S-structure and Logical Form (henceforth LF) in explaining *any* licensing in preverbal indefinite. Consider the following examples from Uribe-Etxebarria (1995:346-48).

(30) a. A doctor who knew anything about the acupuncture was not
     available.
   b. *A doctor who knew anything about acupuncture was not
     intelligent. (No bleached predicate)
   c. A solution of any of these problems doesn't exist.
   d. *Anybody didn't come.(No indefinite NP in which *any* is
     embedded.)

Following the S-Structure approach, some cases such as (30a, c) are problematic, as the triggered element *any* precedes the triggering element 'not'. In such a case Neg cannot c-commands the NPI but examples in (30a, c) are grammatical. Thus, Uribe-Etxebarria (1995) proposes an LF approach to solve this problem. She proposes that polarity items reconstruct at LF if there is a bleached predicate[3] and *any* is embedded in an indefinite NP such as in (30a, c), in contrast with (30b, d). However, we find the following counter-examples. Observe:

(31) a. The solution(s) to any of these problems does/do not exist.
     (No indefinite NP)
   b. Any rumors about his past disappeared. (No bleached predicate)

In (31a), NPI *any* is licensed inside a definite NP, not an indefinite NP. In (31b), *any* is licensed, although there is no bleached predicate.

---

[3] Szabolsci (1986) introduces 'bleached predicates' to explain the Definiteness Effects in Hungarian. Those verbs that express existence, or changes in the state of existence or availability belong to that category.

Therefore, in our analysis, we basically assume the LF approach to account for *any* licensing in the preverbal position but do not strictly follow these requirements.

3.2.2. NPI *any* licensing: The case of *disappear*

At first, consider the following examples, in which *any* is licensed in the preverbal position.

(32) a. Any rumors/doubt about his past *disappeared(/*appeared.)*
    b. Any possible variation of dose delivered from position to position was *eliminated (/*added)* by rotating the entire assembly at six revolutions per minute. (from BNC)
    c. Rotating the entire assembly at six revolutions per minute *eliminated (/*added)* any possible variation of dose delivered from variation to variation.

In the above examples, *any* is licensed by removal predicates such as *disappear* and *was eliminated* in preverbal positions. However, their lexical antonyms do not license *any,* as they are not negative. Interestingly, passives such as *was eliminated* in (32b) also license *any* in the preverbal position, whereas actives such as *eliminate* in (32c) licenses *any* in the postverbal position. Assuming the Unaccusative Hypothesis (Perlmutter 1978), we consider passives such as *was eliminated* as well as unaccusative predicates such as *disappear* to license *any* in the postverbal position at D-Structure and then, reconstruct at LF so as not to violate the case filter. Keeping this reconstruction idea in mind, consider (33):

(33) a. Any rumors/doubts about his past *disappeared.*
    b. ?*Any rumors/doubts about his past *didn't appear.*
    c. ?*Any rumors/doubts about his past *didn't disappear.*

Presumably, (33b), where overtly negative predicate is used, is stronger in negative force than (33a), where inherently negative predicate is used. However, in (33), *disappear* in (33a) licenses *any,* whereas *didn't disappear* and *didn't appear* do not license the NPI *any.*

Examples in (33) support our reconstruction idea. That is, in (33a) *any* phrase is preceded by *disappear* in D-Structure and LF it moves to the subject position so as not to violate the case filter. On the other hand, the reason why (33b) and (33c) are awkward is that overt negation 'not' blocks movement and becomes a barrier. Parallel to this, we can search no phrases such as *didn't avoid any* and *didn't dislike any* in the corpus, whereas we can easily find the phrases such as *avoid any* and *dislike any* in the same corpus.[4]

---

[4]Native speakers say that double-negative sentences such as (33c) are difficult

4. Morphological-/Collocational Characteristics of Removal Predicates

4.1. Serial Verb Construction: *-peri*-(K), *-tesimau*-(J)

Consider the following Korean and Japanese examples.

(34) a. pakoyhay-/cwukie-/saracie-peri-ess-ta (Korean)
  destroy/kill/disappear- get through-PST- DEC
  '(They) destroyed/kill/disappeared (some-one/-thing).'
 b.* kenselhay-/kwucohay-/natanay- peri-ess-ta
  construct/rescue/appear -get through- PST-DEC
  'constructed/rescued/appeared.'
(35) a. hakaishi-/koroshi-/kie-tesima-tta (Japanese)
  destroy/kill/disappear- get through-PST
  'destroyed/kill/disappeared.'
 b.* kensetushi-/suku-/araware-tesima-tta
  construct/rescue/appear -get through- PST
  'constructed/rescued/appeared.'

In Korean and Japanese, removal predicates occur with auxiliaries such as *-peri*-(K) and *tesimau*-(J) 'throw away; get through', respectively. By contrast, generative predicates are not allowed to co-occur with those auxiliaries.

4.2. Removal vs. Generation affixes/particles/prepositions

Following affixes, particles and prepositions from English and Korean occur with removal and generation predicates, respectively. Observe:

(36) a. Removal morphemes: off, of, from away, out, ex-, de-, dis-, ob-,
  -eyse 'from'(K), *myel-/pak-/so-/sak-/tal-/ke-*'root up'(K)
 b. Generation morphemes: on, into, to, at, *-ey* 'to; on' (K)
(37) Removal Predicates with Removal Morphemes
  sakceha-'eliminate'(K), *semmyelha-*'annihilate'(K), *pakthalha-*
  'rob of', 'rip off'(K)

4.3. Negative Adverbs

There is a list of adverbs that precede our removal predicates. Generation predicates are not likely to occur with these adverbs. Consider such negative adverbs in (38) and further observe the relevant sentence in (39), below:

(38) *mocori*(K)/*kotogotoku*(J) 'with no exception'; *mwuchapyelcekuro*

understand and that they would not use such sentences in everyday life.

(K) and *musabetuni*(J) 'indiscriminately'; *utterly, indiscriminately, flatly* in English

(39) a. Soldiers indiscriminately killed citizens. (negative adverb)
b. *Soldiers indiscriminately rescued citizens.

In English, *indiscriminately* easily occurs with ethically negative verbs such as *kill* and does not easily occur with ethically positive verbs such as *praise* and *rescue.*

5. Conclusion

In this paper, we identified a unique type of weakly negative predicates, i.e., removal predicates. The process-involved ones yield implicature suspension but are not monotone decreasing unlike other stronger types of negative predicates. The absence-state-involved ones, on the other hand, reveal monotone-decreasingness in Korean, Japanese and English. The absence-state removal predicates can license *any* in English.

References

Chierchia, G. 2000. Scalar implicatures and polarity items, Abstract for a colloquium at UCLA.

Giannakidou,A.1998.*Polarity Sensitivity as (Non)Veridical Dependency*, John Benjamins Publishing Company.

Hoeksema and Klein. 1995. 'Negative Predicates and Their Arguments', *Linguistic Analysis* 25.

Horn, L. 1989. *A Natural History of Negation*. Chicago: Chicago U. Press.

Ladusaw, W.1996. 'Negation and Polarity Items. In S. Lappin (eds.), *The Handbook of Contemporary Semantic Theory*, Blackwell. Oxford.

Lee, Chungmin. 1999. 'Types of NPIs and nonveridicality in Korean and other languages'. *UCLA Working Papers in Linguistics, 3: Syntax at Sunset 2,* ed. by G. Storto, 96-132. Dept. of Linguistics, UCLA.

Lee, Chungmin. 2000. 'Contrastive Predicates and Conventional Scales', *CLS* 36.

Perlmutter, D. M 1978. 'Impersonal Passives and the Unaccusative Hypothesis', *Proceedings of the fourth Annual Meeting of the BLS,*157-189.

Szabolsci, A.1986. 'Indefinites in Complex Predicates, *Theoretical Linguistic Research 2.*

ter Meulen, A.G.B. 1995. *Representing Time in Natural Language: The Dynamic Interpretation of Tense and Aspect*, The MIT Press.

Uribe-Etxebarria, M.1995.'Negative Polarity Item Licensing, Indefinites and Complex Predicates' in Simons, M. (ed.), *SALT* V, 346-361.

Yoon, Youngeun. 1996. 'Total and partial predicates and the weak and strong interpretations.' *Natural Language Semantics.* 4/3: 217- 36.

Semantic Co-Composition of the Korean Substantival Nouns- *ha(ta)* Construction: Evidence for the Generative Lexicon*

JONG SUP JUN
Brandeis University

1. Introduction

In the current literature on Korean linguistics, much of the discussion of the light verb *-ha(ta)* has been focused upon the well-known fact that *-ha(ta)* combines with verbal nouns (*phakoy* 'destruction'), adjectival nouns (*swunswu* 'purity'), and predicate nominals (*tochak* 'arrival'; See Urushibara 1993). On the other hand, Korean also has a number of *-ha(ta)* expressions with concrete or substantival nouns (henceforth SNs) like *namu-hata* 'wood-hata', *pap-hata* 'rice-hata', *khemphywuthe-hata* 'computer-hata', etc. A standard assumption on these SN-*ha(ta)* examples, attributable to C-S Suh (1994, 1996, inter alia), is that these expressions are exceptional/idiomatic lexical units, where *-ha(ta)* functions as a proform for various verbs. I have

---

* This paper is an adaptation and modification of Chapter 4 of J. S. Jun (2000). My special gratitude goes to Ray Jackendoff, James Pustejovsky, Joan Maling, and Edgar Zurif for discussion and valuable comments. I also thank Sook Whan Cho, Soowon Kim, Chungmin Lee, the 8th ISOKL participants at Harvard Univ. in 1999, the 10th J/K Conference participants at UCLA in 2000, and my Brandeis colleagues in Pustejovsky's graduate seminar in the fall of 1999 for critical comments and various objections. Of course, any possible errors in this paper are due to my personal biases and imprudence.

argued against this standard assumption, showing that in colloquial speech *-ha(ta)* productively combines with substantival nouns like *chimtay* 'bed', *cangnong* 'wardrobe', *phullayswi* 'flashlight', etc. as shown in (1) -- (4) (J. S. Jun 1999).

(1) Inho-ka   chimtay-ha-le-ka-ss-ta
    Inho-NOM bed-obtain/buy-to-go-PST-DC
    'Inho went to obtain/buy a bed'   (OBTAIN)

(2) oppa!   wuri chimtay-ha-ci-mal-ko phuthon-ha-ca!
    darling we bed-buy-Neg-CONJ   futon-buy-let's
    'Darling! Let's buy a futon rather than a bed!'   (OBTAIN)

(3) onul   emma-lang   cangnong-ul(-)hay-ss-ta
    today mom-together chest/wardrobe-ACC-obtain/buy-PST-DC
    'Today, I bought a chest together with my mom'   (OBTAIN)

(4) yeki-ey   phullayswi-lul(-)hay-la!
    here-DAT flashlight-ACC-use-IM
    'Give here(= this spot) a flashlight! /
    Shine the flashlight over here!'   (USE)

Here, the descriptive generalization is that *-ha(ta)* has two base meanings, namely, USE and OBTAIN, when combining with SNs. What is central to this proposal is that SN-*ha(ta)*s are not exceptional/idiomatic expressions, but lexically derived constructions. I called this suggestion the Lexical Derivation Hypothesis of the SN-*ha(ta)* construction.

Now, several questions arise. One most-important question is concerned with the exact compositionality of a particular SN-*ha(ta)* expression as a whole. For instance, substantival nouns like *khemphywuthe* 'computer', *phullayswi* 'flashlight'; *chalhulk* 'clay'; *monopolli* 'Monopoly Game'; *kamyen* 'mask', and *masukhala* 'mascara'; etc. all form -*ha(ta)* constructions to mean 'to use that particular SN'. Nevertheless, this rough semantic generalization cannot explain anything about the strict compositionality of all these particular expressions. For instance, *phullayswi-hata* does not simply mean 'to use a flashlight'. Rather, it means 'to turn on a flashlight'. *Chalhulk-hata* does not and cannot mean 'to use clay to hit somebody by throwing it to him/her'. Rather, it means 'to make something out of clay'. Likewise, *monopolli-hata* means 'to play Monopoly Game'; and not 'to use a particular Monopoly game board to spank a child'. In other words, SN-*ha(ta)* expressions do not simply refer to any kind of use of the SN in question. Rather, it always refers to a very specific use of the particular SN. Having noticed this, Soowon Kim (p.c.) suggested an alternative pragmatic approach, in which the exact meaning of a particular SN-*ha(ta)* might be determined by pragmatic context, and not by the principle of the strict compositionality.

There is another important question, which is to some extent theory-internal. The two base meanings suggested in Jun (1999), i.e. USE and OBTAIN, are illustrated in the ambiguity of *sayngsen-hata* 'fish-hata' in (5).

(5) a. ca,   sayngsen-hay-se pap-ul   mek-e-la!
      well,   fish-eat/with   rice-ACC eat-IM
      'Well, eat rice while eating fish!'   (USE)
   b. onul   cenyek-ey sayngsen-ul(-)hay-ya-ci
      today supper-in fish-ACC-cook-DC
      'I will cook fish for supper today'   (OBTAIN)

In (5a), *sayngsen-hata* means 'to eat a dish of fish'; that is, 'to USE a dish of fish for its proper or intended function'. On the other hand, in (5b), *sayngsen-hata* means 'to cook fish'; that is 'to OBTAIN a dish of fish'. Aside from the first question of the exact compositionality for either of these ambiguous meanings, the base meaning generalizations of USE and OBTAIN invoke some theoretically mysterious questions. Is this distinction between USE and OBTAIN reducible to homophony or polysemy? In other words, is the *-ha(ta)* with the meaning of USE a really different word from the *-ha(ta)* with the meaning of OBTAIN? If they are two separate lexical entries, are they also different from the *-ha(ta)* combining with verbal nouns? Also, if these *-ha(ta)*s have two distinct meanings, namely USE and OBTAIN, then can we still call them light verbs? If they are heavy in semantic contents, why do they behave so differently from other semantically heavy verbs in complement choices?[1] These theoretical questions are crucial in maintaining the Lexical Derivation Hypothesis of the SN-*ha(ta)* construction.

In short, this paper aims to answer two research questions, one empirical and the other theoretical. The empirical question is concerned with the exact compositionality of a particular SN-*ha(ta)*. The theoretical question is concerned with the valid lexico-semantic relationships between various *-ha(ta)*s. In what follows, I will argue that both the empirical and the theoretical problems are neatly explained when we look at these question from the perspective of the generative lexicon (henceforth GL) theory proposed by Pustejovsky (1995, 1998).

---

[1] See Jun (1999) for details about Pinkerian (1989) narrow class memberships in the various complement choices for *-ha(ta)*.

2. Co-Composition between the Telic^{SN} and the Agentive^{HATA}

2.1. Basic Machinery

In the GL theory, every lexical item α has a qualia structure, where the Telic quale specifies α's purpose and proper function, and the Agentive quale specifies the factor involved in α's origin. These quales, together with some other quales like Constitutive and Formal, interact dynamically to derive a specific compositional meaning. (6) shows Putejovsky's (1995: 122) favorite data.

>   (6) a. John *baked* the potato. (Change of State)
>   b. John *baked* the cake. (Creation)

In (6a), the exact compositional meaning of *baked the potato* involves the change of state. That is, by baking a potato, you just change the state of the potato from its raw state to the cooked state. On the other hand, the exact compositional meaning of *baked the cake* in (6b) involves the creation of the cake. There is no change of state in (6b), since before baking you do not have any cake. Hence, *bake* in (6a) and (6b) is logically polysemous. To explain this verbal logical polysemy, Pustejovsky assumes that *bake* has the change of state meaning. Then, how is the creation sense in (6b) possible? Pustejovsky argues that it is possible only through selecting a specific type of object NPs. In (6b), *bake* selects *cake*. The lexical representation for *cake* assumed by Pustejovsky (1995: 123) is (7).

$$(7) \quad \begin{bmatrix} \textbf{cake} \\ \\ ARGSTR = \begin{bmatrix} ARG1 = x : food\_ind \\ D-ARG1 = y : mass \end{bmatrix} \\ \\ QUALIA = \begin{bmatrix} CONST = y \\ FORMAL = x \\ TELIC = eat(e2, z, x) \\ AGENTIVE = bake\_act(e1, w, y) \end{bmatrix} \end{bmatrix}$$

(7) states that w (somebody) bakes y (possibly, flour) in order for x (which is *cake*) to exist for the purpose of z (somebody)'s eating the x. The qualia roles in (7) unifies with the qualia roles of *bake*. *Cake*'s qualia specification, where 'bake_act' results in the Formal value x, is co-composed with the

qualia roles of *bake*, so that the appropriate creation sense in (6b) is derived. This is the basic idea of co-composition.

Now, it is time to solve our first empirical problem. Let us go back to our *sayngsen* example in (5). In English, *fish* is lexically ambiguous between *fish (alive in the water)* and *fish (for dish)*. In Korean, however, these two concepts are lexicalized separately. That is, *fish (for dish)* is lexicalized as *sayngsen*, whereas *fish (alive in the water)* is lexicalized as *mulkoki*. Thus, *sayngsen* in Korean must have a lexical representation which is distinct from that of *mulkoki*. *Mulkoki* is a kind of Pisces, whereas *sayngsen* is a kind of foodstuff.[2] Consequently, the lexical representation of *sayngsen* is assumed as in (8), where the Telic quale refers to the eating event.

$$(8) \begin{bmatrix} \textbf{sayngsen} \\[2ex] \text{ARGSTR} = \begin{bmatrix} \text{ARG1} = x : \text{dish/foodstuff} \\ \text{D} - \text{ARG1} = z : \text{raw fish} \end{bmatrix} \\[3ex] \text{QUALIA} = \begin{bmatrix} \text{FORMAL} = x \\ \text{AGENTIVE} = \text{cook}(e, y, z) \\ \text{TELIC} = \text{eat}(e', y/w, x) \end{bmatrix} \end{bmatrix}$$

If we assume an inheritance of the Telic value of *sayngsen* to *-ha(ta)* in *sayngsen-hata*, we can simply explain why the compositional meaning of (5a) is 'to eat *sayngsen*'. In order to achieve this formally, what we need is simply to assume the lexical representation of *-ha(ta)* as in (9).

$$(9) \begin{bmatrix} \textbf{-ha(ta)1} \\[1ex] \text{EVENTSTR} = \begin{bmatrix} \text{E1} = e1 : \text{process} \end{bmatrix} \\[2ex] \text{ARGSTR} = \begin{bmatrix} \text{ARG1} = <1> \begin{bmatrix} \text{animate\_ind} \\ \text{FORMAL} = \text{physobj} \end{bmatrix} \\[2ex] \text{ARG2} = <2> \begin{bmatrix} \text{physobj} \\ \text{FORMAL} = \text{entity} \end{bmatrix} \end{bmatrix} \\[2ex] \text{QUALIA} = \begin{bmatrix} \text{AGENTIVE} = \phi(\text{TELIC}, <2>)(e, <1>, ...) \end{bmatrix} \end{bmatrix}$$

---

[2] Joan Maling (p.c.) has pointed out that the same lexicalization pattern holds for English word pairs like 'pig--pork', 'cow--beef', etc.

In (9), the phi notation 'ϕ(TELIC, <2>](e,<1>,...)' means 'Import the Telic event from the LCS of <2>, and make <1> one of its arguments in the argument structure of the Telic event specification of <2>'. This co-composition between the Agentive of -*ha(ta)* and the Telic of the SN derives the exact compositional meaning of *sayngsen-hata*. Likewise, what we see in expressions like *masukhala-hata* 'mascara-hata' and *congichalhulk-hata* 'paper mâché-hata' is co-composition of quales between the Agentive of -*ha(ta)* and the Telic of the complement SNs. Since the Telic specifies α's proper function, *masukhala* and *congichalhulk* have Telics 'wear_act(e, x, z=mascara)' and 'make_act(e, x, w)' respectively. If we co-compose these quales with the Agentive of -*ha(ta)* in (9), we would safely and accurately land at our intended interpretations. In this way, the principle of compositionality can be preserved, which is not achieved by an alternative pragmatic approach in all cases.

2.2. Empirical Justifications

One crucial question is if there is any independent motivation for a highly specific lexical representation like (8) other than the co-composition with a light verb. The answer to this question is, I believe, empirical in nature. That is, if we can achieve great empirical coverage with lexical representations like (8), then our theory is empirically sound. In the GL theory, the qualia structure is motivated by three generative mechanisms, which allow us to achieve variety of empirical consequences in semantic interpretations. They are co-composition, type coercion, and selective binding. In this section, I argue that lexical representations like (8) are empirically motivated by type coercion and selective binding as well as the co-composition with -*ha(ta)*.

First, a typical true type coercion occurs when there is a mismatch between the actual complement type and the complement type expected by lexical governors.

(10) John began a book. (Pustejovsky, 1995: 115)

In (10), the predicate *begin* licenses an event-type complement, which is in reality occupied by a physical object *book*. This mismatch is resolved by coercing the actual type of *book* (i.e. physobj) into an event-type. This is possible through a formal mechanism called type coercion on the qualia structure of a lexical item. As for *book*, one of the qualia specifications -- possibly, Telic -- should be 'read(e,x,a_book)'. λ-extraction on this quale yields an event-denoting expression like '$\lambda x \lambda e$[read(e,x,a_book)]'. It is this λ-extracted event variable that enables the type coercion from physobj to event in the semantic interpretation of (10).

Predicates like *want, begin,* and *enjoy* take an event-type complement. A crucial test for lexical representations like (8) is to see if a coerced reading is possible when event-taking predicates are combined with SNs in Korean.

(11) a. Inho-nun sayngsen-ul wenhay-ss-ta
    TM fish-ACC wanted
   'Inho wanted to eat a dish of fish'
  b. Inho-nun ceckalak-ul   tulko sayngsen-ul/puthe
      chopsticks-ACC with fish-ACC/from
   sicak-hay-ss-ta
    began
   'Inho began to eat a dish of fish with chopsticks'
  c. Inho-nun sayngsen-ul culki-ess-ta
         enjoyed
   'Inho enjoyed eating a dish of fish'

(11) shows that a true type coercion from physobj to event is systematically possible on the λ-extracted Telic event of *sayngsen* 'fish'; i.e. $\lambda w\lambda e[eat(e,w,fish)]$.

The other empirical justification for the qualia structure of a lexical item is selective binding. According to Pustejovsky (1995: 129-30), *a long record* in *John bought a long record* is not a record whose physical shape is long, but 'a record whose playing time is long'. Assuming that the attributive adjective *long* has 'an interpretation as an event predicate', the desired reading is only possible when *long* selectively binds the λ-extracted Telic event of *record*; i.e. $\lambda x[...Telic=\lambda e[play(x)(e) \wedge long(e)]...]$.

It is not difficult at all to find cases of selective binding between SNs like *sayngsen* 'fish', *masukhala* 'mascara', and *congichalhulk* 'paper mâché' and event-modifying adjectives like *convenient* and *spraying*. Look at (12).

(12) a. (kasi-ka eps-ese) phyenhan sayngsen
    thorn not.exist convenient fish
   'fish convenient to eat (because there is no fishbone)'
  b. ppwuli-nun masukhala
    spraying mascara
  c. (son-ey puthci anh-ase) phyenhan congichalhulk
    hand-to stick not-since convenient paper mâché
   'paper mâché convenient to work with (because it is not sticky)'

The selective binding in (12) systematically occurs with the λ-extracted Telic event of SNs. These two pieces of evidence -- type coercion and selective binding -- provide empirical support for the qualia based analysis of the SN-*ha(ta)* construction.

3. Co-Composition between the Agentive^{SN} and the Agentive^{HATA}

3.1. Basic Machinery

Let us look the other interpretation of *sayngsen-hata*. In (5b), *sayngsen-hata* means 'to cook fish / to OBTAIN a dish of fish'. In order to arrive at this particular interpretation, we simply need to assume a co-composition between the Agentive of the SN and the Agentive of -*ha(ta)* in (13).

$$(13) \begin{bmatrix} -\textbf{ha(ta)2} \\ \text{EVENTSTR} = \begin{bmatrix} \text{E1} = \text{e1} : \text{process} \end{bmatrix} \\ \text{ARGSTR} = \begin{bmatrix} \text{ARG1} = <1> \begin{bmatrix} \text{animate\_ind} \\ \text{FORMAL} = \text{physobj} \end{bmatrix} \\ \text{ARG2} = <2> \begin{bmatrix} \text{physobj} \\ \text{FORMAL} = \text{entity} \end{bmatrix} \end{bmatrix} \\ \text{QUALIA} = \begin{bmatrix} \text{AGENTIVE} = \phi(\text{AGENTIVE}, <2>)(e, <1>, ...) \end{bmatrix} \end{bmatrix}$$

Since the Agentive event of *sayngsen* is 'cook(e,y,z)' in (8), we will get (14) in the next page by plugging (8) into the ARG2 of (13). (14) shows the exact interpretation of *sayngsen-hata* in (5b) as a strictly compositional meaning.

The empirical power of this GL machinery is further tested by trickier cases as in (15).

(15) hoysa ttaylyechi-ko thayksi/pesu/*catongcha-na hay-yakeyss-ta
     job   resign-and taxi/bus/*vehicle-just   ha-will-Dec
     'I want to resign my current job in order to be a taxi/bus-driver'

(15) is problematic in two respects. First, -*ha(ta)* in (15) is not easily reducible to either USE and OBTAIN. Rather, it is more like DO-FOR-A-LIVING as indicated by Jun (1999). Secondly, if we consider the generation of an SN-*ha(ta)* as constrained by Pinkerian narrow class memberships, it is

(14)

$$
\begin{bmatrix}
\textbf{sayngsen} - \textbf{ha(ta)} \\[4pt]
\text{EVENTSTR} = \begin{bmatrix} \text{E1} = \text{e1} : \text{process} \\ \text{E2} = \text{e2} : \text{state} \\ \text{RESTR} =< \infty \end{bmatrix} \\[30pt]
\text{ARGSTR} = \begin{bmatrix}
\text{ARG1} =<1> \begin{bmatrix} \text{animate\_ind} \\ \text{FORMAL} = \text{physobj} \end{bmatrix} \\[20pt]
\text{ARG2} =<2> \begin{bmatrix}
\textbf{sayngsen} \\
\text{ARGSTR} = \begin{bmatrix} \text{ARG1} = \text{x} : \text{dish/foodstuff} \\ \text{D} - \text{ARG1} = \text{z} : \text{raw fish} \end{bmatrix} \\[16pt]
\text{QUALIA} = \begin{bmatrix} \text{FORMAL} = \text{x} \\ \text{AGENTIVE} = \text{cook}(\text{e}, \text{y}, \text{z}) \\ \text{TELIC} = \text{eat}(\text{e}', \text{y/w}, \text{x}) \end{bmatrix}
\end{bmatrix}
\end{bmatrix} \\[30pt]
\text{QUALIA} = \begin{bmatrix} \text{AGENTIVE} = \text{cook}(\text{e1}, <1>, \text{z}) \end{bmatrix}
\end{bmatrix}
$$

not clear why *taxi/bus* should belong to a different semantic class from *vehicle/car*. These problems, which are left as residual issues in Jun (1999), are neatly solved in my current GL approach.

The GL theory is the theory of syntagmatic processes with reference to paradigmatic relationships (Pustejovsky 2000, forthcoming). To put it differently, a syntagmatic process like co-composition is achieved by referring to a paradigmatic hierarchy like a formal type system (Pustejovsky 1995; Copestake & Briscoe 1992; Copestake 1992; Pustejovsky & Boguraev 1993). Seen from a hierarchical type-lattice widely assumed in computational linguistics, *taxi* and *bus* are subtype examples of a higher type *vehicle*. Pustejovsky (forthcoming) has formally developed a subtype relationship 'θ[taxi ⊆ vehicle]: taxi → vehicle', where *taxi* inherits the qualia structure of its higher type, and at the same time has the subordinate qualia structure deeply embedded in the inherited qualia structure. That is, if we assume a lexical representation of *vehicle* as in (16a), by a subtype relationship θ, *taxi* inherits the qualia structure from *vehicle*, and keep(s) its own fine distinction from *vehicle* by having a subordinate qualia structure as in (16b).

$$(16)\ a.\ \begin{bmatrix} \textbf{vehicle} \\ ARGSTR = \begin{bmatrix} ARG1 = x : physobj \end{bmatrix} \\ QUALIA = \begin{bmatrix} FORMAL = x \\ TELIC = drive/ride(e, y, x) \end{bmatrix} \end{bmatrix}$$

b.

$$\begin{bmatrix} \textbf{taxi}\ (esp.\ Korean\ \textbf{thayksi}) \\ \\ ARGSTR = \begin{bmatrix} ARG1 = x : physobj \end{bmatrix} \\ QUALIA = \begin{bmatrix} FORMAL = x \\ TELIC = \begin{bmatrix} TELIC = use\_for\_a\_living(e', y, x) \\ AGENTIVE = drive/ride(e, y, x) \end{bmatrix} \end{bmatrix} \end{bmatrix}$$

In (16b), the embedded Telic quale 'use_for_a_living(e',y,x)' is not stipulative as it seems to be, and is motivated by independent evidence. That is, when *thayksi* is coerced into an event reading due to the complementation for an event-taking predicate like *sicak-ha(ta)* 'begin', the composite meaning of the entire VP *thayksi-lul sicak-ha(ta)* 'begin a taxi' refers to the event of USE-FOR-A-LIVING.

One interesting consequence of (16b) is a recursive qualia structure, and in this case *taxi*'s specific (embedded) Telic role is defined recursively under the (superordinate) Telic role inherited from *vehicle*. The recursive qualia structure is informally defined in (17).

> (17) Recursivity in Qualia Structure: When β is α's subtype entry, and α has a qualia structure θ, β inherits θ, and can further specify δ (delta), which specifies β's subordinate qualia structure, for its qualia structure, which is distinct from θ.

Given the recursive qualia specification as in (16b), we can co-compose the Telic role of *thayksi* with the Agentive role of *-ha(ta)* to get a particular compositional meaning 'to drive a taxi for a living'. Now, our immediate questions have been settled. First, we do not have to posit any base meaning like DO-FOR-A-LIVING. Rather, co-composition between the Telic of the SN and the Agentive of *-ha(ta)* simply guarantees the exact meaning of *thayksi-hata*. Secondly, we have a good reason to exclude *vehicle* from the Pinkerian narrow class which *taxi* and *bus* belong to; that is, *taxi* and *bus* are different from *vehicle* in their subordinate qualia structures.

3.2. Empirical Justifications

In 2.2, I presented independent empirical motivations other than co-composition for the Telic quale of SNs like *sayngsen* 'fish'. In this section, I will show that there is also independent empirical motivation for the Agentive quale of SNs like *sayngsen* to provide support for the co-composition analysis of the SN-ha*(ta)* construction. The Agentive quale of SNs like *sayngsen* also displays type coercion and selective binding. (18) shows type coercion when combined with event-taking predicates, and (19) shows selective binding with event-modifying adjectives.

> (18) Mina-nun kwuk-ul   ollye nohko
>   TM soup-ACC put.on after
>   sayngsen-ul sicak-hay-ss-ta
>   fish-ACC   began
>   'Inho began to cook fish after making soup'

> (19) a. (yoli haki-ey)   pulphyenhan sayngsen
>   dish making-at inconvenient   fish
>   'fish inconvenient (to make a dish)'
>   b. (mantulki-ey) elyewun umsik
>   make-at   difficult food
>   'food difficult (to make)'
>   c. tongchimi-nun mas nayki-ey swiwun kimchi-ka   anita
>   TM taste make-at easy   NOM not.be
>   'Tongchimi is not a kind of kimchi which is easy to make good'

In (18), the SN *sayngsen* coerces its type from physobj to event in semantic interpretation when it is in the complement position of an event-taking predicate *begin*. This is only possible when the λ-extraction of an event variable occurs with the Agentive quale of *sayngsen*. Also, in (19), event-modifying adjectives all modify λ-extracted event variables of SNs like *sayngsen*, *umsik*, and *kimchi* in semantic interpretations. These two pieces of evidence provide independent motivation for the qualia structure of SNs.

4. HATA as a Light Verb

One great advantage of the GL approach to the SN-*ha(ta)* construction is that it provides a nice solution to the other question I introduced in the beginning. This question can be summarized into two major issues. One: Is the -*ha(ta)* with the meaning of USE a different word from the -*ha(ta)* with the meaning of OBTAIN? Two: If they really mean either USE or OBTAIN, are they still light verbs? To the first question, my current approach answers that we do not have to posit two different lexical entries for these two different uses of -*ha(ta)*. In (9) and (13), I treated the two -*ha(ta)*s with actually the same lexical representation except for the co-composition of the Agentive with specific quales of the SN complements. In terms of the present assumptions of the GL theory, the choice of specific quales in co-composition is lexically specified for each complement-verb pair. Preserving my claim that only some semantically narrow class items participate in generating the SN-*ha(ta)* construction from the Pinkerian perspective, the choice of the Telic in (9) and the Agentive in (13) for co-composition is not the matter of -*ha(ta)*, but the matter of particular SNs. Hence, the first -*ha(ta)* with the meaning of USE and the second -*ha(ta)* with the meaning of OBTAIN can be considered as one and the same lexical entry, which is a very desirable result for the economy of the theory.

Here's one corollary of this position. Unlike Jun (1999), this GL approach does not attribute the lexical meaning of USE and OBTAIN to the lexico-semantic property of -*ha(ta)*. Rather, the base meanings of USE and OBTAIN are reflections of the primitive concepts of Telicity and Agentiveness. As a consequence, we do not have to consider our -*ha(ta)*s semantically heavy verbs. That is, the -*ha(ta)* combining with SNs maintains its status as a light verb. The relationship between this -*ha(ta)* and the light -*ha(ta)* combining with verbal nouns is certainly beyond the scope of this paper, and we will need a thorough investigation of a broad range of data. I leave this question to a future research.

5. Conclusion

So far, I have shown that the SN-*ha(ta)* construction in Korean can be well explained by the GL theory. We do not need an unconstrained theory of pragmatics to account for the recalcitrant composition of various SN-*ha(ta)*s. With a generative device like co-composition, we can explain the exact semantics of various SN-*ha(ta)*s while preserving strict compositionality. Also, the two base meanings of USE and OBTAIN advocated in Jun (1999) turn out to be some reflections of the interaction between qualia structures. Overall, I believe that this GL approach provides strong support for the Lexical Derivation Hypothesis of the SN-*ha(ta)* construction.

6. Post-Script

One possible line of inquiry regarding my present approach to the Korean SN-*ha(ta)* construction is what can be correlates in other languages. During the presentation of this paper (at the 10th J/K Conference at UCLA), there were some interesting discussions about this issue, which I think are worth mentioning in this paper as a guideline for a future research.

A possible correlate of the SN-*ha(ta)* construction in English is, I think, innovative denominal verbs. In Clark and Clark's (1979: 768) classical discussion, 'the parent noun of each verb ... denote[s] a palpable object or property of such an object', which concept is consistent with the notion of SNs. One striking consequence of Clark and Clark's study is that their semantic analysis of English denominal verbs is very similar to my GL approach to the Korean SN-ha*(ta)* construction. For instance, they think that 'the commonest denominal verbs ... depend mainly on generic knowledge about concrete objects (p. 789)', and that the generic knowledge people are assumed to have comprises an object's ontogeny (i.e. Agentive quale), its potential roles (i.e. Telic quale), and so on. Obviously, Clark and Clark's study was done before Pustejovsky developed a formal theory dealing with this generic knowledge. It is not surprising that their way of putting things is much different from the GL formalism. But the fact that Clark and Clark's intuition about semantics of English denominal verbs is not very far from the GL intuition renders support for the GL theory and the correlation between English denominal verbs and the Korean SN-*ha(ta)* construction. A recent study by Joh (2001) uses the GL formalism to explain semantics of English denominal verbs. I think this remark suffices to post a future research goal on this field.

References

Clark, E. & H. Clark. 1979. When Nouns Surface as Verbs. *Language* 55-4: 767-811.

Copestake, A. 1992. *The Representation of Lexical Semantic Information*, CSRP 280, Univ. of Sussex.

Copestake, A. & T. Briscoe. 1992. Lexical Operations in a Unification-Based Framework. In J. Pustejovsky & S. Bergler (eds.), *Lexical Semantics and Knowledge Representation*. Berlin: Springer Verlag.

Joh, Y. K. 2001. The Semantics of Innovative Denominal Verbs in English. MA Thesis. Seoul National Univ.

Jun, J. S. 1999. Productive Combinations of Substantival Nouns with -ha(ta) in Korean: Evidence for the Design of the Lexicon. In S. Kuno et al. (eds.), *Harvard Studies in Korean Linguistics, VIII*. Cambridge, Mass.: Harvard Univ.

Jun, J. S. 2000. *Semantics of "Substantival Nouns-ha(ta)" in Korean and its Implication about the Design of the Mental Lexicon*. Ms. Brandeis Univ.

Pinker, S. 1989. *Learnability and Cognition: The Acquisition of Argument Structure*. Cambridge, Mass.: MIT Press.

Pustejovsky, J. 1995. *The Generative Lexicon*. Cambridge, Mass.: MIT Press.

Pustejovsky, J. 1998. Generativity and Explanation in Semantics: A Reply to Fodor and Lepore. *Linguistic Inquiry* 29-2: 289-311.

Pustejovsky, J. 2000. Syntagmatic Processes. In A. Cruse (ed.), *Handbook of Lexicography*. Berlin: Mouton De Gruyter.

Pustejovsky, J. forthcoming. Type Construction and the Logic of Concepts. In P. Bouillon and F. Busa (eds.), *The Grammar of Word Meaning*. Cambridge: Cambridge Univ. Press.

Pustejovsky, J. & B. Boguraev. 1993. Lexical Knowledge Representation and Natural Language Processing. *Artificial Intelligence* 63: 193-223.

Suh, C-S. 1994. *Kwuke Munpep (Korean Grammar)*. Seoul: Ppulikiphun Namu.

Suh, C-S. 1996. *Kwuke Munpep (Korean Grammar)*. Seoul: Hanyang Univ. Press.

Urushibara, S. 1993. Nonagentive Light Verb Constructions: Korean vs. Japanese. In S. Kuno et al. (eds.), *Harvard Studies in Korean Linguistics, V*. Cambridge, Mass.: Harvard Univ.

Two Positions of Korean Negation*

AE-RYUNG KIM

Kanda University of International Studies

1. Introduction: Contrasts in Negations

Negation is realized in two different ways in Korean as shown in (1).

(1) a. Mary-ka computer-lul **ani** sa-ssta.   S(hort-form) Negation
       M-nom   computer-acc **neg** buy-past
       'Mary did not buy a computer'
    b. Mary-ka computer-lul sa **ci-ani** ha-ssta.   L(ong-form) Negation
                            buy **neg** do-past

The negation marker *ani* can come before a verb as in (1a) or after a verb accompanied by a particle *ci* and so called light verb *ha* as in (1b). Among several terminologies suggested to distinguish the two types of negation, I will use short form negation (henceforth S negation) and long form negation (henceforth L negation) to refer to negations of (1a) and (1b), respectively.

Negation has been studied on many aspects. One aspect is whether the negation marker *ani* is an adverb or Spec/head of NegP (Han and Park (1994), Yi (1994), Yoon (1990), among others). Another aspect is of the categorical status of the particle *ci* occurring in L negation, which leads to a discussion of whether L negation is mono-clausal or bi-clausal (Song 1967, Jung 1991). Whether S and L negations are identical semantically and/or syntactically is another big issue (Song (1973), Yoon (1990), Han and Park (1994), Park (1998), among others).

* I would like to thank Yun-jin Nam and Sandra Stjepanovic for the valuable discussions and suggestions. This research is supported by Postdoctoral Fellowship Program of Japan Society for the Promotion of Science (JSPS).

This paper intends to build a structure with two positions of negation in Korean and explains contrasts manifested in two types of negations. One contrast is of scope interaction as shown in (2).

(2) a. Mary-ka computer-*man*   **ani** sa-ssta.   only>neg (3a)[1]
         M-nom   computer-*only* **neg** buy-past
    b. Mary-ka computer-*man* sa **ci-ani** ha-asst.   only><neg (3a&b)
                              buy **neg** do-past
    c. Mary-ka computer-*man* sa **ci-<u>nun</u>-ani** ha-assta.   only<neg (3b)
                              buy <u>**foc-neg**</u> do-past
(3) a. It was only Mary who did not buy a computer.   only > neg
    b. It was not the case that only Mary bought a computer.   only<neg

It is well known that a scope-bearing item (henceforth SBI), such as NP-*man* 'only', takes wide scope over *ani* in S negation as in (2a), while its scope is ambiguous in L negation as in (2b). There is a third pattern of scope interaction. When the focus/topic marker *nun* is inserted between *ci* and *ani* in L negation as in (2c), *ani* takes wide scope over an SBI. Two types of negation show another contrast when an NPI *amu(ket)-to* precedes an SBI as in (4).

(4) a. **Amu-to* computer-<u>man</u> **ani** sa-ssta.
         No one computer-only neg buy-past
         'No one bought only a computer.'
    b. *Amu-to* computer-<u>man</u> sa **ci-ani** ha-ssta.

I will illustrate how the proposal of two negation positions can explain the three-way scope contrast in (2) and the contrast involving *amu-to* in (4).

In section 2, I briefly introduce previous proposals for a structure with negations. In section 3, I propose a structure with two positions of negation and show how the proposal accounts for the scope contrasts. In section 4, I provide evidence for the proposal. Section 5 discusses the contrast in (4) and reduces the contrast to an intervention effect pointed out by Beck and Kim (1997).

2. Structure with Negation
2.1. Previous Analyses

There are two opposite approaches to a structure with negation. One approach assumes a single structure for a sentence with S negation and its counterpart with L negation. To illustrate how a single structure can account for both types of negation, let me introduce a structure (5) suggested by Y-J Yoon (1990).

---

[1] The wide scope of an SBI over negation in (2a) has been observed in the literature (C-H Cho 1975, S-H Ahn 1990, Han and Park 1994, Park 1998, among others). Although the ambiguity of (2b) is commonly acknowledged (H-S Han 1987, S-C Song 1988, among others), J-H Suh (1989) takes subject-object asymmetry position: an SBI in the object position is ambiguous with respect to negation but subject takes unambiguously wide scope over negation.

(5)

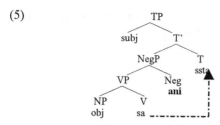

The structure (5) includes NegP under TP with *ani* as its head or Spec. Yoon (1990) assumes **optional** verb movement. If a verb moves to T, S negation is derived. If it does not move, *ha* 'do' is inserted in T for the stranded tense, resulting in L negation. Without going into further detail, we can predict (5) cannot explain why (2a) and (2b) show different scope interaction.

Han and Park (1994) point out a similar problem with (5) with respect to scope. To explain the scope contrast they propose distinct structures for sentences with S negation and L negation as in (6a) and (6b), respectively.

(6) a. S negation   b. L negation

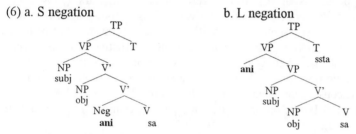

According to Han and Park (1994), negation marker *ani* originates adjoined to the lowest V', lower than the object in S negation and adjoined to VP, higher than the subject in L negation. Although (6a) correctly predicts the wide scope of an SBI in S negation, (6b) cannot predict ambiguous scopes in L negation.

To explain the ambiguity of (2b), we could consider an account in which negation *ani* originates in a position higher than VP and an SBI quantifier-raises (QR) either to TP or VP as suggested in Heim and Kratzer (1998). On this account, if an SBI QRs to TP, it takes wide scope over negation. If it QRs to VP, the relative scope is reversed. If Han and Park's (1994) analysis adopts two different positions for QR, the ambiguity of (2b) is explicable. Their analysis, however, does not assume QR of an SBI.

3. Proposal: Two Positions of Negation
3.1. How to Derive Two Types of Negation

The aforementioned proposals have an explanatory merit. The single structure analysis can distinguish (2a) from (2b) in terms of PF structure; the distinct structures explain the wide scope of an SBI in S negation; optional positions for QR explain ambiguous scopes in L negation. None of the accounts, however, is comprehensive enough to explain all of the observed facts.

In this paper I propose a hybrid account to combine the merit of the aforementioned proposals. I adopt Chomsky (1995) for the structure of a sentence in which vP is the complement of T and VP is the complement of v. In this struc-ture I assume two different positions of negation as in (7).

(7)

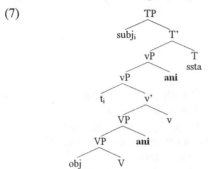

In the proposed structrure (7), negation *ani* can originate in a vP-adjoined position or in a VP-positioned. These positions are equivalent to V'-ajoined and VP-adjoined poisitions of (6), respectively, in Han and Park (1994). Two positions of negaiton is semantically motivated. It is acknowledged that what can be negated is either a sentence (sentential negation) or one of its constituents (constituent negation), though two negations are not distinctive in terms of truth-condition in most cases. I suggest that two semantic negations are mapped onto different syntactic positions in Korean: vP-adjoined *ani* is sentential and VP-adjoined *ani* is constituent, negating a constituent of VP including VP.[2]

Let me first elaborate on how different types of negation are derived as in (2), repeated in (8).

(8) a. Mary-ka computer-*man* **an(i)** sa-ssta.   only>neg
    b. Mary-ka computer-*man* sa **ci-an(i)** (ha)-assta.   only><neg
    c. Mary-ka computer-*man* sa **ci-<u>nun</u>-an(i)** (ha)-assta.   only<neg

Yoon (1990) attributes the different position of *ani* in S and L negations to op-tional verb movement. In this paper, I attribute it to different numerations of two types of negations. As manifested in (8a) and (8b), lexical items are different: while in S negation only *ani* is added to the numeration of the counterpart af-firmative sentence, in L negation the numeration includes a particle *ci*, and light verb *ha* as well as *ani*. Adopting Chomsky's (1995, 98, 99) feature deletion mechanism, I argue that the verb movement is triggered by the necessity of hav-ing an uninterpretable feature checked and deleted. The crucial mechanisms this paper hinges on are summarized as in (9).

(9) a. An uninterpretable feature should be deleted before LF interface.
    b. A feature is deleted by Merge, Agree or Move (as a last resort).
       (<u>Agree</u> is a relation between an LI and a feature in some restricted search

---

[2] Ernst (1992) suggests two positions for English *not*. In his suggestion, constituent negation is an adjunct below the highest VP (vP in our structure), and sentential negation is the head of NegP which is higher than VP. For instance, *not* in (ia) is constituent and *not* in (ib) is sentential.
(i) a. Ken could *not* heard the news.
    b. Ken could *not* have heard the news.

space.)
c. Phase Impenetrability Condition (PIC)
   The domain of H is not accessible to operations at ZP (the next strong phase), but only H and its edge.

The fact is that all Korean verbs should be suffixed by a tense morpheme, or a morpheme ci or, ki, which must be attached to a predicate. Based on the observation, I assume that a verb bears a feature, say [+pred], which need to be deleted by Agreeing with one of the morphemes.

Given Chomsky's feature deletion and different numerations of S and L negations, a verb obligatorily moves or stays. In S negation, [+pred] of a verb should be deleted by tense. In order for a verb to be in the domain of tense without violating PIC as described in (9c), it should be under head or an edge of vP. I will assume the verb moves to the head as shown in (10). In the structure with a verb under v, ani should originate in a VP-adjoined position to conform PF structure of S negation, in which ani should be preverbal.

(10) a. Mary-ka computer-lul **ani** sa-ssta
      b.

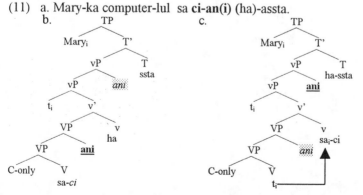

On the other hand, the numeration of L negation includes a particle ci, which can delete [+pred] of a verb. The particle ci has to be attached to a verb, but it is flexible when the attachment occurs as shown in (11b) and (11c).

(11) a. Mary-ka computer-lul sa **ci-an(i)** (ha)-assta.
      b.   c.

If ci is attached to a verb under V, the feature [+pred] is deleted by Merge of ci. Then the verb should be frozen under V and v is filled by the light verb ha. In this derivation, *ani* must originate in a VP-adjoined position to conform PF structure of L negation, i.e., to be postverbal as in (11b). On the other hand, if *ci* does not attach to a verb under V, the verb has to move to v to have [+pred] checked without violating PIC and the attachment of *ci* occurs at this point as shown in (11c). In this derivation, *ani* must originate in a vP-adjoined position.

L negation can be accompanied by a topic/focus marker *nun* which precedes *ani* as in (8c). In this structure *ani* must originate higher than *nun*. Where then does *nun* originate? Sohn (1996) characterizes such *nun* as putting negative focus on an item. The focus targets subject, object, VP or just verb as is illustrated in (12).

(12) Mary$_i$-ka [$_{vP}$ t$_i$ computer-lul sa **ci**]-<u>nun</u>-**ani** ha-ssta.
     M-nom   computer-acc   buy   <u>foc</u>-neg do-past
     a. '[$_F$ Mary] did not buy a computer.' b. 'Mary did not buy [$_F$ a computer].'
     c. 'Mary didn't [$_F$ buy] a computer.   d. Mary didn't [$_F$ buy a computer]

Jackendoff (1972) restricts focus to be associated with an item in its c-command domain (range in his terms). Given the restriction, the c-command domain of *nun* should be vP since focus can be associated with the subject. Hence we can conjecture that *nun* is generated higher than vP in (8c). If this conjecture is right, *ani* in (8c) must be vP-adjoined to be higher than *nun*.

In the proposed analysis a verb has to move in S negation to have [+pred] checked without violating PIC. In L negation the verb movement depends on when *ci* is attached to a verb. The position of *ani* is determined by PF structure, whether it is preverbal or postverbal. According to this proposed structure, *ani* is constituent in S negation, sentential in L negation with *nun* and ambiguous in L negation.

3.2. Analysis of Scope Contrast

Under the proposed structure with negation, the scope contrasts in (8) are explained straightforwardly from their LF structure, represented as in (13) if we make general assumptions regarding scope interpretation as in (14).

(13)

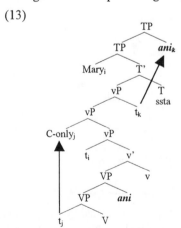

(14) a. SBIs QR to a minimal projection of a proposition, vP or TP at LF.
    b. Sentential negation should be in the position to c-command its argument, the highest TP at LF.
    c. The c-command relation at LF determines relative scope.

An SBI, *computer-only* c-commands constituent negation but is c-commanded by sentential negation, whether it QRs to vP as in (13) or it QRs to TP.

The LF structure (13) illustrates the three-way scope contrasts trivially. In S negation like (8a), *ani* is constituent and thus c-commanded by *computer-only*, which explains the wide scope of an SBI. In L negation with *nun* like (8c), *ani* is sentential and it c-commands *computer-only*, which explains the wide scope of negation. In regular L negation like (8b) *ani* could be constituent and sentential, and hence it can be c-commanded by or c-command *computer-only*, which explains ambiguous scopes.

4. Mapping Semantic Negations to Configuration

The analysis of the scope contrasts in (8) crucially hinges on the assumptions that *ani* is fixed as constituent in S negation, as sentential in L negation with *nun*, and ambiguous in L negation. In this section I intend to justify those assumptions.

4.1. Sentential Negation of *ani* in L negation with *nun*

I will show that *ani* in L negation with *nun* is sentential by disproving that it is constituent. For this purpose, I will employ an NPI NP-*pakkey*, which must be licensed by negation like Japanese NP-*sika*.

(15) a. Mary-ka computer-*pakkey* **ani** sa-ssta
      M-nom computer-ONLY neg buy-past
      'Mary bought only a computer.'
    b. Mary-ka computer-*pakkey* sa **ci-ani** ha-ssta
    c. *Mary-ka computer-*pakkey* sa **ci-nun-ani** ha-ssta

An NP-*pakkey* is licensed in S negation and regular L negation as in (15a) and (15b), but not in L negation with *nun* as in (15c).

NP-*pakkey* is interpreted as NP-'only', canceling the meaning of negation. It is conjectured that the meaning NP-'only' obtains from semantic incorporation of NP-*pakkey* and negation. A sentence (proposition) forms a meaning (sense) by combining the meanings of its constituents. Hence for a sentence with NP-*pakkey* to have a meaning, it must contain a constituent negation so that NP-*pakkey* is meaningful. The incompatibility of *ani* and NP-*pakkey* in (15c) indicates that *ani* is not a constituent negation in L negation with *nun*.

For a second test, I use *because*-clause discussed in Linebarger (1987). *Because*-clause cannot be under the scope of negation if there is an NPI predicate such as *budge an inch* as shown in (16a).

(16) a. *He didn't <u>budge an inch</u> because he was pushed, (but because he fell).
      'It was not the case that he moved a little because he was pushed.'
    b. He didn't <u>move</u> because he was pushed, (but because he fell).

To negate subordinate *because*-clause *not* must be sentential in (16a) and (16b). The ungrammaticality of (16a) indicates that an NPI predicate *budge an inch* cannot be licensed by sentential negation. In other words, it requires a constituent negation. We can find a similar Korean NPI, *kkomcakto hata.*[3]

(17) a. *John-i,   mil-ye-se,   <u>kkomcakto ha</u> **ci-ani** ha-ssta.
        J-nom, push-be-because, budge   neg do-past
     b. John-i,   mil-ye-se,   <u>umciki</u> **ci-ani** ha-ssta.
        J-nom, push-be-because, move   neg do-past
        'John did not move because he was pushed.'

Since Korean sentences show the same contrast as (16), we can claim that an NPI *kkomcakto ha* must be licensed by a constituent negation. This NPI, however, is not compatible with *ani* in L negation with *nun* as shown in (18c).

(18) a. John-i *kkomcak-to* **ani** *ha*-ssta.
        'John did not move a bit.'
     b. John-i *kkomcak-to ha* **ci-ani** ha-ssta.
     c. *John-i *kkomcak-to ha* **ci-<u>nun</u>-ani** ha-ssta

We have seen two cases which show that *ani* in L negation with *nun* is not compatible with an NPI which requires a constituent negation. If *ani* is not constituent, it is sentential negation.

4.2. Constituent Negation of *ani* in S negation

I will show that *ani* in S negation is constituent by disproving that it is sentential. Let me exploit *because*-clause again. We saw that to negate *because*-clause, negation in the main clause must be sentential. *Ani* in S negation, however, does not seem to negate it as in (19a).

(19) a. #John-i, mil-ye-se,   **ani** umciki-ssta.
        J-nom, push-be-because, neg move-past
        'It was not the case that John moved because he was pushed.'
     b. John-i, mil-ye-se,   umciki **ci-ani** ha-ssta.
        J-nom, push-be-because, move   neg   do-past

(19b) is acceptable only when *ani* is sentential and negates *because*-clause. If *ani* is constituent, (19b) would be interpreted as 'because John was pushed, he stayed still', which does not sound sensible. The sentence (19a) is interpreted in the same way as is (19b) with the odd interpretation. It indicates that *ani* in S negation is not sentential.

Another test for constituent negation of *ani* in S negation is compatibility with an NPI adverb *celtaelo*, which must occur with *ani* as shown in (20).

---

[3] An NPI predicate *kkomcak ha* without *to* can be licensed by *if*-clause as in (i).

(i) <u>Kkomcak ha</u>-myeon, sson-ta.
    Budge an inch-if   shoot-will
    'I will shoot you, if you budge an inch.'

(20) *Mary-ka *celtaelo* computer-lul sa-ssta.
    M-nom absolutely computer-acc buy-past
    'Mary absolutely bought a computer.'

It is also pointed out that *celtaelo* is an adverb modifying a sentence which has
sentential negation in Song (1973) and Cheng and Park (1997).

(21) a. Mary-ka, apa-seo, hakkyo-ey ka ci-ani ha-ssta.
    M-nom, sick-because, school-to go neg do-past
    'Because Mary was sick, she didn't go to the school.'
    b. #Mary-ka *celtaelo*, apa-seo, hakkyo-ey ka ci-an ha-ssta.

For the sentence (21a) to be sensible, *ani* must be constituent not sentential. This
sentence is not compatible with *celtaelo* as in (21b). It indicates that the adverb
celtaelo requires a sentential negation.

We can see that the adverb *celtaelo* is not compatible with S negation as easily as with L negation as in (22).

(22) a. ?*Mary-ka *celtaelo* computer-lul **ani** sa-ssta.
    M-nom absolutely computer-acc neg buy-past
    'Absolutely, Mary did not buy a computer.'
    b. Mary-ka *celtaelo* computer-lul sa **ci-ani** ha-ssta.
    c. Mary-ka *celtaelo* computer-lul sa **ci-nun-ani-ha-ssta.**

In an assertive sentence with past tense, an S negation is marginal with *celtaelo*.[4]
Then *ani* in S negation does not function as a sentential negation required by
celtaelo. Hence it is a constituent negation.[5]

---

[4] In fact, an NPI adverb *celtaelo* is not a clear test for our purpose. If a sentence with S negation is
imperfect with present or future tense, the sentence sounds fine with *celtaelo*.
(i) Mary-nun *celtaelo* computer-lul **ani** sa.   (Y.J. Nam p.c.)
    M-top absolutely computer-acc neg-buy-pres-dec
    'I bet Mary will never buy a computer.'

[5] Cheng and Park (1997) argues that *ani* in S negation is sentential, showing that *ani* takes scope over
conjoined subject as *ani* in L negation.
(i) a. *John-kwa Mary*-ka **ani** wa-ssta.   (John-man wa-ssta.)
    J-and M-nom   neg come-past   J-only   come-past
    'It is not the case that John and Mary came. (Only John came.)'
    b. *John-kwa Mary*-ka wo **ci-ani** ha-ssta.   John-man wa-ssta.
(ii) a. John-kwa Mary *tulta* **ani** wa-ssta.   (#John-man wa-ssta.)
    J-and-M-nom   both neg come-past J-only   come-past
    'It is not the case that John and Mary came. Only John came.'
    b. John-kwa Mary *tulta* wo **ci-ani** ha-ssta.   (John-man wa-ssta.)
If we insert *tulta* 'both' after the subject as in (ii), however, contrast emerges and *ani* in S negation is
lower than the subject. Though the examples (i) involving conjoined NP challenges the claim that *ani*
in S negation is constituent, it cannot be a counter example to the claim because of the contrast in (ii).

5. Consequence
5.1. Another Contrast between S and L negation

I hypothesized that constituent and sentential negations originate in different positions to account for the scope contrast in (2/8). There is another type of contrast, which must rely on this hypothesis to be accounted for. In sentences in (4), repeated in (23), a certain linear order between an NPI *amu-to* and an SBI NP-*man* 'only' is prohibited.

(23) a. **Amu-to* computer-<u>man</u> **ani** sa-ssta.
　　　 No one　computer-only neg buy-past
　　　 'No one bought only a computer.'
　　 b. *Amu-to* computer-<u>man</u> sa **ci-ani** ha-ssta.

When an NPI *amu-to* precedes NP-*man*, the sentence is grammatical in L negation as in (23b), but ungrammatical in S negation as in (23a). This contrast cannot be explained if we assume the single position of *ani* in S and L negations, because two sentences have the same LF structure, no matter whhat kind of LF movement we adopt.

Given the hypothesis of two different positions of *ani*, we can distinguish the configurations of (23a) and (23b). I have claimed that *ani* in S negation originates VP-adjoined, while it originates VP-adjoined or vP-adjoined in L negation. At LF, vP-adjoined *ani* moves to the highest TP, while VP-adjoined *ani* stays in situ. Hence LF structures of (23a) and (23b) would be represented as in (24a), and (24a) or (24b), respectively.

(24) a. $[_{TP}$ **amu-to**$_i$ $[_{TP}$ t$_i$ $[_{vP}$ computer-<u>only</u>$_j$ $[_{vP}$ t$_i$ $[_{VP}$ **ani** $[_{VP}$ t$_j$ buy]]]]]]
　　 b.$[_{TP}$ **ani**$_k$ $[_{TP}$ **amu-to**$_i$ $[_{TP}$ t$_i$ $[_{vP}$ computer-<u>only</u>$_j$ $[_{vP}$ t$_k$ $[_{vP}$ t$_i$ $[_{VP}$ t$_j$ buy]]]]]]]

Let me assume (23a) is not grammatical because (24a) is an illegitimate structure. An attempt to account for the illegitimate (24a) is that *amu-to* is not c commanded by *ani* at LF. This accoun is, however, immediately disproved by (25).

(25) a. *Amu-to* computer-lul **ani** sa-ssta.
　　　 No one　computer-acc neg buy-past
　　　 'No one bought a computer.'
　　 b. Computer-<u>man</u> *amu-to* t **ani** sa-ssta.

A grammatical sentence (25a) is same as (23a) in configuration, with *amu-to* not c-commanded by *ani*. The difference between (23a) and (25a) is elimination of an SBI, NP-*man*. If the SBI scrambles before *amu-to* as in (25b), the two items become compatible in S negation. It is inferred that (23a) is ungrammatical because of NP-*man* intervening between *amu-to* and *ani* at LF. This inference is confirmed by the acceptable structure (24b) of (23b), in which *ani* and *amu-to* is not interrupted by NP-*man*.

The hypothesis of two positions for Korean negation provides a clue to the contrast between (23a) and (23b). They have different configurations at LF as in (24a) and (24b). Remember that L negation (23b) can be ambiguously represented as in (24a) and (24b) because *ani* can be either VP or vP-adjoined. If (23a) is ungrammatical because (24a) is illegitimate, (23b) should not allow an interpretation with constituent negation. The judgment, however, is intuitively not clear, since native speakers of Korean tend to incorporate *amu-to* with negation in the interpretation. Hence we need to establish a way to interpret *amu-to* and negation analytically.

It is common practice to interpret *amu-to* and negation as incorporated into 'no one' and represent them as '¬∃' as we interpret NP-*pakkey* as NP-'only' incorporated with negation. *Amu-to*, however, behaves differently from NP-*pakkey* when it cooccurs with another NPI.

(26) a. ***Amu-to*** <u>kkomcak-to ha</u> **ci-ani** ha-ssta
       no one   budge   neg do-past
       'No one budged an inch.'

   b. *Mary-***pakkey*** <u>kkomcak-to ha</u> **ci-ani** ha-ssta
       M-ONLY   budge   neg do-past
       'Only Mary budged an inch.'
       'Only Mary didn't budge an inch.'

While NP-*pakkey* cannot cooccur with *kkomcak-to ha*, *amu-to* can. Although *amu-to* and NP-*pakkey* are classified as strong NPIs as in Nam (1994) in the sense that both can be licensed only by negation, the contrast shown in (26) requires them to be distinguished. While NP-*pakkey* is incorporated with negation, I suggest that *amu-to* should be interpreted in the same way as is *anyone* in English. *Anyone* is interpreted as '∃x' (an NPI) if it is c-commanded by its licensor as in (27a) and as '∀x' (a free choice) if it is outside the c-command domain of its licensor as in (27b).

(27) a. Mary did **not** insult <u>anyone</u>.
   a'. ¬∃x [Mary insult x]
       'There is no x such that Mary insulted x.'
   b. <u>Anyone</u> **can** fool Jack.
   b'. ∀x POSSIBLE [x fool Jack]
       'For every x, it is possible for x to fool Jack.'

Along this line I will interpret *amu-to* as '∃x' or '∀x' depending on c-command relation with its licensor *ani* at LF. Since the licensor of *amu-to* is only negation, the interpretations '¬∃x' and '∀x¬' are equivalent in truth condition. With this two ways of interpretations, (26a) would be represented as in (28a) and (28b).

(28) a. ∀x [person(x) ∧ ¬[x budged an inch]]
   b. *¬ [∃x [person(x) ∧ [x budged an inch]]

If *ani* in (26a) is constituent negation, it is represented as in (28a). If *ani* is sentential, (28b) represents the sentence. The latter interpretation, however, is not acceptable because sentential negation cannot license an NPI predicate *kkomcak-to ha* as we saw in section 4.1.

With analytic interpretations of *amu-to*, let us go back to the sentence (23b).

(29) a. *∀x > only computer > ¬
   b. ¬ > ∃x > only computer

(29a) represents (23b) with constituent negation, whose interpretation should be disallowed we saw in (23a), and (29b) represents (23b) with sentential negation.

(30) ***Amu-to*** computer-<u>man</u> sa **ci-ani** ha-ssta.
　　No one computer-only buy neg do-past
　　a. *'For everyone, it was only a computer that he did not buy.'
　　b. 'It was not the case that there was someone who bought only a computer.'

Between two interpretations of (23b), repeated in (30), only (30b) with sentential *ani* is acceptable. The other interpretation with constituent *ani* is not available. Now we can confirm that an LF structure is illegitimate where an SBI NP-*man* intervenes between *amu-to* and constituent negation *ani* at LF.

We can also observe the same effect in the reversed linear order as in (31).

(31) a. Mary-<u>man</u> ***amuket-to*** **ani** sa-ssta.
　　　M-only　　nothing　　neg buy-past
　　　'It was only Mary such that for everything, she did not buy it.'
　　b. Mary-<u>man</u> ***amuket-to*** sa **ci-ani** ha-ssta.
　　　i) 'It was only Mary such that for everything, she did not buy it.'
　　*ii) 'It was not the case that it was only Mary who did not buy something.'

In (31) an SBI originates in the subject position and an NPI *amuket-to* in the object position. In this order, we obtain interpretations opposite to (23): S negation is grammatical, and L negation is interpretable only with sentential negation. The LF structures of the two sentences would be represented as in (32a) and (32b).

(32) a. [$_{TP}$ only Mary [$_{TP}$ [$_{vP}$ $\forall$x [$_{vP}$ [$_{VP}$ ***ani*** [$_{VP}$]]]]]
　　b. *[$_{TP}$ ***ani*** [$_{TP}$ only Mary [$_{TP}$ [$_{vP}$$\exists$x [$_{vP}$]]]]

The subject SBI adjoins to TP and the object *amuket-to* adjoins to vP. In (32a) negation adjoins to VP, while in (32b) it adjoins to the highest TP. Since an SBI does not intervene between *amuket-to* and negation in (32a), S negation is grammatical and L negation is only interpreted as having a constituent negation. Since negation and *amuket-to* is separated by an SBI in (32b), sentential negation does not obtain from L negation.

In this section we have witnessed two related phenomena: *amu-to* cannot precede an SBI in S negation; scope ambiguity between negation and an SBI in L negation disappears if *amu(ket)-to* is added. The hypothesis of two negation positions captures the two phenomena uniformly such that an SBI cannot intervene between *amu(ket)-to* and *ani* at LF.

5.2. Intervention Effect

Beck and Kim (1997) point out an intervention effect occurring in wh-questions.

(33) a. *Nuku*-ka　　amuket-to sa ci-ani ha-ss-ni?
　　　Person-nom nothing　buy neg do-past-Q
　　　'Who did not buy anything?'
　　b. ***Amu-to** *mues*-ul sa　ci-ani ha-ss-ni?
　　　No one　thing-acc buy neg　do-past-Q

'What didn't anyone buy?'

(34) a. *Nuku*-ka   computer-**man** sa-ss-ni?
    Person-nom computer-only buy-past-Q
    'Who bought only a computer?'
  b. *Mary-**man** *mues*-ul sa-ss-ni?
    M-only   thing-acc buy-past-Q
    'What did only Mary buy?'

In (33) and (34) we can see that *amuket-to* or NP-*man* 'only' cannot precede a wh-phrase. Beck and Kim (1997) describe this phenomenon in terms of a barrier named Quantified Induced Barrier (QUIB), which defines that an SBI (quantifier) functions as a barrier to binding between a wh-phrase and its LF trace.

If the analysis of two positions of negation is on the right track, the intervention effect in the negation is a phenomenon exactly on a par with the intervention effect in wh-questions except the involvement of LF movement. Can we reduce the intervention effect in negation to Beck and Kim's (1997) QUIB? We might consider LF movement of *amu(ket)-to* to negation (with elaboration on the structure of NegP). Then an SBI intervening between *amu(ket)-to* and *ani* becomes a barrier between *amu(ket)-to* and its trace. A problem with this option is that *amu(ket)-to* c-commands *ani* when it is interpreted as '∀x' and it cannot move to negation, unless we allow lowering.

It still seems to be possible, however, to unify the two intervention effects if we adopt an alternative analysis of in-situ wh-questions. Aoun and Li (1993), Kim (2000) among others, analyze wh-questions as involving wh-operator in CP and in-situ wh-phrases as variables. Under this approach, wh-phrases do not move at LF, but they need to be associated with wh-quantifier for proper interpretation. Then the sentences (33-34a) and (33-34b) would be represented as in (35a) and (35b), respectively.

(35) a. [$_{CP}$ **WH-OP** [$_{TP}$ **wh**-phrase [$_{vP}$ *amuket-to*/NP-*only* [$_{vP}$]]]]
  b. *[$_{CP}$ **WH-OP** [$_{TP}$ *amuket-to*/NP-*only* [$_{TP}$ [$_{vP}$ **wh**-phrase]]]]

In (35a) an SBI does not intervene between wh-operator and wh-phrase, while in (35b) it does and this structure is not acceptable. If we can draw a common property from the relation of *amu(ket)-to* and *ani* and that of wh-operator and wh-phrase, we can unify the two intervention effects.

Under the binding approach to in-situ wh-questions, a wh-phrase does not have an inherent interrogative interpretation. To be interrogative it has to be bound by wh-operator. Thus it is heavily dependent on wh-operator. Likewise, *amu(ket)-to* is dependent on negation to be properly interpreted. There seems to be a constraint on two semantically related items as in (36).

(36) Anti-Intervention
    An SBI cannot intervene between an item α and an item β on which α semantically depends.

The constraint (36), however, is no better than Beck and Kim's (1997) QUIB. Both QUIB and (36) point out a problem to be solved. Though this paper cannot suggest a solution to that problem, it shows that the intervention effect is a general phenomenon not restricted just to wh-questions.

6. Summary

I suggested a hypothesis that Korean negation marker *ani* originates either vP-adjoined or VP-adjoined and that *ani* generated in different positions represent different semantic negations. I have shown that this hypothesis cannot only explain three-way scope contrast as in (2/8), but also accounts for the contrast of *amu(ket)-to* as in (4/23) in S and L negations. The proposal of two negation positions reduces the contrast in (4/23) to Beck and Kim's (1997) intervention effect.

(Selected) References

Beck, Sigrid and Shin-sook Kim. 1997. On Wh- and Operator Scope in Korean. *Journal of East Asian Linguistics* vol. 6. 339-384.

Cheng, Daeho and Hong-keun Park. 1997. NPIs Outside of Negation Scope. *Japanese/Korean Linguistics* vol. 6. 415-435.

Chomsky, Noam. 2000a. Derivation by Phase. *Researching and Verifying an Advanced Theory of Human Language*. ed. K. Inoue, 1-45. Kanda University of International Studies.

Chomsky, Noam. 2000b. Minimalist Inquiries: the Framework. *Step by Step: Essays on Minimalist Syntax in Honor of Howard Lasnik*. eds. R. Martin, D. Michaels and J. Uriagereka, 89-155. The MIT Press.

Ernst, Thomas. 1992. The Phrase Structure of English Negation. *The Linguistic Review* vol. 9. 109-144.

Han, Ho and Myung-Kwan Park. 1994. The Syntax of Negation in Korean and Its Development in Child Language. *ESCOL '94* 152-162.

Kim, Ae-ryung. 2000. *A Derivational Quantification of "WH-Phrases"*. Ph. D. Diss. Indiana University

Linebarger, Marcia C. 1987. Negative Polarity and Grammatical Representation. *Linguistics and Philosophy* vol. 10. 325-387.

Nam, Seungho. 1994. Another Type of Negative Polarity Item. *Dynamics, Polarity and Quantification*. Eds. M. Kanazawa, and C. J. Pinon. CSLI.

Park, Myung-Kwan. 1998. Negation and the Placement of Verb in Korean. *LanguageResearch*. Vol. 34. 709-736.

Sohn, Kewn-won. 1996. Negative Polarity Items and Rigidity of Scope. *Japanese/Korean Linguistics* vol.5. 353-368.

Song, Seok Choong. 1973. Some Negative Remarks on Negation in Korean. *Language Research* vol. 9. 252-263.

Suh, Jinhee. 1989. Scope Interaction in Negation. *Havard Studies in Korean Linguistics III*. 527-536.

Tanaka, Hidekazu. 1997. Invisible Movement in *Sika-Nai* and the Linear Crossing Constraint. *Journal of East Asian Linguistics* vol. 6. 143-188.

Yi, Eun-Young. 1994. NegP in Korean. *Cornell Working Papers in Linguistics* 12. 193-208.

Opacity in Japanese and Korean*

AE-RYUNG KIM & YOSHIHISA KITAGAWA

Kanda University of International Studies, and Indiana University & Yokohama National University

1. Introduction

Rizzi 1990: 7, 26 made the celebrated claim that certain types of intervention effects arise because government is subject to **relativized minimality**, which can be characterized by three major properties. First, government must be **minimal** (or local) in that no other governor may intervene between the intended governor and governee. Second, 'intervention' is **relativized** in that it takes place only with respect to the **same type of government** — between two instances of: (i) head-government, (ii) antecedent government for A'-chains, (iii) antecedent government for A-chains, and (iv) antecedent government for X^0-chains, respectively. Finally, 'intervention' is **GT-compatible** in that minimality can be established by mere presence of a **potential** rather than actual governor. That is, whether an element is an 'intervening governor' or not is determined simply in terms of its configurational property irrespective of its content. To qualify as an intervening potential **head**-governor, for instance, there is no need for an element to have any of the substantive contents like 'nominal, verbal,

* Thanks to Daisuke Bekki, Greg Carlson, Leslie Gabriele, John Paolillo and Steven Franks for their comments and judgments. This work was partially supported by Postdoctoral Fellowship from Japan Society for the Promotion of Science and Indiana University COAS Faculty Research Grant.

agreement or tense' features. Likewise, to qualify as an intervening potential **antecedent** governor, there is no need for an element to have **actual coindexation** — all that is required is mere presence of **any** c-commanding **head** or **specifier** of a relevant type.

As the Minimalist Program evolved out of the Government and Binding Theory, researchers ceased to analyze syntactic relations in terms of government, and accordingly, relativized minimality has come to be rarely taken up in its original form. It seems reasonable to state, however, that the essence of relativized minimality captured in terms of the three properties described above is still widely regarded as a useful and possibly correct generalization. In this paper, we would like to present various 'intervention effects' which are similar to but are crucially different from those captured by relativized minimality in that they seem to require a condition distinct from GT-compatibility. In particular, 'intervention' they involve seems to be defined in terms of the notion of an **actual** rather than potential 'antecedent' or 'licenser'.

2. Problems

2.1 Kim 2000 on K-binding in Korean

Kim 2000 proposed and argued for a novel approach to the interpretation of what are often referred to as wh-words in Korean. Let us first summarize the research presented there, out of which our main topic emerged. As shown in (1), nominals like *nuku* and *mues* provide a constant interpretation as a quantifier when they are accompanied by a particle. *Nuku*, for examples, is interpreted as existentially quantified with *-inka* but is interpreted as universally quantified with *-ina*.

(1) a. nuku-**inka** / -**ina**   'some*one* / every*one*'
    b. mues-**inka** / -**ina**   'some*thing* / every*thing*'

When the same words appear in an interrogative sentence as in (2) without being accompanied by any such particle, however, they can be ambiguously interpreted either as wh-questioned or as existentially quantified.

(2) John-i   **mues**-ul   sass   -**ni**?   (i) **'What** did John buy?'
    -NOM   -ACC   bought   **Q**   (ii) 'Did John buy **something**?'

When more than one such nominal appears in sentences like (3) and (4) below, however, a puzzling restriction emerges — both nominals can be interpreted as wh-questioned or as existentially quantified in an across-the-board (henceforth ATB) fashion as indicated in (3 i) and (3 ii). Mixture of the two readings as in (3 iii) and (3 iv), however, is not permitted in either combination. ('#' indicates the unavailability of the intended interpretation.)

(3) [$_{CP2}$ John-i [$_{CP1}$ **nuku**-ka **mues**-ul sassta-ko]   malhaess-**ni**]?
    -NOM   PERSON   THING   bought-that   said   **Q**

(i) **Who** did John say had bought **what**?

(ii) Did John say **someone** had bought **something**?

(iii)#**Who** did John say had bought **something**?

(iv)#**What** did John say **someone** had bought?

(4) [$_{CP2}$ **Nuku-ka** [$_{CP1}$ Mary-ka computer-lul sassta-ko] **nuku**-eykey malhaess-**ni**]
    PERSON   -NOM computer-ACC bought-that PERSON-DAT said   Q

(i)   '**Who** told **whom** that Mary had bought a computer?'

(ii) 'Did **someone** tell **someone** that Mary had bought a computer?'

(iii) #'**Who** told **someone** that Mary had bought a computer?'

(iv) #'**Who** did **someone** tell that Mary had bought a computer?'

Given the flexibility of the interpretation of *mues* in (2), the restriction here is surprising. To deal with this and many more puzzling phenomena, Kim proposed an analysis centered around the notion 'K-binding'. First, this approach captures the flexible interpretation of nominals like *nuku* and *mues* by regarding them as some type of underspecified nominals denoting only basic semantic properties like 'human (= PERSON)' and 'non-human object (= THING)', reminiscent of Kuroda's 1965 'indeterminate pronouns' in Japanese. Such nominals are labelled as 'K-nominals', 'K' standing for 'kernel'. K-nominals, being underspecified, must enter an operator-variable relation to have their semantic content fully specified. Second, complementizers in Korean are regarded as quantifiers, which bind K-nominals and establish an operator-variable relation. This process is referred to as 'K-binding'. There are two types of complementizers in Korean. One type must bind a K-nominal. As the ungrammaticality of (5) indicates, it is mandatory for the wh-quantifier (**WH$_C$**) *-no* to bind a variable, once it appears in a sentence.

(5) *John-i   computer-lul   sass-**no**?
    -NOM   computer- ACC   bought-**WH$_C$**

K-nominals bound by **WH$_C$** function as its variables and are wh-questioned. All other complementizers in Korean (e.g. *ko*, *na* in the Kyungsang dialect) are assumed to belong to the second type and function as a default existential quantifier which can, but need not, bind K-nominals. K-nominals bound by these existential complementizers ($\exists_C$) come to be existentially quantified in a way similar to Heim's 1982 'Existential Closure'. The notion K-binding was also combined with the **derivational** approach to quantification developed along the lines of Epstein, et al. 1998, in which K-binding proceeds in a bottom-up fashion, **derivationally** and **unselectively** at each point when Merge introduces a complementizer, whether it is a wh-complementizer (**WH$_C$**) or an $\exists$-complementizer ($\exists_C$) (cf. Chomsky 2000). This approach allows us to predict all of the patterns of K-binding observed in (2)-(4) and more. In order to keep the dis-

---

[1] See also the notion 'phase' by Chomsky 2000b and Chomsky 2000a.

cussion simple, however, let us disregard here one source of ambiguity of K-nominals by employing the wh-complementizer *-no* in the Kyungsang dialect as in (6) instead of the ambiguous complementizer *-ni* in the standard Korean.

(6) [$_{CP2}$ **Nuku**-ka [$_{CP1}$ John-i **mues**-ul sassta-**ko**] Mary-eykey malhaess-**no**]?
    　　PERSON　　　　THING　　　$\exists_c$　　　-DAT　said　**WH$_c$**
    (i)　'**Who** told Mary **what** John bought?'
    (ii) #'Did **someone** tell Mary that John had bought **something**?'
    (iii) '**Who** told Mary that John had bought **something**?
    (iv) #'Did **someone** tell Mary **what** John had bought? '

Suppose in (6), the $\exists$-quantifier in the lower CP, binds *mues* and yields the existential reading 'something'. When the derivation proceeds to the matrix CP, the matrix **WH$_c$** *-no* must bind the other K-nominal *nuku* and yield a wh-interpretation 'who'. The mixed reading in (6 iii) therefore is expected to be available. When $\exists_c$ in the lower CP does not apply, on the other hand, — recall that the default quantification by $\exists_c$ is optional — both of the K-nominals must be bound by **WH$_c$** in the matrix, and the ATB wh-interpretation in (6 i) is also expected. Since *nuku* is yet to be introduced when $\exists$-quantification may take place in the lower CP, it can never be interpreted as 'someone', and neither of the interpretations in (6 ii) and (6 iv) is available.

2.2 'Recycling' Problems

When we continue to deal with the interpretation of K-nominals in this fashion, however, one set of facts remains unexplained. In sentence (7) below, for instance, we correctly predict that the two K-nominals can obtain the ATB wh-interpretation in (7 i) but not the ATB existential interpretation in (7 ii). If $\exists$-quantification does not apply in the lower CP, both K-nominals must be bound by the matrix wh-complementizer, yielding (7 i). If $\exists$-quantification does apply in the lower CP and bind both K-nominals, on the other hand, the matrix wh-complementizer would not be able to bind a variable, which makes the derivation crash and makes (7 ii) unavailable.

(7) [$_{CP2}$ John-i [$_{CP1}$ **nuku**-ka **mues**-ul sassta-**ko**] malhaess-**no**]
    　　　　　　PERSON　THING　bought-$\exists_c$　said　**WH$_c$**
    (i) **ATB**-reading:　'**Who** did John say bought **what**?'　　　(Expected)
    (ii) **ATB**-reading : #'John said that **someone** bought **something**.'(Expected)
    (iii) **Mixed** reading:#'**Who** did John say bought **something**?'　(Unexpected)
    (iv) **Mixed** reading:#'**What** did John say **someone** bought?'　(Unexpected)

In another possible derivation, however, $\exists$-quantification may apply in the lower CP and bind only one of the K-nominals. Therefore, when the derivation reaches the matrix CP, the wh-complementizer should be capable of binding the other K-nominal, thereby yielding either of the mixed readings in (7 iii) and (7 iv). These interpretations, however, are not allowed in reality.[2] The restrictions here can be schematically described as in (8), which poses an interesting problem.

(8)

a. $[_{CP2} \ldots [_{CP1} \mathbf{K} \ldots \mathbf{K} \, \exists_C] \ldots \mathbf{WH}_C]$ b. $[_{CP2} \ldots [_{CP1} \mathbf{K} \ldots \mathbf{K} \, \exists_C] \ldots \mathbf{WH}_C]$

Here, non-local K-binding is prohibited which involves only one of the two K-nominals in the lower CP and the wh-complementizer in the matrix CP. It does not seem appropriate to reduce this restriction to relativized minimality since the ∃-complementizer *ko* as a potential binder of K-nominals does intervene and still permits non-local K-binding, as can be verified by the ATB wh-interpretation in (7 i). Possibility of this non-local wh-quantification also suggests that it is not a matter of cyclicity alone. Kim 2000 stipulated a condition as in (9), which prohibits CP_1 in (8a-b) as the lower cycle from being used more than once as the domain of quantification.

(9) A domain of quantification cannot be 'recycled'.

We now believe, however, that the crucial factor creating the restriction here is the presence of another instance of K-binding in the lower CP, and it intervenes the other instance of K-binding, which leads us to offer a generalization as in (10).

(10) When one instance of K-binding takes place in its domain, that domain becomes **opaque** for other instances of K-binding from outside.

CP_1 in (8a-b) thus becomes an opaque domain for the non-local wh-quantification due to the presence of the local ∃-quantification. When the local ∃-quantification does not take place, on the other hand, CP_1 is not an opaque domain for the non-local wh-quantification, and the ATB wh-interpretation like (7 i) is permitted.

Interestingly, if long-distance scrambling applies to one of the K-nominals in (7) as in (11), it alters the possible range of available interpretations in a peculiar way.

(11) $[_{CP2}$ **mues**-ul$_1$ John-i $[_{CP1}$ **nuku**-ka t_1 sassta-**ko**] malhaess-**no**]
     THING   PERSON | $\exists_C$ $\mathbf{WH}_C$

(i) **ATB**-reading: 'Who did John say bought **what**?'
(ii) **Mixed** reading : '**What** did John say **someone** bought?'
(iii)**Mixed** reading: #'**Who** did John say bought **something**?'

That is, along with the ATB wh-interpretation in (11 i), we can now obtain one mixed interpretation in (11 ii) while the other mixed interpretation in (11 iii) still remains

---

[2] The same observation has been also made with respect to Chinese by Li 1992.

unavailable. This puzzling situation, in fact, is exactly what we predict given the restriction in (10). Although local $\exists$-quantification took place in the lower CP in (11), scrambling has brought *mues* outside the opaque domain, it therefore may now undergo wh-quantification in the matrix CP without causing the opacity effect and interpreted as 'what'. The other mixed reading in (11iii), on the other hand, is not permitted because when *mues* 'THING' is existentially quantified in the subordinate clause, CP_1 becomes an opaque domain and *nuku* 'PERSON' cannot be non-locally wh-quantified to be interpreted as 'who'.

2.3 Reflexive Binding in Japanese

The question to be asked at this point is if the condition like (10) is peculiar to K-binding in Korean or if it is something of a more general nature. A quest for the answer to this question led us to pay attention to the observation made by Howard and Niyekawa-Howard 1976 with respect to the interpretation of a reflexive pro-form *zibun* in Japanese. To begin with, it has been often noted, with a sentence like (12), that *zibun* can take either local or non-local antecedent.

(12) **Taroo**$_1$-wa [Ziroo$_2$-ga **zibun**$_{1/2}$-ni toohyoo-suru to] omoikondeiru (rasii)
     -TOP   -NOM   self-DAT   vote   that believe   (seem)
     '(It seems that) Taro believes that Jiro would vote for himself / him.'

Howard and Niyekawa-Howard (henceforth HNH) 1976: 229-230 report, however, that such flexibility is eliminated in a very peculiar way in some contexts.

(13) karera$_x$-wa/ga [watasi-tati$_y$-ga **zibun**-no syasin-o   **zibun**-no heya-ni
     they$_x$-TOP/NOM   we$_y$-NOM   **self**'s   photo-ACC **self**'s   room-in
     kazaroo-to-siteiru   koto]-o   imadani   siranai
     plan.to.display   fact-ACC   yet   don't.know
     'They don't know yet that we are planning to display **each of our/their** portraits in **each of our/their** rooms.'
     (i) **ATB**-binding: karera$_x$ ... watasi-tati$_y$ ... zibun$_y$ ... zibun$_y$
     (ii) **ATB**-binding: karera$_x$ ... watasi-tati$_y$ ... zibun$_x$ ... zibun$_x$
     (iii)**Mixed**-binding: #karera$_x$ ... watasi-tati$_y$ ... zibun$_x$ ... zibun$_y$
     (iv) **Mixed**-binding: #karera$_x$ ... watasi-tati$_y$ ... zibun$_y$ ... zibun$_x$

The two instances of *zibun* in (13) can take either the subordinate subject or the matrix subject in an ATB-fashion, as indicated in (13 i-ii). On the contrary, neither of the mixed antecedents is possible (as in (13 iii) and (13 iv)).[3] HNH offer the generalization in (14), which they label as the Reflexive Coreference Constraint (RCC).

---

[3] Unless we add some narrow focus accompanied by an emphatic stress. We will deal with such phenomena in an extended version of the present work we are preparing.

(14) Multiple instances of the reflexive pronoun within a given domain must share the same antecedent. (Howard and Niyekawa-Howard 1976: 231)

In (13), unlike in HNH's example, we used plural antecedents in order to ensure that a formal process of binding is involved. Accordingly, we pay attention only to the distributive interpretations arising from such a formal process, and endorse RCC only as a valid generalization on the formal binding of *zibun*. We can obtain the same observations concerning *caki* in Korean (cf. Kim 2000), and the same warning applies.

There does not exist any problem in the mixed binding of multiple *zibun* per se, as illustrated by the availability of a distributed interpretation in (15 iv).

(15) **watasi-tati$_x$**-wa [masaka   **karera$_y$**-ga **zibun$_{x/y}$**-ni toohyoo-suru
     we$_x$-TOP   improbably **they$_y$**-NOM **self$_{x/y}$**-DAT vote
     hazu-ga- nai to]   **zibun$_x$**-ni omoikomase-yootosita.
     wouldn't COMP] .self$_x$-DAT attempted.to.persuade
     'Each of us tried to make **ourselves** believe that they would never vote for
     themselves / each of **us**.'
     (i) **ATB**-binding: #watasi-tati$_x$ ... karera$_y$ ... zibun$_y$ ... zibun$_y$
     (ii) **ATB**-binding: watasi-tati$_x$ ... karera$_y$ ... zibun$_x$ ... zibun$_x$
     (iii)**Mixed**-binding: #watasi-tati$_x$ ... karera$_y$ ... zibun$_x$ ... zibun$_y$
     (iv) **Mixed**-binding: watasi-tati$_x$ ... karera$_y$ ... zibun$_y$ ... zibun$_x$

The RCC effect observed in (13) has many significant implications. First, possibility of non-local binding in (13 ii) indicates that similar non-local binding in (13 iii) and (13 iv) in principle is possible. Furthermore, it also suggests that the RCC effect **cannot** be reduced to relativized minimality since non-local binding in (13 ii) is taking place across the subordinate subject NP$_y$ as a potential antecedent of *zibun*. We can, on the other hand, capture the contrast between (13 ii) and (13 iii-iv) when we recognize the blocking effect of non-local reflexive binding arising from the presence of another instance of more local reflexive binding in (13 iii-iv), that is, due to the intervention of NP$_y$ as the **actual** rather than a potential antecedent. We can, in other words, reduce the RCC effect to the generalization in(10) above when we extend it from K-binding to reflexive binding.

Scrambling one instance of *zibun* out of the subordinate clause as in (16) below again permits one type of mixed interpretation ('each of **their** portraits in each of **our** rooms') but not the other ('each of **our** portraits in each of **their** rooms').

(16) **karera$_x$**-wa/ga   **zibun**-no-syasin$_1$-o [ano-ziten-de-wa   **watasi-tati$_y$**-ga t_1
     they$_x$-TOP/NOM **self**'s.portrait$_1$-ACC at.that.point   **we$_y$**-NOM |
                ↑_____|

     zibun-no heya-ni kazaroo-to-siteita koto]-o imadani siranai
     self's   room-in plan.to.display   fact-ACC yet   don't.know

'They don't know yet that we were planning to display each of **their** portraits in each of **our** rooms at that time.'

Let us also point out here that, even when we combine reflexive binding with negative polarity in the subordinate clause as in (17), we do not detect any negative island effect on non-local reflexive binding.

(17) **aitura**$_x$-wa-hutaritomo [daRE-*MO*^{y} **zibun**$_x$-nitoohyoo-si-*nai*^{y} to]
 those.brats$_x$-TOP-both *anyone*^{y} **self**$_x$-DATvote-*NEG*^{y} COMP]
 omoikondeiru (rasii)
 believe (seem)
 '(It seems that) each of those brats believes that nobody will vote for him.'

The long-distance binding of *zibun*, in other words, is insensitive to a barrier of the type argued for by Beck and Kim 1997. This observation therefore urges us to refrain from pursuing an analysis in which the intervention effect observed in (13) arises when *zibun* undergoes LF-movement and crosses over a barrier of some sort.

3. Proposals — Relativized Opacity

We now propose that the opacity effects observed in both K-binding and reflexive binding are captured in terms of the notion '**relativized opacity**' defined in (18).

(18) a. Opacity: One **actual** instance of head-licensing makes the licensing domain opaque.
 b. Domain: The maximal **projection** of the **licensing head** is the domain of licensing.
 c. Relativization: This opacity prohibits the **same type of licensing** from outside the domain.

First, K-binding involves quantification of K-nominals by a complementizer head. It therefore can be regarded, rather straightforwardly, as involving a type of licensing by a head item. As illustrated in (8) above, when an actual instance of such 'head-licensing' (by $\exists_C$) takes place, the maximal projection of this licensing head (CP_1) becomes an opaque domain, and other instances of the same type of licensing, i.e. K-binding by WH_C in CP_2, is prohibited out of this domain. This yields the intervention effect we have observed above. Reflexive binding can be also regarded as involving 'head-licensing', though it is somewhat more complex. As illustrated in (19) below, to begin with, the verb as licensing head establishes a selectional relation with its external argument (NP^i) located in its Spec position. The same licensing head then pairs its

Spec with the licens**ee** (*zibun*^{i}) and completes the licensing. The licensing here, in other words, is accomplished by the mediating role of the head verb.[4]

(19) Reflexive binding:

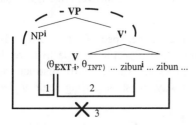

Finally, since an actual instance of head-licensing for reflexive binding (involving *zibun*^{i}) has taken place, the maximal projection of this licensing head (VP) becomes an opaque domain, and other instances of the same type of licensing, i.e. reflexive binding involving other instances of *zibun*, is prohibited out of this domain. Here, the Internal Subject Hypothesis has been adopted for VPs, which can be replaced by *v*Ps if one opts for such an analysis. We will examine the relativized nature of the opacity in question ((18c)) in Section 5 below.

4. Further Motivation

In this section, we will attempt to demonstrate the generality of relativized opacity by further extending our observations. In particular, we will identify two further cases of intervention effects, this time in English, and argue that they too can be reduced to relativized opacity.

4.1 Wh-pairing in English

Our first topic of interest is the interpretation of 'wh-in-situ'. First, a sentence with an embedding CP like (20) is known to permit the wh-in-situ *what* to be paired with the wh-phrase in the Spec of either matrix or subordinate CP (Baker 1970).

(20) [$_{CP}$ **Who** knows [$_{CP}$ **where** we bought **what**]]?

   (i) Ans: *John* knows **where** we bought **what** (for instance, *he* knows that we bought the **book** in **Amsterdam**, the **CD** in **Groningen**, etc.)

   (ii) Ans: *John* knows **where** we bought the *book* (for instance in Amsterdam), *Mary* knows **where** we bought the *CD* (for instance in Groningen), etc.

---

[4] A similar mediating role of the verbal head in binding is also implied in Reinhart and Reuland 1993's rendition of the conditions A and B of the binding theory. In the diagram (19), the linear order of constituents has been altered solely for ease of presentation.

When *what* is paired with *where*, the wh-phrase in the lower CP, it can be felicitously answered as in (20i). When *what* is paired with *who*, the wh-phrase in the higher CP, on the other hand, it will be felicitously answered as in (20ii) (Pesetsky 1987: 99). We will refer to the association of wh-phrases that induces answers like (20i) and (20ii) as '**Wh-pairing**'.

Now in (21) below, we have two wh-phrases in the Spec of CP, **who** and **when**, and two whs-in-situ, *what* and *whom*. We therefore expect to be able to have the pairing of whs (or more precisely, the forming of a set of whs) in **four** distinct ways. In reality, however, **two and only two** distinct ways of such pairing seem to be possible for (21).

> (21) [$_{CP}$ **Who** knows [$_{CP}$ **when** George received **what** from **whom**]]?
> (i) **ATB**-pairing (= both **what** and **whom** paired with **when**)
> Ans: *Al* knows **when** George received **what** from **whom** (for instance, *he* knows George received **money** from **a tobacco company** in **1998, a piece of real estate** from **the American Rifle Association** in **1999**, etc.)
> (ii) **ATB**-pairing (= both *what* and *whom* paired with *who*)
> Ans: *Al* knows **when** George received *money* from *a tobacco company*, and *Joe* knows **when** George received *a piece of real estate* from *the American Rifle Association*, etc.
> (iii) **Mixed** pairing (= *what* paired with *who*, and **whom** paired with **when**)
> Ans: #*Al* knows **when** George received *money* from **whom**, *Joe* knows **when** George received *a piece of real estate* from **whom**, etc.
> (iv) **Mixed** pairing (= *whom* paired with *who*, and **what** paired with **when**)
> Ans: #*Al* knows **when** George received **what** *from a tobacco company, Joe* knows **when** George received **what** from *the American Rifle Association*, etc.

In particular, the two whs-in-situ can be paired with either one of the wh-phrases in the Spec of CP in an across-the-board fashion. Each of the two whs-in-situ, on the other hand, cannot be paired with a distinct wh-phrase in the Spec of CP. Thus, both *what* and *whom* can be paired with *when* in the lower CP, and felicitously answered as in (21i). Similarly, *what* and *whom* can be paired with *who* in the higher CP, and felicitously answered as in (21ii). On the other hand, it seems impossible to interpret the sentence in (21), pairing *what* with *who* and *whom* with *when*, or pairing them in the other mixed fashion. Neither of answers in (21iii) and (21iv) therefore can be provided.

Note that the restriction here cannot be reduced to the superiority effect holding between two whs-in-situ since both instances of mixed pairing described in (21iii) and (21iv) are prohibited. The restriction does not seem to be due to relativized minimality, either, since long-distance pairing across a wh-phrase in the lower CP is possible as in (21 ii). Furthermore, possibility of long-distance pairing also suggests that the intervention effect observed in the mixed pairing is not caused by the wh-island constraint. This observation in fact invites us to speculate that the pair- (or set-) interpretation of whs-in-situ in general may not involve LF-movement but a type of binding by a complementizer head acting as an operator (cf. Baker's 1970 'Q-morpheme').[5]

We may consider, however, that otherwise puzzling restrictions on Wh-pairing observed in (21) arise due to relativized opacity. All we must do is to reinterpret Baker's 1970 'Q-morpheme' on the head complementizer by recognizing the mediating role it plays in wh-pairing. This mediating role is similar to that played by the verbal head in reflexive binding in (19) above. As illustrated in (22) below, the head COMP in the subordinate clause of (21) establishes a relation with a wh-phrase in its Spec (Wh_1^i), possibly via some kind of agreement process involving a [+WH] feature (or 'Q-morpheme') as often assumed. The same head COMP then pairs a wh-in-situ (Wh_2^i) with its Spec and completes the licensing.

(22) Wh-pairing:

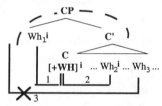

Since an actual instance of head-licensing for a wh-in-situ (involving Wh_2^i) has taken place, the maximal projection of this licensing head (CP) becomes an opaque domain, and the same type of licensing, i.e. Wh-pairing involving another wh-in-situ (Wh_3), is prohibited out of this domain.

4.2 *Differentiation* in English

We can observe still another case of an intervention effect in English with respect to the interpretations of a quantifier-like element *different*. First, as Carlson 1987 points out, sentences involving control as in (23) permit both transparent and opaque interpretations of *different* as indicated in (23 i) and (23 ii), respectively.

(23) **John and Mary** want [**PRO** to visit **different** places next Sunday].

    (i) Transparent : *different places* = the place desired by John and the place independently desired by Mary, which happened to have been distinct like a museum and a library.

    (ii) Opaque : *different places* = any place that is distinct from the other person's choice, whichever place that may be

Carlson further points out that the licensing of *different* for these distributive interpretations involve the implicit comparison between two or more elements appearing in

---

[5] Pesetsky 1987: 109 claims that whs-in-situ move at LF only if they are non-D(iscourse)-linked. We will not take this interesting factor into consideration in this work.

plural eventuality induced by the presence of a plural or distributive NP, which I will refer to as the process of 'Differentiation'. What this observation suggests, therefore, is that the transparent reading of *different* in (23a) is licensed non-locally by the plural eventuality induced by the matrix subject *John and Mary* and the opaque reading is licensed locally by the plural eventuality induced by the subordinate subject *PRO* controlled by the matrix subject. Before we proceed further, let us emphasize here that we are paying attention to the two distinct **distributive** interpretations licensed in these particular ways, and not to a locally-licensed transparent interpretation or any other collective interpretations, which can be detected even in a transitive sentence like 'John and Mary saw different movies'. Here, *different* could mean something like 'distinct from the previous choice', 'distinct from other people's choice', 'novel or unusual choice', and so on. With this background, observe now the sentence (24), which contains two instances of *different* in a similar control structure.

(24) John and Mary want [PRO to visit **different** places on **different** weekends].

    (i)   **ATB-transparent**: John wants to visit a museum this weekend, and Mary wants to visit a library next weekend.

    (ii)   **ATB-opaque**: John and Mary each wants to visit a place that is not the choice of the other on the weekend that is not the choice of the other.

    (iii)**#Mixed**: John wants to visit a museum, and Mary wants to visit a library, and they each wants to do that on the weekend that is not the choice of the other.

    (iv) **#Mixed**: John and Mary each wants to visit a place that is not the choice of the other, and John wants to do that this weekend and Mary wants to do that next weekend.

Since each instance of *different* is subject to the ambiguous interpretations we saw in (23), (24) is expected to exhibit, in principle, four distinct combinations of interpretations. It seems to be the case, however, that the sentence yields an across-the-board transparent reading as in (24i) or an across-the-board opaque reading as in (24ii), but neither of the mixed interpretations as in (24 iii-iv). As illustrated by (25) below, mixed readings of *different* per se are available in certain discourses with or without the appearance of two instances of *different*.

(25) [John and Mary are breaking up.] Mary wants to move out of their apartment this weekend, but John wants to move out of their apartment next weekend. They do, in other words, want to move out of their apartment on **different** weekends. And they certainly want to live in **different** cities thereafter.

This suggests that the restriction observed in (24) is not due to pragmatic factors. It seems natural, therefore, for us to regard the restriction here as arising from the syntactic interaction of the two instances of the licensing of *different*, i.e. as a type of intervention effect arising in *Differentiation*. Note, however, that an across-the-board transparent reading as in (24i) is possible, and it involves non-local licensing of *different* crossing over *PRO* as an potential licensor. This again suggests that the intervention effect here is not due to relativized minimality. We can, however, capture the intervention effect here as a case of relativized opacity when we assume that *Differentiation* is a licensing process in which a verb as the licensing head plays a mediating role of associating *different* with a plural NP located in its Spec position, in a way similar to reflexive binding — the actual instance of head-licensing involving the head (V), its Spec (plural NP) and the licensee (*different*) turns the maximal projection of this licensing head (VP) into an opaque domain, out of which another instance of *Differentiation* is prohibited. This licensing can be visually illustrated by simply replacing *zibun* in (19) above with *different*.

5. Relativization of Opacity

The relativized nature of the opacity effect in question ((18c)) can be confirmed when we observe that distinct types of head-licensing do not interact with each other. First, as illustrated in (26), the reflexive proform *zibun* in the lower clause can be bound by the matrix subject *John* despite the presence of wh-pairing for whs-in-situ in the lower clause.

(26) *John to Bill$_x$*-wa [$_{CP}$ Mary-ga **nani-o doko-de** *zibun$_x$*-no-tame-ni
  John.and.Bill$_x$-TOP   -NOM **what   where** *self$_x$*-for
  katta **ka**] sit-te-iru.
  bought **Q** know
  'John and Bill knows where Mary bought what for each of them.'

Likewise, in (27) below, the wh-in-situ in the lower clause and the wh-phrase in the higher CP can be paired even when reflexive binding takes place within the lower clause, permitting an answer like '**Bill** knows where *she* bought a **jewel** for *herself* (for instance in Hong Kong), **Al** knows where *she* bought a **dress** for *herself* (for instance in Paris), etc'.

(27) **Who** knows [$_{CP}$ **where** *Hillary$_1$* bought **what** for *herself$_1$*]?

The transparent interpretation of *different* induced by *Differentiation* involving the matrix verb in (28) is also possible even when reciprocal binding satisfies the condition A of the binding theory within the lower clause.

(28) *John and Mary* want [**PRO** to hire *different attorneys* for **each other**].

It should be noted here that the notion 'same type of licensing' in relativized opacity is defined in more strict terms than 'same type of government' in relativized minimality since we identified all cases of licensing taking place in (26)-(28) as head-licensing. Tentatively, we identify 'same type of licensing' as 'identical type of licensing' — reflexive binding for reflexive binding, wh-pairing for wh-pairing, and so forth.

References

Baker, C. L. 1970. Notes on the Description of English Questions: The Role of an Abstract Question Morpheme. *Foundations of Language*. 6: 197-219.

Beck, S. and S.-s. Kim. 1997. Oh WH- and Operator Scope in Korean. *Journal of East Asian Linguistics*. 6: 339-384.

Carlson, G. 1987. *Same* and *Different* : Some Consequences for Syntax and Semantics. *Linguistics and Philosophy*. 10:

Chomsky, N. 2000. Minimalist Inquiries: the Framework. *Step by Step: Essays on Minimalist Syntax in Honor of Howard Lasnik*, eds. R. Martin, David Michaels, and Juan Uriagereka, 89-155. Cambridge, Massachusetts: The MIT Press.

Epstein, S. D., et al. 1998. *A Derivational Approach to Syntactic Relations*. New York: Oxford University Press.

Heim, I. 1982. Semantics of Definite and Indefinite Noun Phrases. Doctoral dissertation, University of Massachusetts, Amherst.

Howard, I. and A. M. Niyekawa-Howard. 1976. Passivization. *Syntax and Semantics 5: Japanese Generative Grammar*, ed. M. Shibatani, 201-237. New York: Academic Press.

Kim, A.-R. 2000. A Derivational Quantification of "WH-Phrase". Doctoral dissertation, Indiana University.

Kuroda, S.-Y. 1965. Generative Grammatical Studies in the Japanese Language. Doctoral dissertation, Massachusetts Institute of Technology.

Li, Y.-H. Audrey. 1992. Indefinite Wh in Mandarin Chinese. *Journal of East Asian Linguistics*. 1: 125-156.

Pesetsky, D. 1987. Wh-in-Situ: Movement and Unselective Binding. *The Representation of (In)definiteness*, eds. Eric Reuland and Alice ter Meulen, 98-129. Cambridge: The MIT Press.

Reinhart, T. and E. Reuland. 1993. Reflexivity. *Linguistic Inquiry*. 24: 657-720.

Rizzi, L. 1990. *Relativized Minimality*. Cambridge, Massachusetts: The MIT Press.

Intervention Effects are Focus Effects*

SHIN-SOOK KIM
Universität Konstanz

1 Introduction

Beck (1996) and Beck & Kim (1997) discuss the interaction between *wh*-in-situ and negation and other quantifiers and propose the Minimal Quantified Structure Constraint (MQSC) which basically says that an intervening quantifier blocks LF movement of *wh*-in-situ (I will call this type of blocking effect an "Intervention Effect", following terminology of Hagstrom 1998 and Pesetsky 1999).

In this paper, I will show that the MQSC is too strong a constraint in the sense that not every quantifier seems to show the Intervention Effect in Korean. Analyzing negative polarity items in Korean as focus phrases, I argue that what produces an Intervention Effect is not negation or quantifiers in general, but rather focus phrases. Assuming with Reinhart (1998) that the

---

* For helpful comments and discussion, I would like to thank Josef Bayer, Miriam Butt, Lansun Chen, Regine Eckardt, Hanneke van Hoof, Manfred Kupffer, Aditi Lahiri, Gereon Müller, and the audience at the 10th Japanese/Korean Linguistics Conference. The work was supported by DFG grant to the SFB 471 "Variation und Entwicklung im Lexikon".

wh-in-situ is a function variable bound by the question existential operator (Q-operator), I propose that a focus phrase may not intervene between a Q-operator and the *wh*-in-situ bound by that Q-operator.

2   LF Intervention Effects

The generalization made by Beck (1996) and Beck & Kim (1997) is that an intervening quantifier blocks LF movement of *wh*-in-situ to an operator position.[1]

2.1   German

In German, sentences are ungrammatical when the *wh*-in-situ is c-commanded by a quantifier at surface structure.

(1) is a normal multiple *wh*-question in the unmarked order with the subject preceding the adjunct.[2]

(1)   Wen   hat Karl   wo   getroffen?
      whom has Karl   where met
      'Who did Karl meet where?'

However, sentences are ungrammatical when a quantifier c-commands the *wh*-in-situ. When the *wh*-in-situ is scrambled over the intervening quantifier, the sentences become grammatical. This contrast is illustrated in (2) – (4) (the quantifiers are marked in boldface, and *wh*-in-situ is underlined).[3]

---

[1] Beck's (1996) Intervention Effect applies not only to *wh*-in-situ, but also to the stranded restriction of the overtly moved *wh*-phrases and *wh*-scope marking constructions. In this paper, however, I will only concentrate on *wh*-in-situ cases.

[2] Unlike Korean, which optionally allows *wh*-scrambling, German does not allow *wh*-scrambling in normal contexts (see Fanselow 1990, Müller & Sternefeld 1993, among others). So, the example (i), which is minimally different from (1) in that the *wh*-in-situ *wo* 'where' is scrambled in front of the subject, is ungrammatical:

(i)   *Wen   hat   wo$_i$ Karl   t$_i$ getroffen?
       whom   has   where   Karl   met
       'Who did Karl meet where?'

It is interesting to note that there are some contexts in which German allows *wh*-scrambling. The intervention context is one of those, and the otherwise impossible *wh*-scrambling is allowed to repair the ungrammaticality. I would like to refer the reader to Heck & Müller (2000) for a promising optimality-theoretic analysis of the "repair-driven movements".

[3] Beck (1996) notes that the judgments for sentences like those in (2) – (4) are somewhat subtle: "The '??' means that the data are incomprehensible (uninterpretable) rather than

(2) a. ?? Wen   hat **niemand** <u>wo</u>   gesehen?
         whom   has nobody   where seen
     b.   Wen   hat <u>wo</u>   **niemand**   gesehen?
            whom   has where   nobody   seen
            'Who did nobody see where?'
(3) a. ?? Wen   hat **nur**   **Karl**   <u>wo</u>   getroffen?
         whom   has only   Karl   where   met
     b.   Wen   hat <u>wo</u>   **nur**   **Karl**   getroffen?
            whom   has where   only   Karl   met
            'Who did only Karl meet where?'
(4) a. ?? Wen   hat **fast**   **jeder**   <u>wo</u>   getroffen?
         whom   has almost   everyone   where met
     b.   Wen   hat <u>wo</u>   **fast**   **jeder**   getroffen?
            whom   has where   almost   everyone met
            'Who did almost everyone meet where?'

Based on this, Beck (1996) proposes the generalization that an intervening quantifier blocks LF *wh*-movement. So the following configuration is ruled out where t_i^{LF} stands for a trace created by LF-movement.

(6)   *[... X_i ... [Q ... [... t_i^{LF} ...]]]

This constraint on LF movement is formalized as follows:

(7) a. *Quantifier-Induced Barrier (QUIB)*:
         The first node that dominates a quantifier, its restriction, and
         its nuclear scope is a Quantifier-Induced Barrier.
     b. *Minimal Quantified Structure Constraint (MQSC)*:
         If an LF trace β is dominated by a QUIB α, then the binder of
         β must also be dominated by α.

To put it in plain words, LF movement of *wh*-in-situ may not cross a c-commanding quantifier.
     To show how the MQSC works, we take the cases (2a-b) and look at the LFs which are given in (8a-b). At LF, the *wh*-in-situ *wo* 'where' moves to the SpecC position and leaves an LF trace t_j^{LF}.

---

simply ungrammatical." The same effect is observed with the Korean data (which I marked with '?*') to be discussed in the next subsection.

(8) a. LF for (2a):

[$_{CP}$ wen$_i$ wo$_j$ [$_{C'}$ C [$_{IP}$ niemand t$_i$ t$_j^{LF}$ gesehen hat]]]
whom where   nobody   seen   has

    b. LF for (2b):

[$_{CP}$ wen$_i$ wo$_j$ [$_{C'}$ C [$_{IP}$ t$_j^{LF}$ [$_{IP}$ niemand t$_i$ t$_j$ gesehen hat]]]]
whom where   nobody   seen   has

The crucial difference between the LFs (8a) and (8b) lies in the positions of the trace left by the LF movement of the *wh*-in-situ (*wen* 'whom' is moved already at S-Structure in both cases, so its trace does not carry the superscript LF and is not subject to the MQSC). In (8a), the LF trace is located in a position c-commanded by the negative quantifier *niemand* 'nobody', and in (8b), it is outside the c-command domain of the quantifier. In (8a), the intervening negative quantifier *niemand* 'nobody' induces a QUIB, the IP. The LF trace t_j^{LF} of *wo$_j$* is dominated by this QUIB, but the binder of that trace is not. Thus (8a) violates the MQSC. On the other hand, in the grammatical LF (8b), there is no intervening quantifier between *wo$_j$* and its LF trace t_j^{LF}, thus there is no violation of the MQSC.

2.2 Korean

Discussing the scope of *wh*- and quantifier scope in Korean, Beck & Kim (1997) propose that Beck's (1996) generalization applies to Korean, too, which is a *wh*-in-situ language (see Hoji 1985 for a similar conclusion for Japanese and S.-W. Kim 1991 for Korean).

(9a) is a normal *wh*-question in the unmarked word order. In addition, Korean allows optional *wh*-scrambling as in (9b). Both options are grammatical.[4]

(9) a. Suna-ka   <u>muôs-ûl</u>   sa-ss-ni?
        Suna-Nom   what-Acc   buy-Past-Q
    b. <u>muôs-ûl</u>$_i$ Suna-ka t$_i$ sa-ss-ni?
        what-Acc   Suna-Nom   buy-Past-Q
        'What did Suna buy?'

When a negative polarity item (henceforth, NPI) *amuto* 'anyone' c-commands the *wh*-in-situ, however, the sentence is ungrammatical. When the *wh*-in-situ is scrambled to a position that is higher than the NPI, the sentence becomes grammatical, as shown in (10b).

---

[4] Throughout this paper, I use the McCune-Reischauer system of romanization to transcribe Korean examples, except that I will use the diacritic ˆ instead of ˇ.

(10)   a.   ?* **amuto** <u>muôs-ûl</u>   sa-chi   anh-ass-ni?
           anyone   what-Acc   buy-CHI   not do-Past-Q

       b.   <u>muôs-ûl</u>$_i$ **amuto**   t$_i$ sa-chi   anh-ass-ni?
           what-Acc   anyone   buy-CHI   not do-Past-Q
           'What did no one buy?'

Phrases with focus particles such as *man* 'only' or *to* 'also' also show the same effects, and we observe the same repair effect by scrambling.[5]

(11)   a.   ?* **Minsu-man**   <u>nuku-lûl</u>   manna-ss-ni?
           Minsu-only   who-Acc   meet-Past-Q

       b.   <u>nuku-lûl</u>$_i$ **Minsu-man**   t$_i$ manna-ss-ni?
           who-Acc   Minsu-only   meet-Past-Q
           'Who did only Minsu meet?'

(12)   a.   ?* **Minsu-to**   <u>nuku-lûl</u>   manna-ss-ni?
           Minsu-also   who-Acc   meet-Past-Q

       b.   <u>nuku-lûl</u>$_i$ **Minsu-to**   t$_i$ manna-ss-ni?
           who-Acc   Minsu-also   meet-Past-Q
           'Who did Minsu, too, meet?'

And finally, universal quantifiers such as *nukuna* 'everyone' seem to show a similar effect, although the effect is much weaker.[6]

(13)   a. ?(?) **nukuna-ka**   <u>ônû kyosu-lûl</u>   chonkyôngha-ni?
           everyone-Nom   which professor-Acc   respect-Q

       b.   <u>ônû kyosu-lûl</u>$_i$ **nukuna-ka** t$_i$ chonkyôngha-ni?
           which professor-Acc   everyone-Nom   respect-Q
           'Which professor does everyone respect?'

Based on this observation, Beck & Kim (1997) conclude that in Korean, too, quantifiers seem to block LF *wh*-movement.

---

[5] See König (1991) for a broad comparative study of focus particles and Bayer (1999) for a recent syntactic analysis of focus particles such as *only* and *even*.

[6] It is well-known that the corresponding English question is ambiguous. The universal quantifier *everyone* can take either narrow scope below the *wh*-phrase (yielding a single answer) or wide scope over the *wh*-phrase (yielding a pair-list answer). Interestingly, questions with a universal quantifier in Korean do not allow pair-list answers. What is available is only a single answer or a functional answer. This seems to imply that the universal quantifier cannot take scope over the *wh*-phrase in Korean.

Reasonable as this generalization may seem, however, a closer scrutiny reveals some problems with it, which will be discussed in the following section.

3   Not Every Quantifier Shows the Intervention Effect

One problem with the claim by Beck & Kim (1997) is overgeneralization. As briefly mentioned above, we have a somewhat weaker effect with the universal quantifier *nukuna* 'everyone' (see (13a)). More problematic is the fact that no intervention effect is observed with some quantifiers. For example, the quantifier phrase *taepupun-ûi N* 'most N' and quantificational adverbs such as *hangsang* 'always' and *chachu* 'often' in Korean do not show any intervention effects. The following sentences with these quantifiers c-commanding the *wh*-in-situ are all grammatical.

(14)   **taepupun-ûi hansaeng-tûl-i** <u>nuku-lûl</u>   hoichang-ûlo
        most-Gen   student-PL-Nom   who-Acc   president-as
        ch'uch'ônha-ôss-ni?
        recommend-Past-Q
        'Who did most students recommend as president?'
(15)   Minsu-nûn   **hangsang/chachu** <u>nuku-lûl</u> p'at'i-e   teliko ka-ss-ni?
        Minsu-Top   always/often   who-Acc   party-to   take-Past-Q
        'Who did Minsu always/often take to the party?'

Beck & Kim (1997) already mentioned that it is not the full class of quantificational expressions that blocks LF movement in Korean. But a full explanation as to what natural class can be made up out of the interveners in Korean is lacking to date.

Interveners such as NPIs and focus phrases with particles *man* 'only' or *to* 'also, even' show intervention effects without exceptions (see (10) – (12)).[7] It is interesting to note that focused phrases even without any focus particle exhibit the same effect, which is illustrated in (16).

---

[7] Lee & Tomioka (2000) claim that intervention effects disappear in embedded contexts, both in Japanese and Korean. But I myself do not share this intuition about Korean. So the sentence (ia) is still ungrammatical for me:

(i)   a. ?* Suna-nûn [Minsu-to/man   nuku-lûl   ch'otaeha-ôss-ta-ko] saengkakha-ni?
             Suna-Top   Minsu-also/only   who-Acc   invite-Past-Dec-C   think-Q
      b.   Suna-nûn [nuku-lûl_i Minsu-to/man   t_i   ch'otaeha-ôss-ta-ko] saengkakha-ni?
             Suna-Top   who-Acc Minsu-also/only   invite-Past-Dec-C   think-Q
             'Who does Suna think that also/only Minsu invited t?'

(16) a. ?* MINSU-ka <u>nuku-lûl</u> p'at'i-e ch'otaeha-ôss-ni?
     Minsu-Nom who-Acc party-to invite-Past-Q
   b. <u>nuku-lûl</u>ᵢ MINSU-ka tᵢ p'at'i-e ch'otaeha-ôss-ni?
     who-Acc Minsu-Nom party-to invite-Past-Q
     'Who did MINSU (not someone else) invite to the party?'

Taken together with the overgeneralization problem, one question to raise would be whether it is possible to distinguish a natural class among the interveners in Korean. The crucial question seems to be: Why do NPIs and focus phrases show the same intervention effect? What do NPIs have in common with focus phrases? In the next section, I first extend the discussion to include Hindi, and then look at the morphological structure of NPIs in Korean and show that NPIs share an interesting property with focus phrases.

4 The Structure of Negative Polarity Items

4.1 Hindi

Lahiri (1998) observes that negative polarity items (NPIs) in Hindi are morphologically made up of an indefinite existential or a weak predicate and a focus (or "emphatic") particle *bhii* that means 'also' or 'even'. The following list shows the NPIs and the corresponding simple existentials:

(17) The morphology of Hindi NPIs (Lahiri 1998: 58)
   ek bhii   'anyone, even one'   ek   'one'
   koii bhii   'anyone, any (count)'   koii   'someone'
   kuch bhii   'anything, any (mass)' kuch   'something, a little'
   kabhii bhii 'anytime, ever'   kabhii 'sometime'
   kahiiN bhii 'anywhere'   kahiiN 'somewhere'

One interesting property of NPI-licensing in Hindi (and also languages like Japanese and Korean), as opposed to languages like English, is the fact that in Hindi NPIs in subject position are licensed by clausemate negation. This is illustrated in (18) (compare (18a) with the ungrammatical English sentence *Anyone didn't come).

I have no explanation why in Japanese and Korean (for some speakers) the intervention effect disappears when the question is embedded. I refer the reader to Lee & Tomioka (2000) for a critical and interesting reanalysis of the data in Beck & Kim (1997).

(18) a.   koii bhii nahiiN   aayaa
           anyone not   came
           'No one came.'

      b.   maiN-ne ek bhii aadmii-ko   nahiiN   dekhaa
           I-Erg   any   man   not   saw
           'I didn't see any men/man.'

4.2 Korean

NPIs in Korean have a very similar structure to Hindi NPIs. In particular, they also contain the scalar focus particle *to* meaning 'also, even' (see Y.-S. Lee 1993 and C. Lee 1997).[8] Korean exhibits two types of negative polarity items, one based on an indefinite expression and the other based on a *wh*-pronoun. This is illustrated in (19) and (20).

(19) indefinite + *to* 'also/even'
      a.   han salam-to   an   o-ass-ta.
           one person-even   not come-Past-Dec
           'No one came.'

      b.   amu-to   kû ch'aek-ûl   ilk-chi   anh-ass-ta.
           any-even   that book-Acc   read-CHI   not do-Past-Dec
           'No one read that book.'

      c.   Suna-nûn   amu-to   an   manna-ss-ta.
           Suna-Top   any-even   not   meet-Past-Dec
           'Suna didn't meet anyone.'

(20) wh + *to* 'also/even'
      a.   Suna-nûn   nuku-to   an   manna-ss-ta.
           Suna-Top   who-also/even   not   meet-Past-Dec
           'Suna didn't meet anyone.'

      b.   Suna-nûn   ônû   haksaeng-eke-to   kû   ch'aek-ûl
           Suna-Top   which student-Dat-also/even that book-Acc
           chu-chi   anh-ass-ta.
           give-CHI   not do-Past-Dec
           'Suna didn't give the book to any student.'

---

[8] For a detailed semantic analysis of NPIs in Hindi and Korean, I refer the reader to Lahiri (1998) and Y.-S. Lee (1993), respectively.

Taking into consideration that the *wh*-pronouns in Korean can be interpreted as indefinite pronouns in some contexts, it is not surprising to have the NPI type (20).[9]

Given this similarity, it seems reasonable to assume that NPIs in Korean are focus phrases like Hindi NPIs.

5 Focus Phrases and Intervention Effects

After having analyzed Korean NPIs as focus phrases, we can now assume that focus phrases in general show intervention effects in Korean.[10] In the next subsections, I will try to formalize this generalization and give some cross-linguistic evidence for it.

5.1 Interpreting Wh-in-situ without LF Movement

It is a long-standing question whether there is LF movement of *wh*-in-situ or not (from the early pioneering work by Huang 1982 to the recent minimalist program by Chomsky 1995). Beck (1996) and Beck & Kim (1997) assume that for semantic reasons, *wh*-in-situ has to move at LF to an operator position in SpecC. However, there is an alternative way to formulate the Intervention Effect without assuming LF movement of *wh*-in-situ. Discussing the Intervention Effect, Pesetsky (1999) proposes an alternative formulation which does not assume LF phrasal *wh*-movement, which is given in (21):

(21)   *Intervention Effect* (Pesetsky 1999: 88)
       A semantic restriction on a quantifier (including *wh*) may not be separated from that quantifier by a scope-bearing element.

For interpreting *wh*-in-situ without LF movement, we could take the choice function analysis proposed by Reinhart (1997, 1998). The determiner *which*, or the *wh*-expression in general, is interpreted as a choice function variable, which is long-distance bound by the question existential operator Q in SpecC. The existential question operator is introduced in the LF component via a sort of existential closure, so that no LF movement at all is involved.

The description of choice functions is given in (22):

---

[9] Cf. Haspelmath (1997) for the typology of NPIs. The 'indefinite/wh + *also/even*' combination is a very common form of NPI cross-linguistically.

[10] See Sohn (1995) for a similar observation with focus phrases for Korean, and Yanagida (1996) for Japanese.

(22)   A function f is a choice funtion (CH(f)) if it applies to any non-
       empty set and yields a member of that set.

(Reinhart 1997: 372)

According to Reinhart's analysis, the question (23a) is illustrated informally
in (23b), and its semantic representation is given in (23c) (putting aside the
issue of extensionality):

(23)   a.   Which lady t read which book?
       c.   for which $<x, f>$ (lady(x)) and (x read f(book))
       c. $\{P|(\exists <x, f>)$ (CH(f) & lady(x) & $P = ^\wedge$(x read f(book)) &
            true(P))$\}$

The question here denotes the set of true propositions P, each stating for
some lady x and for some choice function f that x read the book selected by
f.

Turning now to *wh*-in-situ in Korean, we can apply the same procedure.
Following Reinhart, I assume an abstract existential question operator in
SpecC of the interrogative clause. Now, the Korean interrogative sentence
(24a) can be semantically represented as in (24b). The choice function bound
by the question operator selects a value from the student set denoted by the
NP *haksaeng* 'student' (**Q** = question existential operator).

(24)   a. $[_{CP}$ **Q**$_i$ $[_{IP}$ Suna-ka   onû   haksaeng-ûl$_i$ manna-ss]-ni]?
                        Suna-Nom which   student-Acc   meet-Past-Q
            'Which student did Suna meet?'
       b. $\{P|\exists f$ (CH(f) & $P = ^\wedge$(Suna met f(student)) & true(P))$\}$

The question here denotes the set of true propositions P, each stating for
some choice function f that Suna met the student selected by f.

5.2   Focus Phrases as Barriers for Q-Binding

Assuming with Reinhart (1998) that the *wh*-in-situ is a function variable
bound by the question existential operator Q in SpecC, I propose that a focus phrase may not intervene between a Q-operator and the *wh*-in-situ bound
by that operator. This is formulated as in (25):

(25)   If a *wh*-in-situ α is c-commanded by a focus phrase β, then the Q
       operator binding α must also be c-commanded by β.

The following structure (26) is then ruled out by the restriction (25) (the boldfaced **Q** is the existential Q-operator and "FocP" stands for Focus Phrase):

(26)   * [$_{CP}$ **Q**$_i$ [$_{IP}$ ... FocP ... wh$_i$ ...]]

Consider now the examples (11a-b), which are repeated as (27a-b).

(27) a. * [$_{CP}$ **Q**$_i$ [$_{IP}$ Minsu-man   nuku-lûl$_i$ manna-ss]-ni]?
              Minsu-only   who-Acc   meet-Past-Q
      b.   [$_{CP}$ **Q**$_i$ [$_{IP}$ nuku-lûl$_i$ [$_{IP}$ Minsu-man   t   manna-ss]]-ni]?
              who-Acc   Minsu-only   meet-Past-Q
              'Who did only Minsu meet?'

In the ungrammatical case (27a), the focus phrase *Minsu-man* 'only Minsu' intervenes between the Q-operator and the *wh*-in-situ bound by it. In the grammatical case (27b), on the other hand, there is no intervening focus phrase.

5.3   Some Cross-Linguistic Evidence for Focus Barriers

In Chinese, another *wh*-in-situ language, ordinary quantifier NPs, frequency adverbials, and negation do not show the Intervention Effect (see Huang 1982: 263–67 and Aoun & Li 1993a,b). The following examples with these quantifiers c-commanding the *wh*-in-situ are all grammatical.

(28)   meigeren dou   mai-le   shenme?[11]
       everyone all   buy-ASP   what
       'What did everyone buy?'
(29)   Zhangsan changchang mai   shenme?
       Zhangsan often   buy   what
       'What does Zhangsan often buy?'
(30)   Zhangsan bu xiang   mai   shenme?
       Zhangsan not want   buy   what
       'What doesn't Zhangsan want to buy?'

---

[11] Aoun & Li (1993b) contrast sentences like (28) with the ungrammatical Japanese sentence (i) from Hoji (1985):

(i)   * Daremo-ga   nani-o   kaimasita   ka?
         everyone-Nom what-Acc   bought   Q
         'What did everyone buy?'

Interestingly, focus phrases (including NPIs) in Chinese do show the Intervention Effect (Lansun Chen p.c.). Moreover, Chinese seems to have a repair strategy to circumvent the Intervention Effect. This is illustrated in the following examples.

(31) a. ?Lili ye kan-le   na-ben   shu?
            Lili also read-ASP which-CL book
      b. na-ben   shu Lili ye   kan-le?
            which-CL book Lili also   read-ASP
            'Which book did Lili, too, read?'

(32) a. ?? lian Lili ye   kan de dong   na-ben   shu?
            even Lili also read DE understand   which-CL book
      b. na-ben   shu lian Lili ye   kan de   dong?
            which-CL book even Lili also   read DE understand
            'Which book could even Lili understand?'

(33) a. ?* zhiyou Lili   kan-le   na-ben   shu?
            only   Lili   read-ASP which-CL book
      b. na-ben   shu zhiyou Lili kan-le?
            which-CL book only   Lili read-ASP
            'Which book did only Lili read?'

(34) a. * shei ye kan bu dong   na-ben   shu?
            who also read not understand which-CL book
      b. na-ben   shu shei ye kan bu dong?
            which-CL book who also read not understand
            'Which book could no one understand?'
            (*shei ye* 'who also' meaning 'anyone')

Notice that the NPI *shei ye* 'who also' in (34) has the same morphological structure as one type of the Korean NPIs (wh + *to* 'also'). Unlike Japanese or Korean, which exhibit a relatively free word order derived by scrambling, Chinese has a rather fixed word order. But exactly in the context where a focus phrase occurs in a position c-commanding the *wh*-in-situ in the unmarked order, the *wh*-in-situ has to be fronted to the sentence-initial position in order to get a grammatical sentence. Irrespective of what kind of movement it could be, it is important to note that focus phrases in Chinese show the Intervention Effect, as well.

6 Conclusion

In this paper I have reviewed the claim made by Beck (1996) and Beck & Kim (1997) that quantifiers block LF movement of *wh*-in-situ. One of the problems with this claim is that not all quantifiers show the Intervention Effect in Korean. This seems to imply that there is some cross-linguistic variation as to what blocks LF *wh*-movement (or Q-binding of *wh*-in-situ in the sense of Reinhart 1998). One question to raise was whether it is possible to distinguish a natural class among the interveners.

It is interesting to note that negative polarity items (NPIs) show the Intervention Effect quite generally (to be observed in Bengali, Chinese, Hindi/Urdu, Korean, and Turkish). Taking into consideration that NPIs in Korean consist of an indefinite expression and a focus particle *to* that means 'also, even', just like Hindi NPIs, the interveners in Korean can be classified as focus phrases. Given this, I proposed that focus phrases (not quantifiers in general) may not intervene between a Q-operator and the *wh*-in-situ bound by that operator. I further provided some evidence for focus barriers from Chinese.

One remaining question is why there is cross-linguistic variation among the interveners. For example, why does the universal quantifier in German show a stronger Intervention Effect than the corresponding Korean quantifier *nukuna* 'everyone'? Why is there no Intervention Effect with the universal quantifier in Chinese? Of course, the analysis I proposed in this paper does not provide a full explanation of the phenomena. But one natural class of interveners that produces the Intervention Effect quite generally could be found, namely focus phrases.

References

Aoun, J. and Y.-H. A. Li. 1993a. *Wh*-Elements in Situ: Syntax or LF? *Linguistic Inquiry* 24: 199–238.

Aoun, J. and Y.-H. A. Li. 1993b. On Some Differences between Chinese and Japanese *Wh*-Elements. *Linguistic Inquiry* 24: 365–372.

Bayer, J. 1999. Bound Focus or How can Association with Focus be Achieved without Going Semantically Astray? *The Grammar of Focus*, ed. G. Rebuschi & L. Tuller, 55–82. Amsterdam: Benjamins.

Beck, S. 1996. Quantified Structures as Barriers for LF Movement. *Natural Language Semantics* 4: 1–56.

Beck, S. and S.-S. Kim. 1997. On *Wh*- and Operator Scope in Korean. *Journal of East Asian Linguistics* 6: 339–384.

Chomsky, N. 1995. *The Minimalist Program*. Cambridge, Mass.: MIT Press.

Fanselow, G. 1990. Scrambling as NP-Movement. *Scrambling and Barriers*, ed. G. Grewendorf & W. Sternefeld, 113–140. Amsterdam: Benjamins.

Hagstrom, P. 1998. Decomposing Questions. Doctoral dissertation, MIT.

Haspelmath, M. 1997. *Indefinite Pronouns*. Oxford: Clarendon Press.

Heck, F. and G. Müller. 2000. Repair-Driven Movement and the Local Optimization of Derivations. Ms., Universität Stuttgart & IDS Mannheim.

Hoji, H. 1985. Logical Form Constraints and Configurational Structures in Japanese. Doctoral dissertation, University of Washington.

Huang, C.-T. J. 1982. Logical Relations in Chinese and the Theory of Grammar. Doctoral dissertation, MIT.

Kim, S.-W. 1991. Chain Scope and Quantification Structure. Doctoral dissertation, Brandeis University.

König, E. 1991. *The Meaning of Focus Particles: A Comparative Perspective*. London: Routledge.

Lahiri, U. 1998. Focus and Negative Polarity in Hindi. *Natural Language Semantics* 6: 57–123.

Lee, C. 1997. Negative Polarity and Free Choice: Where Do They Come from? *Proceedings of the 11th Amsterdam Colloquium*, ed. P. Dekker et al., 217–222. ILLC, University of Amsterdam.

Lee, K.-S. and S. Tomioka. 2000. LF Intervention Effects are Topic Effects: Wh Questions in Japanese and Korean. Talk given at the 10th Japanese/Korean Linguistics Conference, UCLA.

Lee. Y.-S. 1993. Licensing and Semantics of *Any* Revisited. *Harvard Studies in Korean Linguistics V*, ed. S. Kuno et al., 577–592 Seoul: Hanshin Publishing Company.

Müller, G. and W. Sternefeld. 1993. Improper Movement and Unambiguous Binding. *Linguistic Inquiry* 24: 461–507.

Pesetsky, D. 1999. Phrasal Movement and Its Kin. Ms., MIT.

Reinhart, T. 1997. Quantifier Scope: How Labor is Divided between QR and Choice Functions. *Linguistics and Philosophy* 20: 335–397.

Reinhart, T. 1998. *Wh*-in-situ in the Framework of the Minimalist Program. *Natural Language Semantics* 6: 29–56.

Sohn, K.-W. 1995. Negative Polarity Items, Scope, and Economy. Doctoral dissertation, University of Connecticut.

Yanagida, Y. 1996. Syntactic QR in *Wh*-in-situ Languages. *Lingua* 99: 21–36.

Event Sensitivity of Head-Internal Relatives in Japanese*

YUKI MATSUDA

The University of Memphis

1. Introduction

This paper proposes an account of the semantic properties of Head-Internal Relative (HIR) clauses in Japanese. Sentence (1) exemplifies HIR clauses.

(1) Taroo wa [sara no ue   ni ringo ga   atta no] o   tot-te tabeta.
    Taro TOP plate GEN above at apple NOM placed NM ACC take&ate
    'Taro took and ate the apples placed on the plate.'

Sentence (2) exemplifies more productive Head-External Relative clauses.

(2) Taroo wa [[sara no   ue   ni atta] ringo] o   tot-te tabeta.
    Taro TOP plate GEN above at placed apple ACC take&ate
    'Taro took and ate the apples which were on the plate.'

---

* I wish to thank Kaoru Horie, Satoshi Kinsui, Yoshi Kitagawa, Satoshi Tomioka, and especially Yuki Kuroda and Toshiyuki Ogihara for very helpful comments and suggestions which led to various improvements. Any remaining errors are of course my own.

Some attempts have been made in the past to map (1) into (2) at some level of syntactic representation (Ito 1986, Ishii 1991, Watanabe 1992), which we might refer to as Logical Form (LF). Under this analysis, both (1) and (2) have the same syntactic representation at that level. If we assume that the syntactic representation at this level is semantically interpreted, we expect HIR and HER clauses to generate the same meaning. However, as noted by many researchers including Hoshi (1995), Shimoyama (1999), and Kuroda (1975/76, 1999), there are some semantic differences between HIR and HER clauses. For example, Shimoyama (1999) points out that proportional quantifiers interact with them in different ways, as shown in (3) and (4).

(3) Taroo wa [[Hanako ga hukuro ni irete-oita] **hotondo no kukkii**] o
    Taro TOP Hanako NOM bag in put-ASP most GEN cookie ACC
    tot-te tabeta.
    took-and ate.
    'Taro took and ate most of the cookies that Hanako put into the bag.'

(4) Taroo wa [Hanako ga **hotondo no kukkii** o hukuro ni irete-oita no] o
    Taro TOP Hanako NOM most GEN cookie ACC bag in put-ASP NM ACC
    totte tabeta.
    took-and ate.
    Lit: 'Hanako put most cookies into the bag, and Taro took and ate them.'

Both (3) and (4) contain a nominal phrase with a quantificational expression, *hotondo-no* 'most'. As we see from the approximate English translations, (3) and (4) are truth conditionally different. For example, the sentence (3) is compatible with the following situation: Hanako put 10 cookies into a bag, and Taro took 8 cookies from the bag and ate them. Here, the 8 cookies Taro took count as <u>most</u> in relation to the 10 cookies that Hanako put into the bag. By contrast, the HIR counterpart (4) is not compatible with the same situation. Rather, (4) is compatible with the following situation: Hanako bought 10 cookies at a store and set aside 2 of them to take with her. She then put the remaining 8 cookies into a bag for Taro, which counts as <u>most</u> in relation to the 10 original cookies, and Taro picked up all the 8 cookies and ate them. In other words, in (3), 'most' can relate {x | Hanako put x in the bag and x is a cookie} and {x | Taro took and ate x}. By contrast, in (4) 'most' must relate {x | x is a cookie} and {x | x is in the bag}.

This interpretive difference between (3) and (4) is explained in the following way. In (3), the intersection of the two sets of individuals, {x: Hanako put x into a bag} and {y: y is a cookie}, can constitute the restrictor for the quantified expression *hotondo* 'most' and the matrix clause is the nuclear scope of the quantifier. By contrasts, in (4) a set of cookies specified by the context serves as its restrictor and the nuclear scope of the quantifier is the embedded VP, *put x into the bag*. This semantic difference between HIR and HER clauses strongly suggests that the "head noun" in a HIR clause is interpreted *in situ* and that HIR clauses require a semantic analysis different from HER clauses.

2. The E-Type Pronoun Hypothesis

In order to take into consideration such an interpretive difference from HER clauses, Hoshi (1995) and Shimoyama (1999) propose E-type analyses of Japanese HIR clauses. E-type pronouns are pronouns which are interpreted as if they are a bound pronoun but are not syntactically "bound" by a quantified expression (See Cooper 1979, and Evans 1980). These pronouns are definite descriptions which pick up their referent from the given context. Hoshi (1995) and Shimoyama (1999) adopt this E-type pronoun analysis to account for HIR clauses. In their account, a HIR is a closed sentence and is followed by a definite description that denotes a unique individual that has a contextually salient property recovered from the meaning of the HIR. Under this account, sentence (4) is roughly interpreted as *Hanako put most cookies into the bag and Taro picked them up.*

Under their analyses, which consider HIR clauses to be a closed sentence, we can predict that in (4), the domain of the quantified expression *hotondo-no* 'most' is restricted only by a set of cookies and that the nuclear scope of the quantifier is the embedded VP, *put x into the bag* . The E-type pronoun picks up its reference from the HIR clause. Note that HIR clauses are followed by the morpheme *-no*. Shimoyama (1999:167) assumes that the morpheme is similar to the definite article *the* in English, which denotes a function that applies to a property and yields the maximal individual that has this property, as shown in (5).

(5) $[[no]] \in D_{<<e,t>, e>}$
$[[no]](f)$ denotes the maximal individual a such that $f(a) = 1$

Under her analysis, a HIR clause is a CP, which is generated at the specifier position of a DP, and an E-type pronoun is an NP, which is generated at the complement position of a determier *no*. (6a) is her example, and (6b) illustrates her assumption about the structure of the DP containing a HIR clause (Shimoyama 1999: 166 (36a-b)).

(6) a. Taroo wa[[Hanako ga **dono sinbun mo** katte kita]no]o tana ni narabeta.
    'Hanako bought (and brought) every newspaper and Taro shelved *them*.'

b.

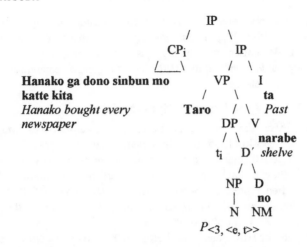

According to Shimoyama's analysis, the entire DP containing a HIR denotes a unique individual that has the property specified by the HIR clause and the context, and this individual becomes an argument of the matrix predicate.

3. Maximality Effect

Both Hoshi (1995) and Shimoyama (1999) point out that HIR clauses have a maximality effect. Maximality refers to a situation in which the largest group of entities with a particular property is chosen.[1] Hoshi (1995: 132) introduces the following example to show the maximality effect in HIR clauses.

(7) #John ga [[Mary ga san-ko no ringo o muite kureta] no] o tabeta.
Sikasi zituwa Mary wa yon-ko no ringo o muita no datta.
'#Mary peeled three apples and John ate them, In fact, however, it was the case that Mary peeled four apples.'

The anomaly of (7) is accounted for by assuming a definite description analysis of HIR DPs. A definite description denotes the maximal individual that has the property in question. For example, under this analysis, the HIR DP in the first sentence in (7) denotes the maximal group of apples that Mary peeled whose cardinality is three. This is contradicted by the second sentence in (7) because it says that Mary peeled four apples. Thus, the entire discourse in (7) is anomalous. In this way, the anomaly of (7) is accounted for.

---

[1] See Grosu and Landman (1998) for examples showing the "maximality effects". They assume a semantic operation, maximalization, to explain these examples.

In sum, Hoshi and Shimoyama's E-type pronoun analysis, which argues that the "head" noun is interpreted *in situ* and that the E-type pronoun picks up its reference from inside the HIR clause, successfully accounts for the semantic difference between HER clause (3) and HIR clause (4). Regarding the DP containing a HIR clause as a definite description seems to lead us in the right direction. However, as it stands, there are some serious problems associated with this analysis. In the next section, I will discuss them.

4. Problems with the E-Type Pronoun Hypothesis

4.1. Predicate Restrictions on HIR clauses

While the E-type analysis due to Hoshi (1995) and Shimoyama (1999) accounts for many relevant examples, there are some crucial problems with this analysis. The problem with the analysis is that it simply overgenerates interpretations. For example, unlike the acceptable example (2), sentences such as (8), (9), and (10) are unacceptable, which is unexpected under the E-type anaphora account.

(8) *[Sara no ue   ni ringo ga   atta   no] wa   oisi-soo-datta.
      plate GEN above at apple NOM located NM TOP delicious-appear-was
    Intended: 'The apples that were on the plate looked delicious.'

(9) *Taroo wa [onna-no-hito ga yuumei-na no] o   sit-te iru.
      Taro TOP woman   NOM famous NM ACC know
    Intended: 'Taro is acquainted with the woman who is famous.'

(10) *Taroo wa [onna no hito ga   yuumei-na no] ni   hanataba o   watasita.
      Taro TOP woman   NOM famous   NM DAT bouquet ACC gave
    Intended: 'Taro gave a bouquet to the woman who is famous.'

Unlike the HIR examples in (8) through (10), their Head-External Relative (HER) counterparts in (11) through (13) are perfectly acceptable.

(11) [[Sara no ue   ni atta] ringo] wa   oisi-soo-datta.
      plate GEN above at placed apple TOP delicious-appear-was
    'The apples that were on the plate looked delicious.'

(12) Taroo wa [[yuumei-na] onna no hito] o   sit-te iru.
      Taro TOP famous   woman   ACC know
    'Taro is acquainted with the/a woman who is famous.'

(13) Taroo wa [[yuumei-na] onna no hito] ni hanataba o watasita.
Taro TOP famous woman DAT bouquet ACC gave
'Taro gave a bouquet to the/a woman who is famous.'

Kuroda (1975/76) posits the pragmatic condition in (14) which HIR clauses are subject to.

(14)   The Relevancy Condition: For a p.i. [head-internal (y.m.)] relative clause to be acceptable, it is necessary that it be interpreted pragmatically in such a way as to be directly relevant to the pragmatic content of its matrix clause. (Kuroda 1992: 147)

I contend that the condition Kuroda introduces is not purely pragmatic in nature. Take (10) for example. As far as pragmatic relevance is concerned, it is easy to imagine a situation in which some woman's being famous is relevant to Taro's giving her a bouquet. For example, her being famous causes him to give her a bouquet. Thus, we cannot claim that a HIR clause is acceptable if and only if its pragmatic relevance for the content of the matrix clause can be established. We can at least see that such relevancy is strongly affected by the types of predicates used in these sentences (c.f. Milsark 1974, and Carlson 1977). Carlson (1977) argues that predicates can be either individual-level or stage-level. Individual-level predicates are used in a sentence which predicates more or less permanent properties or attributes of individuals. Such predicates include *oisii* 'delicious', *sitte iru* 'know' and *yuumei da* 'is famous'. Stage-level predicates are used in a sentence which describes temporary situations or stages of individuals. Such predicates include *watasita* 'gave' and *atta* 'be located'. Sentence (8) and (9) show that HIR clauses cannot occur with an individual-level predicate, in the sense of Carlson (1977), and sentence (9) and (10) show that HIR clauses cannot contain an individual-level predicate. By contrast, the following sentences are acceptable because both the HIR and matrix clauses contain a stage-level predicate.

(15) [Sara no ue ni ringo ga atta no] ga oti-te kita.
plate GEN above at apple NOM was located NM NOM fall
'The apples that were on the plate dropped.'

(16) Taroo wa [onna no hito ga heya kara detekita no] ni hanataba o watasita.
Taro TOP woman NOM room from came out NM DAT bouquet ACC gave
'Taro gave a bouquet to the woman who came out the room.'

From these examples, we can see that the acceptability of HIR clauses is highly sensitive to the temporal and aspectual specifications of both matrix and embedded predicates in the sentence containing a HIR clause. Under the standard E-type analysis, however, we do not expect there to be such a semantic condition on the availability of HIR clauses.

Another problem for the E-type pronoun hypothesis is pointed out by Kuroda (1999). Kuroda observes that HIRs cannot occur in the pre-copular position and points out that pronoun hypotheses cannot predict such a distributional characteristic. First, let us consider a HER clause that is fully acceptable.

(17) Ano otoko ga [[ginkoo kara dete-kita] otoko] da.
      that man NOM bank from came-out man   COP
      'That man is the man who came out of the bank.'

(17) says that man that we are pointing at is the man who came out of the bank. However, as Kuroda's example (18) indicates, when a copular sentence contains a HIR clause, the sentence is anomalous.

(18) *Ano otoko ga [ginkoo kara otoko ga   dete-kita no] da.
       that man NOM bank from man NOM came-out NM COP
       Intended: 'That man is the man who came out of the bank.'
       (Kuroda 1999: 54)

(18) is ill-formed and cannot mean that the subject NP *ano otoko* 'that man' has the same denotation as 'the man who came out of the bank'. Given our earlier observation that the acceptability of HIR clauses is highly sensitive to the temporal and aspectual specifications of both matrix and embedded predicates in the sentence containing a HIR clause, we might be able to let the same constraint take care of the data involving copular sentences. Copular verbs are certainly not a stage-level predicate. We may be able to say that HIR clauses cannot occur with individual-level predicates, including copular verbs. Once again, the regular E-type analysis does not explain why such a restriction should exist.

4.2. HIR clauses do not denote a simple individual

Furthermore, the regular E-type analysis faces a problem in the following case. HIR clauses cannot be used as an answer to a wh-question that clearly asks for an individual in its answer as shown in (19).

(19) a. Taroo wa dare o hoteru e turete-itta no?
     Taro TOP who ACC hotel to   took   Q
     'Whom did Taro take to the hotel?'

   b. Taroo wa [[kuukoo ni tuita] gakusei] o hoteru e turete itta.
      Taro TOP airport at arrived student ACC hotel to took
      'Taro took the student who arrived at the airport.'

   c. *Taroo wa [gakusei ga kuukoo ni tuita   no] o hoteru e turete-itta.
      Taro TOP student NOM airport at arrived NM ACC hotel to took

(19a) asks for the identity of an individual whom Taro took to the hotel.
(19b-c) show that while (19b), which contains a HER, is an acceptable
answer to (19a), (19c), containing a HIR counterpart, is not. If the HIR clause
in (19c) denotes a unique individual, as the E-type pronoun hypothesis
claims, it should be able to be used to answer (19a), contrary to the fact.

4.3. HIR clauses may not be a topic phrase

Kuroda (1999) also points out that in general HIR clauses cannot occur in the
topic position. Given the fact that definite descriptions in general are a good
candidate for a topic phrase, this too is surprising under the regular E-type
pronoun hypothesis.

(20) a. Otoko ga haitte kita.
     man NOM came in
     'A man came in.'

   b. *Sono otoko wa*   itiban ookii isu ni suwatta.
      the/that man TOP most big chair to sat
      '*The man* sat down on the biggest chair.'

The pronoun *sono otoko* 'that man' in (20b) picks up a referent from the
antecedent sentence (20a). It is no problem for this pronoun to be a topic
phrase, as we see in (20b). However, examples (21b) and (22b) show that
HIR clauses cannot be a topic phrase.

(21) a. Taroo wa [doroboo ga ginkoo kara detekita   no] o tukamaeta.
     Taro TOP thief NOM bank from came-out NM ACC caught
     'Taro caught the thief who came out of the bank.'

   b. *[Doroboo ga ginkoo kara detekita no] wa Taroo ga tukamaeta.
      thief NOM bank from came-out NM TOP Taro NOM caught
      Intended: 'The thief who came out of the bank, Taro caught.'

(22) a. [Hon ga   san-satu kirei-ni narande ita no] ga kyuuni   otite kita.
      book NOM three-CL neatly lining was NM NOM suddenly fell
      'The book lined up neatly suddenly came down.'

   b. *[Hon ga   san-satu kirei-ni narande ita no] wa   kyuu ni otite kita.
      book NOM three-CL neatly   lining was NM TOP suddenly fell
      Intended: 'The book lined up neatly suddenly came down.'

(21a) and (22a) are acceptable because each HIR clause is in an argument position (the direct object and the subject position respectively). (21b) and (22b) show that once the HIR clause is topicalized, the entire sentence becomes ill-formed. With the previous E-type pronoun hypothesis, which assumes that HIR clauses are definite descriptions about regular individuals, it is very puzzling why the HIR clauses cannot be a topic phrase.

   In sum, the previous E-type anaphora account of HIR clauses is empirically accurate to the extent that it assumes that a "head" noun is interpreted inside the HIR clause. However, we have seen some empirical problems with it. First, it is not clear why the pronoun should be sensitive to predicate types. Second, it is not clear why the pronoun cannot be used as an answer to a wh-question which asks for the identity of an individual. Third, it is not clear why the pronoun cannot be the topic of a sentence.

5. A Hybrid Entity

We have seen that HIR clauses behave like a definite description but at the same time, we cannot maintain that they denote an ordinary individual such as John or Mary. In this section, I will present an analysis of HIR clauses that explains the behaviors of HIR clauses presented above.

   Following Davidson (1967), many researchers including Higginbotham (1987), Schein (1993), and Kratzer (1995) contend that the semantics of declarative sentences involves existential quantification over events. I adopt this hypothesis and argue that the semantics of a HIR clause necessarily involves both an individual and event.[2] This is stated semi-formally as in (23).

(23) A HIR is a definite description that denotes a plural entity that consists of an individual and an event.

I argue that a HIR clause is a definite description involving a hybrid entity, which is composed of an ordinary individual and an event. I assume that both

---

[2] There are some precursors of my proposal. Vlach (1983) presents a similar proposal about bare infinitive complements of perception verbs in English. Horie (1993) also makes a similar observation about HIRs in Japanese.

ordinary individuals and events are of the same type e but are sorted as e_i and e_{ev} respectively. Following Link (1983), I assume further that plural entities are introduced by putting together any two objects in D_e. We formalize this idea as follows. We first posit as in (24) a syntactic operator that introduces an expression that denotes a "plural entity."

(24) For any expressions α, β of type e, $\alpha \oplus \beta$ is also an expression of type e.

The syntactic operator $\oplus$ defined in (24) is interpreted as in (25).

(25) For any α, $\beta \in D_e$, the operation $\sqcup$ (the "gluing operation") is posited such that $\alpha \sqcup \beta \in D_e$

Given this system, we naturally expect that there would be entities consisting of an ordinary individual and an event. I contend that this is indeed what we want for HIR clauses in Japanese.

(26) Typology of entities

Type	denotation
e_{ev}	Event
e_i	Thing/object/person etc. Ordinary individual
$e_i \oplus e_{ev}$	Individual-event hybrid entity

I assume that existential quantification over an event or a hybrid entity consisting of an individual and an event is introduced only in a non-stative sentence. These assumptions are summarized here in (27).

(27) a. The semantics of non-stative sentences involve existential quantification over events or hybrid entities.
    b. The semantics of stative sentences (including genetics) do not involve existential quantification over events or hybrid entities.

For the purpose of this paper, I adopt Shimoyama's (1999) analysis of HIRs except that the entire DP denotes a hybrid entity rather than a regular (maximal) individual. To take an example, consider (21a) repeated here as (28).

(28) Taroo wa [doroboo ga ginkoo kara dete-kita no] o tukamaeta.
    Taro TOP thief NOM bank from came-out NM ACC caught
    'Taro caught the thief who came out of the bank.'

(28) is analyzed as having the LF structure in (29a). Then the unpronounced proform in N position (indicated by P) receives as its denotation an appropriate hybrid entity consisting of an individual and an event. We assume that the context provides the N with an appropriate denotation only if the HIR involves both an individual and an event. In the case of (29a), the HIR denotes what is given in (29b), which in turn allows the context to assign the property given in (29c) as the meaning of the proform in N (i.e. P). In what follows, x, y, z, etc. are used as variables of type e. When it is necessary to make explicit which sorts are intended, the subscript i is used to indicate individuals, and ev is used for events. For example, x_i is a variable for individuals and x_{ev} is a variable for events.

(29) a. $[_{IP}[_{CP}$ Doroboo ga ginkoo kara detekita$]_i$
         thief   NOM bank from came-out

     $[_{IP}[_{VP}$ Taroo $[_{V'}[_{DP}$ t$_i[_{D'}$ $[_{NP}$ $[_N$ P$]][_D$ no$]]]o[_V$ tukamae$]]][_I$ ta$]]$
       Taro   NM ACC caught   PAST

    b. $\exists x_i \exists y_i \exists z_{ev}[z_{ev}$ is a past event & x_i is a thief or thieves & y_i is a bank or banks & z_{ev} is x_i's coming out of $y_i]$

    c. $\lambda x \in D_e.$ $\exists y_i \exists z_{ev} \exists v_i[x = y_i \sqcup z_{ev}$ & y_i is a thief or thieves & v_i is a bank or banks & z_{ev} is y_i's coming out of $v_i]$

We assume that the denotation of *no* in HIRs is characterized as in (30a). On the basis of this, the denotation of the entire DP is given as in (30b).

(30) a. $[[no]] \in D_{<<e,t>,e>}$ such that for any $f \in D_{<e,t>}$ $[[no]](f)$ is the maximal hybrid entity **a** such that $f(a) = 1$.[3]

    b. The maximal hybrid entity x such that $\exists y_i \exists z_{ev} \exists v_i[x = y_i \sqcup z_{ev}$ & y_i is a thief or thieves & v_i is a bank or banks & z_{ev} is y_i's coming out of $v_i]$ holds.

Some caveats are in order here. We assume that when the context assigns the relevant denotation to the proform P, the relevant information can only come

---

[3] What is a maximal hybrid entity of the relevant sort? We can answer this question by defining *no* in a formal fashion: For any property $P \in D_{<e,t>}$, $[[no]](P)$ = the unique $x \in D_e$ such that there is an individual **b** and an event **c** and a = b $\sqcup$ c and P(a) = 1, and there is no individual **d** or event **e** such that d is bigger than b and e is bigger than c such that $P(d \sqcup e) = 1$.

from the HIR that is associated with the proform; it cannot come from a different source. For reasons of space, I shall not pursue this question further in this paper. Another point worth mentioning is whether the maximal hybrid entity is definable in a given situation. To be more specific, the reader might wonder if there can be a maximal event portion of a maximal hybrid entity. I contend that there is one on the assumption that in a given situation we can assume that there is a uniquely identifiable event associated with some situation described by a stage-level predicate. For example, when a thief or a group of thieves come out of a bank, we assume that there is only one event that describes all relevant aspects of this situation and nothing else. If so, the maximal event is identifiable as the unique event that satisfies the description.

I am now in a position to demonstrate how my analysis accounts for the problematic data introduced above. First, the predicate restriction in (8), (9), and (10) is naturally accounted for by my analysis. (8) and (9) each contains a HIR. Given our assumption in (27b), we can conclude that the HIRs in (8) and (9) contain no hybrid argument consisting of an individual and an event. On the other hand, (23) requires that a HIR denote a hybrid entity consisting of an individual and an event. In this way, (8) and (9) are ruled out. In (10), on the other hand, the HIR clause contains a stage-level predicate, whereas the matrix clause contains an individual-level predicate. In this case, the HIR can denote a hybrid entity because its predicate is stage-level. However, given the assumption in (27b), the matrix predicate cannot have a hybrid argument. Thus, (10) is ruled out.

My analysis also accounts for the paradigm found in the *wh*-questions. In Japanese *wh*-questions, *dare* 'who' is used when requesting information about a person or persons and *nani* 'what' for non-human entities. (31) through (33) show that EHR clauses can be used to answer questions that involve *dare* or *nani*. (31) clearly involves a person, (32) clearly involves a thing. (33) is a little more complicated. Unlike (24), the complement clause of the perception verb *mite iru* 'is watching' in (33) seems to denote an event. We can therefore hypothesize that a simple event can also be questioned by *nani*.

(31) Q: Taroo wa dare o turete kita no.
Taro TOP who ACC brought Q
'Who did John bring?'

A: [Kinoo kissa ten de atta] onna-no-ko] da yo.
yesterday coffee shop at met girl is
'The girl (we) met in the coffee shop yesterday.'

(32) Q: Taroo wa nani o mite iru no?
Taro TOP what ACC watching is Q
'What is John looking at?'

A: [[Ike de oyoide iru] kingyo] o mite iru mitai.
pond at swimming is goldfish ACC watching is look
'It looks like he is watching goldfish swimming in the pond.'

(33) Q: Taroo wa nani o mite iru no?
Taro TOP what ACC watching is Q

A: [Kingyo ga ike de oyoide iru no] o mite iru yoo da.
goldfish NOM pond in swimming is NM ACC watching is look COP
'It appears that he is watching the goldfish swim in the pond.'

By contrast, HIR clause may not be questioned by either *dare* or *nani*, as illustrated in (34b).

(34) Q: Taroo wa {*dare/*nani} o hoteru e turete-itta no?
Taro TOP who/what ACC hotel to took Q
'Whom/what did Taro take to the hotel?

A: Taroo wa [gakusei ga kuukoo ni tuita no] o hoteru e turete-itta.
Taro TOP student NOM airport at arrived NM ACC hotel to took

It seems that there is no single *wh*-word that elicit an answer that provides the requested information in terms of a HIR clause. If we assume that *nani* 'what' can request information about a simple individual or about a simple event but not a hybrid entity composed of an individual and an event, the above data are accounted for.

Finally, we should discuss why HIR clauses are unlikely candidates for topic phrases. We saw above that this would constitute a problem for the Hoshi and Shimoyama's version of E-type pronoun hypothesis. Our modification to their theory would be able to correct this problem if we assume Kuroda's theory (1992) of judgments. Kuroda argues that topicalized sentences express categorical judgment. This judgment reflects our recognition of a predication relation between a property and a preconceived individual entity. Preconceived individual entities include definite descriptions and names. It seems fair to say that a maximal hybrid entity as it is defined here cannot constitute a preconceived individual entity because it consists of two disparate types of entities. By contrast, ordinary definite descriptions and names are used to describe an entity or entities of the same type. Thus, it is arguable that ordinary definite descriptions and names are much better candidates for topics. Obviously what counts as "preconceable" entities must be clearly defined before we can go on to provide a formal solution to this problem. Therefore, I must leave this issue partially unanswered for the purpose of this paper.[4]

7. Conclusion

In conclusion, the proposal we defend successfully accounts for semantic properties of HIR clauses unlike those proposals that are purely syntactic or based upon standard E-type pronoun analyses.

References

Carlson, G. 1977. Reference to kinds in English. Doctoral dissertation, University of Massachusetts, Amherst.

Cooper, R. 1979. The Interpretation of Pronouns. *Syntax and Semantics 10, Selections from the Third Groningen Round Table*, eds. F. Henry and H. Schnelle, 61-92. New York: Academic Press.

Davidson, D. 1967. The Logical Form of Action Sentences. The Logic of Decision and Action, ed. N. Rescher, 105-122. Pittsburgh: University of Pittsburgh Press.

Evans, G. 1980. Pronouns. *Linguistic Inquiry* 11: 337-362.

Grosu, A., and Landman, F. 1998. Strange Relatives of the Third Kind. *Natural Language Semantics* 6: 125-170.

Higginbotham, J. 1983. The Logic of Perceptual Reports: An Extensional Alternative to Situation Semantics. Journal of Philosophy 80: 100-127.

Horie, K. 1993. A Cross-Linguistic Study of Perception and Cognition Verb Complements: A Cognitive Perspective. Doctoral dissertation, University of Southern California.

Hoshi, K. 1995. Structural and Interpretive Aspects of Head-Internal and Head-External Relative Clauses. Doctoral dissertation, University of Rochester.

Ishii, Y. 1991. Operators and Empty Categories in Japanese. Doctoral dissertation, The University of Connecticut.

Ito, J. 1986. Head-movement at LF and PF: the syntax of head-internal relatives in Japanese. *University of Massachusetts Occasional Papers in Linguistics* 11: 109-138.

Kratzer, A. 1995. Stage-level and Individual-level Predicates. *The Generic Book*, eds. G. Carlson and F. J. Pelletier, 125-175. Chicago: University of Chicago Press.

Kuroda, S.-Y. 1975/76. Pivot-Independent Relativization in Japanese II. *Papers in Japanese Linguistics* 4: 85-96.

---

[4] See Kuroda (1995) for some ontological issues about the theory of judgments.

Kuroda, S.-Y. 1992. *Japanese Syntax and Semantics*. Dordrecht: Kluwer.

Kuroda 1999. Syubu Naizai Kankei-setu. *Kotoba no Kaku to Syuuen*, eds. S.-Y. Kuroda and M. Nakamura, 27-103. Tokyo: Kuroshio.

Link, G. 1983. The Logical Analysis of Plurals and Mass Terms: A Lattice-Theoretical Approach. Meaning, Use and Interpretation of Language, eds. R. Bäuerle, C. Schwarze, and A. von Stechow, 302-323. Berlin: Walter de Gruyter.

Milsark, G. 1974. *Existential sentences in English*. Doctoral dissertation, MIT.

Schein, B. 1993. *Plurals and Events*. Cambridge: MIT Press.

Shimoyama, J. 1999. Internally Headed Relative Clauses in Japanese and E-Type Anaphora. *Journal of East Asian Linguistics* 8: 147-182.

Watanabe, A. 1992. Subjacency and S-structure movement of WH-in-situ. *Journal of East Asian Linguistics* 1: 255-291.

Vlach, F. 1983. On Situation Semantics for Perception. *Synthese* 54: 129-152.

Index